A History of the Modern Middle East

A History of the
Modern
Middle East

Second Edition

William L. Cleveland
Simon Fraser University

Westview
PRESS
A Member of the Perseus Books Group

The photograph appearing on the cover shows a street scene in Damascus, October 1918. (Crown copyright, Imperial War Museum)

Copyright 2000 by Westview Press, A Member of the Perseus Books Group

Published in 2000 in the United States of America by Westview Press, 5500 Central Avenue, Boulder, Colorado 80301-2877, and in the United Kingdom by Westview Press, 12 Hid's Copse Road, Cumnor Hill, Oxford OX2 9JJ

Visit us on the World Wide Web at www.westviewpress.com

Library of Congress Cataloging-in-Publication Data
Cleveland, William L.
   A history of the modern Middle East / William L. Cleveland.—2nd ed.
      p.   cm.
   Includes bibliographical references and index.
   ISBN 0-8133-3489-6 (pbk)
   1. Middle East—History—1517–   2. Middle East—History—20th century.   I. Title.
DS62.4.C53   1999
956—dc21   99-36867
                                                                                   CIP

Printed and bound in the United States of America The paper used in this publication meets the requirements of the American National Standard for Permanence of Paper for Printed Library Materials Z39.48-1984.

10   9   8   7   6   5   4

Contents

Illustrations

Photos

Preface to the Second Edition

This book is intended to introduce Middle Eastern history to students and general readers who have not previously studied the subject. In the pages that follow, the term *Middle East* refers to the region from Egypt in the west through Iran in the east, and from Turkey in the north to the Arabian Peninsula in the south. I am aware that sound arguments exist for extending the geographical coverage to include Arab North Africa, the Sudan, and Islamic Afghanistan. However, I have decided to concentrate on the central Middle East, though I have suggested in the final chapter that the recently independent Islamic republics of Central Asia may be in the process of restoring their historic ties to the Middle East region. The primary chronological focus of the book is from the late eighteenth to the late twentieth centuries. I have added a new Part 5 to this second edition that has extensively revised, reorganized, and updated Part 4 of the original work so as to rethink the historical patterns of the past quarter century and to include developments up to early 1999. Part 5 also contains four new maps.

Although I have revised every chapter in this second edition to achieve greater clarity or to reflect new interpretations, the first four parts of the work retain the basic format of the original edition. In Part 1 I offer a general survey of the patterns of Middle Eastern history from the rise of Islam to the eighteenth century. In Chapters 1 and 2 I present the main features of Islamic faith and ritual and examine the emergence of Islamic social and political institutions from the time of the Prophet Muhammad to the end of the Mongol invasions of the thirteenth and fourteenth centuries. In trying to portray Islam in its own terms and in its proper historical setting, I have suggested the importance of the interaction between the Islam of the Quranic revelations and the settled civilizations of the Near East. I have also stressed the global aspects of Islamic civilization and have tried to demonstrate that the dynamic of that civilization cannot be understood by focusing only on the rise and decline of one Middle Eastern Islamic empire but must be seen as a global pattern of several different centers of Islamic florescence, each true to the essentials of the Quranic revelations but each also anchored in economically and culturally unique settings. In Chapter 3 I examine the rise of the Ottoman Empire and the formation of Ottoman ruling institutions, discuss the rise and fall of the Iranian-based Safavid Empire, and conclude with a discussion of the struggle between the Sunni Ottomans and the Shiᶜa Safavids over the lands of Iraq.

In Part 2 I focus on three main centers of political authority—the Ottoman Empire, the autonomous province of Egypt, and the Qajar Empire of Iran—from the early nineteenth century to the peace settlement of 1919–1920. The patterns of transformation in Iran were different from those in Egypt and the Ottoman Empire, and I have attempted to identify and explain the differences and to show their significance for the development of modern Iran. I have approached the modern history of the Ottoman-Egyptian Middle East with the belief that the area was organized by a long-established system based on Ottoman-Islamic practices and values. The Ottoman system had never been either static or uniform throughout the region, and it was again in flux on the eve of its nineteenth- and twentieth-century transformation. Nevertheless, after 300 years, the general objectives and practices of Ottoman rule were understood and their application was predictable to the inhabitants of the various regions of the empire.

One of the prominent themes of the book is that the disruption and eventual destruction of established Ottoman-Islamic ruling practices and social relationships during and after the reforming era was a wrenching and disorienting experience for the peoples of the Middle East. The terminology of this process of change has often been presented under the headings of modernization or Westernization. However, those terms have taken on connotations that are either value-laden or culturally judgmental or both. I have therefore avoided them except in instances where they accurately correspond to the intent of Middle Eastern participants such as Kemal Atatürk, who was, in my opinion, a Westernizer. In place of modernization and Westernization, I have preferred the term *transformation,* which better conveys the objectives of the nineteenth-century reformers and also places the nineteenth-century changes in the context of earlier eras of Middle Eastern transformation. The nineteenth century was not the first instance of externally inspired transformation in the Islamic Middle East, nor was it the first attempt at Ottoman reform. The rise and consolidation of the Ottoman Empire in the fifteenth and sixteenth centuries was itself a transforming process. So, too, was the imposition of Shiᶜism in Iran during the same period. I take the view that nineteenth-century Middle Eastern rulers did not intend to "Westernize" their states but merely sought to adopt selected European technological improvements and organizational methods for their armed forces. However, as greater numbers of influential administrators and military officers became committed to selective borrowing from Europe, the transformation was accelerated and spread to spheres outside the purely military. (I examine this process in Part 2.)

Chapter 4 is a discussion of the early phase of the transformation as embodied in the reform programs of the Ottoman sultans, Selim III and Mahmud II, and Muhammad Ali of Egypt. In Chapter 5 I examine the acceleration of the transformation during the Ottoman Tanzimat and the reign of Ismaʿil in Egypt, showing how the combination of increased expenditures and the loss of local markets to European merchants led to the bankruptcy of the two states and the eventual British occupation of Egypt. I also focus on educational changes and show the patterns by which the so-called French knowers came to be favored over the graduates of religious institutions for positions in the bureaucracy, the teaching profession, and the judiciary. In Chapter 6 I explore the impact of the British occupation on Egypt up to the outbreak of World War I and examine Qajar Iran during the reign of Nasir al-Din Shah. By introducing late-nineteenth-century Iran at this point in the book, I hope to enable readers to grasp the differences between the Ottoman-Egyptian experiences already discussed and those of Iran.

In Chapter 7 I present the perspective of individuals who opposed the transformation or at least wished it to be more firmly grounded in Islamic practices and principles. The Ottoman ruler Sultan Abdul Hamid II and three rural reformist movements, the Wahhabi, the Sanusi, and the Mahdiyyah, are representative of the trend of resistance to European-style reforms that surfaced in the late nineteenth century. I also deal with the ideas of Islamic reform put forward by Muhammad Abduh as well as with the more secular "Arab awakening" sparked by the activities of Christian missionaries and the introduction of the printing press. My discussion in Chapter 8 concentrates on two very different protest movements in favor of constitutional government. The Young Turk revolution restored the Ottoman constitution and brought to power a group of military officers and civil servants educated in the new institutions and determined to reform, and thus to save, the Ottoman Empire. In the first section of this chapter I examine their policies and seek to identify the main currents of communal identity that competed for the loyalties of the Ottoman population on the eve of World War I. In the second section I discuss the Iranian constitutional upheaval of 1905–1911 and compare it to the Young Turk era.

In Chapter 9 I deal with World War I in the Middle East, the various wartime agreements and treaties regarding the disposition of Ottoman territories, and the final peace settlement that divided the former Ottoman Arab lands between Britain and France. In concluding this chapter, I argue that the passing of the Ottoman Empire and of the organizing principles on which it was based was of seminal importance for the peoples of the Middle East, particularly for the inhabitants of the former Arab provinces of the empire. The Arabs had not prepared for a post-Ottoman order, and they had certainly not prepared for one that found them ruled by British and French occupiers. For the quarter century after 1920, the Arab leaders were preoccupied with gaining full independence from the European powers and establishing national identities for their new states. (In Part 2, as in other parts of the book, I have not provided separate chapters for diplomatic and domestic affairs, preferring instead to view international relations as an aspect of internal developments.)

In Part 3 I cover the period from the imposition of the mandate system to the creation of Israel in 1948. The thorny question of how to present Middle Eastern history after the Ottoman collapse and the emergence of several new states has received a variety of answers in other books. I have chosen a state approach, but one that I hope is comparative and brings out the characteristics of special chronological eras or periods. Thus, I believe that there was an interwar era that possessed certain common features that distinguish it from preceding and succeeding periods. For example, I have emphasized the importance of the Ottoman background to this period in Turkey and the Arab successor states and have suggested the existence of continuities in the political leadership that set the tone for the relationship between the local elite and the European occupying power. In Chapter 10 I compare the objectives and impact of the reform programs of Atatürk in Turkey and Reza Shah in Iran. In the treatment of the Arab states, I have tried not only to show the internal continuities and breaks with the late Ottoman era but also to demonstrate that the British and French patterns of administrative control played an important role in shaping the development of the states under their rule. Chapter 11 is a discussion of Egypt, Iraq, and Transjordan, countries in which Britain exercised dominance, and Chapter 12 is an examination of French rule in Syria and Lebanon as well as the special case of the rise of Saudi Arabia. The chapter concludes with an analysis of the major political ideologies of the interwar period—regionalism, Pan-Arab nationalism, and the continuing appeal of Islamic solidarity. Chapter 13 deals with the Palestine mandate and the birth of Israel.

Part 4 is a study of the Middle East from 1945 to the early 1970s. Chapter 14 discusses Turkey to the restoration of civilian government in 1983 and Iran to the eve of revolution in the mid-1970s. In Chapters 15 and 16 I treat the Arab states, and their relations with Israel, during the period I have defined as the Nasser era. I have employed this term in the belief that Nasserism exercised a major influence on the Arab world, not just by the inspiration it provided during the rule of the Egyptian president but also by the despair it left in the wake of its unexpected collapse in 1967. Chapter 17 is new and extensively expands the analysis of Israeli political culture and institutions from 1948 to 1977. I also examine in this chapter the emergence of the Palestine Liberation Organization (PLO) and the impact of that organization's search for a regional base of operations up to Black September 1970.

The new Part 5 contains substantial changes and additions to the first edition. In the introduction to Part 5, I present guidelines for understanding the new historical patterns that have emerged since the early 1970s. Chapter 18 focuses on Egypt and Lebanon during the 1970s and 1980s. I discuss the domestic pressures that influenced President Anwar Sadat of Egypt to launch a war against Israel in 1973 and to sign a peace treaty with that same state in 1979. The chapter also examines the local demographic changes that combined with the activities of Palestinian organizations to plunge Lebanon into a bloody civil war and to prompt Israel to invade the country in 1982. The chapter concludes with a new section on the early years of Husni Mubarak's rule in Egypt.

As of early 1999, presidents Hafiz al-Asad of Syria and Saddam Husayn of Iraq had both dominated their respective countries for nearly three decades. In Chapter 19 I examine their rise to power, their domestic and foreign policies, and the transformation in the social composition of the ruling elite that their rule represented and encouraged. The chapter closes with a discussion of the Iran-Iraq War of 1980–1988. Chapter 20 is divided into two parts: In the first I analyze the Iranian revolution of 1979 and the significance of the creation of the Islamic Republic of Iran; the second part is devoted to an examination of the resurgence of politicized Islam as a general Middle Eastern phenomenon, with a special case study of Egypt. My focus in Chapter 21 is on Saudi Arabia and Yemen from the early 1950s to the 1980s and the oil-producing Arab states of the Persian Gulf from their formation to the 1980s. I stress the effects of the oil price revolution of 1973 and discuss the tensions caused by the ruling families' deployment of vast wealth to create social and technological change on the one hand and to prevent political change on the other hand.

In the new Chapter 22, I examine the Palestinian uprising known as the *intifada* and the origins and outcome of the Gulf War of 1991. The chapter concludes with a discussion of the impact of the prolonged aftermath of the war on Saudi Arabia, Kuwait, Yemen, and Iraq up to early 1999. When the first edition was about to go to press, Israel and the PLO signed the historic first Oslo peace accord. The section I hastily added on that agreement was necessarily tentative. From the advantage of hindsight, I have devoted Chapter 23 to an analysis of the rise and fall of the peace process and have tried to show the linkages between the *intifada*, the Gulf War, and the first Oslo accord. I have also added sections on the social and political consequences of Yasir Arafat's presidency of the Palestinian National Authority (PNA) and the Netanyahu years in Israel. The chapter concludes with the fall of the Netanyahu government and the election of Ehud Barak as Israeli prime minister in May 1999. All of the material in Chapter 24 has been added since the appearance of the first edition. The chapter opens with an analysis of U.S. Middle Eastern policies in the 1990s, then provides a comparative discussion of Turkey and Iran up to early 1999. I also examine the continuing vitality of political Islam in Egypt and conclude with a section on the factors contributing to the reintegration of Islamic Central Asia into the central Middle East. The conclusion to this edition is more pessimistic than was that of the first edition.

The focus of this book is primarily political, but I have tried to weave into the narrative discussions of major social, economic, and ideological currents in the hope that a full and integrated history of the Middle East will emerge. A single book cannot cover everything and should not try to do so. The select annotated and updated bibliography offers guidance to readers seeking further information on topics introduced in this book and on other aspects of the Middle Eastern past that are not treated here.

When I began working on this book, I had taught survey courses on modern Middle Eastern history for twenty years and had published scholarly monographs on the subject. Although I knew that writing a textbook would be a challenge, I believed that my experience as a teacher and scholar would enable me to complete the project in "a couple of years." I was correct about the challenge but very wrong about the time required to meet it. In this regard, I would like to thank Peter Kracht, senior editor at Westview Press, for his patience and tact as first the months, and then the years, rolled by.

I would also like to acknowledge the assistance I have received from others. My greatest debt is owed to the many scholars of the Middle East whose works have guided and informed me throughout the preparation of this book. In the course of attempting to broaden my own knowledge of the field, I have gained a greater awareness of their contributions and a new respect for their achievements. I hope I have appropriately recognized my debt in the notes and the bibliography. Family members, colleagues, and friends outside the academy offered encouragement when it was most needed, and I am grateful to them all, especially my wife, Gretchen. I would like to thank my history department colleagues John P. Spagnolo and Derryl N. MacLean for sharing with me their knowledge and their personal libraries—both often on short notice. I would be remiss if I did not express a special note of gratitude to Robert C. Brown, the former dean of arts at Simon Fraser University, for his unwavering personal and institutional support.

Although computers have eased the task of editing, the production of a manuscript still requires considerable staff work, and I have received generous assistance from Joan MacDonald and Joanna Koczwarski. I would also like to acknowledge the valuable contributions of Donald Malcolm Reid, who offered suggestions and encouragement throughout the preparation of this work and contributed an important critique of the first edition, and James P. Jankowski, who also reviewed the manuscript, correcting errors of fact and making pertinent recommendations for the reorganization of several chapters. It is a pleasure to recognize the skills of Eric Leinberger, the cartographer for both editions. Fabio Lopez-Lazaro and Lliam Grayer were the first graduate research assistants to work on this project, and I acknowledge their help in getting things started. I extend a special word of appreciation to Paul Frederick Horton, the most indefatigable fact-finder of my acquaintance, and Michael James Quilty, both of whom were intensely involved in the long final stages of this work. Their editorial comments, research assistance, and personal friendship did much to sustain this project and make it seem worthwhile.

Four faculty members who adopted the first edition for their courses kindly agreed to provide detailed criticisms of the work and suggestions for revisions that could be incorporated into this second edition. Their comments were invaluable, and it is with the deepest gratitude that I acknowledge the contributions of F. Robert Hunter, James P. Jankowski, Donald Malcolm Reid, and Mary Christina Wilson and thank them for the time and effort they devoted to improving this work. I have also benefited from the judicious advice of L. Carl Brown, the astute observations of Jane Power, and from the outstanding efforts of research assistant Susan Nance, whose role in the preparation of Part 5 was crucial. I should also like to thank Jennifer Chen of Westview Press for her understanding.

The questions raised and the suggestions made by undergraduate students over the years have influenced the organization and presentation of the book. I hope the end result answers most of their questions and incorporates the best of their suggestions. If it serves to make modern Middle Eastern history more comprehensible without reducing complexities to simplicities, it will have served its purpose.

William L. Cleveland

A Note About Place Names
and Transliteration

For purposes of clarity and consistency, I have used the names of modern countries to refer to certain regions during the entire period covered in this book, even if those names were not in use in the past. Thus I refer to the *area of Iraq* or *lands of Iraq* to designate the settled areas of the Tigris-Euphrates river basin; *Greater Syria* to indicate the region currently divided among Israel, Jordan, Lebanon, and Syria; and *Iran* to designate the territory between Iraq and Turkmenistan. I also employ the name *Iran* instead of Persia. Once the modern states of Syria, Iraq, and Iran come into existence, I use their names to refer specifically to the territory embraced within the frontiers of those states.

The transliteration apparatus has been kept to a minimum. *Hamza*s are not indicated, and the Arabic *ayn* is indicated by ᶜ, but only when it occurs in the middle of a word. In most cases, the plurals of words have been formed by adding an *s*. An exception is the plural of *alim,* which is rendered as *ulama*.

The Development of Islamic Civilization to the Eighteenth Century

PART I

⟨I⟩
⟨I⟩

The religion of Islam is often viewed solely in terms of its origins in the barren, sparsely settled Arabian Peninsula. To be sure, it was in the Arabian city of Mecca that Islam was revealed to the Prophet Muhammad in the years A.D. 610 to A.D. 632. However, during the century following Muhammad's death, the Arabs expanded out of the peninsula and conquered a world empire stretching from Spain to present-day Pakistan. The great capital cities of the first Arab-Islamic empires, Damascus and Baghdad, were not located in Arabia but in the long-settled lands of antiquity. To understand the development of Islam and Islamic civilization, we must recognize that the Middle East region into which Islam expanded was a rich repository of centuries of accumulated intellectual exchanges, religious experiences, and administrative practices. Islamic society built upon these existing foundations and was shaped by them. As Ira Lapidus has written, "The civilization of Islam, though born in Mecca, also had its progenitors in Palestine, Babylon, and Persepolis."[1]

Ancient Near Eastern civilization began to develop within the city-states that first appeared in lower Iraq around 3500 B.C. These settled communities developed written alphabets, governing institutions, and elaborate religious rituals. By about 2400 B.C., larger political entities began to emerge in the form of regional empires in which several cities were incorporated into a single state ruled by a dominant monarch. The growth of ever-larger regional empires acted as an integrative force by unifying greater numbers of people under common legal systems and exposing them to shared cultural and religious experiences. Over the course of centuries, improvements in agricultural and military technology, in transportation and communications, and in social and administrative organization enabled empires to dominate increasingly extensive territories. This process reached its first culmination in Egypt's Nile Valley, where an advanced civilization took shape under the rule of the pharaohs. The monuments to gods and kings that line the banks of the Nile testify to the shared religious and dynastic traditions of the ancient Egyptians. A similar unifying effect was achieved by the Iranian-based Acheminid Empire (550 B.C.–331 B.C.), which brought all the Middle Eastern lands from Egypt to the Oxus River into a single imperial framework.

The Acheminid Empire was defeated by Alexander the Great in 331 B.C., but Iranian-based empires continued to provide order and a measure of religious and cultural uniformity to the territories extending from lower Iraq to the Oxus River in the east. In the wake of Alexander's conquests, the Middle Eastern lands lying between Iran and the Mediterranean Sea absorbed yet another layer of tradition as Greek was implanted as the language of administration and high culture. Alexandria and Antioch developed into centers of Greek learning, and Greek became the dominant language of discourse among the urban elite from Egypt to Anatolia.

The absorption of new ideas and techniques continued with the Roman conquest and the consolidation of Rome's efficient administrative practices in Egypt, Palestine, Syria, and Anatolia during the first century B.C. Yet although the Mediterranean lands of the Middle East were administered as provinces of the Roman Empire, their high culture remained more Hellenic than Latin. With the transfer of the imperial Roman capital to Constantinople in A.D. 330 and the fall of western Rome a century later, the eastern identity of the empire was solidified. That identity was represented by the Byzantine Empire, which preserved the administrative practices of Rome within the context of Hellenic civilization.

Formative Islam interacted not only with the existing material cultures outlined above but also with established religious beliefs and practices. At the time of the rise of Islam, local and regional cults, though still in existence, had largely been subsumed by the official religions of the dominant Byzantine and Sasanian empires. It was only natural that the formation of empires contributed to religious uniformity. Subject peoples were expected to abandon their local gods and goddesses and adhere to the officially sanctioned imperial religion. Thus the process of imperial consolidation led also to religious consolidation and to the emergence of monotheism, the belief in the supremacy of one god. By the time of the Arab-Islamic conquests, most of the inhabitants of the Middle East belonged to one of three monotheistic faiths.

Monotheism was first preached by the prophets of ancient Israel and is one of the most significant and enduring legacies of the Jewish faith. Although the Jews had been dispersed from Palestine by the Romans in the first and second centuries A.D., Jewish communities continued to flourish in the Middle East on the eve of the rise of Islam. Other forms of monotheism were also present in the region. In the seventh century B.C., the Iranian prophet Zoroaster preached a doctrine that upheld the existence of a supreme God pitted in a constant struggle against the forces of evil. Zoroastrianism was revived by the rulers of the Iranian-based Sasanian Empire (A.D. 234–A.D. 634) and was adopted as the official religion of their state.

A third monotheistic faith, Christianity, grew rapidly from Roman times onward and was proclaimed the state religion of the Byzantine Empire in the late fourth century. However, differing interpretations over the nature of Christ created divisions among the adherents of the faith and led to the growth of separate churches, each jealously guarding its version of the truth. At the Council of Chalcedon in 451, the main body of the church defined Christ as having two natures, divine and human. But other Christian communities, known as Monophysites, believed that Christ had only a single nature. The Monophysite doctrine was institutionalized in the Coptic church of Egypt, which had its own religious hierarchy and conducted its ritual in the native Egyptian Coptic language. The Armenian church in Anatolia also held to the Monophysite interpretation, as did certain groups in Syria. At the time of the rise of Islam, these regional Monophysite churches, with their vernacular liturgies, were under attack from the Byzantine authorities, who sought to impose the official Greek Orthodox version of Christianity on all the subjects of the empire.

Islam unified the Greco-Christian territories of Byzantium and the lands of Iranian-Zoroastrianism into a single religiously based universal empire. The encounter between the new faith of Islam and the established traditions of the Middle East led to the creation of a new civilization that was profoundly and unmistakably Islamic yet also bore evidence of the centuries of accumulated practices that had preceded it.

Notes

1. Ira M. Lapidus, *A History of Islamic Societies* (Cambridge, 1990), p. 3.

The Rise and Expansion of Islam | 1

On the eve of the rise of Islam, the settled lands of the Middle East were ruled by two competing imperial states, the Roman-Byzantine Empire in the west and the Sasanian Empire of Iran in the east. The Byzantine emperors were successors to the Caesars and presided over an imposing edifice of high cultural and political traditions that blended Greek learning, Roman administration, and Greek Orthodox Christianity. In the early seventh century, the emperor's territorial possessions stretched from the Italian peninsula across southern Europe to the magnificent capital city of Constantinople. The empire's Middle Eastern provinces included Egypt, Palestine, and Syria, as well as parts of Iraq and Anatolia. Supported by a standing professional army, a highly developed bureaucracy, and the priesthood of the Orthodox church, the rulers of Byzantium appeared to be powerful and secure.

In the late sixth and early seventh centuries, however, Byzantium was weakened by challenges to its military, religious, and administrative authority. Beginning in 540, the imperial rivalry between the Byzantines and Sasanians broke out into open warfare that continued almost uninterrupted until 629. Campaign and countercampaign exhausted the military forces of both empires, depleted their treasuries, and inflicted extensive damage to the lands and cities lying between the Nile and the Euphrates. To meet the financial demands of constant warfare, the Byzantine emperors periodically raised taxes, a measure that alienated their subjects, who had already suffered economic hardships from the passage of warring armies back and forth across their lands.

Religious divisions created additional tensions between the Byzantine state and its subjects. Once the Byzantine Empire adopted Greek Orthodox Christianity as the state religion in the late fourth century, the emperors and the church attempted to enforce popular acceptance of this officially approved version of the faith. But peoples within the empire continued to adhere to other forms of Christianity, and to Judaism, and to use their own vernacular languages for scripture and ritual. Unwilling to tolerate these challenges to official orthodoxy, the state branded them as heretical and undertook to suppress them. The persecution of Jews and of Christians outside the Greek Orthodox community caused great disaffection within the empire and explains in part why many Byzantine subjects welcomed the arrival of the more religiously tolerant Muslim rulers.

The Sasanian Empire of Iran, with its capital at Ctesiphon on the Tigris River, contested Byzantium for control of the territories between Iraq and Egypt. Heir to the 1,200-year-old Acheminid tradition of universal Iranian empire, the Sasanian state was based on the principle of absolute monarchy. The emperor was the king of kings (*shahanshah*), a distant and all-powerful ruler living in palatial splendor and surrounded by elaborate ceremonial trappings. Over the centuries, Iranian bureaucratic practices had become refined, and the Sasanian Empire was administered by a large and experienced scribal class. Like their Byzantine counterparts, the Sasanian emperors had at their disposal an effective standing professional army, which was noted for its heavily armed and armored cavalry.

Yet the Sasanian Empire's apparent strength was, like Byzantium's, diluted by popular discontent, much of which stemmed from religious diversity. By the late sixth century, the official Sasanian state religion of Zoroastrianism had become more significant as a ceremonial faith for the ruling elite than as the religion of the population at large. In the western portion of the empire in particular, people were more attracted to various strains of Christianity and Judaism than to the religion of the imperial court. In the absence of a unifying religious affiliation with their ruler, many subjects of the Sasanian Empire lacked feelings of loyalty toward the state.

In 602 the Sasanian ruler Khusrau renewed the long-standing war with Byzantium by launching a campaign that resulted in the capture of Jerusalem and the conquest of Egypt. But in 622 the Byzantine emperor Heraclius began a successful counteroffensive that carried his forces into Iraq and led to the temporary occupation of Ctesiphon. As the two empires of the Middle East waged their wars of attrition, a movement was forming in the sparsely inhabited Arabian Peninsula that would overwhelm them both.

Although the Byzantine and Sasanian empires were in a period of transition when Islam first extended into them, it is important to recognize their impact on the development of Islamic governing practices and religious doctrine. Formative Islam would be influenced by the Greek legacy of Byzantium, by the bureaucratic tradition of Iran, and by the concepts of emperor that had developed in the courts of Constantinople and Ctesiphon. Islam must be understood as a product of the societies into which it spread as well as of the society in which it originated.

Pre-Islamic Arabia

With the exception of Yemen in the south and a few scattered oasis settlements elsewhere, the Arabian Peninsula is a vast desert. It is the home of the

Arabs, an ancient Semitic people whose origins cannot be traced with certainty. In contrast to the rigorously administered domains of the Byzantine and Sasanian empires, the Arabian Peninsula of the early seventh century lacked any central organizing authority. It had no state structure, no common legal system, no administrative center. Tribes were the largest units of social and political organization to which an individual's loyalties were given. Each tribe was an entity unto itself bound by ties of kinship based on a belief in common descent from a founding ancestor. The majority of Arabia's inhabitants were pastoral nomads engaged in raising camels, sheep, or goats. The scarcity of pasturelands in the harsh environment of Arabia required constant movement from one grazing ground to another. Competition for the scarce resources of the land created rivalries among the tribes, and warfare became ingrained as a way of life. All males were expected to be warriors, and accounts of the exploits of the most daring among them became enshrined in tribal culture. The widespread experience of the Arabs in warfare was to be a significant factor in the early expansion of Islam.

Notwithstanding the divisions inherent in the tribal structure of pre-Islamic Arabia, forces of cultural unity were present. The Bedouin ethos of bravery and honor was celebrated in a special style of Arabic poetry known as a *qasidah*. The existence of this poetry, which was recited at market fairs and tribal gatherings, has convinced historians that the Arabs of the seventh century possessed a common poetic language that could be understood in different regions of the peninsula. This was of the utmost significance for the spread of Islam because it meant that the Prophet Muhammad's religious message could be communicated to Arabic speakers across a broad expanse of territory. Although Arabic was a written language by this time, *qasidah*s were recited from memory rather than read from a text. The tradition of memorization and oral recitation played a role in the transmission and retention of the Quran in a mainly illiterate society.

Isolated though it was, the Arabian Peninsula was not completely cut off from the forces that shaped Middle Eastern civilization. In the marches of the north, two Arab kingdoms—Petra (sixth century B.C.–A.D. 106) and its successor, Palmyra—were flourishing centers of commerce before their absorption into the Roman Empire. They served as channels through which ideas originating in the settled regions of the Middle East were transmitted to the Arabian interior. On the eve of the rise of Islam, two Arab tribal confederations, the Ghassan and the Lakhm, guarded the Arabian frontiers as client states of Byzantium and the Sasanians, respectively. Both of these Arab confederations were Christian and provide evidence of the spread of the concept of monotheism among the Arabs before the time of Muhammad.

At the southeastern tip of Arabia, Yemen was another source for the entry of external influences into the peninsula. Unlike the rest of Arabia, Yemen was a fertile and well-watered region able to support a settled agricultural society. Beginning with the establishment of royal authority in 1000 B.C., Yemen developed an elaborate civilization with institutionalized religious practices and a complex social hierarchy. For several centuries the dominant power in Yemen was the Kingdom of Saba, which, in periods of its greatest strength, exercised authority in the Arabian interior and north along the Red Sea coast. With its location at the confluence of the Red Sea and the Indian Ocean, Yemen became a transit center for merchants and travelers bringing not only goods but also a rich variety of religious beliefs from India, Africa, and the Middle East. By the fourth and fifth centuries A.D., Christianity had been adopted by several Arab communities in southern Arabia, and the ruler of Yemen's last pre-Islamic dynasty converted to Judaism. From Yemen, an awareness of monotheistic religions filtered into other parts of the peninsula. Yet despite the fermentation of religious doctrines in the settled regions of northern and southern Arabia, most of the tribes of the interior continued to practice various forms of animism, worshipping local idols or deities.

During the two centuries before Islam, Arabia acquired increasing importance as a commercial transit route between the Middle Eastern empires and Yemen. The wars between Byzantium and the Sasanians disrupted the east-west overland routes and gave rise to a brisk north-south caravan trade through the Hijaz, Arabia's coastal plain adjacent to the Red Sea. The items of commerce were mainly luxury goods transported by sea from the Indian Ocean basin to Yemen, where they were transferred to camel caravans that traversed the Hijaz on their way to Gaza, Damascus, and the cities of Iraq. Caravans also carried goods south from Byzantium to Yemen. The main Arabian beneficiary of this commercial network was the Hijaz city of Mecca, which developed into the most important commercial city of the peninsula. By the early seventh century, Meccan merchants had accumulated sufficient capital to organize their own caravans and to provide payments to an extensive network of tribes in exchange for pledges to allow the caravans to pass in peace.

In addition to its role as a commercial center, Mecca was a religious site of major significance. The city's shrine, the Ka'ba, became the center of an animistic cult that attracted worshipers throughout western Arabia. By the time of Muhammad's birth, the Ka'ba had become the site of an annual pilgrimage during which warfare was suspended, and Mecca's sanctuary became a kind of neutral ground where tribal disputes could be resolved. The city derived considerable income from its religious role, and its leading families recognized the importance of the sanctuary as a source of wealth and influence.

The leading clans of Mecca were all members of the Quraysh tribe that settled the city, established its religious role, and dominated its political and commercial life. Although formal municipal organizations did not exist, the affairs of the city were loosely regulated by a council of prominent Quraysh merchants. Historians have suggested that Mecca was in a state of transition between the vanishing tribal ways and a nascent urbanism spawned by merchant capitalism. The customary tribal values were being displaced, but no fully developed set of communal values suitable for an urban setting had yet emerged.

Muhammad and the Foundations of Islam

Muhammad ibn Abdullah, the future Prophet of Islam, was born in Mecca around 570. His early life gave little indication of the compelling prophet and skillful statesman he would later become. He was born into the clan of Hashim, a subtribe of the Quraysh. His ancestors had acquired prestige as the guardians of Mecca's sanctuary, but at the time of his birth the family's wealth and status had been considerably reduced. Muhammad was orphaned at the age of two and was raised and sheltered by his uncle, Abu Talib. As a young man, he engaged in the caravan trade and may have journeyed to Damascus. His financial position was secured when, in his early twenties, he married a wealthy widow, Khadijah. Khadijah holds an honored place in the history of Islam; she was the first convert to the new faith after Muhammad himself, and she supported him during the difficult early years of his prophethood when he was scorned by most of Mecca's population.

Although Muhammad was widely respected as a decent and trustworthy individual, he lived an otherwise ordinary life as merchant, husband, and father to the four daughters born to Khadijah. But as Muhammad neared his fortieth year, his behavior gradually began to change. He often left Mecca, sometimes for days at a time, to meditate in solitude in the mountains outside the city. Some scholars have conjectured that Muhammad was reflecting on what he saw as the problems that afflicted Meccan society and was seeking ways to resolve them. It was during one of his solitary vigils on Mount Hira that Muhammad was summoned to his prophetic mission, an event known in Islam as the Night of Power. The summons came as a command from God, transmitted through the angel Gabriel, for Muhammad to recite to his fellow Meccans the divine messages that he had been chosen to receive. The Night of Power marked the beginning of a movement that would transform Arab life and lead to the emergence of a universal monotheistic religion.

For the remaining twenty-two years of his life, Muhammad continued to receive revelations, which his companions recorded, memorized, and later collected into a single book, the Quran (Recitation), which constitutes the core of the Islamic faith. The Quran is a sacred work in both form and content. Not only does it contain God's commands, it also represents the direct word of God; its language is therefore divine and unchangeable. Throughout the centuries since the Night of Power, non-Muslims, especially the Christian and Jewish monotheists for whom Islam represented the most direct challenge, have found it difficult to accept the idea that the Quran contains God's words, not Muhammad's. The point here is not to debate the contesting claims to religious truth but to insist on the depth of Muhammad's experience and the utterly convincing language in which that experience was conveyed. The verses of the Quran, especially those from the Meccan period, reveal an individual possessed of a compelling sense of urgency and inspired by a commitment that transcended his previous existence and pushed him into the role for which he believed he had been chosen—as the Prophet of God.

Muhammad's prophethood can be divided into two phases, the period at Mecca (610–622) and the years in Medina (622–632). The difference in the Prophet's circumstances during these two periods of his life is reflected in the style and content of the revelations. The Quran was revealed in a series of chapters (suras) and is organized according to the length of the chapters, with the longest first and the shortest at the end. The shorter chapters are from the Meccan years, when Muhammad concentrated on establishing the theological foundations of the faith. The central element of the Meccan period was an uncompromising monotheism. As an early Meccan revelation insisted,

> *Say: He is God, One, God, the Everlasting Refuge,*
> *who has not begotten, and has not been begotten,*
> *and equal to Him is not anyone.*
>
> *(Sura 112)*[1]

The Arabic word for one supreme God, *Allah,* refers to the monotheistic deities of Judaism and Christianity as well as Islam. It is thus incorrect to employ the term *Allah* in an exclusively Islamic context. The term translates as *God,* and that is how it should be employed and understood.

What did the omnipotent deity of the Quran want from his human creations? In the Meccan revelations, he demanded that they practice prescribed patterns of worship and behavior. They were to submit to his will and show their gratitude toward him as the provider of the bounties of the earth. Islam means submission, and the followers of the faith, Muslims, are those who have submitted to the will of God. In addition to matters of ritual, God also set forth commandments on how human beings should relate to one another in their daily social intercourse. Although the Meccan verses were not as detailed on this subject as were the later revelations at Medina, they nevertheless provided a clear indication of God's preferences. Thus God warned the people of Mecca to pay more attention to the less fortunate in society and to moderate their search for wealth. The following bluntly critical passage demonstrates God's displeasure at practices in the Mecca of Muhammad's day:

> *No indeed; but you honour not the orphan,*
> *and you urge not the feeding of the needy,*
> *and you devour the inheritance greedily,*
> *and you love wealth with an ardent love.*
> *(Sura 89)*

The Quran chastised those who were uncharitable and warned those who felt that their wealth had made them immune from punishment that God would be the final judge of their afterlife. The concept of the Day of Judgment was a central element of the faith. The revelations warned the people of Mecca that their deeds, their attitudes, and even their innermost thoughts would be assessed by the Almighty on Judgment Day. As described in the Quran, it would be a decisive moment:

> *When earth is shaken with a mighty shaking*
> *and earth brings forth her burdens,*
> *and Man says, "What ails her?"*
> *upon that day she shall tell her tidings*
> *for that her Lord has inspired her.*
> *Upon that day men shall issue in scatterings to see their works,*
> *and whoso has done an atom's weight of good shall see it,*
> *and whoso has done an atom's weight of evil shall see it.*
> *(Sura 99)*

The theology of the Quran was straightforward. Humans were instructed to obey the revealed will of an omnipotent God of judgment: Those who accepted him and followed all of his commands would be rewarded paradise; those who rejected God and deviated from his commands would be condemned to the fires of Gehenna.

Muhammad's preaching attracted few converts and aroused considerable opposition during the Meccan period of his mission. After all, he posed a challenge to the social, economic, and religious structure of the city. Not only did he criticize the attitudes of the wealthy Quraysh merchants, he also condemned the religious practices that made Mecca a prosperous pilgrimage center. As the years passed and the Meccan opposition turned from scorn to threats of physical harm, Muhammad and his followers began to search for a more hospitable location. When an invitation came to them to settle in the city of Yathrib (later Medina), Muhammad accepted it.

Located some 200 miles (322 km) north of Mecca, Medina was a fertile oasis city suffering from the ravages of an extended blood feud among its several tribes. Muhammad was invited as a mediator and was promised by Medinan representatives that any Muslims who accompanied him would receive protection. In 622 the small community of Muslims gradually migrated from Mecca to Medina. The event, known as the *hijrah* (emigration), marks a turning point in the development of Islam: 622 is the first year of the Muslim calendar.

During his ten years in Medina, Muhammad's status rose dramatically. From a scorned prophet with few followers, he became the head of a small state and the dominant figure throughout Arabia. This transformation was achieved through a combination of warfare, negotiation, and preaching, the success of which seemed to confirm Muhammad's right not only to prophethood but to political leadership as well. Muhammad consolidated his authority in Medina by convincing influential personalities in the city to embrace Islam and accept his leadership. Once his power base was sufficiently established, he was able to take measures against the groups that continued to refuse his prophetic and political authority. Among the latter were several Jewish tribes whose members would not accept the legitimacy of Muhammad's claim as the Prophet. Muhammad eventually expelled them from Medina and ordered their property confiscated and distributed among the Muslim emigrants.

Even as he was consolidating his position in Medina, Muhammad made plans to bring Mecca into the expanding Islamic community. He was motivated partly out of a desire to see his native city accept the only faith that would ensure its inhabitants of salvation and partly out of a recognition that without the talents and experience of the Quraysh, the horizons of Islam would remain limited. Muhammad's strategy was to disrupt the caravan trade on which Mecca's prosperity depended. Within a year of his arrival in Medina, he ordered the first of what would become an ongoing series of raids on Meccan caravans. The initial raid occurred during one of the sacred pilgrimage months, when, according to established custom, hostilities were suspended. This was disturbing to the many Muslims of Medina who continued to respect existing traditions. However, Muhammad was able to reassure them by a revelation explaining that although fighting during the sacred month was distasteful, the presence of disbelief was even worse. Warfare against unbelievers was thus sanctified through divine revelation, and all Muslims who engaged in spreading Islam through force of arms were designated by God as deserving of special merit.

In retaliation for Muhammad's attacks on their caravans, the Meccans launched several campaigns against the Muslims in Medina, but each time the outnumbered Muslim forces managed to hold their own and even to gain limited victories. Muhammad emerged during these encounters as an innovative military tactician, and his success in thwarting the Meccans enhanced his prestige among the neighboring tribes. Many swore their allegiance to him not because they fully understood or accepted the religious message of Islam but because association with Muhammad's endeavor appeared to guarantee victory, and with victory came the spoils of war. The increasing size of the Prophet's forces and his effective alliances with the tribes enabled him to stifle the trade of Mecca to the point where the city's prosperity was seriously threatened. In 630 Muhammad led a force of 10,000 men to the outskirts of Mecca; demonstrating his qualities as a statesman, he promised the inhabitants that their lives would be spared and their property would remain secure if they surrendered the city and accepted Islam. The Quraysh leadership agreed to the terms, and the Prophet made a victorious entry into the city from which he had fled just eight years earlier. According to accounts of the occasion, Muhammad went to the Kaᶜba and had the idols destroyed, proclaiming the shrine sacred to God. Mecca would remain a pilgrimage center, and the Kaᶜba would become the focal point of the new faith. From 630 to 632, most of the remaining tribes of Arabia submitted to the authority of Mecca and accepted Muhammad's prophetic mission.

In the years between the *hijrah* and the surrender of Mecca, Muhammad's leadership role became more complex. Medina developed into a small city-state with a treasury, a military, and an ever-increasing number of converts. The content of the Quran reflected the changing circumstances by offering instructions on how the expanded functions of the state were to be organized and how human beings should conduct their relations with one another. In these commandments, the all-embracing nature of Islam was established. For example, to contract a debt agreement as the Quran required—in writing before a witness—was a religious duty, and failure to follow the prescription was a sin. In this way, the details of marriage, inheritance, divorce, diet, and economic practice were made part of the religious experience of Muslims. Muhammad created a community (*ummah*) in which the laws of human behavior in daily life were prescribed by God.

It would be an exaggeration to call Arabia a cohesive, unified state after the surrender of Mecca. Nevertheless, the transformation created by the Prophet had been substantial. He had implanted the core concept of a community of believers united in their recognition of a single Supreme Deity and in their acceptance of that deity's authority in their daily lives; he had conveyed notions of social morality that forbade alcohol and the blood feud and that recognized the legal status of women and demanded protection for the less fortunate in society. Muhammad combined in his person the roles of prophet, state builder, and social reformer. Today there is much emphasis on the martial elements of Islam, but to comprehend fully Muhammad's mission, we need consider the importance of Quranic passages like this one:

> Be kind to parents, and the near kinsman,
> and to orphans, and to the needy,
> and to the neighbour who is of kin,
> and to the neighbour who is a stranger,
> and to the companion at your side,
> and to the traveller.
>
> (Sura 4)

The Arab Conquests and the First Empire

Muhammad died in 632, only two years after the submission of Mecca. It would not have contradicted historical patterns if Arabia had rejected the Prophet's summons and taken up the old ways again. Instead, Muslim factions in Mecca and Medina resolved to continue the development of the new religious community and competed with one another to assert their control over it. Because Muhammad had no sons and because the Quran contained no clear instructions on how a successor should be chosen, the question of the leadership of the community was open to different interpretations. Some believed that it should remain within the Prophet's family and supported the candidacy of Muhammad's cousin and son-in-law, Ali. Another view was held by the recently converted Quraysh merchants of Mecca who had once spurned Muhammad and who now hoped to regain prominence by having one of their representatives succeed the Prophet. But a third group, the early converts to Islam who had suffered with Muhammad in Mecca and participated in the *hijrah* to Medina, preempted the other claimants by naming one of their own, Abu Bakr, as the new head of the community. The other factions accepted Abu Bakr's leadership, but the dispute over the first succession sowed seeds of conflict that have affected Islam throughout its history.

Abu Bakr (632–634) was simply called the successor—*khalif*—anglicized as caliph. Eventually the term *caliph* came to designate the religious and political leader of the Islamic community, and the office became known as the caliphate. Abu Bakr and his three successors, Umar (634–644), Uthman (644–656), and Ali (656–661), are known in Islamic history as the Rashidun (rightly guided) caliphs in recognition of their personal closeness to the Prophet and their presumed adherence to Quranic regulations. Although two of them were assassinated and their reigns were filled with political and social turmoil, Muslims of later and even more troubled times looked back with nostalgia on the era when the four companions of the Prophet launched the movement that thrust the Arabs out of the peninsula and into world history.

Abu Bakr was occupied with restoring Meccan control over tribes that broke away from the community at the death of Muhammad. The next caliph, Umar, recognized the need to direct the raiding instincts of the tribes away from intercommunal conflict and authorized attacks against the southern flanks of Byzantium and Sasanian Iran. Thus began the epoch of the Arab conquests and the building of an Islamic empire.

The speed and extent of the Arab conquests were remarkable. In 637 the Arab forces defeated the imperial Sasanian army at the battle of Qadisiyya, an encounter that was quickly followed by the capture of Ctesiphon and the beginning of the difficult Arab campaign across the Iranian plateau toward the Indian subcontinent. Success against Byzantium was equally swift. The

Arabs captured Damascus in 635, Jerusalem in 638, and in 641 they occupied parts of the rich agricultural province of Egypt. By 670 the western campaign against Byzantine and Berber resistance had reached present-day Tunisia, and in 680 the daring Arab commander Uqba ibn Nafi led a small force from Tunisia through Algeria and Morocco to the Atlantic Ocean. The North African territories were by no means occupied and conquered during ibn Nafi's march to the sea, but he had prepared the way for their eventual incorporation into the Islamic empire. The westward expansion of the Arabs culminated in the conquest of Spain in the first half of the eighth century. Within 100 years of the Prophet's death, Arab forces had reached the Indian subcontinent in the east, and in the west they had occupied Spain and crossed the Pyrenees into France before they were finally halted by the forces of Charles Martel at the battle of Poitiers in 732. In this first wave of conquests, the Sasanian Empire was completely destroyed and its territory absorbed within an Arab-Muslim administration. Byzantium, although it suffered the loss of its core Middle Eastern and North African provinces, retained control of Anatolia and the Balkans and presented a formidable barrier to Muslim expansion until it was overcome by the Ottomans in the fourteenth and fifteenth centuries.

Even more stunning than the speed and extent of the conquests was their durability; with the exception of Spain, which retained an Arab-Islamic presence until the fifteenth century, the areas occupied during the first century of expansion have remained Islamic, if not Arabic, to the present day. In North Africa, as in Egypt and the eastern Mediterranean—the heartlands of Hellenism and early Christianity—and in the long-settled region of Iraq, the Arabic language and the Islamic faith became dominant. Persian language and culture eventually reasserted themselves in Iran, but they were expressed in an Islamic idiom.

The conquests would not have been so swift or so durable without the existence of a combination of social, economic, and religious factors that facilitated the local population's acceptance of the new Arab rulers. First, as we have discussed earlier, monotheistic religions were widely practiced among the peoples in the conquered territories, and the Islamic assertion of monotheism placed it within the existing religious traditions. Second, Islam manifested considerable tolerance toward non-Muslims. The Quran commanded Muslims to protect "people of the Book," that is, Jews and Christians who possessed a revealed scripture. In practice, this toleration was extended to the Zoroastrians of Iran and the Hindus of the Indian subcontinent. Forced conversions played a small part in the Arab conquests, and for at least two centuries the majority of the inhabitants of the Islamic empire were non-Muslims. They were known as *dhimmis,* a term meaning followers of the religions tolerated by law. *Dhimmis* were allowed the freedom to practice their religion and to manage their internal affairs through their own religious officials. However, *dhimmis* were not regarded as the equals of Muslims and were required to pay a special poll tax (*jizyah*); they were prohibited from serving in the military and from wearing certain colors, and their residences and places of worship could not be as large as those of Muslims. Although these and other restrictions constituted a form of discrimination, they represented an unusually tolerant attitude for the era and stood in marked contrast to the practices of the Byzantine Empire.

The taxes imposed by the Arab-Islamic state were less burdensome than those levied by the Byzantine and Sasanian empires. Moreover, the Arab rulers tended to leave existing administrative practices undisturbed and did not interfere with local customs. For the most part, the only lands that were confiscated belonged to the Byzantine and Sasanian royal families or to nobles who had fled and abandoned their estates. Because of these lenient practices, the local population generally preferred Arab to Byzantine or Sasanian rule, and there were occasions when Christians and Jews actively assisted the Arab conquests in Syria and Palestine. Although some of the conquered peoples adopted Islam, the Arabs did not encourage conversions during the first century of their rule. This was partly because the *jizyah* constituted an important source of state revenue and partly because the Arabs, at this early stage in the development of Islam, regarded it as an exclusively Arab religion.

The First Civil War and the End of the Rashidun Caliphate

As the conquests continued to bring more territory under Islamic rule, the second and third caliphs, Umar and Uthman, faced the challenge of devising effective administrations, distributing the new wealth, and satisfying and controlling the independent spirit of the Arab tribes. For despite the change from tribal to communal organization, the Arab tribesmen continued to assert their right to independent action and resisted the efforts of the emerging central government to impose its authority over them. Only gradually over the course of the first two Islamic centuries were most of the tribes settled in cities or on the land.

The question of the succession to the caliphate had been largely ignored in the rush of the early conquests. When Uthman was murdered by mutinous Arab tribesmen in 656, however, the succession issue reemerged. It was resolved only after a civil war that left an enduring schism within the Islamic *ummah*. Ali was chosen to succeed the murdered Uthman. Next to the Prophet himself, Ali is the most revered of the founders of Islam: He was the Prophet's cousin, the husband of the Prophet's daughter Fatima, and one of the most dedicated of the early converts to Islam. Indeed, in some quarters of the *ummah,* the belief existed that Muhammad had intended for Ali to be his immediate successor. By the time he was finally selected as caliph, Ali represented a broad coalition of interests calling for greater equality among all Muslims, both Arab and non-Arab, and for the restoration of the leadership of the community to the house of Muhammad. But Ali's right to the caliphate was contested by Mu'awiyah, the powerful governor of Syria and a member of the same clan as the murdered Uthman.

The forces of the two claimants to the leadership met at the battle of Siffin in 657. Because the results of the encounter were inconclusive, Siffin has been the source of lasting divisiveness within the Islamic community. According to accounts of the battle, Ali's forces were on the verge of victory when Mu'awiyah's men placed Qurans on the tips of their spears and appealed for arbitration based on the Quran, calling out, "Let God decide." Ali agreed, but the arbitration settled nothing, leaving both Ali and Mu'awiyah in the same positions they had held before the fighting began. However, a group of Ali's followers, subsequently known as the Kharijites, withdrew their support because of Ali's acceptance of the arbitration. In the Kharijites' view, Mu'awiyah's challenge to Ali's caliphate was an act of unbelief that classified Mu'awiyah as an infidel and required true believers to wage war against him. But they also believed that Ali's willingness to engage in arbitration was an act that usurped God's rightful role in determining the outcome of the battle and thus made Ali also guilty of unbelief. The Kharijites' combination of "rigorous puritanism and religious fundamentalism" forged them into an uncompromising movement that accepted no middle ground in its interpretation of the Quranic injunction to "command the good and prohibit evil."[2] Although the Kharijite vision of Islam did not achieve political fulfillment in the early Islamic centuries, it remained a vibrant force and has, in the years since 1970, resurfaced as the doctrine of militant Islamic opposition groups in Egypt and other countries.

Because of the defection of the Kharijites and the expansion of Mu'awiyah's power in Syria and Egypt, Ali was never able to establish his uncontested right to the caliphate. He set up a capital in Kufa, one of the Arab garrison cities in lower Iraq, but his position continued to deteriorate, and he was murdered by a Kharijite in 661. Ali's caliphate was short and divisive but far from inconsequential. It came to represent the validity of the legitimist position of authority within the Islamic *ummah,* and, as we will see in later chapters, stood as an enduring symbol of the desire of a substantial minority of Muslims to embrace a communal leader directly descended from the family of the Prophet. Indeed, attachment to the memory of Ali and his family and the tragedy associated with them was to be infused with such passion and vitality that it gave rise to a permanent schism within the Islamic community.

From Arab Exclusivism to Islamic Universalism: The Umayyad and Abbasid Empires

Ali's passing marked the end of the first phase in the development of the Islamic community and the beginning of a new period of imperial expansion and consolidation. Mu'awiyah was recognized as caliph throughout the em-

pire and became the founder of the Umayyad dynasty (661–750). Muᶜawiyah was a pragmatic ruler whose principal concerns were the continued
expansion of Islam, the management of the state's resources, and the consolidation of his dynasty. During his caliphate, the political center of the empire was transferred from Mecca, the small caravan city of its origins, to the
ancient city of Damascus, with all its Byzantine associations. Muᶜawiyah
adopted certain Byzantine administrative practices and employed former
Byzantine officials and craftsmen, initiating the transformation of the Arab
empire into a Byzantine successor state and surrounding the caliphate with
the trappings of monarchy.

Although the conquests continued to bring material wealth to Damascus
under Muᶜawiyah's successors, the Umayyad Empire was troubled by internal dissension. Part of the dissent was caused by the policy of Arab exclu-
sivism adopted by the Umayyad ruling elite. They continued to equate Islam with Arab descent and to administer the empire's fiscal and social affairs
in such a way as to favor the Arabs and to discriminate against the growing
number of non-Arab converts to Islam. In addition, Umayyad efforts to establish firm central authority over the Arab tribes was another source of unrest and generated widespread discontent with the ruling dynasty. The discontent culminated in a revolution that overthrew the Umayyad house in
750 and brought to power a new dynasty, that of the Abbasids.

The office of the caliphate remained with the Abbasids from 750 to 1258.
Under the Abbasids, the heroic age of the conquests gave way to the development of administrative institutions, commercial enterprises, and a legal
system. The bureaucrat, the urban merchant, and the learned judge replaced
the Arab warrior as the favored element in society. The consolidation of the
conquests in the geographical center of a centuries-old admixture of cultural
and religious traditions resulted in a complex interaction between the existing cultures and religions of the Middle East and the dynamic infusion of
energy from Arabia. The new and vibrant Islamic civilization that arose
found its first, but by no means its last, expression in the period of the high
caliphate (750–945) of the Abbasid Empire.

The first 150 years of the Abbasid Empire, represented by such caliphs as
al-Mansur (754–775), Harun al-Rashid (786–809), and al-Maᶜmun
(813–833), were a period of relative political stability, immense economic
prosperity, and increasing universalism within the central Islamic domains.
These conditions, in turn, created the possibilities for the flowering of a rich
and diverse civilization. The Abbasids abandoned the Arab exclusiveness
that had generated so much discontent under the Umayyads. In its place,
they adopted a universalist policy accepting the equality of all Muslims, regardless of their racial origins. This attitude, coupled with the revitalization
of urban life and the expansion of commercial activity, led to a growing cos-
mopolitanism within the empire as converts from among the conquered
peoples participated fully in the economic and political life of the state.

The universalism of the Abbasids was symbolized by yet another transfer of the imperial capital, this time from the predominantly Arab city of Damascus eastward to a newly created city, Baghdad, which the caliph al-Mansur established on the west bank of the Tigris near the former Sasanian capital of Ctesiphon. The change of location brought the Islamic political center into more direct contact with Iranian imperial traditions, with their emphasis on royal absolutism and bureaucratic specialization, and added yet another layer of influences to the Arab and Byzantine experiences of the Islamic state. Abbasid administration was modeled on Sasanian government and employed large numbers of converted Iranians in its increasingly elaborate bureaucratic structure.

Sasanian practices also had an impact on the office of the caliphate. During the era of the Rashidun, the caliphs functioned as first among equals and lived modestly on the model established by Muhammad. Umar, the second caliph, entered the newly captured city of Jerusalem clad in a plain brown robe, and Uthman's assassination in 656 was facilitated by his lack of a bodyguard. This emphasis on simplicity changed under the later Umayyads, who distanced themselves from the population, took pleasure from the riches that flowed into the treasury at Damascus, and became less consultative and more authoritarian. The Abbasid rulers, with their more direct exposure to the Iranian idea of an absolute king of kings, carried the evolution of the caliphate to absolutist monarchy further than any of their predecessors. The Abbasid caliphs lived in luxurious palaces, isolated from all but their most trusted inner circle of courtiers and advisers. They came to identify themselves not simply as successors to the Prophet but as "shadows of God on earth," and they exercised vast powers over their subjects. Thus the Abbasid solution to the problem of political authority was to centralize it and to place it in the hands of an absolute monarch who exercised the powers of both secular king and spiritual head of the Islamic *ummah*. For nearly two centuries following the revolution of 750, this Abbasid formula worked reasonably well and brought to the empire unprecedented prosperity, dazzling intellectual achievement, and general political stability based on the widespread acceptance of the benefits of caliphal absolutism.

But no monarch could maintain absolute control of an empire that stretched from Morocco to India. For a time, the Abbasid caliphs controlled the appointment and recall of governors in all the far-flung provinces of their domains. In the late eighth century, however, North Africa slipped away from Baghdad's authority and became a region of autonomous Islamic states. During the ninth century, independent and often short-lived dynasties rose and fell in various parts of Iran. Yet despite the emergence of new centers of power, the Abbasid caliphs remained the dominant rulers of the Middle East until the tenth century, and the imperial court at Baghdad set a style of royal behavior that was imitated in provincial capitals and breakaway dynasties throughout the vast territories in which Islam had become established.

Conclusion

In the historically short span of time from the Prophet Muhammad's death in 632 to the transfer of the imperial capital from Damascus to Baghdad in the 750s, the Islamic *ummah* had expanded from its Arab origins to embrace a universal world empire. The epoch of the Arab conquests constitutes a decisive period in world history, one that transformed a nomadic desert population organized along tribal lines into the ruling elite of an imperial structure concentrated in the heartlands of classical antiquity. Arabic replaced Greek, Persian, Aramaic, and other established literary traditions as the language of administration and high culture; Islam replaced, though it did not eliminate, Judaism, Christianity, Zoroastrianism, and paganism as the dominant religion in the Middle East. This process of replacement raises important questions. In its interaction with the existing literary, religious, and administrative traditions of Byzantium and Iran, how could the Islam of the revelations, the Islam of the Prophet's caravan city of Mecca, survive as a guide to administrative, economic, and social practices? How could the peoples living within the territories of the extensive Arab conquests, with their long-established traditions, be organized to obey the commands on proper human behavior that God revealed to a Meccan merchant in seventh-century Arabia? In developing answers to these questions, or simply in developing certain patterns of living and worship, Muslims affirmed their belief in the validity of Muhammad's mission by creating a civilization centered on the revelations contained in the Quran.

Notes

1. A. J. Arberry, *The Koran Interpreted* (New York, 1955). All subsequent Quranic citations are from this translation.
2. John L. Esposito, *Islam: The Straight Path* (New York, 1988), pp. 47–48.

The Development of | 2
Islamic Civilization to
the Fifteenth Century | ⟨|⟩ ⟨|⟩

An understanding of the modern Middle East depends on familiarity with the main historical patterns and principal social and religious institutions that developed in the period between the consolidation of the Abbasid Empire in the eighth century and the rise of the Ottoman and Safavid empires in the fifteenth century. This chapter presents those patterns and institutions in a highly selective fashion, focusing on the processes that enabled Islam to become an enduring global civilization rather than on wars, famines, and periods of economic recession and civil strife, though they, too, were part of the legacy of these centuries.

Patterns of Islamic History

Islamic history is sometimes treated as the rise and decline of the Abbasid Empire. In this version of the Islamic past, the chronological signposts are presented in the following manner: During the years from 750 to 945, an absolutist empire centered in Baghdad experienced a period of economic growth, cultural richness, and political stability that made it the dominant world power of the era. In 945 an Iranian military dynasty, the Buyids, took over temporal power in Baghdad, reducing the caliph to a figurehead and ensuring that the Iranian ruler exercised decisionmaking authority in the Abbasid Empire. According to this interpretation, the weaknesses that beset the Abbasids in the late tenth century caused Islam to enter into a long period of political and cultural decline that was intensified by the empire's destruction in 1258 and continued until the consolidation of the Ottoman Empire in the fifteenth and early sixteenth centuries.

Although the dates in the above account are correct, this interpretation, with its exclusive focus on the Abbasid Empire and its linking of the decline of that empire with the decline of Islam, is misleading. Even when the Abbasids were at the peak of their power, other Islamic dynasties and cultures were being formed. Their achievements were as important for the development of universal Islam as were those of the Abbasids. In a recent attempt to conceptualize the stages of Islamic history, Marilyn Waldman has suggested that rather than viewing the Abbasid Empire as the core around which a series of lesser Islamic states revolved, we should instead think in terms of a group of regional Islamic empires, each of which developed a particular synthesis of local and Islamic practices.[1] Waldman's perspective enables us to see that at the same time that Baghdad flourished, so, too, did distinctive and wealthy royal courts in Delhi, Ghazna, Cairo, Córdoba, and other regions. There was no single Islamic polity or culture that was tied to the fate of the Abbasids in Baghdad. The regional empires (or regional dynasties, as some prefer to call them) expanded and enriched Islamic traditions in areas that lay outside the Abbasid domains. Thus, although the fall of the Abbasid Empire in 1258 resulted in considerable political fragmentation, it did not lead to a "dark age" of Islamic culture, nor did it create a political vacuum in the central Islamic lands.

This is not to deny the important role played by Baghdad and other leading cities of the Abbasid Empire in nurturing and disseminating Islamic legal, intellectual, political, and religious traditions. However, ideas that originated in Baghdad were often received and applied somewhat differently in the provincial capitals or in the cities of the other regional empires. Scholars who emphasize the significance of regional Islamic empires seek to demonstrate the existence of Islamic pluralism across time and space. Islamic societies were dynamic and diverse, not static and monolithic; they included areas as different as India and Syria, Egypt and Spain. It should again be stressed that the fate of the Abbasid Empire itself was not fully reflective of the fate of Islam in the period from roughly A.D. 1000 to 1500. This is not to suggest that the late and post-Abbasid eras were without political turmoil or economic problems but rather that the durability of Islam as the first truly global civilization demonstrates the existence of a constant process of renewal from one Islamic region to another. Because Islam was universal, a period of stagnation in one segment of the *ummah* might be reversed by an infusion of intellectual, economic, or military energy from another.

There are several examples of this process. In 969 the Shiᶜa Fatimid dynasty based in Tunisia seized Egypt from its Abbasid governor and transformed it into a dynamic Mediterranean empire that challenged the Abbasid caliphs for moral, political, and economic supremacy in the very heartlands of Islam. The Fatimids founded Cairo and ruled Egypt, Sicily, and much of North Africa for 200 years until their ruling house was weakened by internal schisms and replaced by a new dynasty founded by the Kurdish ruler Saladin. To take another example, during a critical period in the late eleventh and early twelfth centuries after the Christian kingdoms of northern Spain had occupied Toledo and were poised to retake the rest of the Iberian Peninsula from its divided Muslim princes, the rulers of two resurgent Islamic dynasties based in Morocco sent their military forces across the Strait of Gibraltar. Their successive interventions halted the Christian advance and were instrumental in assuring Islamic dominance in southern Spain for another two centuries. One final example of the role of a regional empire in preserving Islamic tradition focuses again on Egypt. In 1258 the Mongol forces of Hülagü sacked Baghdad and killed the last Abbasid caliph. They then advanced into Syria, where they were defeated in 1260 at the important battle of Ayn Jalut by the forces of yet another new Egyptian-based Islamic empire, the Mamluks. These and other similar instances demonstrate that in various quarters of the Islamic world a constant process of renewal and preservation was taking place. There is no question that the destruction of the Abbasid Empire and the death of the last caliph were significant historical events, but we should not conclude that they marked the decline of Islam. The Abbasid successor states and the Islamic regional empires preserved and enriched Islamic cultural and religious traditions in the centuries after the sack of Baghdad.

The Creation and Uses of Wealth

The advent of the Abbasid Empire ushered in an era of economic prosperity that led to a revival of urban life and the expansion of trade and industry not only within the Abbasid domains but throughout the world of Islam. Baghdad, nourished by the produce of the carefully controlled irrigation systems of the lower Tigris-Euphrates, grew into a huge cosmopolitan city with a population that may have reached 1 million inhabitants in the ninth century. Referred to by contemporaries as the navel of the universe, the Abbasid capital was the hub of a vast trading network that linked it to China, India, Africa, and the entire Mediterranean region (see Map 2.1). In bringing these diverse regions into sustained commercial contact with one another, Islamic merchants created an international market in which the products of India and Southeast Asia were exchanged for the goods of Spain and the Mediterranean lands. Cities became centers of production and consumption, and urban life flourished in bustling ports like Fustat, Almería in Spain, and Basra, the home of Sindbad the Sailor in the tales of the *1,001 Nights*. The long-distance caravan trade revived existing inland cities such as Damascus and Aleppo and generated tremendous population and commercial growth in Marv, Samarkand, and Bukhara, the eastern cities that acted as way stations along the Silk Route to China. Merchants exploited the commercial opportunities of the expanding international marketplace to acquire huge fortunes. Their wealth gave them status and enabled them to play a prominent role in shaping the contours of Islamic society as it emerged during this period.

Increased agricultural production fostered the rise of large urban centers and contributed to the extraordinary prosperity that characterized the Islamic empires of the eighth through twelfth centuries. The growth in agri-

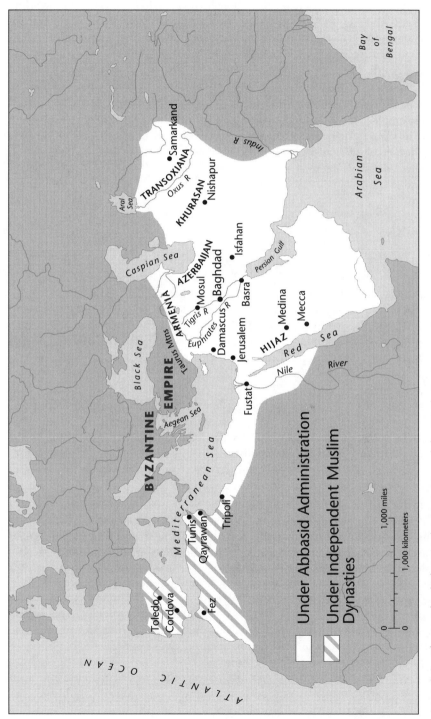

Under Abbasid Administration

Under Independent Muslim Dynasties

1,000 miles

1,000 kilometers

Map 2.1 The Lands of Islam at the Beginning of the Ninth Century

culture was made possible by the transfer of crops from India to the Middle East and the Mediterranean basin, a process that created the most significant agricultural revolution in world history between the adoption of sedentary agriculture and the European discovery of the Americas. Following the Arab conquest of Sind (Pakistan) in the early eighth century, crops from the subtropical climate of India were transported to the Fertile Crescent, Egypt, Africa, and Islamic Spain. In all of these regions, the newly introduced crops became such staples that we tend to think of them as having been part of the cultivated landscape since classical antiquity. But such food crops as rice, sugarcane, lemons, limes, bananas, date palms, spinach, and eggplant as well as the industrial crop cotton were all brought by the Arabs from India to Iraq and then disseminated across North Africa to Spain and to other parts of Europe.

The development of the new crops demanded a major reorientation in the rhythm of peasant life and contributed to significant advances in agricultural methods. In the pre-Islamic Middle East and North Africa, winter was the principal growing season; in the hot, dry summers, fields lay fallow. With the introduction of crops grown in India's hot, subtropical climate, summer became an additional growing season in the Middle East, and the food supply increased dramatically. Peasant cultivators and agricultural laborers had to work the year round; moreover, because the new crops were adapted to the high rainfalls of India, their survival in the drier climates of western Asia and northern Africa depended on the expansion of existing irrigation systems, improvements in hydrological technology, and constant maintenance by the central government. Through their conquests and settlement of diverse climatic regions and the establishment of a trading network connecting those regions, the Arabs, a people whose immediate pre-Islamic existence was not primarily associated with sedentary agriculture, acted as the catalysts for an agricultural revolution that had an impact on the clothes people wore, the foods they consumed, and the ways in which the majority of them organized their working lives.

The wealth generated from the produce of the land and the profits of commerce enabled Abbasid high society to enjoy a refined style of living surrounded by luxuries of regional and distant origin. The royal family established a pattern of patronage that benefited artisans, physicians, and writers, especially Arabic poets. This pattern was imitated by rich merchants and high-ranking functionaries in both Baghdad and the provincial capitals. It contributed to the widespread florescence of a rich literary and scientific culture and imprinted on a certain segment of Islamic society the notion that to be great and powerful involved more than having an army; it also meant having a court of poets, scholars, and physicians. In the centuries to come, local rulers would nurture literature and learning even as they sought political separation from the Abbasid caliph, showing that their aspirations for power were firmly grounded in the high Islamic cultural tradition. Sultan Mahmud (998–1030), head of the Ghaznavid Empire (977–1186) based in Afghanistan, was one such patron of the arts and sciences. The son of a slave and only the second ruler of his dynasty, he tried to establish his credentials as a worthy Muslim ruler by surrounding himself with poets and scholars. His court at Ghazna became one of the principal intellectual centers of the era. That Mahmud may have used force to bring some of the writers to Ghazna and that he certainly held others there against their will shows the importance he attached to patronage as a factor in his right to rule.

The intellectual adventure of high Islamic society was not limited to poetry and the decorative arts. Ideas, like material goods, were transported back and forth along the caravan routes and sea-lanes, and noted scholars were recruited by caliphs and princes alike to adorn their courts. Muslim mathematicians, working within the Indian and Persian traditions, made lasting contributions to algebra (from the Arabic word *al-jabr*) and trigonometry. Muslim astronomers, physicians, and chemists produced works that influenced the development of the natural sciences in European as well as Muslim intellectual circles. The patronage of the Abbasid caliph al-Maʿmun (813–833) helped launch the movement that recovered the works of the noted Greek philosophers and physicians, among them Aristotle, Plato, and Galen, and translated them from Greek into Arabic in state-sponsored translation academies. The presence of the classical Greek tradition in Arabic editions compelled Muslim scholars to grapple with a human-centered philosophical tradition and produced two of the most noted Aristotelian commentators of the middle ages, Ibn Sina (Avicenna in Latin; 980–1037), a physician employed in a number of royal courts in eastern Iran, and Ibn Rushd (Averroës in Latin; 1126–1198), a Muslim jurist from Córdoba. The appearance of Arabic editions of Aristotle in regions as distant from one another as Spain and eastern Iran is evidence of the mobility of ideas within the global civilization of Islam. During the twelfth and thirteenth centuries, the Christian rulers of northern Spain encouraged the translation of the Arabic editions of the Greek philosophers into Latin. Through this channel of transmission, the Greek legacy entered the consciousness of western Europe. The first European commentaries on Plato and Aristotle were not based on Greek texts but on Latin translations of earlier Arabic translations undertaken in Baghdad and other eastern centers.

The diffusion of both secular ideas and Islamic religious doctrine was facilitated by the widespread manufacture and use of paper in the Islamic territories. Paper manufacturing is generally believed to have originated in China in the first century B.C. It entered the world of Islam following an Arab victory over a Chinese force east of the Aral Sea in 751. Among the prisoners taken in the clash were some Chinese papermakers whose skills were transmitted to Muslim craftsmen. Paper was introduced to Baghdad in the late eighth century and made its appearance in Spain by 900 at a time when Western societies still depended on papyrus and parchment. Within another century, the manufacture of paper had spread across the world of Islam, with centers of production located in Samarkand in Central Asia and Valencia in Spain.

From the eighth century onward, Islam became a global civilization in which knowledge, technology, and artistic tastes were transported back and forth across a vast domain. Because of the very diversity and extent of the territories in which Islam became a prominent religious force, a variety of regional practices and interpretations imparted special characteristics to Islamic cultures in different parts of the world. As noted in the introduction to this chapter, no single political or cultural unit embraced the totality of Islam. Some scholars now point to the existence of several Islams coexisting in vibrant diversity yet united in acceptance of the message of the Quran and the core requirements of ritual. It is to those that we now turn.

Islamic Rituals and Institutions

Our account of the Arab conquests and the development of a global Islamic civilization may appear to be a history of secular achievements. But what was the impact of the divine revelations in shaping state and society during these early centuries? It is through an examination of the distinctly Islamic influence on the formation of social and cultural norms that we can understand the emergence of a dynamic and durable Islamic perspective that was able to survive the rise and fall of dynasties.

The view, often expressed in the West, that the organization of Islamic social and political life is based solely on the revelations contained in the Quran is incorrect and ignores the complex historical evolution of Islam. From the very first conquests under the Rashidun caliphs and continuing on through the Abbasids, the emerging class of Islamic scholars made a sustained effort to accommodate the Quranic revelations to the traditions of the long-established cultures over which the caliphs came to rule. This effort at synthesis led to the elaboration of theology and to the development of a comprehensive legal system based on the Quran but not restricted to it. At the popular level, the establishment of a universally accepted set of rituals provided Muslims with a sense of common identity and gave an Islamic dimension to their daily lives. Yet even as Islamic scholars sought to unify doctrine and ritual, the faith continued to attract a great diversity of peoples who brought to the emerging Islamic tradition a rich variety of cultural backgrounds and religious experiences. This interplay between unity and diversity was a constant feature of formative Islam; the faith was flexible enough to embrace new practices and develop regional variations yet rigorous enough to preserve its core identity.

The Five Pillars of Faith

Islamic ritual is the institutionalized form through which all believers submit themselves to God and acknowledge his omnipotence. Although a discussion of ritual cannot convey to an outsider the true meaning of Islam for a practicing Muslim, it can provide insight into the exacting demands and the communal emphasis of Islamic worship. This worship is based on the five pillars of faith:

Proclamation of Faith (*Shahadah*). With the words "I attest that there is only one God and Muhammad is his Prophet," Muslims affirm their faith in Islam. As noted previously, the basic religious principle of Islam is monotheism. The deity of the Quran is an all-powerful, righteous God of judgment whose commands are not to be questioned. The second element of the faith is the acceptance of Muhammad's role as the final Prophet of God. According to the Quran, Muhammad was not only the transmitter of the divine message, he was designated as the Seal of the Prophets, the last in the long line of human beings who had received and transmitted God's word. The Quran recognizes the missions of earlier prophets but contends that the commands they conveyed have been forgotten. Islam was therefore portrayed not as a new religion but as the revival of the true word of God that had been revealed to Abraham and to other prophets throughout the course of human history. Over time, human beings in their weakness either ignored or perverted the revelations of these prophets. Through Muhammad, the all-merciful God for one last time revealed his will to his human creations. There would be no future opportunities to receive God's plan; there would be no prophets after Muhammad. God's designation of an Arab prophet and the Arabic language as the vehicles for his final revelation was of the utmost significance for the Arabs' sense of themselves and their role in human history.

Prayer (*Salat*). Muslims are instructed to perform the ritual prayer five times daily at intervals from dawn to sunset. This is not a casual communication with God but a rigorously prescribed set of movements and recitations during which believers face in the direction of the holy Kaʿba in Mecca and acknowledge total submission to God by touching their foreheads to the ground. The daily prayers are most often performed in the workplace or the home. The Muslim day of communal worship is Friday, and the noon prayer on that day is the moment when the members of the *ummah* gather in the large congregational mosques.

Fasting (*Sawm*). The Quran commands all adult Muslims whose health permits to abstain from food, drink, and sexual activity from dawn to dusk during the month of Ramadan, the month in which Muhammad received the first revelations. Fasting is a time of atonement and a reminder, through abstention, of God's generosity in providing for his human creations.

The Pilgrimage to Mecca (*Hajj*). Muhammad incorporated the Ka'ba, the existing shrine of Mecca, into Islam and made it the key sanctuary of the new faith, associating its origins with the figure of Abraham. According to the Quran, Muslims should make the pilgrimage to Mecca and its shrine at least once in their lives, though the duty is most explicitly directed at those who can afford the journey and whose working lives will not be unduly disrupted by the lengthy travel time required. As with prayer, the rites of pilgrimage are institutionalized; the ceremony occurs during a certain month and involves specific obligations. Throughout the centuries, the pilgrimage has served as a reminder to Muslims the world over of their shared faith. The duty of the caliph and the custodian of the holy cities to keep the pilgrimage route safe has been one of the most sacred administrative trusts.

Alms (*Zakat*). This duty is part of the concept of charity to the less fortunate that appears frequently in the revelations. *Zakat* is an annual wealth tax all Muslims must pay. Although the Quran does not specify the amount of the *zakat,* it developed in practice as 2.5 percent of a person's accumulated wealth and assets and was collected by the central treasury.

Jihad

The obligation of *jihad,* although not a formal part of ritual, constitutes an integral component of Islamic doctrine. The primary meaning of *jihad* is armed struggle against non-Muslims for the purpose of expanding or defending the territory under Muslim rule. The word has a broader meaning than warfare, however, and can refer to an individual's inner struggle against sinful inclinations or to an exceptional effort for the good of the Islamic community. Certain modern Muslim writers have thus emphasized the need to internalize *jihad* in order to achieve religious reform. Yet *jihad* has also been invoked by late twentieth-century movements as an instrument of political protest. These movements have defined the incumbent regimes, whether in Egypt or elsewhere, as irreligious and have claimed that it is therefore necessary to overthrow them by means of a popular *jihad. Jihad* is, then, a nuanced doctrine, and simply to render it as "holy war" is incorrect and should be avoided.

The *Shari'ah:* The Integration of Religion and Society

The five pillars constitute the essential framework of Muslim worship. But the Quranic revelations were intended to direct *all* the affairs of the *ummah,* including relations among human beings. As the Islamic state expanded into a world empire, its leaders encountered new situations and adopted administrative practices not found in the Quran. How was the Quran, revealed in Mecca and Medina and responsive to the needs of those small Arabian cities, to be employed as the code of conduct for an empire stretching from Spain to Central Asia? Conversely, if the reason for the existence of the Islamic *ummah* was to ensure that human society conducted itself according to the commands of God, how could the community justify the use of practices not found in the Quran?

These questions began to receive concentrated attention with the emergence of learned theologians and Quranic experts during the late Umayyad and early Abbasid periods. Muslim scholars were concerned about the existence of differing practices within the *ummah;* they recognized that this diversity threatened the notion of Islam as a single community united by its adherence to the will of one God. From the eighth through the tenth centuries, much of the intellectual energy of Muslim thinkers was directed toward this issue, with the aim of devising a uniform legal system that would recognize the requirements of imperial administration and the value of local customs while remaining true to the concept of a community guided by divine revelation. The result of these efforts was the compilation of the *shari͑ah,* the all-embracing sacred law of the Islamic community. The *shari͑ah* is not a single code of law; rather, it consists of four different sources to which legal experts may refer when assessing the propriety of human actions. The first source is, of course, the Quran. But the Quran, though it sets forth clear moral guidelines and precise instructions on matters of marriage, divorce, and inheritance, does not address all of the practical legal issues that might arise in society. In order to fill in details not directly addressed in the Quran, Muslim jurists came to a general consensus on the permissibility of employing three additional sources of law.

The first and most important of them is the tradition of the Prophet, known as *sunnah.* Muslim scholars agreed that since God had chosen Muhammad to receive the final revelation, he must have possessed exemplary human qualities. Therefore, the words and actions of Muhammad in his daily life were taken as divinely approved guides for human conduct. This source of law became codified as scholars sifted through the many stories (*hadith*) about Muhammad that were in general circulation. Those accounts which could be verified on the basis of the reliability of the original eyewitness and of the individuals who transmitted them over the years were accepted as genuine and were used by legal experts in their assessment of proper conduct.

The second additional source of law is analogy (*qiyas*). When jurists encountered a situation for which there was no direct precedent in the Quran or *hadith* literature, they assessed it on the basis of principles previously accepted for a similar situation. The third supplementary source is the consensus of the community (*ijma*). As consensus developed in practice, it referred to decisions made by the leading scholars and jurists of the community. When they collectively agreed that certain practices were forbidden or permitted, their decisions became part of the *shariʿah*. The exercise of applying informed human reasoning to points not covered in the Quran was known as *ijtihad;* it represented the right of learned scholars to interpret the intent of God's revelations. But by the tenth century, the scholarly consensus was that the principles and details of Islamic law had been fully determined and *ijtihad* was therefore no longer desirable. Henceforth Muslim jurists could not interpret points of law but were constrained to rely on the established legal texts. The closing of the gate of *ijtihad,* as it was known, was based on the proposition that the preservation of existing tradition was preferable to the dangers inherent in the possibilities of permitting multiple and variant interpretations to gain circulation. Although *ijtihad* was still applied in practice and Islamic law continued to evolve after the tenth century, the agreement to limit the application of human reason had the effect of giving more weight in legal matters to tradition than to innovation. Some Muslim thinkers of the nineteenth and twentieth centuries have called for reopening the gate of *ijtihad* as a way of reconciling the conflicting demands of tradition and change.

It is important to recognize that the three supplementary sources of law, even though they involve an element of human reasoning, are based on the principles of the Quran and thus on the will of God. The *shariʿah* is divine law intended to regulate all human activities and to empower Muslim jurists to assess the legality of the actions of individuals on the basis of their compliance with God's commands.

The compilation of the *shariʿah* was accompanied by the parallel elaboration of a practical system of justice with courts, rules of evidence, and properly trained officials. The judges (*qadi*s) who presided over the *shariʿah* courts were appointed by the state, and their application of the sacred law strengthened *shariʿah*-based norms within society. The office of *qadi* became so essential a component of Islamic societies that it virtually defined them as Islamic. Where there was a *qadi,* there was the presence of Islamic law.

The Role of the Ulama

It is often asserted that there is no priesthood in Islam. To the extent that there are no human intermediaries between the individual believer and God, the statement is correct. However, for a religion to survive and retain its vitality, there must exist individuals trained in doctrine and prepared to transmit it. In Islamic society this group is known as the ulama (literally, those who know). Because of the wide scope that Islam plays in the regulation of human affairs, the ulama perform a variety of functions within Islamic society. Since the governing law is God's law, the scholars who compiled the *shari͑ah,* the judges who applied it in the Islamic courts, and the legal experts who advised the judges were considered part of the ulama establishment; and since the most important form of knowledge was knowledge of religion, the teachers in the mosque schools and universities, too, were members of the ulama, as were the mosque preachers and the prayer leaders. This broadly based group of teachers, religious scholars, and legal functionaries occupied a central position in Islamic society. They were the guardians of the high scholarly tradition, the formulators of doctrine, the compilers of the *shari͑ah,* and the transmitters of religious knowledge.

As the ulama emerged as a defined group during Umayyad and early Abbasid times, they acquired their training through the normal channels of the decentralized mosque schools. But in the eleventh century the central government in Baghdad established a formal system of higher education designed to ensure uniformity among the ulama. The schools of instruction, called *madrasah*s, offered standardized training in Arabic, Islamic jurisprudence, Quranic exegesis, and the like. One result of this educational effort was to mold the ulama into a class committed to a standard orthodox vision of Islam and to the state that promised to uphold it. In addition, the spread of the *madrasah* system from Baghdad to other Islamic centers served to provide the ulama with a relatively standard form of training and thus contributed to the maintenance of a certain unity in the Islamic scholarly tradition.

Sufism

The learned Islamic tradition represented by the ulama, though providing a measure of uniformity to law and doctrine, did not necessarily fulfill popular religious needs. The Arab conquests brought peoples of such diverse local cultures and religious experiences into the *ummah* that a mingling of existing forms of worship with Islamic ritual was to be expected. One of the strengths of formative Islam was the recognition that different manifestations of popular piety would have to be tolerated within the *ummah.* The official ulama establishment at first resisted and then accepted the existence of popular religious practices. However, the ulama persisted in their attempts to keep such practices within an Islamic frame of reference.

Sufism, or Islamic mysticism, embodies a rich variety of religious experiences. It began as an ascetic movement among individuals who opposed the worldliness and materialism of the Umayyad court in Damascus. Believing that the Umayyads had abandoned the simple style of living practiced by the Prophet and the Rashidun caliphs, the early Sufis renounced worldly goods and lived as mendicants, dedicating themselves to prayer and meditation in emulation of the Prophet. During the ninth century Sufism evolved into a devotional movement centered on the love of God. Sufi worship acquired ecstatic characteristics, and its practices spread among the population in the central Islamic lands. In place of the formal intellectualism of the ulama, Sufism represented emotional religious experience, an attempt to attain closer communion with God; in the Islamic context, this meant to come as close to God as Muhammad had done.

The development of Sufism followed a general pattern: Groups of devotees would gather around a local religious figure whose stature was based on his or her ability to attain communion with God through special ritual practices that might include breathing exercises, the chanting of phrases from the Quran, or physical movements such as rhythmic dancing, all of which were intended to put the participant in a state to reach out to God. In the twelfth and thirteenth centuries, groups of Sufis who practiced the same ritual and followed the same master formed themselves into structured brotherhoods (*tariqah*s). Although most brotherhood organizations were local, several established regional branches, and a few managed to set up networks throughout the world of Islam. In many locales the brotherhoods became the centers of communal volunteer activities, distributing food to the poor, organizing relief in times of famine or illness, and in general serving as a focal point of social as well as religious life. For the majority of Muslims, spiritual fulfillment was found in the Sufi experience.

As Islam spread across Asia and into Africa, Sufi rituals acquired greater variety and caused concern within the ulama over the adoption of devotional practices that departed from what was prescribed in the Quran. Yet despite ongoing tension between the rigidity of doctrinal Islam and the fluidity of Sufi practices, each side accepted the other as necessary. Because Sufism attracted mass conversions to Islam, the ulama tolerated a variety of Sufi rituals. For their part, the Sufi orders were not opposed to the doctrinaire Islam of the ulama but saw the need for the kind of emotive dimension of the Islamic experience that Sufism offered. As the *shariʿah* bound society together under a uniform legal system, the brotherhoods functioned as a structured subsystem in which diverse local practices found an outlet.

The Status of Women in the Quran

As with other features of Islam during its formative centuries, the social and legal status of women underwent considerable change. Moreover, women's roles in society differed depending on the social class to which they belonged and the region of the Islamic world in which they lived. Although there were many variables shaping the roles of women throughout Islamic history, the Quran set forth guidelines that were intended to improve their status in seventh-century Arabia.

The Quranic reforms concentrated on the areas of marriage, divorce, and inheritance. In pre-Islamic Arabia, women were sold to their husbands by their family or tribe in exchange for a dowry. The Quran prohibited this practice by making the dowry payable to the bride alone, not to her family, thus giving women the legal right to own material wealth. In addition, the wife was allowed to keep the dowry even if the marriage ended in divorce. Another marriage reform was contained in the Quranic injunction that restricted to four the number of wives a man could have and in the admonition that if a husband feared he could not treat each of his wives equally, he should marry only one. This proclamation is often misunderstood because it is not placed in historical context. Polygamy was unlimited in pre-Islamic Arabia, and the Quranic prohibition against taking more than four wives was indeed a reform.

Prior to the advent of Islam, divorce was a completely unregulated male prerogative among the Arabs of the peninsula. In a statement attributed to Muhammad, the Prophet declared that "of all the permitted things, divorce is the most abominable with God," and the Quran introduced modest controls on the practice.[2] In order to provide an opportunity for reconciliation between estranged spouses, the Quran legislated a waiting period of three months between separation and divorce. During this period, the husband was required to provide maintenance for his wife. The waiting period also served to determine whether or not the wife was pregnant; if she was, the husband was responsible for maintaining the mother and child for two years, even though the divorce was finalized. Quranic legislation managed to curtail the unbridled rights of husbands to divorce their wives, but husbands were still able to repudiate their wives without stating a cause, a practice that sustained male domination in marriages. Women, who had no divorce rights in pre-Islamic times, did acquire them through the *shari⁴ah*. However, a wife's ability to initiate divorce remained limited and involved far more complex legal processes than prevailed for husbands.

In the realm of inheritance, the regulations of the Quran instituted major advances for women. Whereas before Islam women were completely excluded from inheriting, the Quran decreed that wives, daughters, sisters, and grandmothers were entitled to fixed shares of the deceased's estate. To be sure, the proportion of the estate assigned to females was less than that to which males were entitled, but the very act of granting women legal status as inheritors represented a profound change from existing Arab practices. Women were acknowledged as having economic rights and were therefore given legal status within the community of Islam.

Notwithstanding the Quran's reformist attitude toward gender relationships, the divine revelations did not accord women equal status with men. For example, the Quran stipulated that if two men were not available to witness the drawing up of a debt contract, then the witnesses should consist of one man and two women so that "if one of the two women errs, the other will remind her" (Sura 2). Similarly, the Quran stated that "men are the managers of the affairs of women for that God has preferred in bounty one of them over another" (Sura 4). And as the expansion of Islam brought the

Arabs into contact with other cultures and required them to adapt to urban life, the reformist tendencies of the Quran were abandoned. In the regulations of the *shariʿah* as well as in the customs of everyday life, the status of women declined.

The custom of veiling, which became common practice among urban Muslim women, illustrates how Quranic prescriptions could be applied in ways that might not have been intended. The Quran stipulates that women—and men—should dress modestly and comport themselves discreetly, but it does not require women to veil themselves. Veiling was introduced after the Arab conquests of Byzantium and Iran, societies in which middle- and upper-class women wore veils to distinguish themselves from the lower classes. The Arabs adopted veiling, and the Muslim jurists, using the Quranic passages on modesty, sanctioned the practice. In the Islamic societies of the Middle East, veiling gradually led to the segregation of women even to the point of excluding them from the communal prayer gatherings.

Two Versions of Leadership:
Sunni Caliph and Shiʿa Imam

The Islamic community is divided into two major branches, Sunnis and Shiʿas (or Shiʿites). The fundamental difference between them is over who should hold the political leadership of the Islamic community and what the religious dimension of that leadership should be. Sunni Muslims accept the legality of the selection of the Rashidun caliphs and their successors, the Umayyads and the Abbasids. They acknowledge the caliphs as mortal beings with no divine powers. Thus, although the caliphs represented the religious leadership of the community, their authority was temporal, and they left matters of doctrine and jurisprudence to the ulama. The caliphs were responsible for upholding the *shariʿah* and ensuring that opportunities for the fulfillment of an Islamic way of life prevailed within the community. The term *Sunni* is derived from the word *sunnah,* meaning tradition or custom, and is used in this context to refer to those Muslims who followed the custom of the community. Sunnis constitute the vast majority of Muslims in the world and are sometimes designated as orthodox Muslims, though that definition is misleading.

The Shiʿas contend that with the exception of Ali and his descendants, all of the caliphs were usurpers. They also hold a much different view than the Sunnis of the religious functions the leader of the community is empowered to exercise. Although Shiʿa doctrine was elaborated over the course of several centuries, the core of the Sunni-Shiʿa split originated in the years immediately following the death of the Prophet Muhammad.

As discussed in Chapter 1, disputes over the succession to the caliphate led to a Muslim civil war that pitted the supporters of Ali, the Prophet's cousin and son-in-law, against the forces of Muʿawiyah, the founder of the

Umayyad dynasty. Although the civil war produced no clear victor, Ali's murder in 661 enabled Mu'awiyah to secure his claim to the caliphate and to make certain that his son, Yazid, succeeded him. During the first year of Yazid's reign (680), the *shi'a* (partisans) of Ali persuaded Ali's son, Husayn, to lead a rebellion against the Umayyads. In the Shi'a version of the history of this episode, Husayn was motivated by a desire to reverse the secularizing and materialist tendencies of the Umayyads and to redirect the community along the path that Muhammad had prescribed for it. But the popular support Husayn had been promised failed to materialize, and in 680 the grandson of the Prophet and his small band of followers were killed by Umayyad forces at the town of Karbala in Iraq.

This was a seminal event in the development of Shi'ism: Shi'as viewed Husayn's rebellion as a protest against Umayyad tyranny, and his death took on the aura of martyrdom. Karbala developed into the holiest shrine of Shi'ism, and the annual rites of mourning for Husayn at that site became the most important religious ceremony in the Shi'a calendar. From a doctrinal perspective, Husayn's death became a symbol of the suffering to which the forces of oppression had subjected the Prophet's family and the usurpation of that family's right to rule. Husayn's martyrdom thus solidified the Shi'as' belief that the individuals most qualified to hold supreme political authority over the Islamic community were the descendants of the Prophet through the line of Ali and his wife, Fatima, the Prophet's daughter. The Shi'as hold that Muhammad had selected Ali as his successor and that each of the Shi'a leaders (Imams) since that time had designated his successor before his death. This process was continuous from Ali, regarded as the first Imam, to the twelfth Imam, who (as is explained below) has been ascribed a major part in Shi'a Islam.

As Shi'a doctrine evolved in the decades after Husayn's martyrdom, it accorded the Imams a special religious role that the Sunni caliphs did not have. Shi'ism maintains that Muhammad was granted divine inspiration that he in turn transmitted to Ali and that was then passed to the designated Imams after him. Even though Sunni dominance prevented these Imams from exercising political authority, Shi'as consider them the vessels through which God provided his uninterrupted guidance to human society. The Shi'a Imams are regarded as having been divinely inspired; they possessed esoteric knowledge not granted to other humans, including knowledge of the hidden meanings of the Quran, and were therefore able to offer infallible pronouncements on religious law and to provide interpretations that took into consideration changing circumstances.

Shi'a doctrine took on added complexity, and added importance for the history of the modern Middle East, by the way it interpreted events involving the twelfth Imam, Muhammad al-Mahdi. According to the majority Shi'a position, sometimes called Twelver Shi'ism, the twelfth Imam entered into a condition of occultation in the year 874. He disappeared but did not die; he was—and, eleven centuries later, remains—concealed by God. At some point before the Day of Judgment, he will return as the Mahdi, the expected one, and will fill the earth with justice.

Shiʿa doctrine accords al-Mahdi the status of the Hidden Imam who, because he is still alive, continues to exercise control over human affairs. However, this notion posed both political and religious problems for the Shiʿa community. How was the community to be guided in the absence of the Hidden Imam? How was his divine inspiration to be communicated to his followers? Chapter 6 examines the process by which the Shiʿa ulama in Iran established their claim to represent the Hidden Imam, a claim that had important consequences for the shaping of modern Iranian society.

The followers of another version of Shiʿism, known as Ismaʿilis or Seveners, differ from the Twelvers in their interpretation of the line of succession between the seventh and eighth Imams. They contend that the imamate has continued uninterrupted to the present day, and they follow the Aga Khan as their infallible Imam.

For most of the Islamic centuries up to 1500, the Shiʿas did not have states of their own and existed under Sunni authority. In the tenth century, however, Shiʿa political power flourished with the formation of the Ismaʿili Fatimid dynasty (969–1171) in Egypt, the establishment of an imamate in Yemen, and the domination of the Abbasid Empire by Twelver military rulers. Yet the Shiʿism of the ruling houses was not adopted by the populations at large, and when the Fatimid dynasty collapsed and the Buyid military dynasty was replaced in Baghdad (1055), the majority of the inhabitants of Egypt and the western Abbasid Empire were still Sunnis and welcomed the restoration of Sunni rule.

The Middle East from the Eleventh to the Fifteenth Centuries: An Overview

During the eleventh century, military power and the ruling authority that went with it passed from Arabs to Turks in the central Islamic lands. Turkish pastoral nomads from Asia had been in contact with Islam from the early period of the Arab conquests, and Turks had served as professional soldiers in the armies of various Abbasid caliphs. Several of the Turkish tribes on the frontier of settlement along the Oxus River had adopted Sunni Islam; when they eventually entered the central Islamic territories they did so as defenders of the faith, not as agents of its destruction.

By the middle of the eleventh century, a confederation of Turkish tribes known as the Seljuks had established domination over Iran, and in 1055 the Abbasid caliph invited the Seljuk leader to assume administrative and military authority in Baghdad. The Turkish Seljuks became the lieutenants of the caliph and the defenders of the high Islamic tradition. In this capacity, the Seljuk sultans (temporal rulers) created a huge empire stretching from northeastern Iran through the Arab lands. In the period of Seljuk ascendancy, other Turkish tribes migrated westward and established a permanent Turkish presence in northwestern Iran and the Caucasus region. Following the Seljuks' defeat of the Byzantine army at the battle of Manzikert in 1071, these migrating tribes moved into Anatolia and began the gradual transformation of that land from a Greek-speaking Christian territory to a Turkish-speaking Muslim one.

Despite the Seljuks' early success at empire building, they were unable to maintain lasting central authority over the territories under their control. By 1157 their empire had broken up into a series of smaller successor states ruled, for the most part, by Seljuk princes. But the Seljuk period had lasting importance. It demonstrated the absorptive qualities of Islam, as the Turks adjusted quickly to urban life and adopted the high cultural traditions of Islam, such as patronage of the arts, the sponsorship of architecture, and respect for the *shari'ah* and the ulama. In addition, the Seljuks were responsible for a rejuvenation of Sunni Islam; it was the Seljuk minister Nizam al-Mulk who founded the *madrasah* system of state-sponsored education for the ulama. Moreover, the Seljuks expanded the domains of Islam into eastern Anatolia, thus laying the groundwork for the emergence of the Ottoman state, the most imposing of all the Islamic empires.

Following the breakup of the Seljuk Empire, western Iran and the central Arab lands were divided among several ruling dynasties. Although these states were not major powers, they were more than mere city-states, commanding sufficient resources to enable their princes to maintain luxurious courts and continue the tradition of offering patronage to poets and scholars. It was into this politically fragmented Middle Eastern world of the eleventh and twelfth centuries that the European Crusaders made their first appearance and established the four Latin kingdoms of Edessa, Antioch, Tripoli, and Jerusalem. After slightly less than 200 years of troubled occupation of the region and the launching of several Crusades, the Europeans were ejected from the eastern Mediterranean. Other than leading to the creation of a spirit of resistance and cooperation among rulers in Syria and Egypt, whose combined efforts led to the Crusaders' defeat, the influence of the Crusades was minimal.

A far more serious threat to the Islamic world came from the east. During the thirteenth century, all of the Islamic lands from India to Syria suffered the effects of the Mongol conquests. Unlike the Arab conquests of the seventh and eighth centuries, which brought a new religious and social order, or the Seljuk expansion in the eleventh and twelfth centuries, which invigorated the existing Islamic institutions, the Mongol invasions appeared to have little purpose other than conquest and destruction. They devastated Iraq and Iran. The first wave of invasions took place under the leadership of Genghis Khan, who became the master of most of northern China in the early thirteenth century. He then sent his armies westward; in the 1220s they vanquished the important commercial cities of Samarkand and Bukhara and brought all of Iran under Mongol influence. In 1256 another Mongol campaign was launched against the west by Genghis Khan's son Hülagü, whose objective was to conquer all of the Islamic lands as far as Egypt. In 1258 his forces defeated the caliph's army and then sacked the city of Baghdad and killed the Abbasid caliph, thus toppling the institution that had served as the symbol of universal Islam for 500 years. The Mongol destruction of Baghdad also brought to an end that city's role as an important center of commercial and intellectual life. Although the rise of other Islamic cities had caused Baghdad to lose its dominance well before the Mongol conquest, it had nevertheless remained the seat of the caliphs and the symbolic center of Islam. After 1258, the once thriving imperial capital was reduced to the status of a provincial city, and its population, economy, and influence declined precipitously.

Hülagü did not achieve his ambition of conquering Egypt. In 1260 the forces of the Mamluks, a new Turkish military sultanate based in Cairo, defeated the Mongols in a battle fought north of Jerusalem. As a result of their victory, the Mamluks became the masters of Syria and ruled it and Egypt until 1517. The rule of the Mamluks was not without turbulence, but its persistence for a period of over 250 years shows once again the significance of the Turkish role in governing Middle Eastern Islamic states from the eleventh century onward.

The Mamluk defeat of Hülagü's forces did not end the wave of invasions from the east. From 1381 to 1404, the armies of Timur Lang (Tamerlane) laid waste large portions of Iran, defeated the Turkish princes of Anatolia, and sacked Damascus. Although Timur was a Turk and a Muslim of sorts, his tactics of terror, massacre, and pillage were modeled on those of the Mongols. The area of central Iran still bears evidence of the devastation wrought by his forces. Timur conquered vast territories, but he did not construct a stable empire. Following his death in 1405, Anatolia and the Arab lands were once again fragmented into several small dynastic states.

Conclusion

Following the military victories of the Arab warriors, the Quraysh administrators and merchants consolidated the conquests and ensured that the production and distribution of resources in the conquered territories were not unduly disturbed. In this process of consolidation, local customs were often allowed to continue, and certain existing practices were incorporated into the Islamic tradition. But throughout this pragmatic creation of an empire, an Islamic impulse guided the organization of state and society. The irreverent behavior of some members of the elite could not disrupt the desire of society at large to sustain the concept of the *ummah* espoused by Muhammad. The moral imperatives of the Quran were elaborated upon and formed the core of the *shariᶜah,* a sacred legal system that made everyday activities religious duties. The Arabic language in which the Quran was revealed became the language of imperial administration, intellectual discourse, and popular exchange. Overseeing the enforcement of the *shariᶜah* and the purity of doctrine were the ulama, a class of scholars, judges, and teachers who set and transmitted the norms by which Islamic society perpetuated itself. On a popular level, religious expression found outlets in the Sufi brotherhoods and the rituals associated with them. Although a certain tension existed between the formal Islam of the ulama and the popular Islam of the Sufis, the views of both were accommodated within the universal *ummah.*

The invasions of Timur and the Mongols were a shock to the existing Islamic order in the Middle East, but they did not succeed in destroying it. Out of the chaos and instability of the fourteenth and early fifteenth centuries, there emerged in the territory from Anatolia to India three substantial Islamic empires that stabilized political conditions in the central Islamic lands, reshaped and reinvigorated cultural and religious life, and launched Islam on a new era of expansion and splendor.

Notes

1. Marilyn R. Waldman, "The Islamic World," *New Encyclopaedia Britannica,* 15th ed. (Chicago, 1990), pp. 102–133.
2. Cited in John L. Esposito, *Islam: The Straight Path* (New York, 1988), p. 98.

The Ottoman and Safavid Empires: A New Imperial Synthesis

3

During the sixteenth century, the central Islamic lands that had been so devastated by the Mongol invasions recovered their political unity and cultural vitality within a new imperial synthesis represented by the Mughal Empire of Delhi in the east, the Safavid Empire of Iran in the center, and the Ottoman Empire in the west. Each of these empires was an expansive Islamic state and each made lasting cultural, political, and social contributions to the region in which it was situated. The emergence of these three states clearly demonstrates that Islam had not reached the limits of its expansion during the classical Abbasid caliphate. Marshall Hodgson has written that a visitor from Mars who arrived on earth during the sixteenth century would probably have concluded that the world was on the verge of becoming Muslim. This conclusion would have been drawn partly because of the extent of Islam and partly because of the power and prosperity of the three central Islamic empires.

The Mughal Empire, whose most familiar architectural monument is the stunning Taj Mahal, lies outside the scope of this book, but its existence should be recognized as evidence of the emergence of a new Islamic imperial synthesis in the sixteenth century. Although the Safavid Empire of Iran collapsed in 1736, the success of its rulers in establishing Shi'ism as the state religion has had far-reaching significance for the entire Middle East. The Ottoman Empire provides a continuous link from the sixteenth to the twentieth centuries. From 1517 until the end of World War I, a period of 400 years, the Ottoman Empire was the ruling power in the central Middle East. Ottoman administrative institutions and practices shaped the peoples of the modern Middle East and left a legacy that endured after the empire's disappearance. At its peak, the Ottoman Empire was a European as well as a Middle Eastern power, and its long rule over the Balkans and its role in Great Power diplomacy have also left a lasting mark on European history.

The Rise of the Ottoman Empire

The future Ottoman Empire originated as one of over a dozen small Anatolian principalities that came into existence in the wake of the Mongol invasions of the thirteenth century (see Chapter 2). These Turkish principalities were Islamic warrior states whose ongoing military confrontations with Christian Byzantium were inspired by religious motives as well as by a desire for material gain. The tradition of *ghaza,* warfare against non-Muslims for the purpose of extending the domains of Islam, was a driving force among the Muslim frontier warriors (*ghazi*s), and the *ghazi* spirit was to play a decisive role in shaping the Ottoman Empire. An Ottoman poet of the fifteenth century described a *ghazi* as "the instrument of the religion of God, a servant of God who purifies the earth from the filth of polytheism; the *ghazi* is the sword of God, he is the protector and the refuge of the believers. If he becomes a martyr in the ways of God, do not believe that he has died—he lives in beatitude with God, he has eternal life."[1]

Although the *ghazi* forces were mainly tribal, the rulers of the Turkish principalities attempted to imitate the court life of settled Islamic empires. They adopted the style of Islamic urban civilization by practicing patronage, by appointing *shariʿah* judges to see that the law was properly applied in their domains, and by establishing institutions of Islamic learning. The admixture of the freewheeling frontier warfare of the *ghazi*s and the efforts of their chieftains to adopt the practices of high Islamic tradition was another factor that shaped the Ottoman Empire.

Much about the early history of the Ottoman state remains obscure, but its beginnings are usually traced to the achievements of a Turkish chieftain named Osman, the ruler of one of the smaller *ghazi* principalities. During the early 1300s, Osman's *ghazi* warriors achieved a series of military successes against the Byzantine forces. These victories enhanced Osman's reputation and attracted other chieftains and tribesmen to his realm. The growing military power at Osman's disposal enabled him and his son Orhon to expand their domains in northwestern Anatolia. In 1326 Orhon captured the city of Bursa from the Byzantines and made it the capital of his emerging state. He asserted his independent authority by striking his own coins, and he affirmed the Islamic impulse behind his conquests by founding a *madrasah* and constructing a mosque that bore an inscription describing him as "*ghazi,* son of *ghazi*." As Orhon's *ghazi* principality made the transition from a frontier society to an established state, his subjects came to be known by his family name, Osmanlis (Ottomans). The sense of belonging to a single dynastic house created sentiments of solidarity and loyalty that gradually transcended tribal affiliations.

By the middle of the fourteenth century, the Ottomans had expanded to the shores of the Sea of Marmara; across the water lay the lands of Christian Europe, which had always been beyond the reach of Islamic rulers.

They were not beyond the reach of the Ottomans. Over the course of the next two centuries, all of southeastern Europe came under direct Ottoman control. The Ottoman expansion of the fourteenth to the sixteenth centuries was no less remarkable than the Arab conquests 700 years earlier. Not only did the Ottomans add new European territories to the domains of Islam, they also extended their rule to the Arab lands where Islam had originated.

Three successful military campaigns can serve to illustrate the transformation of the Ottoman state into a world power. The first of them was the conquest of Constantinople, an achievement that had eluded Muslim commanders throughout the centuries. On May 29, 1453, following a long siege, the forces of Sultan Mehmet II (also known as the Conqueror) entered the Byzantine capital and brought an end to Constantinople's role as the symbolic center of eastern Christendom. Henceforth known as Istanbul, the city became the seat of the Ottoman government and was restored to its former splendor by Mehmet II's program of reconstruction and repopulation. Inhabitants throughout the Ottoman domains were encouraged—and sometimes forced—to resettle in Istanbul, and by the end of Mehmet's reign in 1481 the city was once again a thriving cosmopolitan metropolis with a population of over 100,000.

Istanbul continued to flourish during the Ottoman centuries, and by the late sixteenth century its population exceeded 700,000, making it the largest city in Europe. It was also one of the most architecturally breathtaking cities anywhere. Mehmet II and his successors undertook lavish building programs that endowed Istanbul with monumental religious structures and palaces and made its appearance worthy of the capital of the leading Islamic empire of the era. During the sixteenth century, the royal architect, Sinan, perfected the classical Ottoman style, with its vast domes, towering pencil minarets, and geometric complexes. Istanbul came to possess a visual monumentality that symbolized Ottoman wealth and power.

The occupation of Istanbul provided the Ottomans with an unparalleled strategic base from which to dominate the Black Sea and the eastern Mediterranean. However, in order to take full advantage of their position, the Ottomans required a navy; without one, they could not wrest control of maritime commerce from the well-established Italian city-states, most notably Venice. Mehmet the Conqueror constructed shipyards in Istanbul; gathered skilled carpenters, merchants, and sailors from the coastal regions under his rule; and forged an Ottoman navy that eventually drove Venice from the eastern Mediterranean and established the Ottomans as the supreme maritime power from the Adriatic to the Black Sea. The creation of a fleet also enabled the Ottomans to conquer and occupy the principal strategic Mediterranean islands from Rhodes (1522) and Cyprus (1570) in the east to Crete (1664) in the center and to extend its control over North Africa with the conquest of Algiers (1529) and Tunis (1574).

The creation of a successful navy was accompanied by improvements in the Ottoman land army that made it the most formidable military force of the sixteenth and seventeenth centuries. At the heart of Ottoman military superiority was the development and extensive use of gunpowder weapons. As early as 1453, Mehmet II had deployed huge siege guns to breech the walls of Constantinople. In the decades that followed, the Ottomans adapted artillery technology to serve their special needs, most notably by developing light field guns that could be transported on wagons to distant battlefields. These guns were used with devastating effect against the feudal armies of Europe, whose infantrymen still fought mainly with pikes. In addition, the Ottomans equipped their own infantry, the Janissaries (discussed in the next section), with gunpowder weapons to such an extent that in the sixteenth century they deployed more firearms than any other armed force in the world. These technical advantages enabled the Ottoman armed forces to defeat the armies of both Europe and the Middle East in campaign after campaign.

Although the Ottomans concentrated their efforts on expansion in Christian Europe, they also regularly sent their armies to the east to repel the advances of the Safavid Empire of Iran; these campaigns represent the second example of the growth of Ottoman world power. (The Ottoman-Safavid struggle is examined in a separate section later in this chapter.) When Sultan Selim I led the Ottoman army on an eastern campaign in 1516, his objective appeared to be the occupation of the Safavid imperial capital at Tabriz. However, he decided instead to neutralize the threat posed by another regional rival, the Mamluk Empire, which was centered in Egypt but which also controlled Syria and certain territories in southern Anatolia. The efficient Ottoman military easily drove the Mamluks out of Syria, and in early 1517 Selim marched his forces across the Sinai Peninsula and captured Cairo. This swift action resulted in the Ottoman acquisition of most of the classical heartlands of Arab Islam and brought about the integration of Arab and Ottoman Islamic traditions.

The Ottoman conquest of the Arab lands established the sultans as the supreme rulers within the universal Islamic community. They were recognized as the protectors of the holy cities of Mecca and Medina and therefore assumed the important duty of ensuring the security of the annual pilgrimage. In order to fulfill this responsibility, and also to contain the expansive Portuguese seaborne commercial empire, Selim ordered the creation of a Red Sea fleet. Although the Ottomans proved unable to compete with the Portuguese in the Indian Ocean, their domination of Egypt allowed them to establish hegemony in the Red Sea and to incorporate Yemen into their empire. In addition to having commercial and strategic benefits, Selim's occupation of Egypt enhanced the Islamic standing of the Ottoman sultans by enabling them to gain access to the title of caliph. According to legend, a member of the Abbasid ruling house escaped the Mongol destruction of

Baghdad in 1258 and made his way to Cairo, where he and his descendants were sheltered by the Mamluks and recognized as legitimate caliphs. Following the Ottoman conquest of Egypt, the reigning caliph was taken to Istanbul and allegedly transferred the title to Selim and his successors in the Ottoman dynasty. The sultans did not make extensive use of this rather questionable right to the caliphate until the nineteenth century, when they resurrected the legend of the transfer in order to obtain universal Muslim support for their attempts to ward off European imperialism.

The third example of successful Ottoman expansion concerns the European campaigns of Sultan Süleyman the Magnificent (1520–1566), the most powerful of the Ottoman rulers. Although Süleyman achieved important military victories at sea and on the eastern front, he was primarily a *ghazi*-inspired sultan who concentrated on pushing the Ottoman frontier ever-deeper into Europe. In 1520 Süleyman led the Ottoman forces in the capture of the important fortress city of Belgrade, which became the primary staging ground for subsequent Ottoman campaigns. During the rest of the 1520s, Budapest and most of Hungary were brought under Ottoman control. Then, in 1529 Süleyman shocked all of Christendom by marching an Ottoman army across the Danube and laying siege to Vienna, the Hapsburg imperial capital and the gateway to central Europe. Although the outskirts of Vienna were destroyed and the city walls were breached in several places, the defenders held out until the threat of winter forced the Ottomans to begin their long withdrawal back to Istanbul. In the years to come, Süleyman's European campaigns consolidated Ottoman rule in Hungary and Serbia, but the sultan was unable to mount another siege of Vienna. Central Europe was beyond the limits of Ottoman territorial expansion. But the area that did lie within those limits was so extensive—from the Danube to Yemen, from Albania to the northern shores of the Black Sea, and from Algiers to Baghdad—that the Ottoman Empire was, at Süleyman's death in 1566, the major European, Mediterranean, Middle Eastern, and Persian Gulf power; it was not only the leading Islamic state of the sixteenth century, it was a world empire of vast influence and territorial extent (see Map 3.1).

Ottoman Ruling Institutions and Attitudes

In general terms, the Ottoman sultans ruled over an absolutist, bureaucratic, agrarian-based empire. However, it must be emphasized that an empire as large, diverse, and long-lasting as that of the Ottomans did not have a single and unchanging system of administration. Indeed, one of the reasons for the Ottomans' success was their official recognition that the diversity of the territories over which they ruled required the adoption of flexible administrative practices that could accommodate the needs of different regions and different cultures. It is important for students of the modern

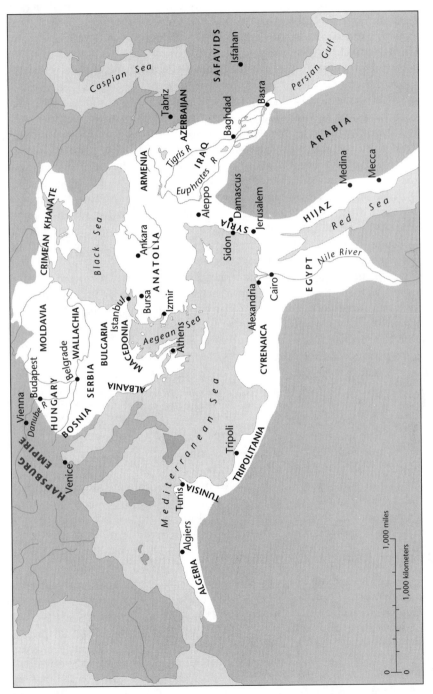

Map 3.1 The Ottoman Empire in the Late Seventeenth Century

Middle East to recognize the skills the Ottoman ruling class employed to entrench among the subject peoples of the empire an appreciation for the benefits of Ottoman rule; this appreciation, though severely tested, continued into the twentieth century.

The principles that guided the Ottoman ruling elite and shaped their attitude toward state and society came from four basic sources. The first of these was the tradition of *ghaza,* holy war against non-Muslims for the purpose of expanding the domains of Islam. Second was the legacy of urban Islamic civilization, which included the notion of dynasty, an elaborate court tradition with the monarch serving as a patron of scholars, and a belief in the ruler's responsibility for instituting and enforcing the laws and values of Islam. The Ottoman sultans accepted their Islamic duties by implementing the *shariʿah* and establishing an Islamic legal system throughout the empire. In addition, they assumed the role of protectors of the universal Islamic community, a role highlighted after the Ottomans took over the administration of such venerated Islamic cities as Jerusalem, Damascus, and Baghdad, as well as the holy places of Mecca and Medina.

A third principle influencing the organization of society was local custom. Ottoman officials developed a shrewd sense of what needed to be changed in the conquered territories and what should be allowed to remain. Any provincial governor whose policies were so heavy-handed that his province rose up in rebellion was as deserving of dismissal as a lenient governor who failed to produce sufficient revenue. As long as taxes were remitted and stability was maintained, the Ottomans were content to tolerate the existence of a wide variety of local practices. This attitude gave rise to an administrative and fiscal mosaic in which subtle shades of difference existed. In this context, it has been accurately noted that the Ottomans were more interested in efficiency than in uniformity. But it was precisely this administrative flexibility that enabled the Ottomans to rule for so long over territories as diverse as Serbia and Egypt or Syria and Greece.

The fourth principle that shaped Ottoman governing attitudes was the division of society into rulers and ruled. The latter, referred to as *reaya,* a term denoting subjects, were expected to produce through labor and taxes the wealth that supported the ruling elite. The state had few obligations toward its subjects aside from the need to assure conditions of stability and order so that the subjects would be able to generate the wealth on which the rulers depended. The Ottoman ruling elite were called *askeris*, literally, the military. However, in practice membership in the ruling class included high-ranking civilian officials and members of the ulama as well as the military. In addition to their elevated status, the ruling elite enjoyed special privileges, the most important of which were tax exemptions.

Within the ruling elite, there was a special group of educated individuals who have been called the true Ottomans. Members of this group not only served the state in high-ranking positions, they also practiced the norms of behavior required of a cultivated, well-bred class. This included having a knowledge of Ottoman Turkish, which was a complex amalgam of Arabic, Persian, and Turkish written in the Arabic script. A true Ottoman was also familiar with the Islamic cultural tradition and could read the Quran in Arabic. Although the Ottoman Empire was founded by Turkish military chieftains, its ruling elite adopted a cosmopolitan outlook and regarded themselves as cultured Ottoman Muslims. The term *Turk* took on pejorative connotations and was used to refer disparagingly to illiterate peasants.

At the pinnacle of the Ottoman hierarchy was the sultan-caliph, an absolute monarch whose right to rule was derived from his membership in the house of Osman. Until around 1600, the reigning sultan chose his successor from among the Ottoman royal princes after they had received military and administrative training in one of the provinces of Anatolia. Succession did not automatically go to the eldest son but rather to the prince who had demonstrated an aptitude for governing and soldiering. In order to prevent rival claims to the throne, the Ottomans adopted the practice of fratricide; once the designated prince had assumed the office of sultan, he ordered his brothers killed. Justification for this practice was encapsulated in the Ottoman political statement that "the death of a prince is less regrettable than the loss of a province." At some point after the reign of Süleyman the Magnificent, fratricide was discontinued, as was the program of training the princes before they assumed the throne. As a result, several of the later sultans were raised within the cloistered walls of the royal palace and had no governing experience prior to becoming rulers.

As the Ottoman state changed from a *ghazi* principality to a world empire, the sultans instituted an imperial council, or divan, to deal with the increasingly complex affairs of government. The members of the divan were responsible for advising the sultan on the military, administrative, and judicial affairs of the empire and were among the highest-ranking members of the true Ottoman elite. The divan was presided over by the grand vizier, the most powerful official in the government hierarchy. He was the absolute deputy of the sultan and acquired the right to exercise executive authority in the sultan's name. During the reigns of weak sultans, the grand viziers sometimes assumed extensive powers and made decisions without consulting the monarch.

Historians have identified numerous fine gradations within the Ottoman ruling elite, but the three major groupings were the military, the civil service, and the religious establishment.

The Military

The *Sipahi* Cavalry. The two main branches of the Ottoman armed forces came from quite different sources. The provincial cavalrymen, or *sipahi*s, were freeborn Muslims who fulfilled an administrative as well as a military function. In an attempt to maintain a large army without making huge cash payments, the sultans awarded *sipahi*s the rights to the income from agricultural lands known as *timar*s. Each *sipahi* was assigned a specific *timar* from which he was allowed to collect the taxes that served as his salary. In return, the *sipahi* was expected to maintain order in his *timar*, to report for military service when called upon by the sultan, and, depending on the size of his income, to bring with him a certain number of armed and mounted retainers. Most of the European and Anatolian provinces were divided into *timar*s, but the practice was uncommon in the Arab territories.

The Janissary Infantry. Although *sipahi*s and their retainers made up the bulk of the Ottoman armies, the most efficient imperial military unit was the professional standing infantry corps known as the Janissaries. The Janissaries were a slave army and represented one of the special ways in which the Ottomans recruited and trained individuals for the most important posts within the empire. At some point in the fourteenth century, the Ottomans institutionalized a method for procuring slaves from among their European Christian subjects. Known as the *devshirme* (collecting) system, it consisted of a levy every few years on adolescent male Christian children from the European provinces of the empire. The children were removed from their families and taken to Istanbul, where they were converted to Islam, tested and screened, and then trained for service in the empire. Most of them were eventually enrolled in the ranks of the Janissary corps, which, at its peak in the fifteenth and sixteenth centuries was the outstanding military unit in Europe. Known for their discipline, morale, and professionalism, the Janissaries were paid regular salaries and were expected to be ready for military duty at all times. Forbidden to marry or to engage in trade, they were quartered in barracks and when not on active campaign were frequently deployed to maintain domestic law and order. By the time of Süleyman the Magnificent, the Janissary corps numbered around 40,000 troops and had expanded from an infantry force to include specialized artillery units.

The Civil Service

As a centralized imperial state, the Ottoman Empire was characterized by an immense and elaborate bureaucracy. The Ottomans drew on the administrative traditions of the Byzantines, the Iranians, and the Arabs to create a highly differentiated civil service in which a veritable army of scribes kept detailed records of census surveys, treasury accounts, official appointments, and the rules and regulations of the government. Most of the middle-level Ottoman civil servants were freeborn Muslims who received on-the-job training as apprentices in one of the several ministries. Often referred to as men of the pen, they were crucial to the efficient functioning of the state.

The Religious Establishment

Along with the bureaucratic and military elite, the ulama formed the third pillar of the Ottoman ruling class. What with the *ghazi* spirit that inspired the Ottoman rulers and their warriors from the early years of frontier warfare against Byzantium, the sultans accorded the ulama a respected place in Ottoman society. To a degree unprecedented in the classical Islamic empires, the Ottomans endeavored to establish *shariʿah* norms of justice by organizing the *qadi*s (judges) into an official hierarchy and arranging for their appointments in the various administrative subdivisions of the empire. Over the course of time, an official known as the *shaykh al-Islam* emerged as the chief religious dignitary of the empire; he oversaw the appointment of *qadi*s and *madrasah* teachers in the far-flung Ottoman territories and acquired status as the official whose legal opinion the sultans sought when they contemplated the introduction of certain administrative and fiscal measures. Despite the influence the ulama exercised on the population at large, despite the importance of the *qadi*s in establishing *shariʿah* norms of justice, and despite the authority of the *shaykh al-Islam,* the entire religious establishment held office at the pleasure of the sultan. The income of the ulama may have been largely independent of the state, but their appointments were not. The *shaykh al-Islam* who dared to issue an opinion that contradicted the sultan's wishes was likely to be dismissed, no matter how well founded his opinion may have been in Islamic legal theory.

The Ottoman Slave Elite

In addition to procuring slave soldiers for the Janissaries, the *devshirme* system also provided the Ottoman state with its top-ranking military commanders and civilian administrators. With the exception of the religious establishment, which was composed entirely of free Muslims, the Ottoman ruling institutions were run by slaves of the sultan. The most promising young men taken in the *devshirme* levy were assigned to special schools within the royal palace complex where they underwent several years of training designed to prepare them for a life of leadership as the Ottoman ruling class. They studied Persian, Arabic, and Ottoman Turkish, and they learned calligraphy and painting as well as military strategy and the handling of weapons. According to a sixteenth-century European observer, the purpose of the palace schools was to produce a "warrior, statesman, and loyal Muslim" who was at the same time "a man of letters and a gentleman of polished speech, profound courtesy and honest morals."[2]

The individuals who successfully completed their palace training were appointed to the most responsible military and administrative positions within the empire. From the mid-fifteenth to the mid-seventeenth centuries, virtually all of the grand viziers, the sultan's designated deputies, were converted

Christians taken in the *devshirme* levy and trained in the palace system. Most other high-ranking ministers, members of the divan, provincial governors, and leading military commanders had similar backgrounds. They managed the affairs of the empire and led its armies, yet they were all slaves of the sultan. In a sense, of course, the term *slave* is misleading. These warrior-statesmen acquired vast wealth, wielded immense power, had household slaves of their own, and married women of their own choosing. But the power they possessed derived from the will of the sultan; they were his creatures, his bondsmen, and he could dismiss and punish them as he chose.

The *devshirme* levy and the palace training system succeeded in severing the ties of young adolescents with their places of origin and creating a trained cadre of officials who were dependent on the sultan and thus totally loyal to him. Their rise in the Ottoman system was determined largely by their own talents (with help from a patron or two), not on the standing of their families. In this way, the Ottoman elite was constantly renewed by the infusion of newly trained and newly committed warrior-statesman-slaves. Because it was forbidden to enslave a freeborn Muslim, the system did not allow for hereditary positions—the offspring of these converted high-ranking officials were regarded as full-fledged Muslims and were, in theory, excluded from holding positions in the Ottoman hierarchy that were reserved for the sultan's slaves. The Ottoman slave system offered such limitless opportunities to the young men who became a part of it that there are recorded instances of Christian—and Muslim—parents attempting to arrange for their sons to be taken in the *devshirme* levies.

The *Millet* System

Readers accustomed to the concept of a homogeneous nation-state in which the inhabitants are united by a shared language and a shared sense of citizenship may find the Ottomans' method of organizing their subjects along religious lines somewhat unusual. As a result of the Ottoman conquests, the sultans came to rule over lands inhabited by millions of Christians and Jews. The religious mosaic of the Ottoman Empire as a whole can be seen in the population of Istanbul. Of the city's 700,000 inhabitants in the sixteenth century, 58 percent were Muslims, 32 percent Christians, and 10 percent Jews. Partly out of the Islamic requirements of toleration and partly for pragmatic reasons, the sultans organized their non-Muslim subjects into religious communities called *millet*s and granted them a considerable degree of autonomy. Each of the three major non-Muslim religions—Greek Orthodox Christianity, Judaism, and Armenian Christianity—was granted *millet* status and placed under the direct authority of the leading church official. The three officials—the Greek Orthodox patriarch, the Armenian patriarch, and the Jewish grand rabbi—were selected with the approval of the sultan and resided in Istanbul, where the Ottoman state kept track of their activities. Recent scholarship has determined that the Ottomans did not attempt to create an empire-wide *millet* structure until the nineteenth century and that up to that point the *millet* system lacked uniformity, differing from region to region and group to group.

It is nevertheless possible to identify common patterns in Ottoman administration of non-Muslims. Christians and Jews were allowed religious freedom and had the right to retain their religious educational systems and religious legal structures. They were directly administered by their own communal officials, who exercised both civil and religious responsibilities. These officials were in charge of tax collection, education, justice, and religious affairs within their religious communities. By permitting non-Muslim subjects to retain their religious laws, educational systems, and communal leadership, the Ottomans were able to administer their diverse peoples with a minimum of resistance. The Jewish community in particular prospered under Ottoman rule, and large numbers of Jews emigrated to the Ottoman domains from Spain following the Christian reconquest. Yet no matter how prosperous or prominent non-Muslims might become, they were not regarded as equal to Muslims. They were tolerated, but they were also subject to social discrimination that barred them from service in the Ottoman armed forces and prevented them from becoming members of the Ottoman ruling elite.

The Loss of Ottoman Superiority

The once prevalent idea that the Ottoman Empire entered into a period of precipitous decline following the reign of Süleyman is no longer accepted. Indeed, some historians now question whether the term *decline* is an accurate description of the process through which the Ottoman Empire lost its dominant position. It is perhaps preferable to view the Ottoman experience from the seventeenth to the twentieth centuries as a period of transformation during which the Ottomans struggled to find a new imperial synthesis in a changing international environment. External factors, most prominent among them the penetration of European merchant capital into the empire, caused a wrenching dislocation of the Ottoman economy. Beginning in the late sixteenth century, Ottoman raw materials, normally channeled into internal consumption and industry, were increasingly exchanged for European manufactured products. This trade benefited Ottoman merchants but led to a decline in state revenues and a shortage of raw materials for domestic consumption. As the costs of scarce materials rose, the empire suffered from inflation, and the state was unable to procure sufficient revenues to meet its expenses. Without these revenues, the institutions that supported the Ottoman system, especially the armed forces, were undermined.

The penetration of European manufactured goods into the empire and the eventual domination of Ottoman commerce by Europeans and their protégés were facilitated by a series of commercial treaties, known as the Capitulations, that the Ottoman sultans signed with the Christian states of Europe. The first Capitulation agreement was negotiated with France in 1536; it allowed French merchants to trade freely in Ottoman ports, to be exempt from Ottoman taxes, and to import and export goods at low tariff rates. In addition, the treaty granted extraterritorial privileges to French merchants by permitting them to come under the legal jurisdiction of the French consul in Istanbul, thus making them subject to French rather than Ottoman-Islamic law. This first treaty was the model for subsequent agreements signed with other European states.

The Capitulations were negotiated at a time of Ottoman military domination and were intended to encourage commercial exchange. However, when the military balance between Europe and the Ottomans tilted in favor of Europe, European merchants, backed by the power of their states, were able to exploit the Capitulations to the disadvantage of the Ottomans. The treaties not only had a devastating effect on the Ottoman economy but also had long-term political implications. By granting the various consuls jurisdiction over their nationals within the Ottoman Empire, the Capitulations accorded the consuls extraordinary powers that they abused with increasing frequency in the course of the nineteenth century.

External economic factors combined with a range of domestic problems to render the various components of the Ottoman system less cohesive than they had been at the time of Süleyman. The rule of incompetent sultans, the presence of struggles over the succession, and the rise of political discord within the court all served to weaken the effectiveness of the central government. The shortage of revenue and the rise of inflation had a devastating effect on the large numbers of state employees on fixed salaries and created an atmosphere that fostered bribery and other forms of corruption. And finally, the government's inability to make regular payments to the Janissaries or to fund the acquisition of new military equipment meant that the Ottoman armed forces lost the absolute dominance that they had earlier possessed.

This loss of dominance was manifested on the battlefield. In 1683 the Ottomans mounted a second siege of Vienna. Although they were defeated outside the city walls, their ability to launch such an ambitious campaign appeared to demonstrate the power of the Ottoman armed forces. However, in the 1690s, the Ottomans engaged in simultaneous wars with Austria and Russia and were defeated on both fronts. The Treaty of Karlowitz, signed with Austria in 1699, ceded most of Hungary to the Hapsburgs and marked the first major surrender of European territory by the Ottomans. The following year, the sultan signed a treaty with Peter the Great acknowledging the Russian conquest of the northern shores of the Black Sea. From this point on, the Ottomans were on the defensive. They were not, however, as moribund a military power as they have sometimes been portrayed. During the eighteenth century, the Ottoman forces held their own in two wars with

Austria and defeated the Russian army in two other wars. These victories may have led the Ottoman ruling elite to conclude that the armed forces of the state were as relatively powerful as ever. That this was not the case was amply demonstrated in the Ottoman-Russian war launched by the Ottomans in 1768. In the course of this conflict, the Russian Baltic fleet entered the Mediterranean and destroyed an Ottoman fleet off the coast of Anatolia. The land war was equally devastating for the Ottomans as the Russian forces drove them out of Romania and the Crimea on the Black Sea. The settlement that ended the war, the Treaty of Küchük Kaynarja (1774), was one of the most humiliating agreements ever signed by the Ottomans. In addition to ceding territory, the sultan granted Russia the right to construct a Greek Orthodox church in Istanbul and to make representations to the Ottoman government on behalf of the Greek Orthodox community. These provisions laid the foundation for Russia's claim to be the protector of the entire Greek Orthodox *millet* within the Ottoman Empire. Russia would use this claim as a pretext for frequent interventions in Ottoman internal affairs in the decades that followed.

The military defeats that led to the ceding of Ottoman territory showed that the armed forces of the empire had lost the technological advantages they once possessed. If the empire was to survive, military improvements had to be undertaken immediately.

The Triumph of Shiᶜism: The Safavid Empire of Iran, 1501–1736

Shah Ismaᶜil (1494–1524) and the Establishment of the State

Just as the Ottomans rose from their humble origins among the tribes of Anatolia to become rulers of a world empire, so their Safavid rivals to the east emerged from a relatively obscure background to found a dynamic and prosperous imperial state. The Safavids were either of Kurdish or Turkish origin. In the late thirteenth century, a member of the Safavid family founded a Sunni Sufi religious brotherhood in Azerbaijan, the Turkish-speaking region of northwestern Iran. The brotherhood attracted an ardent following among the Turkish pastoral tribes of the area, and by the late fifteenth century its influence had expanded into Anatolia and Syria. The heads of the brotherhood led the tribes in a series of expeditions against the Christians of the Caucasus, thereby acquiring temporal power as well as enhancing their reputations as servants of Islam. Their Turkish followers were known as Qizilbash, the Red-headed Ones, after the red headgear they wore to identify themselves as supporters of the Safavid brotherhood.

In 1494 a seven-year-old boy named Ismaᶜil succeeded his brother as head of the order and eventually transformed it into an imperial institution.

Ismaꜥil's forces captured the city of Tabriz in 1501 and Ismaꜥil proclaimed himself shah (king). He then organized a series of campaigns in which the Qizilbash brought areas of eastern Anatolia and Iraq, including Baghdad, under Safavid control. In 1510 Ismaꜥil extended his authority to eastern Iran, defeating a coalition of Turkish tribesmen and establishing the borders of his state at the Oxus River. Ismaꜥil's most ardent followers were located among the tribes of Anatolia, but before he could organize them for further expansion against the Ottomans, the sultan sent a huge army into the region. The Ottoman and Safavid forces met at the battle of Chaldiran in 1514; the gunpowder army of the Ottomans crushed the mounted archers of Ismaꜥil and consolidated Ottoman dominance in eastern Anatolia.

Ismaꜥil's defeat at Chaldiran did not prevent him from founding a dynasty and building an empire into which he introduced revolutionary and far-reaching religious changes: He was responsible for establishing Shiꜥism as the state religion of Iran. The Safavid brotherhood was founded as a Sunni order, and historians are uncertain when its leaders adopted Shiꜥism or even if they did so before the reign of Ismaꜥil. It is known that for a few years during Ismaꜥil's youth, he was sheltered by a local Shiꜥa ruler and may have acquired his Shiꜥa convictions from this experience. Whatever the sources for his belief, Ismaꜥil became a fervent Shiꜥa and was determined to make all of the inhabitants in the territories under his control adopt Shiꜥism. When he proclaimed himself shah in 1501, he also proclaimed Twelver Shiꜥism to be the official and compulsory religion of the state.

Ismaꜥil enforced his proclamation by dissolving the Sunni brotherhoods and ordering the executions of all who refused to accept Shiꜥism. As there was no existing Shiꜥa religious establishment in Iran, Ismaꜥil created one by importing Shiꜥa ulama and legal experts from the Arab lands, especially from Lebanon. These religious officials filled the vacuum at the highest ranks of the religious hierarchy and laid the groundwork for the emergence of a vibrant Shiꜥa ulama class. The version of Twelver Shiꜥism promulgated by Ismaꜥil contained important deviations from previously accepted doctrine. Ismaꜥil claimed to be descended from the seventh Imam, to be divinely inspired himself, and to be the earthly representative of the Hidden Twelfth Imam. He thus portrayed himself as guided by the Imam and empowered to render infallible judgments on religious practices and legal issues. Ismaꜥil's claims were widely accepted, and the religious authority he claimed for himself was acknowledged to be present in his successors as well.

Under Ismaꜥil's successors Shiꜥism became firmly embedded as the religion of the vast majority of the Iranian population. Although this outcome did not, as some have claimed, make Shiꜥism synonymous with Iranian national culture, it did serve to set Iran off from its Sunni neighbors. In addition, because the Safavids ruled over a large and powerful empire, their Shiꜥa beliefs were seen as a threat by their Sunni neighbors, especially the Ottomans. The success of Shiꜥism in the Safavid domains therefore created a new level of hostility between Sunni and Shiᶜa and tended to make precarious the existence of Shiᶜa minority communities within Sunni-administered territories, and vice versa.

The Safavid state was established by the military prowess of the Qizilbash tribesmen. In order to retain their loyalties, Ismaᶜil granted tribal leaders control of vast tracts of grazing land and rewarded the most powerful of them with appointments as provincial governors. This practice did not differ noticeably from the policies followed by the rulers of the dozens of short-lived dynastic principalities that had preceded the Safavids. However, Ismaᶜil introduced new administrative institutions that enabled the Safavid state to become far more durable than any of its immediate predecessors. He began to build a governing apparatus by appointing urban Iranians to the newly created bureaucratic posts within the government. A certain tension developed between the emerging class of Iranian bureaucrats and the Qizilbash tribal leaders, who were largely excluded from the civil administration. At Ismaᶜil's death in 1524, the Safavid Empire was in a stage of transition from tribal military regime to absolutist bureaucratic empire.

From the Reign of Shah Abbas I (1587–1629) to the Collapse of the Safavids

A recurring problem for Ismaᶜil's successors was the factiousness of the Qizilbash tribesmen and their resistance to the imposition of state control. Struggles for prominence among the Qizilbash leaders and their occasional revolts against the government prevented them from effectively defending the Safavid domains. When Shah Abbas ascended the throne, Turkish tribal incursions in the east and Ottoman advances in the west threatened to overwhelm his empire. Abbas reversed the decline in Safavid fortunes, and his reign marked the apogee of the Safavid state. He recovered the lost territories on the eastern and western frontiers (including Baghdad), he introduced radical domestic reforms, and he made his capital, Isfahan, into one of the most beautiful and culturally vibrant cities of the world.

Recognizing the need to control the unruly Qizilbash leaders, Abbas built up a military counterweight to them in the form of a standing royal army composed of converted Christian slaves captured during expeditions to the Caucasus. This was similar to the Ottoman slave system. The new *ghulam* (military slave) army was a gunpowder force that included an artillery corps and infantry armed with muskets. This army, which may eventually have numbered 37,000 troops, was directly financed by the shah and was in turn directly responsible to him.

As we will see in succeeding chapters of this book, rulers who sought to improve their armed forces had to find ways of increasing their revenues in order to be able to pay for the acquisition and maintenance of expensive weaponry. In the case of Shah Abbas, he transferred lands from the tribal leaders to his own royal estates. Over the course of his reign, Abbas converted huge areas of Iran into crown lands, the revenues of which went directly to him, not to the state treasury. With these revenues, he financed the new standing army. Abbas's land transfer policy and his direct control of the new military weakened the power base of the Qizilbash and concentrated centralized royal authority in his person.

In 1598 Shah Abbas designated Isfahan, a city located in the center of Iran, as the new imperial capital. Isfahan was already an established city and had once been the Seljuk capital. However, Abbas transformed the city, lavishing huge sums on the construction of a carefully planned urban center laid out along broad thoroughfares and embellished with richly decorated mosques, a royal palace, luxurious private residences, and a large bazaar, all maintained in a lush garden setting. The material splendor of Isfahan coupled with Abbas's generous patronage attracted artists and scholars, whose presence contributed to the city's rich intellectual and cultural life. As activities from carpet weaving to miniature painting, from the writing of Persian poetry to the compilation of works on Shiʿa jurisprudence were encouraged, Isfahan became the catalyst for an explosion of Persian culture that spread to other Safavid cities and continued after the death of Abbas. Isfahan was also a thriving commercial center whose merchants, prospering under the stable, centralized government established by Abbas, became consumers and patrons themselves. At the time of Abbas's death, the Safavid capital had a population estimated at 400,000; the large size of the city and the impressive achievements of its residents prompted the inhabitants to coin their famous boast, "Isfahan is half the world."

Although the Safavid dynasty had only one effective ruler after Abbas, the centralized machinery of government he had set up enabled the empire to survive his successors' incompetence and provided Iran with another century of political stability. With the exception of a major confrontation with the Ottomans over Iraq, the seventeenth century was a peaceful period in which the economy prospered and cultural life flourished. However, in the absence of external military threats, the Safavid shahs allowed the expensive standing army to decline. Their failure to maintain an effective military force opened the way for a rebellious chieftain based in the territory that is now Afghanistan to seize Isfahan and bring an end to the Safavid dynasty in 1722.

The fall of the Safavids ushered in a lengthy period of decentralization in Iran. From time to time, a powerful military commander was able to establish dominance over the contending tribal confederations and bring large parts of Iranian territory under his control, only to have his fledgling state splinter into factions on his death. Finally, in 1794 a Turkish tribal chieftain named Fath Ali Shah established the Qajar dynasty in central Iran. Although the Qajars were the nominal ruling dynasty of Iran until the 1920s, they never succeeded in recreating the royal absolutism or the bureaucratic centralism of the Safavids. The consequences of the diminished authority exercised by the Qajars is treated in Chapter 6.

Conclusion:
The Sunni-Shiᶜa Struggle for Iraq

From the time of Shah Ismaᶜil's occupation of Baghdad in 1508 until Sultan Murat IV's reconquest of the city in 1638, the Shiᶜa Safavids and the Sunni Ottomans waged a seesaw struggle for control of the lands of Iraq. The results of this confrontation had a significant impact on the region at the time as well as creating the mixture of sectarian loyalties that has survived into the modern era.

Baghdad and the lands of Iraq were under Safavid control when Ismaᶜil introduced Shiᶜism as the compulsory religion for the subjects of his empire. Within Iraq, Sunni shrines were destroyed, the main mosques were turned into Shiᶜa places of worship, and attempts were made forcefully to convert the population. The Ottoman sultans, who considered themselves the protectors of Sunni Islam, could not ignore the imposition of Shiᶜism in the territory that had been the center of the Abbasid caliphate. Nor, for economic reasons, could they tolerate Safavid control of the outlet to the Persian Gulf. In 1534 Süleyman the Magnificent commanded an expedition that succeeded in restoring Iraq to Ottoman control and confirming the Ottoman sultan as the supreme ruler in the world of Islam.

Iraq remained in Ottoman hands until 1624, when the armies of Shah Abbas occupied Baghdad and massacred many of its Sunni inhabitants. Again the Ottomans responded, but despite mounting several sieges of Baghdad, they were unable to capture the city until 1638. Sultan Murat IV, who led the victorious campaign, immediately sent Ottoman military commanders into the countryside to restore Sunni rites among the population and to banish Shiᶜa ulama from the region. From that point until World War I, Iraq remained in Ottoman hands.

Although control of the Persian Gulf port of Basra was an important objective for the Ottomans and Safavids alike, the intensity of their struggle for Iraq suggests that something more profound than economic interests was at stake. The lands of Iraq became the center of a contest for supremacy between Ottoman Sunnism and Safavid Shiᶜism. The territory evoked different historical images for the followers of the two branches of Islam. To the Ottomans, Baghdad was the Abbasid capital city for 500 years, the home of the founders of universal Islam whose legacy the Ottoman sultan-caliphs sought to perpetuate. For the Safavids, Iraq was the home of the two most sacred shrines in Shiᶜism, Najaf, the center of Shiᶜa theology, and Karbala, the site of the martyrdom of Imam Husayn. The commemoration of Husayn's death was the most important ritual event in Shiᶜism, and pilgrimage to Karbala came to be regarded by the Shiᶜa as a legitimate substitute for the pilgrimage to Mecca. In popular Shiᶜa practice, a tablet made from the clay of Karbala and said to be impregnated with the blood of Husayn was a valued talisman; put under a pillow, it was believed to guard the sleeper as if he or she were at Karbala, under the protection of Husayn himself.[3] The Safavid shahs saw the retention of these shrines under Shiᶜa authority as a religious duty; their loss to the Ottomans was a source of profound grief. It is no wonder that the land of Iraq, sacred to followers of both branches of Islam, became a troubled region. Although it remained Arabic-speaking and under Sunni Ottoman control, a majority of its population embraced Shiᶜism. The sectarian divisions implanted during the Ottoman-Safavid struggle would play a significant role in the modern history of Iraq.

Notes

1. Cited in Paul Wittek, *The Rise of the Ottoman Empire* (London, 1965), p. 14.
2. Lord Kinross, *The Ottoman Centuries: The Rise and Fall of the Turkish Empire* (London, 1977), p. 147.
3. Marshall G. S. Hodgson, *The Venture of Islam*, vol. 3 (Chicago, 1974), p. 38.

The Beginnings of the Era of Transformation

PART II

For the Ottoman Empire the eighteenth century marked a period of political and economic disintegration brought about by a combination of declining central authority and intense external pressures. The most prominent feature of this decay was a process of decentralization both within the administration and in the Ottoman state's ability to control its territories. As the absolutism of the sultans waned, other officials within the Ottoman system acquired power and the wealth that went with it. These officials came to have a vested interest in the decentralized status quo and opposed the efforts of sultans and grand viziers to reimpose royal absolutism.

The Janissaries, once the dependable military foundation of Ottoman expansionism, became a threat to the state. The discipline of the corps declined, and its members avoided the restrictions that had confined them to military service alone. Janissaries established lucrative business relationships with craft guilds, engaged in trade and commerce themselves, married and brought their offspring into the corps, and developed a reluctance to engage in combat. The Janissaries were determined to protect the privileges that decentralization provided them; their rebellions in the streets of Istanbul against any attempts to reform their training or curb their civilian activities became commonplace in the course of the eighteenth century.

The diffusion of power was further evident in the formation of other interest groups within the administration. The bureaucracy, once noted for its efficiency and its adherence to the policy of promotion on the basis of merit, became infused with nepotism, and the buying and selling of offices was a common practice. The high-ranking ulama also exercised considerable independent authority.

The decline of central authority also brought opportunities for local leaders to acquire a greater measure of regional power. Throughout Anatolia and the European and Arab provinces of the empire, local valley lords (*dere-*

beys and *a^cyans*) gained increasing degrees of autonomy from Istanbul, setting up what were essentially small principalities. These autonomous rulers did not seek to overthrow the Ottoman state, only to distance themselves from its authority, to collect and control the revenues generated in their territory, and to pass their autonomy on to their heirs. They no longer provided their allotment of armed men to fight the sultan's wars except when they saw some personal advantage in doing so.

The weakness of the central Ottoman state sapped its ability to deal with the military and economic pressures its European adversaries exerted with increasing frequency. As we saw in Chapter 3, permanent territorial losses became commonplace during the second half of the eighteenth century. Such losses were sustained because of the inefficiency of the Ottoman armed forces. Yet even as the state was threatened by the advances of Russia and Austria, the entrenched interest groups within the empire refused to surrender their privileges. The administration was paralyzed by the intransigence of the Janissaries, the self-aggrandizement of the *derebeys*, and the self-serving practices of influential officials and ulama; it was thus rendered incapable of taking the decisive steps required to reverse its fortunes on the battlefield. And with each territorial concession, more revenue-producing land was lost to the Christian enemies.

European gains were not confined to territorial concessions. With the ending of the Napoleonic Wars in 1815, European commerce penetrated the Middle East to an unprecedented extent. The products of the Industrial Revolution, cheap textiles and metal goods, flooded the region, bringing about a change in the pattern of consumption and causing the local handicraft industries to suffer. Because of the incursions of European commerce and capital, the formerly self-sufficient economies of the Middle East became integrated into the world economic system. In response to the hunger of the European industrializing states for cheap raw materials and foodstuffs, certain regions of the Middle East were transformed into exporters of specialized agricultural products—cotton in Egypt, cereals in Syria, silk in Lebanon. However, commercial agricultural production in the Middle East was dependent on the demands of the European market and was thus subject to price fluctuations determined by European needs and tastes. In this way, the Middle East was incorporated into the global economic system as a dependent region, a supplier of raw agricultural commodities and a consumer of European manufactured goods. The institutional and economic transformation of the Middle East occurred simultaneously: As the rulers of the Ottoman Empire, Egypt, and Iran attempted, with varying degrees of effectiveness and determination, to reform their armed forces and their administrative institutions, their states were drawn into the evolving world economy that was largely shaped by Europe.

Even the benefits of expanded commercial activity in the Ottoman world were realized mainly by European merchants or their local agents. In the course of the eighteenth century, the Capitulation agreements were renegotiated and additional privileges granted to the European powers. Among them was the right to grant certificates of protection to non-Muslim Ottoman subjects. These certificates, called *barats*, allowed their holders to receive the same protection that European nationals had. Armed with *barats*, which were freely granted by European representatives, the minority subjects of the empire had a distinct advantage over Muslim merchants and were able to take control of important sectors of Ottoman external trade. Thus, in commerce as in political organization, the empire experienced a marked tendency toward decentralization.

Despite the economic and political difficulties of the eighteenth century, the Ottoman Empire could still draw on considerable human and material resources. Its weakness was relative, not absolute: Huge Ottoman armies still took the field; scribes, bureaucrats, and viziers still conducted affairs of state; and the religious establishment nurtured the Islamic traditions and maintained the *shariʿah* courts. Each of these components of the Ottoman system may have functioned less efficiently than before, but we should not assume that the empire was on the verge of collapse or that it was completely lacking in officials determined to preserve the Ottoman-Islamic values in the face of Christian advances.

For the Ottoman order to recover, though, the central government had to regain control over the institutions and resources of the state, for only by reestablishing central authority could the state in turn undertake the military reforms that were needed for the empire to survive. The failure of Ottoman forces in the field convinced an influential group within the Ottoman ruling class that when it counted, European military technology was superior. If selected elements of that technology could be introduced into the Ottoman armed forces, then perhaps European encroachment would be halted and the Ottoman system would be allowed to revitalize itself without external interference.

The nineteenth century in the Middle East is frequently characterized as a period of tension between forces of continuity and forces of change. On the one hand, the reformers, who advocated the adoption of European institutions and technology, have often been portrayed as the progressive elements of society courageously charting the course toward an inevitably Westernized twentieth century. On the other hand, the adherents of continuity, who viewed with alarm the dismantling of the Islamic order and sought to preserve tradition and retain the values and ideals that had served Ottoman and Islamic society so well for so long, are sometimes portrayed as nothing but archaic reactionaries. We should avoid these simplistic characterizations if we are to appreciate the agonizing and dangerous process of transforming an established religious, social, and political worldview.

Forging a New Synthesis: The Pattern of Reforms, 1789–1849

4

The sixty-year period from the ascent of the Ottoman sultan Selim III to the death of the Egyptian governor Muhammad Ali defines an era of state-sponsored military reforms during which the rulers of the Ottoman Empire and Egypt sought to remake their armed forces in the image of the European powers. The military reformers of this era did not question the cultural norms, social structures, or political relationships on which the Ottoman order rested. However, their efforts to transform their armed forces and reestablish central political authority led them to reorganize the machinery of government and introduce new educational facilities. Military reform was thus the spearhead that led to the reform of civilian institutions and to the creation of a new elite whose status was based on its training in European-style academies. In the course of pursuing their goals, the rulers of this period confronted, and in many cases destroyed, elements of the old order that opposed them. By so doing, they unintentionally undermined the Ottoman system as a whole and opened the doors to a process of transformation that extended far beyond the military.

Selim III (1789–1806): Between Old and New

The policies of Sultan Selim III constituted an intensification of the efforts at military reform carried out by his eighteenth-century predecessors. His goal was not to transform the traditional Ottoman state but to preserve and strengthen it. In this regard, he was a conservative ruler whose vision of the proper Ottoman order was modeled on the system established under Süleyman the Magnificent. But because Selim's programs laid the groundwork for a full-fledged reform movement by his successor, and because his downfall identified the barriers to further change, his reign constituted an important bridge between the old and the new.[1]

When Selim ascended the Ottoman throne, the empire was engaged in yet another losing war with Austria and Russia. To the sultan and a trusted set of advisers, the lessons of the campaign were clear: Unless improvements were made in the military, the Ottoman state could not survive. Once peace was concluded in 1792, Selim embarked on a series of reforms designed to reorganize the existing armed forces along European lines. This involved the employment of European advisers under whose supervision new methods of training and tactics were introduced, new weapons were purchased and deployed, and existing foundries and arsenals were upgraded and new ones constructed. To placate the Janissaries and convince them to accept the new methods, Selim raised their salaries and rebuilt their barracks. However, he only aroused their suspicions, and they successfully resisted his moves toward reform. Frustrated in his attempts to curb their domestic unrest or to improve their military prowess, Selim took steps to bypass them.

To this end, the sultan's most ambitious military project was the creation of an entirely new infantry corps fully trained and equipped according to the latest European standards. This unit, called the *nizam-i jedid* (the new order), was formed in 1797 and adopted a pattern of recruitment that was uncommon for the imperial forces; it was composed of Turkish peasant youths from Anatolia, a clear indication that the *devshirme* system was no longer functional. Officered and trained by Europeans, the *nizam-i jedid* was outfitted with modern weapons and French-style uniforms. By 1806 the new army numbered around 23,000 troops, including a modern artillery corps, and its units performed effectively in minor actions. But Selim III's inability to integrate the force with the regular army and his reluctance to deploy it against his domestic opponents limited its role in defending the state it was created to preserve.

Opening to the West

Although Selim wished to restrict the adoption of European technology and ideas to the military sphere alone, his decision to establish permanent Ottoman embassies in the European capitals had the effect of opening new channels for the transmission of knowledge about the West into educated Ottoman circles. The first mission was sent to London in 1793, and by the end of the century Ottoman embassies had also been set up in Paris, Berlin, and Vienna. The recognition that it was necessary to have permanent representation in Europe marked a departure from previous Ottoman practice. From the beginning of the Ottoman conquests, European commercial and diplomatic agents had been active in Ottoman domains. But the Ottomans, convinced of the superiority of their system, had not deemed it necessary to round out an exchange. If the European rulers needed commercial agreements or peace treaties, they had to send their representatives to Istanbul to seek the sultan's favor there. When an Ottoman ruler wished to discover information about conditions in Europe, he was content to rely on the details provided by one of the European representatives. In the centuries of

Ottoman domination, the drawbacks of this one-sided dialogue may have been minimal; by the time of Selim, they were of major significance.

A similar attitude of superiority prevailed toward the languages of Europe; an educated Muslim Ottoman official of Selim III's era might have known Ottoman, Arabic, and Persian, but he would not have had the opportunity to study a single European language. The Ottoman state communicated with Europe through official court translators (dragomans) employed from the Christian *millet*s. By the eighteenth century, members of the Istanbul Greek community held most of the top dragoman positions in the imperial service.

During Selim's reign, the impact of the new embassies on informing the court about conditions in Europe was slight. The Ottoman ambassadors were ignorant of the languages of the countries to which they were assigned and had to rely on the goodwill of the Greek dragomans they took with them. Nevertheless, these missions provided a small cadre of young Ottoman officials with direct experience of Europe and with a grounding in French, the language of European diplomacy.

The Overthrow of Selim III

The formation and expansion of the *nizam-i jedid* aroused active opposition from the elements of Ottoman society that had benefited from the decline of central authority. From the start of Selim's reign, the Janissaries had viewed his entire program of military reform as a threat to their independence, and they refused to serve alongside the new army in the field. The powerful *derebey*s were alarmed by the way in which the sultan financed his new forces—he confiscated *timar*s and directed the revenue toward the *nizam-i jedid*. Further opposition came from the ulama and other members of the ruling elite who objected to the European models on which Selim based his military reforms.

Led by the rebellious Janissaries, these forces came together in 1806, deposed Selim III, and selected a successor, Mustafa IV, who pledged not to interfere with their privileges. The decree of deposition accused Selim III of failing to respect the religion of Islam and the tradition of the Ottomans. Over the course of the next year, the embassies in Europe were dismantled, the *nizam-i jedid* troops were dispersed, and the deposed sultan, whose cautious military reforms were intended to do no more than preserve the tradition of the Ottomans, was murdered.

A Revived Center of Power: The Egypt of Muhammad Ali, 1805–1848

The Mamluk Restoration and the French Invasion

The diversion of Ottoman resources in wars with European states and campaigns against local warlords reduced the empire's ability to maintain administrative control over several of its provinces. This was evident in the case of Egypt, which by the late eighteenth century had become in reality if not in name an autonomous state under a revived Mamluk order. Although the Ottomans continued to send governors to Cairo, the Mamluk beys had effectively replaced the sultan's representatives as the source of administrative and financial authority in the province. The Mamluk regime was unstable, oppressive, and unpopular. It had no cohesive central government but operated instead through a network of competing Mamluk households, each of which collected taxes, employed troops, and engaged in commercial ventures with local merchants and European agents. Given the absence of an administrative center to provide direction from the top, society was held together by various arrangements worked out among the Mamluks and leading merchants, guildspeople, and members of the religious establishment. From time to time one of the Mamluks was able to attract sufficient clients and men at arms to become dominant in the country. This occurred under Ali Bey al-Kabir (1760–1773), who expanded Egypt's trade with Britain and France and showed a willingness to improve his army by hiring European advisers and purchasing European weapons. However, Ali Bey was overthrown by his own Mamluk military commander, and from 1775 to 1798 Egypt was dominated by a tenuous alliance between two rival Mamluk factions.

Thus, although late eighteenth-century Egypt was not as isolated as it has sometimes been portrayed, the frequent internecine warfare among the Mamluk factions and their heavy-handed tax policies caused order and security in the rural areas to break down. Moreover, the tendency of the Mamluk system to fragment prevented the establishment of any stable central authority through which the country's resources could be organized and its administration regularized. This would change during the governorship of Muhammad Ali.

In the aftermath of the French Revolution in 1789, Britain and France became embroiled in a series of wars that lasted until Napoleon Bonaparte's defeat at Waterloo in 1815. The major battles of the Napoleonic Wars were fought on the European continent, but the Franco-British rivalry extended beyond Europe and brought the two powers into conflict over access to overseas markets and strategic outposts. Egypt became directly enmeshed in this rivalry when an ambitious French expedition led by Napoleon invaded the country in 1798 and administered a decisive defeat to the Mamluk forces at the Battle of the Pyramids. The immediate military objective of the French expedition was to strike at Britain's communications routes with India. Napoleon was also motivated by commercial considerations, hoping to colonize Egypt and to establish it as a reliable source of grain for the French mainland. The British destruction of the French fleet in 1798 at the battle of Aboukir Bay near Alexandria frustrated French goals, and Napoleon soon returned to France.

However, the rest of the expeditionary force, cut off from the outside by the British fleet, remained in troubled occupation of the country for three years. The engineers and scientists that Napoleon had brought with him drew up plans for new canals and communications, and the fledgling French administration attempted to reorganize the landholding and taxation systems. But the occupation was unpopular among Egyptians, and few of the French schemes were actually implemented. The whole episode was brought to an end by a joint British-Ottoman expedition that landed in Egypt in 1801 and eventually arranged for the evacuation of the French forces. One important result of the French invasion was to impress on local Middle Eastern rulers the technological capabilities of a European power that could mount a complex amphibious expedition across the Mediterranean and penetrate to the very heartlands of Ottoman domains.

The Reform Policies of Muhammad Ali

From one perspective, Muhammad Ali can be viewed as another traditional warlord seeking to establish an independent hereditary dynasty at the expense of the weakened Ottoman state. Yet for all the customary features of warlordism and absolutism that characterized Muhammad Ali's rule in Egypt, his regime also represented the first sustained program in the Middle East of state-sponsored Europeanization of the military and of the institutions that supported it.

Muhammad Ali was an ethnic Albanian, born and raised in the Greek coastal city of Kavalla. He arrived in Egypt in 1801 as second in command of an Albanian contingent that was part of the expedition sent by the Ottoman government to evacuate the French. Several factions competed to fill the power vacuum left by the French departure. Muhammad Ali emerged the victor and was recognized by Istanbul as the Ottoman governor of Egypt in 1805. With his position established, Muhammad Ali launched Egypt on a breathtaking forty years of internal development and imperial expansion. He completely refashioned the armed forces, he reorganized the administration and installed a centralized bureaucracy, he changed the patterns of landholding and agricultural production, he introduced heavy industry, and he conquered an empire that by the 1830s included the northern Sudan, the western coast of Arabia, all of Greater Syria, and parts of southwestern Anatolia. All of these administrative, fiscal and personnel changes formed part of a process of state building in which Muhammad Ali transformed the governing structures of Egypt from those of a subordinate province to those of a fledgling state. In the course of making Egypt a military and economic power, Muhammad Ali also brought the country into sustained diplomatic and commercial contact with western Europe.

Muhammad Ali's political objective was to secure independence from the Ottoman Empire and to establish in Egypt a hereditary dynasty for his family. Because he believed that independence could be won and preserved only by means of a powerful army and navy, the main purpose of all of his re-

Muhammad Ali led Egypt through an intense period of transformation and established the dynasty that ruled until 1952.

forms was to strengthen the armed forces. Impressed by what he had seen of British and French troops, he determined that his military would be modeled on European lines. The most immediate barrier to Muhammad Ali's goal of building a European-style army was the continued interference of the Mamluks. Unable to reform them or to win their allegiance, Muhammad Ali destroyed them. In 1811 about seventy-four leading Mamluks were massacred as they left a banquet to which he had invited them in the Cairo citadel. During the months that followed, Mamluk power was decisively broken throughout the country, and Muhammad Ali began the systematic reconstruction of an officer corps based on the European model.

He established an officers' training school in Aswan with European instructors and Turkish and Mamluk students. In a further attempt to produce a cadre of Egyptians with an understanding of European military sciences, Muhammad Ali sent several training missions to Europe, mainly to France. Members of these student groups, returning to Egypt with firsthand experience of Europe and a knowledge of its languages, had an impact on the future direction of their country that extended far beyond the narrowly military origins of their training. In addition to providing for the specific training of combat officers, Muhammad Ali founded educational institutions intended to produce experts in the support services required by the military. During a twenty-year period beginning in the early 1820s, schools of medicine, veterinary medicine, engineering, and chemistry opened their doors. In time these, too, would have influence beyond their initial military intent.

Such an intensive program of higher education oriented toward Western subject matter brought with it a concurrent effort to produce suitable textbooks and instruction manuals. In 1835 Muhammad Ali established the School of Languages for the express purpose of training translators and preparing Arabic textbooks for the state schools. This school exercised an important influence on the direction of Egypt's cultural and educational life until its closure in the 1850s. A related development was the founding of a government printing press that published the translated materials, printed government decrees for distribution, and brought out the first Arabic-language newspaper, *al-Waqai al-Misriyyah* (Official gazette) in 1828. Muhammad Ali's wholehearted acceptance of the printing press was a break from the cautious cultural tradition of the Ottoman world and was of the utmost importance in promoting the spread of Western ideas to the educated elite of Egyptian society.

As he set up his European-style facilities for training officers, Muhammad Ali was faced with the need to obtain large numbers of common soldiers to fill his new army. At one point he thought that the inhabitants of the Sudan could be molded into an effective slave army, and in 1820 he ordered an invasion of the region. Although a portion of northern Sudan was successfully conquered and added to Egypt's domains, an army of Sudanese troops did not materialize. Muhammad Ali then turned to Egypt itself and began conscripting native Egyptian *fellahin* (peasants). Like Selim III's use of Anatolian Turks in the *nizam-i jedid*, this was a departure from the existing norm in the Ottoman world. But Muhammad Ali was not bound by traditional notions of warfare, and though his relentless conscription led to the depopulation of the countryside, he managed to build a peasant army that at its peak numbered over 130,000 troops. The very act of conscription represented a new form of government control over the population. Effective conscription—as well as efficient taxation—required accurate population statistics, and Muhammad Ali endeavored to collect them by establishing conscription registers and later by ordering a national census. Military service was harsh and conscription was dreaded, but Muhammad Ali was determined to support his bid for independence with a credible military machine.

Muhammad Ali recognized that in order to pay for his military, he would have to exploit Egypt's resources to their limits and ensure that the central treasury obtained the maximum possible revenues from all productive sources within the economy. At the time Muhammad Ali became governor of Egypt, the existing systems of land tenure and taxation allowed considerable revenue to be diverted from the state. Mamluks and individuals within the ulama profited from their control of *iltizam*, a tax-farming system in which tax farmers remitted a fixed annual sum to the treasury and retained whatever surplus they could extort from the peasants under their control.

During the first ten years of his rule, Muhammad Ali confiscated the *iltizam* lands and instituted a tax on the extensive *waqf* revenues administered by the ulama. *Waqf* was a practice, approved by the *shari'ah*, that permitted the income from property to be set aside in perpetuity for charitable purposes such as the upkeep of mosques and schools. The revenue from *waqf* endowments was not subject to tax, and by the nineteenth century large portions of productive land in both Egypt and the central Ottoman domains were devoted to *waqf* and thus lay outside the state's control. The ulama acted as trustees for *waqf* endowments and assigned *waqf* revenues to their designated purposes. The centralizing governments of the nineteenth and twentieth centuries sought to break the hold of the ulama over *waqf*s and to gain control of the revenues generated by the endowments. Thus Muhammad Ali's policies served the dual purpose of increasing the state's control over land and revenue and of reducing the wealth and prestige of the Mamluks and the ulama. Over the course of his reign, Muhammad Ali granted land to certain trusted officials who were expected to cultivate it in exchange for tax exemptions, and he gave large tracts of land to his relatives. The net result of these practices was to introduce the concept of private ownership of land and to concentrate enormous holdings into the hands of a few families.

Muhammad Ali's regime also experimented with new crops, by far the most important of them being a special variety of long-staple cotton known as Jumel after the French engineer who helped develop it. Jumel cotton was favored by the European textile industry, and it quickly became Egypt's most lucrative cash crop. To further boost revenues Muhammad Ali brought previously marginal lands into cultivation and increased the yields of existing plots by rebuilding and expanding the irrigation system. Thousands of *fellahin* were put to work dredging canals and constructing barrages so that the annual Nile flood could be stored and used for a full summer growing season when the river was low. These public works projects were carried out through extensive use of the corvée, a levy of forced peasant labor. As with the regime's large-scale conscription practices, the corvée, by uprooting peasants from their lands and forcing them to serve on work gangs, caused a temporary decline in agricultural productivity in those regions most heavily affected by the levy. It was common for foremen on the work gangs to apply the *khurbaj* (whip). Muhammad Ali did not introduce the corvée and the *khurbaj* into the Egyptian countryside, but he did not prohibit their application.

During the first years of Muhammad Ali's rule, Egypt's revenues were derived mainly from the export of agricultural commodities. However, Muhammad Ali did not intend for Egypt to become an exporter of raw materials and an importer of European manufactured products. In an effort to make the country self-sufficient, he began a program of industrialization with an emphasis on war-related materials and textiles for the local market. By the mid-1820s, the arsenal in the Cairo citadel was producing 1,600 muskets a month, and in the late 1830s the new naval complex at Alexandria employed 4,000 workers and was responsible for the construction of nine warships with over 100 guns each.[2] Machinery and managers were imported from Europe, but the labor force was recruited from among Egyptian peasants and craftsmen. Estimates on the numbers of workers vary widely, but it appears that during the late 1830s at least 30,000 to 40,000 Egyptians were employed in industrial enterprises. The products of the war-related industries were of high quality, whereas the textile industry was less successful and could not capture markets that Muhammad Ali did not control directly. The entire program of state-sponsored industrialization was rushed, and many of the factories were abandoned in the 1840s when Muhammad Ali was forced to reduce the size of his army to 18,000 men (see the next section).

Muhammad Ali's ability to direct the Egyptian economy and to control its revenues was attained through a monopoly system. He forced cultivators to sell directly to him at a fixed price, then sold to European buyers at the considerably higher market price. He controlled industrial development in a similar fashion, directing capital investment and collecting the revenues. His domestic monopoly was an irritant to European merchants, who had no opportunity to purchase materials from any Egyptian supplier other than the governor. For most of his reign, Muhammad Ali appears to have defied many of the Capitulation restrictions that were supposed to apply in all Ottoman territories.

One of Muhammad Ali's most lasting achievements, and the one that made the implementation of his other reformist schemes possible, was the reorganization of the central administration. Government was taken away from competing Mamluk factions and centralized under Muhammad Ali's absolute authority. From him there radiated a system of delegated power that at the highest level rested in functionally differentiated ministries. At the middle level there emerged a new group of officials trained in technical and administrative schools and appointed on the basis of their qualifications. Government became more bureaucratized and more predictable. To buttress the state's control over the countryside Egypt was divided into ten provinces, each of which was administered by a centrally appointed governor responsible for law and order and the collection of taxes.

Muhammad Ali's creation of a centralized bureaucracy was one of his most enduring legacies, but the complexities of his government should not be overemphasized. He ran his state in the manner of an extended household; his sons were appointed to key positions, his loyal officials received grants of land, and he made the major decisions himself. Nor should Muhammad Ali's success in Egypt be associated with any identification on his part with Egyptians. He was a dynast, not an Egyptian, and he is reputed to have despised his subjects. The language of his higher administration was Ottoman Turkish, not the local Arabic, and the initial composition of his new bureaucratic and military elite showed his preference for Turks and Circassians over native Egyptians. He also exhibited the traditional Ottoman reliance on minority groups for administrative expertise; his administration contained a high proportion of local Christians, and his most trusted personal adviser and minister of foreign affairs, Boghos Pasha, was an Armenian. Although Muhammad Ali continued to regard himself as a member of an Ottoman ruling elite that was culturally and linguistically separated from the population over which it ruled, his pragmatic educational policies turned out a new elite of native Egyptians who began to assume positions of responsibility in the bureaucracy. The high posts in the military hierarchy continued to be awarded to non-Egyptians, but within the civilian administration the graduates of the new schools began to secure important positions, and within a generation of Muhammad Ali's passing, Arabic replaced Ottoman Turkish as the language of administration.

The Wars of Expansion

Unlike Selim III, who did not have the opportunity to deploy his new army, Muhammad Ali sent his reformed military on wars throughout the Middle East. His military campaigns began in the service of the Ottoman sultan; they concluded with the near conquest of Istanbul.

His first overseas campaign was against the puritanical Wahhabi movement in western Arabia (see Chapter 7). The Wahhabis had captured the holy cities of Mecca and Medina, and the Ottoman sultan, Mahmud II, diverted by European war and domestic turmoil, ordered Muhammad Ali to put down the revolt. The Egyptian forces, led by Muhammad Ali's son Ibrahim, a brilliant commander, landed in Arabia in 1811 and over the course of a difficult campaign captured Mecca and Medina and established an Egyptian presence in the Hijaz. The conquest of the Sudan began in 1820 and brought portions of that region, including its Red Sea coast, under Egyptian dominion (see Map 4.1).

In the meantime events in Ottoman Europe presented Muhammad Ali with an opportunity to expand the Mediterranean base of his empire. In 1821 a nationalist revolt against Ottoman rule broke out in Greece. Neither the rebels nor the Ottoman army was able to achieve a decisive victory, and the revolt dragged on until Sultan Mahmud II requested Muhammad Ali's military intervention. In exchange for his assistance, Muhammad Ali was promised the governorship of Crete. The Egyptian forces, again commanded by Ibrahim, subdued the Greek rebels and helped the Ottomans recapture Athens in 1827. By this time, however, the Greek revolt had become internationalized, and European intervention forced Ibrahim to evacuate his troops and leave Crete under Ottoman sovereignty. Muhammad Ali's support of the sultan had proved costly and had gained him no new territory. His next campaigns would serve his own needs.

In order to obtain raw materials lacking in Egypt (especially timber for his navy) and a captive market for Egypt's new industrial output, Muhammad Ali turned against the sultan and invaded Syria. From fall 1831 to December 1832 Ibrahim led the Egyptian army through Lebanon and Syria and across the Taurus Mountains into Anatolia, where he defeated the Ottoman forces and pushed on to Kuhtaya, only 150 miles from Istanbul.

The Egyptian invasion of Syria triggered a European response that reveals the intricate linkage between the actions of local Middle Eastern rulers and Europe's determination to defend its interests in the area. As Ibrahim's forces pushed the Ottoman armies out of Syria, Mahmud II desperately sought a Great Power ally. Only Russia responded to his appeals, and in 1833 the two states signed a defensive alliance known as the Treaty of Unkiar Skelessi. This treaty overturned a cornerstone of British policy: the aim to keep Russian influence at Istanbul to a minimum. Thus, when the treaty was disclosed, British and French diplomats swung into action in order to prevent further Russian gains in Istanbul. They successfully pressured the sultan and Muhammad Ali to end their hostilities and sign a treaty that recognized Ibrahim as governor of the Anatolian district of Adana and all of Greater Syria. Although Muhammad Ali had failed to achieve international recognition of his sovereign independence, he had expanded his empire and

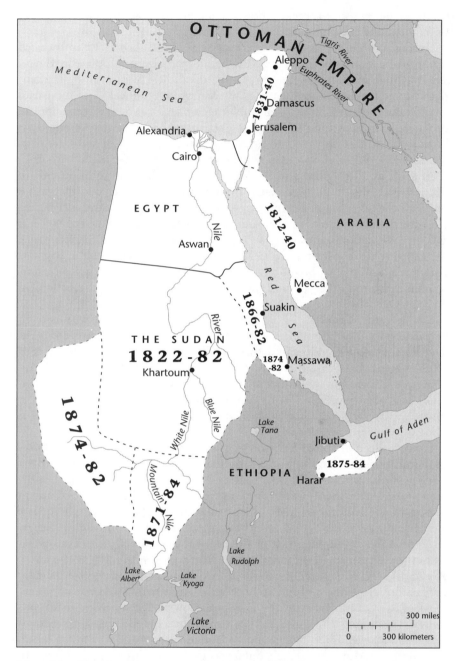

Map 4.1 Egyptian Expansion under Muhammad Ali and His Successors. The dates indicate the years that the various territories were controlled, directly or indirectly, by Egypt.

survived the European intervention his actions had caused. He would not be so fortunate the next time.

During Ibrahim's years as governor of Syria (1833–1840), he introduced many of the domestic programs that had already been adopted in Egypt. The Egyptian monopoly system was also imposed on Syria, making it a captive market for Egyptian textiles. This damaged the local craft industries and, in combination with Ibrahim's imposition of military conscription, produced unrest in the region during the late 1830s. Sultan Mahmud II, hoping to use this unrest to his advantage, sent an army against Ibrahim in spring 1839. But the Ottoman forces were routed at the battle of Nezib, setting off another international diplomatic crisis that brought an end to Muhammad Ali's imperial dreams. Britain, more than ever convinced that the rise of Muhammad Ali's military and commercial power was incompatible with British interests in the Middle East, sent a fleet to Beirut in 1840 and, in joint action with Ottoman forces, landed troops in Lebanon. Once the expedition was ashore, the local hostility that had been building against Ibrahim's administration burst forth in a number of popular uprisings. Ibrahim retreated to Egypt, and the powers of Europe imposed a settlement on the Ottoman-Egyptian conflict.

By the terms of the Treaty of London of 1841, Muhammad Ali was compelled to withdraw from all the territories he had occupied except the Sudan. The treaty also stipulated that the Egyptian army could not exceed 18,000 men. Although these were significant restrictions with important consequences for Egypt, Muhammad Ali managed to achieve at least a portion of his objectives. The Treaty of London stated that the governorship of Egypt was to be a hereditary office held by his family. Indeed, Egypt was ruled by Muhammad Ali's descendants until 1952.

However, the Egypt of his successors was to be in a considerably weaker economic position than it had been during the height of his power. Partly as a result of Muhammad Ali's occupation of Syria and his establishment of the monopoly system there, Great Britain persuaded the Ottoman government to sign a trade convention in 1838 known as the Treaty of Balta Liman. The agreement was to have a profound impact on Ottoman (including Egyptian) economic development. It provided for the abolition of all monopolies within the Ottoman Empire and granted foreign goods entry at the favorable tariff rate of 3 percent. Other European states soon wrested similar concessions from the Ottomans. In combination with a vigorous enforcement of the Capitulations by the European powers and a decline in Egypt's military strength, the Balta Liman agreement helped bring an end to Egypt's industrial development and economic independence. Thus, a significant result of Muhammad Ali's reign was to intensify western European involvement in the affairs of the Middle East as a whole and Egypt in particular. To paraphrase Marshall Hodgson on Europe's determination and ability to defend its developing global interests, if Egypt mattered in London, then London would surely matter in Egypt.

Following the signing of the Treaty of London and the forced reduction of the Egyptian armed forces, most of Muhammad Ali's war-related industries were abandoned, many of his schools were closed, and the public works projects ceased. The military machine for whose needs he had developed the Egyptian economy no longer existed. Yet despite Muhammad Ali's failure to establish complete Egyptian independence, his attempt to create an autonomous state had led him to construct an infrastructure of government that outlasted his rule. He left to his successors the all-important legacies of a centralized administration and a small cadre of trained officials who would continue his commitment to European-inspired reform.

Nationalism and Great Power Intervention: The Greek Revolt, 1821–1829

In addition to outside powers and internal warlords, the Ottoman government faced another threat to its territorial integrity during the nineteenth century: nationalist independence movements by its European subjects. The new ideology of nationalism, with its central principle that peoples speaking the same language and holding shared memories of a common past should form distinct political states, endangered the imperial religious structure on which the Ottoman Empire rested. As nationalism spread among its Balkan subjects, the state was confronted by a continuous series of nationalist uprisings that were often manipulated by the Great Powers for their own ends. The first Balkan independence revolt broke out in Serbia in 1804, but because of the Serbs' difficulties in attracting a Great Power patron, the uprising did not achieve its objectives until 1830, when Serbia was granted autonomy. The Greek revolt, in contrast, generated Great Power support and led to the creation of an independent Greek state.

There were two components of the Ottoman Greek world in the early nineteenth century. The first lay outside Greece proper and consisted of the cosmopolitan Greek intellectual and commercial centers in Istanbul and the Russian Black Sea port of Odessa. Members of the flourishing community in Odessa were prominent in shipping and trade, whereas the Phanariot (from their quarter, Phanar) Greeks in Istanbul dominated the hierarchy of the Greek Orthodox church and held the influential positions of dragomans. Members of this wider Greek community became familiar with conditions in western Europe and with the ideas of the French Revolution, which they communicated to their compatriots in Greece proper. In 1814 a secret society, Philike Hetairia (the Society of Friends), was founded in Odessa for the purpose of coordinating a movement for the independence of Greece from the Ottomans.

Conditions on the Greek mainland were in marked contrast to the world of Phanar and Odessa. As was the case in other regions of the empire, the decline of Ottoman central authority in Greece caused government to become less efficient and more capricious and led to the rise of local Turkish—

and Greek—*derebey*s who controlled the land and exploited the peasantry. The alienation of the population from its Ottoman overlords was increased by the development of nationalism, in this case by a resurgence of Greek literature and a new awareness of the classical Greek past. The Ottomans came to be seen as alien oppressors, not imperial protectors.

The armed revolt broke out in 1821 and briefly occupied two fronts. The Philike Hetairia, led by Alexander Yipsilantis, attempted to foment a rebellion in the Danubian Principalities; this ill-conceived endeavor was quickly crushed by the Ottoman forces. On the Greek mainland, bands of rebels attacked Ottoman installations and killed individual Turkish residents. Although the mainland rebellion lacked coordination and central leadership, it succeeded in driving the Ottomans from the Peloponnesus. However, the revolt soon reached a stalemate; the rebels could not force the Ottomans out of the north, and the Ottomans could not subdue the Greek forces in the Peloponnesus. It was a brutal confrontation, and both sides took bitter reprisals against the civilian populations. The enmity spread to Istanbul, where the Ottomans executed the patriarch of the Greek Orthodox church and the chief dragoman. These executions marked a significant break in the relationship between the Ottoman ruling elite and the Greek elite of the Phanar quarter of Istanbul, on whom the Ottomans had traditionally relied as translators and transmitters of information about western Europe. The Greek revolt would make it necessary for the Ottomans to train their own Muslim translators in Western languages.

Desperate to end the rebellion, Sultan Mahmud II called on Muhammad Ali of Egypt, whose troops, as we have seen, had considerable success against the rebels. When the Egyptian and Ottoman forces linked up in 1827, the revolt appeared doomed. It was at this point that the Great Powers asserted their interests and changed the outcome of events. In Britain public opinion was overwhelmingly in favor of the Greek cause. Russia, using its standard pretext for interference in Ottoman affairs, emphasized its role as the protector of the Greek Orthodox church and asserted its right to intervene on behalf of its coreligionists.

Here was displayed the delicate pattern of diplomacy that developed around what came to be called the Eastern Question. Britain and Russia each feared that the other would use the excuse of the Greek revolt to acquire Ottoman territory. Both powers were eager to gain an advantage at the Ottomans' expense, but they did not wish to antagonize each other and create a situation that could lead to war between them. They therefore applied the unwritten code of Eastern Question diplomacy: They joined together, along with France, and offered to mediate between the Ottomans and the Greeks, hoping that by overseeing the settlement of the crisis they would preserve their respective interests. But Mahmud II refused to play according to the rules of European diplomacy, insisting that the only acceptable settlement was the full restoration of Ottoman sovereignty over Greece. The Great Power alliance responded to the sultan's intransigence by escalating its pressure and sending a fleet to Greece in 1827 to set up a blockade of all supplies bound for the Ottoman-Egyptian forces. Somehow, the European and Ottoman-Egyptian fleets both chose Navarino Bay for their anchorage. Without a declaration of war from either side, one of the largest naval battles of the nineteenth century occurred on October 20, 1827. When it was over, most of the Ottoman-Egyptian fleet was on the bottom of the bay.

The defeat at Navarino prompted Muhammad Ali to withdraw from Greece, but Sultan Mahmud II still refused to concede the loss of the region. Russia then declared war on the Ottoman Empire in 1828, and by the following year its armies had, with considerable difficulty, crossed the Danube and captured Adrianople, the Ottomans' second capital. This was a situation that the checks and balances of Eastern Question diplomacy were supposed to prevent: The empire was facing a disastrous military defeat, and Russia stood to make considerable unilateral territorial gains. Britain considered dispatching a fleet to Istanbul, and war seemed imminent. However, hostilities were avoided when Britain and Russia decided that the dismemberment of the Ottoman Empire was not in the best interests of either power. Put simply, each state concluded that the existence of the empire as a weak buffer state between their competing ambitions was preferable to going to war over the division of Ottoman territories.

The Greek crisis was settled according to this principle. In the Treaty of Adrianople (1829) between the Ottomans and Russians, Russia reduced its original territorial demands and agreed to withdraw to the Danube. The affairs of Greece were regulated by a convention of 1832, which declared Greece an independent state under the protection of Britain, Russia, and France. The Greece that emerged from the revolt was a truncated state of some 800,000 inhabitants, 2.4 million Greeks remaining under Ottoman rule. This was a virtual guarantee that Greek foreign policy would be irredentist.

Joint Ottoman-Egyptian action had defeated the forces of the Greek revolt, but Great Power intervention overturned the results achieved in the local arena. Subsequent Balkan nationalist revolts did not produce exactly the same sequence of Great Power involvement, but all of them did attract external intervention, forcing the Ottomans always to pay attention not just to the rebels themselves but also to the rebels' potential Great Power patrons. That the Ottomans could also find outside patrons and manipulate Great Power rivalries to their own advantage was a lesson that Mahmud II learned well when he used the Russian threat to help create the Franco-British alliance that halted Muhammad Ali in 1833 and again in 1839–1840.

Sultan Mahmud II (1808–1839): Centralization and Transformation

Mahmud II has received bad press from Western diplomatic historians who view him simply as the sultan who ruled during a period of increased dismemberment of Ottoman lands and was overshadowed by his own governor, Muhammad Ali of Egypt. Yet despite the territorial losses suffered during his reign, one might argue that Mahmud II was the most effective of the late Ottoman sultans, a skillful and determined monarch whose rule achieved for the empire what Muhammad Ali's had for Egypt. Like Selim III, Mahmud II was primarily a military reformer. However, he differed from his ill-starred predecessor in that he saw the need to act decisively against the centrifugal political forces that continued to paralyze royal authority.

Given the dominance of the *derebey*-ulama-Janissary coalition that had overthrown Selim III, Mahmud II had to proceed cautiously. The first years of his reign were occupied by a campaign to reestablish central authority within the provinces. Using the Janissaries, whose loyalty he secured with bribes, Mahmud II moved against the *derebeys* and succeeded in breaking their power. By the 1820s, with the Greeks in revolt and Muhammad Ali demonstrating the superiority of his reformed military, Mahmud II ordered the creation of a new European-style army corps to which he intended to attach various Janissary units. The Janissaries, as they had done so often in the recent past, mounted a demonstration against the proposed reforms, but Mahmud II had prepared for the rebellion and used his new troops to crush it. Within the space of a few hours on June 15, 1826, thousands of Janissaries were massacred on the streets and in their barracks, and the military institution that had once been the foundation of Ottoman power was destroyed forever.

The elimination of the Janissaries removed the major obstacle to further reform, and during the final thirteen years of his reign, Mahmud II instituted a rapid-paced program that transformed the traditional Ottoman order. His first priority was the rebuilding of his army along European lines. To avoid the charges of infidelism that had weakened Selim III, Mahmud II called his new force "the triumphant soldiers of Muhammad." It was trained by Prussian and French officers and British naval advisers. Further European influences penetrated the military through the educational infrastructure Mahmud II established; in 1827 a medical school for army personnel was founded in Istanbul; and in 1834 the sultan opened the School of Military Sciences, or war college, modeled on the French officers' training academy at St. Cyr. Instruction at both of these institutions was in French. Following the example of Muhammad Ali, the sultan began sending groups of students to Europe for advanced study, thus ensuring a further commitment to European models among members of the new officer corps. In the same year that the Janissaries were destroyed, Mahmud II also abolished the *sipahi* units and formed a professional salaried cavalry. A related development was the elimination of the *timar* system in 1831.

Mahmud II's reforms were not confined to the military. To increase the administrative efficiency of the state and to reestablish royal authority in the conduct of affairs, the sultan undertook a reorganization of the bureaucracy.

He abolished old offices, introduced new lines of responsibility in an effort to create European-style ministries, and raised salaries in an attempt to end bribery. Just as French uniforms symbolized the post-Janissary army, so the replacement of the turban and the robe by the fez and the frock coat among the bureaucracy represented Mahmud II's efforts to force Europeanization on the civilian branches of government. In 1838 the sultan founded two institutions for the training of higher officials. Both of them offered a mixture of standard and secular subjects and, significantly, included instruction in French. To keep his officials informed of his programs, the sultan founded an official gazette, *Takvim-i Vekayi* (Calendar of events), in 1831. The first newspaper to be published in the Ottoman-Turkish language, it became required reading for all civil servants.

As earlier sections of this chapter have shown, the Ottoman Empire was involved in a series of international diplomatic crises during Mahmud II's reign. The empire's ability to negotiate treaties and alliances was severely hampered by the paucity of officials with knowledge of a European language. Even the customary practice of employing Greek dragomans had to be abandoned as a result of the Greek revolt. In the 1830s Mahmud II moved to fill this void by reestablishing the Ottoman embassies in Europe and by opening a translation office to deal with state correspondence and train Ottoman officials in European languages. Both the embassies and the translation office proved to be important training grounds for the next generation of civil servants.

Under Mahmud II the autonomy of the *derebeys* was curbed, the Janissaries destroyed, and the bureaucracy reorganized and made dependent on the direct authority of the sultan. A more delicate issue was how to limit the power of the leading ulama who had been instrumental in the overthrow of Selim III. Some ulama accepted the military reforms as necessary, but the entire religious establishment was independent of the central state and in command of considerable resources through its control of *waqf* revenues. Mahmud II attempted to circumscribe the authority of the *shaykh al-Islam,* the chief religious dignitary of the empire, by making his office part of the state bureaucracy. The sultan also tried to acquire control of *waqf* revenues by creating the Ministry of Religious Endowments (1826) to administer *waqf* income and direct any surplus to the state rather than allowing it to go to the religious establishment. This centralization measure was not fully implemented during Mahmud II's reign, but it marked the beginning of state intervention in the financial affairs of the religious establishment and weakened the position of the ulama vis-à-vis the central government.

Conclusion

Although the Ottoman Empire suffered territorial losses during Mahmud II's reign, his reforms strengthened the military and administrative arms of the state. His legacy, like that of Muhammad Ali, was the creation of an environment in which the new elite—aptly termed "the French knowers"—were favored. As the sultan became committed to European reforms and as European economic and military pressure on the empire increased, those who knew European ways and European languages received appointments to the highest posts in the military command and the civilian bureaucracy. The opponents of reform were either eliminated or, as in the case of the ulama, gradually bypassed. After Mahmud II's death, the members of this new elite, trained in the translation office, the European embassies, and the military academies, continued his reforms and inaugurated a new phase in the transformation of the Ottoman system.

Notes

1. Stanford J. Shaw, *Between Old and New: The Ottoman Empire Under Selim III, 1789–1807* (Cambridge, Mass., 1971).

2. Roger Owen, *The Middle East in the World Economy, 1800–1914* (London, 1981), p. 71.

The Ottoman Empire and Egypt During the Era of the Tanzimat | 5

During the middle decades of the nineteenth century, the reforms Muhammad Ali and Mahmud II had inaugurated for the purposes of revitalizing their armed forces were extended into nonmilitary areas by their successors. The emulation of European methods of administration, education, and political organization brought about a continued expansion of the role of the state and was accompanied by a pressing need for qualified administrators and technical experts. Europeans filled many of these positions, but the new state-sponsored schools turned out increasing numbers of Ottoman and Egyptian graduates who quickly moved into the top ranks of the state hierarchy. Although the Islamic foundations of society were not openly questioned by the new generation of Western-trained officials, their policies tended to reduce the institutional significance of the religious establishment and to enhance the opportunities available to individuals trained as they were.

Throughout the period, European economic penetration of the Middle East acquired a new and more pervasive dimension. Added to the earlier sales of arms and other manufactured products was the provision of huge amounts of capital investment and easy access to credit. As the local reformers struggled to finance their projects, European banks and financiers stepped forward with loans that seemed, at the beginning, to offer favorable terms. However, as we will see, these loans became the Achilles' heel of the reform movement, and the accumulation of indebtedness led directly to the British occupation of Egypt and to the less obvious but nonetheless equally real loss of economic sovereignty in the Ottoman Empire.

The Tanzimat: Continued Ottoman Reform Under the Bureaucrats

The period from 1839 to 1876 is known in Ottoman history as the Tanzimat (literally, reorganization) and marks the most intensive phase of nineteenth-century Ottoman reformist activity. During these years, the inspiration for reforms came not from the sultans but from Europeanized Ottoman bureaucrats, the French knowers, who were shaped by the institutions established by Mahmud II.

The career patterns of the leading civilian reformers of the Tanzimat era show how different their experiences were from the generation that preceded them and how their rise to power was tied to their exposure to Europe. The first fifteen years of the Tanzimat were dominated by Rashid Pasha (1800–1858), who acquired his credentials for high office through his service as Ottoman ambassador to Paris and London in the 1830s. He rose rapidly in the Ottoman administration and was minister of foreign affairs at the time of Mahmud II's death in 1839. He used this high position to gain exceptional influence and went on to hold the office of grand vizier six times and the position of foreign minister twice. His commitment to remake the governing institutions of the Ottoman Empire in the image of Europe drove him to promote the careers of a number of like-minded younger men, the two most important of whom became his successors as leaders of the reform movement. The career of the first of these disciples, Ali Pasha (1815–1871), serves as a compelling example of the relationship between knowledge of a European language and access to power in the changing Ottoman Empire of the mid-nineteenth century. The son of an Istanbul shopkeeper, Ali became an employee in the translation office at age eighteen, and by the time he was twenty-six he was Ottoman ambassador to London. After five years in London, Ali Pasha returned to Istanbul, where he became minister of foreign affairs in 1846 and grand vizier in 1852, a post he held several more times until his death. Ali Pasha's associate in the last two decades of the Tanzimat, Fuad Pasha (1815–1869), began his higher education at the military medical school founded by Mahmud II and then transferred to the translation office. This educational background opened up an appointment to the Ottoman embassy in London that in turn led to Fuad's promotion in 1852 to the first of what would be five terms as minister of foreign affairs. Fuad Pasha was the most thoroughly Europeanized of the three men and was famous in diplomatic circles for his devastating wit expressed in perfect French. Once, when he was being pressed by an Englishwoman to reveal how many wives he, as a Muslim, had, he replied: "The same as your husband—two, only he conceals one and I don't."[1] Rashid Pasha and his two disciples dominated the Tanzimat and, in collaboration with other bureaucrats whom they sometimes persuaded and sometimes coerced, were the driving forces behind the movement to transform the administrative structure of the Ottoman Empire.

The most striking evidence of the new direction in which the empire was being taken is contained in two royal decrees that defined the very essence of the Tanzimat. The first of them, the Hatt-i Sharif of Gülhane, was issued in 1839 at Rashid Pasha's insistence. The decree was not a piece of legislation but rather a statement of royal intent the sultan issued to his subjects. In it the Ottoman ruler promised certain administrative reforms, such as the abolition of tax farming, the standardization of military conscription, and the elimination of corruption. These sentiments had been expressed previously, but what made the Hatt-i Sharif so remarkable was the sultan's pledge to extend the reforms to all Ottoman subjects, regardless of their religion. In 1856, at the conclusion of the Crimean War, Ali and Fuad Pashas encouraged the promulgation of a second decree, the Hatt-i Hümayan, in which the principles of 1839 were repeated and the guarantees of the equality of all subjects were made more explicit. Thus, Muslim and non-Muslim were to have equal obligations in terms of military service and equal opportunities for state employment and admission to state schools.

The intent of the two decrees was to secure the loyalty of the Christian subjects of the empire at a time of growing nationalist agitation in the European provinces. It appears that during the period of Ottoman decentralization in the eighteenth and early nineteenth centuries, the *millet*s acquired a greater degree of autonomy than they had previously possessed. The decrees of 1839 and 1856 sought to break down the religious and cultural autonomy of the *millet*s and to create the notion of a common Ottoman citizenship, or Ottomanism, which would in theory replace the religious ordering of society in which Muslims were dominant. The pledges were not fully implemented, as much due to Christian preference for new nationalist affiliations as to lingering Muslim feelings of superiority, but the attempt to replace religious affiliation with secular identity continued with the proclamation of a Nationality Law in 1869. This law reinforced the principle that all individuals living within Ottoman domains shared a common citizenship regardless of their religion. The two decrees together with the Nationality Law represent a sharp break with customary Ottoman attitudes and show the extent to which the reformers were prepared to go in attempting to keep the state together. In order to preserve the Ottoman Empire, they introduced the concept of the secular organization of society, which would have the long-term effect of undermining the entire basis of the Ottoman system.

During the Tanzimat, military improvements continued to receive attention, but the sphere of state-sponsored reforms was consciously extended to other areas as well. Thus, whereas Mahmud II's educational policies concentrated on training officers and physicians for the armed forces, the Tanzimat officials established institutions of higher learning for civilians. The two most important of them were the Civil Service School (1859) and the Imperial Ottoman Lycée at Galatasaray (1868). The impact of these two schools, along with the earlier war college, on the formation of the Ottoman political and administrative elite can scarcely be overemphasized. Graduates from the three institutions enjoyed a high success rate in gaining state employment and occupied positions of authority in Turkey and the Arab states until well into the twentieth century.

In addition to their concern with higher education, the Tanzimat reformers drew up proposals for an elaborate system of secondary schools and in 1847 created a Ministry of Education as an arm of the state. Although the secondary schools were slow to develop, the very act of creating them and placing them under the control of a central ministry constituted an expansion of the state's role in an area not previously considered part of its responsibility and marked yet another step toward the establishment of an educational system outside the control of the ulama.

The Tanzimat was also a period for the promulgation of new legal codes. With the French civil code as the model, new penal and commercial codes were introduced, a system of secular courts called *nizame* was established to deal with cases involving Muslims and non-Muslims, and a new civil code, the Mejelle, was compiled. The Mejelle, which was completed in 1876, represents the combination of the new and the customary that characterized so much of the nineteenth-century Ottoman reform movement. On the one hand, it was based on the *shari'ah* and ensured that no matter how much Western law might affect commercial or maritime codes, the civil code for the inhabitants of the empire would remain within an Islamic framework. On the other hand, the organization and arrangement of the Mejelle was inspired by European legal codes and its administration placed under the jurisdiction of a newly created Ministry of Justice.

If the Tanzimat era lacked the dramatic confrontations of the reigns of Selim III or Mahmud II, it nevertheless produced far-reaching changes in the Ottoman system. For this very reason, some members of the Ottoman elite questioned the wisdom of the reforms and warned that the abandonment of long-standing Islamic institutions in favor of the hasty adoption of European ones would lead to disaster for the *ummah* of Muhammad.

The Young Ottomans

One of the results of the increased interaction between the Ottoman Empire and Europe was an Ottoman literary renaissance that found expression not just in established genres like poetry but also in new forms, especially the periodical press that flourished under private ownership in the last two decades of the Tanzimat. Among the main contributors to the new journalism was a group of intellectuals and bureaucrats known as the Young Ottomans. They were not a coherent organization, but they did share certain values they presented in their journals and newspapers.

The Young Ottomans represent an attempt to reconcile the new institutions of the Tanzimat with the Ottoman and Islamic political tradition. They were united in their dislike of the bureaucratic absolutism of Ali and Fuad Pashas and called for the development of a more democratic form of government. In their view, the two reformers had placed the empire in the worst position possible; it had been deprived of its essential Islamic political and social values, but it had not become more efficient through the forced adoption of European institutions. The Young Ottomans sought the best of both worlds; they called for the revitalization of the empire through the incorporation of selected European models and at the same time insisted on the retention of the Islamic foundations of state and society. Theirs was the complex vision of reformers and preservers. The democratic form of government they espoused was found, they claimed, in the Islamic tradition of consultation. This was not the participatory democracy emerging in western Europe but a form of consultation between an absolutist ruler and his ministers. Reform was desirable, but it had to be grounded in the Islamic tradition.

Yet for all their insistence on the need to find sources of change within the Islamic tradition, the most pronounced impact of the Young Ottomans stemmed from their elaboration of the notion of Ottoman patriotism. The concept of the equality of all Ottomans as citizens had been endorsed in the decrees of 1839 and 1856. In the 1860s and 1870s, the most prominent of the Young Ottomans, Namik Kemal, developed this concept to its secular conclusion in his poems and his famous play *Vatan* (Fatherland), all of which extolled the Ottoman fatherland and insisted that all Ottomans ought to share feelings of devotion to this territorial entity above any loyalties they might feel to their religious communities. This was the beginning of territorial patriotism, the belief that there was an Ottoman *patrie* to which its inhabitants owed primary allegiance. Thus, although Namik Kemal held firm convictions about the need to respect the Islamic foundations of Ottoman society, his ideological solution to the problem of Ottoman territorial disintegration was of European inspiration.

The Ottoman Constitution of 1876

In the course of their studies in Europe, some members of the new Ottoman elite concluded that the secret of Europe's success rested not just with its technical achievements but also with its political organizations. Moreover, the process of reform itself had imbued a small segment of this elite with the belief that constitutional government would be a desirable check on autocracy and provide them with a better opportunity to influence policy. These sentiments became more widespread when, following the death of Ali Pasha in 1871, Sultan Abdul Aziz reasserted royal authority. His chaotic rule led to his deposition in 1876 and, after a few troubled months, to the proclamation of an Ottoman constitution that the new sultan, Abdul Hamid II, pledged to uphold.

Although the constitution provided for an elected chamber of deputies and an appointed senate, it placed only minimal restrictions on the sultan's powers. He retained the right to make war and peace, to appoint and dismiss ministers, to approve legislation, and to convene and dismiss the chamber of deputies. Despite the latitude it gave to the sovereign, the constitution provided clear evidence of the extent to which European influences operated among a section of the Ottoman bureaucracy. The constitution also reaffirmed the equality of all Ottoman subjects, including their right to serve in the new chamber of deputies. In a significant omission, the *millet*s were not mentioned. The constitution was more than a political document; it was a proclamation of Ottomanism and Ottoman patriotism; it was an assertion that the empire was capable of resolving its problems and that it had the right to remain intact as it then existed.

It was unfortunate for the framers of the constitution that Sultan Abdul Hamid II did not share their belief in the virtues of limited monarchy. In 1878, after only two sessions of the chamber of deputies, he dissolved the assembly, suspended the constitution, and inaugurated thirty years of autocratic rule. His important reign is discussed in Chapter 7.

Ottoman Finances

As the Ottoman Empire expanded its administrative apparatus and sought to maintain a modern army and navy supplied with weapons and warships purchased abroad, the strain on its finances became acute. The problem confronting the Tanzimat reformers was that they inaugurated expensive new programs while the sources of state revenues remained fairly constant. In order to cover its annual budget deficits, the empire began to take out loans on the European money markets. The first loan, for 3.3 million Ottoman lire, was arranged in 1854 during the Crimean War. Over the next twenty years, the Ottomans contracted an additional fifteen loans totaling over 200 million Ottoman lire (about 180 million sterling). As was to happen in Egypt, the increased level of debt meant that more and more funds had to be diverted away from the operating budget of the empire and directed instead to paying the interest on the loans. By 1874 about 60 percent of the state's total expenditure was devoted to servicing the debt.[2] This was an impossible burden, and in 1876 the government failed to make all of its payments. In effect, the Ottoman Empire was bankrupt.

European diplomats rushed in to protect European creditors. The immediate crisis was finally resolved by the Decree of Muharram (1881), which authorized the establishment of an Ottoman Public Debt Administration and pledged to reserve certain state revenues to service the debt. The real effect of the decree was the surrender of Ottoman financial independence to European interests. The Public Debt Administration was composed of representatives of the main creditors and was authorized to collect designated revenues and use them to pay the interest on the debt. These payments were given priority over all other Ottoman expenditures. The debt continued to be a burden on the empire and its successor states, and only in 1954 did the government of Turkey fully repay its share.

The Diplomacy of the Tanzimat: Patterns of European Pressure on the Ottoman Empire

The numerous crises of the Eastern Question exercised a significant influence on Ottoman foreign and domestic policies during the second half of the nineteenth century. The purpose here is not to explore each war and treaty but to depict in broad strokes how the unfolding of the Eastern Question affected the Ottoman Empire.

Although the Ottoman civilian reformers were busy with internal reorganization, they also had to contend with renewed Russian expansion into Ottoman territory. Russia carried this out in three main ways: first, by using its religious ties with the Greek Orthodox subjects of the empire to gain influence in Ottoman internal affairs; second, by allying itself, on the basis of common religious and Slavic cultural bonds, to the Balkan independence movements in an effort to become the Great Power patron of whatever new states might emerge; and third, by direct warfare against the armies of the Ottoman state. The other Great Power neighbor of the Ottomans, the Austro-Hungarian Empire of the Hapsburgs, exercised a more cautious foreign policy than did Russia. Austria, after all, faced a problem similar to the one that confronted the Ottomans; it, too, was a multiethnic state whose subject peoples were responding to the appeal of nationalism. Nevertheless, Austria was always willing to gain territory at Ottoman expense when the right occasion presented itself. One such occasion arose in the circumstances surrounding the Crimean War.

The Crimean War (1854–1856) was precipitated by Russian attempts to gain direct authority over the Orthodox Christian subjects of the Ottoman Empire. For centuries, Orthodox and Catholic priests, supported by Russia and France respectively, had competed with one another over the rights to supervise the holy shrines in Jerusalem. The Ottomans regarded these matters as trivial and granted various privileges to the clergy of both faiths. The issue resurfaced in the 1840s and reached a climax in 1853 when Russia presented an ultimatum to the Ottoman government demanding that it sign a joint accord guaranteeing the position of the Orthodox Christians in the empire. This would have given Russia the right to intervene on behalf of approximately 8 million Ottoman subjects, and the sultan rejected the ultimatum. Russia then sent troops into the principalities (Moldavia and Wallachia), which prompted France and Britain to rally to the cause of Ottoman resistance to Russian advances. Such a response was in keeping with the principle of the balance of power that characterized Eastern Question diplomacy: No Great Power (Russia in this case) was to be allowed to acquire unilateral territorial gains at Ottoman expense. If the powers could not agree on an equal division of Ottoman spoils, then groups of them (France and Britain in this case) formed coalitions to prevent one of their members from gaining a unilateral advantage. This pattern of behavior was also designed to avoid warfare among the Great Powers over Ottoman lands. However, in the case of the 1853 crisis, the system broke down. When war was finally declared, it was fought on Russian territory in the Crimea, where the British, French, and Ottoman allies bungled their way to an indecisive victory over the Russian forces. While the armies of the four powers were fighting it out in the Crimea, Austria occupied the principalities.

The Treaty of Paris (1856) brought an end to the hostilities and arranged for the readjustment of boundaries. Among other things, the signatories pledged to respect the territorial integrity of the Ottoman Empire, a pledge that came rather late because, as a result of the war, the principalities were well on their way to becoming independent as a united Romanian state. The treaty further arranged for the demilitarization of the Black Sea and the withdrawal of Russian troops from the Danube. These were severe blows to Russian ambitions, and for the next twenty years Russian foreign policy was directed toward overturning the restrictions imposed by the Treaty of Paris.

An opportunity to do so presented itself during the series of wars and revolts known as the Great Eastern Crisis of 1875–1878. By the time of the crisis, the doctrine of Pan-Slavism had gained adherents in Russian political and intellectual circles as well as among Slavic Balkan nationalist leaders. Pan-Slavism was a mixture of Orthodox Christian and Slavic cultural sentiments that combined to create the idea of a Russian mission to liberate the Slavic peoples—Serbs, Croatians, Slovenes, and Bulgarians—from Ottoman rule and unite them into a vast federation. Slav nationalists who wanted nothing to do with a Russian-dominated Slavic federation could nonetheless use Pan-Slavism as a means of obtaining Russian support for their independence movements.

When anti-Ottoman rebellions broke out in Bosnia in 1875 and in Bulgaria the following year, both movements sought Russian intervention. However, the Ottomans responded quickly to the Bulgarian revolt and suppressed it with exceptionally harsh measures. This provided Russia with an excuse to take up the cause of its fellow Slavs, and in 1877 Russia declared war on the Ottoman Empire. The reformed Ottoman military fought well at the start of the campaign, but the Russian forces gradually drove the Ottomans out of Bulgaria. In early 1878 the Russian army captured Adrianople and imposed a harsh treaty on the Ottomans. At this point, Britain, seeing its entire Middle Eastern policy threatened, prepared for war with Russia. Hostilities were averted by the intervention of Chancellor Otto von Bismarck of Germany, and instead of fighting over control of Ottoman territories, the powers met at the Congress of Berlin in 1878 to find a more peaceful method of dismantling the Ottoman Empire. That is precisely what was achieved in the various agreements reached by the congress—the European powers kept peace among themselves by awarding one another bits of Ottoman territory. In this instance, the principle of the balance of power operated as the Great Powers intended it to. The Ottoman losses were considerable. Serbia, Montenegro, Romania, and part of Bulgaria were recognized as independent states; Russia gained Kars and Batum in eastern Anatolia; and Austria was granted the right to administer the province of Bosnia. In addition, Britain, the ally of the Ottomans, demanded control over Cyprus in exchange for continued British support. The Ottomans were not pleased with the request, but their permission was not really necessary; Britain had already occupied the island in order to use it as a base from which to protect its interests in the eastern Mediterranean.

The Berlin settlement was announced during the second year of Sultan Abdul Hamid's reign. It is no wonder that for the remainder of his long sultanate he was suspicious of European promises and hostile to Europeans in general. Nor should it be any wonder that the Tanzimat officials, for all their concern with administrative reform, should have continued to devote huge sums to military modernization. The development of effective armed forces was not a luxury but a basic requirement for survival.

The Arab Provinces of Greater Syria During the Tanzimat

Although the Tanzimat reforms brought greater efficiency to the Ottoman administration of the Arab provinces, they also disrupted the political and social arrangements that had meant relative communal harmony for nearly 300 years. Adding to the disruption of long-established patterns of life was the European economic penetration of Greater Syria during the second half of the nineteenth century.

From the Egyptian Occupation to the Riots of 1860

Greater Syria (which included the present-day states of Syria, Lebanon, Israel, and Jordan) contained the largest concentration of Ottoman Christian subjects outside of Europe. The governorship of Muhammad Ali's son Ibrahim (1831–1840), affected the relations between Muslims and Christians throughout the region, but especially in Mount Lebanon, the local name for the entire Lebanon mountain range, except for its most northern parts. Because of its isolation from administrative control, Mount Lebanon had long served as a place of refuge for dissident religious groups. In the early nineteenth century, political power in the region was shared between two sects, the Maronite Christians and the Druze. The latter group was a dissident offshoot of Shiʿism dating from the eleventh century. Although less numerous than the Maronites, the Druze were fierce defenders of their sectarian identity, and their chieftains were accepted as equal members of the social order. Over the centuries, the two communities had worked out informal arrangements that allowed for a rough-and-ready tolerance between them. Ibrahim's notions of interventionist administration would destroy those arrangements.

Ibrahim insisted that the government treat all the religious communities in Greater Syria equally, and he issued decrees abolishing the special taxes that Jews and Christians had to pay on their places of worship. However, his most disruptive policy was the introduction of universal conscription and the simultaneous attempt to disarm the local population. When certain Druze communities refused to surrender their weapons in 1837, Ibrahim armed a force of several thousand Christians and sent them against the Druze. The Christian forces took advantage of this opportunity to enlarge the territory under their control. In 1839 Ibrahim had a change of heart and ordered the Christians to return their arms. They refused and took part in a general uprising of all the religious communities against Ibrahim, an event that helped force the Egyptian evacuation.

Greater Syria returned to Ottoman rule, but sectarian relations had been profoundly changed. The Maronites had acquired increased power within Mount Lebanon and a new freedom in Syrian society as a whole that they were not inclined to surrender. Encouraged by the promises of equality contained in the Ottoman decrees of 1839 and 1856, Maronites and other Christians expanded their commercial activities, entered into lucrative relationships with European representatives, founded new educational institutions, and generally asserted themselves in a manner that the Druze and Sunnis saw as overstepping the bounds of what was permitted to minority subjects in a Muslim state. The smoldering Muslim resentment over this change in the accepted social and political order erupted into a brutal civil war. It began in 1860 with Druze attacks on Christian villages in Mount Lebanon and soon spilled over into the quarters of Damascus, where several thousand Christians were massacred and European consulates were burned.

To restore order and forestall direct European intervention in the crisis, an Ottoman military force was dispatched to Damascus and Fuad Pasha himself arrived in the city to make certain that the Muslims deemed responsible for the massacres were punished. These actions failed to satisfy the European powers, and in 1861 a conference of European representatives met in Istanbul to work out a formula that would ensure the safety of the Christian population. The proposed solution was the creation of an autonomous administrative status for Mount Lebanon. This involved the establishment of a small political unit, called the *mutasarrifiyyah*, which was to be governed by a non-Lebanese Ottoman Christian subject and protected by a guarantee of the European powers (see Map 12.1). The governor worked through an advisory council in which the religious communities of the district were represented. Although the *mutasarrifiyyah* appeared to be an awkward political entity, it provided its inhabitants with peace and prosperity until its abolition in 1914. However, because it was organized along sectarian lines, it did not soften communal distinctions but rather served as a daily reminder of their existence.

The Social and Economic Impact of the Tanzimat

From the beginning of Ottoman rule in the Arab lands, the officials from Istanbul and the local urban notables alike recognized the need to cooperate with one another. A pattern of interaction emerged that has been termed the politics of the notables.[3] Most pronounced in the cities of Syria, the politics of the notables was based on the satisfaction of mutual interests. An Ottoman governor could not exercise effective authority without the assistance of the local dignitaries, who had their own independent power base. The local notables, in turn, required access to the governor and through him to Istanbul if they were to satisfy the needs of their clients. In this delicate relationship, the notables played the role of intermediaries, gently reminding the governor of their interests while helping him see that the demands of government were also met. The Tanzimat policy of adopting codes of administrative conduct that took precedence over personal relationships threatened to upset the balance between the notables and the state and to undermine their privileges. How could the notables retain their power and status in the changing political climate?

One way was to take advantage of the economic opportunities that were made available by the European commercial penetration of the Levant. Beginning in the 1830s, European commercial activity along the Syrian coast expanded enormously, mainly through the port of Beirut, which rapidly grew into a major economic and cultural center. As the Ottoman Empire was drawn into the international market, its economic survival depended on the development of exports that were needed in Europe. In the case of Greater Syria, this meant increasing the cultivation of such agricultural products as wheat and barley. To make the switch from subsistence to commercial agriculture, the urban notables brought large tracts of new land under cultivation. They were aided in their acquisition of new holdings by their ability to use one of the major reform decrees of the Tanzimat to their own advantage.

The Ottoman land code of 1858 was a centralizing measure designed to regularize landholding patterns and to increase the tax-collecting efficiency of the central government. It was also supposed to protect the peasant cultivator by allowing him to register his lands and thus deal directly with the state instead of with tax farmers. The law required all landowners to register their land with the government, and they would receive in return a written title deed. It further permitted individuals to purchase and register previously unoccupied state lands. Although the impact of the land law varied from region to region within the empire, in parts of Greater Syria it led to the creation of vast private estates. Individual notables bought huge tracts of uncultivated state lands with the intention of developing them for commercial agricultural purposes. In other instances, peasant cultivators, distrustful of the aims of the law, chose to register their lands in the name of their local notable patron—who would, they assumed, see things right with the government. They were, of course, mistaken. By these and other means, the local notables acquired ownership of large tracts of valuable commercial land, thus expanding their wealth and influence. They successfully subverted a reform decree that was intended to limit their power.

Although the local Arab notables generally opposed the Tanzimat, they could see that positions of administrative authority in the changing Ottoman state were going to young men trained in the government schools. Beginning in the 1870s, many of the leading Arab families adopted the practice of enrolling their sons in the higher academies of Istanbul. Upon completing their studies, these young Arabs obtained positions in the Ottoman bureaucracy and thus gave their families access to the government. Indeed, throughout the Tanzimat, the Arab urban elite managed to preserve their privileges and to make themselves indispensable to the Ottoman officials sent out from Istanbul. The politics of the notables survived the centralizing reforms.

Egypt During the Era of Civilian Reform

From Muhammad Ali to Isma^cil, 1848–1863

Of Muhammad Ali's two immediate successors, Abbas (1848–1854) lacked his father's ruling skills as well as his commitment to reform, and Sa^cid (1854–1863), though he intensified Egypt's contacts with Europe, was an ineffective ruler. Nevertheless, the momentum of Muhammad Ali's administrative reforms carried over to their reigns, and the central government continued to broaden and to become more functionally specialized with the creation of new ministries and councils. And as was the case in the central Ottoman Empire, the administrative positions required to carry out the increased range of state activities were filled by a new elite of officials trained in Europe or in European-style Egyptian institutions.

This trend is illustrated by the career of Ali Mubarak (1823–1893), one of the most influential and talented of Egypt's nineteenth-century reformers. Born in a Delta village, Mubarak attended a government preparatory school before being admitted to the Cairo School of Engineering. As the top student in his class, he was chosen to be a member of a student military mission Muhammad Ali sent to France in 1844. He studied for two years in Paris and was then assigned for an additional two years to the school for artillery officers and military engineers at Metz. When he returned to Egypt in 1849, he was given a modest appointment as instructor in the artillery school. But after only one year in that post, he received a remarkable promotion to become director of the entire system of government schools. Ali Mubarak was the first native Egyptian Muslim to obtain such a high-ranking position. It marked the start of his rich career of public service that spanned nearly four decades and included appointments as head of the ministries of education, public works, and railways. In each of these capacities, Mubarak demonstrated extraordinary skills as an educator, engineer, and administrator. His opportunity to shape the development of several areas of Egyptian life was made possible in part by his transit through the state-sponsored educational system of local and European technical schools.

This was also the case with another native Egyptian, Rifaʿa al-Tahtawi (1801–1873), who exercised a major influence on the direction of his country's cultural life. Al-Tahtawi was educated at the traditional Islamic university, al-Azhar, and appeared headed for a career as a member of the ulama until Muhammad Ali chose him to accompany one of the early missions to Paris in 1826. Al-Tahtawi's official role was imam, or religious guide, but he persuaded the Egyptian authorities to allow him to study with the other members of the mission. By the time he left Paris five years later, al-Tahtawi had absorbed the principal works of French political thought and had become a shrewd observer of French customs. Upon his return to Egypt he was instrumental in persuading Muhammad Ali to found the School of Languages (1835), an institution that played in Egypt a role similar to the translation office in the Ottoman Empire. As director of the school for fifteen years, al-Tahtawi supervised the translation of 2,000 works from foreign languages into Arabic. He also wrote several books, including an account of his student days in Paris that contained favorable comments on French society.

For both Mubarak and al-Tahtawi, the path to state employment passed through Paris. Other members of the new administrative elite would have similar experiences. The cumulative effect of this training was to create a group of officials who were not only familiar with the West but who also, as in the case of Mubarak and al-Tahtawi, admired certain aspects of European civilization and used their positions of authority to encourage the spread of Western ideas and the adoption of Western systems of education and administration.

With the elimination of Muhammad Ali's monopoly system and the abandonment of his policy of industrialization, Egypt's economic development came to be shaped by the needs of the European market. In effect, the country became integrated into the international economic order as a virtual plantation economy, exporting raw materials, most notably cotton, and importing European manufactured goods. The massive export of cotton required a dependable transportation system, and in 1852 Egypt entered the railway age with the completion of the first rail link between Cairo and Alexandria. At the same time that the country's internal communications were being improved, it became more closely linked to the international commercial network by the establishment of regular steamship lines between Alexandria and several Mediterranean ports. The project that, above all others, was to consolidate Egypt's linkage to international shipping had its beginnings in 1854, when the Egyptian ruler Saʿid granted the French engineer Ferdinand de Lesseps the concession to construct a canal across the Isthmus of Suez from the Mediterranean to the Red Sea. The agreement was a financial disaster for Egypt and contributed to the country's plunge into bankruptcy. In addition, bitterness over de Lesseps's manipulation of Egypt and its rulers became embedded in the national consciousness.

But de Lesseps was not the only European entrepreneur attempting to profit from the economic opportunities that Egypt offered in the years after Muhammad Ali. Reputable firms and marginal operators, skilled technicians and common laborers, all attracted by the wealth to be made in transport construction, the cotton exchange, and concession hunting poured into the country in the 1850s and 1860s. By 1872 an estimated 80,000 Europeans, over half of them Greeks and Italians, were resident in Egypt. Made exempt by the Capitulations from taxation and from the jurisdiction of the Egyptian government, they sought and received protection from their consuls whenever their scandalous social behavior or irregular financial dealings attracted the attention of the Egyptian authorities. The consuls themselves exercised extensive political and economic influence in Egyptian affairs, and their offices became centers of nearly autonomous power in Cairo and Alexandria.

Some of the Europeans who came to Egypt obtained employment in the state service, mostly as skilled technicians such as train drivers, steamship pilots, and mechanics. Others received more lucrative positions—in 1855 Saʿid appointed an Englishman as minister of railways and communications, and in 1861 he named an Italian to the same post. These appointments of foreigners occurred just as Egyptian officials like Mubarak and al-Tahtawi were demonstrating their own qualifications for high office. The result was tension between Egyptians eager for the influence and rewards they felt they deserved and Europeans equally determined to cash in on an advantageous economic opportunity. By the time of Saʿid's death in 1863, Europeans, with their economic privileges, their diplomatic protection, and their often patronizing manner, had become a source of irritation at all levels of Egyptian society. The situation would become exacerbated with the rule of Ismaʿil.

Ismaʿil the Magnificent (1863–1879)

Ismaʿil is one of the most controversial figures in modern Egyptian history, a foolish spendthrift to some and a farsighted if extravagant reformer to others. Whatever judgment one may pass on this grandson of Muhammad Ali, there can be little doubt that his policies affected Egyptian domestic development and external relations until well into the twentieth century. Ismaʿil's objective was nothing less than the complete Europeanization of Egypt in as short a time as possible. Personally familiar with the Paris of Napoleon III and the Istanbul of the Tanzimat, Isma'il made little attempt to blend his reformist programs into long-standing Egyptian-Islamic traditions. "My country," he is said to have proclaimed, "is no longer in Africa, it is now in Europe," and he set out to make this statement true.[4]

With a thoroughness never envisaged by Muhammad Ali, Isma'il encouraged the development of a European-educated Egyptian elite. He increased the budget for education over tenfold and embarked on a program to expand the primary and secondary school systems and to found specialized technical and vocational institutions. Two of the latter deserve special mention. Dar al-Ulum, founded in 1872 at Ali Mubarak's urging, was intended to retrain graduates of the religious schools to become teachers of Arabic in the new national primary and secondary system. As the principal modern teacher training college in the country, Dar al-Ulum became one of the largest and most successful of the new postsecondary institutions. The School of Languages, reopened in 1868, was far more elitist and European-oriented. By 1886 the institution had evolved into the Cairo School of Law, offering its students a French-based legal education that made them among the most sought-after candidates for state employment. Isma'il also revived the practice of sending student educational missions to Europe and began the process of turning female education into a responsibility of the state. In addition to making these educational reforms, Isma'il founded a national library in 1871 and later established a number of learned societies and museums.

Although Isma'il encouraged the formation of a Western-trained elite, he made no attempt to alter the relationship between the monarchy and the people. He remained an authoritarian ruler, dispensing and withholding royal patronage at his pleasure. Much attention has been given to his establishment of a consultative chamber of delegates in 1866. But Isma'il did not surrender any of his prerogatives to the chamber, and he created it as much out of tactical considerations as for the purpose of consultation. On another political issue, the question of Egypt's relationship to the Ottoman Empire, Isma'il secured some modest gains. Whereas Muhammad Ali had attempted to establish his independence through warfare, Isma'il's method was to shower Ottoman officials with gifts and bribes. When Sultan Abdul Aziz paid an official state visit to Egypt in 1863, the first Ottoman sultan to set foot in the country since Selim I conquered it in 1517, Isma'il spared no expense in entertaining his sovereign. These efforts were rewarded when the sultan elevated Isma'il to khedive, a Persian term meaning lord or master and implying something closer to royalty than the position of governor does. In addition, Egypt was granted the right to expand its army, to issue its own currency, and to contract foreign loans without the sultan's approval, a privilege Isma'il pursued with relish.

In the realm of legal reform, the most significant development during Isma'il's reign was the introduction of the Mixed Courts. The increase in the number of foreigners conducting business in Egypt brought a concurrent increase in the number of disputes between foreigners and Egyptians. Under the terms of the Capitulations, which sheltered foreign nationals from Egyptian law, the usual method of dealing with such disputes was to have the consul of the foreigner hear the case and render a decision based on the law of the foreigner's country. In these circumstances it was rare for foreigners to be convicted, no matter how grave the offenses they may have committed. To protect Egyptians from this abuse and to bring uniformity to a practice in which dozens of different consuls rendered judgments based on the legal codes of several different countries, the Mixed Courts were established in 1876. They were empowered to deal with all civil and commercial cases to which foreigners were party. Remaining in existence until 1949, the Mixed Courts were governed by the French civil code and staffed by judges who were appointed for life and thus free from dismissal for political reasons. An important related development was the opening of the National Courts in 1884. These courts had jurisdiction over all Egyptians in matters of civil, commercial, and penal law and, like the Mixed Courts, operated on legal codes drawn from French law. Although some Egyptian judges were employed in the new justice system, they tended to be overshadowed by the European judges, who received the choice appointments.

With the establishment of the Mixed and National courts, the Egyptian system of justice was dominated by European judges and European lawyers applying legal codes derived from European law. The *shari'ah* courts continued to exist, but since their jurisdiction was confined to the areas of personal status and *waqf*, the field of ulama legal activity was severely restricted. At the same time, however, splendid opportunities became available for Egyptians trained in French law, and those who could afford it rushed to enroll in the Cairo School of Law or to pursue legal studies in France. Thus was Egyptian society set in conflict with itself.

Isma'il's determination to transform Egypt into a European country drove him to devote enormous sums to copying the external trappings of European civilization. Sections of Cairo were refashioned on the model of Paris and provided with boulevards and parks serviced by waterworks, gaslights, and tramways. Isma'il also poured huge sums into the construction of railways, bridges, and new facilities at the port of Alexandria. The crowning achievement in the field of transport was the completion of the Suez Canal in 1869, an occasion Isma'il celebrated by entertaining European royalty and dignitaries in lavish ceremonies. In a gesture that was intended to testify to his appreciation of European culture, he commissioned the Italian composer Giuseppe Verdi to write the opera *Aida* for the opening festivities and ordered the construction of an opera house in which to stage the performance. Verdi was two years late with his composition, but the Suez Canal flourished

During the reign of Khedive Ismaᶜil, the port of Alexandria (shown here circa 1875) became one of the busiest in the eastern Mediterranean. (The Middle East Centre, St. Antony's College, Oxford)

nonetheless. It quickly became a major international waterway benefiting all maritime states by reducing the distance and thus the costs of transporting goods and passengers between the East and Europe. Britain, with its imperial possessions in India and the Far East and its position as the leading overseas trading nation of the time, gained the most from the canal: The waterway cut the distance from London to Bombay in half, and by 1881 over 80 percent of the traffic through the canal was British.

Ismaᶜil's vast expenditures were in effect fueled by cotton. The Northern blockade of Confederate ports during the American Civil War forced British textile mills to turn almost exclusively to Egypt for their cotton supply. The country experienced a tremendous economic boom that saw its income from cotton exports rise from 918,000 sterling in the early 1850s to over 10 million in the late 1860s.[5] In these circumstances, land became a valued economic asset, and the officials who received grants of land from Ismaᶜil used their profits from cotton to purchase additional holdings. An increase in the size of private landholdings was a prominent feature of Ismaᶜil's reign, and he himself controlled one-fifth of all the cultivated land in the country.

But even the large revenues generated by the cotton boom could not keep pace with Ismaᶜil's expenditures. To finance his ambitious schemes and his expensive personal tastes, the khedive was forced to borrow huge sums from European financial institutions. The practice proved disastrous. Brokerage commissions and various hidden charges reduced the value of the loans before they were paid out. In addition, the high interest rates (usually around 10 percent) the European lenders charged diverted funds from the Egyptian economy. As Egypt sank into debt, Ismaᶜil took desperate measures to keep his creditors at bay. In 1872 he issued the *muqabala* law, which allowed landholders to pay six times their annual land tax in advance in exchange for being relieved of all future land tax obligations. In 1875 Egypt sold its 44 percent interest in the Suez Canal Company to the British government for £4 million, but this sale provided only stopgap revenue. By the 1870s new loans were being used simply to meet the interest payments on previous loans. In 1876 the Egyptian government announced that it intended to suspend interest payments on its debt for three months, a statement that amounted to a declaration of bankruptcy. It was the same year that the Ottoman government defaulted on its interest payments.

However, the consequences for Cairo were to be more severe than they were for Istanbul. Over the course of the next six years, Egypt's economic problems led to its loss of political independence. European financial houses pressured their governments to take actions that would prevent Egypt from defaulting on its loan payments. Recognizing the need to placate his creditors, Isma'il agreed in 1876 to the establishment of a body known as the Caisse de la Dette Publique (Public Debt Commission). Composed of four representatives from the European creditor nations, the commission was charged with ensuring that the Egyptian debt was serviced. In addition, two controllers, one from Britain and one from France, were appointed to the Egyptian government to supervise the expenditure of Egyptian revenues. This system of dual control, as it was known, amounted to direct European intervention in the financial affairs of Egypt. When Isma'il attempted to preserve his financial independence by dismissing the two controllers and rallying popular support, the European powers decided that his reign must end and called upon the Ottoman sultan to exercise the authority he still possessed over Egypt. Sultan Abdul Hamid II, not sorry to see the removal of such a troublesome and ambitious prince, issued a formal decree deposing Isma'il in 1879 and appointing his son Tawfiq as khedive.

The Urabi Revolt, 1879–1882

The deposition of Isma'il and the accession of the weak Tawfiq gave the European powers freedom to arrange the disbursement of Egyptian revenues as they saw fit. In 1880 Tawfiq issued the Law of Liquidation, which established Egypt's consolidated debt at the staggering total of £98.4 million (it had been £3 million when Isma'il assumed the throne) and set up a procedure for making regular annual payments on the debt. These payments were given priority over all other state expenditures and amounted to over 60 percent of Egypt's annual revenue; Isma'il had mortgaged his country to European financiers.

The deposition of Isma'il may have brought a measure of financial order to Egypt, but it did not bring political stability. Discontent within various sectors of the elite and among elements of the population at large led to a reaction against European interference and to the emergence of a figure who is regarded in some circles as Egypt's first nationalist hero.

Ahmad Urabi was an Egyptian of peasant origins who had risen to the rank of colonel in the army. Not one of the European-educated officers, he had studied first at al-Azhar and then gone into the army. Perhaps because of his peasant background and his traditional training, he came to be seen in some quarters as representing the authentic voice of the Egyptian people. It was the voice of a peasant population whose labor and taxes had produced the wealth for Isma'il's grandiose schemes, the voice of impoverished rural discontent against tax-exempt foreigners and wealthy local landlords. The Urabi movement began with a relatively minor incident within the officer corps. In early 1881 Colonel Urabi and a group of fellow Egyptian officers protested an impending law that would prevent Egyptians of *fellah* (peasant) origin from rising through the ranks to officer status. When it became clear that Urabi was supported by large portions of the army, Khedive Tawfiq rescinded the offensive law. But the movement did not stop there. What began as an internal protest on an army matter was elevated by Urabi and his supporters to a national campaign against European domination of Egypt's affairs.

The politics of Urabi's movement was made exceedingly complex by the shifting coalitions of notables and high-ranking officials who alternately opposed and endorsed him. However, the movement had two essential purposes: to eliminate foreign control of Egypt's finances and to curtail the autocracy of the khedive by establishing constitutional limits to his authority. Referring to himself as a delegate of the people, Urabi gained the support of the army, a group of reformist notables, and the peasantry, who looked upon him as the leader who would free them from their bondage of taxation and indebtedness. In 1882 Urabi was appointed minister of war and began to make provisions for the formation of a national assembly that would be empowered to determine Egypt's budget and spending priorities. While Urabi and his supporters asserted their rights to manage the affairs of their country, Khedive Tawfiq was forced to depend on foreign support to preserve his throne.

To the governments of Britain and France, the Urabi movement represented a double-edged threat. They refused to believe that a government dominated by Urabists would honor its international financial obligations. In addition, they were alarmed at the prospect of a nationalist government's restricting their access to the Suez Canal. They preferred the rule of the pliable Khedive Tawfiq to the difficulties of dealing with an Urabist government that was responsive to the needs of Egyptians. Reacting to an outbreak of antiforeign rioting in Alexandria in June 1882, the British government authorized the commander of the fleet anchored off Alexandria harbor to bombard the city. In August came the fateful decision to land a British expeditionary force at the canal zone. On September 13, 1882, the British forces defeated Urabi's army at the battle of Tel al-Kebir, and two days later Urabi was captured and his movement brought to an end. In ordering the invasion of Egypt, the British government intended only a brief interventionist action to restore Khedive Tawfiq's authority; instead, it inaugurated an occupation that lasted until 1956. Egypt had indeed become a part of Europe, but not in the way that Isma'il had intended.

The British and the khedive portrayed Urabi as a traitor to his government; he was tried and sentenced to a life of exile in Ceylon. But to the Egyptians who supported him at the time and for those to whom he later became a legend, Urabi was a patriot whose goal was to preserve his country's independence from foreign economic control. The popular cry of his followers, "Egypt for the Egyptians," would be heard again.

Conclusion:
The Dualism of the Nineteenth-Century Reforms

The reforms in the Ottoman Empire and Egypt created an institutional dualism in Middle Eastern society. With the notable exceptions of the destruction of the Janissaries and the Mamluks, most traditional institutions were retained alongside the newly created ones. Thus, although the Ottoman and Egyptian governments introduced new legal codes and new court systems, they did not eliminate the *shari'ah* courts; and though both governments devoted considerable funds to the development of elite European-style academies, they did not close the doors of the religious schools. These schools, despite a decline in their prestige, continued to preserve the Islamic learned tradition, to transmit Islamic values, and to provide educational opportunities for large numbers of students.

The problem arose when the graduates of the Islamic schools sought employment in administrations that were committed, for better or for worse, to policies of Westernization. No matter how extensive these students' knowledge of the Quran or the *shari'ah* may have been, they did not have the qualifications to compete with the students trained in Europe or in European-style schools. At the same time, the opportunities for employment in the traditional elite sector of society were shrinking as the new courts, new schools, and new concepts deriving from European thought reduced the role of the ulama to the more narrowly religious sphere of activity. The favored new elite of French knowers, small though it may have been, exercised an increasing dominance in the direction of the affairs of state, whereas the religiously educated found their once respected training to have limited application. The wrenching nature of imposed change is captured in the remark of Fuad Pasha, the Ottoman minister, to a European diplomat: "Our state is the strongest state. For you are trying to cause its collapse from the outside, and we from the inside, but still it does not collapse."[6]

This dualism had a divisive effect on society as a whole. There had, of course, always been a wide gap between educated officials and the population at large. But as the educated officials came increasingly from Westernized schools, the gap widened. An illiterate conscript from rural Anatolia and his commanding officer who might have been trained in Paris inhabited two different universes. So, too, did an al-Azhar shaykh and a professor in the Cairo Medical School. Nor was the gap between the new elite and the traditional sectors of society bridged by the transmission of any obvious benefits to the latter group. To the Egyptian *fellahin*, the transformation of society meant conscription in Muhammad Ali's armies or Isma'il's public works gangs; it meant heavy taxes and increased indebtedness; it meant abandoning the family plot of land and joining the growing ranks of rural laborers working for atrociously low wages on the vast estates of the emerging class of private landowners.

The impact was similar in the rural heartlands of the Ottoman Empire. As the nineteenth-century transformation brought certain advantages to Egyptian and Ottoman society, it also brought economic hardship, social disruption, and political exploitation.

Notes

1. Cited in Roderic H. Davison, *Reform in the Ottoman Empire, 1856–1876* (Princeton, 1963), p. 90.

2. Roger Owen, *The Middle East in the World Economy, 1800–1914* (London, 1981), p. 109.

3. Albert H. Hourani, "Ottoman Reform and the Politics of Notables," in William R. Polk and Richard L. Chambers, eds., *Beginnings of Modernization in the Middle East: The Nineteenth Century* (Chicago, 1968), pp. 41–68.

4. P. J. Vatikiotis, *The History of Modern Egypt: From Muhammad Ali to Mubarak*, 4th ed. (Baltimore, 1991), p. 73.

5. Owen, *World Economy*, p. 136.

6. Cited in Davison, *Reform in the Ottoman Empire*, p. 9.

	6
Egypt and Iran in the Late Nineteenth Century	◁▷ ⧓ ◁▷

During the final decades of the nineteenth century, the major European powers expanded their overseas empires and, whenever possible, protected their principal imperial possessions by entering into agreements among themselves or by neutralizing the rulers of territories bordering on those possessions. Britain, for example, had started to secure the route to India by annexing Aden in 1839 and by establishing treaties with some of the Arab shaykhdoms in the Persian Gulf. Additional shaykhdoms were brought under British control as first Bahrain (1880), then Muscat (1891), and finally Kuwait (1899) signed treaties pledging not to deal with any foreign power except through Britain. The French North African empire, begun with the conquest of Algiers in 1830, was made more secure with the occupation of Tunisia in 1881; Morocco would be incorporated into this empire in 1912. Italy, in a desperate search for overseas possessions, invaded the Ottoman North African province of Tripoli in 1911. And Russia, though continuing to seek territorial gains in Ottoman Europe, was also in the process of acquiring a huge Asian empire. As will be seen in this chapter, Egypt, Iran, and the Sudan were all drawn into this Great Power rivalry, usually to the detriment of their own interests.

England on the Nile: The British Occupation of Egypt, 1882–1914

The Cromer Years, 1883–1907

The British occupation of Egypt produced one of the most significant colonial encounters of the modern era. It shaped Egyptian economic development for several decades, it had an impact on the formation of the country's political leadership, and it became the focus of an antiimperial nationalist movement that affected Egyptian (and British) politics for the first half of the twentieth century.

102

Britain occupied Egypt in order to safeguard the Suez Canal, to restore Egypt's political and financial stability, and, in the context of the imperial competition of the era, to prevent France from occupying it first. Britain did not intend to engage in a prolonged occupation, and it certainly did not intend to get involved in the task of governing Egyptians. Until the outbreak of World War I, Britain could not even define its relationship to Egypt; the country was not declared a colony or a protectorate, but remained in theory an autonomous province of the Ottoman Empire ruled by a hereditary khedive. Although undefined, however, the British presence was, as its critics pointed out, simply a veiled protectorate.

The individual who presided over the occupation with absolute authority for its first quarter century was Evelyn Baring, later Lord Cromer, a colonial administrator with several years' service in India. Cromer's attitude toward non-Western, non-Christian peoples was typical of many British officials in the late Victorian era. Convinced of the innate superiority of Western civilization, Cromer believed that "Orientals" could never improve their lot until they had mastered the ways of the West, and for this they required a long apprenticeship under the enlightened tutelage of "advanced" countries like Great Britain. Throughout his long tenure as British consul general, Cromer disparaged Egyptian demands for independence and assured his superiors in London that direct British guidance would be necessary for years to come.

Cromer's priorities were to restore Egypt's credit by meeting the debt payments and to maintain domestic tranquillity by supporting the rule of Khedive Tawfiq and discouraging political agitation. Because he was completely opposed to the development of any local industrial base that might offer competition to the British textile industry, Cromer sought to increase Egypt's revenue by expanding its agricultural production. He authorized a massive effort to improve the Nile-based irrigation system through such projects as the construction of the Aswan Dam, completed in 1902; the rebuilding of the Delta Barrage; and the excavation of still more canals. In addition, Egypt went through another railway boom as its already extensive network of track was doubled. These improvements brought about a substantial rise in Egypt's agricultural output, especially cotton, which remained the main source of revenue. Indeed, during the Cromer years Egypt became more dependent than ever before on the export of this single crop.

In terms of Egypt's international financial standing, Cromer's policies must be considered a success. By the mid-1880s, the budget showed a surplus, and there appeared to be no danger of defaulting on the debt payments, which during most of Cromer's period amounted to between 25 and 35 percent of annual government revenues. In addition, the British administration's concern with agricultural development brought with it a rise in the general standard of living in the countryside. Taxes were reduced and such practices as forced labor and the use of the whip were abolished. Despite this progress, the needs of the Egyptian *fellahin* were still largely neglected. The Egyptians who benefited most from Cromer's investment in public works were the large landholders who saw their property values and their profits grow. Although they may not have liked the British occupation as such, they came to have a vested interest in the social and economic advantages it brought them, and they would attempt to preserve those advantages even as they demanded British evacuation.

The British governed Egypt through a rather cumbersome arrangement that was often frustrating both to them and to Egyptians alike. Since Egypt remained nominally an Ottoman province, the Egyptian governmental structure was retained, and Egyptian personnel continued to occupy their posts as ministers and civil servants. Over the years, this practice expanded the cadres of Egyptian officials who had experience in the state bureaucracy, though it cannot be said to have increased their experience in decisionmaking. For if Egyptian officials had some latitude in day-to-day office management, they did not govern their own country. The British adviser attached to each ministry, in consultation with his British staff, determined policy, and Lord Cromer, with his control over the budget, determined funding priorities. By the turn of the century, hundreds of British officials, army officers, engineers, and teachers—many unqualified by either training or experience—dominated all areas of important decisionmaking within Egypt. Their salaries, several times higher than those of their Egyptian counterparts, were paid by the Egyptian, not the British, government, and their air of cultural superiority, emphasized by their memberships in exclusive British sporting clubs, contributed to growing tensions with the Egyptian educated classes, who believed they were qualified to govern their own country.

Although Cromer's programs were designed primarily to serve British imperial and financial interests, they brought certain material advantages to Egyptians. However, in many areas of social development his policies were regressive. This was particularly true in the field of education, where he reversed the trend toward a state-supported school system that had been such a pronounced feature of Isma'il's reign. The reasons behind Cromer's restrictive educational policies were financial and political. During his first years in office, Egypt's uncertain financial situation and Cromer's predilection for investment in revenue-enhancing public works projects led him to reduce the budget for education. Many of the specialized postsecondary institutions founded by Isma'il were closed, and enrollments in the government primary and secondary schools declined. Even after Egypt's finances improved, Cromer provided only limited funding to the Department of Public Instruction. Moreover, whereas Isma'il's government school system had borne the costs of instruction, Cromer's administration introduced tuition fees at all levels, a measure that severely restricted the general public's access to state education. The political aspect of Cromer's educational policies was shaped by his experiences in India and led him to believe that the growth of Western-style educational institutions, especially universities, would create a group of Egyptian intellectuals imbued with nationalist ideals and a sense of frustration over their inferior status. Accordingly, the consul general attempted to confine the Westernized schools to the training of future civil servants and to direct the bulk of primary school graduates into vocational institutes.

One of the factors that prolonged the British occupation and generated tension between Cromer and the Egyptian nationalists was the question of the Sudan. Ismaᶜil had completed the conquest of the Sudan that was begun by Muhammad Ali and had strengthened the Egyptian military and administrative presence there. But when a figure calling himself the Mahdi (see Chapter 7) mounted a rebellion in the Sudan against the Egyptian occupation in 1881, his forces quickly overran the scattered Egyptian garrisons. Determined to hang onto the Sudan, the Egyptian government sent an ill-prepared expeditionary force into the Mahdi's territory in 1883; it was massacred. General Charles Gordon's relief force fared no better, and following Gordon's death at Khartoum in 1885, the Sudan was abandoned to the Mahdi and his successors for the next ten years. Neither Cromer nor the government in London wished to mount an expensive military campaign that would put a strain on both the Egyptian and the British treasuries.

As the scramble for territories in Africa heated up in the 1890s, however, the British cabinet reconsidered its position on the Sudan. When rumors of the presence of a French force in the southern Sudan reached London, the cabinet authorized a joint Anglo-Egyptian expedition under General Herbert Kitchener. Kitchener's difficult reconquest of the Sudan began in 1896, and it was not until 1898 that his forces were able to enter Khartoum and restore what the Egyptian government believed would be Egyptian control over the Sudan. But Cromer and the British government had other plans for the region. They had drawn up provisions for the creation of an Anglo-Egyptian condominium that would make Britain the effective ruling power in the Sudan. Even though Egyptian troops had participated in the reconquest and the Egyptian treasury had contributed over half the cost of Kitchener's campaign, Britain essentially separated the Sudan from Egypt and arranged for the territory to be administered by a British governor general. British prime minister Lord Salisbury told Cromer that Britain intended to have "a predominant voice in all matters connected with the Sudan" and expected the Egyptian government to follow any advice it might receive from London regarding Sudanese affairs.[1] Egyptian opinion was outraged by Britain's action, and demands for the restoration of Egypt's role in the Sudan remained a central plank in the nationalists' platform until 1955, when the Sudanese themselves voted to become independent rather than affiliate with Egypt.

The primary medium through which Egyptian opinion was expressed was the periodical press. In what may seem like a paradox, journalism flourished during the British occupation and assumed an increasingly important place in Egyptian political and cultural life. Although many of the leading journals of the Cromer era, from the daily newspapers *al-Muqattam* and *al-Ahram* (The pyramids) to the monthly magazine *al-Hilal* (The crescent), were founded by Syrian-Christian émigrés who came to Egypt to escape the harsh rule of Sultan Abdul Hamid II, they all addressed the question of Egypt's relationship with Britain. But the Egyptian press served a larger purpose than the presentation of political opinions. It was a forum for the propagation of ideas on the major cultural and social issues of the era. Islamic reformers and Christian secularists, supporters of parliamentary democracy and of khedival autocracy, advocates of Swiss educational methods and of the reform of al-Azhar found an outlet for their views in the lively Egyptian periodical press. Educated Egypt had found a voice, or perhaps many voices, and its echoes reverberated across the political landscape.

Of the leading newspapers of the time, *al-Liwa* (The standard), founded in 1900, probably best represented the rising current of Egyptian protest. It was published by Mustafa Kamil (1874–1908), whose education reflects the path to upward mobility chosen by other ambitious Egyptians of his generation. Kamil enrolled in the Cairo School of Law in 1889 and received his law degree from the University of Toulouse in France. A skillful political journalist and a spellbinding speaker, Kamil gained popularity for his demand for the immediate end of the British occupation. When Cromer and some members of the Egyptian landholding class responded to Kamil's attacks with arguments about the prosperity that British administration had brought to Egypt, Kamil retorted, "The chains of slavery are still chains, whether they be forged of gold or of iron."[2] Though Kamil sometimes claimed that Egypt had Islamic bonds with the Ottoman Empire, he also began to move away from the concept of Egypt as part of a wider Islamic or Ottoman world. More clearly and more directly than his contemporaries, he articulated sentiments of Egyptian patriotism, arguing that Egypt was a unique territorial entity with its own special characteristics and urging its inhabitants to offer it their deepest affection. The following lines are representative of Kamil's patriotic message: "My country, to you my love and my heart, my life and existence. . . . For you, you are life, and there is no life without you, O Egypt."[3] Kamil was not a systematic thinker, but his writings and his oratory contributed significantly to the awakening of the political consciousness of the Egyptian public and to the emergence of the idea of territorial nationalism.

The Egyptian political atmosphere became more highly charged with the death of the accommodating Tawfiq and the accession of his eighteen-year-old son, Abbas II (1892–1914). Though schooled in Switzerland and Vienna, Abbas II was an Egyptian nationalist and aspired to be more than a mere figurehead ruler. He directly challenged Cromer's authority and provided funds for anti-British newspapers like Kamil's *al-Liwa*. To the mix of a vocal press and an independent-minded ruler was added a severe international recession in 1907–1911 that drove the price of cotton down and caused severe hardship in the Egyptian countryside. The spark that ignited the flame of anti-British feeling was provided by the Dinshaway incident of June 1906. It is always dangerous for the historian to single out a specific event as the start of a larger movement, but Dinshaway, coming as it did at a time of economic recession and political discontent, seemed to galvanize Egyptian opinion.

The event was simple enough. Five British officers went pigeon shooting in the Delta village of Dinshaway, which, like countless other Egyptian villages, raised pigeons for meat and eggs. In the course of pursuing their sport, the officers managed to wound the wife of the village prayer leader and to set fire to a threshing floor. The villagers protested, and in the altercation that followed two British officers were wounded, one of whom later died. Because of the political and economic tensions that existed at the time, the British authorities were determined to punish the inhabitants of Dinshaway as an example to the rest of the country. A special tribunal was set up, and fifty-two of the villagers were charged with the unlikely crime of premeditated murder. Thirty-two were quickly convicted, and four of them were publicly hanged in Dinshaway. Several others received floggings, and the remainder were sentenced to prison at hard labor.

Egyptian reaction to the sentences was one of shock and outrage. The press, led by Kamil's *al-Liwa,* denounced the verdict, and the peasants of the Egyptian Delta created folk ballads about the incident, one of which included the lines: "They fell upon Dinshaway / And spared neither man nor his brother. / Slowly they hanged the one and flogged the other."[4] Dinshaway created a certain common ground between the *fellahin* and the urban nationalists and demonstrated to both that Britain was not a benevolent protector but an alien occupier. The British show of force was a miscalculation that intensified Egyptian demands for an end to the occupation and hastened the departure of Lord Cromer, who submitted his resignation in 1907.

The Growth of Political Organizations, 1907–1914

Cromer's successors, Sir Eldon Gorst (1907–1911) and Kitchener (1911–1914), addressed some of the immediate political and economic grievances that surfaced in the aftermath of the Dinshaway incident. Gorst achieved a conciliation of sorts with Khedive Abbas and opened up more high-ranking administrative posts to Egyptians. Kitchener sought to restore Egyptian confidence in Britain by reviving the public works program and legislating the Five Feddan Law (1912), which was supposed to protect small landholders by prohibiting the seizure of properties of five *feddans* or less for debt (1 *feddan* equals 1.04 acres, or .416 ha). But neither of these consul generals could stem the growth of Egyptian opposition to the British presence.

This opposition was expressed through three main organizations, all of them founded in 1907. They consisted of groups of Egyptian thinkers and activists associated with a particular vision of their country's future that they promulgated in various widely circulated newspapers. The opinions of the groups' leaders reveal the broad range of social perspectives that had developed among the Egyptian elite. The Constitutional Reform Party, grouped around Shaykh Ali Yusuf (1863–1913), an al-Azhar graduate, and his newspaper, *al-Muayyad*, advocated Egyptian independence within an Islamic framework. Such well-known Islamic reformers as Muhammad Abduh and Rashid Rida contributed to the columns of *al-Muayyad* (see Chapter 7). At the other end of the political and cultural spectrum was the People's Party. Its leading spokesman was Lutfi al-Sayyid (1872–1963), a graduate of the Cairo School of Law and editor of the paper *al-Jaridab*. The People's Party introduced a tone of secular liberalism into the debate on Egypt's future, and though it advocated independence, it stressed a more cautious approach and reminded Egyptians that they must demonstrate their worthiness for self-government. The third grouping, the National Party, was led by Mustafa Kamil and regarded *al-Liwa* as its official organ. Kamil, as mentioned above, demanded immediate British evacuation and argued that Egypt was a distinct territorial entity to which its inhabitants owed their devotion. The public debate on these important issues was abruptly terminated with the outbreak of World War I; Britain declared Egypt a protectorate, imposed martial law on the country, and deposed Abbas II in favor of his more malleable uncle, Husayn Kamil.

Iran During the Second Half of the Nineteenth Century

European influences came to Iran later than they did to Egypt and the Ottoman Empire and had far less impact there than in those two states. In part this was because powerful forces of decentralization had taken root in Iran during the chaotic period between the fall of the Safavids in 1722 and the consolidation of the Qajar dynasty in 1794 (see Chapter 3). Unlike Muhammad Ali and Mahmud II, the Qajar shahs were never able to gather together sufficient resources to destroy, or even to limit to any measurable degree, the centrifugal elements within society.

Changes in Iranian Shiᶜism After the Safavids

One of the primary factors militating against the centralization of state authority in Iran was the prominent and independent position that the Shiᶜa religious establishment had achieved within Iranian society. As noted in

Chapter 3, the Safavid shahs were accepted as the divinely inspired representatives of the Hidden Imam. Their recognized religious authority assisted them in legitimizing their temporal power. However, with the fall of the Safavids and the emergence in the late eighteenth century of the Qajar shahs, who made no claims to divinity, the question of the right to exercise religious authority in the absence of the Hidden Imam was reopened. The Shiʿa ulama maintained that since the Qajars were merely temporal rulers, the ulama had the exclusive right to provide interpretations on issues of law and religious practice. They established their claim to be the legitimate interpreters of the will of the Hidden Imam by assuming the right to exercise *ijtihad* (see Chapter 2).

What this meant in practice was that those members of the religious establishment whose piety and depth of learning were deemed by their peers to be superior were empowered to render judgments on matters of law and religious practice; they were, in short, entitled to recognition as *mujtahids*, learned individuals qualified to exercise *ijtihad*. In the late eighteenth century, there were never more than three or four *mujtahids* at any given time. This changed during the first half of the nineteenth century, when the religious establishment won popular acceptance of two concepts: first, that all believing Shiʿa Muslims should attach themselves to a *mujtahid* and accept his rulings as valid on matters of religious observance and legal practice and, second, that the rulings of living *mujtahids* were preferable to all other existing rulings. The acceptance of these principles generated a need for an increase in the ranks of recognized *mujtahids*. With the proliferation of *mujtahids*, an informal hierarchy emerged that recognized certain *mujtahids* as possessing such high qualities of learning and understanding that their rulings should take precedence over those of their contemporaries. These individuals bore the title *marja al-taqlid,* the source of emulation, and were the dominant figures within the Shiʿa religious establishment. During the twentieth century, it became customary to refer to an individual who had achieved the status of a *marja al-taqlid* by the term *ayatollah,* the eye of God.

With the fall of the Safavid dynasty and the rise to power of rulers who had no divine attributes, the previously close association between Shiʿa Islam and the state ended, and the Shiʿa religious establishment functioned independently of the government. Backed by a population that granted them extensive authority in religious and legal matters, the ulama could function as a powerful force of support or opposition to the policies of the shahs. By the time of the Qajar dynasty, popular belief held that the rulings of *mujtahids* were more authoritative statements of the will of the Hidden Imam than the proclamations of the shahs. Thus, if a *mujtahid* denounced a royal decree as incompatible with the teachings of Islam, then believers were enjoined to accept the *mujtahid's* decision. In this way, the ulama gained a powerful voice in Iranian political life.

The Reign of Nasir al-Din Shah (1848–1896)

The Qajar shahs established their court at Tehran and surrounded themselves with the pomp and ceremony associated with the long-standing Iranian monarchical tradition. Although individual rulers lived in great personal luxury, the appearance they gave of firmly established royal authority was deceiving. On several occasions during the nineteenth century, the Qajar shahs controlled little beyond the gates of Tehran. They have been described during this period as "having no military security, no administrative stability and little ideological legitimacy."[5] These limitations are illustrated in the long reign of Nasir al-Din Shah (1848–1896). When he assumed the throne, the standing army of the state was pitifully small, numbering as few as 3,000 troops. Real military power rested with the tribal chieftains, who often commanded more armed men than the shah. Since the military forces of the state were so weak, Nasir al-Din had to depend on tribal levies. When he was unable to pay them, which was often, the tribal armies disbanded. Given these circumstances, the tribal chieftains enjoyed a considerable degree of political and financial autonomy. Because the state could not destroy them, as Muhammad Ali had the Mamluks or Mahmud II the Janissaries and the *derebeys*, it resorted to manipulating rivalries among them in order to survive. In these circumstances, the tax-collecting abilities of the government were severely limited, and Nasir al-Din's treasury was chronically short of funds.

Early in his reign, Nasir al-Din did undertake a modest program of military reform, increasing the size of the standing army, introducing new training procedures, and changing the pattern of recruitment. But these measures were hesitant and foundered on the shah's inability to pay the new recruits. The only lasting improvement in the armed forces during Nasir al-Din's reign was the creation of the Cossack Brigade in 1879. Commanded by Russian officers and supplied with Russian arms, the Cossack Brigade was the most effective military arm of the government. However, it remained small (2,000 to 3,000 mounted men), and its control by Russian officers had obvious disadvantages. Iran, then, did not engage in a sustained program of European-inspired military reform, with all the offshoots that this produced in Egypt and the Ottoman Empire.

Nor, in the realm of administration, did the role of the government appreciably expand to create a demand for the recruitment of a cadre of civil servants trained for new tasks. The offspring of the royal family and the semiautonomous local chieftains received most of the choice provincial governorships, a practice that discouraged the rise of a professional bureaucracy with defined duties and written codes of conduct. A further obstacle to the emergence of administrative professionalism was Nasir al-Din's habit of replenishing his treasury by selling offices and tax-farming privileges to the highest bidders on an annual basis; the successful buyers, knowing their tenure in office was likely to be short, sought to recover their costs and to make a profit by whatever means they could. Bribery and extortion were commonplace. The most obvious victims of these abuses were the peasant classes, who were subjected to arbitrary acts on the part of local chieftains and government officials alike. Large landlords, encouraged by the absence of any government regulations, seized small peasant holdings and reduced their inhabitants to laborers. Although it may be true that the peasantry has traditionally resented centralizing governments for their conscription and tax-collecting efficiency, it is also the case that effective regimes have afforded rural society a measure of security and stability. In the Iran of Nasir al-Din, the government came to be resented not only for its inability to provide protection from regional exploiters but also for the rapacious practices of those few official government representatives who did manage to exercise authority in the rural areas.

Nasir al-Din did make an initial but hesitant attempt to improve both his bureaucracy and his officer corps by opening a new institution of higher learning, Dar al-Funun (1851). Staffed by Europeans and offering instruction in European languages and applied sciences, Dar al-Funun stood alone as the only state-sponsored school of its kind. Although some of its graduates pursued further education in Europe and obtained positions in the bureaucracy and the military, the institution did not have an immediate impact on the conduct of Iranian statecraft. Because of the presence of the Qajar princes and tribal dignitaries in the most important government posts, training at Dar al-Funun did not become an established route to status and power. In the absence of any other state-sponsored institutions, all levels of education were dominated by the ulama.

The influence of the Shiᶜa ulama was not confined to the field of education. As we have seen above, during the eighteenth century, the power of the religious establishment increased vis-à-vis the authority of the temporal government. Throughout the nineteenth century, the ulama successfully asserted their right to intervene with religious interpretations of political acts. They also kept their grip on the educational and judicial reins of society; no new elite emerged to replace them in the school system, and there were no major secular challenges to the *shariᶜah* or to the ulama's role in the administration of justice. In contrast to the changing attitudes in Cairo and Istanbul, in Qajar Iran it was still considered a sign of greater status to be admitted to the ranks of the ulama than it was to become a member of the civil service.[6]

The ability of the religious establishment to maintain its independence from the central government was based to a large extent on its financial autonomy. Nasir al-Din could barely collect enough taxes to keep his small administration running, whereas the ulama amassed considerable wealth. In Shiᶜa Islam the temporal government was not allowed to collect the *zakat*, the charitable donation Muslims must pay; instead, the ulama received the *zakat.* A major source of revenue, the funds were used to sustain the members of the religious establishment, to operate *madrasahs* and support the students attending them, and to provide social assistance to the underprivileged. In addition to *zakat* taxes, the ulama received income from teaching, administering *waqfs,* registering deeds and titles, and maintaining mutually advantageous ties with urban merchants. The Shiᶜa religious outlook, so dominant in Iran, enabled the ulama of Nasir al-Din's time to deepen their influence over the population at large and to appear as the protectors of the people from a government that was increasingly viewed as corrupt and impious.

Iran Between Russia and Britain

The lack of direct state initiative in introducing European-style reforms did not mean that Iran escaped Western influences. Both Russia and Britain regarded the country to be of the utmost strategic importance, and their repeated interference in Iranian affairs contributed to the administrative paralysis of Nasir al-Din's regime. During the first half of the nineteenth century, Russia occupied territories traditionally claimed by Iran in Turkestan and in the Caucasus region along the Caspian Sea, including portions of the important province of Azerbaijan. By absorbing Turkestan, Tajikistan, and the lands of the Caucasus into the Russian empire, the czars assumed the difficult task of ruling over an ethnically diverse population of Christians and Sunni and Shiᶜa Muslims. Events since the collapse of the Soviet Union in 1991 have demonstrated that the ethnic and religious loyalties of this population survived both czarist and Soviet attempts at assimilation. Russian expansionism in Iran had commercial as well as territorial objectives. Following a decisive military victory over the shah's irregular tribal forces in 1828, Russia imposed the Treaty of Turkomanchai on Iran. The treaty included clauses granting Russian merchants extraterritorial rights and favorable tariff rates similar to the privileges accorded western Europeans in the Ottoman Capitulations.

In the opinion of British policymakers, the Russian advances in Iran posed a threat to the security of India and offered unwelcome competition to British industry's search for overseas markets. The commercial challenge was met by a treaty signed in 1857 in which the shah granted British merchants the same low tariff advantages and extraterritorial privileges previously accorded Russians. As happened in the Ottoman Empire and Egypt, the capitulatory agreements opened the way for the economic penetration of Iran and drew that country into the European-dominated global economy. Although the volume of Iran's international commercial exchange was much less than that of Egypt and the Ottoman Empire, the country's economic transformation followed a pattern similar to theirs. Iran exported raw agricultural commodities—cotton, silk, wheat—and imported manufactured goods—primarily textiles and hardwares—from Britain and Russia. Iran's traditional textile industry declined in the face of competition from cheap foreign imports. However, one area of production, carpet making, did prosper from Iran's economic opening. As Persian carpets became popular in the West, production was increased to meet the new demand.

Britain's alarm over Russia's territorial advances toward the borders of India led the British to inform St. Petersburg that they would not stand by if Iran were dismembered. Since neither power wanted war over Iran, they tacitly agreed to allow the country to exist as a buffer state between their strategic interests, an arrangement similar to the one made in the case of the Ottoman Empire. Still, both imperial powers continued to compete for influence over the Iranian government. Russian policy aimed at keeping Iran weak and undeveloped, whereas Britain encouraged economic improvements that might strengthen the country and enable it to resist Russian encroachment. Nasir al-Din Shah, caught in the middle of this rivalry, sought to play the two powers off against one another through the use of the only leverage he had: the granting of economic concessions. This device was also a way for Nasir al-Din to acquire much-needed cash with which to finance his taste for imported luxury goods and his expensive trips to Russia and western Europe.

In 1863 the shah awarded the concession to build a telegraph line to a British company and later tried to counterbalance this by giving other concessions to Russian subjects. The shah's court was soon besieged by European concession hunters, the most successful of whom appeared to be a British subject, Baron Julius de Reuter. In 1872 Nasir al-Din awarded Reuter a concession that was quite possibly the largest ever negotiated. Reuter won the exclusive right to construct all railways, canals, and dams in Iran as well as extensive privileges in mining and agricultural development. The shah, desperate for funds, surrendered the economic development of his country in exchange for a relatively modest initial fee and future royalties. Objections to the concession, both within Iran and from the Russian government, were so strong that Nasir al-Din was compelled to cancel it in 1873. Russia and Britain continued to compete for economic concessions from the shah, especially over the rights for railway construction. Their pressure and counter-pressure so stalemated any activity in this area that by 1900 Iran had less than 20 miles (32 km) of functioning railway.

The Tobacco Protest of 1891

The corruption and inefficiency of Nasir al-Din's government, combined with its policy of opening Iran to foreign economic exploitation, created a current of popular unrest that finally broke into open revolt. In 1890 the shah granted an English company the exclusive right to produce, sell, and export Iran's entire tobacco crop. This award, which affected a product widely consumed and marketed by Iranians, brought all the elements of discontent together in a series of mass protests against the concession and the ruler who had granted it. Significantly, the protest was organized and led by members of the Shiᶜa ulama. They urged the population to join them in preserving the dignity of Islam in the face of growing foreign influences; they portrayed the shah's concession policy as a transgression of the laws of Islam and used their independent power base to denounce the government. In 1891 a *mujtahid* from Shiraz issued a decree declaring the use of tobacco unlawful until such time as the concession was canceled. The decree was framed in the context of Twelver Shiᶜism and warned that the use of tobacco in any form was an offense to the Hidden Imam. The *mujtahid* thus employed his power of interpretation to counteract a policy of the central government. The Iranian people, already alienated by the shah's accommodation of European economic interests, followed the *mujtahid*'s ruling by engaging in a statewide boycott of tobacco products. Throughout 1891 several huge demonstrations against the concession were held in Tehran and other major cities. Unable to enforce his will on a public that had rallied behind its religious leaders, the shah canceled the concession in 1892. For the ulama, the experience of the tobacco protest showed that the Iranian people were receptive to calls for political activity based on Islamic frames of reference.

The last years of Nasir al-Din's rule were notably unproductive. The protest against his use of concessions was a financial handicap as well as a personal humiliation, and he found it necessary to contract loans from Russia to keep the state afloat. Iran thus joined Egypt and the Ottoman Empire as a debtor state. During this final period of his long reign, the shah became openly hostile to contact with the West, prohibiting the establishment of new schools and preventing Iranians from traveling to Europe. The isolationism of Nasir al-Din's regime is encapsulated in his boast that he preferred to appoint ministers who did not know whether Brussels was a place or a cabbage.[7] His assassination in 1896 was not a cause for widespread grief.

Conclusion

Throughout the second half of the nineteenth century, the Middle Eastern economic order was restructured by the penetration of European capital and commerce into different parts of the region. The Capitulations, which originated as enticements to western European merchants from a militarily dominant Ottoman Empire, were transformed into instruments of European economic and political control in the age of expansive European capitalism and dominant European military technology. In an effort to recover Middle Eastern military strength and thus to prevent both provincial rebellion and European imperial encroachment, the rulers of Egypt and the Ottoman Empire started to purchase European military technology and to fund European-style training facilities. But the expenditures associated with these endeavors exceeded the capacities of the two states' revenue-producing abilities, and they were forced to seek loans from European lenders. Eventually, the unfavorable economic environment of the Capitulations, which limited the revenue-raising opportunities of the two states, forced them into bankruptcy. In the case of the central Ottoman Empire, bankruptcy led to European control of the distribution of Ottoman revenues but not to European occupation of the Ottoman capital city. The rivalries inherent in the Eastern Question were too intense and the territory involved too strategic to permit one Great Power to dominate the empire at the expense of the others. Nor was the Ottoman Empire a passive state.

In the case of Egypt, however, Britain deemed its interests so important that it defied all potential European resistance and occupied the country in 1882. During Lord Cromer's long tenure as administrator of the occupation, he managed Egypt's economic, political, and social development so as to further British, not Egyptian, interests. Cromer's primary concern was financial stability, and although he presided over an impressive expansion of the Egyptian economy, he ensured that the economy remained geared to the export of raw materials for British industry. And in an effort to justify the continuing British presence in the country, Cromer insisted that Egyptians were unprepared for independence and sought to perpetuate this condition by limiting the educational opportunities available to them. Yet the British occupation itself fostered the growth of Egyptian nationalism, and by the eve of World War I secular and religious leaders alike took up the call that had first been heard during the Urabi revolt—"Egypt for the Egyptians."

Although Iran shared certain historical trends with Egypt and the Ottoman Empire, it diverged from them in others. In the realm of economic development, for example, Iran, like the other regions, was drawn into the global economy as an exporter of raw materials. And the Qajar shahs granted capitulatory privileges and economic concessions to Britain and Russia, thus placing the transformation of Iran's economy in the hands of foreigners. Yet Iran had not experienced the governmental centralization that was such an important precondition for the transformation of Egypt and the Ottoman Empire. Therefore, when Iran entered the first stage of its intense encounter with an expansive western Europe, the ruling Qajar dynasty exercised authority only over portions of the country. The most organized institution within society was the powerful and independent Shiʿa religious establishment, which possessed greater influence among the population than did the monarchy. This combination of factors—a decentralized government and a potent religious organization—caused Iran to take a different course in its interaction with Europe and European ideas than did the Ottomans or Egyptians.

Notes

1. Cited in M. W. Daly, *Empire on the Nile: The Anglo-Egyptian Sudan, 1898–1934* (Cambridge, 1986), p. 13.

2. Cited in Afaf Lutfi al-Sayyid, *Egypt and Cromer: A Study in Anglo-Egyptian Relations* (London, 1968), p. 161.

3. Cited in ibid.

4. Cited in ibid., p. 173.

5. Ervand Abrahamian, *Iran Between Two Revolutions* (Princeton, 1982), p. 41.

6. Nikki R. Keddie, *Roots of Revolution: An Interpretive History of Modern Iran* (New Haven, 1981), p. 32.

7. Abrahamian, *Two Revolutions,* p. 74.

The Response
of Islamic Society

7

By the end of the nineteenth century, nearly all of the major political units of Islam, from Indonesia to northern Nigeria, were under some form of European control. Those that had escaped direct occupation—Iran, the Ottoman Empire, Afghanistan, and Morocco—found their sovereignty restricted by European control of their economies. The domination of Islamic lands by the states of western Europe posed a terrible dilemma for Muslims. Why did the divinely ordained Islamic community suffer such defeats at the hands of the infidels? The general Muslim consensus was that the divine message revealed to the Prophet remained valid. It was not Islam that was flawed; rather, the flaw lay with Muslims themselves and their failure to follow the commands of God. In this view the abandonment of the *shari*c*ah* for secular constitutions and man-made legal codes was symptomatic of the errors of the Western-educated elite, whose eager embrace of alien institutions not only had failed to save society but had hastened its ruin. But the French knowers were not the only targets of criticism. Muslim intellectuals and political activists argued that Islamic practices had become degenerate and had deviated from the true path as set forth in the revelations.

In this atmosphere of self-criticism, a current of reaction against the adoption of European ways accompanied a reassertion of Islamic values. Especially prominent in Egypt was a movement of intellectual inquiry that sought to rediscover the essential principles of Islam and to explain their application to the changing world of the twentieth century.

Religious Assertiveness and Authoritarian Reform: The Era of Abdul Hamid II

Abdul Hamid II (1876–1909) was the last Ottoman sultan to exercise unrestrained royal authority. Within two years of coming to power, he suspended the constitution he had pledged to uphold and shifted control of the machinery of government from the bureaucrats back to the royal palace in order to enforce his autocracy. His reign of thirty-three years, the third longest

117

in the history of the Ottoman dynasty, began with a cautious mixture of reform and conservatism but ended in an oppressive reaction against European institutions and ideas. The sultan used the vastly expanded powers of the central government to impose restrictions on the political and intellectual activity of Ottoman subjects.

The reaction against the wholesale adoption of Western-inspired reforms was symbolized by Abdul Hamid's stress on the Islamic heritage of the Ottoman Empire. In contrast to the secularism of the Tanzimat, he surrounded himself with the trappings of the caliphate and catered to the religious establishment. Abdul Hamid also turned away from Ottomanism, with its acceptance of the equality of all religions, and adopted in its place the doctrine of Pan-Islam. This doctrine was closely linked to Abdul Hamid's emphasis on his position as caliph and his claim to be the protector of Muslims throughout the world. The idea of a revived Islamic *ummah* under the rule of a single caliph had little likelihood of being realized, but Abdul Hamid's exploitation of the concept enhanced his status and drew further attention to the possibilities of casting off European domination through a renewal of Islamic solidarity. Pan-Islam also served as a useful instrument of diplomacy in the sultan's dealings with Britain, France, and Russia. If he could convince the European imperial powers that he possessed a measure of authority over the millions of Muslims in their colonies, he would gain leverage in negotiations with them. From a domestic standpoint, Abdul Hamid's stress on Islamic ties was intended to secure the continued loyalty of the Arab inhabitants of the empire. Many of the leading Muslim Arab notable families enjoyed increased prestige and easier access to important administrative posts during Abdul Hamid's reign, and certain privileged Arab ulama became part of his palace entourage. The crowning material symbol of Pan-Islam was the Hijaz railway from Damascus to Medina, opened in 1908. Constructed to facilitate the annual pilgrimage, it was financed by private subscriptions from Muslims throughout the world and was thus free from the taint of European investment capital.

Despite its outward display of anti-Westernism and traditional religiosity, the first decade of Abdul Hamid's reign witnessed an acceleration of certain Tanzimat programs. This was particularly true in the field of higher education. Several new professional schools were founded, the Civil Service School and the war college were reorganized and their enrollments enlarged, and the network of teacher training colleges was expanded. A major achievement in higher education was the opening of the University of Istanbul in 1900. In addition, there was a rapid development of the empire's communications and transportation systems. Istanbul was linked to Vienna by rail in 1883, and soon thereafter the fabled Orient Express began to offer regular service from Paris. Other lines brought the cities and towns of Ottoman Europe and Anatolia into closer contact with Istanbul, and an extensive telegraph network reached out to the most distant parts of the empire.

These improvements tightened the central government's control over the hinterlands.

One of the significant results of the transportation boom was a strengthening of ties between Germany and the Ottomans. In 1882 the German general Colmar von der Goltz was employed as head of a mission to reorganize the armed forces, continuing a long-standing tradition of Prussian involvement in Ottoman military modernization. During the Hamidian era, German investment capital played a leading role in the construction of railways, most notably in the development of the Berlin-to-Baghdad line across Anatolia, a project that caused Britain such unease that it became as much a diplomatic issue as an engineering challenge. The German-Ottoman connection was made closer by Kaiser Wilhelm II's two state visits, in 1889 and 1898, and by his much-publicized declaration during the latter occasion that Germany was the friend of the world's 300 million Muslims.

Notwithstanding the improvements in education and transportation, the reign of Abdul Hamid had its dark side. The insecure sultan, haunted by memories of his predecessor's deposition and convinced of the dangers of constitutionalism, tried to impose total control over the information available to his subjects and the activities in which they could engage. The press was tightly censored, the school curricula were subjected to close scrutiny, and the public discussion of politics was forbidden. An internal network of government spies and informants, aided by the new telegraph system, infiltrated all levels of the administration; its reports led to the imprisonment and exile, often on the most dubious evidence, of many loyal Ottoman officials and intellectuals. Others escaped the tyranny by voluntary exile or immigration. Away from the reach of Abdul Hamid's police in Paris and Berlin, they formed protest groups and published pamphlets, which were smuggled into Istanbul, denouncing the sultan and his autocracy. And the institutes of higher learning, which Abdul Hamid tried so desperately to control, became breeding grounds of discontent as students and teachers alike chafed at the clumsy restrictions of the censors.

Abdul Hamid's regime was also marked by the ruthless suppression of national separation movements. The harshest measures were directed against the Armenian community. In the opinion of the sultan and his advisers, the loss of territory in the Balkans was bad enough, but the creation of an independent Armenian Christian state in the heartland of Anatolia was unthinkable. When confronted with a series of Armenian nationalist activities in the 1890s, the sultan struck back with a vengeance. The brutal Ottoman response to Armenian nationalist agitation did not distinguish between political militants and the Armenian population at large. In the rural areas of Anatolia, Abdul Hamid unleashed Kurdish irregulars against Armenian villages, and many innocent people were massacred. In Istanbul the state security apparatus harassed and intimidated respectable merchants and clergymen. In 1897 Abdul Hamid used such ferocity to crush an uprising against Ottoman rule in Crete that Greece declared war on the empire. Although the Ottomans easily won the military contest, they lost the diplomatic one; intervention by the European powers forced the sultan to accept the autonomy of Crete, confirming the already suspicious ruler in his distrust of the West.

During the final years of his reign, Abdul Hamid became increasingly isolated in the royal palace. His Pan-Islamic policy was not unpopular with the Muslim subjects of the empire, but it had proved no more successful than the programs of his Tanzimat predecessors in preventing the loss of Ottoman territory. The graduates of the very schools he had founded came to see the sultan as an impediment to progress, and the movement that would overthrow him began to form within the officer corps and the exile communities in Europe.

Islamic Puritanism on the Tribal Frontiers: The Wahhabi, Sanusi, and Mahdiyyah Movements

European expansionism was not the only inspiration for Islamic revivalism. During the eighteenth and nineteenth centuries, an increase in doctrinally based Islamic movements occurred among the rural populations in various Islamic regions. The leaders of these movements often were men educated in the classic Islamic tradition who came to believe that the infiltration of decadent popular practices was causing Islamic society to deviate from the tradition of the Prophet. The rural movements they launched for the purification of the faith helped spread the conviction that Islamic society would have to look within itself for the sources of its own regeneration. The three movements to be examined here were by no means the only ones of their kind. They were, however, among the most influential and the most enduring.

The theological foundations of the Wahhabi movement were set by a scholar from central Arabia, Muhammad ibn Abd al-Wahhab (1703–1792). Educated in the holy cities of Mecca and Medina, Abd al-Wahhab set forth, in writings and preaching, an uncompromising affirmation of *tawhid,* the oneness of God. In this regard he labeled Sufism, with its veneration of saints, as a form of polytheism and branded its practitioners as apostates and thus deserving of death. There was a distinct fundamentalist orientation to Abd al-Wahhab's thought, especially in his insistence that the Quran and the *hadith* were the only reliable sources through which the divine will could be comprehended. Yet coupled with his fundamentalism was an innovative quality that led him to denounce the practice of unthinking adherence to the interpretations of scholars and the blind acceptance of practices that were passed on within the family or tribe. He believed in the responsibility of the individual Muslim to learn and obey the divine commands as they were revealed in the Quran and the *hadith*.

Abd al-Wahhab's preaching attracted the support of a local chieftain from Najd, Muhammad ibn Saʿud. Ibn Saʿud's warriors and Abd al-Wahhab's reformist message merged into a powerful politico-religious force that expanded throughout northern Arabia and succeeded in capturing Mecca in 1803. It was at this point that the Ottoman sultan requested Muhammad Ali to send his Egyptian troops to Arabia to destroy the movement. Although the power of the Wahhabi forces was broken, the reformist ideals of Abd al-Wahhab became ingrained among the tribes of Arabia. The Wahhabi example of self-generated purification had a profound impact in Islamic circles at the time and later became influential among twentieth-century reformers, who adopted many of its principles.

The Sanusi order, which had its base in Cyrenaica (now eastern Libya), was more within the tradition of Sufism than was the Wahhabi movement. Its founder, Muhammad ibn Ali al-Sanusi (1787–1859), was an Algerian who spent several years studying and teaching in Mecca. His views were unpopular there, and he eventually settled in Jaghbub in Cyrenaica, a tribal region that lacked any center of political authority. The aim of al-Sanusi and the order he founded was to recreate the original community of the Prophet. The order rejected the Ottoman and Egyptian forms of Islamic behavior in favor of a more austere desert life. Although the doctrines of the Sanusi brotherhood may not have been as intellectually venturesome or as rigorously puritanical as those of Abd al-Wahhab, al-Sanusi's political achievement was noteworthy. Al-Sanusi and his followers had remarkable success in integrating the surrounding tribes into his religious order and establishing a comprehensive network of brotherhoods and trading posts stretching from northern Cyrenaica into the Sudan. The order survived its founder's death and, as the only organized unit in the region, took part in the struggle against European imperialism. The Sanusis opposed French expansion in Central Africa and resisted the Italian invasion of Tripoli in 1911. The order had its ups and downs during the various phases of Italian rule in Libya, but when the victorious Allied powers were looking for a ruler for the new state of Libya in 1950, they settled on al-Sayyid Muhammad Idris, the head of the Sanusi brotherhood and the grandson of its founder. The Sanusi order thus became the basis for the contemporary Libyan state.

The Mahdiyyah uprising in the northern Sudan has been previously mentioned in the context of Anglo-Egyptian relations (see Chapter 6). Here our concern is with the movement as another example of revived Islamic political activity. The Mahdist revolt was both a rebellion against the Egyptian occupation of the Sudan and a movement for the purification of Islam. Egyptian rule was neither popular nor effective. It had been established by a brutal conquest and could be maintained only by the stationing of thousands of Egyptian troops in the country. Taxes were much higher and more forcefully collected than had been the case previously, and the administrators sent to the Sudan were often corrupt. By the late 1870s, Sudanese discontent with the corruption and the oppressive taxation of the Egyptian administration had reached a breaking point. It was this discontent that

Muhammad Ahmad channeled so masterfully into a mass movement of protest and purification.

Muhammad Ahmad (1844–1885), a Sudanese, had been educated in religion and had established a reputation for asceticism and piety that had gained him a modest popular following. In 1881 he proclaimed himself the Mahdi, the expected one, and to the degree that his followers accepted this claim, he was regarded as directly inspired by God. His goal was to revive the faith and practice of the Prophet through the restoration of the Quran and the *hadith* as the foundations of a just society. He made a virtue of the poverty of the Sudan by renouncing worldly goods and citing the relative luxury of the Egyptian governors as evidence of their impious behavior. He formed an administrative unit, soon to become a full-fledged state, modeled closely on the Prophet's practice in Medina. The Mahdi introduced a military dimension to his movement by declaring a *jihad* against the Egyptian administration, claiming that only by dislodging these lax Muslims from the Sudan could a true Islamic society be established. With remarkable speed, the Mahdi attracted a large and devoted following and conquered most of the northern Sudan, including Khartoum, which his forces captured in 1885.

The Mahdist state survived under his successor (known, significantly, as the *caliph*) until Kitchener's reconquest of the Sudan in 1898. Although the movement spanned less than twenty years, its legacy continues to be a factor in Sudanese politics. During the Mahdi's lifetime, his rebellion attracted considerable attention throughout the Islamic world. His stunning successes in routing the Anglo-Egyptian army and establishing an indigenous Islamic state offered hope to Muslims everywhere that Islamic revival could serve as the weapon to drive out European imperialism.

The Reform of High Islam

The growing concern for the continued survival of the Islamic *ummah* in a world increasingly dominated by Europe also found expression in the urban milieu of high Islam. Here, as in the tribal response, the emphasis was on the need for Muslims to acquire a proper understanding of the original principles of Islam so as to recover the spirit of solidarity and piety that had brought such triumph to the Prophet and his successors. Although some members of the ulama used this period of reevaluation to recommend the rejection of all Western innovations, the most original of the new thinkers recognized the importance of accommodating European achievements in science and technology within the framework of Islam. Theirs was the most difficult task of all—reasserting the universal applicability of the faith while at the same time incorporating ideas that originated outside the revelations.

The activist political dimension of Islamic revival was embodied in the person of Jamal al-Din al-Afghani (1839–1897), who has been described "as a man whose life touched and deeply affected the whole Islamic world in the last quarter of the nineteenth century."[1] Al-Afghani's pronounced influence on Islamic opinion was due less to the originality of his theological formulations than to the appeal of his call for direct action in the name of Islamic solidarity. He was a complex individual, but at one basic level he may be characterized as an itinerant antiimperial activist blessed with exceptional personal magnetism. Raised and educated in Iran, he took up residence in Egypt in 1871 and attracted a group of young men to his ideas of political and religious reform. His activities were unwelcome to Khedive Tawfiq, who ordered him deported to India in 1879. Al-Afghani resurfaced in Paris in 1884; he and one of his disciples, Muhammad Abduh, published an Arabic newspaper, *al-Urwah al-Wuthqa* (The indissoluble bond), that emphasized the importance of religiously based political solidarity. Later al-Afghani became an adviser to Nasir al-Din Shah in Iran, but when the shah granted the tobacco concession of 1890, al-Afghani became one of the leading organizers of the mass protests against it. He was expelled from Iran, but his influence in opposition circles remained strong; Nasir al-Din's assassin was one of al-Afghani's former students. He spent the last five years of his life in Istanbul as a guest of Sultan Abdul Hamid, who was attracted by his Pan-Islamic message but so appalled by his politics that he kept the famous visitor under virtual house arrest.

The purpose in all these wanderings and in the writings in *al-Urwah al-Wuthqa* was to arouse in Muslims a determination to overcome their weaknesses. The Christian West was currently dominant not because it was superior but because Islam had fallen into a state of decadence and stagnation. For al-Afghani, Islam was in accord with the scientific spirit and the demands of human reason, but Muslims had become ignorant of the true principles of their faith. They had to take it upon themselves to rediscover these principles and to discard the superstitions that had corrupted the community. Two elements central to al-Afghani's conception of Islam were unity and action. It was the unity of the *ummah* that had brought such greatness to Islamic civilization in the past. Despite the existence of different races and languages among Muslims, al-Afghani believed that Pan-Islamic sentiment was the most powerful force for bringing the community together. Muslims should use their feelings of communal solidarity to resist European exploitation and to revive their sense of common purpose. However, this revival could be achieved only by effort; it would not come as a gift from God. Al-Afghani deplored all forms of passivity, but he was especially critical of Muslim rulers who allowed European armies to invade their territories and permitted European concession hunters to control their economies. He called for their overthrow and for the return of political authority to pious and uncorrupted leaders. It was al-Afghani's encouragement of action, the sense he conveyed that the status quo could be changed, that generated such appeal among young Muslims of his era. His memory as the first widely publicized figure to explain how a reformed Islamic community could stand as a bulwark against Western subversion of the values of the Middle East has remained inspirational to the present day.

What al-Afghani sought to accomplish through political agitation his most famous disciple, Muhammad Abduh, pursued by the more measured steps of intellectual inquiry and institutional reform. Abduh (1849–1905) is one of the most intensely studied Arab Muslim thinkers of the modern era. Born in an Egyptian village, he went on to become a student and then a teacher at al-Azhar in Cairo. During his student days, he met al-Afghani and became a devoted member of his circle. After al-Afghani's expulsion from Egypt, Abduh became active in the Urabi movement and was exiled in 1882. He was abroad for six years, mostly in Beirut but also in Paris. Upon his return to British-occupied Egypt, he served for a time as a judge and then was appointed mufti of Egypt in 1899. As the chief Islamic official in the country, he initiated reforms in the *sharicah* court system and tried with little success to introduce changes in the organization and curriculum of al-Azhar. A dignified and respected man, Abduh was as inspirational in his quiet way as the more charismatic al-Afghani. His numerous disciples came to occupy prominent positions in the Egyptian political and religious establishment, and his far-reaching proposals for the reformulation of Islamic doctrine generated a debate among the Muslim clergy and laity that has lasted from his time to ours.

Abduh's proposals, contained in his major scholarly work, *Risalah al-Tawhid* (A treatise on the oneness of God), and in his decrees as mufti, represented his response to the challenge posed by Europe's success. His purpose was to demonstrate that Islam was compatible with modernity and that an educated Muslim did not have to choose between being modern and being Muslim; the two went hand in hand. In broad summary, Abduh attempted to reconcile the unquestioning obedience demanded by divine revelation with the freedom of independent human reasoning. Like Abd al-Wahhab and al-Afghani, he saw that local superstitions and administrative practices dating from earlier centuries had become accepted as integral parts of Islamic doctrine and were robbing the *ummah* of its intellectual vigor and social dynamism. Abduh believed that the eternally valid requirements of Islam were found in the Quran and the verified *hadith* and had been most rigorously observed during the period of the Rashidun caliphs, the four immediate successors of the prophet. Thus, the reformist tendency associated with Abduh's name, the Salafiyyah movement, stems from the Arabic word for ancestor, *salaf,* and is tied to Abduh's contention that the study of the early community provided the surest guide to divinely approved behavior. Practices that had been incorporated into the community since the time of the Rashidun, ranging from political theory to judicial organization, were the products of human reason and were designed to meet specific historical circumstances. It followed that such practices could be modified by human reason to meet new circumstances; they were not part of the eternally valid revelation. In Islamic theological terms, Abduh was calling for the reopening of the gate of *ijtihad,* the application of informed human reason to new situations (see Chapter 2).

If, after the passage of nearly a century, Abduh's proposals seem somewhat contrived and conservative, we must attempt to appreciate how bold they were at the time. Abduh was both a preservationist and a reformer. He could accept, for example, Muhammad Ali's administrative reforms, and he was a strong advocate of broadening the curricula of the Islamic educational institutions. Change did not frighten Abduh. But the thought that some Muslims and Europeans might conceive of change as possible only outside the framework of Islam did concern him. Thus he sought to demonstrate that positive change was not the preserve of the Christian West but was also permissible, even encouraged, in a properly understood interpretation of Islam. In this way he managed both to constrain and to open the receptivity of Islamic society to new ideas and practices. The new had to be measured against the standards of the Quran, the *hadith,* and the practice of the Rashidun; if it was acceptable on those grounds, then it could be applied on the basis of informed human reason. Abduh's disciples took his thought to extremes in both areas: Some considered him the founder of a rigid school of interpretation, and others regarded him as the sponsor of the unbounded application of human reason.

Emerging Currents of Arab Cultural Distinctiveness

Within the Ottoman domains, Abdul Hamid's stress on his role as caliph was a recognition of the importance of Islam as the primary bond between the Arabs and the Ottoman state. The subject peoples of the Balkans had more readily discovered their national distinctiveness because they were also religiously distinct. But for Arab Muslims, the ties of the *ummah* were paramount, and these ties were represented by the Ottoman state. As long as loyalty to the empire appeared to be consistent with loyalty to the best interests of Islam, most Arab Muslims accepted the legitimacy of Ottoman rule. However, when a Syrian reformer, Abd al-Rahman al-Kawakibi, suggested that the Ottomans were responsible for the corruption of Islam, he introduced a nationalist argument that had profound implications for the Ottoman-Islamic order in the Arab provinces.

Al-Kawakibi (1854–1902) was from a distinguished family in Aleppo. His career as a journalist and a municipal administrator in his native city brought him into frequent conflict with Abdul Hamid's censors, and in 1899 he finally emigrated to Egypt, where he became a prominent figure in the intellectual circles of Cairo. In his two published works, *Taba'i al-Istibdad* (The nature of despotism) and *Umm al-Qura* (The mother of cities: Mecca), he analyzed the causes for the degeneration of Islam and offered suggestions for its regeneration. Both books contained extensive criticism of Abdul Hamid's oppressive rule.

At its most basic, al-Kawakibi's defense of Islamic civilization was a glorification of the Arab role in the development of that civilization. The virtues of Islam—its language, its Prophet, its early moral and political order—were Arab achievements. In his view, the decadence of Islam was caused by practices the Turks and other non-Arab peoples had introduced into the *ummah,* and he went so far as to express regret that the Turks had ever embraced the faith. The Arabs were the true protectors of Islam, and al-Kawakibi called for the Ottomans to relinquish their unjustified claim to the caliphate and to restore the office to its rightful possessors, the Arabs. In his opinion, the regeneration of Islam would begin with the establishment of an Arab caliph in Mecca whose responsibilities would be confined to purely religious matters. Al-Kawakibi was not an Arab nationalist, but in suggesting that the Arab version of Islam was the only pure one, he provided an ideological opening through which Arabs, as Muslims, could oppose Ottoman rule.

Muslims did not, of course, constitute the only Arab grouping within the empire. Large Christian minority communities were present in Syria and Mount Lebanon. How did they respond to the new currents of Islamic reformism, and what role did they see for themselves in a state that increasingly emphasized its Islamic heritage? During the second half of the nineteenth century, the Arab Christians of Syria and Lebanon experienced an economic and literary renaissance that is known as *al-nahdah,* the awakening. This resurgence also affected the Arab Muslims of the region, but its greatest impact was on members of the Christian communities. The main catalysts for the awakening were foreign Christian missionary activity and the printing press.

Beginning at the time of the Egyptian occupation of Syria (1831–1840), activity by U.S. Protestant, French Catholic, and Russian Orthodox missionaries increased dramatically. The original missionary impulse to convert the local Christians to mainstream Western versions of the faith quickly shifted to a concern for lay education and to a heated competition, especially between Presbyterians and Jesuits, to enroll members of the local Christian communities in their schools. This competition had fortunate side effects: By 1860, the Presbyterians had founded thirty-three schools in Beirut, Jerusalem, and the villages of Lebanon. This was capped in 1866 by the opening in Beirut of the U.S.-sponsored Syrian Protestant College (later the American University of Beirut), an institution that was to produce a glittering list of alumni in the fields of politics, medicine, and literature. The Jesuits were equally industrious, founding schools in Beirut, Damascus, and Aleppo as well as in the villages. The Reverend Daniel Bliss, the founding president of the Syrian Protestant College, was keenly aware of the competition between the Protestant and Catholic missions and is reported to have claimed during the ceremonies marking the opening of the Syrian Protestant College that he was, in effect, establishing two universities. His prediction came true nine years later when the Jesuits opened the Université St. Joseph in Beirut. In addition to their concern with establishing schools, the U.S. and Jesuit missions imported Arabic printing presses, which they used to produce textbooks and religious materials. In time, these presses published new editions of classical Arabic texts and served as the inspiration for the development of a lively journalistic tradition.

Throughout Lebanon and parts of Syria, this extensive educational effort, conducted largely in the Arabic language, contributed to an Arabic cultural renaissance. There was a revived interest in the classical literary tradition as well as much experimentation with new forms and styles. The career of Butrus al-Bustani (1819–1883) exemplifies the Arab cultural awakening. Born a Lebanese Maronite Christian, al-Bustani was so favorably impressed by his early contacts with American missionaries that he converted to Protestantism. He taught for a time in the missionary schools and in 1863 founded his own institution, the National School, which taught Arabic and contemporary scientific subjects. Al-Bustani's prodigious literary effort included the compilation of an Arabic dictionary, the founding and editing of several periodicals, and, in collaboration with his sons, the production of eleven volumes of an Arabic encyclopedia. His objective was to spread knowledge and appreciation of the Arabic language, and the cumulative impact of his life and work "contributed to the creation of modern Arabic expository prose, of a language true to its past in grammar and idiom, but made capable of expressing simply, precisely, and directly the concepts of modern thought."[2] Al-Bustani also encouraged a receptiveness to the scientific discoveries made in Europe, believing that only through a willingness to acquire modern knowledge would the Middle East recover its proper place in the world.

The influence of al-Bustani and others who shared his enthusiasm for blending the Arabic cultural heritage with contemporary political and scientific thought generated a lively intellectual atmosphere among the growing numbers of educated Arabs concentrated in Beirut. During the 1860s and 1870s, literary clubs and scientific societies became active in that city and served as centers for the discussion of political as well as literary topics. The emphasis on the Arabic language that was at the heart of the *nahdah* led naturally to a heightened awareness of the cultural identity of the Arab community. This was especially marked among the Christian Arabs, the principal beneficiaries of the foreign educational missions. Because of their Christianity, members of this community did not regard the new ideas and institutions coming from Europe as a threat to the foundations of their civilization; they did not have to go through the elaborate intellectual exercises of the Muslim reformers in order to justify change and the acceptance of Western concepts of political and social organization. The success of Europe was an affirmation of the local Christians' faith, and to important segments of them, European intervention and protection offered a tempting route of escape from their minority status under Ottoman rule. Ties between France and the Maronite Christians of Lebanon were especially close.

The reign of Abdul Hamid brought into ever-sharper focus the question of the future of Christians in the Ottoman Empire. However, the Hamidian regime's political repressiveness also affected Muslim Arabs, especially that group of journalists, intellectuals, and nascent politicians who had managed to partake of the educational opportunities offered during the *nahdah*. The Beirut literary societies became increasingly multi-sectarian and began to discuss such subjects as the shared heritage of the Arabs and the notion that solidarity among Arabic speakers had a greater claim on communal loyalty than did religious ties. The idea of patriotism, of the love of a particular territorial entity as an element of social cohesion, also became current. Christian Arabs, as members of a restricted minority community, had a special interest in promoting the concept of equality based on nonsectarian considerations, but the appeal of a shared sentiment of Arabness also attracted Muslims. This current of cultural renewal was by no means a nationalist independence movement, nor did it eliminate deeply rooted feelings of sectarian identity. But it did serve to increase the Arab community's awareness of its distinctiveness and historical achievements. As such, the Arab awakening represented the addition of yet another challenge to the Ottoman system.

Conclusion

By the turn of the twentieth century, the once solid Ottoman-Islamic Middle Eastern order was rendered unstable by the variety of responses emanating from its core components to the challenge of European dominance. There was a growing awareness that the Islamic community had to find within its own traditions the means for regeneration or else face the loss of those traditions. At the center, the Pan-Islamic caliphal autocracy of Sultan Abdul Hamid II generated support from those elements of Ottoman society that had been disadvantaged by the Tanzimat and was endorsed, at least in its Pan-Islamic political dimensions, by Jamal al-Din al-Afghani. In British-occupied Egypt, growing feelings of national distinctiveness and demands for political independence mingled with the country's long-standing role in the Islamic cultural universe as represented by the reformist ideas of Muhammad Abduh. On the tribal frontier, the currents set in motion by the Wahhabi, Sanusi, Mahdiyyah, and other similar movements continued to create waves of unrest against both local corruption and European encroachment and to offer appealing programs of Islamic-based activism as solutions to the problems besetting the *ummah*. And in the Arab center, the *nahdah* generated a vibrant Christian Arab movement of cultural solidarity that also attracted Muslim Arabs and reawakened memories of the central Arab role in the creation of one of history's major civilizations. The Young Turk conspirators who overthrew Abdul Hamid in 1909 attempted to impose a single solution on these diverse trends; in so doing they set them in conflict with one another and unintentionally brought an end to the Ottoman system in the Middle East.

Notes

1. Albert H. Hourani, *Arabic Thought in the Liberal Age, 1798–1939* (Oxford, 1970), p. 108.
2. Ibid., p. 100.

The Era of the Young Turks and the Iranian Constitutionalists | 8

The Young Turk era from 1908 to the Ottoman defeat in 1918 marked a period in which all the trends of the preceding century met in a head-on collision. Adding to the turmoil of these years were proposals for new forms of cultural and political identification that were at odds with the dominant ideology of Ottomanism. The situation in Iran was equally turbulent as that country experienced revolution, civil war, and foreign occupation.

Events within the Middle East unfolded against the backdrop of a changing international order that contained elements of promise—and of danger—for the Middle Eastern region. A promising component of the new order was the emergence of Japan as a modern military power. In a span of barely fifty years, Japan was transformed from a decentralized feudal society to a unified and technologically advanced nation, having acquired the institutions that appeared to lie at the core of European success—a constitution (1889) and a modern military machine. Japan's new status was affirmed by its decisive victory over Russia in the war of 1904–1905, a victory celebrated in many parts of the globe as a triumph of Asia over Europe. The example of Japan was a source of both envy and inspiration to reform-minded activists in the Middle East. To many of them, Japan stood as a symbol of what was possible, indeed of what was necessary, if European dominance was to be resisted.

For Ottoman and Iranian leaders, the urgency of military reform was highlighted by changing configurations within the European alliance system. The changes were primarily caused by Germany's growing strength and Britain's reaction to that development. Germany was a member of the Triple Alliance, a system completed by Bismarck in 1882. The alliance joined Austria-Hungary and Italy with Germany in a mutual defense pact that lasted until World War I. France responded to the Triple Alliance by entering into its own alliance with Russia in 1894. Britain preferred to avoid the entanglements of continental alliances, but increasing industrial and naval competition from Germany forced the British to reconsider their policy of isolation. As a result,

Britain entered into an informal agreement with France, the Entente Cordiale (1904), in which the two powers resolved the overseas disputes that had kept them at loggerheads for more than twenty years. By the terms of the agreement, France finally recognized Britain's occupation of Egypt and the British acknowledged France's preeminent position in Morocco. This dual alliance was expanded into the Triple Entente in 1907 when Britain and Russia reconciled their long-standing differences in Asia. The Anglo-Russian accord was reached at the expense of Iran. The two powers agreed to reduce their competition for influence in Iran by recognizing mutual spheres of influence in the country: Russia would be dominant in the north and Britain in the southeast. The independent center was to be neutral. However, as we will see later in this chapter, the two Great Powers did not hesitate to violate that neutrality when it served their interests.

The relative speed with which Britain and Russia agreed to partition Iran presented an ominous threat to the Ottomans. Throughout the nineteenth century, the rivalries among the Great Powers had served to restrain any one of them from occupying large portions of Ottoman territory. But the formation of the Triple Entente raised the specter of Great Power cooperation in dismembering the empire. The Ottoman leaders responded in two ways: They reemphasized military reform in the hope that they, like the Japanese, could ward off Europe by developing more effective European-style armed forces; and they strengthened the empire's economic, military, and diplomatic ties with Germany, a potential ally in any confrontation with the Triple Entente.

The Revolt of 1908 and the Young Turks in Power

The movement that became known as the Young Turks was an amalgam of three separate protest groups, one an exile community of long standing, the second a collection of discontented civil servants and students, and the third a coalition of disaffected army officers stationed in Ottoman Europe.

From the time of the Young Ottomans, an active Ottoman exile community existed in Paris and Geneva. This community grew during Abdul Hamid's reign and in the 1890s attempted to exercise a direct influence on Ottoman political life. The program of the exiles consisted of demands for the restoration of the constitution of 1876 and a condemnation of the sterile obscurantism of Abdul Hamid's regime. In 1902 a member of the Ottoman royal family organized a congress of Ottoman liberals in Paris that repeated the demand for a constitutional regime. However, these patriotic, European-oriented exiles had no power base and were frequently divided among themselves. Their major contribution to the growing wave of anti-Hamidian sentiment was to revive the idea of a constitution as a means to curb royal autocracy and preserve the territorial integrity of the Ottoman Empire by restoring the principle of Ottomanism.

Within the empire itself, students in the military-medical academy founded a secret protest society in 1889. Known as the Committee of Union and Progress (CUP), it soon attracted other students and some civil servants. In common with the exiles, the participants in the CUP were largely the products of European-style schools and viewed the Hamidian repression as an impediment to the reforms needed to preserve the empire. They believed in the urgency of restoring a constitutional regime and endeavored to establish cell groups to further their program. However, in 1895 and 1896 Abdul Hamid's spies uncovered the movement and arrested and exiled its members. Although a clandestine opposition continued to exist, it had little chance of developing as the sultan increased the scope of his security operations and introduced new measures of censorship.

Abdul Hamid's nearly paranoid distrust of all organized institutions extended to the armed forces. During the last years of his reign, the quality of military equipment deteriorated and salaries, which the early reformers had attempted to raise and to pay regularly, were allowed to decline and to fall into arrears. This caused widespread disaffection among line officers, some of whom began to form secret protest groups that became linked to the CUP. Opposition to Abdul Hamid was especially pronounced among officers of the Ottoman Third Army stationed in Salonika. These officers, educated in European-style military institutions, were loyal to the empire and its proud military tradition and confident that their training had prepared them to carry on that tradition. They believed that Abdul Hamid's attitude toward the army was undermining its strength and reducing its abilities to defend Ottoman territory in Europe. This patriotism, firmly grounded in Ottomanism, led a group of officers from the Third Army to stage a revolt in summer 1908 and to demand that Abdul Hamid restore the constitution; they warned the sultan that if he did not act, they would march on Istanbul and restore the constitution themselves.

Choosing not to challenge the power of an uprising within his armed forces, the sultan accepted the demand from Salonika, and on July 24, 1908, the constitution was declared once again in effect. Abdul Hamid's gesture temporarily restored his popularity, and there was a general rallying behind the sentiments of Ottoman solidarity and political liberty. Elections to the new parliament were held in fall 1908, and by the end of the year representatives from all areas of the empire gathered in Istanbul, where Abdul Hamid formally convened the chamber of deputies that he had dissolved thirty years earlier. But not everyone shared the enthusiasm for European political institutions. In spring 1909 a counterrevolution broke out against the new government. It was led by common soldiers and theological students in Istanbul who voiced their resentment against the influence of the Europeanized army officers by chanting slogans calling for the restoration of the *sharicah*. This time the Third Army acted directly. Styling itself "the army of deliverance," it marched on Istanbul, put down the disturbances, and gave its support to the parliamentary government. Abdul Hamid was accused of fomenting the counterrevolution, and the chamber decided to remove him from office. The way in which the sultan was deposed reveals the crosscurrents of opinion swirling through the Ottoman Empire at this crucial moment in its history: In order to satisfy the Muslim sentiments Abdul Hamid had so skillfully exploited, the traditional method of deposition was followed, the *shaykh al-Islam* issuing a formal decree declaring that the sultan was deposed. However, in order to give voice to the spirit of Ottomanism and political liberty that had inspired the events of 1908–1909, a four-member parliamentary delegation, including an Armenian and a Jewish representative, was sent to inform Abdul Hamid that he had been removed from office. Abdul Hamid was exiled to Salonika, the birthplace of the revolution, and replaced as sultan by his younger brother, Mehmet V (1909–1918), who was little more than a figurehead.

The first phase of the Young Turk period, from 1909 to 1913, witnessed a struggle for power between the CUP, with its base of junior and middle-level army officers and civil servants, and shifting coalitions of liberals and conservatives who had little in common but their opposition to the CUP. Through the manipulation of parliamentary elections and sheer ruthlessness, the CUP gradually gained full control of the government. By 1913 it was able to consolidate its rule as a virtual military dictatorship under the triumvirate of Enver, Talat, and Jamal Pashas. Each of these three men was talented, patriotic, and ambitious; each was also deeply flawed, and together they led the Ottoman Empire to its final dissolution. Enver (1881–1922) and Jamal (1872–1922) embodied the opportunities for social mobility made possible by the new educational institutions; both were from modest origins, both attended the war college in Istanbul, and both became staff officers in the Third Army in Salonika. Talat Pasha (1874–1921), the most competent of the triumvirate, followed a career in the new civilian communications branch of the empire. He rose from a poor family to assume a position in the post and telegraph service in Salonika, and in 1917 he became grand vizier of the Ottoman Empire.

Although the CUP became increasingly oppressive after 1913, it was at heart a reformist movement, and its first years were marked by an intellectual freedom unparalleled in Ottoman history. With the lifting of Abdul Hamid's censorship, the periodical press underwent a resurgence in the major cities of the empire. It was an exhilarating period, as ideas so long denied public expression poured forth in an exuberant torrent. The government, when it was not distracted by wars and the struggle simply to stay in power, concentrated on the expansion of the primary and secondary educational system and the improvement of the military, which had been badly neglected during Abdul Hamid's last years. As pragmatic reformers, the CUP leaders believed that the population would respond favorably to more efficient government. This conviction led them to attack the bloated bureaucracy, pensioning off incompetent officials and generally reducing the number of personnel on the state payroll. Although the logic behind this policy may have been sound, its implementation alienated many members of the civil service and several Arab notable families whose members had occupied posts in the provincial administration on an almost hereditary basis. This was typical of the kind of mistakes that the inexperienced CUP leaders made; they were usually well intentioned, but their policies often offended key groupings within Ottoman society.

Ideology and Politics: The Debate on Identity

The deposition of Abdul Hamid accelerated the public debate over the political and cultural loyalties of the peoples of the Ottoman Empire. At one level, the debate focused on achieving the proper mix between European and indigenous ideas and institutions. At another level, it concerned the troubling issue of national identity. Individuals often found themselves torn between one or another of the alternatives that surfaced during the years before World War I, years that were at once stimulating and perplexing.

When the Young Turks seized power in 1909, they were determined to save the Ottoman Empire. However, in order to pursue this objective, they had to decide what the essential character of the empire was to be. Was it principally an Ottoman state committed to a program of transformation and equal rights for all its ethnically diverse inhabitants? Or was it an Islamic state dependent for its survival on the rediscovery of properly interpreted Islamic traditions? Or, finally, given the composition of its political and military leadership, was it really a Turkish state to which certain minority nationalities were attached?

The CUP leaders were committed to the concept of Ottomanism. Much like the Young Ottomans forty years earlier, they believed that the best way to restore the vitality of the empire was through constitutional government that would limit the power of the monarch and guarantee the rights of non-Muslims by incorporating them into the framework of Ottomanism. One of the government's first acts after the deposition of Abdul Hamid was to abolish the *millet* system, thereby stressing its commitment to Ottomanism and to the ideal of preserving all Ottoman territory. At the same time, however, the regime could not abandon the Islamic foundation on which imperial legitimacy had rested for so many centuries. Thus, the CUP continued to stress the role of the sultan as caliph and to use Islamic symbols to buttress its own claims to legitimacy. In this, as in other aspects of its rule, the CUP was caught on the horns of a dilemma. In order for the ideal of Ottomanism to be realized, the religious distinctions between Muslim rulers and non-Muslim subjects had to be abolished in substance as well as in theory. It was also necessary to eliminate the factors that encouraged national separation movements within the empire and for the international community to respect the territorial integrity of the Ottoman Empire. None of these conditions came close to being fulfilled.

Shortly after the restoration of the constitution in 1908, Bulgaria proclaimed its final independence, Austria annexed the province of Bosnia, and Crete declared union with the Greek mainland. Further contempt for Ottoman sovereignty was shown by the Italian invasion of the North African province of Tripoli in October 1911. The Ottoman government sent reinforcements to support the Sanusi resistance in Tripoli, but pressures from other crises prevented Istanbul from offering serious opposition to the Italians; in October 1912 the Ottomans signed a treaty ceding Tripoli and some of the Dodecanese Islands, including Rhodes, to Italy. This eventful year also witnessed devastating Ottoman setbacks in Europe, as Albania proclaimed its independence and an alliance consisting of Bulgaria, Serbia, Greece, and Montenegro drove the Ottoman forces out of most of Europe during the First Balkan War. In spring 1913, the erstwhile Balkan allies began quarreling over the division of the territories they had taken, providing the Ottomans with an opportunity to regain portions of Thrace. Yet this final victory was a hollow one; in 1912, Ottoman domains in Europe totaled 65,350 square miles (169,910 sq km) inhabited by an estimated 6.1 million people. When the last treaty of the Balkan Wars was signed in September 1913, Ottoman Europe had been reduced to 10,882 square miles (28,293 sq km) and a population of 1.9 million people.[1] In terms of manpower, revenue, and productivity, these losses were staggering. They were also damaging to the CUP, which had committed itself to the preservation of the empire and instead presided over the loss of the heartlands on which the *ghazi* state was founded. Adding insult to injury was the humiliation of the Ottoman military by the armies of the small states inhabited by former subject peoples.

The events of 1908–1913 called into question the policy of Ottomanism. They demonstrated once again that neither the Great Powers nor the Balkan successor states were willing to respect the territorial integrity of the Ottoman state, they showed that minority people preferred national affiliations to Ottoman citizenship, and they undermined the proposition that Muslim and Christian could share in a common Ottoman bond. The CUP leaders were far from perfect, but they faced almost insurmountable odds in their patriotic goal of preserving the imperial domains.

Although the upheavals did not prompt the CUP to abandon its policy of Ottomanism, they did generate a new awareness of the importance of the Anatolian Turkish core to the identity of the empire. The empire had been made much more homogeneous by the loss of 80 percent of its European domains, and it was only natural that in the wake of the Arab *nahdah* and the Balkan nationalist movements, a specifically Turkish cultural movement would also emerge. The movement contained several elements, but it can be broken down into two main, often overlapping currents. The first current,

Pan-Turkism, originated among Muslim Turkish exiles from Russia, several of whom achieved prominence in Istanbul intellectual circles at the turn of the century. Pan-Turkism stressed the existence of unifying bonds among all speakers of Turkish. To advocates of Pan-Turkism, the Ottoman Turks were just one branch of the several Turkish-speaking peoples who inhabited a vast expanse of territory from Anatolia to China. Even if they spoke different dialects, they shared the same basic language and therefore constituted a single and distinctive people. And as one people, they should have their own state made up of all the Turkish speakers in Anatolia, Russia, Iran, Afghanistan, and China. The grandiose political program of the Pan-Turkists may have stimulated Ottoman Turkish intellectuals to rediscover their own Turkish past, but it did not attract sustained support.

More appealing to the Turks of the empire was a doctrine that became known as Turkism and focused more directly on the Ottoman situation. The doctrine stressed the crucial Turkish contribution to the success of the Ottoman Empire and posited the notion that there was a special pre-Islamic, pre-Ottoman cultural heritage that distinguished the Turks from the other inhabitants of the empire. In a marked departure from Ottomanism, the writer Mehmet Emin published a poem in 1897 that began, "I am a Turk, my religion and my race are noble."[2] Although Emin's statement contained an element of ethnic distinctiveness, it still equated Turkishness with Islam.

The formation of a Turkish cultural club in Istanbul in 1912 and its association with a journal, *Türk Yurdu* (Turkish homeland), aided the transformation of the once pejorative word *Turk* into a positive force of cultural identity. It is significant that the leading spokesman of this trend, Ziya Gökalp (1876–1924), was born and raised in eastern Anatolia. A member of the CUP inner circle, Gökalp argued that Turkish national traditions, what he called the soul of the nation, had become submerged under the cultural practices of the people over whom the Turks ruled. His self-proclaimed mission was to rediscover this soul by examining the history of the pre-Islamic Turks and by studying popular culture, which he believed had held fast to authentic Turkish traditions. For Gökalp, language was the essence of nationality, and he disdained the hybrid Ottoman language in favor of a modified Turkish vernacular that he claimed was a more accurate reflection of the original Turkish soul. In seeking a place for Islam as a component of Turkism, Gökalp argued that the Turks had borne the burden of Islamic greatness for centuries and that a reformed Islam was an essential part of the Turkish nation. The combination of nationalism, Islamism, and modernism that circulated among the Ottoman elite during the Young Turk era is captured in Gökalp's statement, "We belong to the Turkish nation, the Muslim religious community and the European civilization."[3] During the prewar years, the doctrine of Turkism did not develop into a coherent ideology defining a specifically Turkish national state. However, the discussions of a

Turkish cultural heritage as distinct from the Ottoman one sowed the seeds for a full-blown Turkish nationalist movement in the postwar era.

The CUP and the Arab Provinces

The CUP's policies toward the Arab-speaking provinces were determined by the regime's quest for political security and centralized administrative control. Like any government with a questionable claim to legitimacy, the CUP sought to purge the administration of officials from the old order and replace them with appointees loyal to and dependent upon the Young Turk regime. Those who suffered most from this practice were the long-established Arab notable families. For example, the al-Abid family, perhaps the wealthiest in Damascus at the turn of the century, was represented in Abdul Hamid's palace entourage, in the central Ottoman government, and in the local Syrian administration. The CUP dismissed the al-Abids from their posts, confiscated some of their lands, and pushed them into self-imposed exile in Paris. Another distinguished Damascus family, the al-Azms, thrived politically and financially under Abdul Hamid. An al-Azm representative sat regularly on the provincial and municipal councils of Damascus, and in the 1890s two members of the family served as ministers in the Ottoman cabinet in Istanbul. The CUP purged the al-Azms from the administration and replaced them with loyal supporters of the new regime.

By denying the Arab notable families their traditional access to the government, the CUP undermined the notables' ability to satisfy their local clients and upset the established social and political order in the Arab provinces. Increasingly, the Arab elite came to perceive the CUP as a Turkifying government. The leadership of the party was dominated by Turks, and many of the officials appointed to replace Arabs in the provincial administrations were also Turks. Although the intentions of the CUP leaders were to centralize the government, not necessarily to Turkify it, their policies caused important segments of the Arab population to become disaffected from the regime. Frustrated at their exclusion from power and angered at seeing their carefully laid plans for advancement within the Ottoman system destroyed by young army officers who failed to appreciate the advantages of mutual cooperation, some members of the Arab elite began to contemplate alternatives to the CUP's brand of Ottomanism.

Although Arab grievances did not coalesce into an organized political movement for national independence, they did take on the coloring of Arabism, a protonationalist outlook that served both political and cultural purposes. On the one hand, Arabism was a means through which some members of the Arab notable families protested against the CUP's attacks on their political and economic status; on the other hand, it represented an affirmation of Arab cultural identity and a desire for that identity to receive greater recognition by the government. Arabism manifested itself in the formation of a variety of literary clubs, reform societies, and clandestine organizations among Arabs in Istanbul and throughout the Arab provinces. The twin strands of political protest and cultural affirmation became intermingled in the programs of these societies, which called for the recognition of Arabic as an official language, the appointment of Arabs to administrative posts within the Arab territories, and greater political autonomy for all the Arab provinces. These demands show that the proponents of Arabism were fully prepared to accept Ottoman rule, but they wanted it to be decentralized. Their grievances were directed against the CUP regime that had deprived them of their proper role within the Ottoman order, not against the Ottoman state itself.

The largest of the Arab organizations formed during the Young Turk era was the Party of Ottoman Administrative Decentralization. Founded in early 1913 and headquartered in the safety of Cairo, the Party established branches in most of the Arab cities of Greater Syria. Its president was Rafiq al-Azm, a member of the Damascus family mentioned earlier, and its agenda was dominated by Syrian urban notables. The name of the party suggests that its membership was willing to reach an accommodation within the framework of Ottomanism but that any such accommodation had to provide scope for a return of the notables to their former status. The willingness of the discontented Arab elite to find a common ground with Ottomanism can be seen in the resolutions passed by the Arab Paris Congress of 1913. Organized jointly by the Decentralization Party and a society of Arab students in Paris, the congress is often seen as the starting point of Arab nationalism. Although the congress certainly provided a forum for the expression of Arab discontent, the tone of its resolutions was strongly Ottomanist, not separatist. The delegates expressed a desire for reforms and decentralization but stated clearly that they did not wish to separate from the Ottoman Empire.

Even though the Paris Congress was decidedly moderate, it did prompt CUP leaders to realize that they had to take steps to satisfy the demands of the most important non-Turkish Muslim people within the empire. The government appointed an Arab, Saʿid Halim, as grand vizier (1913–1917) and adopted a number of other conciliatory measures that turned out to be more superficial than substantive. Among them was the appointment of the president of the Paris Congress and four other Arab notables to the Ottoman senate. These gestures were accompanied by a determined—and successful—CUP effort to co-opt leading Arab dissidents by securing their appointments to provincial administrative posts. Thus, by the eve of World War I, the voice of Arabism had been muffled if not stilled.

The CUP was able to quell Arabism with such ease because it was advocated by so few. It is important to recognize that from 1908 to 1918 the vast majority of the Arab inhabitants of the empire supported Ottomanism. Deeply ingrained habits of loyalty to the Ottoman state and perceptions of the sultan-caliph as protector of the Islamic *ummah* were the chief elements of this support. Too often, the years from the Young Turk revolt to the outbreak of World War I have been viewed from the perspective of the postwar era, which portrays the period simply as the gestation phase of Arab nationalism or as the preparation for the end of a doomed empire and the rise of separate nation-states in the Middle East. But the historian must attempt to reconstruct an era as it was for those who lived through it, and for most members of the Arab elite, the Young Turk era was a time to plan for a future within the political framework of the Ottoman Empire. Despite the CUP's campaign against certain Arab notables whose prestige stemmed from their service in the Hamidian regime, many distinguished Arab families retained their power, and others acquired new standing under the Unionist regime. Thus, during the Young Turk era, Arabs continued to attend the advanced academies in Istanbul and to occupy high-ranking positions in the civilian bureaucracy and the officer corps.

Sati al-Husri and Shakib Arslan represent the diversity of Arab beliefs that could be accommodated within the framework of Ottomanism. Al-Husri (1880–1968) was the epitome of the Europeanized professional. Upon graduating from the civil service college in 1900, he was posted to the Balkans as a schoolteacher and later as a district administrator. An avid reformist and constitutionalist, al-Husri engaged in CUP activities before 1908 and was one of the young professionals who rose to prominence as a result of the CUP triumph. In the years following the deposition of Abdul Hamid, his work in Istanbul as teacher, as director of the teacher training college, and as editor of journals on educational reform gained him the reputation as the founder of modern Turkish pedagogy. Al-Husri was a Syrian Arab, but he was also a cosmopolitan member of the Ottoman elite, and his successful career was based on service to the Ottoman state; he had a vested interest in the preservation of that state, a goal he attempted to realize through educational reform and the spread of the idea of Ottoman patriotism.

At the other end of the spectrum of Arab Ottomanism was Amir Shakib Arslan (1869–1946). A Druze prince from a powerful family in Lebanon, Arslan was influenced by the ideas of al-Afghani and Abduh and became a strong supporter of the Pan-Islamic policy of Abdul Hamid. As a journalist, poet, and local political figure, Arslan advocated the proposition that the survival of the Ottoman Empire was the only guarantee against the division of the *ummah* and its occupation by the European imperial powers. For him, Ottomanism and Islam were closely bound together; the reform of Islam would naturally lead to the revival of the Ottoman Empire. Although he regretted the overthrow of Abdul Hamid, he was able to accept the CUP regime because of what he perceived as its commitment to the preservation of the Islamic core of the Empire. The CUP, in turn, recognized the advantages that the support of an established family like the Arslans could bring and rewarded them accordingly. Arslan was elected, with CUP backing, to the Ottoman parliament in 1914 and was later joined by two of his brothers. The Arslans saw that Ottomanism had its political benefits and represent an example of an Arab notable family that retained its status under the CUP regime.

Neither al-Husri, the secular professional educator, nor Arslan, the Pan-Islamic notable, believed that Arab separatism served his ideological goals or his personal interests. As a result, both supported Ottomanism, albeit of a somewhat different variety. For al-Husri, Ottomanism meant the adoption of European concepts of territorial patriotism, constitutional government, and secular citizenship; whereas for Arslan, it meant the retention of the Islamic foundations of the Ottoman order and an emphasis on the bonds of Islamic solidarity. Most of the Arab subjects of the empire accepted some form of Ottomanism, whether al-Husri's Europeanist version, Arslan's Islamic orientation, or some combination of the two. The demands of Arabism—political decentralization, cultural autonomy, and the replacement of the CUP regime—and the various options that existed within the dominant ideology of Ottomanism were all strands of the complex pattern of identity of the Arabic-speaking peoples. But for all the ideological turbulence and political restlessness of the period from 1908 to 1914, the majority of Arabs—both the elite and the population at large—entered World War I committed to the preservation of the Ottoman Empire.

The Period of the Iranian Constitutional Revolution

The years of political upheaval from 1905 to 1911 mark a new phase in Iranian history and are generally referred to as the period of the constitutional revolution. As with the Young Turk revolt of 1908, the introduction of constitutional government in Iran was used as a weapon to attack royal autocracy. However, whereas the Ottoman constitutional movement had been founded on a transformed bureaucratic elite and a reform-oriented officer corps, the Iranian movement was led by an awkward coalition of interests that contained contradictory ideas of what constitutional government was to achieve. The three main components of the coalition—traditional bazaar merchants, ulama, and a small group of radical reformers—were each convinced that if they could find a way to limit the shah's authority, they could then take the lead in guiding the country in the direction they thought it ought to go.

The popular protests that culminated in the constitutional decree of 1906 were directed against the policies of Muzzafir al-Din Shah (1896–1906), a weak and ineffective ruler. Facing the customary Qajar problem of how to generate enough income to keep the royal court in luxury, Muzzafir al-Din reintroduced the practice of concession granting. In 1901 the shah awarded a British subject, William D'Arcy, the concession for oil rights in the entire country except for five northern provinces. In exchange the Iranian government was to receive 16 percent of the company's annual profits. This proved to be a costly surrender of Iran's resources. Oil was discovered in commercial quantities in 1908, and in 1914 the British government became the major shareholder in the company holding the concession. Iran's vast oil reserves were placed at the disposal of Britain, and the preservation of British control over Iranian oil became a central factor in Britain's Middle Eastern policy. Muzzafir al-Din also had recourse to foreign loans, borrowing money from British, French, and Russian financial institutions. The income from the loans, rather than being deployed in economic development or military improvements, was used to meet payments on earlier loans or was squandered on Muzzafir al-Din's three hugely expensive trips to Europe between 1900 and 1905. In reopening Iran to foreign economic penetration, Muzzafir al-Din made himself vulnerable to the same charges that had been leveled at his father during the tobacco protest of 1890.

The renewal of foreign economic activities in Iran struck hardest at the bazaaris, the urban class of merchants, guild masters, and moneylenders that had traditionally been the hub around which most of Iran's economic life revolved. By granting foreigners favored customs rates in both the import and export trade, the government made it impossible for local merchants to compete successfully. In addition, the import of low-cost manufactured items, especially textiles, destroyed the local craft industries. For the bazaaris, the shah's practice of selling Iran to foreign Christian economic interests was not only offensive to their religious sensibilities, it was a threat to their economic survival.

Another group instrumental in coordinating the protest against the shah was composed of a small but active circle of European-oriented reformers. They were not part of a common employment group—the activists included aristocrats, civil servants, army officers, and even some royal princes. Their experiences of the West were also diverse—some had traveled and studied in Europe, others had witnessed the Ottoman reforms from Istanbul, and still others had acquired their understanding of European institutions and ideas from translated books. What united them was their opposition to royal corruption and foreign exploitation; they believed that Iran was stagnating under the Qajars and that radical reforms were needed to shake the country from its doldrums and restore its position in the world. Motivated by sentiments of patriotism and liberalism, the reformers believed that constitutional government was a key ingredient to building a strong and progressive Iranian nation.

The reasons for the ulama's participation in the constitutional movement are more difficult to determine. Although the ulama were by no means united in their support for the movement, several leading *mujtahid*s and large numbers of lesser ulama played a major part in the antigovernment demonstrations of 1906. The ulama were closely tied to the bazaaris, and it is likely that members of the religious establishment suffered financially from the influx of foreign business activity. In addition, the policies of Muzzafir al-Din tended to reproduce the conditions that had sparked the protest of 1890 during which the ulama had accused the ruler of violating the tenets of Islam. Finally, although Muzzafir al-Din was hardly a centralizer, the Shiᶜa religious establishment continued to guard its independence from the state and may have viewed the constitutional movement as an opportunity to guarantee that independence into the future. Hence, the important ulama role in the constitutional revolution was not based on demands for more reform and transformation but on demands for less. In the Ottoman Empire the ulama generally opposed a constitution because they thought it would reduce their power; in Iran the ulama supported one because they thought it would increase theirs.

The first phase of the constitutional revolution began with a large protest movement in Tehran in December 1905 and concluded in August 1906 when the shah, faced with huge antigovernment protests led by the bazaaris, the ulama, and the reformers, capitulated to the demonstrators' demands and signed a decree convening a constituent assembly. The first assembly (Majlis) met in October 1906 and drafted two constitutional provisions that completely restructured the allocation of political authority within Iran. The first provision, the Fundamental Law, reduced the powers of the monarch by giving the elected legislature final authority over loans, concessions, treaties, and budgets. Muzzafir al-Din signed the Fundamental Law a few days before his death. In the second provision, the Supplementary Fundamental Laws, the rights of Iranian citizens were defined and the legislature granted additional powers, including authority over the appointment and dismissal of ministers. But this had not been a secularizing constitutional movement, and the ulama's triumph was ensured by constitutional clauses that stated that Twelver Shiᶜism was the official religion of the state and provided for a supreme committee of *mujtahids* to review all new legislation to verify that it conformed to the *shariᶜah*. When the new shah, Muhammad Ali, reluctantly approved the Supplementary Fundamental Laws in late 1907, it appeared that the long tradition of authoritarian Iranian monarchy had come to an end.

However, Muhammad Ali Shah was determined to restore Qajar authority. A deteriorating economic situation accompanied by inflation and high prices for basic foodstuffs created lower-class discontent with the government of the Majlis and encouraged mass support for a Qajar restoration. The royalists used ulama loyal to the shah to denounce the constitutionalists as atheists and to arouse popular sentiment in favor of the monarchy. At this critical juncture, external forces played an important role in determining the fate of the fragile constitutional experiment. In August 1907 Britain and Russia signed the entente in which they agreed to divide Iran into spheres of influence; Britain would be dominant in the southeast, Russia would control the north, and a neutral zone would be allowed to exist in the center. The royalists could show that the constitutional government had been even less effective than the shahs in preserving Iranian sovereignty. With popular unrest increasing and more members of the ulama denouncing the constitutionalists, the royalist position became more favorable. Muhammad Ali staged his counterrevolution in June 1908; he sent the Cossack Brigade to close the Majlis, arrested and executed leading members of the constitutionalists, and reestablished royal authority in Tehran. Iran was plunged into civil war and economic chaos.

The eleven months of civil war demonstrated clearly the inadequacy of the government's armed forces. The shah was able to hold Tehran, but other areas of the country loyal to the constitutionalists refused to submit to his authority. During summer 1909, an armed rebel force from the province of Azerbaijan advanced on Tehran from the north while a confederation of Bakhtiyari tribesmen moved up from the south. The two forces entered the capital in July and restored the constitution. Muhammad Ali Shah, who had taken refuge in the Russian legation, was deposed in favor of his young son, who became shah under a regency. The second Majlis convened in August 1909. The constitution had been successfully defended, but it remained to be seen whether a constitutional regime representing such diverse interests could govern effectively.

Over the next two years, the Majlis was the scene of constant friction between the reformers and an alliance of bazaaris and ulama. The coalition that had been united in opposition to the Qajar regime broke apart over such issues as the relationship between the state and the religious establishment, the question of equal rights for non-Muslims, and the extent and pace of social reform. (These same issues resurfaced in the aftermath of the 1979 revolution.) The verbal arguments in the Majlis were transformed into armed clashes on the streets of Tehran between supporters of the various political factions. Once again, government became paralyzed, and an age-old pattern repeated itself. With the central government torn apart by internal disputes, the tribal confederations reasserted their independence and refused to pay taxes; law and order completely broke down in the rural areas.

As the tribes roamed and looted at will, the British landed troops at Bushire in October 1911 in order to protect the stability of their sphere of influence. This had become all the more urgent with the discovery of oil by D'Arcy's exploration company in 1908. When the British occupied southern Iran, Russia invaded the north and in November threatened to occupy Tehran unless the government accepted an ultimatum demanding the dismissal of a newly appointed U.S. financial adviser. When the Majlis refused to accept the ultimatum, it was dissolved by the prime minister and the cabinet. The Russian demands were then granted, and the period of the constitutional revolution was over.

On the eve of World War I, the Majlis remained suspended, and Iran was governed by a conservative group of ministers whose actions were closely monitored by Britain and Russia. In addition, the northern and southern halves of the country were under foreign military occupation. The occupying powers dealt with tribal leaders and local merchants in their spheres of influence without any consideration for the government in Tehran. Iran had gained a constitution and eliminated the authority of the Qajar shahs, but in the process it had become divided against itself. Not only did the coalition of bazaaris, ulama, and reformers break down under the pressures of governing, but the objective that had brought them together in the first place—the reduction of the foreign presence in Iran—had been thwarted. The casting aside of traditional institutions, no matter how desirable it might appear, was a painful process that did not always produce the intended results.

Conclusion

Under the twin pressures of European economic and imperial expansion and mounting domestic discontent, members of the Ottoman and Iranian elite sought to readjust the governing institutions of their states. In the Ottoman Empire, the Young Turks restored the constitution of 1876, hoping that its promises of equality for all Ottoman citizens would generate a spirit of unity and a willingness to cooperate in the implementation of new reform programs. However, the Young Turks pursued a policy of Ottomanism at a time when the various ethnic communities within the empire demanded either independence or a greater measure of political and cultural autonomy. The attempts by the CUP government to balance Ottomanism with stricter central controls alienated the groups that had benefited from the long reign of Abdul Hamid II. Yet despite the centrifugal forces at work, the majority of the Arab and Turkish inhabitants of the empire retained their loyalty to the Ottoman state and shared the belief that European encroachment on Ottoman domains should be resisted.

Iran, which had not undergone as intense a transformation as the Ottoman Empire, nevertheless experienced a constitutional revolution that had the same larger objective as the Young Turk revolt: To preserve the state from internal collapse and external aggression. But within Iran, the forces favoring a constitution had very different ideas about what the constitution was supposed to achieve in terms of the domestic social and political order. For the ulama and the bazaaris, the new regime was to reduce European economic activity and preserve their customary position in the social hierarchy. But the European-inspired reformers hoped for a more thorough transformation that would lead to the introduction of secular laws and a strong legislative assembly. Once the constitution was proclaimed, the differences among the coalition members burst into the open and made effective governance impossible. Moreover, the central state and the armed forces were so weak and the treasury so depleted that neither a royal regime nor a constitutional one could exert authority within the country. As the situation in Iran deteriorated, Britain and Russia attempted to keep order in their zones of influence by occupying them. This was the first of several twentieth-century violations of Iran's sovereignty by outside powers, and it contributed to the growth of the intense Iranian resentment against foreign intervention.

Notes

1. L. S. Stavrianos, *The Balkans Since 1453* (New York, 1963), p. 540.

2. Cited in Uriel Heyd, *The Foundations of Turkish Nationalism* (London, 1950), p. 108.

3. Cited in ibid., p. 149.

World War I and the End of the Ottoman Order 9

The assassination of Austrian Archduke Ferdinand in Sarajevo on June 28, 1914, led to Austria's invasion of Serbia. The Austrian invasion activated the European alliance system, and by August the Continent was at war. The alliance of the Triple Entente—Britain, France, and Russia—was pitted against the Central Powers: Germany and Austria-Hungary. As Europe prepared for the conflict, the Ottoman cabinet remained divided on what action to take. Although the majority of CUP leaders favored a policy of neutrality, some within the government wished to use the European war as an opportunity to strike at Russia, the traditional enemy of the Ottomans. In the end, the empire's fateful decision to join the Central Powers was determined by a small group within the CUP led by Enver Pasha, a committed Germanophile. On August 2, 1914, Enver concluded a secret Ottoman-German alliance against Russia; the alliance was activated on October 29, when the Ottoman fleet bombarded several Russian ports on the Black Sea. The empire had entered what would turn out to be the last of its many wars.

Although the Ottoman Empire was defeated in the conflict and dismembered by the peace treaties, its ability to endure four years of total warfare testified to the tenacity with which its population, civilian and military alike, defended the Ottoman order. Over 1 million Ottoman soldiers were mobilized, and the Ottoman armies achieved impressive successes on several different fronts. In domestic affairs the CUP government introduced programs that had not only an immediate transforming impact but also significant long-term effects on the future development of the Turkish republic. The CUP's attempt to break the empire's economic dependence on foreigners and local religious minorities represents an important example of these changes. The wartime economic policies were necessary in part because so much of the empire's trade and investment was in the hands of firms from the Entente powers whose governments were at war with the Ottomans. Thus, in 1914 the CUP renounced the Capitulations, introduced protectionist tariffs, and adopted measures bringing foreign enterprises under Ottoman jurisdiction and making them subject to Ottoman taxes. This assertion of economic independence was carried a step further by the CUP's policy of granting government contracts to Turkish Muslim entrepreneurs, some of whom reaped enormous wartime profits in trade and transportation. This did not in and of itself create a Turkish Muslim bourgeoisie, but it did serve to create more favorable investment opportunities for Muslim businessmen and to reduce the advantages held by Europeans and their local Christian associates.

The war also served to accelerate the transformation of the Ottoman social order. With large numbers of men mobilized for military service, more women began to enter the civil service and the mainstream professions. The CUP recognized the changing circumstances by legislating a major new family law in 1917. The law placed the *shariʿah* courts under the authority of the Ministry of Justice, thus giving a secular state agency control over family law and personal status, the last important areas of jurisdiction that had remained to the religious establishment. The transfer from religious to secular authority was emphasized in those sections of the new law recognizing the right of women to initiate divorce and restricting the grounds for the practice of polygamy.

The war resulted in the division of the Ottoman Empire and the occupation of its Arab provinces by Britain and France. In Anatolia, however, an independent Turkish republic emerged out of the Ottoman defeat. The survival of the new republic owed much to the Ottoman war effort, which not only enlarged the pool of trained soldiers, officers, and civil servants but also produced an atmosphere in which the public was accustomed to social change and therefore receptive to the sweeping reforms of the 1920s.

The Middle East in the War: An Overview of Military Operations

The Ottoman armies performed much more effectively throughout the war than their opponents had anticipated. Following the military debacle in the Balkan Wars of 1912–1913, the CUP made a determined effort to improve the armed forces. In early 1914 the German general Liman von Sanders arrived in Istanbul at the head of a large German military mission. The CUP granted the mission extensive powers, and its efforts, combined with the government's willingness to introduce far-reaching military reforms, had begun to produce noticeable results by the outbreak of the war. Although von Sanders and other German officers occasionally commanded Ottoman armies during the fighting, the overall direction of the war effort remained in Ottoman hands.

Because of its extensive borders, the empire was vulnerable to attack at a variety of different points, a problem that necessitated posting troops on several fronts simultaneously. In eastern Anatolia and the Caucasus region, Ottoman and Russian armies engaged in constant warfare until 1917. The eastern campaign was launched by a reckless offensive, personally led by

Enver Pasha, in winter 1914–1915. Although Enver experienced some early success, he exposed his troops to such an irresponsibly high casualty rate that what was left of his army was in no condition to resist a Russian counterattack in spring 1915. As the Russians pushed the Ottoman eastern army back from Erzurum, Enver retired to Istanbul. He remained in charge of the Ottoman war effort, but he did not again command an army in the field. The Ottoman forces on the eastern front adopted a defensive posture until the Russian withdrawal in the aftermath of the Bolshevik Revolution of 1917. At that point, after four years of fighting, the Ottomans still retained sufficient resources to mount an offensive that retook most of their prewar territory.

It was in this eastern theater that the CUP carried out its notorious operations against the Armenian community. Although most Armenians remained loyal to the Ottoman state, nationalist organizations in both Russia and Anatolia looked upon the war as an opportunity to create an independent Armenia. Armenian volunteer units served in the Russian army, and there was agitation for a homeland in and around the Anatolian city of Van. On the grounds that some Armenians were collaborating with the Russians, an influential faction within the CUP decided that the Armenian villagers within Anatolia constituted a behind-the-lines threat to the Ottoman forces in the field and ordered collective reprisals against the entire Armenian population. Beginning in early 1915, the regime instituted a systematic policy of forced evacuation of Armenians from eastern and southern Anatolia. Hundreds of thousands were uprooted from their villages and sent south toward the Syrian desert in what amounted to a death march. Countless numbers perished of starvation and illness along the deportation routes, and there can be little doubt that many others were killed before they left Anatolia. The survivors found a refuge—though not always a welcome one—in Lebanon, where they tended eventually to congregate in Beirut. Nor were Armenians in Istanbul spared; on April 15, 1915, about 200 prominent members of the capital's Armenian community were arrested, deported, and, according to some sources, later executed.[1] It would be pointless to enter the debate that rages today between members of the Armenian community in Europe and the United States who accuse the Ottomans of genocide and the Turkish government, which insists that the excesses have been overemphasized. Any episode in which as many as 1 million civilians may have lost their lives is an appalling one, whether it is calculated or the unintended result of internal security measures.

Once the Russian counterattack on the eastern front gained momentum, the Allies opened two new fronts against the Ottomans: The first was aimed at Istanbul, the second at Mesopotamia. The Ottomans repulsed them both. The famous Gallipoli campaign began in February 1915. Its objective was to force open the Dardanelles and capture Istanbul, thereby cutting the Ottomans off from Germany and opening Russia to Entente supply lines through the Black Sea. When the Allied naval squadron was prevented from penetrating the Dardanelles by Ottoman shore-based artillery, an expeditionary force of British and French troops, numbering 200,000, was put ashore on the Gallipoli peninsula. But the Ottoman defenses held and inflicted heavy casualties on the Allied troops, eventually forcing their evacuation in January 1916. It was during the Gallipoli campaign that a young Ottoman colonel, Mustafa Kemal, the future Atatürk, gained a reputation as a resourceful military commander.

At the other geographical extreme of the empire, the head of the Persian Gulf, two compelling imperial concerns shaped British military strategy: One was the ever-present imperative to defend the approaches to India; the second was the need to protect the oil fields of Iran. The former was a cornerstone of British policy; the latter had become equally important with the conversion of the British navy from coal to oil fuel in 1912. Thus, even before the onset of the Ottoman-Russian campaigns on the eastern Anatolian front, an army from British India occupied the port city of Basra in late 1914 and began to advance toward Baghdad. However, the commander of the Anglo-Indian expedition, General Charles Townshend, was deceived by his initial successes and underestimated the resourcefulness of his Ottoman adversaries. Advancing beyond his supply lines, Townshend allowed the Ottomans to surround his forces at the village of Kut. After suffering a lengthy siege, Townshend was forced to surrender an entire British army to the Ottomans in April 1916. But the Mesopotamian front was too important for the British to ignore. Less than a year after Townshend's surrender, another expeditionary force captured Baghdad (March 1917) and brought southern Iraq under British control.

Another important and as it turned out decisive front was the one existing between the borders of Ottoman Syria and British-occupied Egypt. As the key to the Suez Canal, it was recognized by all the belligerents as being of vital strategic significance. In January 1915, at the same time that Enver was engaged in his costly campaign in eastern Anatolia, Jamal Pasha led an Ottoman army of 80,000 men across the Sinai Peninsula for a quick strike against the Suez Canal. The concept of an attack on the unprepared British defenses in Egypt was militarily sound, but the campaign was poorly coordinated, and the Ottoman forces were driven back before they could cross the canal. Alarmed by the near success of Jamal Pasha's attack, the British began a massive buildup of troops in Egypt. By early 1917 a large army had been assembled, and the British launched their own offensive. Under the command of General Edmund Allenby, the British army moved in a wide front against the Ottoman forces in Palestine. It was aided in the campaign by the irregular forces of the Arab Revolt, which operated on its right flank and conducted guerrilla operations behind Ottoman lines. Although Jerusalem was captured in December 1917, the Syrian campaign was by no means over. Ottoman resistance stiffened in 1918, and it was only Allenby's superb supply lines to Egypt that kept the British offensive from bogging down. By autumn the British were able to renew their offensive, and the Ottoman collapse came quickly. On October 1, the forces of the Arab Revolt captured Damascus; a few days later the French fleet took Beirut; and by the end of the month the Ottoman armies had retreated to Anatolia, where they prepared to make another defensive stand. It proved unnecessary. On October 31, 1918, the government in Istanbul signed the Armistice of Mudros, a document of unconditional surrender that brought an end to the war in the Middle East and with it the end of the Ottoman Empire.

As the Ottoman troops began laying down their weapons, the victors swooped in to divide the spoils. Less than a month after the armistice was signed, an Allied fleet anchored off Istanbul, and the imperial capital was brought under British military occupation. With Britain in occupation of most of the Arabic-speaking provinces and a French force stationed in Beirut, the Allies were in full control of the disposal of Ottoman territory. But they were also bound, or so some parties thought, to honor the treaties and agreements they had entered into during the course of the war.

Ottoman Wartime Administration in Greater Syria

In an effort to rally the Muslim population of the empire to the cause of the war and to arouse Muslim opinion against Britain and France, the CUP government mobilized all the Islamic symbols it could muster. In November 1914 the sultan-caliph issued a call to *jihad,* urging Muslims the world over to unite behind the Ottoman Empire in its confrontation with the Triple Entente. The caliph's proclamation portrayed the Entente powers as states bent on destroying Muslim sovereignty around the globe and warned Muslims that unless they responded to the *jihad,* Islam faced extinction. This action showed that the Ottoman Empire still viewed itself as the universal protector of Islam. And the support the vast majority of Ottoman Muslims gave to the empire's war effort demonstrated that even though the CUP government was not particularly well liked, its devotion to the defense of the Ottoman-Islamic order against European ambitions was shared by the population at large.

For its part, despite the absence of any overt antigovernment agitation, the CUP remained suspicious about the loyalties of the Arab population of Greater Syria, especially the inhabitants of the urban centers. The government's suspicions stemmed from the formation of Arab political and cultural societies before the war and the close ties that some members of the Arab Christian community maintained with France. In order to ensure the stability and loyalty of Greater Syria, the CUP adopted a special wartime regime for the region by placing it under the direct supervision of Jamal Pasha, one of the ruling triumvirate.

The Ottoman army in 1917. The product of a century of reforming efforts, the sultan's military enjoyed significant successes at Gallipoli, Kut, and the eastern front during World War 1. (The Trustees of the Imperial War Museum, London)

Jamal Pasha arrived in Damascus shortly after the outbreak of war entrusted with extensive military and civilian powers; he was the commander of the Ottoman Fourth Army stationed in Damascus as well as the governor of the provinces of Greater Syria. By the time he left Damascus in early 1918, Jamal Pasha was known among the local inhabitants as *al-Saffah*, the Blood Shedder, and his policies had alienated large segments of the Arab population from the CUP regime. Jamal Pasha's administration began cordially enough. The governor was committed to the cause of Islamic solidarity, and he announced his appreciation for the Arab contribution to Islam. However, following the failure of his attack on the Suez Canal, he changed his methods for maintaining tranquillity in the Syrian provinces: In place of conciliation he adopted repression.

Convinced that some Arab leaders were in secret contact with Britain and France, Jamal Pasha deported large numbers of them to Anatolia and placed several dozen others under house arrest in Jerusalem and Damascus. In 1915 he began to imprison Arab notables whom he suspected of disloyalty and to send them before military tribunals to be interrogated and tried. Using information contained in documents left behind in the French consulate in Beirut in 1914, Jamal charged his prisoners with treason. Eleven of those convicted were publicly hanged in Beirut in August 1915; another twenty-one were similarly executed in Beirut and Damascus in May 1916. The hangings were a shock to Arab society. The victims included an Arab senator, three Arab parliamentary deputies, several leading journalists, and members of some of the most distinguished notable families of Greater Syria. A few of the accused may have been involved in prewar political discussions with French diplomats, but most were singled out because of their earlier activities in the Ottoman Decentralization Party. The coincidental timing of the second wave of executions—one month before the proclamation of the Arab Revolt—gave all of the victims an aura of martyrdom, and their deaths came to be associated with the cause of Arabism.

If Jamal Pasha managed to arouse intense anti-CUP sentiments in the provinces under his control, he nevertheless succeeded in preventing those sentiments from receiving public expression. The Arabs of Greater Syria, most of whom had been loyal to the Ottoman cause from the start, were cowed into fearful and sullen submission. There was no uprising in Syria and very little anti-Ottoman activity for the duration of the war. Moreover, Jamal Pasha did not completely abandon the Ottoman practice of using local notables as intermediaries between the government and the population. Those notables favored by Jamal viewed the hangings as regrettable but necessary security measures, and they continued to serve the Ottoman war effort as members of parliament and as local administrators. Although Syria had been the source of the first expressions of prewar Arabism, Jamal Pasha's harsh repression and the continuing Ottoman loyalties of many important members of the Arab elite meant that any organized movement for Arab separation would have to originate elsewhere.

Jamal Pasha, one of the CUP ruling triumvirs, and members of his staff, Damascus, 1915. As the Ottoman governor of Syria during World War I, Jamal became known in certain circles as the Blood Shedder for his acts of repression against the Arab population. (The Trustees of the Imperial War Museum, London).

Sharif Husayn ibn Ali and the Arab Revolt

One of the principal concerns that the Ottoman entry into the war aroused in British circles was the question of Islamic solidarity. The sultan-caliph's proclamation of *jihad* against the Entente had the potential to cause much unrest along Britain's imperial route to India as well as within India itself. British officials sought out a Muslim dignitary who might be persuaded to ally with the Entente powers and thus serve as a counterweight to the prestige of the Ottoman sultan-caliph. They thought they had found him in the person of Sharif Husayn ibn Ali, the amir of Mecca. Since much of the his-

Sharif Husayn ibn Ali, the amir of Mecca, proclaimed the Arab Revolt in 1916. In return, Sharif Husayn expected the Allies to recognize him as the king of an independent Arab state once the war ended. (The Trustees of the Imperial War Museum, London)

tory of the post–World War I Middle East has revolved around interpretations of the promises Britain made to Sharif Husayn, it is important to understand the development of the proposals, the context in which they were made, and the actions that resulted from them.

The office of amir of Mecca was the most prestigious Arab-Islamic position within the Ottoman Empire. Its holder was the guardian of the holy cities of Mecca and Medina. Although the Ottoman governor of the Hijaz was actually in charge of administrative affairs and military security in the region, the amir of Mecca held a curiously autonomous position as the individual responsible for maintaining the sanctity of the two holy cities and ensuring that the annual pilgrimage was properly and safely conducted. In addition, the amir of Mecca was selected from among those families claiming direct descent from the Prophet and thus bore the honorific title of sharif. Husayn ibn Ali (1855–1931), a sharif from the family of Hashim, was appointed to the office of amir by Abdul Hamid II in 1908. An ambitious man who distrusted the CUP on both political and religious grounds, Husayn devoted his first years in office to the construction of a network of tribal alliances that would enable him to obtain a greater degree of autonomy from Istanbul. In the manner of an'eighteenth-century warlord, he hoped to secure sufficient power to make the office of amir of Mecca hereditary within his family. These traditional—and limited—objectives were catapulted onto the stage of international diplomacy by the outbreak of World War I.

The CUP government, as wary of Husayn as he was of it, endeavored to persuade him to declare his support for the caliph's *jihad* and to commit contingents of his tribal levies to the Ottoman war effort. The sharif hedged. He did so because he was in the midst of deciding whether his personal ambitions could best be served by supporting Ottomanism or by pursuing other alternatives. In July 1915 Husayn sent a letter to the British high commissioner in Egypt, Sir Henry McMahon, setting forth the conditions that might persuade him to enter into an alliance with Britain and to launch a revolt against his own Ottoman government. This was the beginning of the famous Husayn-McMahon correspondence (July 1915–March 1916), an exchange of ten letters that lie at the root of an immense controversy over whether Britain pledged to support an independent Arab state and then reneged on the pledge.

Britain was receptive to the idea of an Arab rebellion against the Ottomans as well as to the opportunity of acquiring a Muslim ally of Husayn's distinction; McMahon was instructed to follow up on Husayn's initiative. The thorniest issue in their correspondence concerned frontiers. Husayn, claiming to represent all the Arab people, requested British recognition of an independent Arab state embracing the Arabian Peninsula, the provinces of Greater Syria (including Lebanon and Palestine), and the provinces of Iraq—essentially the Arabic-speaking world east of Egypt—in exchange for his commitment to lead an armed rebellion against the Ottomans. Britain sought to protect its own future interests in the region as well as those of its ally, France. Husayn was informed that the area lying west of a line from Damascus, Homs, Hama, and Aleppo (see Map 9.1) could not be included in the proposed Arab state because its inhabitants were not purely Arab. This was stretching a point; the real reason McMahon refused to offer Husayn control over the Syrian coast was because it was claimed by France.

Throughout the exchange of notes, Husayn rejected this exclusion and McMahon insisted on it. In the end, the matter was postponed for further discussion until after the war. However, Husayn made it clear that he would not abandon the Arab claim to coastal Syria. McMahon also attempted to secure Husayn's agreement to a special British position in the Iraqi provinces of Baghdad and Basra. Husayn insisted that these territories were

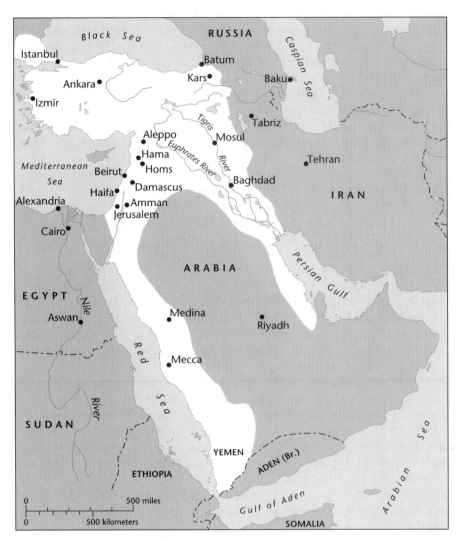

Map 9.1 The Ottoman Empire in 1914

an integral part of the Arab heritage, but he did consent to a temporary British postwar occupation of them until a stable administration could be established. McMahon accepted the territorial demands of Husayn, subject to future negotiations over Syria and the British presence in parts of Iraq, and pledged that "Great Britain is prepared to recognize and uphold the independence of the Arabs in all the regions lying within the frontiers proposed by the Sharif of Mecca."[2]

In addition to agreeing to recognize an independent Arab state after the war, Britain promised to provide Husayn with supplies, weapons, and funds for his revolt against the Ottomans and to recognize an Arab caliphate should one be proclaimed. Husayn, in turn, committed himself to an all-out armed uprising and to a denunciation of the Ottoman regime as an enemy of Islam. Both parties appeared to have attained their objectives. Husayn's ambitions had been secured by a Great Power guarantee, and Britain had acquired a well-placed Muslim ally. However, the imprecision of certain territorial agreements made future disputes over the true intention of Britain's pledge inevitable. Sharif Husayn was aware of this imprecision: He knew that he had asked for a larger Arab state than the Allies were prepared to recognize and that the final boundaries of that state would be subject to future negotiations. Nevertheless, even if he took into account all the reservations and qualifications of McMahon's letters, Husayn had reason to believe that he was promised an independent Arab state (albeit one in which Allied advisers would play an important role) in Arabia, interior Syria, parts of Iraq, and possibly Palestine. McMahon's language was so ambiguous and so vague that it has given rise to widely conflicting interpretations over whether Palestine was included as part of the future independent Arab state. Palestine was not specifically mentioned in the correspondence, but British officials later claimed that the region was part of the coastal Syrian territory that had been reserved for France and was thus excluded from the Arab state, even though it lay south of the Damascus-Aleppo line McMahon mentioned. However, this argument had its flaws. Because Palestine was indeed located south of Damascus, proponents of the Arab claim to the region argued that it could not possibly have been part of the territory lying west of the Damascus-Aleppo line and that it must therefore have been included in the Arab state promised to Husayn. It is likely that at the time of his negotiations with Husayn, McMahon did not pay much attention to Palestine as a distinct region and probably intended it to be part of the Arab state. It may seem as though questions over who was promised what specific territory were rendered irrelevant by the postwar peace settlement, yet they continue to be raised because perceptions are often as important as legalities—and among politically aware Arabs the perception existed, and deepened after the war, that Britain had made a pledge it did not honor, that the Arabs had been misled and then betrayed.

The Arab Revolt began on June 10, 1916, when Husayn's tribal forces attacked the Ottoman garrison at Mecca. By September most of the principal towns of the Hijaz were in Husayn's hands, with the exception of Medina, which was placed under siege for the duration of the war. In the proclamations justifying the revolt, Husayn appealed primarily to the cause of Islamic solidarity. Aware of his delicate position in leading a rebellion against the Ottoman sultan, he tried to portray his action as a duty to Islam. He called on all Muslims of the empire to join him in overthrowing the CUP regime, which was, he claimed, made up of a group of atheistic adventurers who ignored the Quran and the *shariᶜah*. Careful not to attack the caliph, Husayn urged Muslims to rise up and liberate their caliph from the clutches of the CUP. This type of Islamic-oriented propaganda dominated the sharif's proclamations throughout the two years of the revolt. He was not an Arab nationalist and did not think in terms of the ideology of Arabism. He was instead an ambitious dynast who used his Islamic status as a sharif and the amir of Mecca in an attempt to acquire a hereditary kingdom or principality for his family.

Although clandestine support for the revolt existed in some parts of Syria, Husayn's call failed to generate any organized response in the Arabic-speaking provinces. Indeed, many Arab public figures accused Husayn of being a traitor and condemned his actions as dividing the Ottoman-Islamic Empire at a time when unity was most needed. The Arab Revolt did not constitute a popular uprising against the Ottoman Empire. Rather, it was a more narrowly based enterprise relying on tribal levies from Arabia and dominated by the Hashimite family. There can be no question, however, that Arabs applauded the final triumph of the revolt—the capture of Damascus in 1918—and that it laid the foundations for the Arabs' claim to an independent state.

The Arab Revolt's road to Damascus led from the Hijaz through the port city of Aqaba (captured in 1917) and then along General Allenby's right flank in the final offensive of 1918. Sharif Husayn's tribal forces were commanded by his son, Amir Faysal, who was assisted by a group of Iraqi ex-Ottoman officers and a small contingent of British military advisers, among them Captain T. E. Lawrence. Faysal generally tried to avoid pitched battles with the Ottomans and concentrated instead on disrupting enemy communications and supply lines. When he led his troops into Damascus on October 1, 1918, it marked the culmination of the Arab war effort. Faysal immediately began to set up an administration, believing that he was acting in accordance with the pledge that Great Britain had given his father.

Pledges and Counterpledges: Allied Plans for the Partition of the Ottoman Empire

During the course of the war, the Entente powers signed a number of agreements among themselves on the future disposition of Ottoman territories. These agreements did not take into consideration the needs of the Entente's Arab allies but were designed solely to serve the interests of the European members of the alliance by arranging for what one scholar has called "expansionist bookings-in-advance."[3] The purpose of the treaties was to keep the Entente intact by resolving potential postwar disagreements before they surfaced. This was achieved by providing advance territorial compensation to the alliance members.

The "army" of the Arab Revolt, composed mainly of irregular tribal forces, at Wejh, Arabia, 1917. (The Trustees of the Imperial War Museum, London)

In 1915, when Russian armies were being battered by the Ottomans in eastern Anatolia and by the Germans in Poland, Britain and France became concerned that Russia's willingness to pursue the war might evaporate. They therefore decided to offer the czar the most desirable "advance booking" possible. In what would have been an unthinkable proposition at any time before the war, Britain, France, and Russia signed the Constantinople Agreement in March 1915 awarding Russia the right to annex Istanbul and the Turkish Straits. The Constantinople Agreement was never implemented, and it was no doubt with some relief that Britain and France received Lenin's statement following the Russian Revolution in 1917 that the Bolshevik government was renouncing the czarist regime's previous treaties with the Allies.

By far the most vexing interallied Middle Eastern issue was the constant tension between Britain and France over France's claims to Ottoman Syria. As France was bearing the brunt of the horrible trench warfare on the western front, it was unable to directly protect its Middle Eastern interests and viewed with alarm Britain's growing military involvement in the region. To resolve this matter, negotiators from the two countries drew up a secret treaty in May 1916 in which they divided up most of the Arab Middle East between them. Known as the Sykes-Picot Agreement, the treaty is one of the most controversial documents of the war, for it appeared to contravene portions of the pledge that Britain had given to Sharif Husayn. The agreement recognized long-standing French claims to Syria by awarding France a large zone of "direct control" stretching along the Syrian coast from southern Lebanon into Anatolia. In addition, France was granted a sphere of exclusive indirect influence in the Syrian interior. The British position in Iraq was similarly guaranteed; Britain gained the right to exercise "direct control" over the southern portion of Mesopotamia and was granted a huge zone of exclusive indirect influence stretching from Gaza to Kirkuk. The independent Arab state promised to Husayn was, in the Sykes-Picot Agreement, designated as a state or confederation of states lying in the two zones of British and French indirect influence. Under the terms of the agreement, Palestine was to be placed under international administration.

Finally, Great Britain made yet another "advance booking" for yet another interested party. In an effort to appeal to U.S., Russian, and German Jewry and also to secure control over the territory adjacent to the Suez Canal, Britain agreed to favor the establishment of a Jewish national home in Palestine. This agreement—the famous Balfour Declaration of November 1917—was conveyed in a letter from Foreign Secretary Arthur Balfour to Lord Rothschild, a prominent British Zionist (see Chapter 13). If the British pledge to support, however indirectly, Jewish settlement in Palestine was to be implemented, Britain would have to remain in occupation of Palestine. In Arab eyes, any such action would constitute a violation of the promise made to Husayn.

When the war ended, most Ottoman territory had been pledged to one or another of the Allied partners. Since some of the pledges contradicted one another, they could be implemented only by compromise or the exercise of armed force.

The Peace Settlement

An Overview

The impact of the peace settlement on individual Middle Eastern states will be examined in future chapters. The purpose here is to review the process that led to the division and occupation of most of the former Ottoman territories. In January 1919, representatives from twenty-seven nations gathered in Paris to construct a peace settlement that they hoped would eliminate the possibility of future wars. For most of the delegates, European issues had the highest priority, and during the year 1919 four separate treaties (with Germany, Austria, Hungary, and Bulgaria) were drawn up and signed. However, the formulation of a postwar settlement for the Middle East required a longer period of negotiations and involved the Allies in frequent disputes among themselves. Terms of an Ottoman settlement were finally agreed upon at the San Remo Conference (April 1920) and incorporated into the Treaty of Sèvres, which the Ottoman government reluctantly signed on August 10, 1920.

The portions of the treaty that dealt with Anatolia were extremely harsh and amounted to a virtual partition of the original core of the Ottoman Empire. Although the victors intended for an Ottoman state and government to remain in existence, the territory over which the state was to exercise sovereignty was severely circumscribed. The straits between the Black and Mediterranean seas were removed from Istanbul's authority and placed under the jurisdiction of an international commission. The treaty awarded spheres of influence in southern Anatolia to France and Italy. Greece, which had not joined the Entente until 1917, received the Ottomans' last European province, Thrace; Greece was also authorized to establish a military and administrative presence in the major Anatolian port city of Izmir. In drawing up the settlement, the Allied negotiators were compelled to take into consideration the new principle of national self-determination—yet they chose to apply the principle only when it furthered their own interests or coincided with their sympathies. It was doubtless for the latter reason that the Treaty of Sèvres recognized an independent Armenian state in eastern Anatolia and Russian Caucasia. The Allies also agreed that the Kurdish regions of eastern Anatolia should have a semiautonomous status. In approving self-determination for the Armenians and partial self-determination for the Kurds, however, the Allies made it clear that they would not provide military or financial assistance to these two fledgling nations. They did not, therefore, endure for long.

The decisions reached at the San Remo Conference detached the Arab provinces from Ottoman authority and apportioned them between Britain and France. The former provinces were divided into entities called mandates, a term that will be discussed in more detail in the introduction to Part 3. It can be noted here that the mandate system was little more than nineteenth-century imperialism repackaged to give the appearance of self-determination. Britain received the mandates for Iraq and Palestine, France the mandate for Syria. Iraq was a completely new state created out of three Ottoman provinces—Basra, Baghdad, and Mosul—that had little in common. By acquiring control over this new entity, Britain enhanced its position in the Persian Gulf, secured the approaches to India, and gained access to petroleum resources. The third Arab state over which Britain exercised direct influence, Transjordan, did not exist at the time the Treaty of Sèvres was drawn up. The hasty creation of Transjordan was a result of the manner in which France took control of its Syrian mandate and is best understood in the context of that event.

The Rise and Fall of Faysal's Syrian Kingdom, 1918–1920

While the Allies gathered in Paris to sort out their conflicting interests, Amir Faysal was forming an Arab government in Damascus. All the currents of the Ottoman past and the conflicting visions of the Arab future came together in Faysal's fledgling administration.

Amir Faysal, field commander of the Arab Revolt and later king of Syria, at the Paris Peace Conference, 1919. After the defeat of his Syrian forces by the French in 1920, he was exiled; he was then selected by the British to become the first king of Iraq. (The Trustees of the Imperial War Museum, London)

It was staffed by young Arab activists with dreams of a united Syria and Palestine, by ex-Ottoman officials and military officers who converged on Damascus once there was no longer an Ottoman state to serve, and by prominent local Syrian notables who wished to preserve their customary positions of influence. Added to the mix were leaders of the sharifian forces who felt that their military contribution to the Arab Revolt merited the reward of political office. Although these competing factions tended to limit the effectiveness of Faysal's administration, there were nonetheless high hopes for the new state. In March 1920, representatives from throughout Syria met at a general Syrian congress and proclaimed Syria an independent state with Faysal as its king. In many, if not all, quarters of the Arab world, this action seemed to signify the rebirth of an Arab kingdom on the site of the former Umayyad imperial capital.

To France, however, the declaration of Syrian independence signified a usurpation of French claims to the region and a violation of the Franco-British agreement to divide the Arab areas more or less equally between them. In this instance, the wartime agreements were enforced. Despite the pleas Faysal made during his frequent appearances before the peace conference, Britain and France were determined that the satisfaction of their regional interests and the preservation of their alliance should take precedence over all other considerations. This meant that the French claim to Syria had to be recognized; put another way, it meant that Britain had to renounce any support it may have been prepared to give Faysal and his Syrian kingdom. These conditions were realized in the decisions of the San Remo Conference, which, as noted above, assigned the mandate for Syria to France.

Within Syria, the reaction to the San Remo pronouncements was one of anger and confusion. The Arab nationalist bloc in the government urged Faysal to defy the Allied powers, whereas more cautious voices counseled him to seek a compromise that might somehow satisfy French demands and still preserve the Syrian kingdom. Uncertain what advice to follow, Faysal endeavored to open negotiations with the French commander in Beirut, General Henri Gouraud. But Gouraud was in no mood for compromises and ordered his troops to march on Syria. On July 24, 1920, the French forces easily defeated Faysal's army, occupied Damascus, and forced the king of Syria into exile in Europe. The independent Arab state was eliminated only five months after it was proclaimed.

The French occupation of Damascus produced a response from Sharif Husayn's family that necessitated one final bit of territorial allocation. In the aftermath of Faysal's expulsion from Syria, his brother, Amir Abdallah, led a tribal contingent from Mecca to Ma'an, a desert town east of the Jordan River. Abdallah had no clear-cut objective, and his forces posed no direct threat to the Anglo-French position in the Arab world. However, his presence in Ma'an had the potential to rally dissident tribes in the region. The British therefore decided to integrate Abdallah into their informal imperial network, hoping that he would serve as a source of stability in the unoccupied region east of the Jordan and that his presence as a British client would prevent the spread of French influence south from Syria. Accordingly, Abdallah was offered the opportunity to set up an administration in Amman under British administrative guidance; his territory would be part of the Palestine mandate, but it would be exempted from the stipulations of the Balfour Declaration. Abdallah accepted the terms, additional frontiers were penciled in on the map of the Middle East, and in 1921 the unusual desert amirate of Transjordan came into existence.

With the creation of Transjordan, the apportionment of the Arab territories of the defeated Ottoman Empire was complete. The Arab provinces, once part of an imperial whole, were divided into a group of regional states administered by Britain and France (compare Maps 9.1 and 9.2). Sharif Husayn remained in Mecca, but he would soon be discarded as an ally when the British discovered another Arab chieftain who appeared more able to serve their interests. For the Arabs, the aftermath of the war produced feel-

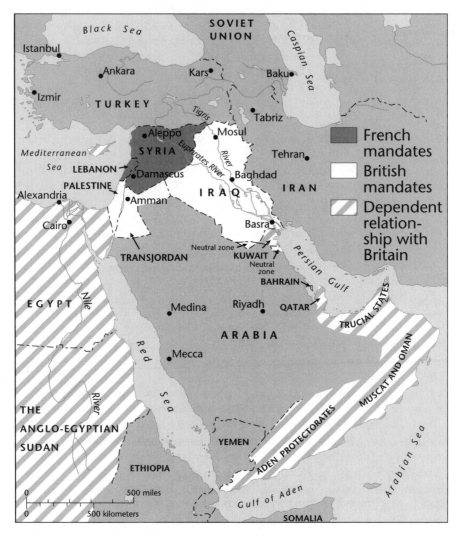

Map 9.2 The Middle East in the Interwar Period

ings of bitterness toward the Western powers and a deep-seated conviction that they had been betrayed. Although it may be argued that Husayn was well aware of the ambiguities in Britain's pledges and that he knew Anglo-French claims would have to be satisfied, it is also true that he and other Arab leaders expected a much different postwar settlement than the one that was imposed on them. From the Arab perspective, the British pledges to Husayn had been sacrificed to the requirements of Allied harmony and imperial self-interest. Arab opinion tended to be distrustful of Anglo-French intentions in the years that followed, and the mandate period was marked by recriminations over secret diplomacy and haunted by lingering visions of what might have been if Faysal's Syrian kingdom had been allowed to survive.

Conclusion:
The End of the Ottoman Order in the Middle East

For the Arab peoples who had lived within the sultan's domains, the dismemberment of the Ottoman Empire marked more than just the end of a particular state; it also marked the end of a political, social, and religious order that had shaped their patterns of public behavior for 400 years. Ottoman rule had been applied with differing degrees of intensity in various regions of the Arab provinces. That kind of adaptability was the very essence of the Ottoman system: It governed directly the areas that could be efficiently controlled and allowed a certain degree of latitude to chieftains and feudal amirs in more remote locations. Even in such areas of direct control as the urban centers of Greater Syria, the Ottoman governors exercised their authority in association with the local Arab notables. The latter retained some degree of local power in exchange for cooperating with the representatives of the central Ottoman state. As well as permitting a measure of regional political autonomy, the pragmatic Ottoman rule tolerated a rich diversity of religious and cultural practices throughout the Arab provinces. But the governments of the postwar successor states, first under European control and later under independent Arab regimes, would not be so accommodating. Practicing what their rulers believed were modern methods of government, the new states would seek to impose strict central control over rural tribes and urban dwellers alike and to instill in all their citizens a measure of cultural uniformity. This is not to suggest that the Ottoman system was superior; rather, it is to point out the stresses to which former Ottoman peoples would be subjected in their new capacity as citizens of emerging nation-states.

The Ottoman Empire had also provided its subjects with a secure sense of belonging to a larger universal order. That order was represented on the one hand by the Ottoman dynasty and its ruling sultan and on the other by the Islamic institutions and practices the sultans made such a point of upholding. The empire achieved legitimacy in the eyes of its subjects not just because of its ability to provide stable government but also because of its rulers' determination to ensure that the political and social order was based on the enforcement of *shari*ʿ*ah* justice, respect for the role of the ulama, patronage of religious education, and protection of the holy cities. In summary, the Ottoman Empire not only embodied the achievements of the Islamic past, it also offered hope, through its continued existence and independence, that a distinctly Islamic state could survive in a world of expansionist European powers. A Muslim Arab subject of the sultan could be comfortable in such a state. But by 1920, neither that state nor its Islamic institutions held sway in the Middle East, and its former Arab and Turkish subjects were left adrift.

The Ottoman system had never been static, but in its final century it underwent considerable transformation. As we have seen, the reform movement served to strengthen the administrative efficiency and the military capability of the empire; but at the same time the reforms, by their very nature, were bound to undermine certain of the foundations on which the Ottoman order rested. Yet despite the institutional changes and the spread of nationalist revolts in the Balkans, the Arab inhabitants of the empire neither wished for, nor anticipated, its collapse and replacement by a regional Arab state system. As has been shown in Chapter 8, the doctrine of Arabism had surfaced before the war, but it was not so much a program for political independence as it was a demand for Arab autonomy within an Ottoman framework. Thus, at the outbreak of the war, Ottomanism, with its Islamic associations, remained the dominant ideology in the Arabic-speaking provinces. And for all the attention that Jamal Pasha's repression and Sharif Husayn's revolt later received, they did not detach the majority of Arabs from their Ottoman loyalties during the war years. But by the end of the war in 1918, Ottomanism was irrelevant. What forces of political loyalty and cultural identity could replace it?

For a time, it appeared that Faysal's Syrian kingdom, with its Pan-Arab orientation, might fill the void left by the Ottoman defeat, but that dream proved illusory. With the French occupation of Damascus and the creation of regional states, the Arab elites were compelled, almost by default, to focus their attention on developments in their own new states. Whereas previously the Arabs had been inhabitants of Ottoman provinces, they now had to forge new identities as Iraqis, Syrians, and Palestinians. This represented a major change from Ottomanism. However, one element in the post-Ottoman Middle East remained constant—the individuals who rose to political prominence in the new mandate states were mainly those who had held positions of influence within the Ottoman system, whether they were local notables or ex-Ottoman civil servants and military officers. The continued domination of this Ottoman-era elite ensured that certain patterns of Ottoman-style political behavior and social attitudes would prevail in the postwar era. How these established patterns of thought and action responded to the demands brought about by changed circumstances is examined in the next part of this book.

Notes

1. Richard G. Hovannisian, *Armenia on the Road to Independence, 1918* (Berkeley, 1967), p. 50.

2. Sir Henry McMahon to Sharif Husayn, October 24, 1915, in J. C. Hurewitz, ed., *The Middle East and North Africa in World Politics: A Documentary Record,* vol. 2, *British-French Supremacy, 1914–1945,* 2nd ed. (New Haven, 1979), p. 50.

3. Elizabeth Monroe, *Britain's Moment in the Middle East, 1914–1971,* 2nd ed. (London, 1981), p. 26.

The Struggle for Independence: The Interwar Era to the End of World War II

The Middle East becomes a much more complicated area of study after the end of World War I. During the nineteenth and early twentieth centuries, three centers of authority—Egypt, the Ottoman Empire, and Iran—controlled the region. To be sure, European powers exercised various degrees of influence within each of these centers, but Cairo, Istanbul, and Tehran were the capital cities for most of the inhabitants of the Middle East. However, following the peace settlement and the establishment of the mandates, a new regional state system came into existence. The core of the Ottoman Empire was fragmented into six states: Turkey and the five new Arab states of Syria, Lebanon, Palestine, Iraq, and Transjordan. Saudi Arabia and Yemen also emerged as distinct political entities. The three centers of authority had been expanded to ten, each with its own domestic and foreign policy. But the policies of most of these new states were determined by European occupiers. Of the ten core Middle Eastern states, only Turkey, Iran, Saudi Arabia, and Yemen exercised full sovereignty during the interwar era, and the latter two were allowed independence solely because they were isolated and because Britain and France regarded them as relatively unimportant. Even Iran's interwar sovereignty was temporary. For a time, it appeared that Reza Khan, the military commander who seized the throne and proclaimed himself shah, was following Turkey's pattern of national self-assertiveness. With the onset of World War II, however, Britain and the Soviet Union invaded Iran and quashed any expectations for Iranian sovereignty. Among the populous and strategically significant new states, only

169

Turkey, the core of the Ottoman Empire and the main beneficiary of the nineteenth-century reforms, was able to definitively defy the imposed peace settlement and pursue its own foreign and domestic policies from the early 1920s to the end of World War II.

The interwar era in the Arab territories was a period of Anglo-French dominance. Britain retained control in Egypt, and between them Britain and France administered the five new Arab states carved out of the Ottoman Empire. The League of Nations sanctioned the division of the former Ottoman Arab provinces into new states and granted Britain and France the right to administer them as mandates. According to the patronizing language of the league's covenant, mandates "were inhabited by peoples not yet able to stand by themselves under the strenuous conditions of the modern world." They were therefore to be placed under the tutelage of the "advanced nations," which would assist them "until such time as they are able to stand alone." It was thus the responsibility of the mandatory powers to prepare these regions for self-government. By phrasing the matter in this way, the league attempted to gloss over the fact that mandates were simply another name for imperial control. The mandate system provided Britain and France with an opportunity to secure their strategic interests in the Middle East while paying lip service to the widely publicized principle of self-determination. However, the mandate system differed from prewar imperialism in that the mandatory power was responsible for preparing its charges for self-government and was thus bound to terminate its control at some unspecified time.

For most of the interwar period, Arab political activity was primarily devoted to achieving independence from foreign control. Other considerations, such as land reform or social welfare legislation, received comparatively little attention. One reason for this focus on gaining sovereignty was that the Arab political leaders of the interwar period came mainly from the established landed or professional classes. The war years had not produced a social upheaval, and the same elite that had enjoyed power and prestige before 1914—the European-educated landed and professional classes in Egypt and the traditional notables in Syria, Lebanon, and Palestine—continued to exercise their privileges during the 1920s and 1930s. Iraq was perhaps an exception to this pattern, but even in Baghdad the political elite was drawn largely from former Ottoman military officers who upheld the tradition of Ottoman ruling-class behavior. These ruling groups sought to maintain their local bases of support while heading the campaign against Britain or France. This necessitated occasional compromises. Local political leaders in a situation of foreign imperial control were dependent for their positions on the goodwill of the occupying power. Thus, even as the Arab political leaders demanded independence, they tried to remain in the good graces of the European authorities. They practiced the politics of the notables in a new setting.

The replacement of the Ottoman political order by the creation of separate states forced wrenching economic and ideological readjustments upon the inhabitants of the region. What had once been an integrated economic unit under a single imperial authority was parceled into fragments. Each new Arab state had its own tariff and customs regulations, its own currency, and its own form of economic ties with its European overlord. Patterns of commercial exchange were also altered as the new frontiers cut off cities such as Aleppo, which had been the entrepôt for produce from the Anatolian hinterland, from their sources of supply. Conflicting ideological appeals competed for the loyalties of the Arab population. As the rulers of each emergent state endeavored to create specific symbols of national identity, advocates of Pan-Arab unity or Islamic solidarity condemned the imposed fragmentation of the Arab world and called upon the rulers to renounce their local power in favor of a larger confederation. And throughout the interwar and World War II years, a new issue—Zionist immigration into Palestine—added to the confusion and tensions created by the end of the Ottoman order.

Just as World War I served to loosen the grip of the Ottoman Empire on its Arab provinces, so World War II hastened the end of Anglo-French dominance in the Middle East and led to the granting of official independence to all the major states of the region. Although neither Britain nor France surrendered its imperial aspirations easily or completely, they were so weakened by the war that they could no longer sustain the overseas commitments required for empires.

Yet if the end of the Second World War brought independence to the Middle East, it was an independence clouded with uncertainties arising out of the embittered ending to the Palestine mandate. In the immediate aftermath of the war, the question of Palestine assumed a special urgency. The revelation of the horror of the German concentration camps and the existence of thousands of displaced Jewish refugees made the Zionists more determined than ever to establish a state in which Jews would be secure. The creation of Israel in the war of 1948 represented the achievement of the Zionist objective. However, it also represented failure on the part of the Arab regimes that had resisted the formation of Israel. The leaders of those regimes were shaken by the events of 1948, and they entered the era of independence discredited and vulnerable to the currents of discontent their policies had spawned.

Authoritarian Reform | 10
in Turkey and Iran

⟨I⟩
⟨I⟩

In the years immediately following World War I, both Turkey and Iran cast out their existing monarchies and embarked on vigorous programs of state-sponsored reform. In Turkey the new policies were carried out under the auspices of a republican form of government within which presidential authority was dominant. Although President Atatürk acquired virtual dictatorial powers, he was legally elected, and he attempted to implant in Turkey the institutions and attitudes that would enable full-fledged democracy to flourish under his successors. In Iran the Qajar dynasty was replaced by the Pahlavis in the person of Reza Shah, a former officer in the Cossack Brigade who seized the royal crown and placed it on his own head. This military officer and self-proclaimed shah continued the absolutist traditions of the Iranian monarchy and sought to ensure the hereditary succession of his son. Both Atatürk and Reza Shah promoted an unprecedented degree of secularism in public life, and both tried to buttress their reforms by the promulgation of new symbols of national identity. In doing so, they attempted to separate the institutions of the state from those of religion and thus to create a primary loyalty to the nation and its emerging secular structures.

The Atatürk Era in Turkey

Postwar Partition, the Greek Invasion, and the War of Independence

By the end of 1918, Istanbul and the Ottoman government were controlled by the victorious Allies. The CUP leaders had fled the country, and such imperial governmental authority as existed was exercised by the sultan, Mehmet VI Vahideddin, who dismissed the Ottoman parliament in December 1918 and thereafter ruled by decree. In the opinion of the sultan and his closest advisers, cooperation with the Allies was the policy most likely to salvage some morsel of independent Ottoman territory in the postwar settlements. This stance opened the sultan's government to charges of collaboration with the foreign invaders.

The Allies were determined to punish the Ottomans as a defeated power, to grant the demands for self-determination put forward by Christian subjects of the empire, and to secure their own strategic objectives in Anatolia. These goals were incorporated into the Treaty of Sèvres in 1920. Although we examined them in Chapter 9, the terms of the treaty deserve to be repeated here: Italy and France were to divide southwestern Anatolia between them; an independent Armenian state, centered around Erzurum, was to be created; and Greece was to receive territory in Thrace that would bring its borders within 25 miles (40 km) of Istanbul. In addition, Greece was awarded the right to administer the port city of Izmir and its adjacent regions. Even in the limited territory left to it by the Treaty of Sèvres, the sovereignty of the Ottoman government was severely restricted: The Turkish Straits were to be administered by an Allied commission; the finances of the government were placed under Allied control; and the hated Capitulations, abolished by the CUP at the start of the war, were restored. But the Istanbul government, in its desperation not to lose everything, signed the treaty.

Even before the treaty was signed, however, events were under way in Anatolia that would render it null and void. Local Turkish resistance groups, calling themselves societies for the defense of rights, rose up to oppose the occupation and division of Turkish soil. This spontaneous resistance, represented by the formation of volunteer militia units and roving guerrilla bands, took on the aura of a national war for independence with the arrival in 1919 of three experienced Ottoman field commanders who assumed the task of organizing the forces. One of these commanders, Mustafa Kemal, gradually asserted his leadership of the emerging national movement. When the sultan's government learned of his activities, it dismissed him from service (June 1920); he became a rebel army officer acting against the policies of the legally constituted government in Istanbul. But he was not alone; other Ottoman commanders accepted his authority and joined his cause, redefined as the preservation of Turkish national independence. The act that unified the resistance forces and made the Turkish population of Anatolia aware of the danger facing it was the Greek invasion of Anatolia.

In the course of the Allied negotiating sessions, Greece's prime minister, Eleutherios Venizelos, persuaded the Allies to support the establishment of a Greek presence in Izmir and its environs. An Allied squadron landed an entire Greek division in Izmir on May 14, 1919. The Greek forces quickly secured the city and then embarked on a brutal campaign, marked by atrocities against Turkish noncombatants and the desecration of mosques, to bring a large portion of Izmir's hinterland under their control. By 1921 the Greeks had captured the former Ottoman capital of Bursa and penetrated so deeply into Anatolia that they posed a threat to Kemal's fledgling national movement.

For his part, Kemal attempted to broaden the base of the resistance and to devise a means by which the nationalists could replace the Istanbul government as the legitimate representative of the Turkish people. His efforts resulted in the convening of a body of representatives in Ankara in spring 1920. Composed of delegates chosen by local resistance groups throughout Anatolia and Thrace and also including several members of the dissolved Ottoman parliament, this body called itself the grand national assembly. On April 23, 1920, the deputies agreed to form a government with Mustafa Kemal as its president. The assembly justified its actions on the grounds that the Istanbul government was controlled by foreign occupiers and no longer represented the will of the Turkish people. Adopting principles of popular sovereignty, the assembly asserted that the national will was embodied in the delegates gathered in Ankara. In January 1921 the assembly adopted a constitution that contained the National Pact, which has formed the basis of Turkish foreign policy ever since. Renouncing any territorial claims to the former Arab provinces, the National Pact went on to affirm the right of full Turkish sovereignty over the remaining portions of the empire inhabited by a Turkish majority.

As far as Mustafa Kemal and the national assembly were concerned, the right of full Turkish sovereignty extended to the portion of Anatolia awarded to the new Armenian republic in the Treaty of Sèvres. The first organized gathering of the Turkish nationalist movement (the Congress of Erzurum, 1919) passed a resolution stating that no privileges that might impair Turkey's political sovereignty would be granted to the Christians. The existence of an Armenian state was regarded as such an impairment. In autumn 1920, Turkey and the Soviet Union invaded Armenia and divided its territory between them, an act that marked the first stage in the dismantling of the Treaty of Sèvres. In the process of dividing Armenia, Turkey and the Soviet Union established cordial relations with one another, freeing the nationalists from concerns over Soviet intentions and enabling them to concentrate their forces against the Greeks.

The year 1921 was a turning point for the nationalists. Both the Soviet Union and France recognized Ankara as the legitimate government of Turkey, and Italy agreed to withdraw its forces from southern Anatolia. In the meantime the resistance forces were being molded into a national army in Ankara. With Mustafa Kemal assuming full command of military operations, the Turkish forces turned back the Greeks during the three-week-long battle of Sakarya in August and September. When the campaign resumed the following year, it quickly turned into a rout as the Greek army broke and fled back toward Izmir. Kemal's forces entered the city in September 1922 and then headed north for Istanbul, where the Allied garrisons were stationed. Kemal was determined to enforce the terms of the National Pact—full Turkish sovereignty—even if it meant engaging the British troops in combat. However, both sides agreed to negotiations, and on October 11, 1922, Turkey, Greece, and Britain signed the Armistice of Mudanya, which arranged for the withdrawal of the Greek armed forces and called for a peace conference to renegotiate the terms of the Treaty of Sèvres.

The preliminaries to the conference brought a final resolution to the problem of the existence of two Turkish governments. The British invited both Ankara and Istanbul to send representatives to the forthcoming negotiations. Kemal used this as an excuse to bring before the assembly legislation that would abolish the sultanate and turn the caliphate into a religious office with no political authority. Although some deputies opposed this proposal, Kemal bent them to his will, and on November 1, 1922, the assembly passed a resolution that separated the caliphate from the sultanate and eliminated the sultanate. Mehmet VI Vahideddin, the thirty-sixth and last sultan of the line stretching back six centuries to Osman, left Istanbul under British protection. The assembly then designated his cousin, Abdul Mejid, as caliph. The abolition of the sultanate represented the end of the Ottoman political era, and the selection of the caliph of Islam by a democratically elected body of national delegates marked the beginning of the Turkish one.

When the Lausanne Conference convened in late 1922, Ankara was represented by Ismet Inönü, whose performance has become a classic in the annals of international diplomacy. Already partially deaf, Inönü simply turned off his hearing aid when the chairman of the conference, British foreign secretary Lord Curzon, launched into lengthy speeches against the Turkish demands. Once Curzon had completed his objections, Inönü restated his original insistence on recognition of the National Pact as though the British foreign secretary had never uttered a word.

Although Inönü's stubbornness exasperated the delegates, it helped assure success for Ankara's position. When the Treaty of Lausanne was finally signed (July 24, 1923), Turkish sovereignty was recognized over all areas claimed by the National Pact with the exception of Mosul in northern Iraq. This was a remarkable turnabout for the Anatolian portion of the Ottoman Empire; from being partitioned and occupied in 1920, it emerged three years later as the internationally recognized independent nation-state of Turkey, free of restrictions on its domestic policies, on its finances (except for the continuing obligation incurred by the loans taken out in the nineteenth century), and on its jurisdiction over foreign nationals. A new nation had been forged in the crucible of a national war of independence. The one area where sovereignty was limited was the Turkish Straits, which remained under international supervision until 1936, when full Turkish control was recognized. A separate agreement between Greece and Turkey arranged for the forced exchange of populations between the two states. In an operation that caused severe hardships to those involved, about 1.3 million Greeks living within Turkey were transported to Greece and about 400,000 Turks were uprooted from Greece and resettled in Turkey. The age of nationalism had arrived with a vengeance.

The Reforms of the Atatürk Era

With independence firmly established, it was possible to concentrate on shaping the institutions of the new Turkish state. The Westernizing direction and rapid pace of the reforms were determined in large measure by the forceful leadership of Mustafa Kemal, known as Atatürk. His surname, meaning father of the Turks, was bestowed on him by the national assembly in 1935. Born into modest circumstances in Salonika in 1881, Atatürk attended the military preparatory school in his native city and went on to graduate from the war college in Istanbul. He was involved with the CUP movement against Abdul Hamid but disassociated himself from the political intrigues and repressive policies of the Young Turk regime. His direct experience of Europe was limited to brief postings as military attaché in Sofia and Berlin. During World War I, he served with great distinction at Gallipoli and on the eastern and Syrian fronts; his prestige was further enhanced by his leadership in the war of independence. A fervent admirer of European institutions and attitudes, he was determined to mold the new Turkey in the image of the West.

The first task facing his government after Lausanne was to determine the political and administrative character of the state. In an immediate break with the Ottoman past, the capital of the country was transferred from Istanbul to Ankara in 1923. This move of the government from the cosmopolitan capital of the former empire to the heartland of Anatolia symbolized the Turkishness of the new state. In the following year, a new constitution was passed in which the principles of republicanism and popular sovereignty were reaffirmed. All males eighteen and over were given the right to vote; their sovereign will was exercised through the grand national assembly. The president of the republic was chosen by the assembly from among its members. Atatürk held this office until his death in 1938. Throughout most of Atatürk's presidency, his comrade at arms Ismet İnönü served as prime minister. The political instrument through which Atatürk ruled was the Republican People's Party (RPP), the sole party in the state. The president was able to acquire enormous power within the framework of democracy because of his control of the RPP and, through it, of the assembly. An important legacy of this early organizational phase was the civilianization of political life. In 1924 the assembly, following Atatürk's example, passed a law requiring that all military personnel wishing to stand for public office would have to resign their commissions.

Once the essential mechanisms of government were established, Atatürk led Turkey through an intensive period of reform designed to root out the Ottoman past and replace it with a Western orientation in all areas of national life. As innovative as some of the reforms appeared to be, they were largely a continuation of the transformation begun in the nineteenth century. Atatürk was, himself, a product of the Ottoman reform era, and much of the legislation adopted during his presidency had its origins in the preceding decades. Though the intensity of change was heightened under Atatürk, the process of change itself was not new and should be viewed in the context of a historical pattern that extended from Sultan Mahmud II

Mustafa Kemal Atatürk, president of
Turkey, circa 1930. (AP/Wide World
Photos)

through the Tanzimat and Young Turk eras. The reforms can be examined
through the six principles that Atatürk designated as the foundations of the
doctrine known as Kemalism: reformism, republicanism, secularism, nationalism, populism, and etatism. Reformism pervaded the entire Atatürk era; it
stood for an openness to innovation and the acceptance of nonviolent
change. The second principle, republicanism, was, as we have seen, made
part of the fabric of the Turkish state from its very beginnings. This contained antecedents dating from the Ottoman era, but the constitutions of
the empire and of the republic differed markedly in their emphasis on popular sovereignty.

Secularism was a central element in Atatürk's platform, and the impatient
Westernizer pursued it with a thoroughness unparalleled in modern Islamic
history. The policy was inaugurated when the grand national assembly
voted in March 1924 to depose Caliph Abdul Mejid, to abolish the
caliphate, and to banish from Turkey all members of the Ottoman royal
family—in effect sweeping aside thirteen centuries of accumulated Islamic
tradition. Other secularizing legislation quickly followed. The office of
shaykh al-Islam was abolished, the religious schools were closed, and the
Ministry of Religious Endowments was eliminated. In 1926 the assembly
went much further and voted to abolish the Mejelle and the *shariᶜah*. In
their place, the Swiss civil code was adopted, along with penal and commercial codes modeled on Italian and German examples. This was a direct

break with the past. Even with the introduction of new legal codes during the Tanzimat and Young Turk eras, the civil code—which included family law—continued to be based on the *shariʿah*. But with the legislation of 1926, the laws of God were replaced in all spheres of human relationships by secular European laws. The new civil code forbade polygamy and broadened the grounds by which wives could seek divorce. As a result of these reform measures, the ulama lost the final vestiges of their role in affairs of state, and their numbers declined.

Secularism affected not only official institutions but also the religious practices of the Turkish people. The Sufi orders were dissolved, and worship at tombs and shrines was prohibited by law. Atatürk launched a personal attack on the fez, the brimless headgear that enabled a worshiper to touch his forehead to the ground during prayer. To Atatürk, the fez symbolized a tie to the Ottoman past, and he was determined to force its abandonment. In summer 1925 the president took to wearing a panama hat during his public appearances, explaining that hats were the headgear of civilized nations. In November the assembly endorsed the president's practice and passed a law that made it a criminal offense to wear a fez. Hats became a prime symbol of Turkey's drive to Westernize. Other measures of Europeanization included the replacement of the Muslim lunar calendar by the Gregorian (1926) and the adoption of Sunday in place of Friday as the weekly day of rest. One of the most controversial acts of secularization involved the translation of the Quran. Because the divine revelations were in Arabic, translations were prohibited, for they were seen as tampering with the direct word of God. But Atatürk commissioned a translation of the Quran into Turkish and had it read publicly in 1932. In the same year legislation made obligatory the issuing of the call to prayer in Turkish instead of Arabic. Unlike the Tanzimat reforms, which allowed for a certain dualism, Atatürk's programs did not leave traditional institutions intact.

Although Atatürk made secularism a central feature of his reform program, his intentions may not have embraced the full meaning of that word. Atatürk's goal was to reduce the influence of Islamic organizations on political and social life and to redirect popular loyalties toward symbols of nation and state. He sought not to abolish Islam as a personal belief system but, rather, to remove it as an institutionalized regulating agent in the affairs of state and society. His program was "secular" in that it envisaged the development of a civil society constructed on human, not divine, legislation, but it allowed scope for religious observance. The impact of secularism was most pronounced in the urban centers, for in rural areas Turks found ways to evade the laws and to participate in Sufi rituals and to practice forms of folk Islam that were technically forbidden.

Two additional principles of Atatürk's platform, nationalism and populism, had overlapping objectives. Nationalism involved the attempt to create pride in Turkishness and to promote symbols of cultural identity for the new state. With this in mind, Atatürk introduced a policy of language reform that had far-reaching consequences. He ordered a commission to develop a phonetic Turkish alphabet using the Latin alphabet in place of the existing Arabic one. The new alphabet was revealed in 1928, and its public use was made compulsory the following year. Atatürk was not worried, as some were, that adoption of the new alphabet would cut the younger generation off from access to the rich heritage of Ottoman literature; that was precisely his aim.

Atatürk also encouraged the development of a nationalist orientation in historical studies. The Turkish Historical Society, founded in 1925, publicized the notion that the Turks were one of the world's preeminent peoples before their association with Islam and the Ottoman Empire. The Turkish nationalist interpretation of history was joined to some rather extreme theories of linguistic nationalism, one of which, the sun letter theory, propounded the idea that Turkish was the first spoken language of the human race. Such ideas, stressing purely Turkish accomplishments, were designed to overcome the pejorative connotations that had been associated with the term *Turk* during the Ottoman period.

Atatürk's efforts to forge a uniform Turkish national identity left no room for cultural pluralism and caused him at times to strain the institutions of republicanism. This is evident in his response to the widespread Kurdish rebellion that lasted for several months in 1925. The rebellion was inspired by a mixture of Kurdish nationalism and Islamic revivalism, two sentiments that were anathema to Atatürk. He persuaded the assembly to pass a law for the maintenance of order that granted the government extraordinary power for two years. Using the latitude provided by the new law, the government established special independence tribunals that were empowered to prosecute and sentence the rebels. When the Kurdish rebellion was crushed in late 1925, the leader and forty-six of his followers were executed by order of one of the tribunals. Neither Atatürk nor his successors were prepared to acknowledge the ethnic and cultural distinctiveness of the Kurdish minority, and the government officially referred to them as "mountain Turks."

Populism was embodied in the establishment of people's houses throughout the country. A combination of adult education centers, sports clubs, and political indoctrination units, the people's houses were the outcome of the government's efforts to take the revolution to the masses. As well as offering recreational facilities, they provided forums for government representatives to explain the new legislation and to promote the cause of Turkish solidarity. They also served a political function. The people's houses were managed by Atatürk's RPP and were used to generate support for the president and his reformist programs. Although a certain element of total state control was inherent in this organizational interconnection, the people's houses were instrumental in establishing the principle of popular participation in government.

Populism and nationalism were further combined in a massive program of educational expansion. Atatürk was driven by the belief that one of his major tasks was the formation of an educated cadre of Turks committed to his reforms and capable of administering them after his passing. In addition, since sovereignty now rested with the people, it was important to develop a literate and informed public. Although the battle against illiteracy, especially in the rural areas, was to be long and difficult, Atatürk broke away from the elitist educational tradition of the Ottoman era and established the principle of free and compulsory elementary education. Between 1923 and 1940, the number of schools in the country doubled, the number of teachers increased by 133 percent, and the number of students increased by nearly 300 percent.[1]

The entire corpus of reformist legislation had an effect on the status of women. Although the practice of veiling was not directly addressed, the reforming tendency of the state created an environment leading toward greater equality between the sexes. Atatürk was fond of the company of emancipated women and encouraged Turkish women to acquire the social graces of Europeans. In what might be regarded as a step in this direction, if hardly as progress by today's standards, beauty pageants were introduced into Turkey, and in 1932 a Turk was crowned Miss Europe. More substantive advances were provided by the adoption of universal education, which enabled women to acquire the training necessary to enter public life. By 1933 there were thirteen female judges in Turkey. In 1934 women were given the right to vote for, and to stand as, candidates for the national assembly; the elections of 1935 returned seventeen female delegates to the assembly.

The final Kemalist principle, etatism, was a development of the 1930s. During the early years of the Atatürk revolution, economic policy was not a high priority. However, with the onset of the worldwide depression in the 1930s, Turkish planners concluded that the country would have to become less dependent on imports and that this could be achieved through the development of an industrial base. Local private capital was insufficient for this purpose, so the government decided to intervene directly in the economy and to divert state funds to the construction of major projects. Etatism, usually defined as state capitalism, began with the announcement of a five-year plan in 1933. Over the course of the plan, large-scale textile and steel plants were constructed, along with such light industries as paper, glass, and cement factories. Although etatism provided Turkey with a modest industrial infrastructure that it might not otherwise have established, the location of the plants was often ill conceived and the operation of some of the factories was inefficient. More serious was the neglect of agricultural development that marked the Atatürk years. Mechanization was limited, productivity rose only marginally, and rural standards of living remained low. Etatism was not a resounding success.

Turkey's foreign relations during Atatürk's presidency were excellent, fostering an extended period of peace in which Turkish leaders could focus on domestic issues. Turkish nationalism concentrated on building internal solidarity and was not expansionist. Atatürk repeatedly renounced any intent of seeking the recovery of former Ottoman territory outside the National Pact boundaries, and he disavowed the Pan-Turkish schemes propounded by some intellectuals and politicians. Turkey was admitted to the League of Nations in 1932 and joined the Balkan Pact in 1934, a sign that workable relations had been reestablished between Ankara and the nations over which the Ottomans once ruled. Because of Atatürk's restrained foreign policy, Turkey exerted little influence in the capitals of the Arab successor states. The most contentious regional issue during the interwar years involved a dispute with France over the Alexandretta peninsula, an area of mixed Arab and Turkish population that had been under French administration since 1921. Because Atatürk believed that Alexandretta was a predominantly Turkish region (a disputable assumption), he contested France's decision to include it as part of a proposed independent Syrian state in 1936. The matter then became the subject of continuous negotiation until 1939, when France agreed to the Turkish annexation of Alexandretta, much to the annoyance of the Syrians (see Map 12.2).

The inauguration of the debate over Alexandretta was Atatürk's last decisive act as president. He died in November 1938 at the age of fifty-seven. His passing was deeply mourned. He was an inspired and inspirational leader, one of those rare figures whose exceptional talents were available to meet a challenge to which they were perfectly suited. A member of the Ottoman military elite whose reputation was established on the battlefields of World War I and the war for independence, he renounced grandiose schemes of glory and accepted the less rewarding task of pragmatic nation building. He used the immense powers he acquired as president to establish respect for the law and to lay the groundwork for popular participation in government. To be sure, his reforms were too abrupt for some, and his creation of a state that sought to regulate individuals' lives more directly than had the Ottomans caused resentment and occasionally led to resistance. His sweeping secular measures, which attempted to cut the Turks off from their Islamic past and to sever their ties with the rest of the Islamic world, alienated segments of the population, especially in the rural areas. And his goal of remaking Turkey in the image of Europe was offensive in certain quarters; he was not a selective reformer but a committed Westernizer. The authoritarian features of Atatürk's republic aroused suspicions in the West, but the democratic institutions he established have endured. Perhaps his most important legacy was the smooth transition of power to his successor, Ismet Inönü, who came to the presidency in 1938 determined to further the principles of Kemalism.

Iran Under Reza Shah

From the End of the War to the Consolidation of the Pahlavi Dynasty

The events of World War I further weakened the authority of Iran's central government, compromised the state's sovereignty, and devastated its economy. Although the Qajar ruler, Ahmad Shah, presided over his court in Tehran, real authority in the country was exercised by the two occupying powers, Britain in the south and Russia in the north. The Russian threat was temporarily removed with the withdrawal of Russian troops in the aftermath of the revolution of 1917. The limitations that the presence of foreign armies placed on the authority of the central government were considerable and contributed to a renewed wave of tribalism and to the rise of a series of provincial political movements aimed not so much at separation from Tehran as at reducing the foreign influence that pervaded the country.

From 1918 until 1921, Britain, determined to protect its oil interests and to contain the new threat of Bolshevism, increased its already prominent role in Iranian affairs. British subsidies kept the government in Tehran afloat, and British military and administrative advisers attempted to reorganize what was left of Iran's army and to manipulate the various political factions within the country to Britain's advantage. When Britain offered to grant Iran a loan in exchange for exclusive advisory privileges, antiforeign demonstrations broke out in several cities and added to the widespread discontent with the government, which was seen as ineffective and pro-British. This chaotic situation was finally brought to an end by the actions of a determined military commander.

On February 21, 1921, Reza Khan, a colonel in the Cossack Brigade, led a contingent of 3,000 men into Tehran, arrested a number of prominent politicians, and requested that the shah appoint a young civilian reformer, Sayyid Zia Tabatabai, as prime minister. The shah agreed, and Sayyid Zia formed a new cabinet and named Reza Khan to the post of army commander. In May Reza Khan forced Sayyid Zia to resign and over the next four years consolidated more and more power into his own hands. The Majlis, recognizing the urgent need to restore order to the countryside, authorized huge budget increases for the armed forces. Reza Khan used these resources to enlarge the military, modernize its weaponry, and send it on relentless campaigns against the tribal rebellions. By 1925 the major areas of dissidence had been subdued, and Reza Khan had become a respected, if not beloved, national figure.

Nor was his authority confined to the military sphere. In 1923 he assumed the office of prime minister; he then suggested to Ahmad Shah that the monarch might enjoy a European vacation. The shah understood the thinly veiled threat and left Tehran for Paris, never to return. Two years later, Reza Khan persuaded the Majlis to depose the Qajar dynasty and to convene a constituent assembly. When this body met in 1925, it voted to entrust the crown of the oldest monarchy on earth to Reza Khan's family. Another local military commander had become king of kings, and in 1926 the Pahlavi dynasty began. It would last but fifty-three years.

The Reign of Reza Shah, 1926–1941

Although Reza Shah never articulated his goals with the clarity of Atatürk, his reforms were intended to accomplish in Iran results similar to those that Atatürk was achieving in Turkey. Indeed, Reza Shah borrowed many of his programs directly from the Kemalist experience. The two rulers have often been likened, but Reza Shah's background and political attitudes were more akin to those of Muhammad Ali of nineteenth-century Egypt than they were to Atatürk's. Born to a Turkish-speaking family in the Caspian province of Mazandaran in 1878, Reza Shah had a limited education and joined the Cossack Brigade at an early age. He may have known some Russian, but he was unschooled in any European language and rose through the ranks to become a colonel. His unusual height and proud bearing endowed him with a commanding presence and made him a successful officer and a formidable autocrat.

He is rightly regarded as a reformer, but his reforms were selective and were not intended to restructure the existing political order. Although elections to the Majlis were held regularly, Reza Shah's manipulation rendered them meaningless. He controlled the entire political system and reduced the Majlis to a rubber stamp for his legislation. Rather than revising the constitution, he left it in place and simply ignored it when that suited his purpose. His personal power was enforced by the use of censorship, the abolition of opposition parties, the banning of trade unions, and the arrest and occasional murder of high-ranking officials who incurred his displeasure.

The institutional bases of Reza Shah's authority rested with his control of the army and the bureaucracy and his skillful use of court patronage. In 1926 the Majlis passed a universal conscription law that required every Iranian male to serve for two years in the armed forces. The shah used this legislation to build up a military force of over 100,000 that included armored brigades, an air force, and a navy. He emphasized his close personal relationship to the armed forces and effectively catered to the officer corps, providing them with high salaries, a sumptuous club in Tehran, and the opportunity to purchase land at reduced prices. In the civilian sphere, Reza Shah's centralizing policies led to a rapid expansion of the state bureaucracy and thus to the creation of a cadre of civil servants dependent for their positions on the Pahlavi regime's continued commitment to reform. A third source of the shah's control over the elite was his ability to dispense court patronage. During the course of his reign, Reza Shah acquired vast private landholdings, the revenues from which he used to establish hotels, casinos, and charitable foundations. Since all of these enterprises required managers and staff, the shah could award such posts to those who were prepared to support his regime.

Although Reza Shah might appear to be a traditional authoritarian monarch in a twentieth-century setting, he was also a reformer committed to strengthening Iran through forced measures of Westernization and centralization. He deployed the army to establish state authority over the tribal leaders with a firmness the Qajars never envisaged. Once the postwar insurrections had been crushed, the shah institutionalized central control by stationing military garrisons in the tribal areas, forcibly disarming the tribes, confiscating their lands, and restricting their migration patterns. These policies achieved the shah's objectives but resulted in the general impoverishment of the tribal population.

As was the case in Turkey, secularism was a central component of Reza Shah's reign. The secularization of state institutions was most marked in the legal and judicial sphere. In 1928 the Majlis voted to adopt a new civil code modeled on that of France. Although the code retained aspects of *shariʿah* law in matters of personal status, many of its provisions contravened the Supplementary Fundamental Laws that had been adopted in 1907 at the insistence of the ulama (see Chapter 8). This supplement prohibited the enactment of any laws that contravened the *shariʿah*. Reza Shah's legal reforms did not change the supplement; they simply ignored it. The role of the ulama in national judicial life was further reduced by the establishment of a hierarchy of state courts in which secular officials replaced the ulama as judges. The state judges were given the power to decide which cases should be referred to the religious courts and which belonged under the jurisdiction of the state courts. The *shariʿah* and the *shariʿah* judicial system were not directly abolished; rather, they were bypassed through new legislation and confined to increasingly narrow fields of jurisdiction—specifically, to matters of family law. Moreover, the ulama were firmly placed outside the new judicial system by a law adopted in 1936 requiring judges in the new state courts to hold a degree from the recently founded Tehran University Faculty of Law or from a foreign university showing that they had undergone at least three years of legal study.

Reza Shah also attacked the financial independence of the religious establishment. A law of 1932 eliminated the ulama's right to register legal documents, and in 1939 the state announced a seizure of all *waqf* lands. The powerful Iranian religious establishment was shaken by Reza Shah's assaults on its position in society, but it was not broken.

Reza Shah's program of secularism, like Atatürk's, imposed the outward symbols of Westernization on the population. In 1928 a law was passed that required males to dress in the European manner, and in 1935 the wearing of a hat became compulsory. (In remote villages expenses were kept to a minimum by the purchase of a single communal fedora, to be worn by whoever was engaged in a venture that might bring him to the attention of the authorities.) Although Reza Shah also introduced legislation regarding women, his policies in this regard were designed more to increase their participation in national life than to improve their legal status. Going even further than Turkey, Iran officially banned the wearing of the veil in 1936, and government employees were encouraged to appear at official receptions with their unveiled wives. Segregation of the sexes in such public places as cafés and cinemas was forbidden as well. Yet women were never granted the right to vote, and the *shariᶜah* provisions permitting polygamy were retained in the civil code of 1928, as were the established provisions making it easy for men and difficult for women to initiate divorce proceedings.

The most successful reforms occurred in education. Because of Iran's limited educational development in the nineteenth century, the central government suffered from a shortage of trained administrators in its attempts to accommodate the expanded role that Reza Shah demanded of it. The regime endeavored to correct this deficiency by devoting more funds to education. As a result, the number of students enrolled in primary and secondary schools increased dramatically. The government opened an indigenous secular institution of higher learning, Tehran University, in 1935 and each year awarded 100 special government scholarships for study in European universities. The majority of secondary and university graduates entered government service, forming a distinctive bureaucratic class whose members had similar educational backgrounds and possessed shared attitudes toward reform. The religious schools were not abolished as they were in Turkey; in fact, even though the Iranian secondary-level *madrasah*s experienced an enrollment decline, the religious primary schools had more students at the end of Reza Shah's reign than they did in 1926.

With its vast and rugged terrain and its multitude of ethnic groups, Iran did not readily lend itself to the creation of a uniform national secular culture. However, Reza Shah tried to force one into being. Like Atatürk, he constructed the national symbols of the new Iran around the pre-Islamic achievements of the ancient Iranian empires. The name of the country was officially changed from Persia to Iran so as to emphasize its Aryan origins. The state school curricula fostered the development of patriotic attitudes, and a scouting movement, for both boys and girls, was formed to inculcate nationalistic sentiments among the youth. Reza Shah supported laws that banned the use of minority languages, outlawed ethnic costumes, and reduced the number of Arabic and Turkish words in the Persian language. In addition, the government established the Society of Public Guidance to promote Iranian national sentiment through radio broadcasts and the dissemination of pamphlets and journals.

As Reza Shah guided Iran from the turmoil of the immediate postwar years into a period of stability, the implementation of his programs required an increase in revenue. Reza Shah generated it by collecting taxes more efficiently than the Qajars had done, by raising tariffs on imports, and by introducing indirect taxes on such consumer items as tea, sugar, and tobacco, a practice that was particularly burdensome to the poor. He devoted a large proportion of the state's revenue to improving the country's internal transportation system, both in an attempt to encourage domestic trade as well as to assist the army in maintaining control of outlying areas. The long-delayed trans-Iranian railroad was given a high priority, and in 1938 the route linking the Caspian Sea to the Persian Gulf via Tehran was completed—financed without recourse to foreign loans. As was the case in Turkey, the Great Depression prompted the Iranian state to participate in industrialization projects. This involved the direct financing of plant construction, the provision of low-interest loans to fledgling local industrialists, and the creation of state monopolies. Although Iran's version of etatism spawned a number of major industrial establishments such as textile mills, sugar refineries, and tea-processing plants, the development process was overly subject to government control and suffered from inefficiencies. Nevertheless, the drive toward industrialization did bring into existence a new wage-earning labor force and changed the character of the major cities, especially Tehran, which grew from a population of 196,000 in 1922 to approximately 700,000 in 1941.

If the urban centers were changing under Reza Shah, the rural areas were not. This was not just a case of neglecting agricultural development but of directly fostering conditions that strengthened the power of the large landowners over their tenants and depressed the quality of peasant life. The regime introduced measures that permitted landowners to increase their holdings at the expense of peasant proprietors to such an extent that by the mid-1930s as much as 95 to 98 percent of the agricultural population was landless.[2] In part, these practices were designed to assist the shah in his drive to become an accepted member of the landed aristocracy. Although he dispossessed certain leading families, he courted others by offering them posts in the government and ensuring their election to the Majlis. Through confiscations and direct seizures, the former Cossack Brigade officer became the largest landowner in the country, and he attempted to cement his ties to the landed aristocracy by making one of their members his third wife and marrying his daughter to another. In these circumstances the relationship between landlord and tenant remained as it had been, one of brutal exploitation. There was no populism in the Iran of Reza Shah. His regime coerced rural dwellers into adopting European forms of dress; it did not seek to advance their welfare or to encourage their participation in national life.

In general, Reza Shah's efforts to free Iran from the economic bondage in which the Qajars had placed it were successful. However, one foreign enterprise he was unable to control was the Anglo-Iranian Oil Company (AIOC), which functioned as a virtual state within a state in the Persian Gulf province of Khuzistan. The company's influence was made all the greater because it was by far the largest industrial employer in the country, with over 30,000 Iranian workers on its payroll. The shah endeavored to renegotiate the infamous D'Arcy concession of 1901 (see Chapter 8), but the company showed no inclination to offer major revisions. After four years of embittered discussions, the parties signed a new agreement in 1933 that provided Iran with a modest increase in the annual royalty payments (from 16 percent to 20 percent of the company's worldwide profits) and the guarantee of a minimum annual payment of £750,000. In return, Iran agreed to extend the concession from 1961, when it was originally due to expire, to 1993. This agreement did little to improve Iran's economic gain from its oil resources or to advance its claims to sovereignty over them; it was to become the source of acrimonious disputes between Iran and Britain in the years after World War II.

Britain's continued dominance in the oil-producing region and her ongoing influence in the south were sources of annoyance to Reza Shah, and he tried to counter them by cultivating diplomatic and commercial ties with Germany. During the late 1930s, Germany became Iran's largest trading partner, and German technicians and agents were active throughout the country. When World War II began, Iran proclaimed its neutrality, but Reza Shah's known pro-German sympathies caused the Soviet Union and Britain to view Iran with suspicion. With the German invasion of the USSR in June 1941, Iran once again became a pawn in the hostilities between outside powers. In order to keep a supply corridor open to the Soviet Union, the British and the Soviets invaded Iran in August. The pampered Iranian army quickly collapsed, the government surrendered on the day after the invasion, and on September 16, 1941, Reza Shah made a desperate attempt to preserve the Pahlavi dynasty by abdicating in favor of his son, Muhammad Reza. The former shah then left Iran under British supervision, eventually settling in South Africa, where he died in 1944. Iran entered World War II just as it had World War I—partitioned and occupied by outside powers.

Turkey and Iran During World War II: Sovereignty and Occupation

If one defines a successful foreign policy as the pursuit of national self-interest, then President İnönü's conduct of Turkish diplomacy during World War II must be judged a triumph. Resisting pressures for an alliance by both the Allies and the Axis, İnönü guided his country along a cautious path of friendly neutrality until the outcome of the war was decided. Finally, on February 23, 1945, less than three months before the armistice, Turkey declared war on Germany, thus qualifying for charter membership in the United Nations.

By contrast, as we have seen above, Iran's declaration of neutrality was not respected. British and Soviet forces remained in occupation of the country from 1941 to 1946, dividing it into zones of influence resembling those established in 1907. From the perspective of the Allies, the occupation of Iran was a routine wartime necessity: Iran produced oil vital to Allied needs, it lay adjacent to other oil-producing regions in the Persian Gulf, and it offered an overland supply route to the beleaguered Soviet Union. However, from the Iranian point of view, the Anglo-Soviet action constituted yet another violation of the country's sovereignty and an insult to its national dignity. The Allied invasion provided postwar Iranian nationalism with a ready-made issue on which to build a case against the intentions of outside powers.

For the duration of hostilities, Iran was harnessed to the Allied war effort with little regard for the effects this might have on the local economy and social structure. The country became a massive supply line to the Soviets, and the trans-Iranian railway, intended by Reza Shah to stand as a symbol of Iranian unity and self-sufficiency, was completely diverted to Allied use. Spending by thousands of foreign occupation troops produced an inflationary spiral that devastated civil servants and others on fixed salaries. Shortages of vital commodities were common and led to hoarding and profiteering by individuals who operated beyond the reach of the government's timid regulatory controls.

When the United States entered the war, it joined the occupying forces by sending thousands of troops to assist in the transport of supplies to the Soviet Union. In addition, U.S. civilian and military personnel assumed influential positions as advisers to the Iranian government and began to direct reforms in such key areas as financial administration, domestic security, and military organization. The groundwork for U.S. involvement in postwar Iranian affairs was thus established.

Conclusion

Reza Shah and Atatürk have sometimes been viewed as similar. Although it is true that many of their state-sponsored reforms were directed toward the same goals, there was a substantial difference between their regimes. Atatürk was an established member of the Ottoman ruling elite who sought to enshrine the principle of popular sovereignty in the new Turkish constitution, whereas Reza Shah was a military usurper whose political objective was to consolidate his own power and to secure his son's succession to the throne. Atatürk controlled Turkey through the Republican People's Party and sowed the seeds from which a popular democratic system took root. His government acquired legitimacy by virtue of its electoral victories, its establishment of the rule of law, and its adherence to the constitutional provisions adopted in 1924. Reza Shah, in contrast, ruled through the army and the institutions of the monarchy; his power was based on coercion rather than consensus, and he chose not to seek the popular mandate that would have given his regime legitimacy. He also ignored the need to establish the political organizations and to foster the political education that would enable his reforms to survive his departure. And though Atatürk sought and used power, he did so—and was seen to do so—solely to further his vision of Turkish progress. Reza Shah was also fiercely patriotic, but he was not above using the powers of the monarchy for his personal gain; when he abdicated, his personal bank account had reached the equivalent of £3,000,000, and his landholdings amounted to over 3 million acres (1.2 million hectares).[3] The people viewed him as avaricious and self-serving and applauded his abdication. Thus, although both rulers introduced radical reforms by shock treatment, the legacies they left to the political cultures of their two countries were bound to be different.

Notes

1. Stanford J. Shaw and Ezel Kural Shaw, *The History of the Ottoman Empire and Modern Turkey,* vol. 2 (Cambridge, 1977), p. 387.

2. Nikki R. Keddie, *Roots of Revolution: An Interpretive History of Modern Iran* (New Haven, 1981), p. 103.

3. Donald N. Wilber, *Riza Shah Pahlavi: The Resurrection and Reconstruction of Iran* (Hicksville, N.Y., 1975), p. 244.

The Arab Struggle for Independence: Egypt, Iraq, and Transjordan from the Interwar Era to 1945 | 11

⟨|⟩
⟨|⟩

In the immediate aftermath of World War I, Britain's attempts to retain control of Egypt and establish a mandate in Iraq were met with widespread popular resistance. Although Britain managed to crush the revolts in the two countries, the costs were high and could not be sustained. Britain therefore formulated a system of alliance building that has been called empire by treaty. In this system, Egypt and Iraq were granted a limited form of "independence" that provided them with freedom to conduct domestic political affairs as they saw fit yet required the two states to allow the presence of British military bases on their soil and to adopt a foreign policy that was acceptable to Britain. By this means, Britain secured its essential strategic needs without incurring the expenses of directly governing the territories. But the restrictions that this system imposed on the full exercise of national sovereignty created a source of conflict between local political leaders and Great Britain and produced continuous tension throughout the period.

The Struggle for Power in Egypt

Although Egypt was spared from becoming a battleground during World War I, its population nevertheless suffered severe hardships in the years 1914–1918. The British decision to make Egypt the launching point for both the Gallipoli and Syrian campaigns meant that the material and human resources of the country were harnessed to the service of the Allied war effort. Farm animals and crops were requisitioned and thousands of *fellahin* conscripted into a civilian labor corps and forced to accompany the British army in its invasion of Ottoman Syria. Rural and urban dwellers alike suf-

190

fered from the effects of inflation and from shortages of basic consumer goods.

With the British declaration of a protectorate over Egypt and the imposition of martial law in 1914, domestic political activity came to a standstill. The establishment of the British protectorate terminated four centuries of Ottoman sovereignty. Egyptian rulers had long worked to distance themselves from Istanbul's authority, but they had not intended to have the sultan's control replaced by that of the British high commissioner. Nor did Egyptians welcome their forced participation in a war against another Islamic state with which they continued to have strong bonds of religious affinity.

When the war ended, the discontent it had spawned created a simmering restlessness at all levels of Egyptian society. Among the Egyptian elite, strong sentiments for self-government were spurred on by U.S. president Woodrow Wilson's pronouncements on the virtues of self-determination. Yet because the war had shown British policymakers how vital Egypt was to the defense of British imperial interests, there was no likelihood of a voluntary British withdrawal from the country. As Lord Lloyd stated to the House of Commons in 1929, "The only place from which the Suez Canal can be economically and adequately defended is from Cairo."[1] However, the actions of a few members of the Egyptian elite ignited the existing anti-British feeling into a national uprising that caught the British by surprise and forced them to seek a negotiated agreement for their continued presence in Egypt.

The Formation of the Wafd and the Revolution of 1919

In November 1918 seven prominent Egyptians from the landed gentry and the legal profession formed a delegation, or *wafd,* that had as its express goal the complete independence of Egypt. The delegation approached the British high commissioner with a request that it be allowed to represent Egypt at the Paris Peace Conference. When the request was denied, the *wafd* organizers took their demands to the Egyptian people. Traveling throughout the country with their message of independence, they sought to rally popular support for their claim that they, and not the British-backed ruler and his ministers, represented the will of the population at large. Thus was founded one of the most widely supported political parties in modern Egyptian history.

The original Wafd was led by Saʿd Zaghlul (1857/60–1927). Like many of the other party founders, Zaghlul was raised in a rural environment and then went on to acquire a European-style education, in his case a degree from the French law school in Cairo after he had studied at al-Azhar. His was a classic career of upward mobility made possible by the educational and career opportunities provided by Egypt's transformation; he gained his

Saᶜd Zaghlul, leader of the Wafd Party and the Egyptian independence movement after World War I. In 1924 Zaghlul became the first popularly elected prime minister of Egypt. (The Middle East Centre, St. Antony's College, Oxford)

wealth and status through his work as a Europeanized lawyer, judge, and government administrator, but he owed much of his success as a national political leader to his familiarity with the idiom of the Egyptian countryside and al-Azhar. During the Wafd's tour of Egypt in early 1919, Zaghlul proved to be a captivating orator and demonstrated a special ability to communicate with rural Egyptians. He quickly became the focus of popular adulation and, with his colleagues, succeeded in arousing popular discontent at Britain's refusal to lift the protectorate. The British authorities responded to the Wafd's campaign by arresting Zaghlul and three other leaders and exiling them to Malta in March 1919.

The exile of Zaghlul unleashed the pent-up emotions of the Egyptian population and created a wave of support for the Wafd. Riots and demonstrations in favor of independence first broke out in the urban areas. When the British attempted to contain them by force, the intensity of the demonstrations increased, eventually exploding into a nationwide upheaval known as the revolution of 1919. In Cairo student demonstrators from the law school and al-Azhar were joined by tram workers and veiled women in demanding the return of their leader and the independence of their country; lawyers and government workers went on strike, shutting down the courts and the bureaucracy. In the countryside angry peasants tore up train tracks, burned railcars, and killed British soldiers. The British met the civilian demonstrators with armed force, and by the end of 1919, more than 800 Egyptians had been killed and 1,400 wounded. The situation was eventually defused with the decision of the new British high commissioner, General Allenby, to allow Zaghlul and his companions to appear before the Paris Peace Conference. The Egyptian people, through their sacrifice, had elevated the Wafd, a group of private citizens, to the role of national representatives.

The Egyptian delegation did not receive a sympathetic hearing in Paris, but the British decided to include Zaghlul in discussions on the future of the Anglo-Egyptian relationship. The negotiations dragged on for two years, largely because the Wafd demanded full and complete independence, whereas the British insisted on imposing conditions that would restrict Egyptian sovereignty. The deadlock was finally broken not by agreement between the two parties but by the unilateral declaration of independence Britain issued in 1922. The declaration abolished the protectorate, proclaimed Egypt independent, and elevated the status of the Egyptian ruler to king. However, the declaration also contained four reserved points that made a mockery of the term *independence.* By these points, the British government remained responsible for the security of imperial communications in Egypt, the defense of Egypt against foreign aggression or interference, the protection of foreign interests and foreign minorities in Egypt, and the Sudan and its future status. The British military presence in Egypt was thus assured, the Capitulations continued to be enforced, and Egypt still did not control its own foreign policy. The British had imposed their version of independence on Egypt against the will of the Wafd and its popular leader, thereby setting the stage for the confrontations that would define interwar political life in Egypt.

Egypt's Liberal Experiment, 1924–1936

In the minds of the Wafdist politicians, the ideas of independence and constitutional government were closely linked. These wealthy, European-oriented Egyptians assumed that the very existence of a constitution and a parliament would somehow resolve Egypt's domestic problems and hasten British recognition of unfettered independence. Britain supported the constitutional ideal, if not the concept of true independence, and in 1923 a constitution was proclaimed. Elections for the first parliament were held in January 1924. The Wafd Party demonstrated its popularity by winning 90 percent of the seats and providing Saᶜd Zaghlul with the opportunity to become Egypt's first elected prime minister. Thus began Egypt's troubled and short-lived experiment with parliamentary democracy, the only time in the country's modern history that a genuine attempt to establish parliamentary institutions along European lines was made.

Among the many factors that militated against the efficient functioning of Egypt's democracy, four may be singled out as particularly debilitating. The first was the nature of the constitution. It awarded extensive powers to the king, including the right to appoint the prime minister and dissolve parliament, and so created an institutionally weak legislature. King Fuad (1917–1936) was determined to protect his royal prerogatives and did not hesitate to dismiss governments whenever it suited his purpose. Second, the British continued to interfere in Egyptian politics, thus undermining the integrity of the parliamentary system. Third, neither the Wafd nor any of the smaller parties adopted the principles of compromise and respect for the opposition that are essential for the proper conduct of parliamentary government. Zaghlul was every bit as authoritarian as the king; he regarded the opposition members of parliament with contempt and stacked the bureaucracy with Wafdist supporters regardless of their qualifications. And finally, the question of Egypt's independence and the existence of the four reserved points caused political life to revolve around a continuous struggle for power among the Wafd, the monarchy, and the British. The Wafd demanded complete independence and more power for parliament at the expense of the king. King Fuad, in turn, sought to preserve his powers by catering to the British, who tended to support him against the Wafd. The British also supported civilian politicians who were prepared to undertake negotiations on the basis of the four reserved points, something the Wafd would not do.

These factors combined to create short-lived governments interspersed with periods of royal rule. Politics was reduced to a power struggle among competing factions of the elite, and the serious domestic issues facing Egyptian society at large were not addressed. The consuming desire for independence was partially fulfilled in 1936, when Britain, alarmed by Italian expansionism in Ethiopia, agreed to renegotiate the 1922 declaration. The result was an Anglo-Egyptian treaty of alliance that recognized Egypt's independence, though it also provided for a British military presence in the Suez Canal zone and reaffirmed Britain's right to defend Egypt in case of attack. Britain, then, retained the advantages of the 1922 declaration. The difference was that the 1936 treaty was signed by an elected Wafdist government, thus giving formal Egyptian consent to the continued deployment of British troops on Egyptian soil. As a corollary to Egypt's new independence, the European states signed the Montreux Convention (1937) that at long last abolished the Capitulations and provided for the phasing out of the Mixed Courts by 1949.

The achievement of a greater degree of internal sovereignty did not bring about a substantial change in the pattern of Egyptian politics. King Fuad died in 1936 and was succeeded by his son Faruq, a young monarch whose early popularity was gradually eroded by his personal indulgences. The politicians, with their preference for secular political institutions and their self-serving devotion to their own needs, became increasingly isolated from the urban and rural masses. The imported parliamentary system inspired little loyalty from the population, especially as the wealthy professional and landowning politicians who operated it were unwilling to direct their attention to the social legislation that Egypt so desperately needed. Nor was there a single national leader capable of inspiring popular confidence. Following Zaghlul's death in 1927, the Wafd, under the leadership of Mustafa al-Nahhas, became factionalized and corrupt. Although it continued to attract a large popular following, it had lost its former élan.

The political leaders were further distanced from the population by their whole-hearted acceptance of European values and their attempts to impose them on Egyptian society. One observer has labeled this dimension of the liberal experiment "the attack upon tradition."[2] It was represented by the diminution of religious values and religious institutions in the regulation of legal affairs and personal relationships. Egyptian society underwent a severe dislocation as liberal leaders endorsed the belief that European civilization, with its supposedly rational foundations, was superior to the divinely ordained Islamic order. Ideas of European origin, ranging from Darwinism to socialism, from feminism to Freudianism, received widespread circulation in the lively periodical press of the era.

For some of the interwar intellectuals and politicians, Egypt's new path toward modernity required a reshaping of its cultural identity. In their eagerness to portray Egypt's cultural legacy as deriving from the liberal traditions of Europe, writers like Taha Husayn (1889–1973), who held an advanced degree from the Sorbonne, downplayed the country's Arab and Islamic heritage in favor of symbols culled from its Greek and pharaonic past. Thus the doctrine of pharaonism glorified the Nile River, the major symbol of Egyptian territorial nationalism, and the rich pre-Islamic civilization to which it had given birth. In his book *Mustaqbal al-Thaqafah fi Misr* (The future of culture in Egypt), published in 1938, Taha Husayn stressed Egypt's Mediterranean heritage and asserted that Egypt had shared in, and contributed to, the same Greek civilization to which Western Europe owed much of its political and intellectual strength. Such deliberate omission of Islam further alienated the population from the parliamentary regime and the politicians and intellectuals who claimed to speak for the people but ignored their economic grievances and insulted their Islamic sensibilities.

The attack upon tradition was also evident in the emergence of an Egyptian feminist movement. Originating among women from Cairo's upper classes, Egyptian feminism coalesced around the leadership of Huda Sha'rawi (1879–1947) and the Egyptian Feminist Union she founded in 1923. The union initially focused on such issues as women's suffrage, equal access to educational opportunities, and the reform of marriage laws. The union supported complete independence from Britain, but, like the upper-class male leaders of the Wafd Party, promoted European social values and had an essentially secular orientation. The objectives of the feminist movement were symbolized by the well-publicized gesture of social freedom made by Sha⁽rawi and her associate, Saiza Nabrawi, who removed their veils as they stepped off a train at Cairo's main railway station in 1923. Some of the Egyptian Feminist Union's educational demands were met: In 1925 the government made primary education compulsory for girls as well as boys, and later in the decade women were admitted to the national university for the first time. The union's campaign for the reform of family law, however, was unsuccessful.

The attack upon tradition was led primarily by educated members of the middle and upper classes who were not representative of the vast majority of Egyptians. Beginning in the late 1920s, disaffected elements of the population began to seek practical solutions to their economic problems and sustenance for their spiritual needs by joining organizations that operated outside the structured party system. This popular reaction against the foreign-inspired parliamentary regime was also a reaction against the secularism it represented. Many of the voluntary organizations that sprang up in the 1930s were associated with one form or another of Islamic activism. By far the most significant of them—and one of the most significant organizations in recent Egyptian history—was the Muslim Brotherhood.

Founded in Isma⁽iliyya in 1928 by Hasan al-Banna, a layman educated at the Teachers' Training College, the brotherhood grew dramatically during the 1930s, and by the end of the decade it had 500 branches throughout Egypt and a membership numbering tens of thousands. The program of the brotherhood was a mixture of the traditional and the innovative. It was traditional in that al-Banna believed that the social and political regeneration of Egypt was intimately tied to the restoration of Islam as a guiding force in national life. To this end, he called for the reimplementation of the *shari⁽ah*, arguing that the ills from which Egypt suffered could be traced to the replacement of Quranic principles by secular legal and political institutions. However, al-Banna's insistence on the restoration of the *shari⁽ah* did not imply a simplistic resurrection of the past. As Muhammad Abduh had done earlier, al-Banna sought to find a way for Muslims to take advantage of the technological advances of the twentieth century without feeling that they were compromising their commitment to Islamic values. He argued, much as Abduh had, that the *shari⁽ah* was originally formulated to meet a specific set of historical circumstances and was thus a product of informed human reasoning. In al-Banna's view the restored *shari⁽ah* would be subject to interpretation and would hence be fully compatible with the needs of a modern society. The lack of specificity in al-Banna's political proposals should not detract from the power of his vision; he called forth not so much an Islamic state as an Islamic order that—precisely because of its Islamic basis—would ensure social justice, economic well-being, and political harmony.

The brotherhood's direct appeal to Islamic-based social reform and social responsibility constituted part of its attraction. While the politicians bickered, the brotherhood acted and made its presence felt across a broad spectrum of Egyptian society. Al-Banna advocated such economic reforms as land redistribution, the introduction of social welfare programs, and the replacement of foreign capital by local investment. The brotherhood forged close ties with Egypt's emergent labor movement and defended workers' demands for union protection and unemployment benefits. It also established enterprises of its own, most notably in the fields of weaving, transportation, and construction, and granted workers shareholding rights in these companies. In an effort to bridge the gap that split Egyptian society into secular and religious spheres, al-Banna's followers founded primary schools that tried to combine religious instruction with training in scientific and technical subjects. The organization also provided material assistance to society's underprivileged by establishing free medical clinics and setting up soup kitchens to feed the urban poor during the height of the depression. In this extensive range of activities, the Muslim Brotherhood manifested al-Banna's belief that social justice was more than a matter of legislation; it was in effect part of a social ethos that could be realized only by a return to Islamic values.

The appeal of the Muslim Brotherhood was widespread and cut across class lines. It became the focus for those who were marginalized by Egypt's disruptive transformation. To the urban poor, and especially to the large number of them who were recent migrants from the countryside, the organization offered material assistance, communal associations, and spiritual comfort. The brotherhood also attracted a large following among university students, who faced the prospect of low-paying civil service jobs and a lifetime of frustrated expectations. The young were drawn as well by the brotherhood's intransigent stand on complete independence and its denunciation of the treaty of 1936 and all the compromises associated with that agreement. And to all who felt adrift in a world of changing values and increasingly complex relationships, the brotherhood represented the stability of Islamic values and offered the hope that they could be incorporated into the uncertain future. This powerful combination of appeals allowed the Muslim Brotherhood to emerge from World War II as a potent force in Egyptian politics.

Despite the outward trappings of secularism that were so much in evidence during the years of the liberal experiment, Egyptian society as a whole remained firmly committed to its Islamic roots. And despite the symbolic recognition of the country's sovereignty in the treaty of 1936 and its admission to the League of Nations in 1937, the presence of British troops in the canal zone suggested that in times of crisis for the British Empire, London, not Cairo, would chart Egypt's course. World War II was to present such a crisis.

An Overview of World War II

In this chapter and the two that follow, we examine the impact of World War II on the individual Arab countries. In order to place the conflict in its Middle Eastern context and illustrate the crucial role that the region assumed in the Allied conduct of the war, we present at this point a brief overview of the chronology of the Second World War.

During the month of June 1940, France fell and German forces occupied most of Western Europe. The main theater of war then shifted to the skies above Britain, where, during summer and fall 1940, the Battle of Britain raged between the German Luftwaffe and the Royal Air Force. The British pilots prevailed, and for the moment Britain seemed secure from invasion. However, the overseas communication routes and oil fields that were vital to continued British participation in the war remained vulnerable and were drawn into the arena of battle.

During the two years following the Battle of Britain, a giant Axis pincer movement gradually closed on the British positions in the Middle East. By 1942, the pincer seemed ready to squeeze shut. In the north the Wehrmacht, already in occupation of the Balkans up to the Turkish border, had Stalingrad under siege and was penetrating through the Caucasian oil fields toward the Caspian Sea. In the south the seesaw Western Desert campaign appeared to have swung in favor of the Axis forces. During summer 1942, General Erwin Rommel's Afrika Korps penetrated into Egypt, driving the British forces back to al-Alamain, only 70 miles (112 km) from Alexandria and within striking distance of the Suez Canal.

Then, in October 1942, the British launched a counteroffensive at al-Alamain that swept Rommel's forces out of Egypt and across Libya to Tunisia, finally defeating them in spring 1943. At the same time—the winter of 1942–1943—the Germans suffered a catastrophic defeat in the Battle of Stalingrad; it marked the start of their long retreat from the Soviet Union. The Allies followed up their triumph in North Africa with the invasion of Italy in 1943 and with the massive seaborne landing at Normandy in June 1944. On May 8, 1945, Germany surrendered. The war in the Pacific came to an end in September, hastened by the U.S. decision to drop atomic bombs on Hiroshima and Nagasaki.

The Axis pincer had not clamped shut on the Middle East after all. During the troubled years from 1940 to 1942, however, the Allied victory was by no means a foregone conclusion. This period of uncertainty for Britain and of humiliation for France presented their imperial subjects with an opportunity to escape their control. But the crisis years also offered a chance for individuals who had been elevated to positions of power by the forces of imperialism to express their gratitude. The regional responses to the Allied predicament were not uniform and illustrate the complexity of the relationships that had developed during the interwar period.

Egypt During World War II:
Pivot of the British Defense System

The British war correspondents who regularly gathered at the grand bar of the Cecil Hotel in Alexandria needed no wire reports to tell them how the campaign in the Western Desert was faring; the speed, or lack of it, with which the Egyptian bartenders served their drinks told them of the day's results on the battlefield. During spring 1942, thirsty British correspondents grew impatient at the length of time it took for their drinks to arrive. The barmen at the Cecil were not the only Egyptians to show a certain ambivalence toward the British cause. Many of Egypt's political leaders offered only a hesitant endorsement of Britain's war effort, and some among them maintained contacts with Axis agents just in case the outcome of the war should find German troops replacing British ones in the streets of Cairo.

When Britain entered the war in 1939, the Egyptian government fulfilled its treaty obligations by imposing martial law and breaking diplomatic relations with Germany. Egypt was not required to declare war and did not do so; the country's ruling politicians wished to keep Egypt out of the conflict, but this proved impossible. As the Axis pincer closed on the Middle East, Britain made Egypt the pivot of its Mediterranean defense. During the course of the war, as many as 500,000 British and Commonwealth troops passed through Egypt. Cairo, as the headquarters of the Middle East supply center and the main urban attraction for soldiers on leave, swarmed with British military and civilian personnel. Because of the importance of Egypt to Britain's war effort, the country became the target of Axis military operations. In concert with Rommel's land-based invasion from the Western Desert, the Axis powers mounted persistent air raids on Alexandria harbor and tried to infiltrate the Egyptian armed forces and political institutions.

These and other related wartime developments affected the course of Egyptian political and economic life. Inflation was rampant, and basic foodstuffs were in such short supply that bread riots broke out in Cairo in 1942. Egyptians blamed the shortage of grain on the presence of the Allied troops. Because the country's trading capabilities were restricted by wartime conditions, Egypt was forced to improve its industrial base. By the end of the war, local self-sufficiency had been achieved in the manufacture of such goods as sugar and tobacco products, and production of shoes, cement, cotton thread, and glass had increased notably. As a result of the expansion of Egyptian enterprise and the employment of more than 200,000 Egyptians in war-related jobs, the local labor force experienced considerable growth, and the trade union movement gained momentum.

In the realm of politics, the events of the war discredited the whole range of institutions—monarchy, parliamentary government, and the Wafd party—that had governed Egypt since 1923 and led to the political paralysis that lasted until the revolution of 1952. At the outbreak of the war, Egypt was governed by a coalition cabinet headed by Ali Mahir, a known Axis sympathizer and a close personal adviser to King Faruq. When Mahir resigned in 1940, a succession of unstable coalition cabinets held power and tried to keep Egypt's future diplomatic options open by avoiding an overt break with the Axis yet maintaining correct relations with Britain. In winter 1942 the ruling coalition broke up and resigned.

That set the stage for the event known as the February Fourth Incident. Like the hangings at Dinshaway thirty-six years earlier, it was one of those episodes in Anglo-Egyptian relations that had repercussions far exceeding the scope of the event itself. King Faruq was eager to have his confidant, Mahir, assume the vacant premiership. But with Rommel's forces within striking distance of Alexandria, Britain was in no mood to countenance a government headed by the pro-Axis Mahir. Instead, the British embassy decided that a Wafdist government under longtime party leader Mustafa al-Nahhas would be most likely to cooperate during this period of extreme crisis. In order to make his government's position known, the British ambassador, Sir Miles Lampson, arranged for an audience with King Faruq on the evening of February 4, 1942. Before calling on the king, Lampson ordered British tanks and troops to surround the royal residence at Abdin Palace. He then presented Faruq with an ultimatum: The king could invite the Wafd to form a government, or he could abdicate. Faruq chose to appoint a Wafdist cabinet.

Lampson's heavy-handed tactics during the February Fourth Incident emphasized Britain's control over Egyptian domestic affairs and infuriated nationalist sympathizers. In addition, the incident discredited the local participants and accelerated the demise of Egypt's enfeebled parliamentary system. The king was humiliated and became more determined than ever to curtail the power of the Wafd, whereas the Wafd itself was compromised. As in 1936, when a Wafdist government signed the independence treaty that allowed for a continued British military presence in Egypt, the party once again appeared ready to abandon its nationalist principles and cooperate with Britain in exchange for political power. Over the course of the next decade, the Wafd continued to suffer from the fact that in 1942 it took office under the protection of British tanks.

In an attempt to shore up its reputation and gain control over the new forces spawned by the wartime economy, al-Nahhas's government enacted long-neglected social and labor legislation, including laws granting legal recognition to trade unions. The Wafd also took the initiative in encouraging the formation of a loose federation of Arab states, commonly known as the Arab League, which came into existence in 1945. Created to promote regional economic, political, and cultural cooperation, the Arab League quickly became a forum in which the Arab member states expressed their disapproval of the creation of a Jewish state in Palestine. Headquartered in Cairo and directed by an Egyptian, Abd al-Rahman al-Azzam, the organization served as a symbol of Egypt's growing involvement in the affairs of the Arab world.

As the war in Europe wound down, the Egyptian political situation remained unsettled. The Wafd, undisputed champion of independence in 1919, was now regarded as a corrupt and bloated party of privilege that had been co-opted by the British. The splinter opposition parties stood no higher in popular esteem. Born more out of personality clashes among Wafdists than out of ideological differences, they failed to generate widespread support. In the absence of credible parties, the monarchy and the extraparliamentary organizations, most notably the Muslim Brotherhood, moved to the forefront of Egyptian politics in the immediate postwar years.

Iraq Between the Wars

From the Establishment of the Mandate to Independence

At the time of the Ottoman surrender in 1918, Britain was in occupation of the three Mesopotamian provinces of Basra, Baghdad, and Mosul. These provinces, which became the state of Iraq under a British mandate in 1920, did not constitute a political community in any sense of the term. They were among the most ethnically and religiously diverse Arab regions of the Ottoman Empire, and their amalgamation into a single country posed exceptionally difficult obstacles to nation building.

The Arab majority was divided along religious lines, with slightly over half the population professing Shi'ism and having close ties with the ulama of neighboring Iran. Because the Ottoman presence in the region had been confined to the major cities, large areas of the countryside were dominated by tribal confederations accustomed to freedom from governmental interference. Further potential for discord came from the large Kurdish and Assyrian Christian minorities in the north and a substantial Jewish community in Baghdad (see Map 11.1).

The difficulties that would be faced in molding these diverse peoples into a single state were brought home to the British occupying authorities by a huge uprising that broke out among the tribes of the Euphrates in June 1920. Lasting for several months, the uprising was a localized rebellion against Britain and the British attempt to replace the decentralized Ottoman system with centralized governmental structures. But even though the rebellion was not a self-consciously nationalist movement, it was inspired by anti-British sentiments and became enshrined in Iraqi national mythology as the first symbol of the new state's rejection of foreign rule. Britain finally managed to quell the uprising, but only at the enormous cost of the lives of perhaps as many as 10,000 Iraqi tribes-people, 450 British soldiers, and an expenditure of £40 million. The combination of a war-weary British public

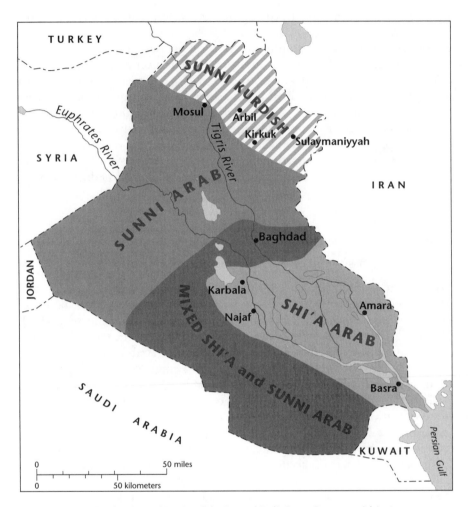

Map 11.1 Distribution of Major Ethnic and Religious Groups within Iraq

and an exhausted British treasury convinced London that such costs should not again be incurred.

The issue for British policymakers thus became how to guarantee British interests in the country—the security of imperial communications with India and the protection of the Iraqi and Iranian oil fields—without assuming the costly and onerous burden of directly governing the volatile population. The solution was to deal with Iraq on a treaty basis and to reduce expenses by placing as much responsibility in the hands of the Iraqi government as an imperial power could bear to do. With this general policy in mind, the

British set out to identify a ruler with whom they could work and who was likely to be acceptable to a broad cross-section of the Iraqi population.

Their choice was Amir Faysal, the field commander of the Arab Revolt, the son of Sharif Husayn, and the monarch of the recently dismembered Syrian kingdom. In selecting Faysal, the British may have been guided in part by a sense of guilt over their abandonment of Husayn and his family after the war. However, they also believed that Faysal would be moderate and that his reputation as an Arab figure of international stature would prove attractive within Iraq. Faysal was brought to the country in 1921, confirmed as king in a carefully managed national referendum, and coronated in ceremonies held in Baghdad—during which a military band played "God Save the King," there being as yet no Iraqi national anthem. Nor were there systems of government, education, military command, or any of the institutions by which a nation is defined and administered. Faysal faced a daunting challenge in guiding the dissident amalgam of peoples, who were Iraqis in name only, to statehood.

The form of government was embodied in the Organic Law of 1925 in which Iraq was defined as a hereditary constitutional monarchy with an elected bicameral legislature. According to the Organic Law, Islam was the state religion, and the *shariᶜah* courts, for both Sunni and Shiᶜa, retained jurisdiction over personal status and *waqfs*. Other basic national institutions were quickly brought into existence. The Iraqi army, which was to be both a national symbol and an essential instrument of state authority, was founded in 1921. Originally limited by the British to 7,500 men, the army was expanded after independence in 1932 and came to number slightly over 26,000 men by the late 1930s. Another of Iraq's pressing needs, both to assist in developing a sense of national identity as well as to train government officials, was the establishment of a public school system. Iraq had a much less developed educational infrastructure under the Ottomans than did Syria; in 1920 the entire secondary student population numbered less than 200. To correct this situation, Faysal arranged for Sati al-Husri, the former Ottoman official, to become director general of education in 1921. Under al-Husri's energetic direction, a secular state school system was quickly set up, and by 1930 primary enrollment had doubled and the number of secondary students had increased to nearly 2,000. Al-Husri also made sure that the curriculum promoted the development of patriotism and national culture.

Following the coronation of King Faysal, Britain had to be careful not to compromise him by making him appear to be a British puppet. His regime needed the continued support of the British army and air force to maintain any semblance of central control, but it also needed to distance itself from the British embrace and to forge ties to the local population. Britain recognized the delicacy of Faysal's position and revised the terms of the mandate so as to allow Iraq an increased degree of autonomy in the administration of its internal affairs. This was done through a series of treaties, the first signed in 1922 and the last in 1930. By the terms of the 1930 treaty, Iraq was to gain full independence within two years, whereas Britain was to retain military and security privileges similar to those that prevailed in Egypt. Thus, Britain was bound to come to Iraq's aid in case of war, and Iraq was bound to grant Britain full use of all communications facilities required for its defense. The treaty also allowed Britain to control the development of the Iraqi armed forces by requiring that any Iraqi military personnel trained abroad had to be trained in Britain, that all foreign military instructors in Iraq be British, and that all the arms for the Iraqi military be supplied exclusively by Britain. To make doubly sure of imperial concerns, Britain was also granted the right to maintain two air bases in the country. In 1932 Iraq duly received formal independence and was admitted to the League of Nations. The least likely, and one of the least prepared, of the Ottoman successor states was the first to achieve international recognition of its sovereignty.

One additional element influencing Britain's attitude toward Iraq was the existence of an important new factor in international relations: the contest for control of oil resources. Europe's scramble for colonies in the late nineteenth century became a scramble for oil concessions in the 1920s. This produced a contradiction in British policy; at the same time Britain was encouraging the appearance of Iraqi independence, it was also trying to wrest a favorable oil concession from Faysal's government. The Iraqis, in desperate need of the funds that would come from royalty payments, reluctantly conceded to British pressures and in 1925 signed a seventy-five-year concession with the firm that became the Iraq Petroleum Company. The agreement provided for Iraq to receive modest royalties at a specified sum per ton of oil but excluded Iraq from having any ownership in the company. Although the rich oil fields of northern Iraq were not brought into full production until after World War II, their existence, and Britain's control of them, were a constant irritant in Anglo-Iraqi relations.

Independent Iraq, 1932–1939

The unstable polity that Britain had created out of three disparate Ottoman provinces somehow survived its first decade of independent nationhood. However, Iraq's difficulties showed the results of grafting European institutions of government onto an ethnically and religiously fragmented society and of then importing a ruler who was expected to make the imposed system work. When Faysal assumed the Iraqi throne in 1921, he had only the most tenuous ties to his new country. He was foreign to the region, and his monarchy had been brought into existence by Britain, the alien occupier, not by popular demand. Faysal recognized the importance of identifying himself with Iraqi interests and was reasonably successful in doing so. By encouraging Britain to move rapidly toward granting independence, he demonstrated his loyalty to his adopted kingdom and convinced the majority of the population of his devotion to their welfare. Most historical accounts give Faysal credit for skillfully accommodating the almost impossible pressures placed upon him. However, his untimely death in 1933 deprived the country of his experienced leadership and virtually removed the monarchy as a factor in Iraqi politics. Faysal's twenty-one-year-old son and successor, Ghazi (1933–1939), was inept and uninterested in affairs of state.

In the absence of leadership from the palace, the government came to be dominated by a narrow clique of individuals without previous experience in civilian administration. They were an unlikely group of politicians, differing markedly from their counterparts in Egypt, Syria, and Palestine. Of the four men who among them held the premiership thirteen times from 1921 to 1941, all were native Iraqis born between 1880 and 1888, all had graduated from the war college in Istanbul, all had joined Faysal in the Arab Revolt before 1918, and all were from lower-class backgrounds. A fifth figure, Yasin al-Hashimi (1884–1937), who was twice prime minister and exercised a towering political influence in the 1930s, was also a graduate of Istanbul's war college. He differed from the other four in that he served in the Ottoman forces throughout World War I, rising to the rank of major general. The prestige derived from their Istanbul education, combined with the support they received from Faysal and the British, elevated this coterie of former Ottoman officers of humble origins to positions of authority from which they dominated Iraqi politics during their lifetimes. The most durable of them was Nuri al-Sacid (1888–1958), who was prime minister five times during the 1930s and was again holding that office when the monarchy was overthrown in 1958. The consolidation of power in the hands of this particular elite represented a significant sectarian trend in Iraqi politics. All of the individuals mentioned above, and most of the other figures who controlled Iraqi political life, were Sunni Muslims. Thus, even though the Shica constituted a majority of Iraq's Arab population, they were excluded from power during the country's formative years and have remained underrepresented in the political structure.

The former Ottoman officers began their Iraqi political careers as salaried civil servants and ended them as wealthy landed proprietors and industrial entrepreneurs; they came to regard themselves as equals to the established notable families, whose expectations of political power they had usurped. Whatever reforming ideals they may have possessed when they returned to Iraq after the war tended to vanish with their acquisition of power and influence. As one of the most astute scholars of modern Iraq has noted, instead of the ex-Ottoman officers subduing the old social order, it subdued them and gave them a stake in its perpetuation.[3]

With the loss of Faysal's mediating skills, Iraq's emergent political elite fell out with one another. Politics degenerated into a series of power struggles revolving around possession of the prime ministership, and govern-

The coronation of Amir Faysal as king of Iraq in 1921 was a very British affair. The prominence of the British role in the ceremony was capped when Faysal received the crown of Iraq to the strains of the British anthem "God Save the King." (The Middle East Centre, St. Antony's College, Oxford)

ments rarely lasted more than a few months. Because the former officers had become committed to the preservation of the existing social order, they were not so much divided by ideological differences as by a desire for personal influence. What distinctions there were among them involved their attitudes toward Iraq's relationship with Britain. Some, like Yasin al-Hashimi, were impatient to end the country's dependence on British arms and to become more active in promoting Arab unity. Others, most notably Nuri al-Saʿid, were more moderate, recognizing their debt to Britain and reluctant to undertake activities that might prompt British intervention and deprive them of their newfound positions.

The infighting among the politicians, the accommodating attitude of many of them toward Britain, and the tight monopoly they exercised over political power disaffected large segments of Iraqi society. Most prominent among the opposition were the younger military officers, who regarded themselves and their organization as the true symbols of the new Iraqi nation. Imbued with sentiments of nationalism and Pan-Arabism, the army leaders were eager to assert Iraq's role in the Middle East as an independent nation. In 1933 the army and its northern commander, General Bakr Sidqi, gained a dubious reputation for protecting the national interest by engaging in a systematic massacre of members of the Assyrian Christian community. General Sidqi, enamored of the fame he had gained in the Assyrian affair,

brought the army into Iraqi political life by leading a coup d'état that overthrew the government in 1936. This initiated a round of military coups—
there were six more of them through 1941—that made the army the arbiter
of Iraqi politics. Yet aside from adding to the already considerable instability
of political life, the coups changed very little. They were unusual in that the
military did not take over the government or abolish the parliamentary system. After each coup, one of the established civilian figures who had dominated Iraqi politics since 1921 emerged as the head of a new government.
These old-line politicians managed to cling to power by allying with one or
another of the many factions within the officer corps. In the process politics
was more than ever reduced to intrigue, and constructive legislation became
impossible.

The army, in its self-appointed role as the guardian of Iraqi nationalism,
imparted a glorification of martial qualities to society at large. As Britain
prepared for war with Adolf Hitler's Germany in 1939, a politically unstable
Iraq was gripped by a wave of Fascist-inspired paramilitary youth movements and increasing anti-British sentiment. Britain's empire by treaty
would be severely tested in the ensuing world conflict.

Iraq During World War II

The wartime experiences of Iraq illustrate the two poles of local reaction to
Britain's role in the country. One powerful segment of Iraq's ruling elite
sought to use the war as a means to chart a path toward true sovereignty,
whereas a second group of established politicians believed that their own
positions would be improved by retaining ties to Britain. The result of this
domestic conflict was an armed confrontation, the Anglo-Iraqi war of 1941,
which further divided the elite and left an enduring legacy of bitterness toward Britain.

At the outbreak of the European war in 1939, Iraqi political life was still
controlled by shifting coalitions of military officers and civilian politicians.
As a result of the military's grip on power, the civilian institutions of government, including the monarchy, were weakened. When King Ghazi was killed
in an automobile accident in 1939, his three-year-old son took the throne as
Faysal II. The infant king was placed under the regency of Abd al-Ilah, a
prince of the Hashimite family and a close political ally of Nuri al-Saʿid.
Nuri, still the most prominent of the civilian politicians, was heading his
fifth government when the war broke out. Despite the British setbacks in
the early stages of the conflict, Nuri continued to believe that Iraq's long-
term interests would be best served by cooperating with Britain and supporting the Allied cause. However, he found his pro-British stance unpopular with the military officers and resigned the premiership in 1940.

In that same year, a loose alliance of patriotic officers known as the Four
Colonels gained political ascendancy and attempted to free Iraqi foreign

policy from its British orientation. Motivated by sentiments of Iraqi nationalism and Pan-Arabism, and impressed by the success of German arms, the Four Colonels intended to take advantage of Britain's precarious military position to assert Iraq's full independence. They struck on April 1, 1941, staging a coup d'état that brought Rashid Ali al-Gaylani to the premiership. Rashid Ali (b. 1892) was a Baghdad-trained lawyer who had served as prime minister on three previous occasions. Although a committed nationalist, he also had a reputation for opportunism and was chosen to head the government mainly because of his willingness to cooperate with the dominant officers. Nevertheless, however much an instrument of the Four Colonels Rashid Ali may have been, his name became linked to the most concerted effort of any Arab state to achieve independence during the war years.

Within a month of Rashid Ali's installation as prime minister, Britain and Iraq entered into hostilities. The crisis was precipitated by two issues: The first was the apparently pro-Axis orientation of Rashid Ali's government; the second was a disagreement over the interpretation of the Anglo-Iraqi treaty of 1930—in short, over whether Iraq was a truly independent nation with the right to exercise its sovereignty by denying Britain the right to establish a supply base at the port of Basra. In the pressing circumstances of 1941, the British government was not interested in discussing the niceties of treaty language, especially with Rashid Ali's government, and went ahead with plans to expand the facilities at Basra. On May 2, 1941, the Four Colonels retaliated by ordering the Iraqi army to surround the British air base near Baghdad, an act that brought Britain and its former mandate to a state of war.

The British Middle Eastern command put together a relief force that marched from Palestine across the Transjordanian desert to Iraq. By the end of May 1941, the Rashid Ali revolt was defeated, and its leaders had fled Baghdad. Britain placed Iraq under military occupation for the remainder of the war, enforcing the Iraqis' belief that Britain was treating their country as an imperial possession, not as a sovereign state. Britain also moved quickly to reestablish the old pro-British ruling coalition. Nuri al-Saʿid and the regent set about consolidating their hold on the machinery of government. Nuri headed two wartime cabinets and made sure that his political opponents were crushed: He arranged for the extradition and execution of the revolt's leaders and forced Rashid Ali to remain in exile. Although Nuri and the regent, Abd al-Ilah, were to dominate Iraqi politics until 1958, both were tarnished by their return to power in the wake of the British invasion and were cast as opponents of nationalism. In this regard, their position was similar to that of the Wafd party of Egypt after the February Fourth Incident.

Although the Rashid Ali revolt was a minor episode in the overall scope of the Second World War, it was an important event in Iraqi history and revealed the measure of frustration and disillusionment felt in both civilian and military quarters over Britain's continuing interference in Iraqi affairs. The British reoccupation of the country from 1941 to 1945 heightened these sentiments and added luster to the image of Rashid Ali and the movement associated with his name. The young officers who succeeded in toppling Nuri and the regent in 1958 claimed that they were only carrying out the unfinished business of 1941.[4]

Transjordan: The Desert Mandate

Because of the circumstances surrounding the establishment of Transjordan, it is difficult to disagree with the statement that Transjordan was an artificial state created to accommodate the interests of a foreign power and an itinerant prince in search of a throne.[5] The foreign power, Britain, decided that it would be useful to set in place a dependent regime that might bring order to the tribal regions east of the Jordan River rather than attempting to do so itself; and the itinerant prince, Abdallah, obtained the throne that he believed had been stolen from him in Iraq by his younger brother, Faysal.

Like Iraq, Transjordan had no previous existence as a political community. During the late Ottoman period, it was a neglected portion of the province of Syria, a desert region inhabited by Bedouin tribes over whom the Ottomans exercised little, if any, control. When Amman became the capital of this new British mandate in 1921, it was scarcely more than a large village with a population of between 2,500 and 5,000. It was in this underdeveloped and previously marginal territory that Amir Abdallah and his British advisers attempted to create a state.

Britain's principal interest in Transjordan was to use it to preserve the Anglo-French postwar settlement in the Middle East. The mandate's free-wheeling tribes were indifferent to international borders and were accustomed to conducting raids into the territory that now formed part of the French mandate for Syria. It was to prevent such raids as well as to bring order to the region that Abdallah was given his throne and provided with a British subsidy and the support of British civilian and military personnel.

At the time of its creation in 1921, Transjordan's long-term status was uncertain. By 1928, however, regional circumstances convinced Britain that the mandate served a useful purpose, and in that year an Anglo-Transjordanian agreement was signed to clarify the mutual rights of Abdallah and his Great Power patron. As was the case in Egypt and Iraq, British rule was indirect, but British interests were protected; the agreement reserved to the British resident the final word in such matters as foreign relations, the armed forces, the budget, and all other essential government activities. A constitution was also proclaimed in 1928, but it cannot be said to have played a very significant role in the evolution of Transjordan's political life. It provided for a small legislative council but made the council so completely subordinate to royal authority that Abdallah could easily control its members and rule more in the manner of a traditional monarch than a constitutional one.

Because Transjordan was created for the purpose of bringing stability to a decentralized tribal region, the British placed special emphasis on building a reliable armed force. The Arab Legion policed the frontiers of the mandate, and internal security was made the responsibility of a special desert patrol formed in 1930 and led by Captain John Glubb. Deploying armored cars, airplanes, and other modern weapons, the desert patrol wing of the Arab Legion was successful in subduing the tribes and halting raids. Although commanded by British officers, the troops of the Arab Legion were recruited from among the local population, especially the Bedouin tribes. Glubb molded them into a well-disciplined fighting force whose intense loyalty to the monarch made them a reliable instrument of Abdallah's rule.

With Transjordan's basically tribal composition, the development of a civilian bureaucracy depended on bringing in trained administrators from outside the mandate. The central positions in the new administration were staffed mainly by British and Palestinian officials, to whom were added a smattering of Hijazis and Syrians. Having no local family or regional power bases, these officials were not likely to engage in oppositional political activities. Indeed, throughout the interwar period, there was little in the way of political life; national parties were not formed, and Abdallah was content to build tribal alliances through the use of bribes or, if that failed, to eliminate tribal opposition by means of the Arab Legion.

The chief regional impact of Transjordan during the mandate era was caused by Abdallah's restless search to expand his influence. The amir's ambitions exceeded the boundaries of his desert mandate, and he constantly schemed to obtain more territory, offering himself on various occasions as a candidate for the thrones of Syria and Iraq. He also tried to carve out a role as a mediator in Palestine, but his willingness to work with Zionist leaders made him suspect in Arab eyes. Abdallah's well-known personal ambitions, his close ties to Britain, and his family's control of the throne of Iraq caused most other Arab leaders to keep him at arm's length.

However much Abdallah may have chafed at his limited regional role and his dependence on Britain, he was shrewd enough to recognize that Britain had provided him with a territory and the means by which to make it a state. When World War II broke out, he did not hesitate to declare his allegiance to Britain. In the troubled early years of that conflict, he and his efficient army rendered invaluable service to the British cause in the Middle East.

During the Rashid Ali crisis in Iraq, Abdallah placed his well-organized Arab Legion at Britain's disposal. It played a useful role in guiding the relief force across the desert and in conducting raids in northern Iraq. Although Abdallah's deployment of his army in a British campaign against another Arab state added to his already clouded reputation in Arab nationalist circles, he hoped that his unequivocal support of Britain would be rewarded once the war was over. He was not disappointed. In 1946 Transjordan was granted independence, and Abdallah was elevated from prince to king. The awkward desert principality that had been created almost as an afterthought of the post–World War I settlement became, in the years following World War II, a prominent military and diplomatic force in the region.

Conclusion

Elizabeth Monroe used the phrase "Britain's moment in the Middle East" to describe the interwar period of British dominance in the region.[6] Yet even as Britain exercised control over mandates, protectorates, and quasi-independent states, the foundations for British expulsion were being laid. Iraqis and Egyptians chafed at the restrictions that made their countries' "independence" less than complete, and many among them expressed growing disenchantment with local politicians who benefited from British rule and therefore failed to oppose it. The Rashid Ali movement in Iraq, led by young military officers, was a manifestation of discontent with British rule and with the British-backed civilian politicians who monopolized power. Britain managed to restore a friendly regime in Baghdad, to bring one to power in Cairo in 1942, and to emerge from World War II with its Middle Eastern base intact. But the war weakened Britain and emboldened those under British imperial control to challenge its authority. Although it may not have been obvious in 1945, Britain's moment in the Middle East was coming to a close.

Notes

1. Cited in Elizabeth Monroe, *Britain's Moment in the Middle East, 1914–1971*, 2nd ed. (London, 1981), p. 118.

2. P. J. Vatikiotis, *The History of Modern Egypt: From Muhammad Ali to Mubarak*, 4th ed. (Baltimore, 1991), chapter 14.

3. Hanna Batatu, *The Old Social Classes and the Revolutionary Movements of Iraq* (Princeton, 1978), p. 322.

4. Phebe Marr, *The Modern History of Iraq* (Boulder, 1985), p. 86.

5. See Naseer H. Aruri, *Jordan: A Study in Political Development (1921–1965)* (The Hague, 1972), p. 3.

6. Monroe, *Britain's Moment in the Middle East.*

The Arab Struggle   12
for Independence:
Syria, Lebanon,
and Saudi Arabia from
the Interwar Era to 1945

The British ensured their Middle Eastern position during the interwar years by means of indirect rule; the French employed a different policy. From the moment General Gouraud's forces drove Faysal from Damascus in 1920, French control of Syria and Lebanon was supported by the presence of a large military contingent and a complex hierarchy of French civilian administrators. France's policy of direct rule placed decisionmaking authority in the hands of the high commissioner and provided little scope for local politicians to practice self-government. The result in Syria was that neither the political leaders nor the population at large gained a stake in the preservation of the French-imposed parliamentary system. The system was without local legitimacy and did not long survive the withdrawal of the French in 1946. The situation was slightly different in Lebanon, where the local leadership contributed to the development of a unique confessional political system and acquired an interest in making the system function.

In contrast to the British and French mandates, the new state of Saudi Arabia managed to achieve full independence during the interwar era. Like Turkey, the Saudi state was shaped in the image of its dominant ruler, Ibn Saʿud. However, whereas Atatürk imposed a relentless secularism on interwar Turkey, Ibn Saʿud founded his new state on the doctrines of Wahhabi Islam.

Arab proposals to develop new bonds of communal loyalties during the interwar years were diverse, ranging from an emphasis on regional identities to pleas for Arab and Islamic unity. As was the case before World War I, no single organizing principle predominated. The notion of Arab unity had great appeal, but the frontiers that Britain and France had drawn on the map of the Arab Middle East proved to be more enduring than many Arab leaders would have wished.

The French Mandate in Syria and Lebanon

The Policy of Divide and Rule in Syria

The French claim to Syria was based on a combination of religious, economic, and strategic interests. As the self-proclaimed protector of the Christian communities in the Levant—and especially of the Catholic Maronites of Mount Lebanon—France professed a moral duty to continue its long-standing religious and educational activities in the region. Such a religious justification for imperial intervention only served to intensify the alienation the Muslim majority felt toward France.

The economic rationale for a French presence in the Levant stemmed from the extensive investments in railways, port facilities, and commercial exchanges that French enterprises had undertaken during the last Ottoman decades. The strategic needs to counterbalance British influence in the Middle East were intertwined with the beliefs held in influential French imperial circles that France would never be a true Mediterranean power until it acquired a Levant possession to go with its North African empire. As we have seen, France backed these claims with a military expedition that ousted Faysal's Arab government from Damascus and replaced it with a mandate sanctioned by the League of Nations.

Instead of encouraging the formation of indigenous administrative institutions to prepare Syria for independence, the French created conditions that would prolong their rule. They did so by adopting a policy of divide and rule that emphasized and encouraged the existing religious, ethnic, and regional differences within Syria. Thus, rather than promoting national unity, France promoted regional and ethnic fragmentation.

The first political division France imposed was the creation of Greater Lebanon in 1920. To the old *mutasarrifiyyah* of Mount Lebanon, France added the coastal cities of Tripoli, Tyre, Sidon, and Beirut; in addition, France removed the fertile Biqa Valley from Syrian jurisdiction and placed it within the frontiers of the expanded Lebanese state (see Map 12.1). The main beneficiaries of this territorial reallocation were France's clients, the Maronite Christians, who remained the single largest religious community within the new Lebanon. French policy increased the possibilities of sectarian conflict. With the exception of Beirut, the areas added to Lebanon contained a predominantly Muslim population whose members objected to being placed within a Christian-dominated polity. The manner in which the evolution of Lebanese political life was affected by the competition between conflicting sectarian interests is discussed later in this chapter.

Within the area of the Syrian mandate proper, France carved out a series of separate political units the existence of which was designed to hinder the development of Syrian national identity (see Map 12.2). Thus, in 1920 Damascus and Aleppo were divided into two separate states, each with its own governor and its own set of French advisers. In a further effort at polit-

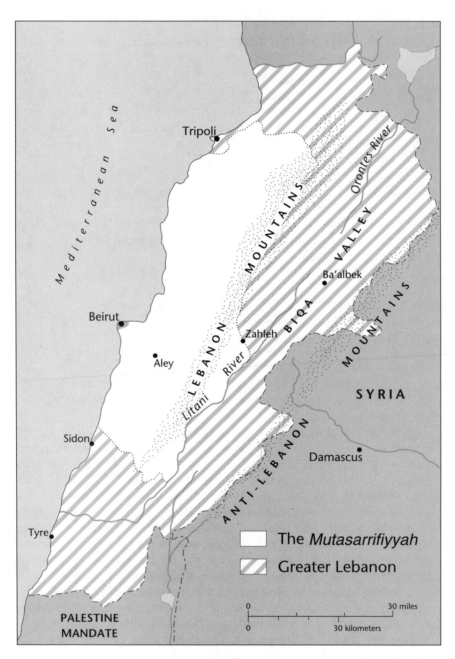

Map 12.1 The creation of Greater Lebanon under the French Mandate in the 1920s

A street scene in Damascus, October 2, 1918, the day after units of the Arab and Allied forces entered the city. Less than two years later, the French took Damascus and imposed twenty-five years of mandate authority on its inhabitants. (Crown copyright, Imperial War Museum)

ical fragmentation, France stressed the distinctiveness of Syria's two regionally compact minority groups, the Alawites (adherents of a form of Twelver Shiʿism) and the Druze, by providing each of them with a separate state in 1922. The Alawite state was situated around the northern coastal city of Latakia; that of the Jabal Druze was located in an area of Druze concentration south of Damascus. Except for a brief period from 1936 to 1939, both of these states were administratively separate from Syria until 1942. In 1924 France introduced a new political arrangement by combining the states of Damascus and Aleppo into a single unit called the State of Syria. In addition to Damascus and Aleppo, the reconstituted State of Syria comprised the cities of Homs and Hama, the next two largest urban centers in the mandate. Social and political life in these four cities was dominated by Sunni Muslim merchants and landowners. In effect, France had isolated the Druze and the Alawites from national politics and had ensured that whatever Syrian political life might exist would be dominated by a propertied and conservative class of urban Sunni Muslims. The destructive political instability that came to characterize Syria after independence in 1946 must be traced,

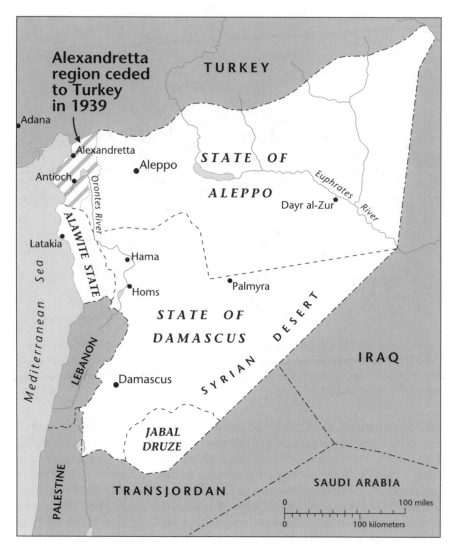

Map 12.2 The Division of Syria under the French Mandate, 1920–1923

in part, to the institutionalized fragmentation practiced by the French mandate authorities.

French policies in Syria were implemented through a large, costly, and often cumbersome bureaucracy supported by an all-pervasive intelligence service and a standing garrison of 15,000 troops of the Armée du Levant. Holding supreme decisionmaking authority at the apex of the administrative structure was the high commissioner for Syria and Lebanon, whose headquarters were in Beirut. The frequent shifts and turns that marked the early years of the French mandate were caused by the rapid turnover in the powerful office of high commissioner—the position was held by four different individuals between 1923 and 1926.

The French method of governing Syria discouraged the acquisition of political responsibility and administrative experience by the local population. Procedures for electoral politics were slow to be introduced, and the top bureaucratic positions in the high commissioner's office were reserved for French staff. Moreover, although there were local Syrian governors and district commissioners, they were not granted independent decisionmaking authority. Hovering beside every Syrian official was a French adviser who had veto power over even the smallest details. There appears to have been more attention devoted to the formation of an indigenous Syrian officer corps than to the bureaucracy. In 1920, the first year of the mandate, a military academy was founded. Employing French instructors, the academy produced a cadre of Syrian officers who were attached to the newly formed Syrian Legion, a locally recruited force that came to number around 6,000 by the mid-1930s. The social composition of the legion's officer corps was to have long-term implications for Syrian politics. Because the Sunni urban notable families tended to regard a military career with disdain, they refrained from enrolling their sons in the academy. This opened the way for other social and religious groups, for whom a career in the armed forces provided an avenue for upward mobility, to dominate the officer corps. With independence in 1946, these officers from minority religious groups brought the army into political life and changed the pattern of Sunni dominance (see Chapter 18).

The imposition of French authority met with local resistance in various regions of Syria during the first two years of the mandate. However, the French army was able to isolate these uprisings and subdue them before they spread to other areas of the country. This was not the case with the great revolt of 1925–1927. Beginning as a localized rebellion, the revolt soon engulfed most of Syria and became a symbol—one of the few—of the common Syrian objection to the mandate and all that it represented.

The revolt originated in July 1925 in the State of Jabal Druze when the French governor attempted to implement a rapid restructuring of Druze political relationships and landholding patterns. Led by the Druze chieftain, Sultan Atrash, the armed uprising succeeded in driving French forces from the Jabal Druze. The enthusiasm with which the news of Atrash's military victories was received in the urban centers of Syria prompted the normally cautious urban notables to cast their lot with the rebels. By autumn 1925, Homs and Damascus were in full revolt as the political leaders of the cities joined with the Druze chieftains of the rural south to create a nationwide resistance movement. The French military commanders, frustrated by their inability to contain the uprising, resorted to an ill-conceived display of imperial force; beginning on the evening of October 18, 1925, they subjected the venerable city of Damascus to an air and artillery bombardment that lasted for forty-eight hours and may have killed as many as 1,400 people. Despite such measures, the revolt raged on until spring 1927, when massive French military reinforcements managed to quell it. In human and economic terms, the revolt left a devastating legacy: Some 6,000 Syrians died, many thousands more were left homeless, and parts of the commercial center of Damascus were reduced to rubble. France also paid a high price in lives and money; the revolt convinced French policymakers to revise, but not to renounce, their plans for controlling Syria.

The Nature of Syrian Politics from the End of the Revolt to 1939

In the aftermath of the great revolt, prominent Syrian leaders formed a new political organization, the National Bloc, that became the focal point of Syrian political life for the remainder of the mandate. An examination of the social backgrounds of the founding members of the National Bloc shows a strong element of continuity in the possession of local political power between the Ottoman and mandate periods. The leaders of the National Bloc were from the same families, and in many cases were the same individuals, who had exercised authority during the Ottoman era. They were representative of the class of landowning urban notables and local government officials who had managed to flourish under the Ottomans, as they were to do under the French, by practicing the style of political behavior known as the politics of the notables. This political style, called "honorable cooperation" by the National Bloc leaders, required the notables to maintain influence over their local client base. To do this, they had to adopt the anti-French sentiments that had become increasingly widespread among the Syrian urban population. At the same time, the notables had to persuade the French that they could control their clients and could convince them to accept compromise solutions to the question of Syrian independence. In short, they presented themselves to the French, much as they had to the Ottomans, as necessary intermediaries in the process of governing. Eager to avoid a repetition of the revolt of 1925–1927, the mandate administration was willing, within limitations, to work with the National Bloc.

The National Bloc leaders were nationalists in that they called for the independence and territorial integrity of Greater Syria. However, their nationalism was of a socially and politically conservative variety. They sought to preserve the existing patterns of social, economic, and political relationships from which their wealth and power derived. Thus, although they demanded French withdrawal, they also wished to retain their dominant local positions so that they could step in and replace the French when the time came. This required them to balance their anti-French proclamations with sufficient cooperation to avoid being exiled or thrown in jail. In their social goals and political behavior, they were not unlike the Egyptian Wafdists or the Nuri al-Saʿid wing of the new Iraqi elite.

The National Bloc leaders acquired very little experience in governing during the mandate. France's refusal to negotiate a treaty spelling out its future intentions in Syria and its reluctance to allow the development of institutions of local self-government created frustration and uncertainty within Syrian political circles. A duly elected Syrian constituent assembly drew up a constitution in 1929, but France rejected the document. A year later, France imposed its own constitution on Syria; it upheld France's role as the mandate authority and thus prevented Syria from adopting any measures that might impinge on French mandatory privileges. For the next six years, Syrian presidents and prime ministers held office, and Syrian legislatures met in annual sessions. But France's power to veto legislation made a charade out of Syrian political life and lent it an aura of unreality.

Hopes for an end to the stalemate in Franco-Syrian relations were raised with the victory of Léon Blum's Popular Front coalition in the French elections of 1936. The hopes seemed justified; by the end of the year, representatives of both countries had signed a draft treaty. The treaty was similar to the Anglo-Iraqi agreement of 1930; it provided for an alliance between France and Syria and granted France the right to defend Syrian sovereignty and to maintain air bases and military garrisons on Syrian soil. Syria was also to achieve the hallmark of independence, admission to the League of Nations.

Upon the ratification of the draft treaty by the Syrian parliament in 1936, the National Bloc prepared to assume power in a semiindependent country. But Syrian expectations of sovereignty were bitterly disappointed. Blum's leftist coalition unraveled in 1938, and the French chamber refused to ratify the Franco-Syrian treaty. Instead of achieving independence, Syria was once again placed under firm French control. In 1939 the high commissioner suspended the Syrian constitution, dissolved parliament, and reestablished the autonomy of the Alawite and Druze states. The French further offended Syrian opinion by ceding to Turkey the district of Alexandretta, a region Syrians regarded as an integral part of their nation (see Map 12.2).

After nearly twenty years of the mandate, Syria remained without independence, without institutions of self-government, and without territorial unity. Moreover, the leaders of its principal political organization, the National Bloc, found themselves discredited by the failure of their moderate approach to achieve any measure of success. The French legacy to Syria was almost a guarantee of political instability.

Lebanon Under the Mandate: The Establishment of Confessional Politics

Lebanon, in the words of one observer, was "born schizophrenic."[1] When General Gouraud proclaimed the creation of Greater Lebanon in 1920, his objective was to safeguard the Maronite community by making sure it would not be absorbed into a Syrian Muslim state. Greater Lebanon was brought into existence to provide the Maronites with a distinct political entity in which they were the single largest religious community. However, they did not compose a majority of the population. By adding several predominantly Muslim areas to the new state, the French reduced the Maronites to about 30 percent of the population. This ensured that the Maronites would be dependent on French backing if they were to retain their political dominance within the frontiers of the new state.

It also ensured the existence of a volatile political mix in which competition for power would be based on sectarian affiliations. The Maronites viewed Lebanon as their own special Christian homeland and assumed that political and economic preeminence was theirs by right. With the support of their French patrons, they envisaged the state developing as a Christian enclave with a Franco-Mediterranean cultural orientation. The face of Lebanon would point westward toward Europe, and its back would be turned to the Arab world. However, the Sunni Muslims, who became part of Lebanon by French decree, not of their own volition, had different expectations. They demanded unity with Syria and looked toward the wider Arab world for their source of cultural identity.

Lebanon's uncertain relationship with its Arab neighbors was not the only source of communal tension within the new state. The nature of the existing political culture and the geographical distribution of the various religious communities posed problems for the creation of a cohesive national system of government. In Lebanon, as elsewhere in the former Ottoman Arab provinces, the individuals' primary loyalty was to their religious communities. But in Lebanon, with the exception of the Maronites in Mount Lebanon and the Druze in the Shuf, the religious communities tended to be scattered throughout the country, creating a sectarian mosaic in which various religious groups lived side by side. Lebanon also had in common with adjacent Arab territories a political culture based on the relationships between groups of local notables and their clients. What imparted a special twist to the Lebanese situation was the religious diversity of the local notables. In Syria, for example, the local notable politicians possessed common economic and religious characteristics: They were mainly urban dwellers who adhered to Sunni Islam. But in Lebanon local notables were as likely to have a rural as an urban power base, and they were of mixed sectarian composition, ranging from Druze princes to Maronite merchants to Sunni landowners. These notables endeavored to further the interests of their clients, who were also their coreligionists, at the expense of other groups. If Greater Lebanon was to survive as a state, it would have to develop a political system within which all these competing interests could be accommodated.

Because Lebanon, with its pro-French Maronite community, was more receptive to the mandate than was Syria, it experienced a smoother passage toward internal autonomy. In 1926 a constitution was approved creating the Lebanese republic. The constitution provided for a single chamber of deputies that was elected on the basis of religious representation, a principle that had been accepted during the period of the *mutasarrifiyyah*. The precise formula for determining this representation was specified in the National Pact of 1943. The constitution also provided for a president who was elected by the chamber. The president was granted extensive authority, including the right to appoint the prime minister and the cabinet. The constitution did not imply Lebanese independence, nor was it accompanied by a bilateral treaty between France and Lebanon. The mandate was firmly in force, and France retained control of Lebanese foreign relations and military affairs. The high commissioner also had the right to dissolve parliament and suspend the constitution, privileges he exercised on two occasions (1932 to 1934, and again in 1939). In addition, the ever-present network of French advisers within each ministry further limited the freedom of the Lebanese to control their own domestic affairs. Despite these restrictions, Lebanon was at least provided with a constitutional framework within which electoral politics and some measure of self-government could be practiced.

The crucial political issue facing Lebanon during the 1930s was the need to reconcile the conflicting aspirations of the Christian and Muslim communities and persuade them to work together in the construction of a distinctly Lebanese polity. The attitudes held by two leading Maronite politicians, Emile Eddé and Bishara al-Khuri, on the issue of Muslim-Christian cooperation can serve to illustrate why Muslims were reluctant to accept the Lebanese state and to suggest the ways in which Muslim suspicions were overcome. Eddé was a Paris-trained lawyer with political experience dating from before World War I. During the mandate period, he held the premiership once and served as Lebanon's president from 1936 to 1941. A man of French taste and culture, Eddé was not displeased by the presence of the mandatory power on Lebanese soil. For him, Lebanon was above all else the Maronite Christian homeland, and he believed that the basic purpose of the state was to preserve Maronite dominance. Distrustful of Muslims and able to speak only imperfect Arabic, Eddé sought to link Lebanon's interests with those of France, not with the surrounding Arab states.

His bitter political rival, Bishara al-Khuri, was also a Paris-trained lawyer. Although he shared Eddé's belief in Lebanon's place as the Maronite homeland, al-Khuri was more sensitive to the needs of the Muslim community and much more insistent in demanding that the French terminate the mandate. Recognizing that the state could not survive without Muslim-Christian cooperation, al-Khuri sought to build alliances with the Muslims based on common opposition to the French presence. His political organization, known as the Constitutional Bloc, actively agitated for complete independence. He hoped that by forming a united front against France, Muslims and Christians would bridge the gulf that separated them and establish mutual interests within the framework of a separate Lebanon.

It is ironic that it was Eddé who was given the opportunity to take an important first step in bringing Muslims to the center of political power. In 1936, French and Lebanese representatives agreed on a treaty similar to the one that France and Syria had signed earlier in the year. The Franco-Lebanese treaty contained an annex that guaranteed "the fair representation of all the country's sects in the government and high administration."[2] Expecting independence to follow shortly, the Lebanese chamber of deputies met in early 1937 and elected Eddé as president. Eddé then proceeded to pick a Muslim, Khayr al-Din al-Ahdab, as his prime minister. This was a key moment in Lebanese political life. It established the principle that the president of the republic would be a Maronite and the prime minister a Sunni Muslim. This pattern of power sharing remained an integral part of the Lebanese political system until the late 1980s.

Al-Ahdab's appointment also served another important purpose. It prompted some Muslim leaders to realize that they could secure greater benefits by working within the system than by remaining outside it. With a Muslim as prime minister, Muslim notables gained easier access to the high commissioner's office, acquired more opportunities to dispense political patronage, and obtained increased support for their commercial ventures. Muslims' gradual reconciliation to the existence of Greater Lebanon was achieved through the evolution of a political system that recognized the sectarian diversity of the country. Confessional politics allowed all communities to obtain representation in the chamber, and by allocating the presidency and the premiership to a Maronite and a Sunni, respectively, it made sure that no single community would dominate all the others.

This is not to suggest that sectarian tensions suddenly vanished in the late 1930s. Maronites continued to regard Lebanon as a specifically Christian homeland and to stress Mediterranean over Pan-Arab ties; Muslims just as vigorously resisted these concepts and insisted that Lebanon was part of the wider Arab world. But despite ongoing communal conflict, the existence of Greater Lebanon was confirmed during the interwar years. The state survived under a distinctly Lebanese form of politics. The state did not, however, achieve the independence that was promised in the 1936 treaty with France. As happened in the case of Syria, the French chamber refused to ratify the treaty. At the onset of World War II, the high commissioner once again suspended the constitution and dissolved parliament. Lebanon's independence, like Syria's, had to await the fortunes of war.

Syria and Lebanon During World War II: The Troubled Path to Independence

The fall of France in 1940 and the establishment of the collaborationist Vichy regime under Marshal Philippe Pétain had repercussions for all of France's overseas territories. In Syria and Lebanon the administration was taken over by officials loyal to Pétain's government, thus bringing the two Levant states within the Axis sphere of influence and making them the center of a complex diplomatic struggle involving the Vichy regime, the British government, and the Free French movement led by General Charles de Gaulle. In the course of this struggle among external powers, the local population was subjected to economic deprivation, armed invasion, and political repression.

During the first two years of the war, domestic political activity came to a virtual standstill. The frustrations caused by the suspension of the constitutions of both countries were exacerbated by worsening economic conditions; the British blockade of the Vichy-controlled eastern Mediterranean made itself felt in a shortage of food supplies. Hunger marches took place in the major Syrian cities and were accompanied, in spring 1941, by demonstrations demanding the restoration of political life. These demonstrations quickly spread to the coastal cities of Lebanon and made the Levant a seething cauldron of political unrest aggravated by economic hardship.

In the meantime Rommel's advance into Egypt and Rashid Ali's revolt in Iraq highlighted the danger posed to Britain's position in the crucial Middle Eastern theater by the presence of the Vichy-commanded French army in the Levant. Determined to prevent Syria and Lebanon from becoming bases for German activity, Britain, immediately after crushing the Rashid Ali revolt, engaged in a joint invasion of the two countries with the Free French. By the end of July 1941, the operation had defeated the Vichy forces and placed the Free French in control. On the eve of the invasion, Britain and Free French leader de Gaulle had agreed on the future status of the two states: Syria and Lebanon were to be granted immediate and unconditional independence. When de Gaulle's representative arrived in Beirut, the inhabitants of Syria and Lebanon prepared, yet again, for independence.

And yet again they were to be disappointed. The Free French regime was no more willing to confer sovereignty on the two Levant states than its predecessors had been. De Gaulle's belief in the imperial grandeur of France and his distrust of British motives in the Middle East prompted him to restore the mandate administration and to ignore the proclamation of independence he had approved in summer 1941. This brought the Free French administration into conflict not only with the people of Syria and Lebanon but also with the British. The combination of popular unrest and British pressure finally compelled the French to restore the constitutions of both countries and to hold elections in 1943. The results were resounding victories for anti-French, pro-independence forces.

In Syria the old National Bloc was returned to power and Shukri al-Quwwatli was elected president. Al-Quwwatli (b. 1891) was from a prosperous merchant-landowning family of Damascus and was representative of the political notables who had dominated Syrian politics for several decades. He was a figure who straddled two eras: His postsecondary education in Istanbul stamped him as a member of the Ottoman order, whereas his participation in the Arab Revolt and his involvement in nationalist politics during the mandate marked him as an activist of the national period.

The Lebanese elections also brought established politicians to power; Bishara al-Khuri, a Maronite, became president and selected as prime minister his Sunni Muslim ally from the interwar years, Riyadh al-Sulh. Together, these two worked out a compromise solution to the problem of Lebanese sectarianism and regional identity. Their agreement, known as the National Pact of 1943, attempted to assuage the Christians' fears of being absorbed into a larger Arab-Islamic state by recognizing Lebanon as a distinct entity; at the same time, the pact sought to satisfy Muslims by proclaiming that Lebanon had an Arab identity and that it would exist as part of the Arab world. Through this compromise, the Christian community accepted Lebanon's Arabness, and the Muslims acknowledged the country as a separate state and implicitly renounced any plans to seek a merger with other Arab states. The National Pact—in combination with the constitutional agreements of the late 1920s and the practices established in the 1930s—served as the framework for Lebanon's regional posture and domestic political structure until its assumptions were undermined by the civil war of 1975.

In addition, the National Pact spelled out the formula for sectarian representation in the chamber of deputies. The formula was based on the census of 1932, a document nearly as important in Lebanese political life as the constitution itself. No further official census was taken, and political representation was frozen at the 1932 figures, despite the profound demographic changes that later occurred. The census determined that all Christians outnumbered all Muslims (including the Druze) by a ratio of six to five. Political power was then allocated according to this ratio. Thus, for every six Christian deputies in the chamber, there were five Muslim ones. Sectarian criteria were also used to determine the composition of the cabinet; Maronites and Sunni Muslims were guaranteed two and sometimes three positions, and the other religions one position each. In this way, confessional politics became enshrined as the basis of the Lebanese system. From the very beginning, the Shiᶜa, with some 20 percent of the population, were underrepresented in the power-sharing structure, and they became even more so as their numbers increased faster than the other communities.

Even though the elections of 1943 constituted a popular renunciation of any continued French interference in the domestic affairs of Syria and Lebanon, the French authorities refused to transfer power to the new local governments. In taking this position, France inaugurated a round of confrontations that did not end until 1945. General de Gaulle simply could not accept the possibility of the termination of France's mission in the Levant, and his representatives applied continuous pressure on the governments of Syria and Lebanon to sign treaties that would guarantee the primacy of French interests in the two countries. As late as May 17, 1945, several days after the war in Europe had ended, France began to reinforce its garrisons in the Levant. If this act was intended to coerce Beirut and Damascus into concluding favorable treaties, it failed miserably. The specter of French troops disembarking on the Lebanese coast awakened memories of 1920 and was met with outbreaks of anti-French violence. The French forces retaliated in kind, most notably by subjecting Damascus to a lengthy air and artillery bombardment during which 400 inhabitants were killed. Active intervention by Britain brought about an armistice, and France agreed to drop its treaty demands and withdraw its forces. Syria was evacuated in spring 1946, and in December of that year the last of the French troops finally left Lebanon.

Syria and Lebanon, formally recognized as independent in 1941, had been forced to wrest their sovereignty from a reluctant France. De Gaulle's efforts to prolong the mandate structure made the two states more determined than ever to assert their independence. Although both countries entered the postwar era with members of the old elite in power—al-Khuri and al-Sulh in Lebanon, al-Quwwatli in Syria—France's manipulation of domestic politics since the establishment of the mandates had denied these individuals the opportunity to acquire experience in the practice of self-government and had not prepared them to deal with the challenges that lay ahead.

New Kingdom in Arabia:
The Rise of the Saudi State

Beginning in the late eighteenth century and continuing through the interwar years, Great Britain was the dominant European power along the shores of the Arabian Peninsula. As we have seen, Britain sought to protect its imperial communications by entering into a series of treaties with the ruling shaykhs of Kuwait, Bahrain, Qatar, and Oman and by bringing the strategic southern tip of the peninsula under direct British control as the Aden Protectorate. Britain cared little about the interior so long as its shifting tribal confederations did not threaten the stability of the rulers along the coast.

At the conclusion of World War I, the British system of empire by treaty appeared to be fulfilling its goals in Arabia. Britain's most important ally, Sharif Husayn, emerged from the war as king of the Hijaz, a much lesser status than he thought he had been promised but one he was forced to accept. However, Husayn's shortcomings as a ruler soon made him unpopular among the inhabitants of the Hijaz. Moreover, as the unwelcome mandate system replaced Ottoman rule in the Arab territories, Husayn came to be viewed as a traitor whose rebellion against the sultan-caliph had weakened the Ottoman Empire and contributed to its defeat and to the occupation of its Arab provinces by Britain and France. Husayn's reputation suffered further when, a few days after Turkey's abolition of the caliphate in 1924, he claimed the title for himself. This unilateral act was denounced by Muslims throughout the world, whose leaders proclaimed Husayn unworthy of the most exalted position in Islam. Britain became increasingly disillusioned with Husayn, regarding him as more of a troublesome liability than a useful ally. When his Hijazi kingdom was threatened by a powerful force from the Arabian interior, Britain limited its assistance to escorting Husayn into exile.

The origins of the new Arabian political order are to be found in the revival of the Wahhabi movement under the vigorous leadership of a remarkable warrior-statesman, Abd al-Aziz ibn Saᶜud (1881–1953). The eighteenth-century alliance between Abd al-Wahhab's puritanical reformist doctrine and the military prowess of the house of Saᶜud was discussed in Chapter 7. Although the movement was dispersed by Muhammad Ali, it was not eliminated. The political revival of Wahhabism began in 1902 when Ibn Saᶜud seized the city of Riyadh, the stronghold of his principal rivals in the province of Najd. Ibn Saᶜud's capture of Riyadh launched the twenty-year epic that brought this minor tribal chieftain to international stature as the ruler of a kingdom that bore his name.

During the period from 1902 to the end of World War I, Ibn Saᶜud brought most of the tribes of Najd under his authority. His success stemmed from his ability to combine his secular position as victorious tribal leader with his religious status as head of the Wahhabi order. First, as tradition demanded, the tribes were loyal to him in his capacity as a victorious commander. However, the history of Arabia had shown that this form of loyalty could be quickly withdrawn with any reversal in the military fortunes of the tribal leader. Ibn Saᶜud's formula was to provide another, higher level of commitment in the form of the puritanical Wahhabi doctrine. He achieved this by forcing the tribes to settle in small agricultural oasis communities within which he undertook the twin tasks of religious indoctrination and alliance building. He built mosques for the communities, he sent ulama into them to disseminate the Wahhabi doctrine, and he compelled the tribal shaykhs to attend a Wahhabi religious institute in Riyadh. At the same time, Ibn Saᶜud provided the communities with material assistance in the form of agricultural supplies and arms. In return, the men of the settlements were expected to be at Ibn Saᶜud's call for military operations whenever he needed them. By persuading the tribes to adopt the practices and outlook of Wahhabism, Ibn Saᶜud provided them with a sense of communal loyalty that was more all-encompassing than the customary tribal alliances. The Ikhwan (Brethren) became imbued with a sense of mission, a desire to extend the Wahhabi doctrine and way of life to other areas of the peninsula. Their commitment to Ibn Saᶜud's success was intimately bound to their commitment to the expansion of Wahhabism.

The postwar settlement, in particular Britain's installation of Husayn's sons on the thrones of Iraq and Transjordan, aroused Ibn Saᶜud's suspicions that he was being hemmed in by a Hashimite federation. In 1924 he led his Ikhwan warriors into the Hijaz, seizing Mecca and Medina and driving

Sharif Husayn into exile. Arabia had a new ruler, the head of the house of Saᶜud and the head of the Wahhabi religious order; it has remained under the direction of those forces to the present day.

Britain, quickly responding to the new realities of Arabian politics, negotiated an agreement with Ibn Saᶜud in 1927. Known as the Treaty of Jiddah, it recognized Ibn Saᶜud as the sovereign king of the Hijaz and sultan of Najd and its dependencies; he, in turn, acknowledged Britain's special relationships with the coastal rulers and pledged to respect their domains. In 1932 the name of the state was officially changed to the Kingdom of Saudi Arabia. By that time, it had received international recognition from the community of nations.

For the remainder of the interwar period, Ibn Saᶜud concentrated on consolidating his rule and establishing the instruments of central authority. His success in doing so has prompted one scholar to place him "among the modern world's greatest nation-builders."[3] With consummate skill, the king utilized force, negotiation, marriage alliances, religious values, and the powerful appeal of his personal example to forge a territorial state out of warring tribal factions. He was a tall and imposing figure, a warrior-king out of an earlier, more heroic era. As astute as he was brave, he proved to be a fair and judicious ruler whose piety, dignity, and accessibility won him the allegiance of his subjects. He was a masterful tribal politician, ruling less as an absolute monarch than as a first among equals. Respectful of existing customs, he consulted regularly with the tribal shaykhs, preferring to resolve disputes through persuasion rather than coercion.

A rudimentary governmental apparatus was formed in Riyadh, and such instruments of central control as the radio, mechanized transportation, and aircraft were introduced. The administration was staffed by bureaucrats from other Arab countries and members of the Saᶜudi family. The king's own marriage alliances alone produced forty-one sons and enabled him to make the royal family a true ruling house whose members viewed their welfare and that of the kingdom as identical. During these formative years, there were few luxuries for the monarch and his offspring. Today's image of Saudi Arabia as a nation awash in oil wealth does not apply to the interwar era. Ibn Saᶜud ruled over an impoverished kingdom whose main source of revenue was derived from the annual pilgrimage to Mecca. Sustained oil exploration began only in 1933 when the government signed a concession agreement with Standard Oil of California, the future Arabian American Oil Company (ARAMCO). Oil was not discovered until 1938, and the outbreak of World War II delayed the development of the Saudi petroleum industry until the late 1940s.

During World War II, Saudi Arabia remained officially neutral until March 1945, when Riyadh declared war on Germany. However, as early as 1940, Ibn Saᶜud announced his support for Britain, and his kingdom cooperated with the Allied countries in a variety of ways. Such cooperation was due, in part, to Arabia's dependence on the Allies. The war years were terribly difficult for Saudi Arabia, as the number of persons making the annual pilgrimage to Mecca declined precipitously, causing revenues to plunge. Britain provided direct subsidies to keep the country afloat, and the United States provided indirect ones. Indeed, the hardships of the war may have led to the prosperity of the decades that followed. The U.S. government became concerned over the depletion of U.S.-based oil supplies during the war and renewed its efforts to expand the scope of its oil operations in Saudi Arabia.

In the years following World War II, Ibn Sa'ud's status differed from that of other Arab rulers and conferred on him a legitimacy they did not possess. He had won his kingdom through his own efforts and was not tainted, as were his Hashimite rivals, by association with European support. Nor could he be accused of allowing an imported European secular constitution to be imposed on his domains. His rule was founded on the indigenous traditions of Wahhabi Islam and tribal politics. Although the administrative structure of the kingdom emerged from decrees Ibn Sa'ud issued on a variety of subjects, the Saudi legal system was based on the *shari'ah*. Saudi Arabia's reputation as an exemplary Islamic state was enhanced by the attention the king devoted to the upkeep of the holy cities and the care he took to facilitate the annual pilgrimage to Mecca. Each of the king's attributes worked together to enable him to fashion a unitary state in Arabia. That state remained tribal, conservative, and inward-looking, but its very existence was an achievement, and its durability is a tribute to the foundations laid by Ibn Sa'ud.

The Search for Identity: Regionalism, Arabism, Islam

The interwar situation in the Middle East required a refashioning of the political and communal loyalties of the Arabs. Ottomanism had been defeated and the institutions of Islam—including the unifying symbol of the caliphate—were under attack by Atatürk's relentless secularism. But what was to replace these established pillars of communal identity? What elements of the Arab heritage could best be used as symbols around which to rally popular resistance to the European occupation and to construct a positive image of Arab identity? During the interwar period, three broad responses to these questions—regionalism, Pan-Arab unity, and Islamic solidarity—dominated political and intellectual discourse.

The regionalists frequently sought to construct a local nationalist mythology by showing the links that a specific region had to its ancient pre-Islamic past. We have already seen the example of pharaonism, which found certain Egyptian authors arguing for the existence of a distinct Egyptian identity based on the heritage of the Nile Valley. In Syria a similar current of regional nationalism appeared in the writings of Antun Sa'adah (1904–1949), a

Lebanese Christian who founded the Syrian Social Nationalist Party (SSNP) in Beirut in 1932. Saʿadah deplored the divisions the French had imposed on Greater Syria and called for the reunification of the country. At the same time, however, he insisted that Syria was a distinct nation in itself with a rich history dating back to the ancient Phoenicians and it should therefore not become part of a unified Arab state. He was a Syrian regional nationalist, believing that Syrian history transcended Arab, Islamic, and Christian history and that Syria, as a separate national entity, was the product of unique geographical and historical features that had interacted in the region since ancient times.

Regionalism of a more pragmatic kind was evident in the policies adopted by the ruling elite of the mandate territories. Seeking to solidify their fragile hold on power, these ruling groups, whether Faysal and the ex–Ottoman officers in Iraq or the urban notables of Syria, believed that their primary task was to generate popular feelings of identification with and support for their fledgling regimes. In order to achieve this, they not only had to establish regional administrations, they also had to create new symbols of regional nationalism to reflect the changed realities. Thus, the introduction of flags, postage stamps, and national anthems emphasized the distinctiveness of each state and solidified the political divisions Britain and France had imposed on the Arab world.

Some thinkers condemned the regional nationalist programs of the politicians as self-serving and argued that the continued fragmentation of the Arabs would condemn them to perpetual weakness in the international order. In the opinion of these opponents of regionalism, what was needed was the unification of the separate Arab states into a single political entity. The most intellectually compelling spokesman of Arab unity was Sati al-Husri (1880–1968), a former Ottoman educator (see Chapter 8) who spent the interwar years in Baghdad overseeing the establishment of the Iraqi educational system. In numerous articles and speeches, and later in books with such titles as *Arabism First, On Arab Nationalism,* and *What Is Nationalism?* al-Husri argued that the Arabs constituted a nation and ought therefore to be united into a single state. For him, the fundamental criteria of nationhood were a shared language and a common history. Different peoples could therefore form a cultural nation even if they were politically divided. Of the two prerequisites for nationhood, the more significant was language, which al-Husri regarded as the critical spiritual bond among human beings. United culturally by the Arabic language and by shared memories of their glorious past, the Arabs possessed all the components of nationhood, even if the Arab nation was at the time divided into several political states. Using examples drawn from European history, al-Husri attempted to demonstrate the inevitability of cultural nationalism to create unified nation-states. What was needed in the present circumstances—and what al-Husri endeavored to provide—was an awareness of shared Arabism. Once this awareness was developed, Arabs would be inspired to seek political unification. Profoundly opposed to the regionalism of Taha Husayn and Antun Saʿadah, al-Husri ridiculed the notion of pharaonism, contending that Egypt was an integral part of the Arab nation and proposing that it act as the Prussia and Piedmont of Arabism.

Al-Husri's definition of Arab nationalism was noteworthy for its clarity and for its uncompromising secularism. Refusing to employ Islamic symbols in his call for unity, he argued that the Arabic language had existed before Islam and that all who spoke Arabic, whether they were Muslim or Christian, should have but one loyalty: to the Arab nation. Although al-Husri's doctrine of nationalism was widely endorsed and helped to keep alive the ideal of a unified Arab nation toward which all Arabs should strive, it has remained a largely unfulfilled vision.

A third major focus of Arab political and cultural identity during the interwar period was Islamic solidarity. Throughout most of the 1920s, the voices of Islamic activism were muted. This was the decade of the secular Wafdist triumph in Egypt, of Atatürk's reforms in Turkey, and of domestic uncertainty in the mandate states. Toward the end of the decade, however, popular disillusionment with the imported constitutional systems and with the politicians who manipulated them led to a search for more representative ideologies. At the same time, the full impact of Atatürk's secularist program had become alarmingly obvious, as had the determination of Britain and France to retain various forms of long-term control over their mandate territories. The Islamic order appeared to be in danger of extinction. In these circumstances, appeals for the defense of Islamic values against Europe and against the actions of local Europeanized politicians found a receptive audience. The success of the Muslim Brotherhood in Egypt and the satisfaction voiced over Ibn Saʿud's triumph in Arabia are evidence of this renewed current of Islamic awareness.

One intellectual dimension of interwar Islam was represented by the Salafiyyah reformist movement in Egypt. Its leading spokesman, Rashid Rida (1865–1935), was a disciple of Muhammad Abduh. In his journal *al-Manar* (The beacon), Rida continued Abduh's practice of seeking an accommodation between Islamic principles and practical innovation. But he became more protective of tradition than receptive to reform. Although *al-Manar* continued to be received throughout the Islamic community as an authoritative voice on issues of religion and society, the Salafiyyah movement as a whole lost touch with Abduh's efforts to reconcile Islam to modernism and adopted instead an outlook more akin to Wahhabism and to the conservatism of al-Azhar.

Rida's writings were theological and did not inspire popular emotions. That task was filled in the field of Islamic activism by Amir Shakib Arslan (1869–1946), the Lebanese Druze notable whose strong pro-Ottoman stance was examined in Chapter 8. Exiled from his homeland by the French mandate authorities, Arslan passed most of the interwar years in Geneva serving as the unofficial representative of Syria and Palestine at the League of Nations and writing a constant stream of articles for the periodical press of the Arab countries. Less a theologian than an activist in the tradition of Jamal al-Din al-Afghani, Arslan advocated a militant Islam charged with political and moral assertiveness. He sought to reconstruct the bonds of Islamic solidarity by reminding Muslims from Morocco to Iraq that despite their diversity, they were united by virtue of their common adherence to Islam; if they would but recognize this bond and act on it, they would achieve liberation from their current oppression and restoration of their splendid past. His Islamic-inspired antiimperial propaganda campaigns were a constant irritant to British and French officials and helped create an awareness among the inhabitants of the different regions of the Arab Islamic world of their common cause.

In addition to his belief in the value of Islamic solidarity as a bulwark against European imperialism, Arslan also defended Islam as an essential component of social morality. A staunch opponent of Atatürk, Arslan wrote that the callous disregard of cultural tradition would undermine the spiritualism that made Eastern civilization superior to the shallow materialism of the West. He deplored the neglect of *shariʿah*-inspired moral commandments and claimed that only by adhering to the true tenets of Islam would Muslims experience the regeneration necessary to recover their proper place in the world. Arslan's message, with its call to action and its defense of traditional values at a time of great uncertainty, was well received and attracted widespread attention during the 1920s and 1930s.

Conclusion

These three expressions of identity—regionalism, Pan-Arab nationalism, and Islamic solidarity—suggest the variety of alternatives that circulated through the Arab Middle East in the aftermath of the collapse of the Ottoman-Islamic order. In the end, neither Pan-Arab unity nor Islamic solidarity could subsume the regional nationalisms favored by the new political elite seeking to build their own bases of local power. Whether arriviste monarchs or insecure prime ministers, the members of this elite maintained their positions by walking a narrow tightrope between resistance and cooperation, knowing always that their failure to oppose the European presence exposed them to popular resentment and possible overthrow, and that their failure to cooperate with the all-powerful high commissioner made them susceptible to dismissal at his pleasure. With few exceptions, the regional political elite eschewed Pan-Arabism, endorsing it in principle only, in favor of constructing local alliances that might at least perpetuate their dominance in the event of the withdrawal of the high commissioner and his staff.

Notes

1. Michael C. Hudson, *The Precarious Republic: Political Modernization in Lebanon* (New York, 1968), p. 37.
2. Kamal S. Salibi, *The Modern History of Lebanon* (London, 1965), p. 182.
3. Michael C. Hudson, *Arab Politics: The Search for Legitimacy* (New Haven, 1977), p. 169.

The Palestine Mandate and the Birth of the State of Israel　13

The territory that composed the British mandate for Palestine was only slightly larger than the state of Massachusetts. Yet the repercussions of developments in and attitudes toward this small piece of southern Syria have reverberated throughout the Middle East and the world at large, shaping regional and Great Power relationships, influencing U.S. and European domestic politics, generating five wars, creating over 1 million refugees, and producing misunderstanding and bitterness among the various parties involved. Historians have offered numerous perspectives on why the mandate became the source of so much discord. To some, the failure to resolve the conflict between Jewish immigration and the preservation of Palestinian Arab rights rests with the indecisiveness and biases of the various British governments that held power during the twenty-eight years of the mandate (1920–1948). Others argue that the question is not one of failure but of triumph—the triumph of the Zionist immigrants and their supporters in overcoming Arab resistance, British opposition, and European anti-Semitism to forge the state of Israel against seemingly overwhelming odds. Another group of historians poses a different set of questions: Why did the solidly established indigenous Arab inhabitants, settled on the land and dominant in the urban administration of Palestine for centuries, and possessing a population majority of approximately eight to one in 1922, become a minority within the new Israeli state in 1948? Why did Zionism, not Arabism or Palestinian nationalism, win the day in Palestine? Did the Palestinian Arab leadership perform its tasks adequately, were its members prepared to cope with the multitude of international issues with which they were confronted, and were they credible representatives of the Palestinian Arab population at large?

The purpose here is to examine the interactions among the British, the Zionists, and the Palestinian Arabs in order to illustrate the main issues of the mandate era. We should keep in mind from the outset the unique premise on which the mandate for Palestine was founded: A small territory that had been inhabited by an Arab majority for some 1,200 years was

233

promised by a third party (Great Britain) as a national home to another people (the international Jewish community), the majority of whom lived in Eastern Europe. The oppressed conditions in which East European Jews lived prompted the Zionists among them to take up Britain's promise and to attempt to construct in Palestine a Jewish national home; at the same time, the established Arab community of Palestine opposed the notion of turning its homeland into a Jewish state and, to the extent that it was able to do so, resisted the process. The Zionist claims to the same territory inhabited by Palestinian Arabs lay at the root of the conflict over Palestine.

The Emergence of Political Zionism

Throughout the centuries since their dispersion from Palestine by the Roman conquest of the first century, the Jewish communities of Europe kept alive the idea of a return to the Holy Land. Palestine occupied so central a place in Jewish religious culture because of the belief that the establishment of the Kingdom of Israel after the Exodus represented the fulfillment of God's promise to the Jews that they were chosen to complete their destiny in Zion. Historical memories of the reigns of David and Solomon intermingled with aspects of religious belief and ritual to create a sustained vision of the ultimate redemption of the Jewish people through a return to the Holy Land. The dream of the return was also kept alive by more tangible needs. Discriminated against by governments and private individuals alike, European Jews were subject to restrictions forbidding them from entering certain professions, denying them access to universities, barring them from state employment, and confining them to specific areas of residence. In the face of oppression and prejudice, the visionary belief in an eventual return to Zion offered Jewry a measure of hope with which to endure the hard reality of the Diaspora. Yet although the sentiment of Zionism was deeply ingrained in Jewish religious life, it received little organizational expression until the late nineteenth century.

The forces that eventually gave rise to organized political Zionism were spawned by conditions in nineteenth-century Europe. During the era of liberal nationalism, the states of western Europe gradually adopted legislation to provide for the legal emancipation of the Jews. With emancipation came assimilation, as Jews moved into middle-class occupations and increasingly identified themselves as citizens rather than members of a distinctive religious community. Although many Jews, especially in Germany, where emancipation had made the most progress, looked upon assimilation as the process that would bring an end to anti-Semitism, others regretted the dilution of the bonds of communal identity and the decline of religious observance that resulted.

If developments in western Europe appeared to favor the integration of Jews into national life, the situation in eastern Europe was considerably different. In Russia and Poland, the main centers of Diaspora Jewry, active persecution of the Jewish communities intensified during the last decades of the nineteenth century. The reigns of Alexander III (1881–1894) and Nicholas II (1894–1917) were marked by a series of pogroms tacitly encouraged by the government. Faced with continuing oppression and harassment, millions of east European Jews sought a new life by immigrating to the United States. For others, Zionism offered an alternative hope for escape from persecution; it was not the spiritual Zionism of centuries past but a new, political Zionism inspired as much by nationalism as by religious belief.

Modern political Zionism—Jewish nationalism focusing on Palestine—originated in Russia, where anti-Semitism was most virulent. Following the pogroms of the early 1880s, Jewish groups were formed with the specific objective of assisting Jewish settlement in Palestine. In 1884 these scattered groups were organized under a central coordinating agency and took the name the Lovers of Zion. During the 1880s and 1890s, the Lovers of Zion sponsored small agricultural settlements in Palestine, but the enterprise suffered from lack of funds and the settlements were not very successful. Despite the difficulties experienced by this early settlement movement, it has assumed a prominent place in the historical consciousness of modern Israelis and is regarded as the first of several aliyahs, or waves of settlement, that contributed to the eventual creation of the state of Israel. In 1882, at the height of the pogroms, a seminal treatise in the history of political Zionism appeared. Entitled *Autoemancipation* and written by Leo Pinsker (d. 1891), the booklet argued that anti-Semitism was so deeply embedded in European society that no matter what the laws said about emancipation, Jews would never be treated as equals. To end their perpetually alien status, Jews could not wait for Western society to change; they had to seize their own destiny and establish an independent Jewish state. Pinsker was more interested in issues of national identity than of religion, and he did not insist that the Jewish state be in Palestine. However, his call for action was appealing to young Russian Jews, and in the 1890s a variety of Zionist organizations emerged, each with its own solution to the problems of Jewish identity and persecution. At this stage in its development, Zionism was an uncoordinated movement without direction.

Theodor Herzl (1860–1904) did not originate the idea of Zionism, but through his energy and determination he forged the existing strands of the ideology into a coherent international movement. Born into a middle-class Jewish family in Budapest, Herzl grew up in an assimilated environment. After obtaining a law degree from the University of Vienna, he worked as a journalist for a prestigious Viennese newspaper. Herzl's experiences as a correspondent in various western European cities convinced him that anti-Semitism was such a deeply rooted prejudice that it could never be eliminated by legislation. He saw emancipation as a facade designed to mask, but not to remove, anti-Jewish sentiments. Driven by this belief, Herzl wrote *The Jewish State* (1896), which provided the ideological basis for political Zionism. Perfectly suited to its era, *The Jewish State* was as much a treatise on nationalism as on religion. Herzl's thesis was that the Jews constituted a nation but lacked a political state within which they could freely express their national culture. These two factors—the existence of a Jewish nationality and the absence of a Jewish state—combined to make the Jews aliens in the lands in which they lived and contributed to their oppression by the dominant cultural majority. In Herzl's opinion the only resolution to this problem, and to the problem of anti-Semitism in general, was for the Jews to acquire political sovereignty in a state of their own, thereby liberating their nationality from its perpetually subordinate status. Like his predecessor, Pinsker, Herzl was motivated more by the pragmatic considerations of nationhood than by the religious associations of the Old Testament, and he did not specify Palestine as the location of the future Jewish state.

The Jewish State had an electrifying effect on East European Jewry and provided Zionism with a clearly stated political objective. Encouraged by the response to his book, Herzl undertook to organize the various strands of Zionism into a single unified movement. Largely because of his efforts, the first Zionist Congress was convened in Basel in 1897. It attracted over 200 delegates and represented a milestone for the Zionist movement. The congress adopted a program that stated that the objective of Zionism was to secure a legally recognized home in Palestine for the Jewish people. Equally important, the Basel congress agreed to establish the World Zionist Organization as the central administrative organ of the Zionist movement and to set up a structure of committees to give it cohesion and direction. In the years following the meeting at Basel, branches of the central congress were set up throughout Eastern Europe, and a grassroots campaign to gather popular support was undertaken. The Zionist Congress met annually after 1897, and although the sessions often revealed deep divisions within Zionism, Herzl's success in attracting more and more delegates to each congress revealed the increasing appeal of the movement he headed.

Notwithstanding the growing participation of east European Jewry in Zionist activities, Herzl recognized that the movement would not be successful until it secured the diplomatic support of a Great Power and the financial assistance of members of the Western Jewish community. Herzl was to be disappointed on both counts. The assimilated Jewish establishments in western Europe and the United States feared that the assertion of Jewish distinctiveness, which was an integral part of Zionism, would produce an anti-Semitic backlash that might threaten their position in society. Moreover, Sultan Abdul Hamid II was opposed to the idea of large-scale European Jewish settlement in Ottoman territory, and none of the European powers was inclined to support a movement that offered no apparent diplomatic advantages. Thus, by the time of his death in 1904, Herzl had managed to infuse Zionism with his own energy and to provide it with an organizational structure that enabled it to survive his passing, but he had not been able to obtain the external governmental backing needed to fulfill the Basel program of establishing a legally recognized home for the Jewish people in Palestine. During World War I, however, the diplomatic status of Zionism improved dramatically.

The Balfour Declaration

As noted in Chapter 9, the Ottoman decision to enter the war on the side of Germany prompted Britain, France, and Russia to plan for the partition of Ottoman territories in the event of an Allied victory. The British pledge to Sharif Husayn of Mecca and the Sykes-Picot Agreement between Britain and France constituted two of the principal proposals for dividing the Ottoman Empire among the Allies. The Balfour Declaration was another partition scheme; it was made all the more complex in that it was issued unilaterally by Britain and was viewed by France and Sharif Husayn as contravening the agreements Britain had already made with them.

During the course of World War I, several factors contributed to bring the question of Zionism to the attention of the British cabinet. The most pressing of them was the belief, held by several key government officials, that Jewish groups in the United States and Russia had the capacity to influence their respective governments' attitudes toward the war. Until the United States declared war on Germany in April 1917, the British cabinet was worried that Germany might make a declaration in support of Zionist aims and thus attract a sympathetic response from U.S. Jewry. A similar consideration arose with regard to Russia, which was on the verge of military collapse and social revolution by autumn 1917. Officials within the British government argued that a British gesture of goodwill toward Zionist aspirations might persuade influential Jewish members within the revolutionary movement to attempt to keep Russia in the war. It does not matter that these various beliefs were ill founded; what is important is that they existed and helped determine British policy.

Chaim Weizmann, the Zionist spokesman in London, also played a significant role in British policymaking. The Russian-born Weizmann (1874–1952) was educated at universities in Berlin and Fribourg, Switzerland, where he received his doctorate in chemistry. He had been attracted to Zionism while a student in Berlin and had traveled extensively through the Russian pale of settlement, establishing local branches of the World Zionist Organization. Appointed to the Department of Chemistry at the University of Manchester in 1904, Weizmann continued his activities in the Zionist cause and set up contacts with leading figures among the British political establishment. A persuasive and persistent spokesman, Weizmann was effective in keeping the question of Zionism before the British cabinet and in cultivating ties with well-placed officials and public figures. He was helped immensely in his task by the cabinet's recognition that British support for Zionism had the potential to serve British imperial interests. Britain's sponsorship of Jewish settlement in Palestine would require a British presence in the region and would thus keep France out of an area that was contiguous to the vital Suez Canal zone.

All of these factors—the search to cement wartime alliances, Weizmann's skillful persistence, the existence of a certain sympathy within the cabinet toward the religious and humanitarian aspects of Zionism, and, most importantly, the chance to secure British strategic interests—interacted to produce a British declaration in support of Zionist objectives in Palestine. On November 2, 1917, the British foreign secretary, Arthur Balfour, wrote to Lord Rothschild, a prominent figure in British Zionist circles, informing him that the cabinet had approved the following declaration of sympathy for Jewish Zionist aspirations:

> His Majesty's Government view with favour the establishment in Palestine of a National Home for the Jewish people, and will use their best endeavours to facilitate the achievement of this object, it being clearly understood that nothing shall be done which may prejudice the civil and religious rights of existing non-Jewish communities in Palestine, or the rights and political status enjoyed by Jews in any other country.[1]

This was the fateful Balfour Declaration, a brief document filled with such ambiguities and contradictions that it confused all the parties named in it.

The Mandate for Palestine: British Administration

The territory that became the Palestine mandate was not a distinctive administrative entity during the Ottoman era (see Map 13.1). It was regarded as part of southern Syria and was divided between the provinces of Beirut and Damascus and the special administrative unit of Jerusalem. The British capture of Jerusalem in December 1917 detached Palestine from Ottoman rule and led to its being placed under British military occupation from 1917 to 1920. During these years, Britain sought to reconcile the conflicting aspirations of Zionism and Arabism by facilitating discussions between Weizmann and the leading Arab personality of the time, Faysal of Syria. In an agreement reached in January 1919, Weizmann pledged that the Jewish community would cooperate with the Arabs in the economic development of Palestine. In return, Faysal would recognize the Balfour Declaration and consent to Jewish immigration, provided that the rights of the Palestinian Arabs were protected and the Arab demands for the independence of Greater Syria were recognized. Faysal did not, as some have claimed, agree to the creation of a Jewish state in Palestine. When the French occupied Syria, the provisions of the Faysal-Weizmann agreement were violated and the document was rendered void.

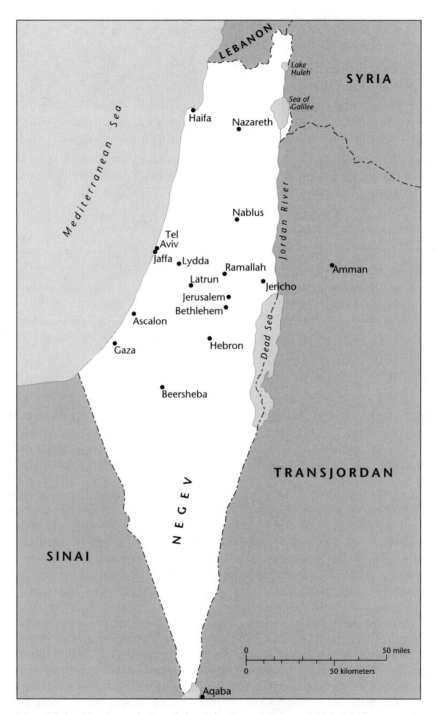

Map 13.1 The Boundaries of the Palestine Mandate, 1924–1948

Meanwhile, the San Remo Conference (1920) awarded Britain the mandate for Palestine, and the military government was replaced by a civilian administration. Two years later the newly created League of Nations gave formal sanction to the mandate and added provisions that raised Zionist expectations and alarmed the Arab inhabitants; the terms of the league mandate incorporated the Balfour Declaration and recognized Hebrew as an official language in Palestine.

The appointment of Sir Herbert Samuel as civilian high commissioner in 1920 offered further encouragement to the Zionists. Samuel was Jewish and an ardent Zionist, and he interpreted his task as facilitating the establishment of the Jewish national home. But what, precisely, was meant by that term? Weizmann had no doubts: At the Paris Peace Conference, he stated that the Zionist objective was gradually to make Palestine as Jewish as England was English. In short, the Zionists interpreted the term *national home* to mean a Jewish state, and they expected the British administration to cooperate in the creation of such a state. But Britain had not committed itself to the establishment of a Jewish state in Palestine. For, after all, in the Balfour Declaration Britain had also pledged to uphold the rights and privileges of the "existing non-Jewish communities in Palestine," a dismissive way of referring to the 668,258 Arab inhabitants who constituted over 85 percent of the population. This was the duty of equal obligation, and it became the insoluble contradiction in the Balfour Declaration. How could Britain facilitate the establishment of a Jewish national home on the one hand and ensure that the rights of the Arab majority would not be threatened on the other? For the full twenty-eight years of the mandate, this question haunted British policymakers; in the end, they could not find a satisfactory answer.

In an attempt to clarify its future plans in Palestine, the British government issued a white paper in 1922 that served as the basis for policy during most of the 1920s. The document illustrates the balancing act that Britain attempted to perform. To placate the Arab community, the white paper stated that the development of a Jewish national home did not mean the imposition of Jewish nationality upon the inhabitants of Palestine as a whole. However, it also conceded certain Zionist demands by declaring that the Jewish people had a right to be in Palestine and that Palestine should become a center in which the Jewish people as a whole could take pride on the grounds of religion and race. If the white paper was intended to remove the ambiguities contained in the Balfour Declaration, it failed utterly to do so.

In conjunction with the special administrative difficulties posed by the existence of the policy of dual obligation, the Palestine mandate presented Britain with the challenge of fulfilling the essential obligations of a mandatory power, namely, to establish the instruments of self-government that would enable the mandate to achieve independence. But what was independent Palestine to be? High Commissioner Samuel held that the most desirable outcome was the creation of an integrated political community, and he proposed several schemes for the development of a unitary state. He believed that without Arab political participation, the mandate would be unworkable. Moreover, if the Arab leadership could be persuaded to participate in the governance of the mandate, it would imply Arab acceptance of the Balfour Declaration. The high commissioner was also motivated by a sincere belief that Jewish-Arab cooperation would improve the Arab standard of living.

His first proposal, the constitution of 1922, called for the creation of a legislative council composed of elected Muslim, Christian, and Jewish representatives plus eleven members nominated by the high commissioner. However, the Arab leaders rejected the plan, declaring that they would not serve in any constitutional government that did not annul the Balfour Declaration. Samuel tried to forge ahead with elections, but the Arab community boycotted them, and the constitutional plan was shelved in 1923. Samuel then attempted to form an advisory council consisting of ten Arab and two Jewish representatives nominated by the high commissioner. This proposal also failed, as the Arab nominees were pressured into refusing to serve.

The Arab rejection of Samuel's various proposals for unitary representation was of the utmost significance in determining the future course of the mandate. It meant that Palestine was governed by the high commissioner and his officials alone. Institutions representing the population as a whole were completely lacking: Palestine never had a constitution, a parliament, or mandatewide elections. The Arab and Jewish communities, rather than jointly participating in the development of "national" institutions, became increasingly isolated from one another. Each community developed its own political apparatus and engaged in its own separate spheres of economic activity. These practices strengthened the communal solidarity within each community but widened the gap between them.

The Palestinian Arab Community: Leadership and Institutions

The Arab Executive

In the interwar period, the leadership of the Palestinian Arabs was assumed by local urban notables, whose power and prestige were based on their ownership of land and their domination of religious and municipal offices. As was the case with other interwar Arab politicians in the British and French mandates, the Palestinian notables sought to preserve their social and political preeminence by adopting a policy of moderate opposition to and cautious cooperation with the British authorities. They were aided in retaining their influence by the British preference for working within the existing social order and using the established notable families as intermediaries between the government and the population at large. Thus, in Palestine as elsewhere in the former Ottoman Arab provinces, the politics of the notables survived into the post-Ottoman era.

However, the existence of the Balfour Declaration and the encouragement of Jewish immigration made Palestine considerably different from the other Arab mandates and created an enormously complex challenge for the Palestinian elite. Not only did they have to confront British imperialism, Zionist determination, and the demands of their own constituents within the frontiers of the mandate, they also had to present the Palestinian case in the corridors of power in London, where none of them commanded the respect and influence that were accorded Weizmann. They were provincial notables into whose hands was placed one of the most intractable problems of this century. Although their numbers included individuals of outstanding talent and dedication, their collective leadership was weakened by factionalism and a tendency to overlook the importance of forming a cohesive political organization that could attract popular support.

The first organized Palestinian Arab response to the postwar settlement came from local branches of Muslim-Christian associations that were formed in large towns during 1918 and 1919. About thirty delegates from these associations gathered in Jerusalem in late 1919 and constituted themselves as the first Palestinian Arab Congress. Thereafter, the congress met annually and adopted resolutions on matters affecting the relationships among the Arab community, the Zionists, and the British. At the Third Congress, held in 1920, a standing Arab Executive was created under the presidency of Musa Kazim al-Husayni, a former mayor of Jerusalem. The Arab Executive claimed to represent all Palestinians, but the British refused to accept it as a properly elected body and only occasionally acknowledged its legitimacy. This British attitude undermined the ability of the Arab Executive to act as an effective channel of communication between the Arabs and the mandate government. An additional problem for the Arab Executive was its lack of structure. Both the standing executive and the branches of Muslim-Christian associations remained essentially loose coalitions of notables without an extensive administrative apparatus or instruments of popular mobilization. As a result, the Arab Executive failed to secure either mass support or formal access to the high commissioner's office. When Musa Kazim al-Husayni died in 1934, the Arab Executive ceased to exist.

The Arab Executive, and Palestinian political activity in general, was further weakened by the existence of a bitter rivalry between two of the leading Muslim notable families of Jerusalem, the Nashashibis and the al-Husaynis. Their competition for power within Palestine dated from the nineteenth century and was intensified during the mandate, adding a destructive factionalism to the politics of the Arab elite. This factionalism was not entirely self-induced; the British, aware of the rivalry, used their power over appointments to maintain the divisions between the two families. Thus, in 1920

Raghib Nashashibi replaced an al-Husayni as mayor of Jerusalem. In the following year, the British counterbalanced this Nashashibi gain by securing the selection of Hajj Amin al-Husayni as mufti of Jerusalem. It is reported that Raghib Bey responded to Hajj Amin's appointment by declaring that he would oppose any position that the mufti took. He and his supporters carried out this threat, even when it was clearly detrimental to the Palestinian cause.

Hajj Amin al-Husayni and the Supreme Muslim Council

As mufti of Jerusalem, Hajj Amin (1895–1974) occupied the most prestigious religious office in Palestine, and he used it to build a political network that made him the acknowledged leader of the Palestinian Arab community during the interwar period.

The mufti of Jerusalem was traditionally responsible for regulating Islamic affairs within the greater Jerusalem district. With the termination of Ottoman authority and the creation of the Palestinian mandate, the British expanded the mufti's jurisdiction to include all of Palestine, thus providing the office with considerable influence in the Muslim community. Raised in his native Jerusalem, Hajj Amin studied at both al-Azhar in Cairo and the war college in Istanbul. He served behind the lines in Anatolia during World War I and eventually became an officer in the Ottoman army. Deeply shocked by the Balfour Declaration, he became active in organizing anti-Zionist demonstrations in the immediate postwar period. Despite his opposition to the Balfour Declaration, he appeared willing to cooperate with the British administration in preventing acts of violence and was thus Samuel's preferred candidate for the office of mufti.

The mufti's authority was greatly expanded by Samuel's creation in 1921 of the Supreme Muslim Council, an autonomous body charged with the management of the entire range of Islamic institutions within the mandate. Hajj Amin was elected president of the council in 1922. In his twin capacities as mufti of Jerusalem and president of the Supreme Muslim Council, he acquired control of a vast patronage network. The council was responsible for the supervision of the *shariᶜah* courts and the appointment of court officials and judges; for the management of *waqf*s, the assignment of *waqf* funds, and the appointment of *waqf* trustees; and for the system of Islamic religious schools, including the selection of teachers. The council paid the salaries of these officials out of an annual budget (ranging from £50,000 to £60,000 during the 1920s) provided by the mandatory government. Hajj Amin used his powers of appointment and dismissal to secure positions for his supporters and to prevent his opponents, especially the Nashashibi family and its clients, from obtaining employment within the religious establishment. In this manner, the mufti was able to transform his religious authority into the most extensive Arab political organization in Palestine.

Although Hajj Amin has been vilified by Zionists and glorified by certain Arab nationalists, his political behavior was more moderate than either group acknowledges. He was too pragmatic a politician to allow his opposition to Zionism to deceive him into thinking that an Arab uprising could dislodge the British. He also recognized that his own continued tenure in office depended upon British goodwill. Therefore, until the outbreak of violence in 1936, the mufti urged restraint on his followers and demonstrated a willingness to cooperate with the British in seeking a negotiated solution to the question of Jewish immigration.

The Jewish Community: Leadership and Institutions

The Jewish Agency and the National Council

Zionist organizations were considerably more extensive than those of the Arabs and reflected the differences in the resources, both human and fiscal, that the two communities could marshal. The Jewish community was better organized, better financed, and better connected than the Arabs. There was no formally recognized body of Arab representatives empowered to present the Palestinian Arab case to the high commissioner, whereas Zionist access to British authority was sanctioned by the terms of the mandate, which authorized the formation of a public body to consult with the mandatory government on matters affecting the establishment of the Jewish national home. To fulfill this function, the World Zionist Organization created the Palestine Zionist Executive in 1921, reorganized as the Jewish Agency in 1929. The Jewish Agency became the quasi government of the Jewish community in Palestine, managing an impressive array of services that ranged from banking systems to health care and immigrant settlement. The chairman of the Jewish Agency had regular access to the high commissioner and other British officials.

Jewish communal affairs were conducted through a hierarchy of representative organizations. The national assembly, constituted in 1920, was an elected body of some 300 delegates who selected from among themselves the members of the national council, or Vaᶜad Leumi. The council was empowered to make administrative decisions on behalf of the Jewish community and was treated by the mandate government as the legitimate representative of Palestinian Jewry.

Histadrut: The Political and Ideological Impact of the Labor Movement

Of the various organizations formed to generate self-sufficiency within the Yishuv (the name of the Jewish community in Palestine before 1948), the most important was Histadrut, the Federation of Jewish Labor. Founded in

1920 to promote Jewish trade unionism, Histadrut gradually expanded its role during the interwar years and came to engage in an extensive range of entrepreneurial activities and to exercise a decisive influence on the ideology and politics of both the Yishuv and the future state of Israel. In order to provide employment for its members, Histadrut created public works projects and founded companies that by the 1930s included such enterprises as shipping, agricultural marketing, road and housing construction, banking, and insurance. Since one of its objectives was to ensure the self-sufficiency of Jewish labor and produce, Histadrut instituted a boycott of Arab workers and Arab products.

In addition to its control over traditional trade union activities, Histadrut also had interlocking ties with the kibbutz workers in the agricultural sector. The kibbutzim were collective agricultural settlements in which all property belonged to the community and all responsibilities were shared equally by the members. They became a symbol of the cooperative communal order that many of the early Zionists hoped to build in Palestine. Together, Histadrut and the kibbutz movement also represented the ideal of Jewish rejuvenation through the dignity of labor and working the land. This was a significant impulse within the Yishuv and imparted to the community a socialist economic orientation and a glorification of the new Jewish self-image in which the passive and oppressed ghetto dwellers of Europe gave way to the self-confident, physically active workers, farmers, and soldiers of Palestine capable of determining their own destinies.

Histadrut's influence on the development of the Yishuv was made all the more extensive by its control of the Jewish defense force, Haganah. Formed in 1920 in response to the Arab riots of that year, Haganah was to provide a trained and centralized military arm capable of defending the Jewish community against Arab attacks. It gradually evolved into a permanent underground reserve army with a command structure that was fully integrated into the political institutions of the Jewish community as a whole. The British authorities disapproved of the organization (especially its method of procuring arms by stealing them from British bases) but made no concerted effort to disband it.

As Histadrut's membership and functions expanded, the organization was placed in the unusual position of acting as both a trade union and the largest employer within the mandate, a combination that gave its leaders considerable power in the decisionmaking councils of the Yishuv. In 1930 two labor groups merged to form the Mapai Party, the body that dominated the political life of the Yishuv and the state of Israel until 1977. Holding the view that the interests of labor and Zionism were identical, Mapai was the perfect representative of the socialist egalitarian ideal that was so important in shaping the outlook of the Yishuv during its formative years. Among the individuals responsible for Mapai's enduring hold on political power, David Ben-Gurion (1886–1973) was especially prominent. Ben-Gurion's experiences and attitudes were typical of his generation of Zionist leaders in Palestine. Like the vast majority of Jewish immigrants who arrived in Palestine before 1933, he was from Eastern Europe. He came to Palestine from Poland in 1906, first working on a kibbutz and then becoming involved in the inner circles of labor Zionism. He was a founding member of Histadrut and served as its executive secretary for several years before being elected chairman of the Jewish Agency in 1935. He was also active in the creation of the Mapai in 1930 and soon became the party's leader. As both Mapai Party head and Jewish Agency chairman, Ben-Gurion was the acknowledged leader of the Yishuv and a popular choice as Israel's first prime minister in 1948.

The Zionist cause was aided not only by the institutions established within the mandate but also by political and financial support from individuals and organizations operating outside of Palestine. The most influential contacts between Zionism and British officialdom were those maintained by Weizmann. In 1920 the World Zionist Organization transferred its headquarters to London, and Weizmann became its president. His ready access to prime ministers, cabinet members, and journalists afforded him the opportunity to intervene quickly, and often decisively, on behalf of the Zionist cause whenever British policy toward Palestine veered from the course he thought it should take. Another source of outside support was provided by elements of the Jewish community in the United States. The Zionist Organization of America was founded in 1917 and, under the leadership of the noted lawyer and future justice of the Supreme Court Louis Brandeis, became a factor in U.S. political life. By the late 1930s, U.S. representatives played an important role in the deliberations of the World Zionist Organization, and private contributions from the United States made up a significant portion of the funds donated to the Zionist cause. With the rise of the United States to global power during World War II, American Jewry would play a vital role in shaping the outcome of the Palestine conflict.

Divisions Within the Yishuv:
Jabotinsky and Revisionist Zionism

Notwithstanding the settlers' success in establishing social and political institutions within Palestine, Zionism remained a fractious movement in which a broad spectrum of opinions found expression. One of the most heated of the interwar disputes concerned the territorial objectives of Zionism and the tactics best suited to obtain them. During the mandate period, when the creation of a Jewish state was still very much in doubt, most Zionists accepted Weizmann's strategy of relying on Britain to bring about the fulfillment of Zionist objectives. However, a splinter group, eventually called the revisionists, condemned Weizmann's approach as too hesitant and too dependent on Britain. The founder and leading spokesman of revisionism was a Russian Zionist named Vladimir Jabotinsky (1880–1940). Jabotinsky called for massive Jewish immigration into Palestine and the immediate proclamation of a Jewish commonwealth. He argued that Britain was quite capable of abandoning the Zionists and that the only way to achieve the Jewish majority required for independent statehood was by encouraging 50,000 immigrants to Palestine a year. Jabotinsky's territorial demands were even more controversial. He claimed that historic Palestine included Transjordan and insisted that large-scale Jewish colonization take place in that territory. At the annual Zionist Congress of 1929, he addressed the delegates with these words: "What does the word Palestine mean? Palestine is a territory whose chief geographical feature is this: that the River Jordan does not delineate its frontier, but flows through its center."[2]

The revisionist movement attracted enthusiastic support among Zionist youth groups in Eastern Europe, where Jabotinsky's followers made him the object of a leadership cult. In 1933 the revisionists formed a separate movement within Zionism, and shortly thereafter they set up their own military force in Palestine, the Irgun, which operated independently of Haganah and the Jewish Agency. Although revisionism lost much of its force with Jabotinsky's death, two of his disciples, Menachem Begin and Yitzhak Shamir, later became Israeli prime ministers and revived the uncompromising Zionism of their former leader.

In growing isolation from one another, the Arab and Jewish communities in Palestine built up their political and social organizations. Both communities were terribly insecure throughout the interwar years. The Arabs were frustrated in their attempts to gain legal recognition as the rightful inhabitants of Palestine. At the same time, they rejected any overtures to participate in national organizations, believing that to do so would validate the mandate and imply their acceptance of the Balfour Declaration. Likewise, Zionist leaders were convinced that the British intent to be fair to Arabs as well as Jews was blocking the establishment of a Jewish national home. Accordingly, they intensified their efforts to promote immigration, develop self-sufficient communal organizations, and confront what they regarded as British lack of cooperation.

Immigration and Land

Jewish immigration and land acquisition lay at the heart of the communal tension in Palestine. The Zionist objective was to build up the Jewish population of the mandate through unrestricted immigration so as to have a credible claim to the existence of a national home. In order to settle and feed the immigrants, it was necessary to acquire as much cultivable land as possible. In pursuit of these twin objectives, Zionism resembled a project of settler colonialism undertaken at the expense of the local Arab population.

The Arabs of Palestine recognized that the goals of Zionism represented a threat to their existence, and they opposed them by attempting to negotiate with Britain to restrict immigration and land transfers; when that tactic failed, they turned to armed revolt.

Jewish immigration to Palestine occurred in a series of waves called aliyahs. The first two took place before World War I. The third, from 1919 to 1923, was composed of about 30,000 immigrants mainly from Eastern Europe. An additional 50,000 immigrants, primarily from Poland, arrived in the fourth aliyah between 1924 and 1926. The influx of immigrants then slowed considerably until 1933, when the rise of Hitler and the Nazi party precipitated the flight of thousands of Jews from Germany and central Europe. Although many of these refugees were not Zionists, the restrictive immigration quotas imposed by such countries as the United States and Canada compelled them to seek refuge in Palestine. In the years of the fifth aliyah, from 1933 through 1936, about 170,000 Jews immigrated to Palestine, suddenly doubling the size of the Yishuv and creating widespread alarm within the Arab community. The composition of the fifth aliyah differed from the others in that the German immigrants included a significant number of educated professionals and businesspeople who often brought with them substantial amounts of capital. Less interested than their pioneering predecessors in working the land, they tended to settle in the coastal cities and to engage in professional or entrepreneurial pursuits.

As shown in Table 13.1, the Jewish community in Palestine numbered approximately 382,000 by the end of 1936, a dramatic increase from the 93,000 recorded in 1922. During the same period, the Arab population grew from around 700,000 to 983,000. Thus, in less than fifteen years, the number of people living in Palestine increased by more than 400,000. It is little wonder that in a region of limited agricultural potential, the ownership of arable land became a matter of contention.

The Zionist organization chiefly responsible for negotiating land purchases was the Jewish National Fund, which bought land it then regarded as belonging to the Jewish people as a whole and leased it exclusively to Jews at a nominal rate. The Jewish National Fund also provided capital for improvements and equipment, a practice that enabled impoverished immigrants to engage in agricultural pursuits immediately upon arriving in Palestine.

Zionist interests usually acquired land by purchasing it from absentee Arab owners. The first and largest such purchase under the mandate was from the Sursock family of Beirut, which sold 50,000 acres in the fertile Jezreel Valley to the Jewish National Fund in 1920. But even leading Palestinian notable families, attracted by the high prices the Zionists were willing to pay, sold cultivable land to agents of the Jewish National Fund or other Zionist purchasing organizations. By 1939 some 5 percent of the total land area of the mandate, making up approximately 10 percent of the total cultivable land, was Jewish-owned.

TABLE 13.1 Population of Palestine by Ethnic Group, 1931–1946

	Arab	%	Jewish	%	Other	%	Total
1931	864,806	82	174,139	16	18,269	2	1,057,601
1936	983,244	71	382,857	28	22,751	2	1,388,852
1941	1,123,168	68	489,830	30	26,758	2	1,639,756
1946	1,310,866	67	599,922	31	31,562	2	1,942,350

Source: Justin McCarthy, *The Population of Palestine* (New York: Columbia University Press), p. 36.

The transfer of cultivated land from Arab to Jewish ownership had a devastating effect on the Palestinian peasantry, which in 1936 still composed two-thirds of the Arab population of the mandate. The usual outcome of such a transaction was the eviction of the Arab tenant farmers and their addition to the growing ranks of the unemployed. The conditions of small proprietors also worsened during the mandate. British taxation policy, which required direct cash payments in place of the customary Ottoman payment in kind, forced peasant farmers to borrow funds at high rates of interest from local moneylenders—who were frequently the large landholders. As a result of the crushing burden of indebtedness, many small proprietors found it necessary to sell their lands, sometimes to Zionist interests but often to one of the landed Arab families. The cumulative effect of land transfers, British policy, and Arab notable attitudes was the increasing impoverishment and marginalization of the Palestinian Arab peasantry. Alienated from their own political elite, who seemed to profit from their plight; from the British, who appeared unwilling to prevent their expulsion from the land; and from the Zionists, who were perceived to be at the root of their problems, they expressed their discontent in outbreaks of violence against all three parties.

Communal Conflict and the British Response

The two major eruptions of communal violence during the interwar years of the mandate—the Wailing Wall disturbances of 1929 and the great revolt of 1936–1939—were directly related to the dislocations caused by immigration and land transfers. Repeated British investigations into the causes of these incidents only served to highlight the unworkable nature of the mandate.

The Wailing Wall Disturbances of 1929

A dispute over the Jewish right of access to the remains of the Western, or Wailing, Wall of the Temple of Herod came to serve as the focal point for all the communal antagonisms that had been building up since the beginning of the mandate. Jews regarded the wall as a holy site and had gone there since the Middle Ages to pray and to lament the passing of the ancient kingdom of Israel. Muslims also had deep religious attachments to the wall and its immediate surroundings, as it formed the western abutment of the Haram al-Sharif (the holy sanctuary) that contained the Dome of the Rock and al-Aqsa mosque, structures associated with Muhammad's nocturnal journey to heaven and two of the oldest and most revered Islamic shrines. At the time of the mandate, the wall was designated as *waqf* and was thus under Muslim jurisdiction.

Although Jews had the right to visit the wall, they were not allowed to set up such appurtenances as chairs, benches, or screens to separate men and women during prayer. The British, in keeping with their policy of maintaining the status quo in religious matters, agreed that these restrictions should remain in effect. However, Jewish activists constantly challenged the regulations, and in late 1928 the British police found it necessary to forcibly remove from the area a screen and the worshipers who had placed it there. The intensity of Jewish objections to this action galvanized the mufti and the Supreme Muslim Council into launching a publicity campaign about the danger that Zionism posed to the holy places of Islam. A year of claims and counterclaims over the status of the wall turned into violent confrontations in August 1929, during which Arab mobs, provoked by Jewish demonstrations, attacked two Jewish quarters in Jerusalem and killed Jews in the towns of Hebron and Safad. By the time British forces quelled the riots, 133 Jews and 116 Arabs had lost their lives. Although the immediate cause of the riots was concern over the fate of a religious site, the real causes lay much deeper. The British decided to find out what they were.

In September 1929 London dispatched the first of what would become a nearly continuous series of royal commissions to Palestine. It was headed by Sir Walter Shaw and was instructed to conduct an inquiry into the reasons for the violence of the previous month. Its report concluded that the main source of tension within the mandate was the creation of a landless class of discontented Arabs and the widespread Arab fear that continued Jewish immigration would result in a Jewish-dominated Palestine. The Shaw Commission went on to recommend that British obligations to the Arab community should be more precisely defined, that Jewish immigration should be brought more directly under British control, and that the practice of evicting Arab tenants following land transfers should cease.

Instead of dealing with the Shaw Commission's report on its own merits, the British decided to send another commission of inquiry to Palestine. The Hope-Simpson Commission conducted its investigation in summer 1930, and its recommendations were incorporated into a statement of British policy known as the Passfield White Paper (1930). The white paper stressed Britain's dual obligation as a mandatory power and stated the government's intention to set aside state lands for the settlement of landless Arab peasants.

It also declared that Palestine had a limited economic absorptive capacity and proposed that restrictions on Jewish immigration be introduced.

The Passfield White Paper addressed some of the Arab grievances, but its proposals to limit immigration were anathema to the Zionists, and they mounted a concerted effort to have the entire document withdrawn. Weizmann, joined by prominent members of the British and U.S. Jewish communities and by British opposition politicians, put tremendous pressure on the government to rescind the policy statement. The campaign was successful. In February 1931 Prime Minister Ramsay MacDonald read to the House of Commons a personal letter he had written to Weizmann in which the Passfield White Paper was effectively repudiated. Known to the Arabs as the Black Letter, it confirmed their belief in the ability of Zionist pressure groups to influence the decisions of the British government.

The General Strike and the Formation of the Arab Higher Committee

Following the Black Letter of 1931 and the decision to ignore most of the recommendations of the commissions of inquiry, the situation in Palestine deteriorated further. The effects of the world depression, coupled with the large-scale immigration of the fifth aliyah, created widespread unemployment among Arabs and Jews alike. Within the Arab community, there was growing disenchantment with the moderate leadership of Hajj Amin and the Supreme Muslim Council. The mufti's preeminent political position was challenged by a new party, the Istiqlal, composed of young Palestinian notables who advocated direct action against Britain and endorsed the development of strong ties with other Arab countries. Although Hajj Amin was able to neutralize the Istiqlal, its demands for greater militancy were representative of sentiments held by increasingly large segments of the Arab population of Palestine. These sentiments, born of despair and frustration, found expression in the events of 1936.

The violence that swept through Palestine in spring and summer 1936 was a spontaneous popular reaction against Zionism, British imperialism, and the entrenched Arab leadership. It was set in motion on April 15 when an armed Arab band robbed a bus and killed a Jewish passenger; the following evening Haganah retaliated by killing two Arab farmers. These incidents provoked both communities into mass demonstrations and mob attacks against each other. In an attempt to channel the popular discontent into an effective weapon against Britain and the Zionists, local Arab resistance committees declared a general strike on April 19, 1936. The strike was to continue until Britain granted the Arabs' demands for restrictions on immigration and land sales and the establishment of a democratic government.

The push of popular resistance from below forced the Arab leaders to act, and on April 25 they formed a national organization, the Arab Higher

Committee, under the presidency of the mufti. Including Christians, Muslims, Nashashibis, al-Husaynis, and prominent members of Istiqlal, the Arab Higher Committee was a belated attempt to unify the factions within the Palestinian elite. Although the committee attempted to coordinate the strike, it lagged behind popular opinion and tended to respond to events rather than to create them. The strike spread rapidly during the summer and was accompanied by attacks on Jews and Jewish property and the destruction of British transport. When various attempts at mediation failed, Britain made a determined effort to crush the rebellion, and in October, after the deaths of 1,000 Arabs and 80 Jews, the strike was terminated by order of the Arab Higher Committee. It had revealed the depth of Palestinian Arab resentment but had resolved nothing; it was thus only a precursor of greater violence to come.

The Peel Commission and the Great Revolt

One of the reasons the Arab leadership called off the strike was Britain's pledge to send yet another investigative commission to Palestine. This commission, chaired by Lord Peel, issued its report in July 1937. It recognized that the premise on which the mandate was based was untenable; a unitary state could not be created out of the contradictory obligations contained in the Balfour Declaration. According to the report, "It is manifest that the Mandate cannot be fully or honorably implemented unless by some means or other the antagonism between Arabs and Jews can be composed. But it is the Mandate which created that antagonism and keeps it alive and as long as the Mandate exists we cannot honestly hold out the expectation that Arabs or Jews will be able to set aside their national hopes or fears or sink their differences in the common service of Palestine."[3] On the basis of these findings, the Peel Commission recommended that the mandate be terminated and that Palestine be partitioned into separate Arab and Jewish states. Britain would continue to exercise mandatory authority in a corridor from Jerusalem to the Mediterranean and in other scattered areas.

This unique solution to the problem of an unworkable mandate satisfied neither of the two parties affected. The Arab Higher Committee opposed partition as a violation of the rights of the Arab inhabitants of Palestine. For their part, the Zionist leaders favored the principle of partition but regarded the territory allocated to the Jewish state as inadequate. This position was adopted at the World Zionist Congress of 1937 and amounted to a Zionist rejection of the Peel Commission's report. Britain's efforts to find a way out of the Palestine labyrinth collapsed in the face of opposition from both Arabs and Jews, and the idea of partition was allowed to fade away.

However, Palestinian Arab discontent would not vanish as easily as a commission report. Upon the announcement of the Peel Commission's proposals in July 1937, Arab violence was renewed. As with the general strike of the previous year, it was spontaneous and locally led rather than premeditated and nationally organized. When the British district commissioner for Galilee was murdered in October, Britain responded by dissolving the Arab Higher Committee and arresting and deporting its members. The mufti escaped to Damascus, where he attempted to reconstitute the committee and to direct the uprising, but his influence over events in Palestine was on the wane. The Arab rebel bands, composed mainly of peasants, concentrated their attacks on railroads, bridges, and British police stations but also destroyed Jewish property and killed Jewish settlers. Although the rebels probably never numbered more than 5,000, they were supported by the bulk of the rural population, and by summer 1938 much of the countryside and several of the major towns were in their hands. Government services came to a virtual halt, and even portions of Jerusalem fell under rebel control.

In addition to its anti-British, anti-Zionist thrust, the revolt contained elements of a peasant social revolution against the established notability. In villages under rebel control, rents were canceled, debt collectors were denied entry, and wealthy landlords were coerced into making "donations" to the rebel cause. Local resistance committees banned the tarbush, the headgear of the Ottoman administrative elite, and insisted that men should instead wear the *kaffiya*, the checkered headcloth that has become a symbol of Palestinian national identity.

In an attempt to put down the uprising, Britain poured 20,000 troops into Palestine and adopted harsh measures of collective punishment on villages suspected of harboring rebels. Jewish forces also engaged in military action against the rebels as well as in retaliatory terrorist attacks against noncombatants. Despite the numerical superiority of their military forces, the British did not manage to restore order until March 1939. The revolt took a heavy toll: More than 3,000 Arabs, 2,000 Jews, and 600 British were killed; the economy of Palestine was in chaos; and the Arab leaders were in exile or under arrest.

If the revolt failed to dislodge Britain from the mandate, it nevertheless succeeded in forcing it to make one more reassessment of its Palestine policy. This was prompted not only by the violence within Palestine but also by the impending war in Europe. In any coming conflict, the oil resources and airfields of the Arab Middle East would be vital to Britain. With the Arab states becoming increasingly involved in the issue of Palestine, Britain recognized the need to placate them in order to secure their future cooperation.

Against this background, the Colonial Office convened an Anglo-Arab-Jewish conference in London in February 1939. However, the conference failed to break the deadlock, and Britain was left to formulate a policy that would inevitably displease one of the parties. This policy, announced in the white paper of 1939, came as a shock to the Zionists. The white paper stated: "His Majesty's Government therefore now declare unequivocally that it is not part of their policy that Palestine should become a Jewish State."[4] The document declared that Jewish immigration was to be limited to 15,000 a year over the next five years, at which point it would cease altogether unless the Arab community consented to its continuation; that land transfers to Jews were to be restricted to certain specified areas; and that in ten years Palestine would be granted independence. It also proposed that an additional 25,000 Jewish refugees be allowed into the mandate. Coming at a time when Jews were fleeing Hitler's terror en masse, the white paper was widely condemned by the international Jewish community. As Zionist leaders marshaled their supporters and prepared for a political campaign against the white paper, Germany invaded Poland, and World War II began. The Jewish community in Palestine, despite its outrage over Britain's statement of policy, could hardly support Hitler's Germany in the conflict; but it could not acquiesce in the terms of the white paper either, for that document meant the end of the dream of a Jewish state. As Ben-Gurion proclaimed, "We shall fight with Great Britain in this war as if there was no White Paper, and we shall fight the White Paper as if there was no war."[5] Although the mufti, in exile in Baghdad, rejected the white paper for not granting immediate independence, most other Palestinian Arab leaders regarded it as a victory of sorts. They now had every reason to believe that they would remain a majority in Palestine.

World War II and the Birth of the State of Israel

Wartime events outside Palestine exercised considerable influence on the future status of the troubled British mandate. The most far-reaching of these events was the Holocaust, the systematic murder of millions of European Jews and others in Hitler's death camps. As the extent of the Nazi atrocities became known, the public conscience of the West came to embrace the notion that the settlement of the surviving Jews in Palestine could atone for the horrors that Western civilization had inflicted upon them. This attitude was especially prominent in the United States. Casting aside the general lack of enthusiasm that had characterized their attitude toward Zionism during the interwar years, many American Jews became ardent supporters of a Jewish state in Palestine. The most forceful public expression of this position was contained in the Biltmore Program, a set of resolutions adopted at a meeting of U.S. Zionists in 1942 calling for open immigration to Palestine and the establishment there of a Jewish commonwealth.

In the wake of the Biltmore gathering, the United States became the center of international Zionist activity, and American and Palestinian Zionists embarked on an intensive publicity campaign to involve the U.S. electorate and U.S. politicians in the issue of Palestine. President Harry Truman, from his arrival in the White House in 1945 through his reelection campaign of 1948, publicly endorsed the Biltmore Program, demonstrating not only humanitarian concerns but also an awareness of the growing power of the Zionist lobby within the Democratic Party. Truman's commitment to the creation of a Jewish state was significant because the United States, with its expanding industrial economy and its unprecedented military might, emerged from the war as a global superpower capable of exerting immense pressure on its allies.

Within Palestine itself, the wartime policy of Britain was intended to keep the mandate tranquil. Seeking to prevent another outbreak of violence like the revolt of 1936–1939, the British administration placed restrictions on Arab political activity and refused to allow the exiled Arab leaders to return. As a result, the Arab community, still reeling from the effects of the British suppression of the revolt, was politically quiescent during the war.

For its part, as we have seen, the Yishuv responded to the circumstances of the war with two conflicting policies: On the one hand, it committed itself to the British war effort against Hitler; on the other hand, it attempted to subvert the white paper of 1939 and to prepare for an armed confrontation with Britain once Germany was defeated.

In support of the Allied cause, thousands of Jewish volunteers joined the British forces, eventually forming a Jewish Brigade that fought as a unit of the British army in Italy. The modern combat experience that the Jewish troops who fought alongside British soldiers gained during the war provided the Haganah with a cadre of trained veterans for fighting against Britain after 1945. In Palestine the Haganah, although technically illegal, was allowed by the British administration to acquire weapons openly and to participate with the British forces in preparations for the defense of Palestine against an anticipated Axis invasion. When the Axis threat subsided after 1942, Haganah members retained their arms as well as their intimate knowledge of the British military network in Palestine.

Notwithstanding the abiding anti-Nazi sentiment within the Yishuv, its leaders continued to regard the British presence in Palestine as the primary obstacle to the fulfillment of their dream of establishing a Jewish national home. In the light of what was becoming known about the fate of European Jewry, Britain's insistence on enforcing the 1939 immigration quotas appeared to be a monstrous injustice, and the Jewish Agency mounted a concerted effort to rescue European Jews and bring them into Palestine illegally. Hiring ships that were often barely seaworthy, the Jewish Agency transported refugees out of ports in southern Europe and landed them on the Palestine coast. When British authorities turned away ships crowded with refugees or apprehended the vessels and sent their passengers to detention camps in Cyprus, they compounded the Yishuv's determination to be rid of British control. These incidents were highly publicized and were used to buttress the Zionist claim that only a Jewish state could provide a haven for the rootless victims of Nazi brutality.

Terror and Civil War

There were three phases of the conflict that brought the state of Israel into being and confirmed its existence: first was the Yishuv's campaign of sabotage against the British administration in Palestine from 1945 to 1947; second was the brief civil war between the Arab and Jewish communities of Palestine in 1947 and 1948; and third was the 1948 war between Israel and the invading forces of the Arab states. Each of these phases was accompanied by a flurry of diplomatic activity that consistently failed to produce an agreement acceptable to both Arabs and Jews.

The first phase of the conflict was part of the strategy contained in the Jewish Agency's decision, made toward the end of World War II, to push for the immediate establishment of a Jewish state. Zionist leaders in Palestine, now more than ever guided by the views of Ben-Gurion, concluded that because Britain would not sponsor the gradual development of a Jewish national home by eliminating immigration quotas, the Jewish state would have to be seized by force. This was to be accomplished by making Britain's position in Palestine untenable.

Ben-Gurion did not intend to confront Britain until the war was over. However, other elements within the Jewish community were impatient. Two irregular armed units that operated independently of Jewish Agency control—though at times with its tacit approval—launched a campaign of terror against British personnel in 1944. The most important of the two units was the Irgun, a fiercely nationalistic organization that served as the military arm of revisionist Zionism. The Irgun consisted of a dedicated core of militant Zionists who advocated a policy of reprisals against Arab civilians and British personnel. Although the Irgun's terrorist tactics often brought discredit to the Zionist enterprise as a whole, its ruthless single-mindedness appealed to a certain segment of the Jewish community that believed that any action taken in the cause of the creation of a Jewish state was justified. In 1943 the Irgun came under the command of Menachem Begin, a recent immigrant from Poland who led the organization until its dissolution in 1948 and who then carried his spirit of uncompromising militancy into Israeli politics. The other dissident military unit, Lehi (often called the Stern Gang after its founder, Abraham Stern), was much smaller and less effective as a combat force but was capable of isolated acts of terror, such as the 1944 assassination of the British minister of state for the Middle East, Lord Moyne.

The Jewish Agency joined the conflict in 1945, when units of the Haganah undertook a series of well-coordinated acts of sabotage against British communications in Palestine. Mainstream Palestinian Zionism had gone to war against Britain. Over the next two years, the combined pressure of Haganah sabotage, Irgun terror (such as the blowing up of a wing of the King David Hotel in Jerusalem in 1946), and U.S. opinion placed Britain in an impossible position. In February 1947 Foreign Secretary Ernest Bevin, recognizing that Britain had lost control of the situation in Palestine, referred the matter to the United Nations.

Bevin's request for the United Nations to formulate a solution to the Palestine mandate was followed by several months of feverish diplomatic activity centered on the United Nations in New York and the White House in Washington. The General Assembly created a United Nations Special Committee on Palestine (UNSCOP) and charged it with investigating conditions in Palestine and submitting recommendations by September 1, 1947. Composed of representatives from eleven nations, UNSCOP arrived in Jerusalem in June and spent five weeks in Palestine. The committee found that Jews were still a considerable minority, constituting only half of the population and owning roughly 6 percent of the total land in Palestine. However, the committee also felt a sense of urgency, both with regard to the deteriorating conditions in Palestine and to the plight of Jewish refugees from Europe. In its report to the General Assembly, UNSCOP unanimously recommended the termination of the British mandate and the granting of independence to Palestine. But the committee was divided, by a vote of eight to three, on what kind of state independent Palestine should be. The minority report called for a federal state. The majority report recommended the partition of the mandate into two states, one Arab and one Jewish, with Jerusalem designated as an internationalized district. Although the provisions of the majority report were far from perfect, they nevertheless offered the possibility of independent Arab and Jewish states within Palestine (see Map 13.2). Zionist leaders endorsed the report; Arab leaders rejected it.

President Truman, fully supportive of the creation of a Jewish state, was determined to achieve the passage of the majority report. Because the proposal required a two-thirds majority vote in the General Assembly and because Washington assumed that the Soviet Union and its allies would oppose it, the vote was expected to be close. Truman—in defiance of the advice of his own State and Defense departments, whose heads recognized the usefulness of maintaining cordial relations with the newly independent Arab states—launched an extensive lobbying effort on behalf of the majority report, and pro-Zionist members of Congress pressured UN delegates with threats of the withdrawal of U.S. economic assistance from their countries if they did not vote for the UNSCOP proposal. When the roll call was taken on November 29, 1947, there were thirty-three votes (including that of USSR) in favor, thirteen against, and ten abstentions: The General Assembly approved the partition of Palestine into separate Arab and Jewish states and accorded international status to Jerusalem. As Charles Smith wrote, "whatever the nature of the Zionist accomplishment in Palestine, the victory at the United Nations was essentially won in the United States."[6] That victory and the policies that flowed from it have colored U.S.-Arab relations ever since.

Throughout the months of negotiations, the Palestinian Arab community was curiously marginal to the discussions. Ever since the British had dismantled the Higher Arab Committee and the Supreme Muslim Council in 1936, the Palestinian Arabs had been without effective leadership. In the absence of unified leadership from within Palestine, the responsibility for presenting the

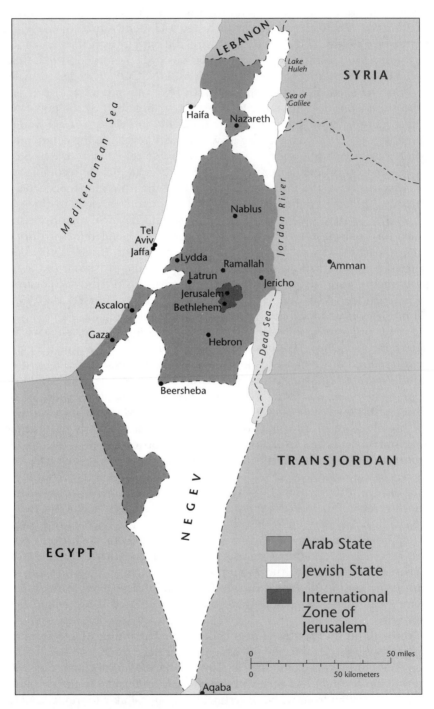

Map 13.2 The UN Proposal for the Partition of Palestine, 1947

Palestinian Arab case came to rest with the Arab League and its member states. However, the postwar Arab regimes, especially those in such key states as Egypt, Syria, and Iraq, faced mounting domestic unrest. The ruling elite of these regimes, anxious to shore up domestic support, adopted a hard-line stance on the Palestinian issue as a means to demonstrate their antiimperialism and to assert their newfound independence in foreign policy. On behalf of the Palestinians, they rejected all attempts at compromise, including the UN partition plan, assuring the Arabs of Palestine that they stood ready to defend them militarily. It was a self-deluding posture.

The disorder within Palestine was intensified by Britain's refusal to assist in the implementation of the UN partition plan. When the UNSCOP report was presented to the UN, Britain did not wait for the General Assembly's vote and immediately announced in September 1947 that the Palestine mandate would be terminated on May 15, 1948. In the months between the announcement and the final British withdrawal, Palestine was plunged into chaos. This was the period of civil war during which the Jewish forces sought to secure the territory allotted to the Jewish state in the UN resolution. Since most of that territory was still inhabited by an Arab majority, there was quite naturally Arab resistance. However, the scattered Arab bands were no match for the disciplined Haganah forces, and by spring 1948 the major centers of Arab population that fell within the proposed Jewish state were in Jewish control and the Arab inhabitants, about 400,000 Palestinians, had fled. During the course of the civil war, the Irgun perpetrated one of its most notorious acts: It massacred the 250 civilian inhabitants of the village of Dayr Yassin near Jerusalem. News of the massacre spread among the Arab population and contributed to the panic that made so many flee their homes. An Arab unit retaliated for Dayr Yassin by ambushing a Jewish medical relief convoy on the outskirts of Jerusalem and killing a number of doctors. Thus did atrocity build upon atrocity in the territory that was still Britain's responsibility.

Throughout the civil war, the British administration made little effort to enforce order, concentrating instead on preparations for its withdrawal. On May 14, 1948, in the midst of the turmoil, the last British high commissioner, General Alan Cunningham, quietly departed from Haifa. As one eyewitness recalled the moment, "The Union Jack was lowered and with the speed of an execution and the silence of a ship that passes in the night British rule in Palestine came to an end."[7] There had been no formal transfer of powers from the mandate authority to a new local government for the simple reason that there was no government of Palestine. Britain had failed to create political institutions in its mandate, instead leaving the Arab and Jewish communities to struggle for supremacy. In this struggle, the Jewish community emerged victorious; a few hours after High Commissioner Cunningham's departure, Ben-Gurion proclaimed the independence of the state of Israel. The new state was immediately recognized by the United States and the Soviet Union.

David Ben-Gurion announcing the independence of the state of Israel, May 14, 1948. The portrait looming over the proceedings is of Theodore Herzl, the founder of the political Zionist movement and author of *The Jewish State*. (AP/World Wide Photos)

The First Arab-Israeli War

On May 15, 1948, units from the armies of Egypt, Syria, Lebanon, Transjordan, and Iraq invaded Israel, launching a regional war, interspersed with several truces, that lasted until December 1948 and that resulted in the defeat of the Arab forces, the enlargement of Israeli territory, and the collapse of the UN proposal for a Palestinian Arab state.

Ostensibly operating under the unified authority of the Arab League, each of the Arab states participating in the invasion in fact placed its own interests first. Thus, the invasion of Israel was hampered from the outset by inter-Arab political rivalries that led in turn to a lack of coordination on the battlefield. In addition, the Arab forces, with the exception of King Abdallah's Arab Legion, were not only poorly prepared, poorly equipped, and poorly led, they were also outnumbered. The legend of a defenseless, newborn Israel facing the onslaught of hordes of Arab soldiers does not correspond to reality. During the first round of fighting from May 15 to June 11,

1948, the combined Arab armies numbered around 21,500, whereas the Haganah and its affiliated units fielded a force of some 30,000. Numbers, of course, do not tell the whole story. The Israeli forces, under the overall strategic command of Ben-Gurion, were motivated by the belief that they were engaged in a life-and-death struggle for the very existence of a Jewish state. They performed exceptionally well, exhibiting the daring and combat improvisation that were to characterize the Israeli military in its subsequent wars. By the time of the first UN armistice in June, the Arab attacks had been repulsed on all fronts except Jerusalem, where the Arab Legion took East Jerusalem and Israeli forces held the new, western portion of the city. Although both sides used the truce to improve their armaments, the Israelis entered the next round of combat (July 9–18) with markedly superior forces. The size of the Haganah was doubled and its firepower substantially increased by the procurement of supplies of small arms, heavy equipment, and even a few aircraft from Europe. When the second armistice took effect in July, the Israeli victory was assured.

Over the course of the next twelve months, each of the belligerent Arab states concluded an armistice agreement with Israel. These agreements were not peace treaties, and they did not constitute recognition of Israel on the part of the Arab signatories; they simply stabilized the cease-fire borders without accepting them as final. Palestine had effectively been partitioned among Israel, Egypt (which remained in occupation of the Gaza Strip), and Transjordan (which had taken the old city of Jerusalem and the territory west of the Jordan River; see Map 13.3).

Not only was there no Palestinian Arab state, but the vast majority of the Arab population in the territory that became Israel—over 700,000 people— had become refugees. The Arab flight from Palestine began during the civil war and was at first the normal reaction of a civilian population to nearby fighting—a temporary evacuation from the zone of combat with plans to re-turn once hostilities ceased. However, during spring and early summer 1948, the flight of the Palestinian Arabs was transformed into a permanent mass exodus, as villagers abandoned their ancestral soil and city dwellers left behind their homes and businesses. Once the Arab flight had started, it was encouraged by the Haganah. In order to secure the interior of the Israeli state and protect Jewish settlements lying outside its UN-decreed borders, the Haganah in April 1948 authorized a campaign against potentially hostile Arab villages. Known as Plan D, the campaign "provided for the conquest and permanent occupation, or leveling, of Arab villages and towns."[8] The Haganah field officers interpreted Plan D as giving them authority to under-take the systematic expulsion of the Palestinian Arabs living within the area allocated to the Jewish state as well as those whose villages were situated just inside the territory awarded to the Arab state. The implementation of Plan D intensified the fears that already existed among the Arab population and contributed to the flight that soon took on an irreversible momentum. As

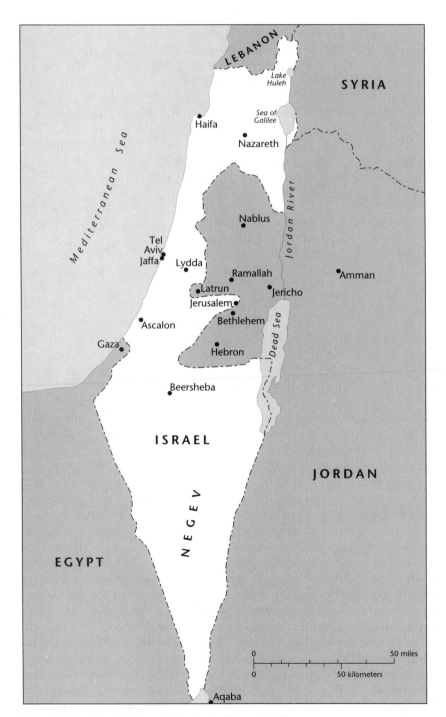

Map 13.3 The Arab-Israeli Armistice Lines, 1949

hundreds of thousands of Arab civilians headed for the frontiers, the Israeli command took advantage of the opportunity that was presented to ensure a contiguous and homogeneous Jewish state with a solid Jewish majority. Throughout the remainder of 1948 and into 1949, there were incidents of forced evacuation of Arabs. As a result, by the time the last armistice agreement was concluded in 1949, there remained only 160,000 Arabs within the borders of Israel.

The majority of those who had fled or been deported were destitute and crowded into refugee camps in various Arab states. The forceful creation of the state of Israel replaced the European Jewish refugee problem with a Middle Eastern refugee problem that has caused great personal suffering and regional political turmoil ever since. (We examine the issue in more detail in Chapter 17.)

In addition to creating the tragedy of the displaced Palestinians, the decisive Israeli military victory—referred to as the War of Independence in Israel—over the invading Arab forces discredited the regimes that had ordered such unprepared units into combat. The Arab defeat took on civilizational overtones, bringing about a critical self-examination of the social and political bases of Arab life. One of the most influential Arab commentaries on the subject, Constantine Zurayq's *The Meaning of the Disaster*, received such widespread circulation that it made the term *disaster* synonymous with the Arab defeat of 1948. That defeat, and its widespread condemnation among Arabs themselves, transformed the original struggle between the Arab and Jewish inhabitants of Palestine into the tragic Arab-Israeli conflict.

Conclusion

From the perspective of relations between states, the decade of the 1940s was a period of profound change in the Middle East. The creation of Israel, the flight and homelessness of several hundred thousand Palestinians, the formation of the Arab League, the achievement of independence by the core Arab states, and the decline of Britain and France and the emergence of the United States and the Soviet Union as world powers clearly represented new and significant developments for the region. Yet in the realm of domestic politics, there was remarkably little change. With the exception of the young shah of Iran, the ruling monarchs of 1949 had been on their thrones in the 1930s, and the men who held office as prime ministers and presidents in 1949 had served in similar capacities in the 1930s.

In several countries, especially the populous Arab states, these ruling elite no longer represented the aspirations of their people. They were seen to perpetuate an old order of corruption and privilege and to owe their political power to their willingness to cooperate with the forces of imperialism. They were also regarded as responsible for creating the circumstances that led to the "disaster" of 1948. They managed to retain their positions during and immediately after World War II, but in the emerging era of national independence, the ruling elite and the social and political order that supported them would be swept aside by new forces of change.

Notes

1. Cited in Walter Laqueur, ed., *The Israel-Arab Reader: A Documentary History of the Middle East Conflict* (New York, 1969), p. 18.

2. Cited in Christopher Sykes, *Cross Roads to Israel* (London, 1965), p. 135.

3. Cited in ibid., p. 205.

4. Cited in Laqueur, *The Israel-Arab Reader,* p. 66.

5. Cited in Sykes, *Cross Roads to Israel,* p. 246.

6. Charles D. Smith, *Palestine and the Arab-Israeli Conflict,* 3rd ed. (New York, 1996), p. 139.

7. Cited in John Marlowe, *The Seat of Pilate* (London, 1959), p. 252.

8. Benny Morris, *The Birth of the Palestinian Refugee Problem, 1947–1949* (Cambridge, 1987), p. 63.

The Independent Middle East from the End of World War II to the 1970s

PART IV

⟨I⟩
⟨I⟩

The end of the Second World War brought to the central Arab states the sovereignty that they had demanded since their creation in 1919. However, the withdrawal of European troops and administrators did not, as the entire Middle East region quickly discovered, mean the end of dependence on outside powers. The emergence of the cold war competition for global supremacy between the Soviet Union and the United States embroiled many of the states of the Middle East in a regional cold war—and sometimes a hot one—as allies of one or another of the two superpowers. Economic assistance and military weapons became the new commodities of alliance building. Countries such as Turkey, Iran, Jordan, and Israel that sided fully with the United States and its European allies against the Soviet Union received generous amounts of U.S. aid and were encouraged to purchase large quantities of Western weapons. Countries that preferred to keep a certain distance between themselves and their former imperial rulers found themselves shut off from Western aid and forced to turn to the Soviet Union for military and economic assistance. The cold war was an essential and basic factor in diplomatic relations and external assistance for virtually all states in the region during the period covered by this section of the book. The United States, in particular, tended to view the Middle East solely through the lens of its rivalry with the Soviet Union for global supremacy, and it neglected to develop policies that might have improved its relations with the core Arab states.

The political leadership of the core Arab countries—Egypt, Syria, and Iraq—changed dramatically during the 1950s. Upper-class civilian politicians educated in European-style institutions were replaced by young military officers from the lower urban or rural strata of society. Motivated by sentiments of nationalism and eager to achieve social justice, economic development, and military superiority over Israel, the officer-politicians adopted ambitious reform programs and initiated weapons purchases that left them indebted to the Soviet Union. The very nature of their objectives led them to expand the role of the state to an unprecedented degree and to introduce planned economies and new networks of social control. Though they endorsed more emphatically than had their predecessors the imperative of Arab unity, they also built up the machinery of state to such an extent that unity was increasingly unlikely; though they denounced the corruption of the bourgeois governments they overthrew, they set up parasitic state bureaucracies that sapped both revenue and initiative; though they embraced the rhetoric of popular democracy, they established authoritarian single-party regimes with sham parliaments and meaningless elections; and though they vastly expanded educational opportunities, they introduced instruments of censorship to limit free expression. The rise of the young military officers to power was greeted with initial popular enthusiasm. But like their predecessors of the interwar era, they were unable to satisfy popular aspirations, and so movements rose in protest against their prolonged rule.

The most obvious manifestation of the failure of the reformist Arab regimes to achieve their stated objectives was Israel's resounding military victory over the combined forces of Egypt, Syria, and Jordan in the June War of 1967. This war was a seminal event in modern Middle Eastern history and ushered in a tumultuous, decades-long period of readjustment. Israel's continued occupation of the West Bank and the Gaza Strip generated intense debate within Israeli society and contributed to the rising influence of religious parties as a political force. The Israeli occupation also contributed to the rise of Palestinian nationalism and to the formation of Palestinian organizations committed to the establishment of an independent Palestinian state. The activities of these organizations added a significant new dimension to regional politics and imparted to the Palestinians greater influence than they had previously exercised.

Democracy and Authoritarianism: Turkey and Iran

14

Turkey and Iran embarked on different courses of political development in the three decades following World War II. In Turkey the authoritarian single-party rule of the Republican People's Party gave way to a multiparty system in which elections were openly contested and voters eagerly participated. Although Turkish democracy had its moments of crisis during this period, they were resolved in favor of a continued commitment to political pluralism and freedom of expression. In Iran, in contrast, Muhammad Reza Shah, after narrowly surviving an oil nationalization crisis in the early 1950s, consolidated an authoritarian monarchy in which political activity was severely restricted. The shah was not without reformist ambitions, but he was unwilling to tolerate challenges to his power; he therefore established a system of government that rested on the narrow base of royal authority supported by the army and the secret police.

The Role of the United States in the Postwar Years

Although the entire Middle East was affected by the cold war struggle between the United States and the Soviet Union, the first states of the region to be drawn into the superpower rivalry were Turkey and Iran, the Soviet Union's immediate neighbors. The United States, as part of its policy of containing the Soviet Union, provided economic and military assistance to the two states. In so doing, the United States inserted itself as an influential force in the domestic and foreign policy considerations of Turkey and Iran. Therefore, before going on to examine domestic developments in the two countries, we should get an overview of the concerns that led the United States to become so deeply involved in their affairs.

In 1945 both Turkey and Iran were confronted with threats to their sovereignty by the Soviet Union. Early in the year, Moscow put forward claims to Turkish territory in eastern Anatolia and demanded a greater share in governing and policing the Turkish Straits. President İnönü's government, encouraged by Britain and the United States, rejected the Soviet demands and asserted its sovereignty. The United States, however, took the incident as an example of Soviet expansionism and was awakened to Turkey's strategic importance and to the desirability of including the country within the emerging U.S. alliance against communism. For its part, the Ankara government recognized that it could not resist Soviet designs by itself and agreed to accept U.S. financial and military assistance and to allow the United States to establish military bases on Turkish territory. This marked the beginning of the durable but sometimes troubled postwar alliance between the two nations.

Iran's crisis with the Soviet Union was occasioned by Soviet behavior in the Iranian province of Azerbaijan. Soviet troops remained in the region after the war was over, a violation of the treaty signed in 1941. In November 1945 the provincial government of Azerbaijan, with Moscow's support, declared its autonomy. A month later, Kurdish patriots followed suit and proclaimed the autonomous Kurdish Republic of Mahabad in the southwestern region of Azerbaijan. The Iranian government, with strong backing from the United States, lodged a complaint with the UN Security Council, and in spring 1946 the Soviet Union agreed to withdraw its forces from Iranian territory. Immediately after the Soviet evacuation, the shah sent Iranian troops into Azerbaijan to crush the local supporters of the autonomy movements.

These two incidents, coupled with Soviet activities in Eastern Europe, contributed to the emergence of the cold war perspective within U.S. foreign policy circles: The Soviet Union was seen as an aggressively expansionist power devoted to the single-minded mission of spreading communism throughout the world. Such an uncomplicated interpretation of Soviet motives led to an equally uncomplicated response; the United States, in order to protect its new global interests, had to commit its resources and those of its allies to the containment of the Soviet Union.

In the eastern Mediterranean region, the cold war view was expressed through the Truman Doctrine of 1947. Formulated in reaction to the Soviet pressures on Turkey discussed above, as well as to the outbreak of a Communist insurgency in Greece, the Truman Doctrine was an early formulation of the domino theory. It was based on the belief that unless the United States intervened, the Soviet Union was likely to gain control of Greece and Turkey, and, once this occurred, the other states of the Middle East would quickly fall under Communist influence. The Truman Doctrine was designed to forestall this eventuality by committing Washington to provide military assistance and economic aid to Greece and Turkey. Between 1947 and 1960, U.S. aid to Turkey totaled around $3 billion, enabling the Turks to maintain an armed force of 500,000 men as a deterrent to Soviet designs. The sheer scale of the foreign aid may also have led to the Turkish government to adopt irresponsible economic policies in the 1950s.

The U.S. policy of containment included plans to construct a network of interlocking alliances among the states of the Middle East. Thus, in 1952 Turkey and Greece became full members of the North Atlantic Treaty Organization (NATO); in 1954 Turkey and Pakistan signed a mutual cooperation treaty; and in 1955 the Baghdad Pact was created by an alliance between Turkey and Iraq to which Britain, Pakistan, and Iran soon became parties. In the process of erecting this shield of alliances against Soviet expansionism, the United States took over Britain's role as the primary Western power in the Middle East. Although the countries of the region appreciated U.S. economic aid, the United States' interference in domestic political life and the presence of U.S. military bases became a cause for resentment in some quarters. The United States had replaced Britain not only as a power but also as a target for criticism by Middle Eastern nationalists.

Turkey: The Transition to a Multiparty System

The end of the war brought to the surface pressures for economic and political change in Turkey. Since assuming office in 1938, President Inönü had followed the lines of economic development laid down by Atatürk. This meant adherence to the principle of etatism, by which the government took a major role in sponsoring industrial development. However, by the late 1940s the Turkish business sector wanted more freedom for private entrepreneurial activity, and the Turkish peasantry, which still made up a majority of the population, was displeased with the government's concentration on industrial development at the expense of agriculture. In addition, intellectuals and politicians alike shared a growing sentiment against the monopolization of political power by a single party. Responding to these currents, Inönü permitted greater freedom for the expression of political dissent. Four members of the national assembly took advantage of this opportunity and defected from the RPP in 1946 to form a new organization, the Democratic Party. Their activities were to bring momentous political change to Turkey.

The new party received the first test of its popularity in the elections of 1946. Although the Democrats won only 65 out of 465 seats in the national assembly, the very presence of an opposition party represented an important development in Turkish political life. During the next four years, the Democrats frequently challenged government policy in the assembly and engaged in heated debate with RPP representatives. The Democrats also concentrated on building an effective grassroots political organization with branches throughout Turkey. Although the Democrats' program did not differ significantly from that of the RPP, they were able to attract support by skillfully exploiting the growing popular disaffection, especially marked in the countryside, with the interference of the state in peoples' lives. Such regulation was the very essence of Kemalism—the establishment of state authority and the intervention of the state to enforce the social and legal changes instituted by the governments of Atatürk and İnönü. The Democratic Party pledged to reduce the interventionist practices of the Kemalist state, portraying itself as the representative of the common Turk on the one hand and the private-sector business community on the other. The elections of 1950 demonstrated the attractiveness of this message to the voters. In what is often referred to as a revolution in modern Turkish politics, the Democrats won 408 seats in the national assembly, the Republicans only 69. The Turkish people had expressed their desire for change, and after twenty-seven years of Republican rule, the party founded by Atatürk was swept out of office. İnönü, whose statesmanship during this period of transition has been widely acclaimed, handed the reins of government over to the Democrats in an orderly manner and joined the national assembly as leader of the opposition. Turkey, only four years after the founding of an opposition party, had undergone a peaceful transition to multiparty democracy.

The Democrats in Power, 1950–1960

The Democratic majority in the assembly turned to the party's founders for the highest national offices, electing Celal Bayar president and Adnan Menderes prime minister. These two individuals dominated Turkish politics during the Democrats' decade in power. Bayar (1882–1986) was a banker with a long record of government service; Menderes (1899–1961) came from a family of large landholders and held a degree from the Ankara College of Law. Neither man had any military background, which has led some scholars to view the rise of the Democratic Party as synonymous with a change in the composition of the Turkish political elite after 1950. Instead of being dominated by government officials and military officers turned politicians, the national assembly came to include a high proportion of professionals and businesspeople. This marked a break with the late Ottoman and early Republican trend, by which a career in the military or the bureaucracy served as a path to political power.

Did the Turkish people's support of the Democrats mean that they desired to overturn the Atatürk-İnönü legacy of secularism? An indication of the policy changes expected of the new government was given when the Democratic victory was announced to the public: The forbidden call to prayer in Arabic was heard from mosques in many regions of the country. The Menderes government knew full well what its mandate was in this regard, and one of its first acts was to legalize the call to prayer in Arabic. Other antisecularization measures quickly followed. Religious instruction was offered to all Muslim students in the primary school system unless their parents specifically requested otherwise; the number of schools for training Muslim prayer leaders was increased; and considerable government expenditures were devoted to the repair of existing mosques and to the construction of some 5,000 new ones. In this more favorable political climate, there was also an expansion in the publication of books and pamphlets dealing with religious subjects as well as a renewed public observance of such Islamic rituals as the Ramadan fast and the pilgrimage to Mecca.

Throughout the 1950s, the public celebration of religious ritual and the official authorization of modest institutional changes in the role of Islam marked a change from previous policy. However, this trend was more representative of a return to a balanced expression of popular religious desires than it was a determined reaction against the policies of Kemalism. People were free to practice what had been restricted for nearly thirty years. Insofar as this contributed to the government's popularity, the Democrats allowed it to continue. Yet if Menderes exploited religious issues for political purposes, he was not in favor of overturning the principle of secularism, only in modifying it.

The economy was the other principal issue on which the Democrats differed from the Republicans. Menderes was committed to reducing the role of the state and allowing more scope for private enterprise and the forces of the marketplace. At the same time, however, his government had also pledged to undertake agricultural reforms and to improve the standard of living of the rural peasantry. These two parts of the Democrats' economic policy were contradictory. Although there is no question that the Menderes government abandoned any semblance of economic planning, it is also true that the state retained a central role in the economy by its fiscal intervention in projects designed to develop Turkey's agricultural sector. Menderes was well aware that the votes of the conservative peasantry had contributed significantly to his electoral victory, and he was careful to nurture this support. His government imported vast quantities of expensive agricultural machinery, especially tractors; built dams and irrigation canals; and constructed a national network of highways that not only helped communication in general but also opened previously remote regions to commercial agriculture. During the 1950s Turkish peasants experienced a decided improvement in their quality of life; the policies of the Menderes government enabled agricultural production to increase by 75 percent and provided cultivators of wheat, cotton, and tobacco with new access to both national and international markets. However, in the mid-1950s the economy began to sour, and the agricultural sector was devastated by a series of droughts that brought a halt to the rural prosperity associated with the Democratic Party. In addition, Menderes's penchant for spending without planning, for importing consumer products and expensive machinery without funds to pay for them, created annual budget deficits that in turn resulted in a mounting national debt.

From the beginning of their tenure in office, the Democrats had been sensitive to public criticism, and once their economic policies came under fire, they introduced a series of repressive measures that allowed the government to censor the press, imprison journalists, and shut down offending newspapers. But such practices could backfire. By removing the outlets for peaceful criticism, the government created a situation in which violent protest became the only means of expressing opposition. This occurred with increasing frequency in Turkey's cities during spring 1960. As violence edged into Turkish political life, Menderes called upon the army to maintain law and order. He also used the armed forces for less orderly purposes, assigning them the task of disrupting Republican Party campaign rallies. This proved to be a mistake. In April 1960, troops blocked the train carrying Inönü to the city of Kayseri, where he was scheduled to deliver a speech. When Inönü disembarked to see what the trouble was, the troops respectfully parted before him; he then reboarded, and his train entered Kayseri between rows of officers and men standing at the salute in tribute to the former companion of Atatürk and hero of the war of independence. The incident at Kayseri should have made it clear to Menderes that the army would not allow itself to be turned into a tool of political repression against the legacy of Atatürk. Nor, as it turned out, would the army allow the government to stray too far from that legacy. A few weeks after the Kayseri incident, with the economy in decline and the government drifting toward authoritarianism, the military intervened and brought an abrupt end to the first Turkish republic.

The Coup d'État of 1960

In the early morning of May 27, 1960, the Turkish armed forces under the command of General Cemal Gürsel seized control of Istanbul and Ankara and arrested leading government officials, including President Bayar and Prime Minister Menderes. Like countless other military juntas throughout the world, the Turkish officers disavowed any intention of remaining in power. Unlike most of their counterparts in newly independent states, they kept their promise and returned the reins of government to the civilian politicians in October 1961. This was not a coup d'état engineered by junior officers ambitious to prolong military rule. Rather, the intervention of 1960 was led by a general and was carried out for the purpose of preserving the principles of Kemalism from which the government of Menderes had, in the opinion of the military, strayed. From the Ottoman reforms of the nineteenth century to Atatürk's role in the foundation of the republic, the military had been in the forefront of European-style change. Men with military backgrounds had not only won the war of independence, they had laid the foundations on which the new Turkey was based. Even though Atatürk had separated the military from politics, the armed forces continued to think of themselves as the guardians of the secular, reformist, and democratic goals proclaimed by Atatürk and followed by his successor, Inönü.

Once the military assumed power, it faced the complex problems of governing and of ensuring that its intervention would produce the outcome it desired. As the instrument of governmental decisionmaking, a National Unity Council made up of thirty-eight officers was formed. General Gürsel became chairman of the council as well as president and prime minister. Within hours of the coup, the council arranged to have a group of law professors from Istanbul University flown to Ankara to begin drafting a new constitution. This act appeared to confirm that the military intervention was indeed temporary and that the leaders of the National Unity Council were committed to preserving Atatürk's principle of separating the military from politics.

The revised constitution was approved in July 1961. It differed from its predecessor in that it replaced the single-house national assembly with a bicameral legislature consisting of a senate and an assembly. It also included clauses protecting the rights of individuals and asserting the principle of secularism. With the constitution in place, the National Unity Council prepared to return the country to civilian rule.

Before elections were held, the military needed to resolve the dilemma of how to deal with the imprisoned members of the Democratic Party. In order to justify their intervention in the political process, the army officers had to demonstrate to the Turkish people that the Democratic leaders were guilty of more onerous crimes than simple misgovernment. Nearly 600 members of the deposed regime were charged with offenses involving political and financial corruption and subversion of the constitution. The trials lasted nearly a year and resulted in the conviction and imprisonment of some 450 individuals for terms ranging from one year to life. Menderes and two of his cabinet ministers were sentenced to death and were hanged in September 1961. This controversial execution of the still-popular Menderes was seen by his followers as a political act, not as an act of justice, and it tarnished the otherwise credible reputation the military earned during its eighteen months in power.

The Second Republic from 1961 to 1983:
Social Change, Political Instability, and Military Intervention

An overview of governmental changes in the two decades after 1961 reveals the instability that characterized Turkish political life during this period. After four years of RPP coalition governments, the new Justice Party won the elections of 1965, but it could not effectively deal with the mounting wave of violence and social unrest within the country and was removed from office by the military in 1971. Two years later the military returned Turkey to civilian rule, but by 1980 the country was once again faced with domestic turmoil, and once again the military intervened to restore order and uphold the principles of Kemalism.

What was occurring in Turkey was a complex process of social, economic, and demographic change. The population nearly doubled in twenty-five years, increasing from 21 million in 1950 to slightly over 40 million in 1975. Turkey, like other Middle Eastern states, went through a phase of rapid urbanization after World War II. In 1950, 8.4 percent of the Turkish population lived in cities of 100,000 and over; in 1975 the figure was 23 percent. The population of Istanbul grew from 1 million in 1950 to over 5 million by the mid-1980s. During the same period, Ankara's population increased from 290,000 to 2.2 million. The major cause of rapid urbanization was the migration of villagers to cities in search of better economic opportunities. They did not always find them, and shantytowns inhabited by unemployed or underemployed migrants became a prominent feature of Turkey's urban landscape.

In response to limited opportunities at home, Turks sought employment abroad. Beginning in the 1960s, a mass migration of Turkish workers to Western Europe took place, and by the late 1980s some 1.8 million Turks resided in West Germany alone. They were called "guest workers" because the host European countries did not intend to grant them permanent residency, expecting them instead to return to Turkey. However, large numbers of Turkish workers stayed in Europe for prolonged periods, raised families there, and sought, against mounting resistance, to become citizens of the states in which they were employed. The issue of the status of the Turks in Europe has become an explosive one, especially in Germany, and is a factor in Turkey's relations with European governments.

It is testimony to the Turkish educational system that during the quarter century of rapid population growth after 1950, the literacy rate continued to rise. By 1975 nearly 75 percent of Turkish men and 48 percent of women were literate, up from 47 percent and 20 percent in 1950. The disparity between male and female literacy rates suggests that the full legal emancipation of women Atatürk had decreed was not translated into practical reality. Nevertheless, in some fields Turkish women played a greater role than their counterparts in other Middle Eastern countries. For example, every national assembly from 1935 (when women were first eligible for election) to 1975 contained female representatives. It is also noteworthy that by 1975, girls made up 46 percent of the students in primary schools, though only 20 percent of university students were women. Statistics of this kind do not, of course, reveal attitudes and opportunities, nor do they explain that notions about what constituted proper social behavior for women varied among regions, generations, and social classes. Although Turkish society as a whole remained conservative on the question of women's social roles, the increasing participation of women in education and public life constituted a significant aspect of the country's social and economic transformation.

The post-1950 social and economic transformation placed severe strains on Turkey's political structure, which had been designed to function as a two-party system. However, the two mainstream parties were unable to accommodate the growing diversity of interests that were spawned by Turkey's transition from a predominantly agricultural to a mixed economy.

Groups that had prospered under the policies of one particular government—industrialists and peasants under Menderes, for example—did not
wish to lose their favored status when new governments came to power.
They therefore formed political parties to represent their particular interests
in the national assembly. At the same time, other groups that believed their
needs were being ignored—industrial workers and university students,
Marxists and Muslim revivalists—formed their own organizations and parties through which they hoped to gain a share of political power. In the
1960s and 1970s, this process of institutionalizing interest groups led to a
proliferation of political parties. Thus, by 1969 the number of parties represented in the national assembly had grown to eight. Although most Turks
continued to support one of the two mainstream parties, the smaller organizations attracted enough voters to prevent either Justice or the Republicans
from gaining an absolute majority. This tended to paralyze the legislative
process and to prompt dissatisfied groups to reject the formal channels of
politics and take their demands to the street.

The circumstances that led to the military overthrow of Prime Minister
Süleyman Demirel's Justice Party government in 1971 illustrate the challenges that the proliferation of political parties posed to Turkish democracy.
During Demirel's term in office, various factions within his party defected
to form splinter groups of their own, gradually reducing his parliamentary
majority and bringing the legislative process to a halt. To add to the administration's difficulties, an economic recession in the late 1960s sparked a
wave of social unrest marked by street demonstrations, labor strikes, and political assassinations. The Justice Party government, like the Democratic
Party regime a decade earlier, was unable to contain the violence. In March
1971, therefore, the Turkish High Command sent an ultimatum to the government charging it with driving the country into political anarchy and economic chaos and demanding the resignation of Prime Minister Demirel.
This military intervention became known as the coup by memorandum because, in contrast to the 1960 coup, the armed forces remained behind the
scenes and did not seize power.

Nevertheless, the civilian politicians who governed Turkey from 1971 to
1973 did so under instructions from the military. The High Command was
motivated by an unrealistic belief that an increasingly complex society could
somehow be purged of its class divisions, its economic disparities, and its
ideological disagreements by the simple expedient of removing discontented activists. Operating under martial law, the government arrested and
imprisoned hundreds of people, especially those identified with the radical
Left. Strikes were banned in certain provinces, and several newspapers were
closed. Yet for all the heavy-handed tactics, few essential changes had been
introduced when the army withdrew from its supervisory role in 1973. Violence had been suppressed, but the social, economic, and political tensions
that were at the root of the violence had not diminished.

The elections of 1973 brought the Republican Party back to power. But because the two-year military interlude had not resolved Turkey's political crisis, the Republicans were again forced to form a coalition government, this time with the National Salvation Party, a conservative, religiously oriented party that advocated the veiling of women and the return of the Arabic script. Prime Minister Bulent Ecevit, the leader of the secularizing party of Atatürk, found himself allied with an avowedly religious party in order to cling to power; it was an arrangement that has been aptly described as "a marriage of inconvenience."[1]

It is not surprising that the marriage did not last. In 1975 Turkey was plunged into the same kind of political turmoil and urban violence that had plagued it in the 1960s. Coalition governments rose and fell, and the minority parties exercised an influence out of all proportion to their electoral support. One analysis of the causes of the social and political turmoil of the 1970s suggests that both of the mainstream parties, Republican and Justice, granted excessive favors to the minority parties in order to attract them as coalition partners. Such favors included the appointment of a number of minority party leaders to cabinet positions. Once the small parties acquired power, they tried to ensure that they kept it by staffing their ministries with supporters. In this manner, the bureaucracy and the law enforcement agencies became politicized, as professional civil servants and police were replaced by patronage appointees. The entrenchment of elements of the extreme Right and Left in the institutions of state polarized the civil service and reduced the ability of the police to deal with the growing violence.

The breakdown of civil order was compounded by two additional elements of discord. The first was increased activity on the part of Kurdish separatists. The second was the rise of Islamic revivalism led by the National Salvation Party. In September 1980 the party held a massive national rally during which the crowds demanded the return of the *shariʿah* and refused to sing the Turkish national anthem. Both of these developments threatened the secular and nationalist principles of Kemalism, principles that the officer corps regarded as the cornerstones of the modern Turkish state. On September 12, 1980, the Turkish High Command, for the third time in twenty years, stepped into the political arena.

The leading civilian politicians were placed under house arrest, and a military-dominated National Security Council took charge of the administrative and legislative functions of government. As was the case in the two previous interventions, the generals did not intend to remain in power, but they did intend to restore order. Martial law was proclaimed, the most militant trade unions were dissolved, and thousands of suspected terrorists and political agitators were arrested and later tried. The leader of the National Salvation Party was charged with violating the secular principles of the constitution and sentenced to a four-year prison term. In an attempt to weed out the politicized elements within the bureaucracy and restore its professionalism, the military purged the civil service and decreed a uniform grooming code intended to eliminate any outward symbols of political loyalty: The code banned "leftist moustaches, rightist sideburns, and ambiguous beards."[2]

The intervention of 1971 had ended the political turmoil but did not address its causes; the generals of 1980 were determined to restructure the political system. They achieved this goal largely through the drafting of a new constitution that strengthened the powers of the president by giving him the authority to appoint the prime minister and to dissolve the national assembly. The constitution also provided for tighter government control of universities, trade unions, and the press. To reduce the influence of the small political parties, a new electoral law denied parliamentary representation to any party that did not receive 10 percent of the total vote. The new constitution was approved in a national referendum in 1982. The National Security Council then named General Evren president for a seven-year term and, hopeful that the reconstructed system contained enough safeguards to prevent a recurrence of disorder, called for elections.

The 1983 elections were won by a new political organization, the Motherland Party led by Turgut Özal. Although the Motherland Party was composed of a potentially disruptive mixture of Islamic revivalists and secular liberals, Özal was able to form a majority government, to enact economic reforms, and to lead the party to another victory in the 1987 elections. For the time being, democracy was restored and politics was back in the hands of civilians.

Despite the three military interventions, Turkey's commitment to a multiparty democratic system endured, and the achievements of the various governments since 1950, albeit uneven, were on the whole impressive, especially if we remember that Turkey was experiencing a major social and economic transformation during these years. A new system of multiparty democracy was introduced just as the country was entering a period of unprecedented change. Turkey was able to survive with its democratic institutions intact, if somewhat battered, because of the Turkish people's commitment to political pluralism and political freedom. This commitment had its origins in the era of stability from 1923 to 1950 during which the principles of Kemalism became embedded in the national consciousness. Other Middle Eastern states that did not have an orderly period of early independence dealt very differently with the kinds of crises Turkey overcame.

Turkish Foreign Policy and the Cyprus Question

The first section of this chapter described the circumstances that led to the establishment of close ties between the United States and Turkey after the Second World War. Those ties were not disrupted by the upheavals in Turkey's domestic politics, and active participation in the Western alliance continued to be a cornerstone of Turkey's foreign policy during the cold war. Within the Middle East, Turkey's relations with the Arab regimes were correct but somewhat uneasy because of Ankara's recognition of Israel in 1949 and its close relations with the United States.

The major stumbling block in Turkey's foreign relations was the Cyprus question. It not only affected Ankara's regional relations with Greece, but it also had repercussions in Washington. The Cyprus question was a legacy of Ottoman territorial expansion and British imperialism. The island, only 50 miles (80 km) off the Turkish coast, was conquered by the Ottomans in 1570–1571. Over the course of three centuries of Ottoman rule, Turks from the mainland settled among the existing Greek inhabitants. By the 1950s, Turks made up 18 percent of the island's population and formed a majority community along portions of the northern coast.

Britain occupied Cyprus in 1878 and was still administering it in the 1950s when Greek Cypriots launched a movement for the independence of the island and its eventual union with mainland Greece. The Turkish government was concerned about the security of the minority Turkish community and alarmed at the prospect of having territory so close to the Anatolian mainland come under the exclusive control of Greece. Negotiations among Britain, Greece, and Turkey eventually produced an agreement that awarded Cyprus independence in 1960. But the political structure of the new state was hedged with so many clauses protecting the rights of the two communities that Cyprus appeared to be governed by the Ottoman *millet* system rather than to be a unitary nation. To add to the volatility of the situation, a document known as the Treaty of Guarantee permitted Britain, Greece, and Turkey to station troops on the island and to intervene if the constitutional order was violated.

It was an arrangement inviting a crisis. In 1964 and again in 1974, Turkey and Greece became embroiled in confrontations over Cyprus that drew in their mutual ally, the United States, and threw the southern flank of NATO into disarray. After each of these episodes, Turkish-U.S. relations suffered a setback.

The crisis of 1964 was sparked by the efforts of the Greek president of Cyprus, Archbishop Makarios, to amend the constitution to limit the political rights of the Turkish community. Such efforts only served to increase communal tensions and finally to cause so much mutual bloodshed that the UN sent an emergency force to patrol a neutral zone between the two communities. However, the presence of UN troops did not convince the Ankara government that the Turkish community in Cyprus was secure, and in early summer 1964, Turkey prepared to invoke its right to intervene on the basis of the clauses of the 1960 Treaty of Guarantee. As the Turkish plans for an invasion of Cyprus unfolded, U.S. president Lyndon Johnson advised Ankara against the expedition. In a bluntly worded threat, Johnson told the prime minister of the time, Ismet Inönü, that if Turkey's planned invasion brought the Soviets into the crisis, then Washington would have to reconsider its NATO obligation to protect Turkey.

The Turkish invasion was canceled, and Inönü suffered a political embarrassment. But beyond that, Johnson's tactless treatment of a loyal U.S. ally created a strain in Turkish-U.S. relations and raised questions within Turkey about the value of its ties with the United States. Many of the political demonstrations of the late 1960s were directed against the U.S. presence in Turkey, a presence that included nearly 20,000 military and civilian personnel. Turkish protesters also expressed their resentment that Turkish foreign policy appeared to be decided in Washington, not in Ankara. The memories of 1964 guaranteed that the next Cyprus crisis would not unfold according to the U.S. plan.

On July 15, 1974, Greek military forces on Cyprus staged a coup that overthrew President Makarios and brought to power a group committed to political unification with the Greek mainland. Turkey responded to this provocation without waiting for U.S. approval; within a week of the coup, Turkish forces landed in northern Cyprus, and by August they had occupied 37 percent of the island and extended their control well beyond the regions in which the Turkish population was concentrated.

Turkey's action prompted the U.S. Congress to suspend all military aid and weapons sales to Turkey. Ankara reacted to the U.S. embargo by closing several U.S. bases in Turkey. The rupture between the two allies was partially healed in 1979 when the U.S. embargo was canceled. However, the U.S. response to the Cyprus invasion awakened Ankara to the dangers of relying too heavily on a single ally, and during the late 1970s Turkey strengthened its diplomatic relations with other countries, including the Soviet Union.

The Turkish intervention brought about the partition of Cyprus into a Greek Cypriot administration in the south and a Turkish Cypriot government in the north. Turkish forces from the mainland remained in occupation of the northern section, and in 1983 the leader of the Turkish Cypriots, Rauf Denktash, proclaimed the independent Turkish Republic of Northern Cyprus. Ankara was the only government to recognize it. Although the UN has sponsored several negotiating sessions in the years since 1974, the Greek and Turkish governments remain at odds over the Cyprus question.

Iran: The Reestablishment of Royal Autocracy

The Ruler and the Opposition, 1945–1953

Reza Shah's abdication in 1941 opened the way for a revival of political activity. The new ruler, Muhammad Reza Shah, was almost overwhelmed by the combination of domestic unrest and foreign pressure to which his government was subjected during the first twelve years of his reign. Had it not been for Anglo-U.S. intervention in 1953, the shah might have lost his throne, and the course of postwar Iranian history would have taken a different direction.

Muhammad Reza (1919–1980) was raised to succeed his father, but his upbringing, by its very nature, removed him from contact with the Iranian people. After spending his early teenage years at the exclusive Le Rosey School in Switzerland, he returned to the royal court, where he received a political and military education closely supervised by his father. When he assumed the throne in 1941, his country was under Anglo-Soviet occupation, and he had little room to maneuver. For the next twelve years, the monarchy was insecure, and the ruler was forced to share power with other institutions.

The elements that had been silenced by Reza Shah's oppression reasserted themselves and sought to recover the status they had enjoyed prior to 1925. Prominent among them were the tribal leaders, the ulama, and the traditional landowning elite. Opposing them were interest groups that had benefited from Reza Shah's rule and were determined to retain the power they had acquired during his reign. The officer corps of the armed forces was the most significant of these groups. At the same time, new social, economic, and ideological interests entered the political arena and pressed for sweeping reforms. The advocates of reform were from diverse social and occupational groupings, ranging from the emergent labor movement and the new middle class of professionals to the older generation of constitutional liberals. The most widely supported reformist organization was the Tudeh (Masses) Party. Founded in 1941 by a coalition of young Marxists, Tudeh directed its appeals to a broad cross-section of the population: It endorsed labor legislation and land reform for workers and peasants, it promised political rights for women, and it supported improved wages for lower-level civil servants. Although Tudeh had a Marxist orientation and adopted a pro-Soviet stance, its leaders avoided labeling themselves Communists so as not to alienate the religious establishment and popular religious sentiment in general. During the 1940s the party expanded its national base and became the largest and most efficiently run political organization in Iran. There were expectations among both Iranians and foreign observers that Tudeh might soon control the government.

Throughout the 1940s, further discord was introduced into Iranian politics by the actions of Britain, the Soviet Union, and the United States, each of which endeavored to cultivate influence among local factions in order to further its own interests. Britain, as it had done in the period before Reza Shah, encouraged cooperation between the monarchy and such status-quo-oriented groupings as the large landowners and the powerful tribes. This was the type of alliance that had served the British so well in the Arab countries, and the one they favored for Iran. The Soviet Union, for its part, supported Tudeh activity, whereas the United States, a relative newcomer to the contest for influence in Iran, tended to back any faction that was opposed to Soviet ambitions. U.S. advisers developed close ties with the Iranian armed forces.

In the face of conflicting pressures from at home and abroad, the inexperienced shah attempted to preserve his throne by satisfying some of the demands of his domestic critics, such as allowing the Majlis to become a forum for open debate. However, the shah had no intention of surrendering all his royal powers. He remained the commander in chief of the armed forces and, in the tradition of his father, curried favor with the officer corps, cementing the ties between the monarch and the military that had proved beneficial to royal rule in the past. The brutal manner in which he crushed the Azerbaijan autonomy movement in 1946 showed that Muhammad Reza, like his father, would not hesitate to employ the military as an instrument of internal security.

As political instability and foreign interference continued to undermine the government and the economy in the late 1940s, the central political question revolved around the issue of who would govern Iran. Would it be the elected parliament and cabinet, or would the shah impose his personal rule, as his father had? At first it appeared that the shah was being forced to move in the direction of establishing a constitutional monarchy. He lacked both personal charisma and religious legitimacy and was still a young and uncertain monarch whose control of the political system and ties to the country at large were tenuous. He was particularly vulnerable to criticism in the one area on which most Iranians, of whatever political coloring, were united—the issue of foreign domination. In the early 1950s, he was to be contested on this issue by the most widespread movement of popular protest in postwar Iran up to the revolution that finally toppled him in 1979.

Muhammad Mosaddiq and the
Oil Nationalization Crisis, 1951–1953

In order to appreciate the appeal of Muhammad Mosaddiq and his National Front organization, we must remember that Iran, although never a colony or a protectorate, was nonetheless denied its sovereignty throughout the first half of the twentieth century. From the disadvantageous concessions granted by the Qajar shahs to the unfavorable oil agreement signed by Reza Shah in 1933, Iran's economic development was placed largely in the hands of European entrepreneurs; from the Russo-British invasion in 1914 to the Soviet-British occupation of 1941, Iran's independence was violated whenever it suited European Great Powers to do so. Cultural disrespect, economic domination, and imperial manipulation characterized Europe's relationship with Iran for much of the century leading up to 1950. Virtually all sectors of Iranian society resented the prominent role played by foreigners, whether they were Soviet engineers, British oil experts, or U.S. military advisers. Many Iranians also directed their discontent at the monarchs, past and present, who had allowed foreign domination to occur in the first place. These sentiments found a spokesman in Muhammad Mosaddiq, whose nationalist beliefs and personal appeal overshadowed the shah and threw Iran into a major international and domestic crisis from 1950 to 1953.

The individual whose name is linked to one of the most significant episodes in modern Iranian history was an unlikely figure to head a populist, antiroyalist movement. Mosaddiq (1882–1967) was born into a landed aristocratic family and studied at universities in Paris and Switzerland, eventually earning a doctorate in law at the University of Neuchâtel. He entered state service in 1915, and for the next several years he led an active political life as cabinet minister, provincial governor, and Majlis deputy. During these years, Mosaddiq earned a reputation as a politician of impeccable honesty and integrity. He also became known for his support of parliamentary democracy and his strong opposition to foreign activities in Iran. In the late 1930s, he was placed under house arrest for his objections to Reza Shah's authoritarianism; he reentered politics as an elected member of the Majlis in 1943.

Throughout the late 1940s, Mosaddiq's impassioned campaign against continued foreign interference in Iran and his warnings about the dangers of abandoning democracy for royal dictatorship attracted widespread support. In 1949 several political parties and interest groups joined together under Mosaddiq's leadership to form the National Front. This broad-based coalition was dominated by elements from both the traditional and the modern middle classes who were united in their opposition to foreign influence and to an increase in the powers of the monarchy. The diversity of the National Front—it contained ulama who advocated a greater role for the *sharicah* and Western-educated professionals who pushed for new measures of secularization—made it difficult for Mosaddiq to satisfy the demands of one faction of the coalition without offending others. However, on the question of national sovereignty, the members of the organization agreed.

The issue that propelled Mosaddiq and the National Front to political prominence was the control of the Iranian oil industry by the British-dominated Anglo-Iranian Oil Company. By the late 1940s, the AIOC had built up such a massive presence throughout the country that it was practically a state within a state. Not only did the AIOC build its own company town at Abadan, site of the world's largest oil refinery, it also supplied its own municipal services, built its own roads and airports, and negotiated its own security arrangements with neighboring tribes. Management and clerical positions were in the hands of foreigners, and Iranians were employed only as laborers. Although the AIOC was a private enterprise, the majority of its stock was owned by the British government; Iranians viewed the company as just another manifestation of British influence in their country.

The Iranian government was displeased with the terms of the concession Reza Shah signed with the AIOC in 1933 (see Chapter 10) and in the late 1940s negotiated revisions. In 1950 the revisions were submitted to the Majlis, where they met with the determined opposition of Mosaddiq and the National Front deputies. Branding the AIOC as an arm of the British government, Mosaddiq called for the cancellation of the concession and the nationalization of the Iranian oil industry. Over the course of the next several months, Mosaddiq and his allies organized demonstrations and gave speeches to win public opinion to their side. One of the ulama members of the National Front equated the oil issue with the very essence of Iran's being, urging "serious Muslims and patriotic citizens to fight against the enemies of Islam and Iran by joining the nationalization struggle."[3] In 1951, amidst the wave of popular enthusiasm generated by the National Front's campaign, the Majlis took two dramatic steps: It passed legislation nationalizing the oil industry, and it invited Mosaddiq to become prime minister. Although Mosaddiq was asked to assume the prime ministership because of his stance on the nationalization of oil, his tumultuous term in office (May 1951–August 1953) was devoted to much more than the dispute between Iran and the AIOC; it was also devoted to a struggle for the political future of Iran.

In response to the passage of the oil nationalization law, the AIOC called for a worldwide boycott of Iranian oil. The British government quickly became a party to the crisis by endorsing the boycott, reinforcing its naval forces in the Persian Gulf, and imposing economic sanctions on Iran. When the United States joined the boycott in 1952, Iran was effectively prevented from selling its oil on the international market, and the country was plunged into a financial crisis by the almost total loss of oil revenues. Despite the economic hardships created by the boycott, Mosaddiq refused to compromise on the nationalization issue, and in October 1952 his government severed diplomatic relations with Britain.

Iran's confrontation with the AIOC and Britain produced a domestic as well as an international crisis. Mosaddiq was determined not only to break the stranglehold of foreign interests in Iran but also to reinstate the parliamentary institutions proclaimed in the 1906 constitution. This involved him in a power struggle with the shah and with the shah's new Great Power patron, the United States. Throughout the months of Mosaddiq's rise to power, the shah had been indecisive. His inclination to accommodate the foreign powers on which his government depended for loans and military equipment provided the opening for Mosaddiq's popularity in the first place; and his reluctance to test his tepid personality in a direct confrontation with the charismatic prime minister allowed the latter to introduce measures that, if carried out, would have reduced the monarchy to a ceremonial role.

In 1952 Mosaddiq persuaded the Majlis to grant him emergency powers, which he used to launch an attack on the monarchy. He obtained a ruling from a special parliamentary committee that placed the armed forces under the control of the government, not of the shah. Mosaddiq also reduced the size of the army, purged the officer corps, and introduced a land reform law. This assault on entrenched interests was part of Mosaddiq's plan to replace the personal rule of the monarch with the rule of constitutional law, to make the military subject to the will of the parliament rather than the sovereign, and to redistribute the wealth and land of the privileged elite.

However, despite general support for his objectives, Mosaddiq was a reformer without adequate revenue, and he found it increasingly difficult to implement the programs on which his continued popularity depended. As Iran's revenues declined because of the worldwide oil boycott, unemployment and prices rose. This provided leftist organizations, especially the Tudeh Party, with opportunities to attract discontented elements of the working class. Moreover, the zeal with which Mosaddiq pursued far-reaching changes within Iranian society alarmed some members of the National Front, especially the ulama, who became suspicious at the secular direction of the reforms. In 1953 the National Front began to disintegrate as the conservative religious parties and other groups on the political right defected from the coalition. The unraveling of the National Front allowed the Tudeh to reemerge as the major political force in the country. At the same time, a group of disaffected military officers formed a secret committee to plot for the overthrow of Mosaddiq and the reestablishment of royal authority.

The goals of the military conspirators coincided with those of the U.S. government. Fearing that Mosaddiq had lost control of the situation in Iran and that the revived Tudeh would lead the country into the Soviet camp, Washington dispatched CIA agents to Tehran to assist the Iranian officers in organizing a coup against Mosaddiq. The shah agreed to the coup in advance and signed a decree appointing the leader of the secret committee, General Fazallah Zahedi, prime minister. When the first coup attempt failed miserably, the shah fled to Rome. However, three days later, on August 19, 1953, the royalist military forces struck again and succeeded in capturing the prime minister. The shah returned to consolidate the monarchy.

During the period from 1951 to 1953, Mosaddiq mobilized Iranian society in an attempt to recover national sovereignty and establish an alternative to royal autocracy. His overthrow marked the triumph of the forces to which he was opposed: The coup of 1953 brought about the return of royal dictatorship and an intensification of U.S. interference in the domestic affairs of Iran.

Consolidation of the Royal Dictatorship After 1953

In the words of one observer, "the 1953 coup brought down an iron curtain on Iranian politics."[4] That curtain remained closed for the next twenty-six years as the shah took steps to make sure that the circumstances that had nearly cost him his throne would not recur.

The oil dispute, which had given Mosaddiq his political platform, was quickly settled by an arrangement that gave Iran a 50 percent share of the profits from petroleum. Iranian oil rapidly recovered its place in the international market and provided the government with ever-increasing revenues. The shah also undertook to improve Iran's standing with the Western powers. Diplomatic relations with Britain were restored in 1954, and the shah proclaimed his commitment to the Western alliance and to a program of economic development on the Western model. Such diplomatic loyalty and economic emulation would, he hoped, result in substantial infusions of U.S. aid. The shah was not disappointed on that score; between 1953 and 1963 the United States provided Iran with $500 million in military aid.

The shah dealt harshly with the groups that had opposed him during the Mosaddiq era. The National Front was disbanded, and its leaders, including Mosaddiq himself, were imprisoned. The regime's security forces made a concerted effort to destroy the Tudeh Party; its underground networks were uncovered, hundreds of its members were jailed, and dozens of its leaders were executed and tortured. In order to prevent the reemergence of organized opposition, the shah, with assistance from U.S. and Israeli advisers, established an internal security organization, SAVAK, that became notorious for its pervasive surveillance operations and its brutal treatment of the political prisoners who packed Iran's jails. From 1953 to 1979, there was no political freedom in Iran. Although there were periods when limited expression was permitted, the overall picture was one of repression, manipulation, and coercion. Elections to the Majlis were controlled, and the two-party system the shah adopted to provide the appearance of democracy was so tightly restricted that Iranians referred to the two organizations as the "yes" and the "yes sir" parties.[5]

A short-lived challenge to this repressive system occurred during 1960 to 1963, when the country experienced one of its periodic economic downturns and the shah, under pressure from the United States to liberalize his regime, allowed the National Front to participate in election campaigns. The criticism of the regime by the National Front candidates, the government's obvious manipulation of the election results, and the worsening economic conditions all combined to provoke an outbreak of strikes and demonstrations. The protest movement reached a climax in 1963 when a relatively unknown member of the religious establishment, Ayatollah Ruhollah Khomeini, began to preach against the regime and its U.S. ally. Khomeini denounced the shah for corruption, for neglecting the rights of the oppressed masses, and for compromising Iran's sovereignty. He further accused the regime of ignoring the country's Islamic beliefs by selling oil to Israel and granting economic concessions to the United States. In June 1963 SAVAK arrested Khomeini. When word of the arrest spread, Tehran and other major cities exploded in a wave of antigovernment demonstrations that continued for three days before the military was able to crush them at the cost of hundreds, possibly thousands, of lives. Khomeini was exiled to Turkey in 1964; a year later he was deported to Iraq, where he continued to write and preach until 1978, when he was forced to leave Iraq for France.

The disturbances of 1963 once again revealed the ability of the religious establishment to mobilize the masses by applying Islamic principles to contemporary conditions. The protests also showed the continued existence of deeply held emotions about foreign economic and political activities in Iran. In this case, the emotions were directed against an oppressive ruler who was charged with binding the country's destiny to an alien power whose interests were not necessarily in harmony with Iran's own.

These were dangerous signs for the regime, and it recognized them as such. Once the disturbances were quelled, the shah paid renewed attention to the institutions on which his power rested. These included an extensive network of court patronage, the government's control of appointments in the expanding civil bureaucracy, and the armed forces. This latter organization was the shah's personal favorite. He viewed the destinies of the military and the monarchy as inextricably linked. He frequently appeared in public in military dress, and his statement "I am the army" encapsulated his view of his relationship to the armed forces.[6] To keep the officer corps loyal, he provided them with well-appointed clubs, access to imported luxury goods, and high salaries. In addition to building up the Iranian armed forces to provide domestic security for his regime, the shah also wished to turn Iran into a major regional military power. He lavished huge sums on military equipment, acquiring some of the most sophisticated and expensive weaponry in the Western alliance's arsenal.

The funds the shah used to satisfy his desires for military equipment came as a result of the quadrupling of oil prices brought on by the oil boycott the Arab producing states imposed during the 1973 Arab-Israeli war (see Chapter 21). The revenue increases were staggering: In the decade from 1964 to 1974, Iran's total oil revenue was $13 billion; in the year 1975–1976 alone, it was $20 billion. The United States encouraged the shah, a loyal ally, to use Iran's oil wealth to acquire advanced weapons. He was allowed to purchase virtually any non-nuclear U.S. weapons system he desired. After expenditures of more than $10 billion on arms between 1972 and 1976, Iran had the fifth largest military force in the world, an army of some 400,000 men equipped with more British Chieftain tanks than the British forces themselves had, and an air force bristling with Phantom fighters, helicopter gunships, and missile-carrying Tomcat aircraft.

As was the case in the nineteenth-century Ottoman Empire and Egypt, the importation of foreign-made weapons systems meant the employment of foreign instructors. The arrival of thousands of agents of U.S. defense contractors, with their high salaries, their access to scarce housing, and their sometimes less than tactful comportment, led to the alienation of those Iranians who, like Ayatollah Khomeini in his sermons of 1963, believed that the shah's fascination with the West was an affront to Iran's cultural integrity and national sovereignty.

Reform from Above:
The White Revolution and Its Effects

Although the shah's primary concern was to consolidate his personal power, he was also committed to the transformation of Iran along Western lines. However, the program of royal reform contained a contradiction: As much as the shah tried to modernize the productive capacities of Iran, he would not permit any challenges to the institution of the monarchy. As a consequence, Iran experienced major economic and social changes but did not witness a corresponding change in the traditional system of royal authoritarianism. This produced conflict between the shah, who determined what would and would not be included in the reforms, and the large portion of the Iranian population that wished to see the political system opened up and freedom of expression permitted.

The shah's proposals for concentrated reform were announced in 1963 as the White Revolution, a term intended to imply reform without bloodshed. Of the twelve points set forth in the original program, the most important from the shah's perspective were land reform and the establishment of a literacy corps. Land reform had a political as well as a social purpose and was therefore among the most contentious goals of the White Revolution. It was designed to strike at the power of the large absentee landlords by limiting their individual holdings to one village. They were required to sell the excess to the state, which then redistributed it to peasant cultivators. The reform achieved its political purpose in that the shah succeeded in introducing the authority of the central state into the countryside and limiting the power of the landed elite. In addition, the traditional peasant role of subservient sharecropper was transformed into that of small private landowner freed from the obligations that had bound him to the will of the landlord.

In the countryside the results of the land reform were mixed. When the program was officially ended in 1971, the shah proclaimed that "there is no longer any farmer in the country who does not own his own land."[7] Although the monarch's claim was a few hundred thousand sharecroppers short of reality, the reforms did bring about a substantial redistribution of Iran's agricultural land. It has been estimated that 92 percent of former sharecroppers—nearly 2 million people—became peasant proprietors under the redistribution program. However, it was questionable whether the new proprietors gained any real economic benefits from their ownership rights. A few did become self-sufficient farmers, but around 75 percent received plots of land that were less than the minimum size needed to sustain a rural family at a basic subsistence level. This latter group, an embittered and disillusioned sector of the countryside, was either forced back into the paid rural labor force or became part of the huge migration to the urban centers. The process of rural migration was further intensified by the large-scale use of mechanized farm equipment, a practice that created rural unemployment by reducing the need for labor.

The literacy corps was part of a campaign to reduce rural illiteracy, which ran as high as 80 percent. The members of the corps were military conscripts who had acquired at least a high school diploma. As part of their mandatory military service, they spent fifteen months in rural villages engaged in such educational activities as teaching primary school and conducting night school classes for adults. Between 1963 and 1978, some 100,000 of these so-called soldiers of knowledge served in the countryside. Similar programs were introduced in the fields of health care and construction.

In addition to the specific projects set forth in the White Revolution, the shah inaugurated ambitious programs for economic and social development. Iran's internal and external communications were improved through the construction of roads and railways and the expansion of port facilities. The state invested heavily in industrial enterprises, and in the years after 1963, Iran's industrial output increased so dramatically that the shah predicted his country would be one of the world's five major industrial powers by the year 2000. Iran's rising industrial capacity was accompanied by a corresponding increase in the number of workers. However, because the state-controlled labor organizations deprived wage earners of true collective bargaining rights, wages tended to remain low while the prices of basic consumer items rose, sowing the seeds for future social discontent.

The shah also used Iran's oil revenues to improve education and health care. Between 1963 and 1977, enrollment in elementary schools grew from 1.6 million to over 4 million; university enrollment increased nearly sevenfold to 154,215. During the same period, the numbers of hospitals, health clinics, and trained physicians rose as well. Improved health care helped to reduce the infant mortality rate and led to a rapid growth in the population from 25.8 million in 1966 to 33.4 million just ten years later. As was the case in Turkey, the overall population boom was accompanied by an even sharper rise in the number of people living in cities. Rural migrants poured into Tehran, where the new industrial enterprises were concentrated, and turned Iran's capital into a sprawling, overcrowded metropolis of nearly 4.5 million people by 1976.

The shah's obsession with Western models of development led him to a grudging acceptance of the usefulness of expanding educational and employment opportunities for women. One of the original points in the White Revolution was the enfranchisement of women. In 1967 and 1975, family protection laws were announced that granted women greater legal equality within marriage. The laws did not abolish polygamy but required the husband to obtain consent from his current wife before taking an additional one. Compared to the legislation passed in Turkey, Iran's efforts to change the status of women were very modest.

Over time, the White Revolution became the justification for the shah's rule. Eager to legitimize his reign on grounds other than the naked use of force, he gave his reformist programs pseudo-progressive labels that masked his dictatorial style and helped to deflect external criticism from his corrupt and repressive regime. To be sure, there was substance to many of the new programs, but their benefits were limited to the privileged few. Land reform was allowed to languish after its promising beginnings, leaving peasants with dashed hopes and landlords with lingering suspicions. The regime's preference for large-scale industrial enterprises and its encouragement of foreign investment undercut the traditional bazaar economy and destroyed the handicraft industry. Thus, despite producing substantial advances in social services and economic performance, the White Revolution did not create popular loyalty to the regime.

In a parallel effort to establish the legitimacy of his rule, the shah placed great stress on the Pahlavi dynasty as the heir to the pre-Islamic Acheminid and Sasanian dynasties. His father had already appropriated for the monarchy the ancient Iranian royal title *shahanshah* (king of kings), to which Muhammad Reza Shah added the term *aryamehr* (light of the Aryans). In emphasizing the achievements of the pre-Islamic Iranian empires, the shah virtually ignored Iran's rich Islamic past and made no convincing connections between his reign and the religious traditions of the Iranian people. His most ambitious attempt to link the glories of Cyrus the Great and the Acheminids to the reign of the Pahlavis came in 1971 in the form of lavish ceremonies held at Persepolis to commemorate 2,500 continuous years of Iranian monarchy. The extravagance of the proceedings, rumored to cost $100 million, attracted ridicule abroad and criticism at home.

Try as he might, the shah was unable fully to establish the political legitimacy of his dynasty or to project the image of a ruler who truly cared about Iran and its people. This failure no doubt came about in part because of the corruption and maladministration that characterized his government. The shah and his family skimmed millions of dollars a year from Iran's revenues for their private use, and favored courtiers extracted small fortunes from foreign firms in exchange for arranging import licenses and contacts in high places. There was lots of money to be made in Iran in the early 1970s, but it was being made mainly by those with connections to the court.

The twin ills of uneven income distribution and political repression alienated broad sections of the population from the regime. However, the closed political system and the ruthless effectiveness of SAVAK denied Iranians any formal channels through which to express their grievances. As a result, opposition movements resorted to violence. Beginning in the late 1960s, ur-

Muhammad Reza Shah and Empress Farah at the tomb of Cyrus the Great during a wreath-laying ceremony marking the start of the celebrations commemorating the 2,500th anniversary of the founding of the Persian Empire. The preponderance of military uniforms suggests the importance of the ruler's ties to the armed forces. (AP/Wide World Photos)

ban guerrilla groups mounted a campaign of terror against representatives of the state and its U.S. ally. The two largest organizations were the Marxist Fadayan-i Khalq and the Islamic leftist Mujahedin-i Khalq. Both groups drew their membership from the young intelligentsia. Although the guerrilla movements were decimated through arrests and executions, their activities throughout the 1970s kept alive a spirit of resistance among Iranians.

A more indirect form of opposition was mounted by the religious establishment. Not all ulama were against the regime, but the majority resented one aspect or another of the shah's policies. Measures such as land reform directly threatened the ulama's livelihood by providing the state with an excuse to appropriate *waqf* lands, the revenues of which contributed to the upkeep of mosques and seminaries. Other programs allowed the state to extend its activities into spheres that had previously been the exclusive domain of the ulama. For example, the literacy corps provided an educational alternative to the primary religious schools, long the sole source of instruction for villagers in remote regions of the country. Other reforms, such as the changes in the status of women, were questioned on religious grounds. The shah attempted to counter the ulama's objections by contending that his reforms were compatible with Islam because they would bring about justice and equality, and he suggested that the ulama should confine themselves to matters of personal piety.

The threat the shah's regime posed to the economic status of the religious establishment constituted one factor in the ulama's opposition. However, they were not motivated by self-interest alone. The activists among them objected to the autocracy of the monarch and the corruption that permeated his regime, noting that these practices contravened Islamic concepts of social justice. They also denounced the shah's total reliance on Western models of development and his encouragement of Western patterns of consumption and living, practices that in the ulama's view promoted inequality and impropriety. Although the repressive organs of the regime made it increasingly dangerous for the ulama to express their opposition openly, their intimate links with the Iranian masses afforded them ample opportunities to make their opinions known.

In 1975, partly as a response to the activities of the urban guerrillas, the shah tightened the reins of repression. He scrapped the two-party system and introduced a single organization known as the National Resurgence Party. This change to a one-party state intensified the totalitarian character of the regime and ushered in a period of harsh police rule involving arrests, censorship, and systematic torture in the prisons. It appeared that the regime, buttressed by a powerful military and a ruthless security force, had taken steps to ensure its survival for decades to come.

Conclusion

Both Turkey and Iran shared a border with the Soviet Union, and both appeared vulnerable to Soviet designs in the immediate aftermath of World War II. This geopolitical situation drew the two countries into the cold war rivalry between the United States and the Soviet Union. The United States, determined to contain the spread of communism, provided economic and military assistance to keep Turkey and Iran politically stable and militarily strong. Both countries accepted U.S. economic aid and participated in the Anglo-U.S. alliance system. However, the U.S. role in overthrowing Mosaddiq and the presence of thousands of U.S. military personnel in Turkey created anti-U.S. sentiment. The United States appeared to be assuming Britain's former role as an imperial power interested in dominating the Middle East for its own ends. The Turks and Iranians who viewed the United States from this perspective came to resent the diminution of national sovereignty that was implied in their governments' readiness to follow the U.S. line in foreign policy.

Although Turkey and Iran had in common certain patterns of social and demographic change during this period, the political institutions through which popular responses to change were expressed were quite different.

Turkey's multiparty democracy contrasted sharply with the shah's royal dictatorship. On those occasions when the Turkish parliamentary system became stalemated, the cause was largely the proliferation of political parties and interest groups. But in Iran the social and economic interest groups created by the shah's modernization programs had no political outlet through which to voice their needs. Even the three interventions of the Turkish military reveal the differences between the two countries. The Turkish armed forces intervened in the political system to resolve parliamentary deadlock and economic turmoil, not to perpetuate military rule. By contrast, the Iranian military was used to maintain the shah's dictatorial control; the military and the monarchy were bound by common interests.

During the 1970s, these two political systems faced growing pressures as a result of the social and economic changes occurring within each state. The Turkish military's inclination to step in whenever the social order was threatened by parliamentary deadlock raised questions about the survival of the civilian multiparty system that was hailed as such an achievement in 1950. In Iran the staggering oil wealth created enormous discrepancies in income and had the potential to generate popular dissatisfaction on the part of those at the lower end of the economic scale. Yet the shah's domestic security forces, backed by the power of the military, appeared to be in a position to crush any popular dissent that might break out.

Notes

1. Dankwart A. Rustow, *Turkey: America's Forgotten Ally* (New York, 1989), p. 98.

2. C. H. Dodd, *The Crisis of Turkish Democracy* (Beverley, UK, 1983), p. 44.

3. Cited in Ervand Abrahamian, *Iran Between Two Revolutions* (Princeton, 1982), pp. 265–266.

4. Ibid., p. 450.

5. Ibid., p. 420.

6. Cited in James A. Bill and Robert Springborg, *Politics in the Middle East,* 3rd ed. (Glenview, Ill., 1990), p. 204.

7. Eric J. Hooglund, *Land and Revolution in Iran, 1960–1980* (Austin, 1982), p. 71. Hooglund's statistics and analysis form the basis for this discussion of land reform.

The Middle East in the Age of Nasser: The Egyptian Base | 15

During the period from 1952 to 1967, Gamal Abd al-Nasser was the embodiment of what the Arab world wanted to be: assertive, independent, and engaged in the construction of a new society freed of the imperial past and oriented toward a bright Arab future. His initiatives were copied in other Arab states, and so dominant was his stature that such terms as *Nasserism* and *Nasserites* became common political currency. Many of his achievements turned out to be more apparent than real, but for a time he presented the Arab world with the image of a dynamic leader who defied the imperial powers and swept away the old ruling elite. He seemed to represent progressive reformism in contrast to the old elite's stagnant immobility; and he projected a spirit of hope that made many believe in the possibility of the rebirth of a new and powerful Arab order capable of avenging the defeat of 1948 and preserving Arab independence in the face of external pressures. For the inspiration that he provided and the influence he exercised, it is appropriate to identify his years in power as the age of Nasser.

The Paralysis of the Old Regime, 1945–1952

The end of the Second World War ushered in a period of renewed Anglo-Egyptian tension. Relations between the two countries were still governed by the treaty of 1936, which placed restrictions on Egyptian sovereignty. A succession of Egyptian governments tried repeatedly to persuade Britain to renegotiate the treaty and evacuate its troops. However, even though Britain conceded independence to India in 1947, it was not prepared to abandon the Suez Canal and was therefore unwilling to grant the Egyptian demands. The government's failure to secure unqualified independence added to the tensions within the country and fueled popular resentment against both the British and the Egyptian ruling class of landowning politicians that had dominated parliament since 1923. The other pillar of the ruling establishment, King Faruq, also failed to inspire popular loyalty. His reputation was discredited by his scandalous personal behavior and his close association with Egypt's humiliating defeat in the 1948–1949 Arab-Israeli war. In the absence of decisive leadership, Egypt drifted into a situation of perpetual political crisis.

One of the main causes of the alienation of the masses from their ruling elite was the growing gap between rich and poor. This was clearly evident in the Egyptian countryside as large private landholdings became increasingly concentrated in the hands of a few owners. By 1952 about 0.4 percent of Egyptian landowners possessed 35 percent of the country's cultivable land. At the other end of the scale, 94 percent of landowners possessed a mere 35 percent of the cultivable land. The average size of the holdings of the first group was 170 *feddans*; the second group owned plots of land averaging 0.8 *feddan*. The massive inequality in land distribution created growing wealth for the large landowners and led to the impoverishment of the small proprietors, who were forced, with greater and greater frequency, to sell their holdings to meet their debts. The landless peasants, who neither owned nor rented land but relied solely on their labor for income, faced even harsher conditions in the years after World War II. Making up more than half of the rural population, they saw their wages constantly depressed as their numbers increased.

This situation cried out for redress, but the leaders of the Wafd and other political parties derived their wealth and social status from their ownership of land and were not inclined to address the issue of rural reform. The festering discontent in the countryside had its counterpart in Cairo and Alexandria, where the expanding labor force lived and worked in substandard conditions, university students organized anti-British demonstrations, and recent migrants from the countryside eked out a bare existence. Although postwar governments did manage to introduce limited social welfare legislation, it was inadequate to ameliorate mass poverty or to allay mass distrust of the ruling politicians.

In this volatile atmosphere, the Muslim Brotherhood expanded its activities and reached the apogee of its power. By the late 1940s it could claim over 500,000 members and many more sympathizers. Egyptians were attracted to the brotherhood by its blending of calls for national independence and the preservation of Islamic values with an appealing program of social reform (see Chapter 11). In the immediate postwar years, militant members of the brotherhood engaged in a systematic campaign of violence against foreigners, foreign business establishments, and Egyptian officials regarded as accomplices of imperialism. When Prime Minister Mahmud Fahmi al-Nuqrashi attempted to clamp down on the organization's activities in 1948, the brotherhood assassinated him. The following year Hasan al-Banna, the founding leader of the Muslim Brotherhood, was himself murdered, most likely by the Egyptian security forces. These acts demonstrate the extent of the political disorder and social disarray into which Egypt had plunged during the final years of the old regime.

In an attempt to return the country to normalcy, King Faruq called for elections in 1950. The Wafd was once again victorious, and its venerable leader, al-Nahhas Pasha, assumed the prime ministership. Hoping perhaps to recover some of the nationalist aura that had once surrounded his party, al-Nahhas in 1951 proclaimed the abrogation of the 1936 treaty. The British government, in the midst of dealing with the Mosaddiq crisis in Iran, was not prepared to make concessions to Egypt. However, the abrogation of the treaty was a popular measure among Egyptians, and armed bands of Egyptian guerrillas began to engage in skirmishes with units of the British army. In one such engagement, British tanks destroyed the Egyptian police barracks at Ismaciliyya, killing fifty policemen and wounding scores more. On the following day, January 26, 1952, known as Black Saturday, the masses of Cairo retaliated for the incident with a wave of demonstrations and riots. During the outbreak, a number of fires were set, and Cairo's central business district was consumed by flames. The angry mobs did not confine themselves to the destruction of British property; they also attacked bars, cinemas, nightclubs, and exclusive boutiques, symbols of the corruption and immorality of the Egyptian upper classes.

The complete breakdown of law and order on Black Saturday hastened the end of the old rule. Although the regime managed to survive for a few more months, it was finally overthrown in the early morning hours of July 23, 1952, when a group of young military officers carried out a coup d'état and seized control of the government. It was more than a brief military intervention; it was the replacement of one regime by another. Two of the officers involved in the coup, Nasser and Sadat, were to govern Egypt for the next twenty-nine years.

The Free Officers and the Coup d'État of 1952

The coup—or the revolution of 1952, as it came to be called—was planned by a group of junior military officers, many of whom had known one another since the early 1940s. Styling themselves the Free Officers, the group coalesced around an executive committee of nine (later fourteen) men headed by Colonel Gamal Abd al-Nasser (1918–1970). Nasser's background and experiences were typical of the Free Officers and can serve to illustrate the influences that shaped the new generation of Egyptian rulers. Nasser's father was a rural villager who moved to Alexandria, where he entered the postal service as a minor clerk and where his first son, Gamal, was born. Nasser did not have a normal family life: His mother died when he was eight, his father was transferred, and the young Nasser grew up living with various relatives in Cairo and Alexandria. During his high school years, he was exposed to all the political crosscurrents of the 1930s and, like so many students of his generation, participated in anti-British demonstrations and was wounded during the protests of 1935.

Adrift and alienated after his high school graduation in 1936, he attended law school for a few months before being accepted at the Egyptian military academy, which had just opened its doors to the sons of the lower and lower-middle classes. He was commissioned in 1938 and spent the war years on postings in the Sudan and the Western Desert, during which time he established contacts with several of the individuals who later formed the executive committee of the Free Officers. Like several members of that group, Nasser fought in the Palestine campaign in 1948. Although his own performance was commendable, he and his fellow officers suffered the humiliation of the Egyptian defeat by Israel, a defeat they believed to have been caused by the corruption of King Faruq, the civilian politicians, and certain figures in the high command. Nasser and his colleagues saw it as part of their patriotic duty to avenge the "disaster" of 1948.

Nasser and several of the core participants in the Free Officers movement were not the scions of the landed or professional elite but the sons of small peasant proprietors, minor government officials, and petty merchants. Others in the group came from families that were more solidly middle class. But they were all from the strata of society that chafed under the British occupation and harbored grievances at the indigenous ruling classes. They also represented the emergence of a new generation into positions of authority—at the time of the coup, they were all junior officers and their ages ranged from twenty-eight to thirty-five, a marked difference from the seventy-five-year-old al-Nahhas, who had headed the Wafd since 1927. Indeed, they recognized that their youth and obscurity might prevent them from winning public support, and before carrying out the coup, they persuaded a respected senior officer, General Muhammad Naguib, to serve as their figurehead leader. Naguib was one of the few Egyptian commanders to emerge from the 1948 conflict with his reputation intact, and he soon became the most popular figure in the regime.

The core group of Free Officers were pragmatic nationalists and "diligent military bureaucrats" with no predetermined views on political organization or ideological orientation.[1] They were motivated by a patriotic desire to end the British occupation and by vague notions of reform and social justice. In 1951, while still a clandestine group within the military, the Free Officers prepared a six-point program to guide their government after the coup. The program called for the destruction of British colonialism and the removal of its Egyptian collaborators, the elimination of feudalism, the ending of the political control of the state by foreign capital, the establishment of social justice, the formation of a strong national army, and the creation of a healthy democratic life.

The military enters politics: A group of Egyptian Free Officers in early 1953. The overthrow of Egypt's ruling dynasty and the Nasser regime's domestic reforms and foreign policy ventures inspired young radicals throughout the Arab east. The three figures seated on the couch are, from right, Major Abd al-Hakim Amr, General Muhammad Naguib, and Colonel Gamal Abd al-Nasser. (AP/Wide World Photos)

Once the officers assumed power, they formed themselves into a Nasser-led organization called the Revolutionary Command Council (RCC) that served as the executive body of the government. Because the RCC had no preconceived plan for administering the country, it tended to respond to situations as they arose, and in this way the regime gradually took shape and found its direction. However, no organization headed by Nasser was ever completely without plans, and in the process of consolidating its power the RCC conducted a twofold campaign: It undertook to do away with rival contenders for power and at the same time tried to gain popular support by proclaiming reforms and introducing a new constitution.

The first rival to be dealt with was King Faruq. Three days after the coup, he was forced to abdicate and sent into exile. The last ruler in the line of Muhammad Ali sailed out of Alexandria harbor on the royal yacht, destined to idle away the remainder of his life on the French Riviera. In 1953 the monarchy itself was abolished, and Egypt was declared a republic. Turning to the Wafd and the other parliamentary parties, the RCC announced a series of sweeping political changes that effectively eliminated the old order: The constitution of 1923 was abolished, parliament was dissolved, and all political parties were banned. The regime went on to declare a three-year transitional period during which the RCC would act as the supreme executive. Naguib assumed the offices of president and prime minister; Nasser remained behind the scenes as minister of the interior. Other RCC members replaced the civilian politicians in the cabinet, and additional officers were appointed to oversee the bureaucracy. The military was assuming complete control of the state. In 1954 another RCC decree prohibited anyone who had held public office from 1946 to 1952 from doing so again. This effectively barred most of the politicians of the old order from participation in public life and opened the way for a new generation from a different stratum of society to assume positions of authority within the bureaucracy. To fill the void created by the abolition of political parties, the RCC organized a mass party called the Liberation Rally. It was not a party in the parliamentary sense of the term but rather a vehicle through which the regime marshaled support for itself and gained control of such interest groups as students and workers. The Liberation Rally was the only party permitted in the country and therefore failed to generate much enthusiasm.

The RCC's main rival for power was the Muslim Brotherhood, which was far and away the most popular political organization in the country. At the time of the coup in 1952, many of the Free Officers had close ties to the brotherhood, and there was an early phase of cooperation between the two organizations, as each hoped eventually to control the other. They could not, however, coexist, and in 1954 the RCC was provided with an excuse to strike when a member of the brotherhood tried to assassinate Nasser. The RCC retaliated by outlawing the brotherhood, executing six of its leaders, and imprisoning thousands of its members. The organization was driven underground, but it was neither forgotten nor eliminated and would be heard from again. The RCC also struck hard against groups on the political left. Shortly after the coup, workers at a large textile plant near Alexandria went on strike and rampaged through the factory in the name of the people's revolution. Expecting sympathy from the new regime, the workers were instead crushed by it. The RCC ordered the army to put down the strike, arranged for the trial and execution of its ringleaders, and took advantage of the existence of labor unrest to imprison leaders of the Communist Party and other leftists.

It was also crucial for the RCC to establish control of the armed forces and ensure their loyalty. To achieve this end, Nasser elevated his close friend and former Free Officer Abd al-Hakim Amr to the post of commander in chief, a position Amr occupied as the regime's political operative within the military for the next fifteen years. Relations between the military and the RCC—and within the RCC itself—were severely strained by the contest for power between Naguib and Nasser that broke into the open in early 1954.

Instead of acting as the purely figurehead president that the RCC intended, Naguib became a popular public personality and began to express his own views on the direction of the revolution, views that often differed from Nasser's. But Nasser was determined to retain control of the revolution, and he waged a bitter public and private struggle against Naguib. Nasser proved the better infighter, and in November 1954 Naguib was accused of supporting the Muslim Brotherhood, removed from office, and placed under house arrest, a restriction he was forced to endure until his death in 1984. Within two years of the coup, Nasser had broken the existing centers of civilian power, purged the military of potential rivals, and maneuvered himself into position as the dominant political force within Egypt.

Concurrent with its consolidation of power, the RCC tried to build popular support through the introduction of reforms. Its most acclaimed achievement was the Agrarian Reform Law of September 1952. The main provision of the law limited the amount of agricultural land a single individual could own to 200 *feddans*. The surplus was to be taken over by the state for redistribution in small plots to tenants or to peasants who owned less than 5 *feddans*. Landlords were to be compensated in Egyptian government bonds. The lands and properties of the royal family were confiscated and included in the redistribution program. In addition to offering benefits to peasants, the regime's purpose in breaking up the landed estates was to reduce the political and economic power of the landholding elite. It can hardly be said that the old landowning classes were stripped of all their wealth, but there is no question that the reduction of their holdings contributed to the decline of their influence within Egyptian society as a whole. Although the land reform laws were imperfectly administered, their very existence showed the new regime's repudiation of the old social, economic, and political order. Land reform became a hallmark of the Nasser era and was the subject of considerable favorable commentary both within and outside Egypt during the regime's early years.

Land reform, coupled with laws that abolished all civil titles (pasha, bey), imparted to the regime a reformist, populist image. Nasser may have hoped to further this image with the new constitution, which was announced at the end of the three-year transition period, in 1956. The document echoed the sentiments of the early Free Officers movement; it stated that the government was committed to the abolition of imperialism and feudalism and to the establishment of a strong army, social justice, and a democratic society. The principle of democracy was, in theory at least, enshrined by providing for an elected, 350-member national assembly. A change from the old order was the inclusion of a bill of rights that protected Egyptians from discrimination on the grounds of race, sex, language, or religion.

Still, the open, pluralistic society proclaimed in the constitution was considerably circumscribed by the manner in which authority was allocated. The Nasserist political system was designed to guide the popular will, not to respond to it. Political parties were banned, and the ineffectual Liberation Rally was replaced by another mass organization, the National Union. All candidates to the national assembly were to be nominated and screened by the National Union's executive committee, headed by Nasser. Decisionmaking authority was further centralized by constitutional provisions that gave extensive powers to the president. In June 1956 a national plebiscite approved the constitution and endorsed Nasser as president; according to the official count, Nasser received 99.9 percent of the votes cast. This helped set a pattern for the use of plebiscites as a substitute for elections. Yet even in the controlled setting of a plebiscite, the regime introduced new populist measures that assured greater mass participation than had been the case previously: Men were compelled to cast ballots, and for the first time women were permitted to vote.

By mid-1956 the Nasser regime had secured its domestic power base and had attracted a certain amount of recognition through its land reform program. But the "revolution" of 1952 seemed to be stalled and to lack any direction that might distinguish it from other military governments that had seized power throughout the developing world. However, a series of foreign policy triumphs soon elevated Nasser to the status of unquestioned leader of the Arab world.

Foreign Relations After 1952

Egypt, Britain, and the Suez Crisis of 1956

The most pressing foreign policy matter facing the RCC in 1952 was Egypt's vexing relationship with Britain. This relationship was all the more complex because it was closely tied to developments in the Sudan. During the final years of the monarchy, the Wafd had demanded the unity of Egypt and the Sudan under the Egyptian crown. Although Britain tried to separate Egyptian issues from the question of the Sudan, Egypt insisted on linking the two. By the time the RCC came to power, Britain had recognized that in order to clear the way for discussions on the status of the Suez Canal, it would have to settle the dispute over the Sudan. The RCC, in an effort to enhance its popularity in the Sudan and to lay the groundwork for future influence there, adopted a new strategy in negotiations with Britain. It replaced Egypt's claims for sovereignty over the Sudan with a demand for the country's self-determination. Since Britain placed a higher priority on settling its outstanding differences with Egypt, it accepted the RCC's terms. The Anglo-Egyptian Agreement, signed in February 1953, recognized the Sudan's right to self-determination and set forth the steps that would achieve that goal. Two years later, the Sudanese parliament proclaimed independence, thus thwarting the RCC's plans to create a political union between the two countries.

Once the Sudan question was resolved, it was possible to discuss Britain's future role in Egypt proper. After several months of negotiations, the two governments signed a treaty in 1954 providing for the evacuation of all British troops from the Suez Canal base within twenty months. Britain did retain the right to reoccupy the base in the event of an attack by any outside power on an Arab League state or Turkey. The British forces were withdrawn on schedule in April 1956, and Nasser appeared to have achieved through patient diplomacy a victory that had escaped his Wafdist predecessors. Why, then, did the Suez Canal become an Anglo-Egyptian battlefield within a few months of the British evacuation?

The answer lies in the coming together of old and new patterns of Middle Eastern and Western relationships. The Suez crisis highlighted the clash between imperialism and the Arabs' desire to exercise their sovereignty, it brought out the difference between the cold war diplomacy of the Western alliance and Nasser's attempt to adopt a policy of nonalignment, and it resurrected the Arab-Israeli conflict and the unresolved issues that had been festering since 1949.

As we have seen in the cases of Turkey and Iran, the United States attempted to construct an alliance system that would serve as a barrier to Soviet expansion. Countries willing to participate in the alliance received generous U.S. military and economic aid. The Baghdad Pact was an attempt to extend the policy of containment to the Arab states through the use of British influence. Participants in the Baghdad Pact were Turkey, Iran, Pakistan, Iraq, and Britain, all of which signed an interlocking series of agreements during 1954 and 1955. Nasser refused to allow Egypt to join the pact, claiming that it was an extension of imperialism aimed at keeping the Arabs in the stifling embrace of the West, and he criticized Nuri al-Saᶜid of Iraq for entering into "imperial alliances." The Egyptian president also began a propaganda campaign to persuade other Arab states to stay clear of the Baghdad Pact. His efforts were successful in persuading the governments of Jordan and Syria to decline membership in the alliance.

Nasser's defiance propelled him into regional prominence, but it further distanced Egypt from the Western alliance. Yet Egypt was in need of the kind of military aid the United States had showered on Turkey and Iran. Ever since the armistice agreements had been signed in 1949, the Egyptian-Israeli border had been the site of frequent hostilities. Palestinian refugees from Gaza conducted small-scale commando raids into Israeli territory. Israel responded with a policy of massive retaliation against Egyptian installations in Gaza. The scale of the Israeli incursions and the ease with which Israeli forces carried out their missions emphasized their military superiority and made the Egyptians aware of the pressing need to replace the outmoded equipment left to them by the British. However, when Nasser approached the West for arms, he was rebuffed. He therefore turned to other sources.

In September 1955 Egypt concluded an agreement with Czechoslovakia to purchase $200 million worth of advanced Soviet military equipment in exchange for Egyptian cotton. The so-called Czech arms deal was really a Soviet-Egyptian arms deal, and it had far-reaching repercussions. With this single agreement, Nasser undermined the laboriously constructed alliance system through which the United States had tried to contain the Soviet Union. The Egyptian president had allowed the Soviet Union to hurdle the Baghdad Pact and to achieve its centuries-old ambition of acquiring a base in the eastern Mediterranean. Once again, Nasser was acclaimed in the Arab press for his successful assertion of independence from the Anglo-U.S. grip. He was acquiring the image of a Pan-Arab leader who not only would break the imperial domination of the Western powers but would also use his country's newfound military strength to avenge the "disaster" of 1948. But there were other views of the Nasser phenomenon; the Czech arms deal caused considerable annoyance in Washington and London.

Egypt's search for financial assistance to develop its agricultural base provided further background to the Suez crisis. After the coup d'état of 1952, Egyptian economic planners resurrected a long-standing scheme to construct a second dam across the Nile at Aswan. The project was viewed as having both political and economic advantages: It would be the kind of spectacular achievement that would enhance the new regime's prestige among the Egyptian population, and it would also have very real economic benefits by increasing the amount of land that could be irrigated and by providing enough hydroelectric power to supply the needs of the entire country. However, the estimated construction costs of at least $1 billion were well beyond Egypt's financial ability. The government therefore sought foreign assistance. In late 1955 the World Bank approved a loan package that involved U.S. and British participation and, because of the irritation that Nasser had caused those two countries, required Egypt to accept certain conditions. While Nasser was deciding whether or not to accept the arrangement, the U.S. government abruptly announced that it was withdrawing its loan offer.

A few days later, Nasser responded with a dramatic act of defiance. On July 26, 1956, Egypt nationalized the Suez Canal, and Nasser proclaimed that the revenues from the canal would be used to fund the development projects the West refused to sponsor. Within Egypt and the Arab world at large, Nasser's bold action was greeted with tremendous enthusiasm. The Suez Canal, built with Egyptian labor but operated by a French company and used as the lifeline of the British Empire, had stood as a symbol of Western exploitation. In seizing it for Egypt, Nasser was seen to have overturned his nation's forced subordination to outside interests.

The reaction in Western capitals was one of extreme hostility. Prime Minister Anthony Eden of Britain regarded Nasser's nationalization of the canal as theft and spoke in ominous terms about teaching the Egyptian president a lesson. Throughout late summer 1956, special international conferences

Nasser's triumphant return to Cairo from Alexandria on July 28, 1956, after announcing the nationalization of the Suez Canal. (AP/Wide World Photos)

were called to seek a resolution of the matter. Although Nasser offered to pay compensation to the Suez Canal Company, he refused to compromise on the Egyptianization of the canal. His position was strengthened by the ability of Egyptian technicians to keep the waterway operating smoothly, something that Britain had claimed would be impossible.

While efforts to reach a negotiated settlement of the crisis were under way, Britain, France, and Israel concluded a secret agreement for joint military action against Egypt. Each country had its own reasons for approving the action, but they all shared a common desire to overthrow Nasser. Their agreement was activated on October 29, 1956, with an Israeli strike into Sinai. On October 31, the British air force began heavy bombing raids on military targets near Cairo and along the canal zone, and Israeli ground forces raced to the east bank of the canal. British and French paratroops dropped on Port Saᶜid on November 5, and on the following day the main Anglo-French force landed at the northern end of the canal and began to advance on Suez City. The advance was halted when, at midnight on November 6, Britain and France agreed to a UN-sponsored cease-fire.

The tripartite attack on Egypt was condemned by both the United States and the Soviet Union. The latter, in the process of crushing an uprising in Hungary, issued a thinly veiled threat to launch a rocket attack on London if

British troops were not withdrawn from Egypt. The U.S. government was particularly upset at the action of three of its close allies and took the position that none of them could be allowed to benefit from the use of force. Under tremendous U.S. pressure, Britain and France withdrew their forces in December, and the Israelis finally evacuated Sinai in March 1957. A special UN emergency force was stationed in Gaza to act as a buffer between Egypt and Israel.

The Suez crisis had important consequences for all the parties involved. Egypt's military defeat was transformed into a political triumph for Nasser. Instead of being overthrown, he emerged from the crisis as an Egyptian and Pan-Arab hero. He had stood up to the two former imperial powers and faced them down, the United States and the Soviet Union had defended Egypt's sovereignty, and when the battlefield was cleared, Egypt retained possession of the Suez Canal. Soviet prestige among the Arabs was also enhanced during the crisis and continued to grow when the Soviets replenished Egypt's battered arsenal. The collusion among the three aggressors reinforced their negative images within the Arab world. If Israel had once again demonstrated the effectiveness of its armed forces, its attack on Egypt confirmed Arab opinion that the country was an agent of the Western powers. As for Britain and France, their decision to ally with Israel in an attack on an Arab state was viewed as a monstrous offense. It had unfortunate repercussions within Egypt; many British and French nationals who had spent their entire lives in the country were expelled and their property seized. Several thousand Egyptian Jews were also expelled or decided to leave because of the strong anti-Jewish sentiment aroused by the Israeli invasion. Of the three invading states, Britain was most severely damaged by its role in the Suez affair. Not only had Britain resorted to the heavy-handed imperialist tactics of earlier years, but it had been forced to abandon its military operation by pressure from two demonstrably stronger superpowers. The epitaph for Britain at Suez was provided in the London *Times'* description of the effect of Prime Minister Eden's decision to invade Egypt: He was "the last British Prime Minister to believe that Britain was a Great Power and the first to confront a crisis which proved beyond doubt that she was not."[2]

Egypt and the Arab World: The United Arab Republic

In his book *Philosophy of the Revolution*, published in 1955, Nasser wrote:

> The pages of history are full of heroes who created for themselves roles of glorious valor which they played at decisive moments. Likewise the pages of history are also full of heroic and glorious roles which never found heroes to perform them. For some reason it seems to me that within the Arab circle there is a role, wandering aimlessly in search of a hero. And I do not know why it seems to me that this role, exhausted by its wanderings, has at last settled

down, tired and weary, near the borders of our country and is beckoning to us to move, to take up its lines, to put on its costume, since no one else is qualified to play it.[3]

As a result of his triumph in the aftermath of the Suez crisis, Nasser stepped into the heroic role he had defined. No other Arab leader approached his status, and no other Arab leader aroused such high expectations. This was a burden as well as an opportunity. Nasser's prestige was based on his successful defiance of the former imperial powers. But in order to retain that prestige, he needed to continue his foreign policy successes and to fulfill the hopes that millions of Arabs outside Egypt placed in him. Nasser responded to the challenge by thrusting Egypt into the turbulent crosscurrents of inter-Arab politics. The impact of Nasserism on the other Arab states is discussed in Chapter 16. The focus here is on Egypt itself.

Although Egypt's Arab heritage was an undeniable reality, prominent writers of the interwar era downplayed that heritage by emphasizing the country's Greek and pharaonic past in an effort to connect it more closely with secular Western culture. Nasser's desire to make Egypt the center of Arabism therefore required a certain amount of cultural reorientation. In place of the multilayered strands of identity posited by pre-1952 intellectuals, the Nasser regime devoted a single-minded emphasis to Arabism and Pan-Arab unity. For example, the 1956 constitution stated that Egypt was an Arab country and a part of the Arab nation. No such declaration had appeared in the 1923 constitution. Nasser's popularity, his endorsement of the concept of Arab unity, and his support for other Arab concerns served to establish Egypt's Arab identity and to place it in the forefront of the Pan-Arab movement. In pursuit of the twin goals of Arab unity and Egyptian hegemony, Nasser interfered in the political affairs of other Arab countries. His involvement in foreign policy ventures following the Suez crisis earned him further esteem but diverted the attention of his government away from pressing domestic problems.

The creation of the United Arab Republic (UAR) in early 1958 appeared to be a major step along the road to Arab unity. The UAR was a total union of Syria and Egypt into a single state. The impetus for the union came from a group of Syrian politicians who were members of the dominant Ba'th Party (see Chapter 16). They feared that a small but well-organized Communist movement within Syria was on the verge of overthrowing their government. They therefore approached Nasser about the formation of a Syrian-Egyptian union, thinking that it would forestall the Communist takeover and preserve their own dominance. Nasser accepted the proposal, and less than a month later, the UAR was announced and Nasser was received by cheering throngs in Damascus.

Despite the acclaim it received at the time of its creation, the UAR was an awkward entity. It was brought hurriedly into existence by an internal Syrian political problem and by Nasser's acceptance of an offer he simply could not refuse. The new state was intended to be an integral union between the two participants, but Egypt quickly became dominant. The Syrian leaders who had requested the merger found themselves forced to live in Cairo, from where they exercised little influence on events in their homeland. Nasser, who became president of the UAR, simply imposed on Syria the single-party military regime that had worked so well in Egypt. Egyptian military and civilian personnel streamed into Syria, replacing their Syrian counterparts in several important functions and behaving with a high-handed arrogance that infuriated the Syrians. One Syrian general later complained that "every Egyptian officer in Syria during the union acted as if he were Gamal Abdel Nasser."⁴ The abolition of Syrian political parties, the dismissal of Syrian officers, and the forced introduction of a modified version of the Egyptian land reform laws alienated powerful sectors within Syrian society. In September 1961, units within the Syrian military rebelled against their Egyptian commanders and brought an end to the UAR and to the first self-conscious experiment in Arab unity.

The breakup of the UAR was a blow to Nasser's prestige and prompted him to reappraise his goals. After 1961 the regime turned inward and introduced a new round of domestic reforms. However, Nasser did not abandon his role as champion of Arab unity and did not hesitate to intervene in the affairs of other Arab states when it served his purposes. This was shown, with disastrous consequences, by Egypt's participation on the rebel side in the Yemen civil war. In 1962 the military ousted the ruler of Yemen and declared a republic. However, the ruler, Imam Muhammad al-Badr, escaped to the mountains and rallied loyal tribesmen to his cause, launching an armed struggle to regain his throne. Imam Muhammad received generous assistance from two other monarchs, the kings of Jordan and Saudi Arabia. It was only natural that the new military regime would turn to Nasser for assistance and that he, as the announced foe of the old order, would respond favorably. By 1965 nearly 70,000 Egyptian troops were engaged on the side of the military regime in Yemen. Bogged down in difficult terrain and harassed by guerrillas, the Egyptian forces suffered heavy losses and were finally withdrawn in 1968. In this case, Egypt's intervention divided Arab loyalties instead of unifying them; it presented the spectacle of Arab fighting Arab and of the heads of state of Saudi Arabia and Egypt hurling insults at one another.

Egypt asserted its leadership of the Pan-Arab movement in other, more subtle ways. Radio Cairo's Voice of the Arabs beamed propaganda broadcasts the length and breadth of the Arab world and beyond. The Egyptian movie industry was the largest in the Arab Middle East and produced films that were seen throughout the region. And the most popular Arab singer of the era, Umm Kalthum, was an Egyptian woman who packed concert halls and enthralled radio audiences in every Arab country. Nasser and Egypt were, it seemed, constantly in the public eye, and much was expected of them both.

Egypt, the Soviet Union, and the United States

Egyptian-Soviet ties were strengthened in the years after Suez. In 1958 the Soviet Union agreed to finance the Aswan Dam project as well as to provide Egypt with increased military and technical assistance. Egypt became increasingly dependent on Moscow for weapons and spare parts. Whereas Muhammad Ali in the 1820s had sent future members of the Egyptian elite to France for training, Nasser in the 1960s sent future flight commanders and civilian technocrats to universities in the Soviet Union. The Soviet-Egyptian relationship had its troubled periods, usually brought on by the ideological differences between the two countries. The scientific socialism and atheism of the Soviet Union contrasted sharply with the nationalistic, Islamic foundations of Egypt. However, Nasser and his Soviet counterparts were pragmatic men who recognized that they needed one another: Nasser received from the Soviets the weapons that gave credibility to Egypt's leadership role, and the Soviets obtained in Egypt a center of influence in the Middle East from which they contested U.S. efforts to contain them.

Soviet-U.S. rivalry in the Middle East was a constant factor in the evolution of Egyptian foreign policy. In the aftermath of the Suez crisis, the United States formulated a new policy to deal with its concerns over the Soviet threat in the region. Known as the Eisenhower Doctrine (1957), the policy contained promises of economic and military assistance to countries resisting communism. In addition, the doctrine authorized the deployment of U.S. forces to protect the independence of Middle Eastern states threatened by armed aggression from any nation controlled by international communism. To Nasser, this smacked of the same kind of Western control embodied in the Baghdad Pact, and he viewed the Eisenhower Doctrine with suspicion. Nevertheless, even as Egypt became more reliant on Soviet military assistance, Nasser kept open his country's ties to the United States. He defined Egypt's foreign policy as positive neutralism. It was a self-interested policy designed to enable Egypt to acquire benefits from both superpowers at the same time while avoiding total reliance on either one of them. U.S. assistance was sporadic and consisted mainly of permitting Egypt to purchase U.S. wheat with Egyptian currency. Two principal factors impeded the improvement of U.S.-Egyptian relations: The first was Nasser's refusal to commit Egypt to the Western alliance and his acceptance of Soviet military aid; the second was the United States' unwavering support for Israel at a time when Nasser was the champion of the Arab cause against Israel.

The Adoption of Arab Socialism

As noted previously, the Free Officers seized power without a predetermined ideology. From 1952 to 1961, the regime acquired legitimacy through its foreign policy ventures and Nasser's immense popularity. But the regime did not establish a set of guiding principles that might have served to inspire popular commitment. Following the breakup of the UAR in 1961, Nasser and his associates reassessed their domestic policies and concluded that Egypt's successful economic development required the adoption of selected elements of socialism. They called their version of the ideology Arab socialism in an attempt to show that it had indigenous roots. Arab socialism became the rallying cry of the regime, the doctrine intended to attract a new generation of Egyptians to the achievement of revolutionary goals.

The government adopted socialism for pragmatic reasons, not out of any long-standing ideological commitment. Indeed, during the regime's early years in power, it offered incentives to foreign and local private investors. However, Nasser's Egypt was not an attractive haven for surplus investment capital, and the regime had difficulty raising funds. Therefore, in order to generate the funds needed for its development schemes, the government decided to take over most of Egypt's enterprises and to become responsible for all capital formation. In this sense, the economic policy of the regime was more a form of state capitalism than Marxist socialism; it was based on the need to raise money, not on the dynamic of class conflict.

The most concentrated wave of socialist decrees occurred from 1961 to 1964. In these years the remaining foreign-owned companies as well as all domestic enterprises, from banks to insurance companies, from import agencies to hotels, were nationalized. Even the media were brought under state control, and Egypt's once lively press became a possession of the central government and was subject to rigorous censorship. Planning agencies were set up to manage the economy, and in 1960 Egypt announced its first five-year plan. The plan placed heavy emphasis on industrial development. During the 1960s, industrial output increased substantially, especially in the production of textiles and food and beverages. Nevertheless, the regime's fascination with large-scale showcase projects, most notably the iron and steel plant at Helwan, resulted in huge expenditures for modest returns. An additional barrier to industrial expansion lay in the very nature of state-run industries: They were subjected to rigid central-planning mechanisms, they were overstaffed at the managerial level, and they had little incentive for quality control because they had no competition. The regime also spent large sums on various land reclamation schemes, none of which proved very successful. However, the completion of the Aswan Dam in 1970 allowed 650,000 *feddans* to be reclaimed as agricultural land. The undeniable benefits of the Aswan Dam, however, have been mitigated by a host of ecological side effects.

Any improvement in the overall Egyptian economy demanded that the government take measures to limit the country's soaring birthrate. Although the 1962 charter (discussed in the following section) made reference to family planning, the government did not pursue the matter in a systematic fashion. As a result, Egypt's population continued to grow at the rate of 2.5 percent a year. In 1960 there were 26 million Egyptians; in 1980 the figure had risen to over 40 million. Overpopulation was and remains one of Egypt's gravest problems.[5] During the Nasser years, the basic consumption demands of an ever-expanding population changed Egypt from a net exporter of foodstuffs to a heavy importer. This situation worsened as the increase in population far outstripped the reclamation of new agricultural land. And for every *feddan* laboriously reclaimed from the desert, valuable chunks of rich soil along the Nile were absorbed by the relentless urban expansion of Cairo and other cities.

In taking over all enterprises within the country, the government created an enormous personnel problem for itself. The state now had to manage and staff the entire range of businesses and industries that had formerly been in private hands. In keeping with its military origins, the regime relied heavily on former officers to direct the various ministries and development agencies. This had the advantage of providing perquisites to the officer corps and cultivating its loyalty; it had the disadvantage of placing individuals in charge of operations for which they were untrained.

The socialism of the Nasser regime also involved far-reaching measures of egalitarianism and social welfare. In 1961 the allowable landholdings per family were reduced to 100 *feddan*s, and in 1969 to 50 *feddan*s. The total land reform program, beginning with the Agrarian Reform Law of 1952, affected only 12 percent of the cultivated area and provided only 9 percent of the rural population with land. Nevertheless, the regime's programs created a dramatic leveling in the distribution of landholdings. Large estates virtually disappeared, and by 1964 small farms (less than 5 *feddan*s) covered 55 percent of the cultivated area, medium farms (5 to 50 *feddan*s) made up 33 percent, and the remaining 12 percent were between 50 and 100 *feddan*s.[6] This more equitable distribution was achieved without major production disruptions; crop yields did not decline and in some years actually increased. Land reform did not eliminate landlessness or rural poverty, but it did enhance the economic and social standing of middle-level peasants, perhaps the main beneficiaries of the regime's agrarian policies.

Other measures of social equity were enacted after 1961. Laws on income distribution struck at the wealthy by limiting individual salaries to a maximum of £E5,000 and by stipulating that all incomes over £E10,000 would be taxed at the rate of 90 percent. These measures succeeded in further reducing the power of the old elite. At the other end of the social scale, the state introduced measures that provided civil servants and workers with such benefits as pensions, minimum wages, and health care.

Institutionalizing Socialism: The Charter and the Constitution

In 1962 Nasser presented to a specially convened congress the Charter for National Action, a document that explained and justified Egypt's new policies. The charter was an attempt to provide ideological foundations for the regime's actions and to create mass identification with the new policies. It proclaimed that Egypt was in the midst of a revolution to achieve freedom, socialism, and unity. The document asserted Egypt's paramountcy in Arab affairs by portraying the country as the vanguard of the Arab revolution. According to the charter, it was Egypt's duty to export its revolution to other Arab countries, a process that would eliminate the reactionary elements within the Arab body politic and pave the way to a durable Arab union. Such statements were hardly welcome to the reigning Arab monarchs.

The instrument through which the goals of the revolution were to be attained was the Arab Socialist Union (ASU), another mass-based single party. The charter defined the ASU as a revolutionary organization open to all Egyptians except feudalists and capitalists. By the late 1960s the ASU had developed into a complex bureaucratic organization of some 5 million members working through branches at the local, regional, and national levels. Nasser headed the ASU, and former military officers dominated the top levels of its administration. The ASU was essentially an arm of the government used to mobilize mass opinion, to train cadres of young Egyptians, and to prevent the formation of antirevolutionary centers. Although the ASU was more successful than its two predecessors (the Liberation Rally and the National Union), it, too, became a cumbersome, patronage-ridden organization that managed, like single parties everywhere, to become an object of resentment.

The political structure of the state was once again redefined in a new constitution, proclaimed in 1964. It did contain some new provisions—such as the requirement that 50 percent of the delegates to the national assembly had to be workers and peasants—but essentially reinforced Nasser's preference for a strong presidential system of government. Despite the trappings of democracy, the national assembly was little more than a consultative body that rubber-stamped legislation originating with the president. Nasser was confirmed in office by another plebiscite held in 1965.

Nasser was averse to sharing power, and his presidency was marked by the centralization of decisionmaking authority in his hands. Institutions mattered little as long as all major issues were referred to Nasser and as long as his decisions became policy. Scholars have described the regime in terms ranging from "guided democracy" to "'soft-hearted' authoritarianism."[7] If the base of popular participation in political life was broadened, the regime made sure that the popular will was controlled from above. Thus, in 1966 the secretary general of the ASU stated that Egypt's political structure was organized to provide "the proper guidance for the masses." But as others have pointed out, it is a short step from the concept of proper guidance to the establishment of a police state that enforces conformity.[8] Nasser's Egypt had its secret police, its spies within the ASU, and its political prisoners. But it lacked the oppressiveness and brutality of the shah of Iran's regime. There was always the belief among Egyptians that Nasser—if not always his associates—had their interests at heart, and with that belief they were willing to grant him immense powers.

The Revolution and Society

The egalitarianism of the Nasser regime extended, in theory, to gender relationships. The charter of 1962 stated that women were equal to men, and other decrees gave women the right to vote and to serve in the national assembly. Moreover, the nationalization of the economy created large numbers of public-sector jobs, many of which were filled by women. As women entered the workplace and the universities in ever-greater numbers, they tended to abandon the veil and to adopt contemporary international dress. However, the changes in appearance were not always reflected in matters of substance. For all the rhetoric about equality, the Nasser regime was exceptionally cautious in its attitude toward family law and did not introduce reformist legislation on such matters as polygamy or divorce.

Like other modernizing regimes, the Nasser government devoted considerable attention to the expansion of education. At the primary and secondary levels, the government's goal was not only to boost the literacy rate but also to give schoolchildren a proper indoctrination in the basics of socialism and nationalism. In terms of raw numbers, the advances in education were impressive: Enrollment in primary schools went up from 1.3 million in 1953 to 3.6 million in 1970. But the enrollment increases exceeded the government's ability to build schools or train instructors and led to overcrowded classrooms and unfavorable student-teacher ratios. And even with all the effort the regime devoted to education, roughly 60 percent of adult Egyptians remained illiterate in 1969.

To encourage students to attend university—and thus to acquire the skills needed to manage a nationalized economy—the state abolished tuition fees at postsecondary institutions and opened several new universities in the provincial capitals. A further incentive for university education was provided by Nasser's famous proclamation of 1962 guaranteeing a government job to every university graduate. Young Egyptians responded to these opportunities in full, and the number of university students nearly doubled during the 1960s. The university system was ill equipped to deal with the influx: Classrooms were packed with students, and teachers, books, and laboratory equipment were all in short supply. These conditions led in turn to a swelling level of discontent on the campuses.

In opening up access to the universities, the regime hoped to persuade students to enroll in scientific and technical fields. Those were the areas in which the state faced the greatest personnel shortages. Throughout the 1960s, however, the majority of students continued to enroll in arts, law, and commerce, the fields in which employment opportunities were most limited. Once they graduated, these students had little choice but to take up

Nasser's guarantee of a job in the expanding state bureaucracy. Such posts were low-paying and offered few rewards other than security. For some, that was sufficient, but for those whose expectations had been raised by earning a university degree, the lack of adequate employment opportunities was a blow to their self-esteem. Their discontent was funneled back to the campuses and contributed to a growing sense of frustration and restlessness on the part of Egyptian university students.

Nasser has sometimes been compared to Atatürk. To the extent that both men were reformers determined to free their countries from foreign domination, the comparison is apt. However, the Egyptian regime's relationship with Islam and the religious establishment was very different from Atatürk's. Rather than seeking to diminish the role of Islam in Egyptian society, Nasser recognized the appeal of Islamic institutions and attempted to bring them under the control of the state and then to use them in the service of the revolution. This is particularly evident in the regime's policies toward al-Azhar University, the venerable institution of Islamic learning and the principal training ground for the Egyptian ulama. Previous governments had either bypassed al-Azhar and its powerful ulama or engaged in bitter and largely unsuccessful attempts to dominate them. The Nasser government had recourse to direct action. In 1961 al-Azhar was reorganized by government decree and forced to accept the addition of four new, nonreligious faculties, medicine, engineering, agriculture, and an Islamic women's faculty. The effect of the reorganization reduced the authority of the rector of al-Azhar and gave the government control over the university's curriculum and the appointment of its administrators and teachers. The government also gained control of *waqf*s and destroyed the last bastion of the ulama's judicial power by abolishing the *shariᶜah* courts in 1955. Through these measures, the regime tried to prevent Islamic functionaries from acting as an independent political force without itself appearing to be an opponent of Islam.

The regime did not hesitate to utilize Islamic institutions to legitimize its policies. The Friday mosque sermons were prepared by government propagandists and contained glowing references to the compatibility of the government's goals with the principles of Islam. Following the nationalization decrees of 1961, prominent government-appointed ulama were persuaded to issue decrees and write articles on the harmony between Islam and Arab socialism. Thus, a book published in 1962 on the compatibility of religion and the charter affirmed that "Arab socialism is guided by the *Shariᶜah* of justice and the *Shariᶜah* of god."[9] Such exploitation of Islam for political purposes illustrates how far removed the Nasser regime was from the secularism of Atatürk.

Conclusion

The Nasser years in Egypt are associated with a number of significant events and policies: the Czech arms agreement, the Suez crisis, the United Arab

Republic, the proclamation of Arab socialism, and the adoption of agrarian reform, to name but a few. However, the sentiment associated with the Nasser phenomenon cannot be fully explained by a list of social reforms or foreign policy ventures. Nasserism was a feeling, a sense of excitement, a hope for a new Arab future. To be sure, it was clear to many that Egypt's bureaucracy was inflated, that its state-run industries were inefficient, and that its educational system was overcrowded. But despite these and other widely recognized shortcomings, Egypt and its dynamic president appeared to have set in motion a positive process of national transformation. The oppressive past had been cast aside through decisive action, and Egypt had gained a measure of independence and pride that at the time seemed enviable and worthy of emulation.

Still, the leadership role that had given Nasser his stature proved a burden as well as a blessing. In order to retain his—and Egypt's—leading place in the Arab movement, he had to renew his image from time to time. In spring 1967 he was presented with an opportunity to stand up to Israel and to bring the other Arab states in line with Egypt's position. Nasser seized the opportunity, and (as we will see in the next chapter) in so doing he exposed his country to a humiliating military defeat that called into question all that he appeared to have achieved.

Notes

1. P. J. Vatikiotis, *Nasser and His Generation* (New York, 1978), p. 109.

2. *Sunday Times,* January 16, 1977.

3. Gamal Abdel Nasser, *Egypt's Liberation: The Philosophy of the Revolution* (Washington, D.C., 1955), pp. 87–88.

4. Cited in Malcolm H. Kerr, *The Arab Cold War: Gamal Abd al-Nasir and His Rivals, 1958–1970,* 3rd ed. (London, 1971), p. 51.

5. A vigorous refutation of the literature on which this paragraph and its conclusions are based is found in Tim Mitchell, "America's Egypt: Discourse of the Development Industry," *Middle East Report,* vol. 21 (March/April 1991), pp. 18–33.

6. Alan Richards and John Waterbury, *A Political Economy of the Middle East: State, Class, and Economic Development* (Boulder, 1990), pp. 152–153.

7. The first term appears in many books; the second is found in John Waterbury, *The Egypt of Nasser and Sadat: The Political Economy of Two Regimes* (Princeton, 1983), p. 11.

8. Derek Hopwood, *Egypt: Politics and Society, 1945–1984,* 2nd ed. (Boston, 1985), p. 92.

9. Cited in Yvonne Yazbeck Haddad, *Contemporary Islam and the Challenge of History* (Albany, 1982), p. 29.

The Middle East in the Age of Nasser: The Radicalization of Arab Politics

16

⟨|⟩
⟨|⟩

The current of discontent that brought an end to the old regime in Egypt was also present in other Arab states. Throughout the 1950s, a wave of coups and countercoups swept the eastern Arab world as a new generation of impatient military officers cast aside the previous order and tried to construct another. But none of these officers had the combination of personal skills, good fortune, and popular support that accompanied Nasser's rise to power. In particular, they proved unable to prevent the division of their armed forces into competing political factions. This politicization of the military led to governmental instability and hampered the new rulers in their efforts to implement their reform programs.

As various regimes rose and fell, Nasser continued his attempts to form a Pan-Arab union under Egyptian control. However, the young military officers of Syria and Iraq, although they admired Nasser and shared many of his goals, did not wish to be dominated by him. The pro-Western governments in Lebanon and Jordan also resisted the call to Arab unity, but in so doing they opened themselves to subversion by Nasserite supporters. The late 1950s and early 1960s were years of intense inter-Arab rivalry and have aptly been called the period of the Arab cold war. In studying this period, we should keep in mind the other cold war between the United States and the Soviet Union that influenced, and was influenced by, developments in the core eastern Arab states.

Syria: The Military in Politics

Syria entered the postwar years with untested parliamentary institutions and a political leadership unfamiliar with the tasks of governing. These impediments to the development of a healthy political life were compounded by the legacy of French mandate policies that stressed the regional and confessional divisions within the country. The individual elected as the first president of independent Syria, Shukri al-Quwwatli (see Chapter 11), added to the burdens of his office by committing the inexperienced Syrian armed forces to the war against Israel in 1948. The patriotic officer corps blamed Syria's defeat on the corrupt civilian regime.

In March 1949 the army took matters into its own hands by staging the first of what would become a series of military coups. Led by Colonel Husni Za°im, the coup ousted President Quwwatli and brought an end to the political domination of the urban notable classes. The wealthy urban politicians who had been educated in Ottoman or European schools were replaced by young men of mainly peasant origins trained in the Syrian military academy. Za°im's seizure of power ushered in a period of extreme political instability marked by two additional coups before the year ended. The second of these coups was led by Colonel Adib Shishakli, who managed to hang onto power until 1954.

Shishakli established a centralized military dictatorship and brought a temporary end to the factionalism within the officer corps. During the first two years of his rule, the order and discipline he imposed on Syrian political life were not unpopular. Shishakli predated Nasser in adopting a neutralist foreign policy and refusing to participate in Western-sponsored defense pacts. His regional policy emphasized Syria's Arabism and was based on the assumption that Syria would be the core of any future Pan-Arab union. Shishakli's popularity declined when, like all dictators, he resorted to repressive measures to keep himself in power. Amidst widespread disaffection with his regime, Shishakli was ousted by a faction within the military in 1954.

Although Syria returned to civilian parliamentary government, the military continued to interfere in politics, and from 1954 until the merger with Egypt in 1958, the Syrian political structure was so fragmented that government could barely function. Syria's political instability can be traced to several factors. First, the divide-and-rule policies of the French had encouraged Syrians to identify with their regional, religious, or ethnic community at the expense of loyalties to the Syrian nation as a whole. After independence, individuals tended to retain their communal loyalties, even when they were members of such national institutions as the armed forces or the civil service. A second source of instability was the factionalization and politicization of the officer corps. Husni Za°im's coup of 1949 weakened the old order and made the military the paramount political force in the country. However, unlike the Free Officers in Egypt, the Syrian military did not produce a figure who was able to secure the loyalty of the entire armed forces for a sustained period of time. Factions within the military continuously maneuvered against whatever officer had most recently seized power and thus prevented the consolidation of a strong military regime.

The emergence of political parties also contributed to the factionalization of Syrian political life. The political style of the urban notables, with its shifting alliances and informal agreements among prominent individuals, was replaced by the rise of broadly based parties committed to specific programs and ideologies. During the mid-1950s the Syrian Communist Party, though not large, became a major force in political life because it was able to attract a following among military officers and minority groups. The party's leader, Khalid Bakdash, was an effective organizer and orator. When he was elected to parliament in 1954, he became the first Communist Party deputy in the Arab world. The Baʿth Party also demonstrated its strength in the 1954 elections. It was to develop as the most significant ideological Arab party of the postwar era and exercised an influence on Nasser and other prominent figures outside Syria.

The Baʿth (literally, resurrection) was founded by Michel Aflaq (b. 1912), an Orthodox Christian, and Salah al-Din al-Bitar (b. 1911), a Sunni Muslim. During their student days in Paris in the early 1930s, the two worked together to formulate a doctrine that combined aspects of nationalism and socialism. Upon their return to Syria, they spent several years as teachers in Damascus secondary schools and attracted a dedicated following among students. The Baʿth became a formal party at the time of Syrian independence in 1946. As defined in the writings of Aflaq, who served as the party's ideologue, the Baʿth was dedicated to revolutionary activism aimed at bringing about a complete transformation of Arab society. A main feature of the party's platform was a belief in the existence of a single Arab nation and a commitment to the achievement of Arab unity. From unity would come the restoration of Arab dignity and the reemergence of Arab virtues. Although Aflaq was a Christian, he made Islam an integral part of Baʿthist ideology. He equated Islam and Arabism, both of which he saw as expressions of the Arab spirit.

Aflaq's doctrine was not confined to vague descriptions of the benefits of Arab unity. In his writings, the Baʿth was given a revolutionary mission to bring an end to social injustice, class exploitation, and tyranny and to establish freedom, democracy, and socialism. Aflaq argued that if independence from imperial control was to be worthwhile, it had to be accompanied by attitudinal change and social reform, it had to involve a national resurrection. Such a resurrection could be achieved only through a social revolution. With its socialist vision, its call for Arab unity, and its compelling appeal to all Arabs to dedicate themselves to a national rebirth, the Baʿth attracted a following among young Arabs that extended beyond the borders of Syria. Nasser later transposed the party's slogan of unity, freedom, and socialism to the Egyptian arena.

Syrian political instability was also fostered by the country's place in the struggle for domination of the eastern Arab world. In the mid-1950s Egypt and Iraq were the main rivals for Arab supremacy. Iraq, under its Hashimite monarchy, represented a conservative, pro-Western orientation, whereas Nasser's Egypt stood for reform and independence from all Great Power alliances. Each of these states sought to bring Syria into its orbit and thereby increase its own regional power. Syrian politicians and military officers were divided over which of the two states would make the best ally, and this division, which Egypt and Iraq were only too happy to exploit, contributed to the political turmoil within the country.

In late 1957 the Syrian Baʿthist leaders, recognizing that they were not strong enough to bring the country under their control and fearing that the continued chaos would benefit the Communists, approached Nasser about a union. They hoped that Nasser, a fellow reformer, would use his influence to keep them in power. The United Arab Republic was proclaimed in February 1958 but, as we saw in the last chapter, was so dominated by Egypt that the Baʿthists played little part in its governance, and the union broke up in 1961. Although the UAR was a failure, in 1958 its creation was regarded as a significant and dramatic development. The combination of Baʿthist ideology and Nasser's leadership seemed to have the possibility of attracting other Arab states to the union and of achieving the Arab rebirth that was so eloquently portrayed in the writings of Aflaq. For these reasons, the proclamation of the UAR produced a widespread reaction among both Arab activists and conservatives.

Iraq: The End of the Monarchy

From the end of World War II to 1958, Iraq remained firmly under the control of the Hashimite monarchy and its agents. King Faysal II came of age in 1953, but the power behind the throne was still Prince Abd al-Ilah, who had been the regent since 1939. Outside the palace, Nuri al-Saʿid, after three decades at the center of power, kept a tight rein on the political process and directed Iraq's foreign policy. The pro-Western, pro-British orientation of this policy was symbolized by Iraq's signing of the Baghdad Pact in 1955.

The complex composition of the Iraqi population (discussed in Chapter 11) continued to have an impact on the country's political development and its relations with other Arab states. The majority Shiʿa community was underrepresented in the political system and resented the concentration of political power and economic benefits in the hands of the Sunnis. The Shiʿas generally opposed Pan-Arabism, knowing that in any Arab federation they would become a marginalized minority. Iraq's most volatile minority group was the largely Sunni Kurdish community. Engaged in a perpetual struggle for political and cultural autonomy, the Kurds opposed Pan-Arabism and warned that if Iraq entered an Arab union, they would demand an independent Kurdish state. To these tensions were added the disparities in the patterns of living between urban and rural inhabitants, between tribes and sedentary peasants, and between the wealthy landowners and the impoverished peasant masses. In the late 1950s about 80 percent of Iraq's population remained rural and lived in abysmal conditions. It has been estimated that as many as 90 percent of the peasants were sharecropping tenants whose relationships with their landlords were of a feudal nature. Individual landholdings were not as large as in Egypt, but the patterns of uneven distribution were similar, with less than 1 percent of all landholders controlling over 55 percent of all privately owned land in 1958.

The Iraqi governments of the postwar era had such a narrow base of support that they were unwilling to address questions of social reform for fear that any alteration of the status quo would alienate the landowners and other groups on whose support the regime's continued existence depended. Nuri al-Saᶜid saw to it that political participation was confined to a small group of loyalists, a practice that alienated the rising generation of reform-minded nationalists attracted by the allure of Nasserism. The regime's stagnation, its pro-British alliance, and its anti-Nasser propaganda were so at odds with prevailing opinion that it could sustain itself only by the use of police repression and censorship, and even that proved insufficient. In July 1958 Brigadier Abd al-Karim Qasim overthrew the regime in a bloody military coup in which scores of people were killed, including King Faysal II, Prince Abd al-Ilah, and Nuri al-Saᶜid. The British-installed Hashimite monarchy, a pillar of the Western alliance system, was terminated after thirty-seven years of existence.

Qasim's coup sent shock waves throughout the eastern Arab world. It ushered in a decade of unstable military rule during which Iraq joined Egypt and Syria in proclaiming revolution at home and neutrality abroad. Qasim established a personal military dictatorship that lasted until 1963, when it was toppled by dissident factions within the military led by Colonel Abd al-Salam Arif, who assumed the title of president. Arif's short rule was ended by his death in a plane crash in 1966; he was succeeded by his brother and fellow military officer, Abd al-Rahman Arif, who held power until 1968.

The successive military regimes announced programs of sweeping domestic reforms, but the political situation was so uncertain and the effort required to hang on to power was so demanding that there was little opportunity for the rulers to implement their reformist decrees. Qasim proclaimed Iraq to be a republic, but it was a "republic" in which neither he nor his successors allowed elections to take place. In Iraq, as in Syria, the end of the old political order was quickly followed by the emergence of ideological parties, the largest and best organized of which was the Communist Party. Its main rival was the Baᶜth, an offshoot of the parent party in Syria, which attracted Pan-Arab nationalists eager to have Iraq merge with the UAR. Qasim at first used Communist support to counterbalance the Pan-Arab nationalists; then, when it appeared that the Communists were about to take over the state, he turned against them, and by 1960 he was well on his way to establishing a personal dictatorship.

Once Qasim overthrew the monarchy, he still had to confront the large landowners who had been among the main supporters and beneficiaries of Hashimite rule. Within a few weeks of coming to power, Qasim issued an agrarian reform law based on the 1952 Egyptian model and intended to serve the same purposes as the Egyptian law, namely, to reduce the wealth and power of the landed elite while improving the living conditions of the peasantry. The Iraqi law allowed individual proprietors to retain up to 620 acres (251 ha) of irrigated land and authorized the state to seize the excess and redistribute it to tenants in lots ranging from 20 to 75 acres (8 to 30 ha), depending on the quality of the land. In the absence of trained personnel and adequate surveys, the law was difficult to implement, and by the end of Qasim's regime the state had distributed only one-third of the acreage it had seized, making the law more a weapon against large proprietors than a means of creating a new class of landowning peasants.[1]

In the area of foreign policy, Qasim withdrew Iraq from the Baghdad Pact and established close ties with the Soviet Union and the Eastern bloc states. Shortly after the coup, Iraq and the USSR reached an agreement providing for Soviet military and economic assistance. With the signing of this agreement, the U.S. policy of containment appeared to be in disarray; the three most powerful Arab states, Egypt, Syria, and Iraq, had, within the space of a few years, rejected the idea of exclusive participation in the Western alliance and had at the same time opened themselves to Soviet influence. The Baghdad Pact was without the country that claimed Baghdad as its capital. Although the three states proclaimed their neutrality in the superpower conflict, they relied on the Soviet Union for their weapons, a relationship that contained the potential for economic and diplomatic dependency.

As for the all-important question of Iraq's role in the Arab world, the regimes of Qasim and the Arif brothers were unable to reach a solution that was acceptable to all the country's political factions. Qasim faced conflicting domestic pressures from two opposing forces: the Pan-Arab nationalists, who demanded an immediate merger with the UAR, and the Communists, who, aware of Nasser's suppression of the Egyptian Communist Party, opposed joining the UAR and advocated instead a sovereign Iraq. Although Qasim proclaimed his support for Arab solidarity, he had no desire to become subordinate to Nasser the way the Syrians had. He therefore chose to retain Iraq's independent status. This produced a rupture with the Nasser regime, which had staked so much on the achievement of Pan-Arab unity. In the final years of Qasim's rule, Iraq and Egypt, two reformist states that shared many of the same goals, again became regional rivals hurling insults at one another through the media.

Despite Qasim's refusal to join the UAR, the Pan-Arab dynamic continued to be a persistent feature of Iraqi politics, as illustrated by the policies of Qasim's successor, Abd al-Salam Arif. Arif participated in a series of summit talks with the Egyptian president, and in 1964 the two countries prepared plans for the integration of their military and economic policies with the intention of achieving full union in 1966. In order to bring Iraq's economic structure into alignment with Egypt's, Arif nationalized all banks and insurance companies as well as several large manufacturing firms. However, even as Arif cooperated with Egypt, he had to placate other factions of officers opposed to unification. He was forced to proceed with such caution that by the time of his death in 1966, little real progress had been made toward the full integration of Iraq and Egypt. Arab unity, so ardently desired by powerful leaders in Syria, Egypt, and Iraq, remained an elusive dream battered by the crosscurrents of political instability, ethnic discord, and personal ambition.

The experiences of the military regimes of Qasim and the Arif brothers revealed the difficulties of establishing reformist governments in Iraq. Not only were the officer corps factionalized and the civilian politicians divided, but Iraqi society as a whole was riddled with so many religious, ethnic, and economic interest groups that mobilization of the population behind a common goal proved impossible. Any program the government announced, whether it was unity with Egypt or agrarian reform, was bound to elicit opposition from one or another of the interest groups. Qasim endeavored to establish a regime based on loyalty to the personality of the ruler, but this alienated the military, which then overthrew him. Arif's use of Pan-Arabism as the doctrine around which to build loyalty to the regime was as divisive as it was cohesive.

The hostility between the government and the Kurds has been a prominent feature of Iraqi history and has, like the question of Pan-Arabism, exercised a considerable influence on the rise and fall of governments during the postwar era. Although the Kurds are mainly Sunni Muslims, they possess a distinct ethnic and cultural identity centered on the Kurdish language. The Allies provided for the creation of a semiautonomous Kurdish state in the Treaty of Sèvres in 1919. The treaty was overturned, however, and the lands promised to the state of Kurdistan were absorbed by Turkey, Iran, and Iraq. Ever since, the Kurds have constituted a restless minority community in each of the three states.

In their resistance to full integration into Iraq, the Kurds have variously demanded cultural autonomy and complete independence. They have attracted so much attention from Iraqi regimes over the years because of their numbers (20 to 25 percent of the country's population) and their concentration around the rich oil fields of the north. In 1958 Qasim took steps to obtain Kurdish support for his new regime by permitting the leader of the Iraqi Kurds, Mustafa al-Barzani, to return from a long exile in the Soviet Union and by issuing a statement guaranteeing Kurdish national rights. Once it became evident to Barzani that the government could not implement its promises, he organized a full-scale Kurdish rebellion against the regime. The conflict raged from 1961 to 1963, with neither side able to secure its objectives. Determined Kurdish fighters prevented the Iraqi army from penetrating their mountain strongholds, but they could not persuade the government to grant their demands. For its part, the Qasim regime struck hard at the rebels, but even its bombing raids against Kurdish villages could not force the Kurds to surrender. The huge cost of the government's military campaign (estimated at $60 million) and its failure to achieve victory were among the factors contributing to Qasim's overthrow in 1963. In the years that followed, cease-fires and promises were made and broken, armed hostilities flared up and cooled off, but the Kurdish separatist movement survived and continued to cause concern among the policymakers in Baghdad.

The Hashimite Kingdom of Jordan: The Survival of Monarchy

In 1946 Amir Abdallah reaped the rewards of his wartime loyalty to Great Britain: Transjordan was granted independence and Abdallah was allowed to proclaim himself king. He soon achieved the important role in regional affairs that he had sought since his state was created, but it came at a high price. The outcome of the Arab-Israeli war of 1948 had profound territorial and demographic implications for Transjordan. Not only did the Palestinian exodus result in the arrival of half a million refugees on Transjordanian soil, but King Abdallah's annexation of the West Bank in 1948 added another 400,000 settled Palestinians to the country's population. Jordan (the new name that Abdallah gave his country in 1948) suddenly contained a population that was two-thirds Palestinian. On the whole, the Palestinians were better educated, more urbanized, and decidedly more politicized than the other inhabitants of the kingdom. Their presence as a discontented majority stimulated the formation of the first organized political opposition to the Jordanian monarchy.

King Abdallah tried to win the allegiance of his new Palestinian subjects by allowing them to acquire Jordanian citizenship and appointing a few of them to his cabinet. However, Palestinians viewed Abdallah as an accomplice of the British and held him responsible for the partition of their homeland. In 1951 the king was assassinated by a Palestinian outside al-Aqsa mosque in Jerusalem. The tribute that Prime Minister Winston Churchill of Britain paid to Abdallah unwittingly revealed one of the causes for the king's murder: "We have," proclaimed Churchill, "lost a faithful comrade and ally."[2]

Abdallah's grandson, Husayn, became king in 1953 and at the age of eighteen assumed responsibility for governing Jordan's volatile population. King Husayn appeared to be the most vulnerable of the Arab monarchs, and his overthrow was regularly predicted. Yet he survived assassination plots, coup attempts, the defeat of 1967, the Palestinian Liberation Organization (PLO) crisis of 1970, and numerous diplomatic setbacks to become one of the most durable monarchs of this century, ruling until his death in 1999. His longevity was due to political astuteness, a loyal army, and substantial economic assistance from the United States. Husayn was educated at Harrow and Sandhurst and communicated to Western audiences in impeccable English. But he also spoke eloquent Arabic and possessed skills as a pilot, horseman, and marksman—all virtues that appealed to the tribally recruited Jordanian army, with which the king cultivated excellent relations.

Shortly after assuming the throne, Husayn faced a crisis brought on by the clash between Nasser and the Western alliance. Within Jordan, Nasserism offered hope to the destitute Palestinians crowded in refugee camps as well as to the Palestinian intellectuals, merchants, and peasants on the West Bank who were unwilling subjects of the Hashimite kingdom. Husayn was pressured from one direction, by Britain, to join the Baghdad Pact and from another, by Nasser and Nasser's supporters in Jordan, to resist the British. Husayn finally decided to reject membership in the pact, resulting in the withdrawal of the British subsidy on which Jordan's economic survival depended. Egypt, Syria, and Saudi Arabia replaced the British subsidy by contributing funds of their own. It appeared at this point that Husayn was prepared to break the ties that bound his kingdom to Britain. However, his flirtation with Nasserist-inspired anti-Westernism was short-lived.

In 1957 the Jordanian regime was rocked to the core by a wave of opposition inspired by a convergence of all of the reformist currents of the era—Nasserism, Ba'thism, and communism. Pressures from Palestinian citizens for a greater share of political power and from high-ranking civilian and military officials for Jordan to distance itself from Britain and participate more actively in the drive for Arab unity threatened to topple the regime. Pan-Arabism, it appeared, was more dangerous to the monarchy than were ties to the West. Husayn struck back at his domestic opposition by suspending the constitution and proclaiming martial law. And in a decision with far-reaching consequences, he requested U.S. military support and economic assistance. Under the terms of the new Eisenhower Doctrine, Washington responded with an immediate grant of $10 million and the dispatch of the Sixth Fleet to the eastern Mediterranean. Husayn had chosen Western aid to save his throne.

It was a choice that made the Jordanian king the target of a steady stream of anti-Hashimite propaganda from Egypt and Syria, the two states that, as we have seen, merged to form the UAR in February 1958. Matters came to a head with Qasim's overthrow of the Hashimite monarchy in Iraq in July of that fateful year. Qasim's coup occurred at a time of increasing tension in Jordan brought on by the activities of Nasser's supporters in organizing a movement against Husayn. Would the last surviving ruler of the British-installed Hashimite dynasty be swept away in the wave of takeovers by re-formist-oriented military officers that had already engulfed Syria and Egypt and now included Iraq? In the tense days of July 1958, Husayn called on his army to keep order and appealed to Britain for additional military assistance. Britain responded by sending a contingent of 2,000 paratroops from Cyprus. They remained in Jordan for over a year, a striking symbol of that country's continued reliance on British assistance.

King Husayn's commitment to the Western alliance was rewarded by a steady increase in U.S. financial aid. By the early 1960s the United States was providing the country with $50 million annually. The skillful applica-tion of these funds enabled Jordan to experience a period of sustained eco-nomic growth. The country's once primitive communications network was modernized; irrigation projects were undertaken on the West Bank; and the tourist industry, centered on Jerusalem and Bethlehem, was developed to the point where it constituted 25 percent of annual revenue. During the 1960s Jordan was changed from the economic dependent of Britain it had been in 1950 to a relatively prosperous developing state with a per capita in-come second only to Lebanon's among the non-oil-producing Arab states.

Following the crisis of 1958, King Husayn was the target of a constant propaganda campaign in which Egypt and Syria branded him as a lackey of Western imperialism. But despite Nasser's charges against him from without and the Palestinians' resentment toward him from within, Husayn was nei-ther overwhelmed by the tide of Pan-Arabism nor overthrown by socialist revolutionaries. Jordan in the late 1960s seemed something of an anachro-nism, existing in the Arab heartland as a free enterprise monarchy allied to the West. But Jordan was also very much engaged in the affairs of the Arab world as a member of the Arab League, as a direct neighbor of Israel, and as the dwelling place of the largest concentration of Palestinians in the world. These factors would influence King Husayn's decisions during the June War.

Lebanon: The Precarious Sectarian Balance

For readers whose only impressions of the city of Beirut are of hostage tak-ings and artillery duels, it is especially important to realize what Lebanon's capital city once was and what its success represented. From the end of World War II to the late 1960s, Beirut was the jewel of the eastern Mediter-ranean, a glittering metropolis that served as an economic and cultural bridge between the West and the Middle East. Beirut's prosperity was, to some extent, made possible by the upheavals in the surrounding Arab states during the 1950s. Faced with nationalization laws in Cairo, Damascus, and Baghdad, Arab entrepreneurs and their capital headed for Lebanon, with its laissez-faire economic system. Lebanese governments did their best to en-courage the movement of foreign capital into the country by deregulating the currency exchanges and adopting banking secrecy laws. These and other measures made Beirut a major international banking center and earned Lebanon the reputation as the Switzerland of the Middle East. The government also removed trade restrictions, thus fostering the import and reexport trade in which the Lebanese excelled and prospered.

In addition to being a bustling financial and commercial center, Beirut was also a home for political exiles and a haven of free expression in an area of the world where government censorship was becoming the norm. A free press in which the most divergent political views were aired, a burgeoning publishing industry, and a university that attracted students from all over the Arab world contributed to Beirut's role as a center of intellectual exchange and political discussion. The city offered other attractions as well. Its luxury hotels, its Las Vegas–style casino, and its flashy nightclubs drew all manner of pleasure seekers. In this regard, it has been remarked that "every region of the globe needs one city where the rules don't apply, where sin is the norm, and where money can buy anything or anyone."[3] For the Middle East, Beirut was that city.

But Beirut stood for something far more important than material prosperity and pleasurable nightlife—the city showed that sectarian pluralism could work. Jews fled Egypt and the Kurds of Iraq were shelled by their own government, but Beirut thrived as a multireligious, multiethnic urban mosaic. The city's long fall into the abyss of communal violence in 1975–1976 sent a frightening question to the Middle East as a whole: If sectarian cooperation had failed in the relatively tolerant atmosphere of Beirut, what chance did it have in the rest of the region?

But even during Beirut's days of glory, deep sectarian differences were never far beneath the surface of Lebanese life. As we have seen in Chapter 11, Lebanon developed a unique political system in which communal loyalties were institutionalized. The constitution of 1926, the census of 1932, and the National Pact of 1943 established the basis of confessional politics and identified Lebanon as an Arab country, but one that would not attempt to federate with any other Arab state. This proposition was put to a severe test in the age of Pan-Arabism. The sum total of the Lebanese system was, then, a balance of sectarian rivalries. Communal differences were not resolved but rather were neutralized in a system that prevented any one sect from achieving dominance. In the absence of a monolithic state, diversity flourished, and Lebanon gave the impression of a peaceful sectarian coexistence.

However, the perseverance of sectarian communal loyalties stultified Lebanon's political development and allowed family and religious ties to prevail over national ones. Politics was dominated by established families whose power derived from economic status and a long-standing tradition of leadership. Within each of the country's electoral districts, a political boss (*za'im*) from the leading family of the region manipulated elections and distributed political favors and financial rewards. The *zaᶜim* might himself be a candidate for parliament, or he might prefer to round up votes for someone else who would then be in his debt. Votes were often obtained by means of bribery and, if necessary, force, which the *zaᶜim*'s armed retainers meted out at will. The individuals who were elected to parliament through the *zaᶜim* system regarded their primary responsibility as serving the needs of their local clients; they lacked any urgent sense of national issues and used parliament for the purposes of furthering their regional-sectarian interests. The *zaᶜim* was in effect a feudal lord dressed in a tailored European suit. The attire misled many outside observers at the time and prompted them to write glowing reports about Lebanese democracy. Such reports were usually filed from Beirut, a city whose ample amenities hid the blunt force that made up Lebanese politics.

The *zaᶜim* system did not give rise to ideological political parties but instead tended to encourage the formation of sectarian-based blocs loyal to a single individual. The bloc that most forcefully represented the Maronite perspective, and that most nearly approximated a national Maronite political organization, was the Kataib, or Phalange. Founded as a Maronite youth organization by Pierre Gemayel in 1936, the Phalange was influenced by the European Fascist parties of the time. Its youthful scouting organization developed into an armed militia controlled by Gemayel and ready to defend the notion that Lebanon was the special Maronite homeland. One of the Phalange's slogans, "Lebanon above all," was an uncompromising commitment to the preservation of a distinctive Maronite-dominated country independent of any Arab federation.

An altogether different bloc was the small but influential Progressive Socialist Party founded in 1949 by the Druze leader Kamal Jumblatt. Although the party was protective of Druze interests, it also reflected Jumblatt's radical reformist ideals and therefore crossed sectarian boundaries, appealing to a broad cross-section of Lebanese who knew they were missing out on the good life enjoyed by the political bosses and the Beirut elite. Jumblatt became an important figure in Lebanese politics; he was a traditional *zaᶜim* who was also a credible social reformer able to put together leftist coalitions that challenged Maronite supremacy and welcomed Pan-Arabism. The Sunni Muslim organizations were fragmented among a number of regional political bosses, some of whom were attracted to Nasser's Pan-Arabism. Lebanon's Sunni Muslims still felt a deep attachment to Syria and chafed at the circumstances that left them with less influence than they felt they deserved. In the age of Pan-Arabism, Lebanon stood out as a Western-oriented, Christian-dominated capitalist state with a discontented Sunni Muslim population.

Any examination of Lebanon's various crises since World War II must take into consideration the institutional role of the president of the republic. The National Pact ensured that the president would be a Maronite Christian, and the constitution conferred upon the head of state exceptionally strong powers relative to the parliament. In order to prevent a powerful president from perpetuating his rule, the constitution limited an individual to a single six-year term of office. The country's first two post-independence presidents—Bishara al-Khuri (1943–1952) and Camille Chamoun (1952–1958)—attempted to alter this constitutional provision. In so doing, both plunged their country into crisis.

Al-Khuri, whose long service to the cause of Lebanese independence has been discussed in Chapter 11, proved to be less adept as an administrator than he was as a negotiator. Although the years of his presidency coincided with Lebanon's economic boom, his inclination to overlook corrupt financial practices by his relatives and supporters contributed to the development of a current of opposition to him. His opponents became more outspoken when al-Khuri, in the *za'im* tradition, manipulated parliamentary elections so that he was chosen for a second consecutive term as president in 1949. He did not, however, serve out his new term. He was forced to resign in 1952 when a coalition of his opponents, including fellow Maronites, called a successful general strike to protest his methods.

His successor, Chamoun, was committed to the Western alliance and the preservation of Lebanon's free enterprise system and was responsible for much of the legislation that made Lebanon's banking regulations so attractive to outside investors. It was unfortunate for Chamoun that Lebanon was attractive to other outside forces as well. Chamoun's presidency coincided with the spread of U.S.-Soviet rivalry in the Middle East, the rise of Nasser, and the emergence of demands for reform by Lebanon's Muslims. The Muslims called for a new census, believing that its outcome would show that they were the largest religious community in the country and deserved a greater apportionment of government positions than they held at the time.

In these circumstances, Chamoun had to face directly the question of whether Lebanon should commit itself to the West or assert its Arab heritage by establishing closer relations with Egypt and Syria. His own Maronite community was strongly committed to Lebanon's Western orientation, but increasing numbers of Muslims were attracted to Nasserist Pan-Arabism. In an attempt to keep both communities satisfied, Chamoun opted not to join the Baghdad Pact, at the same time emphasizing Lebanon's friendship with the West. During the Suez crisis of 1956, Chamoun irritated Nasser and his Lebanese supporters by refusing to break diplomatic relations with Britain and France at the time of their invasion of Egypt.

The tensions created by the conflicting internal and external pulls on Lebanon's loyalties came to a head in the eventful summer of 1958. Chamoun appeared to be contemplating measures that would enable him to obtain a second term in office, a prospect that was unacceptable to the Muslim community. Muslim opposition to Chamoun's plans developed into a full-scale rebellion during which such large cities as Tripoli and Sidon broke away from the control of the central government. President Chamoun ordered the army to put down the revolt, but the commander in chief, General Fuad Shihab, refused to employ the armed forces in an internal political dispute. The Lebanese civil war was still simmering when Qasim overthrew the Hashimite regime in Iraq on July 14. Chamoun immediately requested U.S. assistance to save his country from falling under the control of pro-Nasser forces.

The United States responded promptly. On the day after the Iraqi coup, 15,000 U.S. Marines landed on the beaches of Lebanon. The United States was determined to preserve a friendly regime in Lebanon, whether it was threatened by communism or Nasserism. Chamoun, the target of much of the Muslim animosity, stepped aside after completing his presidential term in September. As his successor the parliament chose Fuad Shihab, the army commander whose deft handling of the military during the civil war met with both Muslim and Christian approval. Once Shihab became president, Muslim-Christian relations improved, and Lebanon returned to business as usual.

However, Shihab differed from his predecessors. A selfless politician dedicated to the interests of Lebanon as a whole, he recognized the source of Muslim discontent and launched an ambitious program of political and economic reforms. His policies were sufficiently unique to acquire the label Shihabism. The goal of Shihab's program was to modernize the state. In the Lebanese context this meant increasing the power of the central government at the expense of the political bosses and installing the basics of a social welfare system. Shihab was aware of the need to reduce the disaffection that had led to the 1958 civil war by providing Muslims with a stake in an independent Lebanon. He ensured that more Muslims received top positions in the administration than had previously been the case. In addition the president sharply increased government expenditures, especially on public works projects such as road building, rural electrification, and the extension of the supply of water to previously neglected rural areas. During Shihab's term in office (1958–1964), the power of the president and of the central government in general expanded noticeably. Although the president did not succeed in achieving all his reforms, Shihabism was a positive force in Lebanese life: It represented a commitment to orderly government, to law enforcement, to social reform, and to sectarian reconciliation. It did not, however, bring an end to sectarian politics. Members of each confessional group still manifested a primary loyalty to their religious community and jealously guarded the privileges they believed were due that community.

As for the external pressures that had contributed to the civil war, the breakup of the UAR in 1961 reduced to some extent the immediate need for Lebanon to make a decision about its Pan-Arab future. Moreover, the socialist policies the Nasser regime adopted after 1961 caused many

Lebanese Muslim entrepreneurs to question whether Arab unity was worth the surrender of the free enterprise system that served them so well. Nevertheless, Lebanon continued to be vulnerable to subversion by Nasserites and Baᶜthists and subject to the perpetual internal divisions of a nation that was in and of the Arab world but inhabited by a population torn between its desires to be assimilated within that world and to be distinct from it.

Israel, the Arab States, and the June War

Origins of the War

Even during periods of non-belligerence, the Arab-Israeli conflict shaped the attitudes of the participants. Israelis lived in constant insecurity, fearing the potential military power of a unified Arab nation. Within the Arab states, the memories of the Israeli victory in 1948 and the Israeli invasion of Egypt in 1956 were an active part of political consciousness. Much of the rhetoric surrounding Nasserism contained promises for the liberation of Palestine from its Zionist occupiers. Arab unity was pictured as a way for the Arabs to acquire the strength needed to achieve a military victory over Israel. From the Arab perspective, Israel was an expansionist arm of Western imperialism, and there was a widespread belief that Israel would sooner or later launch an attack on the Arabs in order to gain more territory for Jewish settlement. Israelis, in turn, accepted the Arab propaganda at face value and watched with alarm as the Soviets poured arms into Egypt, Syria, and Iraq. Although the Arab leaders behaved much more cautiously than their propaganda suggested, there were frequent clashes along the Jordanian-Israeli border during the 1960s. They were instigated by the activities of the fledgling Palestinian resistance organizations that began to form in the late 1950s. Palestinian guerrillas based in Syria conducted raids into Israel through Jordanian territory; Israel would then retaliate in force against targets in Jordan. Despite these incidents, in early 1967 the eastern Arab states were more concerned with inter-Arab affairs than with Israel. The quarrels between the monarchies and the socialist states seemed more likely to escalate into armed conflict than did any of the tensions between Israel and its neighbors. Nasser, his prestige diminished by his failure to bring about a durable Arab union and by his military intervention in Yemen, was preoccupied with retaining his leadership of the reformist bloc of Arab states and rejuvenating Egypt's lagging economy.

In May 1967 Soviet and Syrian intelligence reported that Israel was preparing a large-scale military operation against Syria for its sponsorship of Palestinian guerrilla activities. The reports were incorrect but at the time were taken to be true. Nasser, in order to bolster his Pan-Arab leadership role, responded to the threat to Syria by deploying troops in the Sinai Peninsula. This was posturing, an attempt to demonstrate to the Arab world at large that Egypt stood shoulder to shoulder with other Arab countries against their common enemy. It was a successful gesture, and a wave of pro-Nasser, anti-Israeli demonstrations broke out in several Arab cities. Nasser was thus tempted into escalating his brinkmanship. He requested that all UN forces be withdrawn from Sinai. Probably to his surprise, the request was quickly granted, and the UN forces that had formed a shield between Egypt and Israel were evacuated. The momentum seemed to be with Nasser, and he took the crisis a step further by reoccupying the UN positions at Sharm al-Shaykh and announcing a blockade on Israeli shipping passing through the Straits of Tiran.

In retrospect, it appears that Nasser was bluffing. With a large part of the Egyptian army bogged down in Yemen, Egypt was in no position to go to war with Israel. It is likely that Nasser expected Soviet-U.S. intervention to calm the crisis and permit him to escape with his reputation renewed. However, Nasser had unleashed emotions that were beyond his ability to control. He gave the appearance of preparing for the final showdown with Israel, and other Arab leaders clambered to get on side. On May 30, King Husayn of Jordan, who only a few days earlier had been denounced in the Egyptian press, flew to Cairo to sign a mutual defense pact with Egypt. The Iraqi government joined the alliance a few days later.

The Israeli government of Prime Minister Levi Eshkol could not tolerate the blockade of the Straits of Tiran nor allow the continued buildup of Arab solidarity around Nasser, which, if unchecked, would place Israel under intolerable long-term pressures. The Israeli cabinet decided the situation had to be countered by military action. In the early morning of June 5, 1967, the Israeli air force attacked air bases throughout Egypt and destroyed most of the Egyptian air force while it was still on the ground. Later the same day, after Syria and Jordan had entered the conflict, Israeli pilots effectively destroyed the air forces of those countries as well. With undisputed control of the air, the Israeli forces defeated the Egyptian army in Sinai and advanced to the east bank of the Suez Canal. The two states signed a cease-fire on June 9. In the meantime Jordan engaged Israeli forces in the Jerusalem area on June 5, only to be driven out of East Jerusalem and across the Jordan River, abandoning the West Bank to Israeli occupation. Finally, the Israeli army turned its full might against Syria and wrested the Golan Heights from Syrian control (see Map 16.1). The cease-fire on the Golan front was agreed to on June 11. In a mere six days, Israel had defeated three Arab states. The war was a resounding triumph for the Israeli military, a humiliating disaster for the Arab forces, and a shattering blow to Nasserism.

The Aftermath of the June War

The Arab defeat was costly in both material and psychological terms. Each of the three Arab belligerents surrendered territory to the Israelis. Egypt

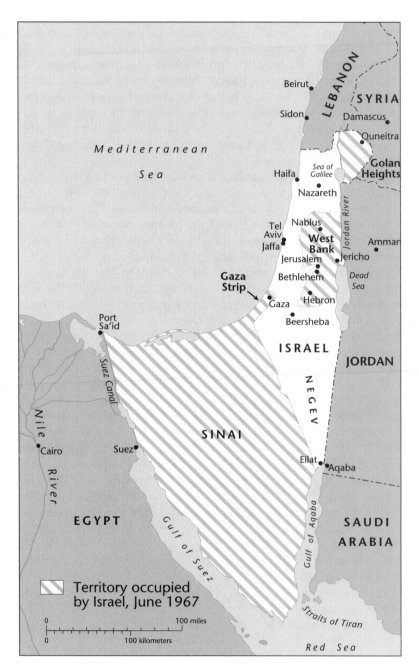

Map 16.1 Israel and the Territories Occupied in the June War. Sinai, but not the Gaza Strip, was returned to Egypt under the terms of the 1979 Egyptian-Israeli treaty.

was deprived of the revenues from the Sinai oil fields and the Suez Canal, which remained closed to shipping from 1967 to 1975. To add to the humiliation, Egypt was forced to make up these lost revenues by accepting subsidies from Saudi Arabia and Kuwait, monarchies Nasser had roundly criticized in the recent past. Jordan lost not only the West Bank, which had been its most productive agricultural region, but also the tourist sites of Jerusalem and Bethlehem. The Golan Heights were not a major economic loss for Syria, but Israel's occupation of them placed the Israeli forces within easy striking distance of Damascus. In addition, the armed forces of the Arab states were decimated. Egypt lost 12,000 men and 80 percent of its air force and armor, Syrian losses were 2,500 killed, and the Jordanian army was temporarily put out of action as a fighting unit. The Arab regimes that had pledged to liberate Palestine were militarily prostrate and deprived of any of the bargaining power associated with armed strength.

Although the war lasted only six days, it created another tragic Arab refugee situation and a complex demographic dilemma for Israel. Jordan, in surrendering the West Bank, lost a large portion of its settled Palestinian population, but at the same time it received 300,000 new refugees fleeing the West Bank and Gaza Strip. In Syria about 80,000 inhabitants were uprooted from the Golan Heights, and in Egypt the continued fighting along the Suez Canal reduced the cities of the canal zone to ruins and forced the evacuation of their inhabitants to other areas of the country. Israel, with the capture of East Jerusalem, the West Bank, Gaza Strip, Sinai, and the Golan Heights, suddenly found itself administering a new Arab population of 1.5 million people. This situation raised important questions about the character of the Israeli state in terms of its religious composition as well as its democratic traditions. Those questions are discussed in Chapter 17.

Another aspect of the war was its revelation of the disparity in the military capabilities of the Arab and Israeli armed forces. The speed and totality of the Israeli victory imparted to the Israeli military an aura of invincibility. Daring young generals like Ariel Sharon became national heroes, and the almost perfect performance of all the components of the Israeli armed forces made them an object of study by envious military organizations throughout the world. The marked superiority of the Israelis gave them a certain arrogance and removed any urgency for compromise and negotiation in the wake of their sweeping victory. By contrast, the Arab armed forces, and especially those of Egypt, were made to appear incompetent. In the aftermath of the war, investigations brought to light a level of corruption and mismanagement in the Egyptian military that disgraced the entire Nasser regime.

It was this psychological shock at the apparent hollowness of the new Arab regimes that was perhaps the most profound effect of the war. Much as the defeat of 1948 had discredited the old regimes of landed elite, urban notables, and wealthy monarchs, so the 1967 debacle tarnished the reputations of the military regimes that had come to power in the 1950s with their programs of social reform and their promises of strength through Arab unity. By June 11, 1967, the new regimes seemed every bit as corrupt, dysfunctional, and inept as their predecessors. What the historian Hanna Batatu has written about attitudes toward the Iraqi regime after June 1967 can also be applied to Syria and, to some extent, Egypt: "In the eyes of the people, the whole concept of the officers' state came into disrepute. For it became obvious that by its entry into politics and its division into factions, the officer corps had not only made a mess of government or become a seedbed of political instability, but had also seriously reduced the effectiveness of the military system. Not to mention the fact that, by transforming itself into a privileged order, it had become psychologically divorced from the rest of the people." Batatu concluded his analysis with the observation "that profound and fundamental social and political changes cannot be realized without long and sustained efforts and sacrifices, and massive popular participation; that, in other words, progressive ideological verbiage is not enough."[4] The disillusionment that Batatu described was widely felt. Arif's Iraqi regime fell to a Baᶜthist coup in July 1968; the Syrian regime survived for a time, but in November 1970 it, too, was overthrown, and Hafiz al-Asad began his long rule in Damascus.

In Egypt President Nasser somehow managed to retain his authority and a large measure of his personal popularity during the bitter, soul-searching aftermath of the war. However, the solidarity of the officer corps on which the regime was built collapsed in the wake of purges, attempted takeovers, and the arrest and suicide of Nasser's longtime confidant and commander in chief of the armed forces in June 1967, Field Marshal Abd al-Hakim Amr. Egyptian cynics explained Amr's demise with the phrase "he was suicided." As the result of an extensive Soviet effort, Egypt's air force and armor were restored to their prewar levels by the end of 1967. At the same time, the Soviets increased their military mission in Egypt to several thousand advisers, making Egypt completely dependent on the Soviet Union for its military survival.

The peace that usually follows wars did not come to the Middle East after 1967. Increased Palestinian guerrilla activity in Jordan met with Israeli retaliation in force. And on the Suez Canal front sporadic artillery exchanges erupted into full-scale combat in 1969 when Nasser, in an attempt to salvage Egyptian pride and to demonstrate that the country's ability to fight was not destroyed, launched what he called a war of attrition. It consisted of heavy artillery shelling of Israeli positions, to which the Israelis responded with barrages of their own, reducing the Suez Canal cities to ruins. By 1970 the war of attrition had escalated to the point where Israel was launching more than 150 air attacks a day, sometimes against targets deep within Egypt.

The problem for the would-be peacemakers was that the Arab states would not negotiate from a position of weakness, and Israel saw no need to make concessions from its position of strength. A basic framework for regional peace was put forth in the famous Resolution 242 adopted by the UN Security Council on November 22, 1967. The resolution asserted "the inadmissibility of the acquisition of territory by war" and called for a just and lasting peace based on the withdrawal of Israeli forces from territories occupied in the June War and the acknowledgment of the right of every state in the area to live in peace within secure and recognized boundaries. The resolution also affirmed the need of achieving a "just settlement of the refugee problem." Although Egypt, Jordan, and Israel endorsed Resolution 242, Syria and the Palestinian organizations rejected it. Because the document was so ambiguous and open-ended, even the accepting parties interpreted it quite differently. Thus the resolution failed to provide a consensual basis for a peace settlement.

However, Secretary of State William Rogers of the United States finally managed to put together a peace plan that Egypt, Jordan, and Israel supported. The plan included provision for a ninety-day cease-fire that went into effect in July 1970. Although the cease-fire was renewed several times and was thus successful in bringing an end to the war of attrition, the United States could not convince Egypt to sign a peace agreement with Israel nor persuade Israel to withdraw from occupied Egyptian territory. But at least the Rogers Plan had silenced the guns along the Suez Canal and given all parties an opportunity to reassess their positions.

Another significant result of the June War was the impetus it gave to the rise of Palestinian military and political organizations (as discussed in Chapter 17). In September 1970, clashes in Jordan between Palestinians and the Jordanian army prompted Nasser to offer his personal mediation of the crisis. An Arab summit meeting convened in Cairo and worked out a cease-fire that was acceptable to the Palestinians and King Husayn. On September 28, the day after the conference concluded, Nasser, who had been involved in round-the-clock negotiations, died of a heart attack. Despite the blows that his prestige had suffered, Nasser's death was greeted with outpourings of genuine grief and shock. At a time of acute crisis and uncertainty, the dominant Arab figure of the past fifteen years was removed from the scene. The Arab world temporarily suspended its rivalries to mourn for Nasser and to ponder its future without him.

Conclusion: The Nasser Era in Perspective

In the opinion of Malcolm Kerr, Nasser "symbolized a range of attitudes and actions reaching far beyond Egypt and beyond the particular things he himself said and did."[5] There is no question that Egypt exercised a profound regional influence during the Nasser years. Not all of the domestic turmoil in the Middle East can be attributed to Nasser, yet it seems clear that his example inspired imitators and attracted followers throughout the

Arab world. His attempts to break away from the Western embrace and its imperial connotations found a responsive echo in Baghdad and Damascus, in Tripoli and Algiers, and the promise of social and political reform associated with his policies became the ideal for reformers elsewhere. And the dream of Arab unity was shared by millions disillusioned at the status of the Arabs in recent history. Yet Nasser's intervention in the affairs of other states was often detrimental to the goals he claimed to have set. Nasser became concerned with external challenges to his leadership of the Pan-Arab movement, and he exhausted Egypt's resources in a series of external adventures ranging from attempts to subvert the Jordanian and Iraqi regimes, to intervention in Yemen, to the final disaster of 1967.

Although the sentiments that infused Nasserism were inspirational, the doctrine may have passed away with its namesake. Arab critics accused Nasserism of "middlism," of trying to satisfy too many conflicting aspirations. In this view, Nasserism was unable to decide whether it was religious or secular, democratic or authoritarian, socialist or capitalist. It contained parts of all of these orientations but took no clear stand on which of them was most important. By contrast, Michel Aflaq provided the Baʿth Party with a much more sharply defined set of principles than was found in Nasserism, but the Baʿth lacked a politician with Nasser's leadership qualities. Perhaps, in the end, the broad appeal of Nasserism was based more on its activism, its encouragement for change, than on any precise doctrine. If this was indeed the case, then there was little in Nasserism that could be transferred to a successor.

The strike by the Israeli air force on the morning of June 5, 1967, marked the true end of the Nasser era. From that point until his death, Nasser focused on political survival and departed from the policies that had defined Nasserism. After June 1967 he allowed the Soviet Union to acquire a dominant influence within the Egyptian military, he dropped the quest for Arab unity, and he worked in tandem with a monarch, King Husayn of Jordan, whom he had vilified on numerous previous occasions. Moreover, Nasser's acceptance of UN Resolution 242 and the Rogers Plan suggested to some that he was prepared to make an accommodation with Israel. At his death, the hopes he had raised were as shattered as the Egyptian cities along the Suez Canal, and the Arab public he had lifted with his promises entered a period of disillusionment and despair.

Notes

1. Hanna Batatu, *The Old Social Classes and the Revolutionary Movements of Iraq* (Princeton, 1982), p. 837.

2. Cited in Mary C. Wilson, *King Abdullah, Britain, and the Making of Jordan* (Cambridge, 1987), p. 210.

3. Thomas L. Friedman, *From Beirut to Jerusalem* (New York, 1989), p. 216.

4. Batatu, *The Old Social Classes,* p. 1066.

5. Malcolm H. Kerr, "The Political Outlook in the Local Arena," in Abraham S. Becker, Bent Hansen, and Malcolm H. Kerr, eds., *The Economics and Politics of the Middle East* (New York, 1975), p. 41. Other observations in this section are based on Kerr's critical assessment of Nasserism.

Israel and the   17
Palestinians from
1948 to the 1970s

⟨⎮⟩
⟨⎮⟩

Following its creation in war, Israel faced enormous peacetime challenges of nation building: Its leaders had to establish a governmental structure, set up a judicial system, and transform the communal organizations of the Yishuv into Israeli national institutions. In addition, because Israel's reason for being was founded on the claim to be a specifically Jewish nation, its ruling elite also had to determine what role religion would play in the institutional life of the state. During the first years of independence, the political leaders were able to reach a consensus on the administrative structure of the state. However, attitudes toward the proper role of Jewish religious law in public life differed widely.

The success of the Israeli military in the June War (1967) brought new confidence, but it also created new problems. With the conquest of the West Bank, the Gaza Strip, and the Golan Heights, Israel became an occupying power, ruling in an often arbitrary manner the million Palestinian Arabs brought unwillingly under its domination. The future of the occupied territories became the focus of a divisive national debate. What some Israelis viewed as an unjustifiable occupation, others saw as a God-given opportunity to hasten the redemption of the Jewish people by laying claim to all the lands of ancient Israel. The tensions between peace activists and settlers, between secularists and advocates of the need to introduce a greater measure of religious law, were sharpened rather than lessened as Israel entered the fourth decade of its existence as an independent state.

While Israelis argued about the future of the occupied territories, groups of Palestinian exiles began to take steps to recover their lands. One of the most far-reaching results of the June War was the rise to prominence of Palestinian resistance groups. Despairing at the failure of the Arab states to achieve their repatriation for them, Palestinians assumed the responsibility of liberating their homeland themselves. Palestinian guerrilla organizations undertook armed action against Israel and engaged in international acts of terrorism designed to attract attention to the plight of the Palestinian people. In the course of establishing an armed resistance movement, the Palestinians became a factor in the domestic politics of the Arab states and forced the entrenched Arab leadership to take their demands into account. Although the commando operations never posed a serious military threat to Israel, they did provoke large-scale Israeli reprisals and contributed to the ongoing tension that has characterized the Middle East from the 1970s onward. Outside the Middle East, the diplomatic initiatives of the Palestinian Liberation Organization (PLO) and its chairman, Yasir Arafat, succeeded in placing the question of Palestinian rights on the agenda of the United Nations and in shining a spotlight on the Israeli occupation of the West Bank and the Gaza Strip.

The Israeli Political System and Political Culture

The high level of communal organization that characterized the Yishuv facilitated Israel's transition to an independent state. The institutions—with in many cases the same personnel—that had administered the Yishuv were transformed into national institutions at Israel's creation. During the years from 1949 to 1977, Israeli politics was dominated by the labor-oriented Mapai Party, the same organization that had played the most prominent role in guiding the Yishuv. David Ben-Gurion, the towering figure of Israel's creation, held the offices of prime minister and minister of defense for most of the period from 1949 to 1963. He stamped the new state with his forceful personality, determined its foundational policies and its political practices, and imbued the office of prime minister with paramount authority within the political system.

One of Ben-Gurion's pressing concerns was to enshrine the authority of the state over the diverse communal organizations that had made up the Yishuv. His pursuit of this goal was most forcefully demonstrated in the *Altalena* affair of June 1948. At Israel's independence, units of the Haganah were reorganized as the Israeli Defense Forces (IDF) and placed under the authority of the civilian minister of defense. However, two dissident military organizations, the Irgun, led by Menachem Begin, and the smaller Lehi, refused to relinquish their autonomy and continued to conduct independent military operations. The crisis of authority was brought to a head when the ship *Altalena* arrived off the Israeli coast with a consignment of arms destined for the Irgun. Ben-Gurion ordered the IDF to prevent the arms from being unloaded. An armed struggle ensued, the *Altalena* was shelled and eventually sank, and several members of the Irgun were killed or wounded. Following this decisive encounter, the remaining autonomous military units were absorbed into the IDF, ensuring that the central state exercised control of all military forces. The affair also had the effect of solidifying an enduring enmity between Ben-Gurion and Begin.

Although a certain fluidity characterized Israel's institutional framework in the early years of state building, the main features of the political system had crystallized by 1949. Israel was established as a parliamentary democracy with a unicameral legislature (the Knesset) composed of 120 elected representatives. Candidates for the Knesset ran on a national slate rather than as representatives from particular districts and were thus elected by the nation at large. All citizens, male and female, received suffrage at age eighteen. Israel's form of parliamentary government provided the prime minister and cabinet with a particularly strong role in policy formulation and decisionmaking. The presidency was intended to be mainly a ceremonial office. In 1949 an ailing Chaim Weizmann left London, where he had been so effective in the Zionist cause for so many years, and made the journey to Tel Aviv to become Israel's first president.

Israel is sometimes referred to as "the party state" in recognition of the decisive influence that Israeli parties have exercised on its political life. Because Israelis voted for parties, not for individual candidates, it was virtually impossible to enter politics except through the mechanism of a party. When elections were announced, the party leadership prepared a numbered list of candidates and presented it to the public. Voters selected the party of their choice, and seats to the Knesset were assigned on the basis of proportional representation. For example, a party receiving 25 percent of the vote would be awarded thirty seats in the 120-member Knesset. These seats would be given to the first thirty names on the party's list. It was crucial for ambitious politicians to secure a high ranking on their party's list. They could do so only if they satisfied the party leaders by adhering rigorously to the party line during Knesset sessions. A maverick party member was likely to be dropped to a lower position on the party list and risked not gaining a Knesset seat. This system endowed party leaders with extensive powers, which they often exercised behind closed doors and with little accountability.

During the mandate years, organizations representing all the diverse strands of Zionism and religious orthodoxy engaged in intense competition for the loyalties of new immigrants. In order to attract adherents, they offered a broad range of social, educational, and recreational services. With independence the state took over some of these services, but the diversity of tenaciously held views remained a feature of Israeli politics. This diversity found expression in the formation of numerous political parties that stamped Israel with a unique, and sometimes troublesome, multiparty structure.

Israel's election law further encouraged the existence of numerous political parties. According to the law, any party that received 1 percent of the vote was entitled to representation in the Knesset. Raising the minimum threshold to 1.5 percent in 1992 did not significantly reduce the number of parties. Under this system, there was no need for political groups to modify even their most extreme positions in order to gain seats in the Knesset. Parties at the far ends of the political spectrum had a good chance of receiving 1 percent of the national vote and possibly joining a coalition government.

Because the popular vote was divided among so many different parties, no single party received an absolute majority in the Knesset. It was—and remains—normal for each Knesset to contain representatives from ten to fifteen different parties. Even during the heyday of Ben-Gurion's popularity, his Mapai Party never held more than 47 in the 120-seat Knesset. As a result of this multiparty system, the party with the most seats could form a government only by seeking out coalition partners. By its very nature, coalition government requires compromise and concession. During the Ben-Gurion era, stable coalitions were constructed between apparent opposites as the secular, moderately socialist Mapai frequently allied with the orthodox religious Right to create a parliamentary majority that endorsed Mapai's overall program while conceding portions of the religious parties' platforms. As a result, small parties that became part of a coalition government were able to exercise an influence on legislation out of all proportion to their share of the popular vote.

The presence of so many competing and intensely held positions in the political arena gave rise to a contentious and vociferous Israeli political culture. Knesset debates, even on seemingly minor issues, were often disorderly affairs filled with name calling, denunciations, and passionate oratory in which opposing factions accused one another of the basest intentions and warned of the gravest consequences if their own position was not upheld.

The Changing Composition of the Israeli Population

In the first years of statehood, Israel's major national effort was devoted to immigrant absorption. From 1948 to 1951, the Jewish population of Israel increased from approximately 650,000 to slightly more than 1.3 million. This was the result of an influx of some 684,000 immigrants, a phenomenon that posed enormous economic, cultural, and social problems for the new state. About half of the new immigrants were from Eastern Europe, the so-called displaced persons uprooted by the Nazis. If life in Israel demanded wrenching adjustments from the existence that many immigrants had known previously, it at least presented familiar patterns of discourse. Eastern European ideologies had shaped Zionism, Eastern European leaders had forged the institutions of the new state, and individuals of Eastern European birth occupied the most prominent positions in the political, judicial, religious, and educational hierarchy of the Israeli state. With the exception of Yitzhak Rabin, who was born in mandate Palestine, all of Israel's prime ministers from 1948 to 1992 were born in either Russia or Poland.

However, the first wave of immigration included at least as many Oriental (Sephardic) Jews from Arab countries as it did European (Ashkenazi) Jews. For a variety of reasons—some related to concerns over their status and safety within Arab society after the 1948 war, others involving active outreach policies by Israel—large numbers of individuals from the long-established Jewish communities in such Arab countries as Egypt, Iraq, Yemen, and Morocco immigrated to Israel. Between 1948 and 1956, roughly 450,000 Sephardic Jews arrived in the country. Speaking mainly Arabic, they possessed different cultural norms, political experiences, and conceptions of Judaism than their European counterparts. They did not integrate into Israeli society as rapidly as did the Ashkenazim. Large numbers of them were settled in new development towns in remote areas or in former Arab housing in the poorer quarters of the major cities. Ignored by the central authorities, underrepresented in the political system, and plagued by low participation rates in education and high rates of unemployment, the Sephardim became an impoverished sector of the Israeli population. Over the decades, the gap in income and social status between the Sephardim (including their offspring born in Israel) and the Ashkenazim widened and generated palpable social tensions. By the late 1970s, the Sephardic community comprised over half of the population of the country and began to make its numerical weight felt in political circles.

The emerging Israeli polity also had to deal with the presence of 160,000 Palestinian Arabs who had remained within the post-1949 borders of the state. The Zionist program had not envisaged the existence of a large, non-Jewish minority population in the future Jewish state, and the question of how to accommodate Israeli notions of social justice with the exclusivity of the Zionist ethos was a vexing one for the Israeli leadership. Finally, in 1952, the Knesset passed the Nationality Law, which, in addition to granting automatic citizenship to any Jewish immigrant, awarded Israeli citizenship to those Arabs who could prove their long-standing residence in Palestine. At the same time, however, Israeli authorities continued to regard their Arab citizens as a potential fifth column and adopted measures designed to prevent them from developing cohesive representative organizations. From 1948 to 1966, areas of Arab concentration were placed under the authority of a Military Administration that required Israeli Arabs to carry special identity cards and to obtain travel permits to go from one village to another. During the first decade of Israeli statehood, the government expropriated thousands of acres of Israeli Arab land and forcibly relocated the displaced inhabitants. Israeli Arabs were further alienated by wage and employment discrimination and by their exclusion, because of their non-Jewishness, from the central mission of the Jewish state.

Until the mid-1970s, Israel's effective system of economic and social controls prevented the Arab minority from forming associations through which it might express its grievances. However, with the rise of a more educated, nontraditional Arab elite and with the dramatic increase in the size of their community (Israeli Arabs numbered nearly 1 million, roughly 20 percent of the population, by the late 1990s), Arab voices began to be heard in the political arena. An additional factor of politicization was the Israeli occupation of the West Bank and Gaza Strip after 1967, which enabled Israeli Arabs to reestablish contact with relatives in the refugee camps and to become more aware of their shared Palestinian Arab heritage.

Nationality, Religion, and the State: The Ongoing Dilemma

The formation of Israeli national identity was a contested process in which proponents of the application of a greater measure of religious law clashed with secular pragmatists and socialist visionaries intent on building a fresh civil society and culture. The disagreements over the proper components of national identity became all the more intense because the participants viewed them as nothing less than a struggle for the very soul of Israel. The contest is far from over, but during the formative years of statehood it produced a form of national identity that was an uneasy combination of secular and religious outlooks.

In the secular sphere, a new Israeli national culture took shape that stamped Israeli Jews as distinctive from Jews living elsewhere. The most important manifestation of this new identity was the establishment of Hebrew as a national language. This development began at the turn of the century and continued through the mandate era, when Zionist organizations undertook an extensive educational effort to teach Hebrew to immigrants and to persuade them to use it in place of the languages they currently spoke. The triumph of Hebrew was a striking achievement of the collective will, and the language became the most significant building block of the new Israeli nationality.

In constructing their national identity, Israelis collectively sought to sever their ties to the European Jewish past, to the Diaspora, with its memories of victimization. One example of this distancing was the practice of replacing traditional Jewish Diaspora family names with distinctively Israeli Hebrew ones. Some of the new last names, such as Galili (of the Galilee) or Shamir (rock), reflected the terrain; others, like Peled (steel) or Oz (might), portrayed images of strength. All of them provided evidence of a fresh Israeli identity freed from the negative images of the Diaspora past.

The reality of the landscape further contributed to the formation of Israeli national distinctiveness. Tel Aviv, Israel's largest city, retains little of the central European urban ambiance that once characterized its fashionable quarters. Instead, the city has grown to reflect its Mediterranean setting as a sun-drenched seaside metropolis pulsing with café life, crowded beaches, and shops selling falafel, a traditional Arab staple food that appears to have become the Israeli national dish. The Israeli symphony orchestra, the national basketball team, and the Hebrew University of Jerusalem are institutions of the new Israeli national culture, Jewish, of course, but also decisively and uniquely Israeli.

The conscious creation of new symbols of secular national identity in the post–World War II Middle East was not unique to Israel. But there the emerging secular culture clashed with historically rooted convictions concerning the role that religious law ought to play in the formation of a Jewish state. In the opinion of one historian, "The question of the relationship between religion and the state is probably the most complex, the most vexing, and potentially the most explosive problem bequeathed to Israel by Jewish history and by the country's own more recent background."[1] This question became so problematic because of the widely differing expectations that were contained within the Zionist movement and then transferred to the arena of Israeli politics and Jewish self-definition. Some Zionists believed that the Jewish nation, once it came into existence, would develop a political culture in which religion would be separated from the state. Others dreamed of creating a Jewish nation in which the sacred laws of the Torah would be adopted as authoritative guidelines for the evolution of state and society; for them, Israel would be Jewish in practice as well as in faith. Most Israelis favored a middle ground between these two positions, but that was difficult to achieve in the face of the determination of the Jewish religious establishment and the nature of Zionism itself.

Political Zionism was founded on the principle that a Jewish state was to serve as a homeland for all the Jews of the world. This principle was made a reality by the Law of Return (1950), a foundational principle of the new state, which gave every Jew in the world the right to immigrate to Israel. Although the Law of Return possessed a compelling logic within the history of Zionism, it gave rise to such difficult questions as: Who is a Jew? Which institution within the state is to authenticate an individual's Jewishness? Is religious law to regulate all of public life? In the contest for the right to decide these matters, the advocates for the application of a greater degree of religious law won several victories. For example, in 1953 the religious courts were recognized as part of the formal judicial system of the state and were awarded exclusive jurisdiction in matters of personal status (marriage, divorce, the confirmation of wills, and the determination of who qualified as a Jew). The religious, or rabbinical, courts were under the supervision of the Supreme Rabbinical Council, which oversaw the training and appointment of the judges. Both the council and the religious courts were exclusively controlled by the Orthodox rabbinical establishment, which applied the strictest interpretations of Jewish law in those areas of public life where religious law was the law of the state. Despite the fact that the other two main branches of Judaism, Conservative and Reform, had more followers within Israel than the Orthodox community, their rabbis were excluded from presiding over several basic religious ceremonies. Thus, for example, the only marriages recognized as legal in Israel were those performed by Orthodox rabbis. Similarly, conversions to Judaism within Israel were not recognized unless they were performed within the Orthodox religious framework. Although less than a third of Israelis regularly observed Orthodox practices, the authority of the Orthodox rabbinical establishment to decide the most sensitive personal status issues extended to the entire population.

The religious basis of the state was further enforced by measures that granted the non-Jewish communities of Israel—made up mainly of Muslim and Christian Arabs—the right to follow their own laws in matters of personal status. In effect, the Ottoman *millet* system was reconstituted in judicial matters. But this was not the case in questions of communal designation: Israeli identity cards defined the nationality of their holders as either "Jewish" or "Arab," not as "Israeli." In this instance, nationality was equated with a specific religion for Jewish Israelis and with a specific ethnicity for Israeli Arabs, an ethnicity that had the negative effect of singling them out as non-Jewish.

The influence of the Jewish religious establishment was felt in other areas of national life as well. On the Sabbath, interurban public transportation ceased, most restaurants and places of public entertainment closed, the national airline did not operate, and municipal bus systems offered only limited service or, in the case of West Jerusalem, none at all. Indeed, the Sabbath was observed in West Jerusalem more rigorously than in Tel Aviv or Haifa. The roads in some of Jerusalem's religious neighborhoods were barricaded against traffic, and residents sometimes threw stones at passing vehicles as a protest against driving, an act that they viewed as a violation of the Sabbath. In addition, all public institutions, including the military, were required to observe kosher dietary laws. In the realm of public education, the state provided funding for both secular and religious schools; parents then selected the type of education they wished their children to receive. As with other spheres of officially sanctioned religious practices, both the teaching positions in the state religious schools and the right to determine if food products were properly kosher became the monopoly of the Orthodox establishment.

Among the many factors that enabled a minority within the Israeli population to impose significant portions of its program of religious identity on society as a whole, the most obvious was the country's multiparty system and the demands it created for coalition governments. As already noted, throughout Israel's formative years a bloc of small religious parties was often essential for the formation of governments and therefore managed to extract a series of concessions from the dominant Mapai Party. Ben-Gurion, like many Zionist leaders of his generation, was convinced that religion and state would eventually separate, and he did not believe that his endorsement of portions of the religious parties' platforms would have significant long-term effects. Over the years, however, the concessions Ben-Gurion granted added up to a formidable list of laws and regulations that have institutionalized the role of religion in Israeli public life and have generated tensions within Israeli society that are persistent, divisive, and intensely political.

Security and Foreign Relations

Israel began its independent statehood with a siege mentality that gave a high priority to issues of defense and security. Surrounded by Arab states that remained technically at war with it and by Arab leaders who made bellicose proclamations about avenging the defeat of 1948, Israeli society was driven to devote a high proportion of its resources, both financial and human, to the rapid buildup of its armed forces. Ben-Gurion proclaimed that to survive, Israel had to become "a nation in arms," and he set out to make that goal a reality. Because of Israel's limited population, the state could not afford, financially or socially, to maintain a standing professional army militarily superior to those of its neighbors. It therefore based its military program on a reserve system that permitted a reduction of the armed forces during peaceful interludes and a rapid expansion through full popular mobilization at times of national emergency. All Israelis were conscripted into the armed forces at age eighteen, men for three years, women for two. Arab Israelis, ultrareligious Jews, and women with special family responsibilities received exemptions. To maintain reservists in a high state of combat readiness, men remained in the active reserve until their late forties, and women, until their mid-thirties. Meeting the security and defense needs of their country thus involved most Israelis in a process of military training that shaped the pattern of their civilian lives for years after they left active service. This was disruptive to advanced education and civilian career planning, but it was so nearly universal and so widely perceived as necessary to the survival of the state that the majority of Israelis accepted reserve training and mobilization for war as among their commonly shared expectations of life. So pervasive were these expectations that parents, when asked how many children they had, sometimes replied: "We are raising three soldiers."[2] Israel's military achievements became a source of national pride and provided evidence, both symbolic and concrete, of the state's determination to survive in hostile surroundings.

In the arena of the Arab-Israeli conflict, Israel's efficient armed forces were used as an instrument of foreign policy. During the Ben-Gurion era, the doctrine of retaliation in force became embedded in official Israeli thinking. This doctrine, sometimes referred to as "Ben-Gurionism," was pursued in the belief that the Arab regimes could be persuaded to abandon their hostility to the existence of Israel only by being subjected to constant reminders of Israel's military power. The core principle of Ben-Gurionism was that every Arab act of aggression against Israel would be met by an armed response well out of proportion to the initial act itself. This policy, regularly implemented in the 1950s, continued to be a standard instrument of Israel's diplomacy by force of arms in the ensuing decades. The most extreme example of Ben-Gurionism in action was an Israeli attack on Egyptian positions in the Gaza Strip in February 1955 in which thirty-eight Egyptians were killed and Egypt's military weakness was exposed. The policy of retaliation in force did not have the result that the Israeli leadership intended. Rather than compelling the Arab rulers to sue for peace, it only heightened their suspicions that Israel harbored expansionist ambitions that had to be countered through the acquisition of advanced weapons. Within months of the Gaza Strip raid, Nasser concluded the Czech-Soviet arms agreement (see Chapter 15), which brought the cold war to the heartland of the Middle East.

As Israel developed its international foreign policy in the early 1950s, it initially adopted a policy of neutrality in the global rivalry between the United States and the Soviet Union. However, with the extension of the cold war to the entire Middle East and with the Soviet Union's efforts to cement ties to the core Arab states by providing them arms, Israel began to pursue a pro-Western foreign policy with special emphasis on relations with the United States. Ties between the two countries had been close from the very beginning, and they became even more so after the June War. As a result of Israel's outstanding military performance in that conflict, U.S. policymakers came to view Israel as a potential strategic asset to U.S. Middle Eastern policy. The Johnson and Nixon administrations increased the delivery of sophisticated weapons to Israel and raised the level of U.S. economic and military assistance from $77 million in 1968 to $693 million in 1975. The reasoning behind the development of this policy was essentially twofold: First, the United States hoped that Israel's absolute military superiority would contribute to regional stability by deterring the Arab states from going to war against Israel; and second, U.S. cold war mentality envisaged a powerful Israel acting as a barrier to Soviet expansionism in the Middle East. In the years that have passed since the adoption of this position in the early 1970s, there is little evidence that U.S. expectations have been fulfilled: Israeli actions have occasionally compromised U.S. strategic interests, Israel's readiness to deploy its armed forces in pursuit of its own security objectives has not been a stabilizing factor in the region, and Syria and Iraq followed Egypt's lead in forming military partnerships with the USSR. Nevertheless, successive U.S. administrations continued to provide ever more generous assistance to Israel, to offer diplomatic backing at the United Nations, and to deepen what has become known as the "special relationship" between the two countries, a relationship that has not been grounded in a formal treaty of alliance but that is nonetheless a fixture of U.S. policy.

The Elections of 1977: Israel in Transition

In the decade from 1967 to 1977, two closely interconnected factors combined to produce a significant change in Israeli political alignments and national priorities. The first was the effect of the continued occupation of the West Bank and the Gaza Strip on Israeli and Palestinian society. We will discuss this issue in the next section. The second factor, made possible by the first, was the surprising outcome of the Israeli elections held in May 1977.

These elections, variously referred to as "the revolt of the Sephardim" or "Israel's earthquake elections," profoundly and dramatically transformed the balance of political power in Israel. In a reversal of the voting patterns that had existed since 1948, the electorate entrusted a right-of-center coalition, the Likud bloc, and its leader, Menachem Begin, with the task of forming a government. Israel's new prime minister was a proponent of revisionist Zionism and had headed the extreme nationalist terrorist organization Irgun from 1943 to 1948 (see Chapter 13). After the state of Israel was established and the Irgun disbanded, Begin was elected to the Knesset as the leading spokesman of the small ultranationalist party known as Herut. With its demand for the creation of Greater Israel on both banks of the Jordan River, Herut was for several years little more than a militant party on the fringe of Israeli politics. However, in 1974 Herut broadened its popular base by forming a political coalition with other, more centrist parties. Its electoral victory in 1977 elevated Menachem Begin, the quintessential outsider, to the apex of Israeli political power.

Begin's election was due in large measure to the support he received from the other outsiders of Israeli society, the Sephardic community. Bitter at their exclusion from mainstream Israeli life and angered over their social and economic marginalization, the Sephardic Jews lashed out at the establishment by voting in large numbers for Begin. The Labor Party, which was the name taken by Mapai after it merged with two smaller parties in 1968, also contributed to Likud's victory. After nearly thirty years in power, Labor had become a stale and bloated bureaucratic party subject to charges of nepotism and corruption. The Israeli public concluded that it was time for a change.

So substantial was the political and social reorientation represented by the election of Begin and Likud that some scholars have termed the years from 1977 to the present "the second Israel." The Begin years (1977–1983) appeared to mark the beginning of a new era in Israeli history, one in which the secular socialist Zionism that had dominated the mandate and early statehood periods was replaced by a highly charged tone of religious militancy. Begin did not create this atmosphere of religious resurgence, but he was in accord with it and used it to further his own political agenda. That agenda was primarily focused on the retention of the territories occupied during the June War.

The Palestinian Factor After 1948

The Palestinian Diaspora Community

The 1948–1949 exodus of the Arab population from the parts of Palestine that fell within the borders of Israel created a refugee problem of immense proportions (see Chapter 13). In 1950, 960,000 Palestinians were registered for relief by the United Nations. As a result of natural population increase and the displacements caused by the June War, the number of refugees rose to 1.3 million in 1968. The refugees lived in makeshift camps located primarily in Jordan, Lebanon, Syria, and the Gaza Strip. The camps were not intended to become permanent; they had been set up as temporary shelters pending a solution to the refugee problem. The solution envisaged at the time was the repatriation of the refugees to the areas from which they had fled. However, actions taken by the Israeli government in the years immediately following 1948 made this an unlikely prospect. The Israeli authorities, faced with a wave of Jewish immigration that totaled more than 600,000 individuals between 1948 and 1951, took over vacant Palestinian villages, urban dwellings, and farmland to house and feed the immigrants. The absorption of Palestinian land and property into the Israeli economy made it next to impossible for Israel to consider the repatriation of the Palestinians.

Destitute and uprooted, the majority of Palestinian refugees had no alternative to the miserable conditions of camp life. To be sure, those with wealth, family connections, or employable skills were able to reestablish themselves in other Arab states, Europe, and North America. In the Gulf states, for example, Palestinians found employment in the expanding economies of the oil-producing countries and eventually formed prosperous communities of businessmen, administrators, and technocrats. However, most of the refugees were of rural background—sharecroppers or peasant proprietors who had fled their land and their homes and left behind most of their family possessions. They were sustained by the UN Relief and Works Agency (UNRWA), which was founded in 1950 to oversee the welfare of the camps. The agency was overwhelmed by the magnitude of the relief task it faced. Its budget was so strained that it could provide an average annual expenditure of only twenty-seven dollars per individual for food, shelter, clothing, and medical services. For the refugees, living quarters consisted of shacks made up of flattened petrol cans or tents in which extended families shared an unprivate existence. Over time, many of the camps took on more permanent features and came to resemble villages, with concrete block dwellings, schools, and a few economic enterprises. But though they resembled villages, they were not the real thing; they were degrading habitations of people on the international dole, people deprived of work, of freedom, and, it appeared, of a future.

It must be appreciated that the majority of the refugees did not seek this situation; rather, it was forced upon them by circumstances. Denied repatriation to Israel, they were dependent on the opportunities that the host countries were prepared to make available to them. These opportunities varied from country to country. Restrictions on employment and freedom of movement were harshest in Egypt and Lebanon. For example, Palestinians

Scene at the Khan Yunis Palestinian refugee camp in the Gaza Strip, 1949. Concrete block dwellings have replaced the tents, but the camp remains and is home to thousands of Palestinian refugees. Khan Yunis and camps like it were the crucible for the formation of Palestinian national consciousness and provided the PLO with its recruits. (AP/Wide World Photos)

registered as refugees in the Gaza Strip were not allowed into other parts of Egypt. In Syria, Iraq, and Jordan, Palestinians were allowed to work and open businesses, but only in Jordan were they granted citizenship. The host countries had a shortage of cultivable land and a surplus of unskilled labor and could not absorb large numbers of uprooted Palestinian peasants. In addition, the host governments feared that Palestinian political activities would bring Israeli retaliation. They therefore viewed the Palestinians with suspicion and prohibited them from forming political organizations.

In these circumstances, it was almost impossible for the refugees from rural backgrounds to break out of their cycle of dependency. Some found seasonal employment as agricultural laborers, others worked as street vendors, and others were employed at low wages in the construction industry within their host country. But mostly they remained trapped in a vicious set of circumstances. The Arab host governments did not wish them to remain on their soil as refugees, but at the same time these governments would not grant them the opportunities that would enable them to break out of their refugee status. Their lack of integration into their host societies and their confinement to the camps served to keep alive their identity as Palestinians and to nurture the idea that their refugee status could be terminated only by a return to Palestine.

The situation in Jordan was somewhat different than in the other host countries. There the Palestinians were granted citizenship, and many found employment—and middle-class status—as civil servants in the Jordanian government. Those who prospered in Jordan became the core of a post-1948 Palestinian exile bourgeoisie, emotionally committed to the ideal of the return to Palestine but practically devoted to the niceties of middle-class existence.

In the period between 1948 and 1967, many Palestinian exiles placed their hopes for repatriation on outside forces. Groups of Palestinian intellectuals in Beirut endorsed various strains of Marxism, Baᶜthism, and Pan-Arabism in the belief that the application of these doctrines would benefit the Palestinian cause by regenerating Arab society as a whole. Many others placed their faith in Nasser as the leader most likely to bring about the liberation of Palestine. But these were non-Palestinian solutions to the Palestine question; they tied the recovery of Palestine to external Arab regimes and outside ideologies. Even the most specifically Palestinian organization of the time was little more than an instrument of the Arab states. The PLO was founded in 1964 under the auspices of the Arab League. Its creation represented an attempt by the Arab states to restrict Palestinian resistance activity and to prevent the Palestinian movement from operating independently. The PLO was based in Cairo, where it was closely scrutinized by Nasser's security agencies. The Arab governments selected Ahmad Shuqayri, a lawyer from one of Palestine's established notable families, to be chairman of the organization. The majority of the members of the PLO's executive council were, like Shuqayri, from the traditional Palestinian notability; they were individuals whose lives as exiles were far removed from the experiences of the refugee camps.

The Impact of the June War

The June War profoundly altered Palestinian circumstances and attitudes. Not only had the Arab states failed to liberate Palestine, they had managed to lose additional areas of Palestinian territory to Israel. Disillusioned with the Arab leadership, groups of Palestinian activists concluded that Palestinians themselves would have to assume the responsibility for liberating their homeland. The Arab defeat in 1967 was the catalyst that transformed the PLO from a body of Cairo-based bureaucratic notables into an independent resistance organization devoted to armed struggle against Israel.

In the immediate aftermath of the June War, several small Palestinian guerrilla organizations became active in the Gaza Strip and Jordan. The most successful of them was al-Fatah, an organization headed by Yasir Arafat. Al-Fatah was formed in the late 1950s by a group of young Palestinian university graduates working in Kuwait. After 1967 it moved its operations to Jordan, where it enjoyed considerable success in recruiting, training, and deploying the flood of Palestinian youths who were attracted to the guerrilla groups. Al-Fatah rapidly emerged as the most formidable of the independent commando organizations, and in 1969 Arafat was elected chairman of the PLO executive committee. The PLO was not a single entity but, rather, an umbrella organization under whose authority several different, and often fractious, resistance groups coexisted. Arafat, as head of the largest group, was able to build coalitions that have endorsed his chairmanship of the entire organization from 1969 to the present. In view of the decisive influence exercised by Arafat and al-Fatah over the years, it is worth considering the sources of their appeal and durability.

From its very beginnings, al-Fatah adopted a straightforward ideology that emphasized Palestinian nationalism above all else. The founders of the organization avoided tying the cause of Palestine to such doctrines as Communism, Baᶜthism, or Pan-Arabism. They stressed the basic objective of recovering the Palestinian homeland and linked the modern resistance movement to such historic Palestinian episodes as the 1936–1939 uprising. This Palestinian-centered focus cut across religious and class lines and provided an appealing and readily comprehensible message to a broad cross-section of Palestinians. In this way, the al-Fatah/PLO leadership succeeded in restoring the Palestinian dimension to the Arab-Israeli conflict and in forging a Palestinian national identity.

Al-Fatah also affirmed the necessity of armed resistance in the struggle to recover Palestine. A further constant in the al-Fatah/PLO position was the refusal to endorse UN Resolution 242. This refusal was based on two considerations: First, the resolution recognized Israel's right to exist, and second, it mentioned the Palestinians only as a refugee problem, not as a people with a right to a national homeland. Over the years, the reality of Israeli power produced certain modifications in the PLO's position. In 1974 the goal of liberating all of Palestine was dropped in favor of creating a Palestinian state comprising the West Bank and the Gaza Strip. This new position implied but did not directly admit Israel's right to exist. Finally, in 1988 the PLO endorsed Resolution 242 and accepted the existence of the state of Israel in its pre-1967 boundaries.

As defined in the Palestinian National Charter of the PLO, the new Palestine was to comprise the whole area of mandate Palestine and to be a democratic, nonsectarian state in which all religions would be recognized and would have equal status. In short, the charter denied the specifically Jewish character of Israel. It is not surprising that Israelis found the document threatening and used it as evidence to support their claim that the PLO stood for the destruction of the state of Israel.

Yasir Arafat in 1971. One of the founders of al-Fatah and chairman of the PLO since 1969, Arafat demonstrated a remarkable ability to survive as the leader of a factionalized resistance organization. (AP/Wide World Photos)

An additional reason for the ongoing prominence of the al-Fatah bloc within the PLO was its continuity of leadership. Despite deaths and defections, four of the group's core founders from the 1950s were still at the center of PLO power in the early 1980s, and other early members remained on al-Fatah's executive committee. The cohesiveness of al-Fatah's founders was due in part to their shared background and experiences. Most of them were part of the 1948 exodus and had direct experience of refugee life. They also had enough talent and ambition to escape the camps—all but one of the individuals who participated in the activities of al-Fatah in the mid-1960s were university graduates. Arafat (b. 1929), for example, obtained an engineering degree from Cairo University, where he was also instrumental in founding a Palestinian Student Union. For Arafat and his colleagues, service to the cause of Palestine occupied most of their adult lives and gave them a credibility within the Palestinian community that the traditional notables lacked. Indeed, when al-Fatah took over the PLO in 1969, the occasion marked the final transfer of Palestinian leadership from the established notability to a new group of full-time activists.

Al-Fatah was not, of course, the only group within the PLO. Among the other commando organizations, the Popular Front for the Liberation of

Palestine (PFLP) and the Democratic Front for the Liberation of Palestine (DFLP) represented challenges to the al-Fatah/PLO mainstream position. Although they never seriously threatened al-Fatah's political dominance, they often embarrassed the PLO by their rejection of its directives and their resort to independent terrorist activities. The PFLP grew out of a pro-Nasser organization that was active in Beirut in the late 1950s and early 1960s. Headed by a Palestinian Orthodox Christian physician, George Habash, the organization was more committed to linking the Palestinian movement to the cause of social revolution in the Arab world at large than was al-Fatah. The DFLP, under the leadership of Nayif Hawatmah, also an Orthodox Christian, was to the political left of the al-Fatah mainstream. It formulated a platform in which workers and peasants were to be the main participants and beneficiaries of the Palestinian movement.

As the PLO gradually acquired the characteristics of a government in exile during the 1970s, it developed a complex network of committees and agencies that were engaged in providing social services to Palestinians. The PLO operated schools and medical clinics in the refugee camps and managed a Lebanese-based conglomerate that was involved in a variety of manufacturing enterprises. In addition, the PLO undertook diplomatic initiatives in its drive to win acceptance as the legitimate representative of the Palestinian people. Within the Arab world, this goal was achieved at the Arab summit meeting held in Rabat in 1974, during which the PLO received recognition as the sole representative of the Palestinians. Later the same year, Arafat addressed the General Assembly of the United Nations, and the PLO was granted observer status in that body. In 1975 France authorized the opening of a PLO information office in Paris, and most other Western European governments soon did the same. Austria took this development one step further in 1980 by according the PLO full diplomatic recognition. Despite its diplomatic successes elsewhere, the PLO was unable to obtain any sort of public recognition from the United States until 1988.

The Failure to Secure a Base of Operations: Black September 1970

The emergence of the guerrilla organizations in the aftermath of the June War provided evidence that the Palestinian cause was being kept alive by the actions of Palestinians themselves. Thousands of young Palestinians sought to escape the dreary confines of the refugee camps by joining the organizations, and in those heady months the aura of activism that had once been symbolized by Nasser was transferred to the Palestinian guerrillas. In search of a heroic historical model suitable to their circumstances, the commandos pointed to the 1954–1962 Algerian revolution against France as an example of how a determined nationalist resistance could overcome seemingly hopeless odds. However, the Palestinian resistance operated in vastly different circumstances than had the Algerian or other successful national liberation movements. The Palestinians were external to the land they hoped to liberate. They therefore required a base of operations in one of the Arab states bordering Israel. The governments of these countries, though, could hardly be expected to welcome bands of armed guerrillas determined to operate independently and to conduct military action against Israel.

The clash between the commandos' desire to establish an independent base of operations and an established government's need to maintain its domestic authority was most acute in Jordan. The post-1967 concentration of guerrilla organizations in that country posed a direct challenge to King Husayn. By 1970 the commandos were operating independently of the king's authority, establishing their own administrative networks in the refugee camps, conducting raids into Israel that provoked the usual Israeli reprisals, and generally behaving as though their organizations were exempt from the jurisdiction of the Jordanian state. The tension reached the breaking point in September, when the PFLP hijacked four civilian airliners and landed three of them in a portion of Jordan that it defined as "liberated territory." As the Jordanian army stood helplessly by, the PFLP threatened to blow up the planes and kill the hostages if any attempt was made to interfere. The PFLP's flaunting of its independence from the government was a signal to King Husayn that he was faced with two unpleasant options: He either had to break the power of the guerrillas or tolerate the further erosion of his authority and the probable takeover of his kingdom by Palestinians. As he had done on previous occasions, the king chose to preserve his throne.

On September 15, 1970, the Jordanian army was commanded to restore order. Thus began the ten-day carnage known as Black September, during which the Jordanian military directed all the force at its disposal against the Palestinian presence in the country. Making no distinction between civilians and armed guerrillas, the Jordanian troops bombarded the refugee camps in and around Amman and relentlessly pursued the commando groups throughout the country. When a cease-fire was finally arranged on September 25, more than 3,000 Palestinians had been killed. The events of Black September brought home to Palestinians the extent of their isolation in the Middle East; Israel was not the only state in which they were unwanted.

In the years immediately following Black September, against a backdrop of international terrorism carried out by Palestinian organizations made desperate by the failure to achieve their political objectives in the Middle East, the PLO transferred its organizational base to Lebanon. Throughout the early 1970s, Palestinian groups, some of them members of the PLO, some not, carried out a series of airliner hijackings, airport massacres, and suicide missions into Israel. The most notorious of these actions was the ghastly 1972 Munich episode, in which members of the Israeli Olympic team were taken hostage and killed during the rescue attempt. At the same time, the

Israeli government conducted operations against Palestinian leaders in Europe and Beirut, and the Israeli air force killed scores of people in Jordan and Lebanon during its frequent raids.

In the meantime, the PLO was able to recover from Black September and reconstitute itself in Lebanon. In Chapter 18 we will discuss the impact that the PLO's activities had on Lebanese society.

Israel and the Palestinians in the Occupied Territories

While activist organizations among the Palestinian exiles engaged in armed resistance and formed communal assistance groups from bases outside Israel, the Palestinian population of the West Bank and Gaza Strip lived under an Israeli occupation regime that controlled the patterns of its existence and shaped its development. The West Bank comprised 2,270 square miles and was inhabited in late 1967 by an estimated 596,000 Palestinian Arabs. The Gaza Strip was only 140 square miles in size, but into it were crowded nearly 350,000 Palestinians, the vast majority of them refugees. Israeli success in capturing the territories raised a vexing series of questions for Israeli authorities about how to deal with the land and its inhabitants. For security reasons, the Israeli military regarded the retention of at least a portion of the territories as essential. Official Israeli political circles at the time believed that most of the occupied lands would eventually be returned in exchange for peace agreements with the Arab states. However, Jewish religious organizations viewed the territories—especially the West Bank, which they referred to by its biblical names, Judea and Samaria—as part of the historic land of Israel and claimed that Israel had a duty to retain them for the Jewish people. But if the territories were to be retained, how were their Arab inhabitants to be treated? If they were granted Israeli citizenship, they would dilute the Jewish character of the state and would, with their higher birth rates, eventually make up a majority of the Israeli population. On the other hand, to deny them citizenship was to accept the proposition that they were to be treated as a permanently occupied people deprived of basic human rights.

Rather than making clear-cut decisions on these matters, successive Israeli governments from 1967 to 1977 maintained the military occupation of the West Bank and Gaza Strip and launched a modest settlement policy designed to establish a Jewish presence in strategically important border areas along the Jordan River (see Map 17.1). Although Israel annexed Arab East Jerusalem in 1967, the Israeli government was not yet committed to a policy of retaining all of the occupied territories and claimed that land might be exchanged for peace. This element of compromise was eliminated with the election of Begin and the Likud bloc in 1977.

The election of Likud coincided with the rise of a religious settlers' movement. In Begin this movement found a prime minister who was publicly

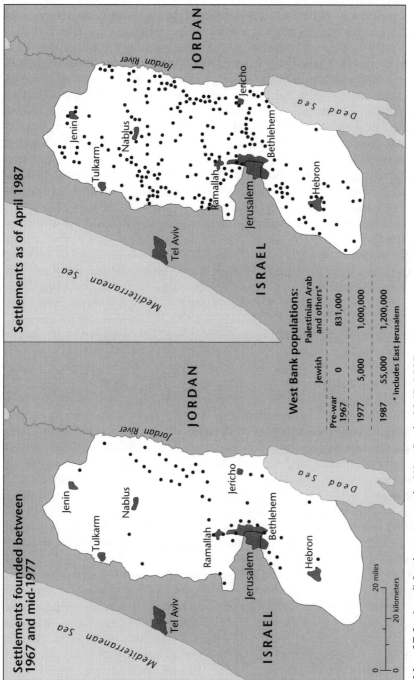

Settlements founded between 1967 and mid-1977

Settlements as of April 1987

JORDAN

Jordan River

Jenin

Nablus

Tulkarm

Ramallah

Jericho

Jerusalem

Bethlehem

Hebron

Dead Sea

Mediterranean Sea

Tel Aviv

ISRAEL

West Bank populations:

	Jewish	Palestinian Arab and others*
Pre-war 1967	0	831,000
1977	5,000	1,000,000
1987	55,000	1,200,000

* includes East Jerusalem

0 — 20 miles

0 — 20 kilometers

Map 17.1 Israeli Settlements on the West Bank, 1967–1987

committed to the annexation of the occupied territories. During his years in power, Begin brought the question of the retention of these lands to the forefront of Israeli politics and permitted organizations favoring increased settlement activities to acquire influence in government and in society at large. At the heart of Begin's strategy was a policy of establishing Jewish settlements throughout the West Bank and Gaza Strip. When he assumed office, there were twenty-four settlements inhabited by 3,200 persons; at his resignation six years later, the number of settlements had increased to 106 and the number of settlers to 28,400. In order to encourage Israelis to move to the occupied territories, the Begin government introduced a suburban settlement policy designed to appeal to commuters from Tel Aviv and Jerusalem. Comfortable, low-cost housing was built to lure to the West Bank white-collar workers who might not be attracted to agricultural settlements. Begin's goal was to create such a large and dedicated Jewish presence in the occupied territories that no future government could possibly relinquish its hold over them.

The settlement policy adopted after 1977 was also intended to break up and isolate areas where the Arab population was heavily concentrated. This tactic was pioneered by a militant religious organization called Gush Emunim (the Bloc of the Faithful), which began to establish illegal settlements on Arab-owned land in the mid-1970s. The Begin government endorsed Gush Emunim's actions and encouraged it and other groups to settle in predominantly Arab centers. The settlement policy was thus used as an instrument to divide Arab society into isolated segments and to prevent the emergence of a collective Palestinian identity.

The land needed for the settlements was acquired in a variety of ways. The military administration that governed the occupied territories used its authority to appropriate private Arab land for security purposes. In 1980 the Begin government declared that unregistered and uncultivated land would be classified as state land to be dealt with as the Israeli authorities saw fit. This measure took advantage of the confused West Bank land tenure system that existed in the wake of Ottoman, British, and Jordanian rule, giving the Israeli government the pretext to acquire 500,000 acres on the West Bank, slightly more than 40 percent of the total land area. In addition, 30 percent of the Gaza Strip was transferred to Israeli state ownership by the early 1980s.

The economic component of Begin's annexationist strategy consisted of an attempt to link the economies of Israel and the occupied territories. Palestinians from the territories were employed as laborers within Israel proper, especially in the construction industry. Even though the wages and benefits they received were low by Israeli standards, they were relatively high by the standards of the territories. The economic well-being of individual West Bank Arabs increased under the occupation, but due to wages earned within Israel, not to improvements in the economy of the West Bank itself. Thus, the inhabitants of the territories became dependent on work from Israeli employers for their continued material well-being. At the same time, the Israeli authorities imposed measures to prevent the territories from achieving their own independent economic development. For example, import duties were levied on certain agricultural products brought into Israel from the West Bank, but Israeli growers faced no such barriers for their produce in the territories.

In order to gain political control of the Palestinians under occupation, the Israeli military administration imprisoned or deported hundreds of activists and tried to break the spirit of those who remained. Collective punishment, house arrest, and the closure of business establishments were but a few of the sentences meted out to the Arab population. The repressive policies of the government were compounded by the aggressive actions of some of the settlers, who practiced their own brand of vigilante justice. The net effect of the Israeli occupation was the simultaneous demoralization and radicalization of the Arab inhabitants of the West Bank and Gaza Strip. On the one hand, they were fearful that they would lose their land and alarmed at their apparent abandonment by the international community. On the other hand, they were made defiant by the policies of an Israeli government that left resistance as the only alternative to annexation. In these circumstances, they turned to the one external body that had consistently acted on their behalf: the PLO. By the late 1970s, links had been forged between the PLO and the inhabitants of the occupied territories, and Arafat had become accepted as the spokesman of the Palestinians of the West Bank and Gaza Strip as well as of the refugees and exiles in the Arab countries.

Conclusion

Despite Israel's diplomatic isolation in the Middle East, and despite the stresses, strains, and occasional contradictions within Israeli society itself, the new state managed to forge an identity, construct a stable democratic political system, maintain an effective military capability, and attract the loyalty and participation of its Jewish citizens in the unique enterprise of building a Jewish nation. However, the election of Menachem Begin in 1977 launched Israel in a new and uncharted direction: It ushered in government-supported currents of Jewish religious militancy that called into question the assumptions of Ben-Gurion and other founders of Labor Zionism and created divisions within Israeli society that were more pronounced than had previously existed. In the intense political struggle to determine the future direction of the Jewish state, ultranationalism and religious fervor, sometimes bordering on zealotry, appeared to be in the ascendancy.

The emergence of an armed and organized Palestinian resistance movement after 1967 renewed the Palestinians' sense of themselves as a distinct national entity deserving of the same recognition as Israel. Yet at the same time, Palestinian militancy sharpened political divisions among the Arab states upon whose support the resistance movement ultimately depended. Although the leaders of the Arab states expressed support for the Palestinian cause, they were reluctant to offer sanctuary to the commando organizations. The example of Jordan in the years from 1969 to 1970 was a vivid reminder that the presence of Palestinian activists posed a threat to the existing Arab regimes. Yet without a secure base from which to conduct operations into Israel, the Palestinian guerrilla organizations would have no legitimacy. In the aftermath of the Black September massacres in Jordan, the PLO found an ideal sanctuary in Lebanon. However, as will be discussed in Chapter 18, that country proved to be a fragile safe haven.

At the same time, the PLO was successful in building support among the inhabitants of the occupied West Bank. Perhaps the principal achievement of the Palestinian resistance was to create a Palestinian consciousness, as a distinctive people entitled to basic human rights, that was too deeply rooted to be eliminated by the brute force of Israeli occupation policies. But it was also noteworthy that in the process of discovering their own feelings of national identity, the Palestinians had awakened the international community to the realization that the Arab-Israeli conflict was, at its core, a matter between the state of Israel and the Palestinian people. Until the two parties central to the dispute recognized this basic reality and agreed to negotiate their differences, there would be no resolution of the conflict.

Notes

1. Nadav Safran, *Israel, the Embattled Ally* (Cambridge, Mass., 1978), p. 200.
2. Yossi Beilin, *Israel: A Concise Political History* (New York, 1992), p. 137.

A Time of Disorder and Renewal: The Middle East from the 1970s to the 1990s

PART V

⟨I⟩
§
⟨I⟩

$\mathbf{A}$t some indefinable point in the early 1970s, the patterns of Middle Eastern history began to take new directions. No single organizing theme can accurately embrace the diversity of these emergent historical trends, but the concept of "disorder and renewal" conveys the disruptiveness of the late-twentieth-century Middle East. Yet despite the contradictions that this term implies, the new historical patterns are not isolated from one another. Rather, they represent parts of a complex, interrelated set of developments whose causes are evident and comprehensible. The same cause-and-effect relationships operate in the Middle East as elsewhere in the world. Recognizing the new patterns, and the changes they represent or the elements of continuity they contain, may place in perspective the specific events discussed in this section of the book and make causal relationships more visible.

One such pattern was the growth of U.S. power and influence in the aftermath of the cold war. As we have seen in Chapter 14, the cold war competition for influence between the United States and the Soviet Union had a significant impact on Middle Eastern regional diplomatic alignments and the distribution of billions of dollars worth of military equipment. Although this competition was financially wasteful and militarily dangerous, it did prevent either superpower from achieving absolute dominance in the Middle East. However, the end of the cold war and the abrupt reduction of Soviet power offered the United States an opportunity to achieve unprecedented influence in the region.

The events that led to the collapse of the Soviet Union began with the economic and political reforms initiated by Soviet president Mikhail Gorbachev in the mid-1980s. Gorbachev recognized that in order to obtain Western assistance for his planned restructuring of the Soviet economy, he would have to diffuse the tensions that existed between the Soviet Bloc and the West and particularly between Moscow and Washington. Through a series of arms control agreements and summit meetings with Presidents Reagan and Bush, Gorbachev succeeded in laying the basis for diplomatic and economic cooperation with the United States. However, Gorbachev's promises of domestic political liberalization unleashed forces that were beyond his control. In the brief period from 1989 to 1991, the Baltic republics asserted their national independence, the east European satellite states overthrew their Communist regimes, and the entire Soviet Union collapsed with astounding speed, disintegrating into a welter of competing ethnic rivalries and regional loyalties.

Throughout the period of the Soviet Union's collapse, Gorbachev and his successor continued to request Western economic assistance and technical expertise. They did not wish to antagonize their potential benefactors in the West by supporting Middle Eastern Soviet client states in anti-Western activities. This meant that Moscow's leading Arab allies, Syria and Iraq, could not be assured of receiving support for ventures directed against America's regional interests. Nor, with the Soviet economy in a precipitous decline, could Moscow's Middle Eastern allies count on receiving the same level of material assistance that they had in the past. The superpower balance had been overturned.

Another feature of Gorbachev's reform program that had far-reaching consequences for the Middle East was the loosening of restrictions on the emigration of Soviet Jews. This opened the way for the eventual immigration of 580,000 Soviet Jews to Israel between 1990 and 1995. Israel's efforts to absorb such an enormous influx of new immigrants placed a severe strain on the country's resources and prompted its leaders to request increased financial assistance from the United States.

Evidence of the unrivaled post–cold war influence of the United States was most striking in the Gulf War of 1991, during which the United States was able to form an international coalition, including Egypt and Syria, to wage war against Iraq and drive it out of Kuwait. Such action would have been virtually impossible during the cold war because of the likelihood of Soviet intervention. In the aftermath of the Gulf War, the United States stood alone as the hegemonic power in the Middle East, and its troops remained stationed in the area as protectors of the oil-producing states of the Gulf.

A second pattern that emerged during the period was the growing centrality of the Arab-Israeli conflict as a factor shaping regional affairs. Following the signing of a peace treaty with Egypt in 1979, the Likud government of Menachem Begin launched a military invasion of Lebanon in an attempt to destroy the PLO infrastructure there and to reshape that country to its liking. In addition, Israel accelerated its settlement activities in the West Bank, and in so doing generated a widespread Palestinian uprising that continued for four years and focused world attention on the harsh realities of the Israeli occupation. The uprising within the occupied territories galvanized the external PLO leadership into undertaking a series of diplomatic initiatives that eventually led to the first Oslo Accord in 1993 and mutual recognition between the PLO and Israel. The so-called peace process that was set in motion by this agreement stalled in the second half of the 1990s, prompting the United States to become directly involved in attempting to preserve the momentum toward peace that Israeli and Palestinian rejectionists threatened to sabotage.

A third far-reaching development during these years was the revolution in petroleum prices and the resulting expansion of the regional influence of such petroleum giants as Kuwait and Saudi Arabia. During the Arab-Israeli war of 1973, the Arab oil-producing states introduced an oil boycott on Western consuming nations. The boycott caused the cost of oil to soar and sped up negotiations that enabled oil producers to acquire marketing and pricing control of the precious resource on which the West was dependent. As the price of oil increased precipitously, dire predictions were made about the collapse of the Western and Japanese economies. However, the industrialized nations were willing to pay whatever the market would bear. Access to oil, not its price, became the driving force behind the West's policies toward the oil-producing states. To ensure access, the West, led by the United States, sought to shore up the friendly monarchies that ruled most of the major oil-producing states and preserve the political status quo in the Persian Gulf. Iraq's attempt to alter that status quo by annexing Kuwait in 1990 was met with a massive armed response that left Iraq devastated and the United States more determined than ever to defend its vital petroleum interests.

A fourth pattern characterizing this period was one of constancy, not of change: Authoritarian regimes, often dominated by the same individual for long periods of time, continued to be the norm in most of the Arab states and Iran. Under these regimes, the power of the central state and its machinery of control increased markedly. In the course of enhancing their power and security, authoritarian rulers in Iran, Egypt, Syria, Iraq, and the Arabian peninsula—and the military in democratic Turkey—took measures to silence leftist opposition forces. Such measures limited the available channels through which the population could express its grievances over economic mismanagement, the maldistribution of wealth, the absence of democracy, and the general failure of the regimes to satisfy popular aspirations and needs. Islamic organizations constituted one of the few remaining avenues of protest.

The search for sustainable ways to resist authoritarian rule was partly responsible for the appearance of a fifth new pattern of events in the independent Middle East: the unexpected emergence of Islamic-based political activity and protest. In the first two decades after World War II, Western development theorists assumed that the Middle East—and the rest of the developing world, for that matter—would become increasingly secular as they became increasingly modern. Yet even as the role of the ulama declined and the jurisdiction of the *shariᶜah* was limited, the Islamic sensibilities of the population as a whole remained intact. When the imported ideologies of the independence era failed to bring economic well-being to society at large, a current of Islamic revivalism came into existence. Its most dramatic manifestation was the Iranian revolution of 1979, but it was—and remains—a persistent feature of the political life of every Islamic country and will figure prominently in this study of the past quarter century of Middle Eastern history.

A sixth pattern was a growing tension in the relations among the Arab states. Egypt's peace with Israel transformed the configuration of the Arab state system as the preeminent Arab army was withdrawn from the confrontation with Israel and the leading Arab state was expelled from the Arab League. In these circumstances, Syria and Iraq made bids for regional dominance and in the process became bitter rivals. Iraq's ambition led it to invade and annex Kuwait, a neighboring Arab state, and resulted in several other Arab states joining the military coalition that waged war against Iraq.

And finally, the roughly twenty-five-year period treated in this section was particularly violent. The consensus holding society together fell apart in some states, and the relations between states sometimes deteriorated into open warfare. Internal violence was exemplified in the civil war that engulfed Lebanon for fifteen years, in the running conflict between Turkey and portions of its Kurdish population, in the brutality of settler actions against Palestinians in the occupied territories and in Palestinian terrorist activities in Israel, in the armed attacks by militant Egyptian Islamists against government personnel and foreign tourists and in the state's counterinsurgency responses, and in the assassinations of an Egyptian president and an Israeli prime minister. In the sphere of the relations between states, this period opened with the longest of the Arab-Israeli wars and continued with Israel's invasion of Lebanon and siege of Beirut, the bloody eight-year war between Iraq and Iran, and Iraq's invasion of Kuwait and the armed response of the U.S.-led coalition. The reasons for such violence can be understood in the context of developing historical patterns.

Changing Patterns of
War and Peace: Egypt
and Lebanon in
the 1970s and 1980s

18

⟨|⟩
⟨|⟩

The discontinuities of the years from the early 1970s onward were strikingly evident in Egypt and Lebanon and in the effects that regional developments exercised on these two states. Nasser's successor, Anwar Sadat, endeavored to break the diplomatic stalemate with Israel and to chart a new direction for the Egyptian economy. In the process of pursuing these objectives, Sadat waged war, negotiated for peace, formed an alliance with the United States, and reintroduced capitalist incentives into Egypt. Sadat's partial reordering of Egypt's economic policies represented a departure from the Nasserist model, and his foreign policy marked a sharp and dramatic break from the goals Nasser had pursued.

The history of Lebanon in the period covered by this chapter is one of internal breakdown closely interwoven with the impact of external forces. The sectarian cooperation that had characterized Lebanon since independence collapsed in a wave of communal violence, and the state that had been the Arab world's symbol of toleration and compromise was plunged into a bloody civil war that lasted for fifteen years. Although the causes of the civil war were primarily internal to Lebanon, regional influences also played a role. Lebanese society was divided over the presence of the armed Palestinian resistance movement in the country, and the civil war was fought, in part, to determine the status of the PLO within Lebanon's borders. Syria and Israel both attempted to shape the outcome of the civil war to their advantage through armed intervention that prolonged the conflict and increased the suffering.

Egypt Under Sadat:
Domestic and Diplomatic Realignments

Anwar Sadat (1918–1981) was not the expected choice to take on the imposing task of filling the void left by Nasser's death in 1970. Although he had been one of the original Free Officers, Sadat did not command the respect of his peers or the Egyptian public. Known in some quarters as "Nasser's poodle," he was viewed as a weak and pliable yes-man who would soon be replaced by a stronger figure. But Sadat showed that he was not to be taken lightly. Although his policies were highly controversial, even his detractors acknowledge that he reoriented Egyptian domestic and foreign policy in ways that were every bit as profound as Nasser's.

Sadat's first task was to secure his domestic political base. This he did in May 1971 by purging the government and the ASU of his rivals. He then proclaimed political and economic liberalization wrapped up in the slogan of "the revolution of rectification." Sadat had gained control of the levers of power, but what was he to do with them? Indeed, what power remained to Egypt in 1971? Sadat had inherited from Nasser a terribly difficult set of interrelated economic and diplomatic problems. The no war, no peace confrontation with Israel required military expenditures that were draining the Egyptian economy of several hundred million dollars per year. As long as Egypt remained in a state of active hostility with Israel, such potential sources of revenue as tourism, Suez Canal tolls, and foreign investment would not materialize. Egypt desperately needed peace to rebuild its economy, but the diplomatic circumstances were not conducive to a lessening of tensions. Israel, made confident by its resounding military triumph in 1967 and kept solvent by generous U.S. assistance, saw no reason to make concessions from its position of strength. Egypt, defeated, indebted, and occupied by Israeli forces from Suez to Gaza, had no leverage with which to bring about a change in Israel's attitude.

Assuming that only the United States had the power to alter the Israeli negotiating position, Sadat endeavored to generate U.S. participation in breaking the diplomatic stalemate. In July 1972 Sadat abruptly expelled most of the 20,000 members of the Soviet military mission to Egypt. This by no means terminated the Soviet-Egyptian relationship, but it was the first step toward a major realignment of Egypt's relations with the superpowers. The dismissal of the Soviet advisers weakened Egypt's military capabilities, a risk Sadat was prepared to take in order to demonstrate to the United States his independence from the Soviet Union and his willingness to entertain the notion of U.S. diplomatic involvement in Egypt's conflict with Israel. As it turned out, Sadat's timing was unfortunate: The expulsion of the Soviets occurred just a few weeks before the Palestinian terrorist operation against the Israeli Olympic team in Munich. The Egyptian president's gesture was wasted on a U.S. public that had no sympathy for Arab causes.

The October 1973 War

Sadat's presidency had achieved little after two years. The measure of despair that affected Egypt generally was reflected in 1972 and early 1973 in outbreaks of student demonstrations that stood as criticisms of the government's apparent lack of resolve. Sadat renewed his efforts to break the diplomatic stalemate. If Egypt could show that Israeli military might was not as all-powerful as assumed, then perhaps the United States could be persuaded to enter the negotiating process and work to soften Israel's hard-line position. In pursuit of this aim, Sadat, with Syria as an ally, undertook war as an instrument of diplomacy.

In the early afternoon of October 6, 1973, Egyptian forces launched an attack across the Suez Canal in coordination with a Syrian offensive against Israeli positions on the Golan Heights. The Egyptians achieved stunning success as they breached the Bar Lev line on the east bank of the canal and overwhelmed the Israeli positions. It was a considerable achievement for Egyptian arms. Soviet advisers had earlier told Sadat that although the operation was possible, it would take four days and result in a 50 percent casualty rate. But in the first twenty-four hours of the offensive, Egypt put 80,000 men across the canal and lost just 200. This episode in the October War became enshrined in Egyptian consciousness as "the crossing" and stood as a symbol of military triumph after a quarter century of unrelenting defeats at the hands of the Israelis.

Although Egyptian forces continued to perform well, they did not again go on the offensive after the crossing. Instead, they stopped their advance and consolidated their positions in a front 8 miles (13 km) deep east of the canal. There was no reason to push further: Sadat's limited objectives had already been achieved. He had restored Egypt's credibility as a military power, he had retaken a certain amount of occupied Egyptian territory, and he had demonstrated to the superpowers that Israeli superiority could not be taken for granted. Thus, Egyptian forces dug in and waited for international diplomacy to take its course. But by failing to press their advantage, the Egyptians gave the Israelis time to stabilize the Syrian front and to mount a counterattack against Egyptian positions.

On October 16, Israeli forces under General Ariel Sharon pierced Egyptian defenses and crossed to the west bank of the Suez Canal. This maneuver entrapped the Egyptian Third Army and brought Sharon's tanks within striking distance of Cairo. The outlook of the conflict had suddenly been altered. Not wanting to lose the advantages that the crossing had provided, Sadat and his Soviet ally were ready to accept a cease-fire. On October 22, Secretary of State Henry Kissinger of the United States and Foreign Minister Andrei Gromyko of the Soviet Union presented a cease-fire agreement that Egypt, Israel, and, later, Syria accepted.

That the cease-fire was arranged by U.S. and Soviet officials demonstrated that Sadat had achieved his purpose of involving the superpowers in the Middle East conflict. Indeed, the October War was to some extent a proxy fight. From October 14 to November 15, the United States airlifted 22,000 tons of military supplies to Israel; the scale of the Soviet resupply to Egypt and Syria was also enormous. There was something grotesque in the willingness of the superpowers to replenish their clients' equipment in order to enable them to continue a war that might otherwise have ended sooner. The essence of the situation was captured in a political cartoon of the time that portrayed Egypt and Israel as two deflating balloons being pumped up by the Soviet Union and the United States, respectively.

Given the scale of the fighting and the eagerness of the superpowers to resupply the combatants, it is not surprising that the costs of the war were staggering. Israel suffered over 2,500 killed, Egypt lost 7,700 men, and Syria 3,500. Egypt and Syria together lost over 2,000 tanks and 450 aircraft as compared to Israeli losses of 800 tanks and over 100 aircraft. As sobering as these statistics were, the war raised the even more chilling prospect of direct superpower engagement in the Middle East. If the Egyptian position had deteriorated further, would the Soviet Union have been compelled to intervene to rescue its client? And if that had occurred, would the United States have been forced to protect Israel? The October War demonstrated that as long as the Arab-Israeli conflict persisted in the form it then had, the potential for superpower conflict was present. This was one reason for the new level of U.S. involvement in Middle East peacemaking after October 1973.

Another reason was oil. The October War completely changed the face of the petroleum industry and provided the oil-producing nations with a level of power that was previously thought impossible for them to achieve. On October 17, in a gesture of sympathy with Syria and Egypt, the Arab member states of the Organization of Petroleum Exporting Countries (OPEC) announced that they would reduce their oil production by 5 percent a month until Israel withdrew from the occupied Arab territories. Two days later Saudi Arabia suspended indefinitely all oil shipments to the United States. The reduction in the international supply of oil sent prices soaring and caused the world community to reassess its previously held assumptions about petroleum production (see Chapter 21). Within the context of the diplomacy of the Arab-Israeli conflict, the use of the oil weapon prompted the governments of Western Europe and Japan to look more favorably on the Arab cause and forced U.S. policymakers to face up to the growing U.S. dependency on imported oil. The oil factor was a major incentive for Washington's intensive efforts to seek a peaceful settlement of the Arab-Israeli conflict.

These efforts were represented by Secretary of State Kissinger's so-called shuttle diplomacy. In January 1974 Kissinger negotiated a disengagement agreement between Egypt and Israel, and in September 1975 he persuaded the two parties to sign a document known as Sinai II, which provided for the withdrawal of Israeli forces from western Sinai. U.S. peacemaking was smoothed by economic assistance. The special relationship between the United States and Israel was reconfirmed during the negotiating sessions and was reflected by an increase in U.S. military aid from an average annual sum of $400 million in the period 1971–1973 to an average of $1.5 billion during 1974–1975. This amounted to 42 percent of Israel's annual defense spending. Egypt also reaped rewards for its willingness to follow Kissinger's lead. The United States contributed to the reconstruction of the Suez Canal, which reopened in 1975, and raised its economic assistance package to Cairo from $8.5 million in 1974 to $750 million by 1976.

From the Crossing to the *Infitah*

Despite the precarious military situation that prevailed at the time of the cease-fire, the October War was a political triumph for President Sadat. Styling himself the hero of the crossing, he basked in the popularity the Egyptian public accorded him. He promised them that the spirit of the crossing would be transferred to the task of restructuring the economy and would bring substantial benefits to the nation at large. Sadat introduced his new economic proposals in the October Paper, a blueprint for dismantling parts of the socialist system introduced under Nasser. No Egyptian leader could afford to tamper with the social welfare portions of Nasserism, but Sadat argued that the public sector had become inefficient and uncompetitive. He therefore sought to liberalize the economy by introducing incentives for capitalist investment, both local and foreign.

The new economic program was called "the opening"—*al-infitah*—and it contained a broad range of proposals designed to encourage foreign investment. For example, foreign banks were invited to return to Egypt and were offered tax exemptions and favorable terms for repatriating their profits. Foreigners were allowed to import equipment with considerable freedom. Even some of the revolution's founding principles regarding agrarian land were modified as the government made it easier to buy and sell land and to raise land rents. The *infitah* offered lucrative opportunities to those private-sector enterprises fortunate enough to enjoy linkages with the public sector. Private contractors reaped significant profits from the rebuilding of the cities along the Suez Canal and from a construction boom that took place in Cairo. But despite the improved investment climate created by the lessening of tensions with Israel, foreign capital was not particularly attracted to Egypt. Investors who did take advantage of the *infitah* tended to put their money into the purchase or construction of apartment buildings and office towers or into tourist-related ventures such as luxury hotels. They chose these low-risk, nonproductive investments over the uncertain performance of Egyptian industry. In those instances where foreigners sought industry-related investments, they were often frustrated by the cumbersome bureaucracy and the resistance of the entrenched public sector.

Adding to the difficulties of Sadat's new economic policies were the same barriers that had constrained Nasser's socialism. Egypt had a staggering foreign debt, mainly to the Soviets for arms purchases; an enormous defense budget; and an inflation rate of over 20 percent. For the ordinary Egyptians who entered the post–October 1973 era with raised expectations, the *infitah* was a bitter disappointment. It favored the wealthy few but brought no tangible benefits to the population at large. In this respect the new economic policy appeared to foster the kinds of income disparities that had been condemned in the socialist decrees of the early 1960s.

One of the existing social welfare programs that benefited the poor was the subsidization of such basic consumer items as bread, sugar, rice, and tea. Subsidies kept the prices of these staples down, but at a cost to the state of $1.5 billion per year. The International Monetary Fund (IMF) warned Sadat that his government would not qualify for further loans until the funds used for the subsidies were invested in more productive areas. In January 1977, without giving advance notice, Sadat reduced the subsidies on certain items and canceled them altogether on others. The Egyptian population expressed its anger in a devastating outbreak of antigovernment riots. In Cairo the mobs attacked police stations and ASU headquarters, symbols of the regime's control. Many of the demonstrators' slogans revealed their disenchantment with the empty promises that Sadat had made so often since 1973. The cry, "O hero of the crossing, where is our breakfast?" stood as a heartfelt rebuke to the state apparatus that could provide propaganda but not food. Sadat finally had to call in the army, the first time it had been deployed against its own civilians since 1952. At least 150 Egyptians were killed as the army crushed the riots. Sadat immediately restored the subsidies in order to prevent further disturbances.

Faced with mounting domestic unrest and the continuing failure of the *infitah,* Sadat renewed his diplomatic initiatives in the hope that a settlement of the conflict with Israel would lead to an improvement in Egypt's economic situation. Within ten months of the January 1977 riots, Sadat was in Jerusalem addressing the Israeli Knesset—a clear indication of the close relationship between Egypt's domestic problems and Sadat's foreign policy ventures.

From Jerusalem to Camp David:
The Unfolding of the Peace Process

On November 20, 1977, a worldwide television audience watched, many in disbelief, as the president of the major Arab military power flew to Jerusalem and proclaimed to the Israeli parliament Egypt's acceptance of peace with Israel. However conflicting the motives may have been that led to the occasion, and however bitter were the disagreements that lay ahead, it was a moving moment, comparable in some respects to the dismantling of the Berlin Wall in 1989.

Sadat's journey to Jerusalem marked the beginning of a new phase of ponderous and sometimes acrimonious peacemaking between Egypt and Israel with the United States acting as a third party. Negotiations were made all the more difficult because Sadat and the newly elected Israeli prime minister, Begin, had different ideas on what they ought to be discussing. Sadat wanted not only to deal with bilateral Egyptian-Israeli relations but also to get agreement on a comprehensive plan for Middle East peace that would include a resolution of the Palestinian issue. Prime Minister Begin, as we have seen above, had no intention of relinquishing Israel's hold on the West Bank and Gaza Strip and therefore sought to confine the discussions to Egyptian-Israeli matters.

When disagreement over the issue of Palestinian self-determination threatened to scuttle the negotiations, President Jimmy Carter invited Begin and Sadat to Camp David for face-to-face negotiations. For thirteen wrenching days in September 1978, the three leaders and their staffs engaged in nonstop discussions. The United States attempted to find a middle ground between Sadat's desires for a comprehensive settlement and recognition of Palestinian rights and Begin's uncompromising stand on the West Bank and Gaza Strip. The end result was a set of documents, the Camp David Accords, that the three heads of state signed on September 17, 1978.

The Camp David Accords consisted of two major documents. The most straightforward of them set forth the conditions for an Egyptian-Israeli peace treaty. The other, entitled "A Framework for Peace in the Middle East," endorsed UN Resolution 242 as the basis for a durable and comprehensive settlement of the Middle East conflict. In spelling out the future status of the Gaza Strip and the West Bank, the framework agreement proposed a staged plan for the achievement of Palestinian autonomy over a period of five years. However, the proposal was open-ended and based on assumptions that never materialized. It was also so vaguely worded that it was subject to differing interpretations, and that was exactly what Begin wanted. The framework for peace was a victory for the Israeli prime minister and a defeat for the idea of a Palestinian state. At Camp David, Israel won the right to deal with the occupied territories as it saw fit, even if that was not immediately apparent to Sadat and Carter.

On March 26, 1979, Sadat and Begin signed a formal Egyptian-Israeli treaty in Washington. During the following year, the two countries exchanged ambassadors, and Israel began its staged withdrawal from Sinai, an operation that was completed in 1982 with the assistance of a $3 billion contribution from the United States. As for the framework for peace, it was never implemented, despite protests and urgings from the United States and Egypt. Begin had managed to exchange Sinai for control of the West Bank and Gaza Strip and had in the process neutralized the most powerful Arab military machine. In the absence of a comprehensive peace settlement, there was no disguising that Sadat had done nothing more than conclude a separate peace with Israel. The U.S. administration was grateful, but the Arab world was shocked.

Egypt paid a high price in inter-Arab relations for its treaty with Israel. Egypt was expelled from the Arab League, league headquarters were transferred to Tunis, and all of the Arab states, with the exceptions of Oman and the Sudan, broke diplomatic relations with Cairo. In addition, the oil-producing states canceled their subsidies, making Egypt economically dependent on the West, especially the United States. Once the driving force behind the movement for Arab unity, Egypt was now isolated from the Arab world.

Politics and Society After Camp David

From the beginning of his term in office, Sadat had proclaimed his intention of liberalizing the political system. There was little change until 1977, when the Arab Socialist Union was dissolved and merged with a centrist government organization called the National Democratic Party. At the same time, two other parties, one on the left and one on the right, were allowed to form and to contest elections to parliament. However, on those occasions when members of the opposition questioned the government's policies, Sadat took offense and tightened the reins of government authority. Sadat's instincts for political liberalization clashed with his desire to be beyond criticism and his need for adulation. Thus, despite the new opportunities that existed for airing divergent opinions, Sadat retained supreme power throughout his presidency and did not allow legitimate political pluralism to take root.

One of the reasons the regime was subject to criticism was the continued failure of the *infitah* to secure material improvement for the majority of Egyptians. Even after the treaty with Israel and the delivery of large amounts of U.S. aid, foreign investment was minimal. Those who did profit from the economic liberalization, many of whom were the president's friends and relatives, engaged in ostentatious displays of wealth that only served to remind the majority of Egyptians how unsatisfactory their own circumstances were. Moreover, Sadat's behavior created a certain distance between him and the Egyptian people and undermined the popularity he had achieved during the crossing of 1973. In contrast to the personally austere Nasser, Sadat enjoyed the trappings as well as the realities of power. He acquired villas and mansions and even set up a presidential office in one of the old royal palaces in Cairo. His extravagances led the masses to refer to him as Faruq II or the khedive, a reference to the nineteenth-century ruler Ismaᶜil. In addition, the prominent public role assumed by Sadat's wife, Jehan, was offensive to some quarters of Egyptian society.

The treaty with Israel provided a further source of discontent. Although the treaty received approval in a national referendum, many Egyptians felt a sense of unease about reaching an accommodation with an Israeli state that continued to occupy the Gaza Strip, the West Bank, and East Jerusalem,

President Anwar Sadat of Egypt and his wife, Jehan, December 15, 1970. Their lavish style of living and their cultivation of a Western image distanced them from the Egyptian people and contributed to their unpopularity. (AP/Wide World Photos)

with its venerated Islamic shrines. There was also popular resentment over Egypt's isolation from the Arab Islamic world and the country's growing dependence on the United States. These various crosscurrents of dissatisfaction found their primary outlet in the formation of Islamic opposition movements (see Chapter 20 for a fuller discussion).

The renewed concern for Islamic principles of justice and social order was in part caused by the failure of imported ideologies to solve Egypt's problems. Nasser's socialism had not prevented the humiliation of 1967, and Sadat's encouragement of capitalism and his reliance on the West were not generating noticeable improvements. Egypt was gripped by a social malaise, a yearning for guidance and hope. In this atmosphere, the Islamic values that had provided the foundations for social harmony in the past were given new attention in the political arena. The Muslim Brotherhood, which Sadat allowed to resume its activities provided it did not become a political party, achieved considerable success in recruiting university students and recent graduates. These were the Egyptians most disillusioned by the gap between their high expectations and the grim realities of the low-paying, unchallenging civil service positions to which they were consigned.

In addition to the public campaign carried out by the Muslim Brotherhood, other, more militant organizations were also active. Bearing names such as al-Jihad (Sacred Struggle) and Takfir wa al-Hijrah (Excommunication and Emigration), they rejected the Sadat regime as impious and claimed that it was an Islamic duty to work for its overthrow and replacement by a government committed to the restoration of the *shariʿah*. The militant Islamic groups were dominated by individuals with university experience who were driven by a mixture of religious belief, social despair, and economic deprivation. Sadat, with his Western ways and his U.S.-brokered treaty with Israel, became the focus of their discontent. He recognized the danger posed by the clandestine Islamic opposition, and in September 1981 he ordered the arrest and imprisonment of over 1,000 individuals suspected of plotting against his regime.

On October 6, 1981, not long after his preemptive political strike against the Islamic organizations, Sadat reviewed a military parade held to celebrate the eighth anniversary of the crossing. When one of the vehicles in the long line of U.S.-made carriers paused in front of the reviewing stand, the hero of the crossing himself stood to salute its occupants. They returned his gesture with a hail of gunfire. The assassins who brought so sudden and perplexing an end to the regime of this flawed but fascinating Egyptian president were affiliated with al-Jihad. Islamic militancy had, it appeared, infiltrated the armed forces on whose support the regime had relied for nearly thirty years.

Sadat was succeeded by his vice-president, Husni Mubarak, whose regime will be examined later in this chapter.

The Lebanese Civil War, 1975–1990

The First Phase, 1975–1976

In the years following the June War, the Palestinian-Israeli conflict intruded on Lebanese political life. This development, in combination with demographic and political changes taking place inside Lebanon itself, upset the country's fragile sectarian balance and plunged it into fifteen years of vicious and destructive civil war. The civil war was not an exclusively Lebanese affair; it was precipitated by the Palestinian presence in the country and soon attracted external intervention by Syria and Israel, thus bringing to an end the attempts of Lebanon's political bosses to insulate their country from the wider regional conflict.

Following the events of Black September, the Palestinian commando organizations moved their base of operations to Lebanon, where they joined 300,000 Palestinian refugees who were already present in the country. The majority of them lived in camps in southern Lebanon, and it was in and around the camps that the bulk of the guerrilla groups settled. The commandos' freedom to undertake military operations against Israel was based on a 1969 agreement in which the Lebanese government turned over the supervision of the refugee camps to the PLO in exchange for the PLO's pledge to obtain the government's consent for any armed incursions it might make.

This latter restriction went largely unheeded, and from 1970 onward, the cycle of Palestinian raids into Israel and Israeli retaliation in force repeated itself countless times. The Israeli bombing attacks affected not only the Palestinians but also the mainly Shiᶜa villagers of southern Lebanon, thousands of whom abandoned their homes and migrated to the squatter suburbs of Beirut, embittered at a government that was unable to protect them from either Palestinians or Israelis. The relative ease with which Israeli forces were able to execute commando raids of their own, exemplified by a strike against Beirut International Airport in 1968 and the assassination of three Palestinian leaders in Beirut in 1973, caused an outcry against the government from Arab nationalists and radical reformers. They accused the authorities of failing to deploy the Lebanese army against Israel and of using it instead to frustrate the activities of the Palestinian commandos. This accusation served to identify the crux of the issue facing the people of Lebanon: Were the Palestinian commandos to be allowed unrestricted freedom to conduct raids against Israel with the inevitable Israeli armed response, or should the Lebanese state attempt to retain control of the commandos' activities? The country was deeply divided on the matter.

Support for the Palestinians came primarily from Muslims alienated by the existing system, which benefited the political bosses and their associates but failed to provide basic social services to broad sections of the population. By the early 1970s, the suburbs of Beirut were surrounded by a poverty belt of at least 500,000 inhabitants, most of them rural migrants. Some had been driven from their villages by the Israeli raids in the south; others were forced to leave the countryside because the government did not fund the irrigation and transportation services that were needed for commercial agriculture. The failings of the central government were particularly evident during the presidency of Sulayman Frangieh (1970–1976), who abandoned the reformist programs of President Shihab and reverted to nepotism and corruption.

The social and economic grievances of Muslims were compounded by the sectarian arrangements that continued to favor the country's Christians. Long before the crisis of the 1970s, Lebanon's political leaders recognized that Muslims outnumbered Christians and that the largest single religious grouping in the country was the Shiᶜa Muslim community. Largely ignored in the distribution of confessional powers during the mandate years, the Shiᶜas in the 1970s asserted their sectarian majority and demanded their fair share of the political and economic pie. The Christians were not inclined to give it to them, insisting that the interwar agreements that set a parliamentary ratio of six Christian deputies for every five Muslim deputies remain in effect. The underprivileged and underrepresented Muslims, both Sunni and Shiᶜa, reacted to the Christian leaders' intransigence by identifying with the Palestinians, a community that was also opposed to the status quo.

With the alteration of its demographic balance and the new pressures placed upon it to assume a role in the regional Arab-Israeli conflict, the Lebanon of the 1970s was no longer the Lebanon of the 1932 census or the 1943 National Pact. The political leader who most clearly recognized these changes was Kamal Jumblatt, the leader of the Druze community. As indicated in Chapter 16, Jumblatt was not just an established *zaᶜim*, he was also a political and social reformer able to attract a following beyond the confines of the Druze community. In 1969 Jumblatt forged a loose coalition of discontented Muslims into a front known as the Lebanese National Movement. Committed to administrative reform, the abolition of the confessional basis of politics, and freedom of action for the Palestinian commandos, the Lebanese National Movement was to be a major factor in the civil war.

Standing in direct opposition to Jumblatt's National Movement and to the Palestinian presence in Lebanon were the Maronite political leaders. The Maronites prospered under the existing confessional political system and were prepared to use armed force to resist changes. The most uncompromising Maronite leaders were Pierre Gemayel, head of the paramilitary Phalange, and former president Camille Chamoun, who had his own private militia, the Tigers. When it became evident to these politicians that the government and the army were incapable of taking decisive action against the Palestinians, they resolved to take it themselves.

In preparation for their confrontation with the Palestinians, the Christian militias embarked on a large-scale program of arms procurement. The PLO and the leftist organizations did the same, and by spring 1975 all factions within Lebanon were armed to the teeth. The spark that ignited this explosive situation came in April, when the Phalange attacked a busload of Palestinians and killed twenty-seven of the passengers. This set off a round of fighting between the PLO and the Maronite militias that lasted until the end of June, at which point the main PLO forces accepted a cease-fire and withdrew from the fighting for the remainder of the year.

However, the disengagement of the PLO did not resolve the differences between the Lebanese themselves, and in August 1975 fighting broke out between Muslim and Christian militias. The Muslim groups in general supported Jumblatt's Lebanese National Movement; the Christian forces were spearheaded by the Maronite Phalange. From their fortified positions in Beirut's high-rise office towers and luxury hotels, the opposing sides engaged in artillery duels that transformed the core of the cosmopolitan city into a war zone and reduced it to blackened ruins. In December the conflict took an even more ominous turn as the Phalange and its allies began expelling Muslims who resided within those areas of Beirut controlled by the

Maronite forces. This action intensified the sectarian divisions within the city and made the possibility of a return to confessional cooperation still more remote.

The PLO, whose presence in Lebanon was one of the main causes of the civil war, had managed to avoid becoming entangled in the fighting after its brief confrontation with the Maronites. But in January 1976 the Phalange and its Maronite allies formed a coalition known as the Lebanese Front and laid siege to the large Palestinian refugee camp of Tal al-Za'tar located in the suburbs of Beirut. Because the PLO's base of support came from Palestinian refugees, the siege of Tal al-Za'tar drew the organization back into the conflict. At the same time, the Lebanese army began to disintegrate into its confessional components, as officers and troops defected in order to join militia organizations that reflected their religious affiliations. Without an army, without an effective central government, Lebanon plunged deeper and deeper into the chaos of civil war.

The war was expanded and then brought temporarily to an end by Syrian intervention. In May 1976 President al-Asad of Syria sent his army into Lebanon to rescue the Christian militias from the battering they were taking at the hands of the PLO and the forces of Jumblatt. Al-Asad's choice of allies was perplexing because it created a situation in which Syrian troops and Maronite militiamen fought side by side against the PLO and the forces of the National Movement. Whatever al-Asad's motives may have been for supporting the Maronite faction, Syria's invasion of Lebanon escalated the fighting and expanded the level of destruction.

On October 18, 1976, Syria and the PLO accepted a cease-fire drawn up by Arab heads of state, and the worst of the fighting came to a halt. The terms of the agreement provided for the stationing in Lebanon of an Arab deterrent force to maintain law and order. In reality, the force was composed almost exclusively of Syrian troops whose presence enabled al-Asad to continue his efforts to shape the Lebanese situation to suit the needs of Damascus. These efforts have continued into the late 1990s, and although they have undergone several twists and turns, their overall objective has remained constant: the establishment of Syrian preeminence in Lebanon. The cease-fire agreement allowed the PLO to retain the same status it had enjoyed before the war. Once the cease-fire came into effect, Palestinian commando units returned to their old bases in southern Lebanon and prepared to resume their activities against Israel.

Although the civil war eroded the power of the central Lebanese state, it did not move Lebanese politicians to abandon the confessional system or to amend the formula by which political representation was allocated. It was as though the destruction of Beirut, the deaths of 30,000 to 40,000 people, and the invasion of Syrian forces had failed to resolve any of Lebanon's prewar problems. In the years from 1976 to 1982, the country disintegrated into a collection of sectarian enclaves, each defended by its own militia orga-

376 | Part V: A Time of Disorder and Renewal

nization. Warfare between militia factions became a way of life, and the name *Lebanon*, which had once stood as a symbol for sectarian harmony, became synonymous with mindless violence. Attempts by President Elias Sarkis (1976–1982) to rebuild the army and to effect reconciliation foundered on the unwillingness of the private militias to disband and on the suspicions and distrust of a people who had experienced the brutalities of civil war. Those brutalities frequently resurfaced, notably with the assassination of Kamal Jumblatt in 1977. His followers assumed the assassin was a Maronite and took vengeance on members of that community. And so it went, moments of hope and plans for reconstruction dashed by the explosion of car bombs and the ring of snipers' bullets.

The 1982 Israeli Invasion of Lebanon

When Israeli troops crossed the border into Lebanon in June 1982, they launched what would become Israel's longest and most controversial war. In the course of the three-month-long operation, the Israeli Defense Forces not only engaged units of the PLO, they also placed an Arab capital city— Beirut—under siege and contributed to the deaths of hundreds of Lebanese and Palestinian civilians. The invasion was planned and conducted by the government of Menachem Begin and was intended to facilitate Begin's goal of annexing the occupied West Bank.

For Begin, the PLO provided the connection between the West Bank and Lebanon. He believed that if Israel could drive the armed factions of the PLO from Lebanon, then the Palestinians in the West Bank would be isolated and more susceptible to Israeli annexation. The situation in Lebanon invited Israel's attention because of the continuing weakness of the Lebanese government, whose authority scarcely extended beyond the capital. As it had done before the civil war, the PLO took advantage of this weakness to assume a degree of administrative autonomy in a belt that stretched from the organization's headquarters in West Beirut south to the Israeli border. It was that belt the Israeli government wished to destroy. Its first concerted effort to do so occurred in 1978, when 25,000 Israeli troops invaded Lebanon as far north as the Litani River. The operation failed to dislodge the PLO from its strongholds, although it did cause large-scale demographic disruptions in south Lebanon as thousands of villagers, mainly Shiᶜas, fled their homelands for the area of Beirut. Pressure from the United States and the UN eventually compelled Israel to withdraw its troops. At the same time, the UN Interim Forces in Lebanon (UNIFIL) were installed in southern Lebanon in an attempt to provide a buffer between Israel and the PLO. For the government of Begin, the 1978 invasion brought home two lessons: First, the presence of Palestinian guerrillas in Lebanon could not be eliminated by military action that confined itself to southern Lebanon alone; second, the influence of the Palestinians in Lebanese affairs could not be eradicated without resolving the broader issue of Lebanon's political instability.

With these lessons in mind, Begin and Minister of Defense Sharon devised a plan they hoped would solve Lebanon's lingering crisis in a way that would work to Israel's advantage. The plan had three main objectives: the destruction of the PLO as a fighting force; the withdrawal of the Syrian occupying troops, whose presence in Lebanon brought them uncomfortably close to Israel; and the forging of a mutually advantageous alliance with the dominant Maronite faction. This faction was led by Bashir Gemayel, who became the instrument through which Israel sought to reconstruct the Lebanese state.

Bashir was the younger son of Pierre Gemayel, the founder and titular leader of the Phalange. In the period of instability following the first phase of the civil war, Bashir became commander of the Lebanese Forces, a military organization made up of several different Christian militias. Determined to perpetuate the Phalangist version of Maronite domination in Lebanon, Bashir engaged in a ruthless and successful campaign to destroy the autonomy of the other militias and bring them under his direct command. During the late 1970s and early 1980s, he had extensive contacts with Israeli officials, with whom he shared a dislike for the Palestinian and Syrian presence in Lebanon. By spring 1982 the groundwork for cooperation between Gemayel and the Israeli government had been laid; what was required was a pretext for military operations.

It was provided by a series of PLO mortar and rocket attacks against settlements in the Galilee sector of northern Israel. In response, Israel launched a huge invasion on June 6, 1982. The operation was called "Peace for Galilee," and its stated purpose was the destruction of the PLO bases in southern Lebanon. However, the real objectives of the Israeli government were far more ambitious than those given to the public. Peace for Galilee was designed not only to clear the PLO bases from southern Lebanon but also to destroy the PLO infrastructure in West Beirut and to ensure the election of Bashir Gemayel as president of Lebanon. In the view of the Israeli cabinet, such an outcome would establish a stable and cooperative government in Beirut and leave Israel with a free hand in the occupied territories.

The deliberate misleading of Israeli and world opinion concerning the planned scope of the military operations was one of the reasons for the strong reaction against the invasion. Another was the terrible toll it took in civilian lives. Within days of launching the invasion, Israeli forces pushed beyond their stated objectives and reached the outskirts of Beirut. At that point, Defense Minister Sharon ordered Lebanon's capital city placed under siege. Throughout summer 1982, West Beirut, the area of PLO concentration, was subjected to intense air, sea, and land bombardments that caused heavy casualties among the predominantly civilian population. The PLO remained defiant in the face of the Israeli siege, and the Israeli government was reluctant to order its forces to take West Beirut in house-to-house fighting because of the high casualty rate that would result.

Finally, international efforts at mediation, mounting domestic criticism within Israel, and deteriorating conditions in West Beirut combined to produce an agreement for the withdrawal of the PLO forces. The agreement, signed on August 18, called for a multinational force headed by France and the United States to supervise the evacuation of the PLO fighters; it also provided guarantees for the safety of the Palestinian civilians who would be left behind. By September 1, the evacuation was completed and the U.S. forces were withdrawn.

When in late August Bashir Gemayel was chosen as Lebanon's president, it appeared that the Israeli government had achieved all of its objectives. Two weeks after his election, however, Gemayel was assassinated, and the Sharon-Begin scheme began to unravel. In the wake of the assassination, Israel violated the evacuation agreement by sending its army into West Beirut. Instead of protecting the civilians as it claimed it was doing, the Israeli military allowed units of the Phalange to enter the Palestinian refugee camps of Sabra and Shatila and to massacre over 1,000 men, women, and children who had been left unprotected by the PLO evacuation.

The atrocities at Sabra and Shatila produced an international outcry against the entire Lebanese invasion and a wave of revulsion within Israel. Members of the Israeli Defense Forces spoke out against the invasion, and large segments of the Israeli population continued to question the reasons for engaging in a conflict that took so many lives at a time when the survival of the state was not threatened. In response to the criticism, the government struck a board of inquiry, the Kahan Commission, to investigate the events at Sabra and Shatila. The commission found that Israeli officials, both civilian and military, were indirectly responsible for the massacres. Defense Minister Sharon's role was singled out, and he was forced to resign his portfolio. The political career of Prime Minister Begin was destroyed by the Lebanon war. Disillusioned by the failure of his plans and troubled by the high casualty rates among the Israeli soldiers who had died in futile pursuit of his goals, Begin resigned the prime ministership in 1983 and withdrew completely from public life up to his death in 1992.

The effect of the Lebanon war on the PLO was profound. Deprived of the autonomous Lebanese base that had sustained it on Israel's northern border for over a decade, the organization moved its headquarters to Tunis, some 2,000 miles (3,200 km) away from the territories it sought to liberate. Although Arafat and his associates retained control of the PLO, the organization was less cohesive and more vulnerable to pressures from the Arab states than it had previously been.

In 1983 the Israelis finally decided to get out of Lebanon. They undertook a protracted evacuation that lasted until 1985 and even then was incomplete. Israel continued to occupy a security zone in the south, a zone that made up roughly 10 percent of Lebanese territory. As long as Israeli forces remained in Lebanon (and they were still there in 1999), they were subject to attacks by local armed groups claiming the right to liberate their country from occupation.

In the aftermath of the partial Israeli withdrawal, the new Lebanese president, Amin Gemayel, brother of the murdered Bashir, was faced with armed opposition from Druze and Shiᶜa militias; feeling abandoned by the United States and Israel, he turned in desperation to the Syrians to save his government. Syria was only too willing to help and began deploying its troops in support of Gemayel. Nothing more vividly demonstrated the failure of Israel's plans to manipulate the situation in Lebanon than this latest twist: In 1985 Syria's position in the country was more firmly entrenched than it had been at any time since the outbreak of the civil war a decade earlier. And in that same year, armed Palestinian guerrillas reestablished themselves in southern Lebanon.

The Taif Accord of 1989

For most of the decade following the Israeli invasion of 1982, Lebanon suffered from armed violence and governmental paralysis. Muslim and Christian militia groups continued their mutually destructive combat, and armed elements of the PLO attempted to reestablish their presence in the country. The dispossessed Shiᶜa community awakened to political self-consciousness and rallied behind two militant organizations, Amal and Hizballah (Party of God), for the achievement of its political and religious goals. Outside forces also contributed to the tension and disorder: The Israeli-occupied zone was a constant source of friction in the south; in the central and eastern regions, 40,000 Syrian troops stood ready to enforce decisions made in Damascus; and the Shiᶜa group Hizballah, operating on funds provided by Iran, called for the establishment of an Islamic state in Lebanon.

The conflict was so prolonged in Lebanon because the Lebanese religious communities could not agree on political reform. The essential problem was that the power allotted to the main religious communities in Lebanon's confessional political system no longer reflected the country's demographic realities. The restoration of government required the reworking of the constitution and the National Pact so as to reflect the Muslim majority (see Chapter 12). Any such reform would diminish the political power of the Maronites, a prospect so unpalatable to some Maronite leaders that they preferred the partition of Lebanon and the establishment of a separate Maronite homeland.

After the failure of several compromise proposals during the 1980s, Lebanon's politicians were brought together under the auspices of the Arab League in 1989. The setting was unusual to say the least. The meeting was not held in Lebanon but in the Saudi Arabian town of Taif. The delegates at

Taif consisted of the surviving members of the last Lebanese parliament (elected in 1972) plus replacements for those who had died in the intervening years. This unique assemblage managed to hammer out a national reconciliation pact that granted Muslims a greater role in Lebanon's political system. The major change was a transfer of some of the powers of the presidency to the prime minister and the cabinet. By reducing the authority of the Maronite president in favor of the Muslim prime minister, the Taif accord recognized the changed composition of the population. A second important feature of the agreement was to change the religious representation in parliament from the existing six-to-five ratio in favor of Christians to an equal number of seats for Muslims and Christians. This was achieved by adding nine new Muslim seats, three of which were assigned to the Shiʿa community. Far from eliminating confessionalism, the Taif accord vigorously affirmed religious identity as the core of Lebanese politics.

The agreement also acknowledged the existence of a special relationship between Lebanon and Syria. It called for the extension of the authority of the Beirut government over the entire country and requested the militias to disband and surrender their heavy weapons to the Lebanese army. This seemingly unlikely development was, according to the language of the agreement, to be facilitated by Syrian assistance. In effect, the delegates at Taif agreed to the use of Syrian armed force to implement the accord. Syria's military presence in Lebanon also gave Damascus extensive influence over Lebanese politics and, for that very reason, convinced elements within the Christian community to resist the Taif agreement with all the force at their disposal.

The Rebellion of General Michel Aoun, 1989–1990

In the months preceding the Taif Conference, the contorted twists and turns of civil war politics produced a situation that was complicated and unwieldy even by Lebanese standards. The term of President Amin Gemayel expired in September 1988, but the quarreling factions of militia leaders and politicians could not agree on a successor. Just before leaving office, Gemayel appointed the commander in chief of the Lebanese armed forces, General Michel Aoun, a Maronite Christian, as acting prime minister. At this point, the sitting Muslim prime minister, Salim al-Huss, declared that he and his cabinet constituted the legitimate government of Lebanon. The existence of two competing governments, one headed by a Maronite Christian, the other by a Sunni Muslim, threatened to create the permanent division of Lebanon. This was the situation that finally pushed the Lebanese politicians to the meeting at Taif and produced the national reconciliation pact. Most of the established Maronite leaders were prepared to accept the Syrian overlordship implied in the Taif accord in exchange for a chance at peace. Aoun was not.

Portraying himself as a Lebanese patriot rather than a Maronite particularist, Aoun proclaimed a war of liberation against the Syrian presence in the country and began a military campaign to drive Syrian troops from Lebanon. His two-year rebellion was the most destructive and deadly episode in Lebanon's fifteen years of civil war. Fierce artillery battles in and around Beirut ravaged the city's residential sections and killed over 1,000 civilians. At first, Aoun's stubborn stand against Syria attracted a certain amount of support from Muslims as well as Christians, but his recklessness and callous disregard for civilian lives soon turned most Lebanese against him. By early 1990 Aoun's forces were fighting not only Syrians and Lebanese Muslims but also gunmen from the major Maronite militia, whose leaders had decided he posed a threat to whatever future Lebanon might have.

This confusing and tragic rebellion was brought to an end in October 1990. While the world's attention was focused on the crisis created by Iraq's invasion of Kuwait, Syrian air and ground forces launched an all-out attack on Aoun's positions. Aoun escaped to asylum in the French embassy as Syrian tanks took control of the rubble-strewn streets of Beirut.

With the defeat of Aoun, the Lebanese temporarily abandoned armed confrontation in favor of mutual cooperation to implement the Taif accord. Under a new president, Ilyas Hrawi, and a pro-Syrian cabinet, the government began the delicate task of disarming the militias and restoring the authority of the Lebanese army. Yet even as Lebanon returned to a semblance of normality and embarked on a phase of postwar reconstruction, two persistent problems threatened the delicate balance that had been achieved at Taif. First, the very nature of the civil war had tended to deepen sectarian identities. In the dangerous conditions of a society at war with itself, individuals sought safety in communities of their coreligionists. Members of other religious communities, no matter how nonsectarian they may have been personally, came to be viewed as enemies. Thus did Lebanon enter its postwar existence with communal identities more solidified than ever. The second problem was in the south. As long as Israel occupied portions of the Shiᶜa heartland in southern Lebanon, the two major Shiᶜa militias, Amal and Hizballah, would not voluntarily turn in their weapons. The situation was rendered more complicated by the PLO's success in restoring a measure of its former autonomy in the region, a development the Shiᶜa opposed. Once again, the wider regional conflict intruded upon Lebanon and made the healing of that country's internal divisions dependent on a resolution of the conflicts that gripped the Middle East as a whole.

Egypt in the 1980s

The 1980s were a difficult decade for Egypt. Sadat's successor as president, Husni Mubarak (b. 1928), faced a daunting series of diplomatic and domestic challenges, few of which he addressed decisively. As a result, Egypt drifted into political and economic paralysis.

When Sadat appointed Mubarak as vice-president in 1975, he proclaimed that the torch of leadership was being passed to the October generation. Like his two predecessors, Mubarak was a military officer from modest origins. Unlike them, he showed no interest in political activity while serving as a young officer; he was a professional soldier instilled with the military's sense of hierarchy and methods of decisionmaking. After graduating from the Egyptian military academy, Mubarak received flight training in the Soviet Union and later rose to serve as commander of the Egyptian air force during the October War. As president, his caution and lack of flamboyance distinguished him from Nasser and Sadat. Yet if he lacked the public dynamism of his two predecessors, he nevertheless demonstrated a remarkable capacity to remain in power—in 1993 he was elected to a third six-year term as president.

The qualities that favored such longevity in office were not those that guaranteed decisive leadership. Mubarak's principal goal was to ensure the survival of the regime by introducing a minimum of structural adjustments while appearing to liberalize political and economic practices. His reluctance to support significant reforms and his inability to present a compelling vision of the country's future brought stagnation to all areas of Egyptian national life.

During his early years in office, Mubarak appeared to be guiding Egypt toward a more democratic political system. The elections of 1984 were the most open since 1952. They took on the appearance of a new era of political freedom by the government's decision to permit the Wafd Party to enter candidates in the election after thirty-two years of banishment. The Wafd gained control of enough seats to become the largest opposition bloc within parliament. However, the Wafd soon became divided within itself, and the excitement that had greeted its return was dampened by the regime's retreat from further political liberalization. After 1984 the state introduced tighter controls over oppositional political activity and used its full range of powers, from patronage to intimidation to blatant electoral fraud, to ensure the election of government candidates. These were not new practices in post-1952 Egypt, but their use by a regime that had no purpose other than to stay in power and by a president who inspired little popular confidence served only to alienate the public and to engender apathy toward the controlled electoral process.

The economic policies of the regime reflected a similar tendency to preserve the status quo. Mubarak continued Sadat's commitment to a mixed public-sector/private-sector economy and resisted pressures from the United States and the International Monetary Fund to accelerate economic privatization. Domestic political considerations made it very difficult for the state to divest itself of the public-sector industries, no matter how inefficient they might have been. The most crucial factor in the public's acceptance of the regime rested in its ability to offer employment. The extent of the state's role as employer is made strikingly apparent by statistics that show that in

1986 4.8 million Egyptians were on the public payroll; this figure constituted 10 percent of the country's entire population and 35 percent of the labor force.[1]

Political constraints also shaped the regime's policies toward the private sector. During the *infitah*, a prosperous entrepreneurial class emerged and acquired sufficient influence within ruling circles to make it politically risky for the state to attempt to curtail its business activities. The result was a growing gap between two groups at the top of the economic ladder, the prosperous private sector and the upper echelons of the state bureaucracy, on the one hand, and the mass of state employees, whose wages shrank and whose working conditions declined, on the other. In this situation corruption became widespread. It was normal for state officials to augment their incomes by entering into arrangements with private-sector entrepreneurs in which the officials would issue special import permits or waive licensing requirements in exchange for a share of the private company's profits. These and other extralegal activities made a mockery of the state's regulatory machinery and contributed to attitudes of cynicism toward the regime as a whole.

The situation was ripe for protest. The most persistent opposition to the regime came from the diverse Islamic organizations within the country. The state deployed force to crush the militant Islamic groups, while at the same time attempting to co-opt the more moderate organizations. However, as will be shown later, attempts to balance factions against one another became more difficult once society as a whole began to embrace portions of the Islamists' program.

The main orientation of Mubarak's foreign policy was determined by the treaty with Israel, the new relationship with the United States, and domestic economic needs. The restrictive nature of these three factors became evident during the Israeli invasion of Lebanon, when Egypt, once the main confrontation state, stood on the sidelines while the Israeli military closed in on Beirut. Mubarak had no choice but to honor the peace treaty and thus preserve Egypt's close relationship with the United States and the generous economic assistance it brought. But in doing so, he highlighted Egypt's diminished regional status and its new international realignment.

During the 1980s, Egypt received $2.2 billion a year in economic assistance from the United States, second only to the amount the United States provided Israel. Critics of Egypt's growing economic dependence on U.S. aid voiced concerns that the country was also losing its foreign policy independence and becoming a puppet of U.S. objectives in the Middle East. The specific projects funded by U.S. economic assistance and the methods by which they were selected also came under criticism. It often appeared that U.S. priorities, not Egyptian ones, were driving Egypt's development strategy. In addition, as Egypt's military was rebuilt in the American image, Egypt began to accumulate a sizable debt for its purchases of advanced U.S. weaponry. Economic necessity drove Egypt into the U.S. embrace, but many opponents of the relationship, both within and outside Egypt, questioned Mubarak's wisdom in turning his country into "America's Egypt."

Despite the obstacles that the U.S. alliance and the treaty with Israel posed to Egypt's reintegration within the Arab world, Mubarak successfully achieved this task. As a result of his patient diplomacy, Egypt was readmitted to the Arab League in 1989, and two years later Cairo regained its designation as League headquarters. But the Arab world that Egypt reentered was much different than it had been in 1979. Egypt was no longer the single most dominant Arab state, and its ability to influence regional events was noticeably weaker than it had previously been.

Conclusion

In October 1973 the Arab world appeared to be united in its support for the Syrian-Egyptian military offensive against the occupying Israeli forces. However, President Sadat's conclusion of a separate peace with Israel in 1979 shattered Arab solidarity and marked the end of the Nasserist vision of Pan-Arabism. In the contest to fill the power vacuum left by Egypt's withdrawal from the anti-Israeli coalition, Syria and Iraq made major bids for regional dominance—the former with its intervention in Lebanon and the latter with its war against Iran (see Chapter 19). At the same time, Saudi Arabia employed its enormous financial strength in an attempt to influence regional developments. Yet none of these three states received universal Arab support for its policies, with the result that the Arab world was once again divided within itself.

The Palestinian military organizations arrived in Lebanon just as that country was experiencing social and demographic changes that weakened the sectarian-based political system and led to a horrible civil war. During the war, the Palestinian organizations retained their autonomy in Lebanon and continued to mount raids into Israel. The Begin government, having secured a peace treaty that neutralized Egypt, invaded Lebanon in hopes of eliminating the PLO as a military force in Lebanon and cutting its ties with the inhabitants of the occupied territories. Although the invasion achieved its military objectives, it did not succeed in ending Palestinian political activity or the chaos in Lebanon.

These concluding remarks have tried to show that although the events and trends discussed in this chapter may appear episodic, they are linked to one another. Taken together, they represent the beginning of a new era of turbulence and uncertainty that extended to other states in the region.

Notes

1. Robert Springborg, *Mubarak's Egypt: Fragmentation of the Political Order* (Boulder, 1989), p. 137.

The Consolidation of Authoritarian Rule in Syria and Iraq: The Regimes of Hafiz al-Asad and Saddam Husayn

19

The Arab defeat at the hands of Israel in the June War prompted a period of soul-searching throughout the Arab world and led, in the cases of Syria and Iraq, to the overthrow of the existing regimes. Prior to 1967, these two states had acquired well-deserved reputations for political instability, but in the post-1967 order, they developed remarkably durable regimes. In Syria Hafiz al-Asad seized power in 1970, and in 1999, at the age of sixty-nine, he was elected to his third seven-year term as president; in Iraq Saddam Husayn emerged as the political strongman in 1971, was officially proclaimed president in 1979, and retained his hold on power even after his country's defeat in the Gulf War of 1991 and despite its struggles under an economic embargo that was still in effect in 1999. Both of these men ruled their countries longer than Nasser ruled Egypt. Each of them distrusted the other, and their two countries became engaged in a smoldering rivalry for regional dominance in the 1970s. Yet despite their clashes over foreign policy, their two regimes had much in common.

In al-Asad and Husayn, both states had rulers whose persons and regimes represented the rise of a new elite of rural origins at the expense of the established urban politicians and merchants. Both regimes were authoritarian, basing their power on the military and the Baʿth Party. In both, the sole ruler held absolute power and became the object of a personality cult. Both regimes adopted socialist economic policies and stood for egalitarian reform. However, a major contrast between them existed in the area of national wealth. Although Syria finally became a net exporter of oil during the al-Asad era, its petroleum revenues paled in comparison with Iraq's. In 1979 Iraq's oil production was second only to Saudi Arabia's among all the oil-producing states of the Persian Gulf.

Hafiz al-Asad, Saddam Husayn, and their comrades in both countries expressed common sentiments of resentment toward the United States for its failure to understand the Arab predicament and for its unwavering support of Israel. Both regimes engaged in enormous expenditures on military equipment in the 1970s and 1980s in order to buttress their claims to regional superiority and to confront their principal regional enemies—Israel in the case of Syria, Iran in the case of Iraq. Their expanded military capabilities might have given them increased diplomatic leverage, but it also prompted Iraq to embark on ill-conceived military ventures.

To focus on the careers of al-Asad and Husayn is not to suggest that it is individual leaders alone who shape the social and political dynamics of a state. However, these two rulers achieved such dominance in the decision-making councils of their countries and retained that dominance over such a long period of time that a knowledge of the forces that shaped them and their policies is crucial to an understanding of the history of the region.

Syria in the al-Asad Era

Hafiz al-Asad: The Rise to Power

Al-Asad was born in 1930 in the impoverished and isolated Alawite region of northwestern Syria. The Alawites were a Shiᶜa sect whose beliefs and rituals diverged so much from mainstream Islam that members of the Sunni establishment occasionally referred to them as infidels. Comprising about 10 percent of the Syrian population, the Alawites possessed long-standing traditions of autonomy and alienation from the rest of Syrian society. Al-Asad was determined to break out of the isolation and poverty that characterized his community. He managed to gain admittance to the secondary school in Latakia, the first member of his family to advance past a primary education, and he consistently finished at the top of his class. Like other young men of his generation, al-Asad was attracted by the Baᶜth Party's doctrine of national revival and social reform. At age sixteen he joined the party and became an active student politician and Baᶜthist organizer.

Upon graduation from secondary school, he faced a problem that was common to many young Syrians of rural origins; he had talent and ambition, but his family was too poor to finance a university education. In al-Asad's case, as for a number of his Alawite comrades, the military academy, with its free tuition, offered an opportunity for a poor country youth to acquire postsecondary training and a state job as an officer in the armed forces. Al-Asad enrolled in the academy in 1951 and was assigned to the fledgling air force division. By all accounts he was a top student and was selected for advanced fighter pilot training in the Soviet Union. By the late 1950s, he had made the breakthrough from Alawite peasant to skilled pilot and commissioned junior officer. But in the highly politicized Syrian armed forces of the era, the officer corps engaged in affairs of state as well as military duties. Al-Asad was no exception. He combined his role as officer and pilot with organizational activities on behalf of the Baʿth Party.

For men of al-Asad's political outlook, the period of the United Arab Republic (1958–1961) was difficult (see Chapter 15). He admired Nasser and supported the notion of Arab unity. However, he was dismayed over Egypt's domination of the union and was especially upset at Nasser's insistence that the Syrian Baʿth Party be dissolved. His outlook was not improved when he was assigned to a meaningless post in Cairo, presumably because the Egyptian authorities regarded him as a potential troublemaker. During al-Asad's time in Cairo, he became involved with other like-minded young Syrian officers in a clandestine organization that plotted for the revival of the Baʿth Party in their homeland. Their opportunity came in the two years of political chaos that followed Syria's secession from the UAR in 1961.

In 1963 al-Asad and his fellow officers carried out a coup d'état that brought the Baʿth back into power. It also brought to power a tightly knit group of young Alawite officers who worked to consolidate their control over Syrian political life. In addition to al-Asad, who at age thirty-three became the commander of the air force, the ruling coterie was composed of Muhammad Umran and Salih Jadid, both from peasant backgrounds similar to al-Asad's. Although the head of state, Amin al-Hafiz, was a Sunni Muslim, the three young Alawites controlled the levers of power. Their domestic policies were designed to consolidate Baʿthist rule and to remake Syrian society along more equitable lines.

The social reforms undertaken by the new Baʿth regime continued the political and economic campaign against the urban notables. In 1965 the regime nationalized 100 companies and began to expropriate and redistribute land from the large privately owned estates. The following year all members of the old influential families were purged from government service. The new military regime was restructuring the Syrian political elite by forging an alliance between individuals of rural origins and the lower middle-class urbanites—schoolteachers, civil servants, and university students—who formed the backbone of the Baʿth.

Al-Asad's faction of young officers led a violent internal coup that ousted Amin al-Hafiz in 1966 and purged the regime of many of the original supporters of the Baʿth, including its cofounders, Aflaq and al-Bitar, both of whom fled their homeland never to return. Although the regime that emerged out of the coup was ostensibly governed by civilians, it was in reality controlled by the military officers who had engineered the putsch. Al-Asad, now minister of defense as well as commander of the air force, became the dominant figure within the armed forces; his fellow Alawite Jadid controlled the Baᶜth Party. The June War, in which Israel destroyed the Syrian air force and captured Syrian territory, discredited the regime and especially its minister of defense. However, al-Asad was convinced that Syria's defeat was caused primarily by the mistakes of his associates, and he resolved to gain control over all aspects of Syrian decisionmaking. In November 1970 al-Asad achieved his goal by ordering the arrest of Jadid and other members of the government. Early in the following year, al-Asad was elected to a seven-year term as president. The ambitious Alawite of peasant origins had risen to the pinnacle of Syrian power; what would he do with that power?

Instruments of Rule

Most scholarly studies of al-Asad portray him as cautious, calculating, and pragmatic. His pragmatism was evident in the moderate way he applied Baᶜthist principles and in the attempts he made to broaden the base of popular support for his regime. Although al-Asad's government pursued the socialist policies enshrined in Baᶜthist doctrine, it was more tolerant of private enterprise than were the radical military regimes of the 1960s.

In another pragmatic gesture designed to gain support for his regime, al-Asad set up institutions of political participation that were more open and more broadly based than any Syria had known in over a decade. In 1973 the government introduced a new constitution that provided for an elected assembly known as the People's Council. Yet the constitution provided the president with such sweeping powers that the assembly was little more than a symbol of democratic government. The most controversial aspect of the constitution was its omission of the usual clause requiring the president of the republic to be a Muslim. To the battered Sunni majority within Syria, this omission suggested that the regime of the Alawite ruler was both secular and sectarian, and they organized protest demonstrations in the major cities. Al-Asad quickly backed down from this confrontation and arranged for the insertion of a clause calling for a Muslim president. He also arranged for a prominent member of the Shiᶜa ulama to issue a decree affirming that the Alawites were Muslims. The protest and al-Asad's response to it showed that sectarian tensions continued to play a role in Syrian political life.

Al-Asad was calculating as well as pragmatic, and primary among his calculations was a determination to retain the power he had worked so hard to acquire. Al-Asad had used the military and the Baᶜth Party as the vehicles for his ascent to the presidency, and once in power he established them as the foundations of his regime. He himself took the office of secretary general of the Baᶜth, thus combining the two roles of head of state and head of the party. With its elaborate hierarchy, its network of affiliated popular organizations, and its branches in the armed forces, the Baᶜth developed into an instrument of political control and indoctrination. The other pillars of the regime, the military and the internal security forces, enforced the state's authority and, when necessary, were deployed to stamp out opposition.

Al-Asad attempted to ensure loyalty to his regime by appointing relatives and trusted associates to key positions in the ruling hierarchy. In this regard al-Asad's personal triumph in attaining the presidency was also a victory for the Alawite community. Alawite officers were promoted to the most prominent commands in the military and security agencies, giving them a stake in the preservation of the regime. In addition, members of al-Asad's family were placed in charge of an array of special forces outside the regular military structure. The most notable of these was an elite praetorian guard, known as the Defense Companies, commanded by the president's younger brother Rif‘at. The regime took on a distinctly Alawite coloring that made it suspect in the eyes of the Sunni majority.

The Sunni Muslims who managed to gain appointments in the new power structure tended to be from modest social backgrounds rather than from the old urban notability. Thus, in addition to its Alawite coloring, the regime also had a decidedly rural composition and represented the rise of the countryside at the expense of the former elite class of urban-based notable families. The new elite of al-Asad's state also differed from the reformers who had built the Ba‘th Party in the 1940s and 1950s. Aflaq and al-Bitar, the founders of the party, were of Damascene origin and developed their ideas while studying European literature and philosophy in Paris. To some extent, they represented a continuation of the nineteenth-century practice of seeking knowledge in the West. But the officials of al-Asad's regime came from rural hamlets and small towns; their educations took place in rudimentary village secondary schools and the national military academy. They were not inspired by the abstract ideas of European philosophers and were not, in most cases, influenced by any sustained experiences in Western Europe.[1] They were, like the Free Officers of Egypt, pragmatic officers and administrators whose goals were focused on the needs of their country in its Middle Eastern context and on keeping the power that had finally come their way.

Domestic Policy: Economy and Society

When al-Asad seized power in 1970, Syria's economy was predominantly agrarian based, and the country's leading cash export was cotton. During the first decade of al-Asad's rule, the economy shifted to one dominated by the service, industrial, and commercial sectors, and oil replaced cotton as the main source of foreign exchange.

The Ba‘thist regimes of the 1960s had reoriented Syria's existing private enterprise economy to an economy based on state control. This was achieved through the nationalization of major business firms, banks, industrial plants, and transportation companies. In addition, the large landed estates were expropriated and a hesitant program of land redistribution was begun. President al-Asad retained the principle of public-sector domination of the economy, but he was less doctrinaire than his predecessors. He made gestures of reconciliation to the Sunni urban business people and merchants by liberalizing the economy and relaxing some of the restrictions on private-sector activity.

The combination of public-sector dominance and private-sector participation was successful for a time, and Syria experienced an economic boom in the 1970s. Financial aid from the Arab oil-producing states, foreign loans from other countries, and increased revenues from Syria's own modest petroleum industry enabled the government to embark on major development projects and to expand the range of state services. However, Syria's economic prosperity was tied to the Middle Eastern political situation, and when al-Asad's foreign policies alienated the oil-rich states, the country's economy plummeted and the government was forced to introduce austerity measures.

Syria's economic development suffered from internal problems as well. The supply of trained managers and technicians was inadequate to staff the rapidly expanding state-run enterprises. In addition top managerial posts were often awarded on the basis of loyalty to the Ba‛th Party rather than on merit, a practice that led to inefficiency. And finally, the regime's economic development became enmeshed in a web of corruption. Although al-Asad lived modestly, some of the high-ranking officials who rode into power on his coattails did not. The luxurious consumption in which certain military officers, government officials, and party functionaries engaged was financed by kickbacks, profiteering, and dealings on the black market. One of the most notorious practitioners of these activities was the president's brother Rif‛at, whose expensive tastes and shady financial dealings were widely known. The corruption associated with such public figures contributed to popular disenchantment with the regime as a whole.

Al-Asad, possibly because of his own rural origins, gave a high priority to improving the living conditions of the peasantry. His government extended educational and medical services in the countryside, developed transportation and irrigation systems, and introduced peasant cooperatives to provide seed, machinery, and credit to the cultivators. Although rural living conditions were improved by these measures, the regime's efforts to manage agricultural production were not particularly successful. Land distribution schemes were set in place, but the majority of Syria's peasants remained landless. Moreover, the introduction of central planning led to the bureaucratization of agricultural decisionmaking, creating situations in which Ba‛th Party functionaries with little understanding of agriculture were empowered to impose decisions on patterns of crop rotation, marketing, and the like. Cotton production increased significantly in the 1970s and 1980s, whereas the cultivation of food crops was sluggish and did not keep pace with consumer needs; Syria was forced to import ever-greater amounts of food.

When al-Asad assumed power, the country's illiteracy rate was around 60 percent. He proclaimed that his government would eradicate illiteracy within ten years, but despite a huge jump in the numbers of students attending public schools, the illiteracy rate was still over 50 percent a decade after the president's proclamation. The problem seemed intransigent in part because of Syria's rapid population growth, which, at 3.7 percent a year, was among the world's highest and outstripped the government's ability to provide teachers and classrooms. For those students who did manage to complete a secondary education, entry into university was encouraged by free tuition and an open admissions policy. Although this policy had the positive effect of expanding the opportunities for university education to all segments of Syrian society, it had the negative impact of creating overcrowded classrooms and reducing educational standards.

Under the al-Asad regime, all levels of the educational system were tightly controlled by the central government, which used the classroom as a forum for indoctrinating students into Baʿthist ideology. The system was designed to instill obedience to authority and devotion to the principles of the party. The regime's manipulation of education was particularly striking at the university level: The party and the security services screened faculty appointments and controlled admissions, making sure that those who had the opportunity to advance in society were individuals who had conformed to the rules of correct political behavior.

For all its restrictions on political and intellectual freedoms, the al-Asad regime pushed ahead with social reforms. It made a public commitment to female equality by legislating equal rights and privileges for women. Women served as parliamentary representatives and began to enter the professions and the judiciary, and al-Asad's minister of culture in 1976 was a woman. However, popular practice did not necessarily conform to the legal code, and conservative social attitudes continued to limit women's participation in the workforce. Moreover, al-Asad's opponents used the regime's encouragement of female emancipation to emphasize the government's secularism and lack of respect for Islamic values.

As the regime sought to implement the original Baʿth principle of social transformation, it also imposed political rigidity, cultural uniformity, and intellectual obedience. This was the contradiction of a government committed on the one hand to principles of reform and on the other to the preservation of an authoritarian military regime. The transformation of Syria was to be controlled by the state, not fueled by the creative energy of individuals. And in the end the state was stifling, inefficient, and oppressive.

Syria in the Middle East: The Bid for Dominance

For al-Asad, the conflict with Israel took precedence over all other foreign policy considerations. In his view, Israel was an expansionist state whose ambitions were underwritten by the United States. He believed that it was

Syria's duty to resist the Israeli threat and to work in the cause of Arab unity. Al-Asad's concern with Israel reflected the opinion of most Syrians, who felt more keenly about the loss of Palestine than did the inhabitants of other, more distant Arab states. During the late Ottoman period, the territory that eventually became the Palestine mandate was regarded as part of southern Syria, and its transformation into the state of Israel stirred strong emotions among Syrians.

Al-Asad realized that if Syria were to lead the Arab struggle against Israel, the country's armed forces would have to be upgraded. He persuaded Syria's principal arms supplier, the Soviet Union, to increase the quantity and quality of weapons it provided. Thus he launched a huge buildup of the Syrian armed forces that saw them grow from 50,000 in 1967 to 225,000 in 1973 to over 400,000 in the early 1980s. Such an unprecedented expansion of the military was costly. By the early 1980s, Syria was devoting over 20 percent of its gross national product (GNP) to military expenditures. The arms purchases strained the country's economy and consumed funds that might otherwise have been invested in domestic projects.

Al-Asad's overriding concern was to recover the Golan Heights, the territory that Syria had lost to Israel in 1967. He was convinced that this could and should be achieved on the battlefield. Only by demonstrating military competence would the Arabs be taken seriously in the international community. Al-Asad found a willing ally for his position in President Sadat of Egypt. Together, they planned the military action of October 1973. Although the war began well for the two Arab allies, it ended in defeat for Syria and a somewhat tarnished triumph for Egypt. Nevertheless, the battle for the Golan Heights had been closely contested, and the new Syrian army had performed capably. Al-Asad had reason to believe that in time an Arab coalition could recover the Israeli-held territories. The possibility of finding credible partners to form such a coalition began to vanish when Egypt abandoned the campaign against Israel.

In Chapter 17 we saw how Sadat engaged in the tortuous negotiations that finally took him to Washington for the signing of an Egyptian-Israeli peace treaty in 1979. From al-Asad's perspective, Sadat had betrayed the Arab cause by becoming a participant in the imposition of a U.S.-Israeli order on the Middle East. The Syrian president was determined that this order not be allowed to prevail. Since there appeared to be no reliable Arab allies committed to resisting it, al-Asad decided that Syria itself would do so by achieving military parity with Israel. This decision led to the enormous arms buildup mentioned above.

In attempting to achieve military parity with Israel, al-Asad was also planning to make Syria the most powerful state in the Arab world. He had, in effect, launched a bid for regional hegemony that would enable Syria to control the Arabs' response to the presence of Israel. This was an expensive policy, but not a reckless one. It fit al-Asad's calculating nature. His goal was to dominate the states that fell naturally within Syria's orbit—Lebanon and Jordan—as well as the PLO. Syria, through its military power, would intimidate these states and prevent them from making peace with Israel as Egypt had done. Syria would also attempt to restrain them, especially the PLO, from engaging in activities that would give Israel an excuse to attack Syria before its arms buildup was completed.

Al-Asad's regional policy was popular within Syria and helped to solidify his domestic position during the early years of his rule. And within the Arab world at large, he was seen as a possible successor to Nasser in the drive for Pan-Arab unity. However, al-Asad's embroilment in the Lebanese civil war undermined his reputation and brought his leadership into question both at home and in the wider Arab world. As we saw in Chapter 17, Syria intervened in Lebanon in 1976 on the side of the Maronite Christians against the leftist Muslim-PLO alliance. Al-Asad had gambled on being able to determine the outcome of the civil strife, but instead Syrian forces had become bogged down in a costly and indecisive military occupation. And by sending his army against the PLO, al-Asad, the supposed champion of the Palestinians, raised doubts about the sincerity of his commitment to their cause.

If al-Asad had risked Arab disapproval with his intervention in Lebanon, he was to take an even bolder step during the Iran-Iraq war of 1980–1988, discussed in the following section. The long-standing rivalry between Syria and Iraq was intensified in the 1970s, when both states came under the rule of different factions of the Baᶜth Party. Each accused the other of deviating from true Baᶜthist principles, and the propaganda machines of Damascus and Baghdad hurled vitriolic insults across the airwaves. The Iranian revolution of 1979 that toppled the shah and brought to power a militant Shiᶜa Islamic regime under Ayatollah Khomeini (see Chapter 20) increased the tensions between Syria and Iraq. Saddam Husayn, president of Iraq, feared that Khomeini's call for Islamic revolution might affect Iraq's restless Shiᶜa majority. Husayn therefore set out to destroy the new Iranian regime by launching an armed invasion in 1980. Most other Arab states supported Iraq in the long war that followed, but not Syria. Al-Asad broke ranks with the Arab world—and with Sunni Arab opinion—and sided with non-Arab Shiᶜa Iran. Al-Asad saw Khomeini's regime as a protest against the U.S.-Israeli order, and he believed the Arabs should support the new government in Tehran. There may have been a certain hardheaded logic to al-Asad's position, but it was lost on other Arab leaders, and Syria became increasingly isolated within the Arab world.

Despite this isolation, Syria, largely because of its new military power, managed to acquire the regional influence that al-Asad had sought. By the mid-1980s, Syria was in a position to ensure that no Arab-Israeli peace settlement could be negotiated without Syria's participation and that any peace proposals that might emerge from other parties could be sabotaged by Syrian action.

The Crisis Within: The Islamic Opposition

The Syrian public objected to al-Asad's intervention against the PLO in Lebanon and his support for Iran in its war with Iraq; an opposition movement arose that nearly overthrew his government. The opposition was also inspired by factors having little to do with foreign policy: It was a conservative Muslim and Sunni protest against an Alawite regime that was overtly secular and reformist; it was an urban protest against a regime that catered to rural and minority groups at the expense of the once dominant urban families; and it was a popular protest against a regime that spawned a new elite of wealthy party and government officials, a regime that was corrupt as well as repressive.

The opposition was concentrated in the old commercial cities—Aleppo, Homs, and Hama—and was spearheaded by young militants associated with the Syrian branch of the Muslim Brotherhood. Ever since the Ba'th took power in 1963, there had been outbreaks of Islamic-inspired protest against the party's secularizing tendencies. The discontent resurfaced in 1976 with a wave of violent attacks on government and party officials, especially on prominent Alawites. The singling out of members of the Alawite sect emphasized the strong Sunni character of the opposition. Throughout the late 1970s, the antiregime forces intensified their activities, mainly through a campaign of urban guerrilla warfare against the government. Various militant organizations formed an Islamic Front with the declared aim of overthrowing the regime and establishing an Islamic state in Syria. The front's proclamations emphasized al-Asad's Alawite origins and labeled him a heretic. The success of the Islamic Front's operations attracted a cross-section of disaffected Syrians who resented the regime's authoritarianism, favoritism, and corruption.

Al-Asad's security forces made hundreds of arrests, but the violence continued to spread. In 1980 the Islamic Front destroyed government installations in Damascus, and the protest movement began to take on the features of a full-scale rebellion. Antiregime forces achieved their most stunning victory in February 1982 when they seized control of parts of the city of Hama and called on all Syrians to join in a *jihad* against the government. Al-Asad responded to the Hama rebellion with ferocious brutality. The Syrian military, under the overall direction of Rif'at al-Asad, launched a deadly campaign against the city and its civilian population. Heavy artillery shelled the old urban quarters where the rebels hid, then tanks smashed their way through the rubble, demolishing whatever structures remained. Churches, mosques, and houses were destroyed and entire districts razed. When the military operation was halted after two weeks, the Asad regime had preserved itself and crushed the rebellion, but at a terrible cost. Large portions of the city of Hama lay in ruins, and at least 10,000 of its inhabitants were dead, killed by the armed forces of their own government. The events at

Hama sent a collective chill of fear through Syrian society. Al-Asad had issued a warning to other potential dissidents that his regime would use all the force at its disposal to remain in power.

The next serious challenge to al-Asad's authority came from within his own ruling group. For several months in 1983 and 1984, the president was recuperating from a heart attack and was rarely seen in public. During this period, his younger brother, commander of the elite Defense Companies, was emboldened to make a bid for power. He placed his Defense Companies in strategic positions in and around Damascus; other generals, loyal to the president, moved their forces to the capital city to oppose Rifʿat. Once again, Syria was on the verge of conflict between factions within the armed forces. However, al-Asad's adroit handling of the crisis prevented violence and enabled him to reassert his authority. Rifʿat was then edged out of power and finally out of Syria altogether.

Al-Asad again stood supreme, but his triumph over the rebels in Hama and over his own brother in Damascus showed that his authority rested not on popular consent or civilian institutions but on the loyalty of the armed forces. In the aftermath of these two crises, the regime became more repressive and more remote, and al-Asad became "more an object of orchestrated adulation" than had been the case previously.[2] The development of a personality cult around the president suggested the existence of a certain insecurity on the part of al-Asad and his advisers, of a feeling that the unpopularity of the regime's policies could be explained away by raising the image of the president to the level of one whose wisdom was beyond the comprehension of the average citizen. Thus were the trappings of dictatorship consolidated.

Iraq in the Era of Saddam Husayn and the Baʿth

The Rise of Saddam Husayn

The coup that overthrew the monarchy in 1958 launched Iraq into a period of political and social instability (see Chapter 16). When another coup d'état occurred in 1968—the third such event of the decade—it appeared to be just another in the series of political convulsions that regularly plagued Iraq. However, the 1968 coup brought to power a determined group of individuals who established a stable regime that endured for over thirty years. The figure who shaped the character of the regime and set its policies was Saddam Husayn.

Like al-Asad of Syria, Husayn was a man of humble rural origins who used the Baʿth Party as a stepping stone to the presidency of his country. Husayn differed from al-Asad in that he came from the Sunni Arab community, which, though a minority, has dominated the central administration of the region from Ottoman times to the present. Husayn was born in 1937 to a family of landless peasants in Takrit, a middle-level administrative town on the Tigris. His father died before he was born, and he was raised in the home of an uncle who had participated in the Rashid Ali uprising against the British in 1941 and was imprisoned when the revolt was crushed. It is reported that Husayn was deeply affected by his uncle's lingering hostility toward the British and the British-backed monarchy.

Husayn's education was confined to Takrit until he was eighteen, at which point he moved to Baghdad to begin high school. His studies were interrupted by his involvement in political activity. He joined the rising tide of protest against the monarchy and in 1957 became a member of the Baʿth Party. In 1959 he participated in a daring and unsuccessful attempt to assassinate the Iraqi president, Abd al-Karim Qasim. Husayn escaped arrest and fled the country, eventually settling in Cairo, where, at age twenty-four, he completed his high school education.

When the Baʿth seized power in Baghdad in 1963, Husayn returned to Iraq but was imprisoned when the Baʿth regime was overthrown in 1964. He spent two years in jail, then escaped and resumed his activities on behalf of the party. At this point, the Baʿth was in the midst of an extensive reorganization directed by Ahmad Hasan al-Bakr (b. 1914), a former military officer and prime minister who was also from the town of Takrit and was related to Saddam Husayn. In 1966 al-Bakr arranged for the appointment of his young relative as the deputy secretary general of the Baʿth.

From 1964 to 1968, Husayn's experiences as political prisoner, party organizer, and conspiratorial plotter shaped his attitude toward political conduct. Because the Baʿth was a banned opposition party, Husayn's duties had to be carried out underground. As a result, he developed a secretive decisionmaking style and a tendency to be suspicious and distrustful of those around him. He also developed a reputation as a man not to be crossed.

In July 1968 the Baʿth and its allies overthrew the regime of Arif and established a new government in which Hasan al-Bakr held the offices of president and prime minister. Al-Bakr was also the chairman of the newly formed Revolutionary Command Council (RCC), an inner circle of close associates that served as the main decisionmaking body within the state. His fellow Takriti Saddam Husayn became vice-chairman of the RCC in 1969. The new regime consolidated its control in the usual manner by purging the officer corps and the higher ranks of civil servants and appointing Baʿth loyalists to the vacated positions. From the very outset, the regime was ruthless in its treatment of those whose loyalties were suspect. Hundreds were sentenced to lengthy prison terms, and others were hanged in public executions intended to remind Iraqis of the fate that awaited any who dared oppose the regime. By the end of 1970, the number of "official" executions stood at eighty-six.

As the regime ferreted out its enemies, it also sought to identify its friends. Just as al-Asad in Syria had depended on his fellow Alawites for support, so al-Bakr and Husayn turned to their associates and kinsmen from

Takrit. In the early years of the regime, Takritis were appointed to key positions in all the organizations that propped up the government. Thus, at one point in 1973, Takritis held four of the nine memberships on the RCC; all the principal posts in the party, army, and government; and the commands of the air force, the Baghdad garrison, and the tank regiment of the Republican Guard. Their role was so critical that one historian was moved to remark that "the Takritis rule through the Baᶜth party, rather than the Baᶜth party through the Takritis."[3] The national prominence of individuals from the same modest-sized town, several of whom were related by blood or marriage ties, gave the politics of the regime a personal rather than an institutional or ideological tone.

The Takriti who cast an increasingly large shadow over the workings of the regime was Saddam Husayn. His power derived from his authority within the civilian ranks of the Baᶜth Party, his control of a new Baᶜth militia, and his position as head of a complex network of security agencies that provided him with information he used to determine who rose and who fell. By the early 1970s, Husayn had emerged as the real force behind the regime. However, al-Bakr continued to play an important role. As a former officer, he had contacts within the armed forces, and he used his presidential powers to expand Baᶜthist influence among the officer corps. By all accounts, the senior al-Bakr and the young Husayn worked together effectively, and their regime carried out some impressive economic and social reforms.

Their political objective during the 1970s was to establish a one-party state, and they effectively extended the Baᶜth into all aspects of Iraqi society. Labor unions, student federations, and women's groups all came under party control. The officer corps was also brought within the orbit of the party, and promotion was determined by party membership. An important transformation occurred in 1977 when all members of the Baᶜthist ruling council became members of the RCC, virtually removing the distinctions between party and state.

In 1976 Husayn, who had no military background, appointed himself a general in the army. Husayn's insertion into the military hierarchy reduced the importance of al-Bakr, and in 1979 he resigned. Husayn immediately succeeded him as president, secretary general of the Baᶜth Party, chairman of the RCC, and commander in chief of the armed forces. Throughout the years of his rule that followed, Husayn concentrated ever-greater powers into his hands until his regime became a one-man dictatorship.

Domestic Policy: Ethnic and Religious Tensions with the Kurds and Shiᶜa

We saw in Chapter 11 that the Iraqi state as created by Britain contained an enormously diverse population. The majority of the inhabitants of Iraq were Shiᶜa Arabs, who lived mainly in the southern part of the country. The Shiᶜa were economically and politically disadvantaged by the system put in place by Britain and perpetuated by the independent regimes since 1932. In addition there was a large minority of ethnically distinct Kurds in the oil-rich north. The post-1968 Baᶜthist regime, for all its aggressive centralization of political authority, had difficulty in controlling Shiᶜa expressions of discontent and Kurdish demands for independence.

The contentious issue of the status of the Kurds within Iraqi society troubled the Baᶜthist regime of Husayn and al-Bakr as much, if not more, than it had the preceding governments. At its most basic, the Kurdish question was a clash between a people who sought autonomy and a government that wished to assert centralized control, a clash between a culturally and linguistically distinct minority who claimed their own nationality and a ruling elite that was committed to the primacy of Arab nationalism.

When the Baᶜth seized power in 1968, the Kurdish region was once again in a state of rebellion. Although in 1970 Saddam Husayn personally negotiated an agreement that recognized Kurdish autonomy, the agreement was not implemented, and by 1974 the on-again, off-again conflict between Baghdad and the Kurds had escalated into full-scale warfare. As had happened in the past, the government forces were able to use their advantage in firepower to make initial gains, but they were unable to penetrate the mountain strongholds, and the conflict reached a stalemate. In this instance, the Iraqi government's position was made more difficult by the attitude of its neighbor, Iran.

The shah of Iran, a conservative monarch, an ally of the United States, and a ruler with ambitions to extend his country's influence in the Persian Gulf region, was alarmed at the emergence in Baghdad of a Baᶜthist regime that mouthed revolutionary slogans, obtained its weapons from the Soviet Union, and had its own designs on controlling the northern Gulf. Iran was only too willing to weaken the Baghdad government by providing aid to the Kurdish rebellion in Iraq. During the 1974–1975 fighting, the shah sent weapons and contingents of Iranian Kurds to assist the rebels; he also offered Iraqi Kurds sanctuary in Iran. Then, in what seemed like a sudden about-face for both states, Iraq and Iran in 1975 concluded a treaty, known as the Algiers Agreement. Iraq conceded a long-standing Iranian demand to redefine the boundary along the Shatt al-Arab waterway; Iran in turn pledged to close its borders to Iraqi Kurds and to cease assisting the rebellion in Iraq.

The agreement was a disaster for the Kurds of Iraq. Denied the opportunity to disperse their forces across the Iranian border—or the Turkish border, which had been closed to them earlier—they were decimated by the Iraqi air force and were compelled to seek a cease-fire in summer 1975. Once the Baᶜthist regime was assured of military victory, it implemented a reconstruction plan that granted the Kurds a limited degree of cultural and political autonomy as well as providing them with considerable funds for local development projects. But there was another, and brutal, side to Baghdad's Kurdish policy. In an effort to reduce the chances for future rebellion, the government uprooted as many as 250,000 Kurds and relocated them in the central and southern regions of the country. The authorities also forced large numbers of Arabs to move to Kurdish territory so as to dilute the Kurdish majority in certain mixed provinces. This was a policy of pacification, not of peace, and it was recognized as such by the Kurdish people. Despite the obstacles facing them, they managed to resurrect their resistance movement by the late 1970s. That movement was given a new impetus by the war with Iran and then burst again into the open in 1991 in the immediate aftermath of the Gulf War (see Chapter 22).

The interactions of the Shiᶜa community with the central government differed from those of the Kurds. Because the Shiᶜa had become diversified, they were not a monolithic community with a common attitude toward the government. In the years after World War II, thousands of Shiᶜa migrated from the rural south to Baghdad, where they became integrated into national life as members of the labor force and the civil service. Whatever grievances this segment of the Shiᶜa community may have had against the regime, they were based more on economic and political considerations than on religious ones.

Among the rural Shiᶜa of the south, however, religious identity continued to be important, and the influence of the ulama remained strong. The leading ulama and their followers opposed the Baᶜth regime on three grounds: its secularism, its refusal to appoint Shiᶜa to the higher echelons of the government or the party, and its attempts to dominate all organizations within society, including religious institutions. Shiᶜa protest was expressed through the formation of a secret, ulama-led organization known as al-Daᶜwa (Islamic Call), which advocated the overthrow of the regime and the establishment of an Islamic government. Large-scale Shiᶜa antigovernment demonstrations broke out in 1977 and again in 1979 during the pilgrimage rites in the holy cities of Karbala and Najaf. The regime was sufficiently alarmed at the extent of Shiᶜa protest that it arrested large numbers of individuals suspected of belonging to al-Daᶜwa and executed a prominent member of the ulama who was one of the organization's leaders. These acts of repression in 1979 occurred just at the time Ayatollah Khomeini took power in Iran and issued his appeal for Islamic revolution. The Baghdad regime's uncertainty over the loyalty of its Shiᶜa population in the face of the ayatollah's appeal was one of the factors that led it to invade Iran in 1980. As shown by the Kurdish rebellion and the Shiᶜite protest movement, Iraq's national unity remained fragile, even after fifty years of statehood.

Domestic Policy: Economic Development and Social Transformation

The total control that Western-owned companies maintained over the production, marketing, and pricing of Middle Eastern oil was a constant reminder of the region's continuing dependence on the West and a constant irritant to Arab nationalists. In Iraq each of the regimes that ruled after the revolution of 1958 attempted to acquire control of the country's petroleum resources from the foreign-owned Iraq Petroleum Company (IPC). IPC was a consortium of several Western companies, Britain having the largest share; it completely dominated all aspects of the Iraqi petroleum industry in the years after World War II and showed little inclination to relinquish its power. But in 1972 the Baᶜth regime, frustrated with IPC's unyielding stance, proclaimed the nationalization of the company. This was an event of major political and economic importance. For one thing, it was far and away the most popular measure that the regime had taken and contributed substantially to its acceptance. From an economic perspective, the nationalization of IPC brought benefits to Iraq that could not have been foreseen at the time. The government gained control of Iraq's oil resources on the eve of the momentous price revolution that accompanied the 1973 Arab-Israeli war. For example, Iraq's 1968 oil revenues amounted to $476 million; in 1980 the figure was $26 billion.

Enriched by the tremendous influx of oil revenues, the regime was able to embark on an ambitious program of industrial development and social reform. The Baᶜthists of Iraq, like their counterparts in Syria, were committed to a socialist economy that allowed some scope for private enterprise. The public sector took the lead with investments in such heavy industries as iron, steel, and petrochemicals. Although Iraqi industry suffered from low productivity because of a shortage of skilled labor and trained management, there was nevertheless sufficient progress to prompt some to predict that by the year 2000 Iraq would join the ranks of the minor industrial powers. But the country's civilian economic sector ground to a halt during the war with Iran, and then the entire infrastructure of the state was destroyed by U.S. bombing raids during the Gulf War of 1991.

The regime undertook extensive reforms in the countryside, striking hard at the remnants of the old rural elite and providing new opportunities for peasants to obtain land. In 1970 a new agrarian reform law placed further limitations on the size of landholdings and authorized the government to expropriate additional acreage from large landowners. Although the government rented out some of the land it seized, it redistributed most to small owners or landless peasants. The redistribution was extensive; between 1970 and 1982, 264,400 farmers received grants of land. The regime also supported the formation of agricultural cooperatives and experimented, unsuccessfully, with large collective farms. Although the land reform measures altered the social structure of the countryside, they did not contribute to an improvement in agricultural production. In Iraq as in Syria, agriculture received a low priority from the regime, and food imports rose steadily as agricultural production stagnated.

Because of its oil wealth, Iraq could afford to pursue the creation of a social welfare state. The government was able to reduce taxes, subsidize basic foodstuffs, establish free health care, and abolish university tuition fees. These measures, when combined with the plentiful employment that accompanied the extensive development schemes, led to an improvement in living conditions and income levels for the population at large. Thus, though the Ba^cth regime of al-Bakr and Husayn may not have been loved, the prosperity that accompanied its consolidation of power in the 1970s at least led to its acceptance.

In keeping with its secular and reformist outlook, the government improved the legal status of women and increased their opportunities to acquire education and employment. In 1978, amendments to the personal status law outlawed the practice of forced marriages, expanded the grounds on which women could obtain divorces, and made polygamy contingent on obtaining the permission of a judge. Women's access to education was also enhanced, and by 1982 over 30 percent of university students were female. The regime sought to attract women into the work force by setting up child care centers, offering paid maternity leave, and requiring equal pay for equal work. Although these may not appear as radical measures, they represented a new direction for Iraqi society.

To improve the productivity of the population, the regime sponsored an extensive campaign against illiteracy. Launched in 1978, the campaign was aimed not just at the school-age population but at older citizens as well. Thousands of literacy centers were established, and Iraqis were required to attend them for a minimum of two years. Similar attention was devoted to the regular school system, and the number of students in primary and secondary schools rose dramatically during the 1970s. The educational system was used to propagate Ba^cth doctrines and to monitor political behavior. Courses in Ba^cthist ideology were mandatory for all university students, and the regime tried to make certain that only party members received faculty appointments.

In the course of the Ba^cth regime's first decade in power, it was responsible for generating a change in the social composition of the ruling elite. The highest positions in the party, the government, and the membership of the RCC itself came to be held by individuals of lower-class rural origins. In this regard, developments in Iraq were similar to those in Syria, and the rise of the Takriti villagers was comparable to the rise of the Alawites. Political authority in Iraq was exercised by men who had rural upbringings and rural educations, men who had little university education and who had rarely studied or lived outside the Middle East. These men and their dominant leader, Saddam Husayn, embroiled Iraq in a series of complicated foreign policy confrontations that revealed how poorly they understood the wider world—and how poorly the wider world understood them.

Foreign Policy

During the period from 1968 to the end of the war with Iran in 1988, Iraqi foreign policy underwent a considerable modification. When the Ba^cth regime came to power, Iraq was isolated from the West and aligned with the Soviet Union, on which it depended for arms purchases and technical expertise. The solid relationship between the two countries was symbolized by the signing of a fifteen-year Iraqi-Soviet friendship treaty in 1972.

Although Iraq maintained its ties to the Soviet Union, it was gradually drawn out of its isolation from the West and into the global economy because of its petroleum industry. Iraq's development projects and social welfare programs relied heavily on the revenues generated by oil. The regime recognized this dependence and sought efficient technical and marketing assistance wherever it could find them, including Japan and the West. According to the Iraqi minister of planning in 1975, "What we want is the best technology and the fastest possible fulfillment of orders and contracts."[4] This pragmatic approach to economic development led the regime to award construction projects to U.S., British, and French firms. By the late 1970s, Western countries were also competing to gain a foothold in Iraq's lucrative arms market. France won a contract to supply Mirage fighter aircraft and 200 tanks, and Italy agreed to provide the regime with sophisticated naval vessels. Despite this diversification in its sources of technical expertise and arms supplies, Iraq continued to rely on the Soviet Union for the bulk of its military purchases. In its official outlook toward the superpowers, the regime took a pro-Soviet, anti-U.S. position. But in terms of economic development, especially within the petroleum industry, the Baᶜth adopted a pragmatic policy and imported as much Western technology and advice as it could buy.

Within the Middle East, the regime at first projected an image of revolutionary radicalism. It rejected UN Resolution 242 on the settlement of the Arab-Israeli conflict, it participated in the 1973 war by sending a contingent of troops to the Syrian front, and it denounced the Egyptian-Israeli treaty of 1979. Yet for all its strident rejectionism on matters concerning Israel, Iraq's real opportunity to exercise regional influence lay in the Persian Gulf. The regime made a clumsy attempt at expansionism in 1973 when, in a preview of the events of 1990, Iraqi forces occupied a post inside the Kuwaiti border and demanded that Kuwait cede two offshore islands to Baghdad. A concerted response by Saudi Arabia and the Arab League averted a major crisis, and Iraq was forced to withdraw. Following the resolution of its outstanding differences with Iran through the Algiers Agreement of 1975, Iraq's relations with its Gulf neighbors improved dramatically; as it increased its economic ties to the West, the regime adopted a more temperate foreign policy within the Arab world. The new policy enabled Iraq to cooperate with the moderate Arab states and to acquire an influence in Arab circles that elevated Saddam Husayn to a position of regional prominence. Husayn's ambition to have Iraq assume the leadership of the Pan-Arab movement did not appear unrealistic in the late 1970s.

The Iran-Iraq War, 1980–1988

In 1979 the shah of Iran was overthrown by a popular revolution inspired by the rhetoric of Ayatollah Khomeini. The regime that emerged out of the revolution, the Islamic Republic of Iran, called for the spread of Islamic revolution in every region of the Middle East. With the advent of the Islamic Republic and its militant Shiʿa vision of Islam, the tensions between Iran and Iraq, papered over in the 1975 Algiers Agreement, were once again brought into the open.

The issues that divided the two countries ranged from the long-standing cultural rivalry between Arab and Persian civilizations to immediate disputes over frontiers and navigation rights, to conflicting interpretations of the role of nationalism and religion in public life. One of the most sensitive questions for Iraq was the northern border. The Kurds had taken advantage of the turmoil surrounding the Iranian revolution to resume their armed insurrection against the regime of Saddam Husayn. The new Iranian government refused to close its borders to Kurds seeking refuge from the Iraqi army, thus violating the terms of the 1975 agreement.

But to the Iraqi regime, the most alarming challenge posed by Khomeini was his direct appeal to the Shiʿa of Iraq to overthrow Husayn. This was not only a political threat to the existence of the regime, it was also an ideological threat that pitted the universalist principles of Islam against the Baʿth's secular nationalism. A year before assuming power, Khomeini had specifically identified Saddam Husayn and his "infidel Baʿth party" as enemies of Islam. In 1980, following Husayn's suppression of Shiʿa disturbances and the execution of a leading Shiʿa clergyman, Khomeini proclaimed that "the people and army of Iraq must turn their backs on the Baʿth regime and overthrow it." In the same speech, Khomeini charged the Iraqi regime with "attacking Islam and the Quran."[5]

It appeared to Husayn that the Iranian government was endeavoring to destabilize his regime by aiding the Kurdish rebellion, encouraging a Shiʿa uprising, and denouncing the legitimacy of Baʿthist rule. He resolved to topple Khomeini's government before it could fully consolidate its power. In this decision Husayn had the support of the oil-rich monarchs of Kuwait, Saudi Arabia, and the smaller Gulf states for whom Khomeini's brand of populist, revolutionary Islam was anathema; he also had the support of the United States.

In an appearance on Iraqi television on September 17, 1980, Husayn announced the abrogation of the Algiers Agreement. To emphasize his point, he ceremoniously ripped up the official copy of the document. Five days later, Iraqi forces invaded Iran in what was intended to be a brief military operation against a foe in disarray. Instead, Husayn launched the longest conventional war of the twentieth century, a horrible conflict that cost hundreds of billions of dollars and took hundreds of thousands of lives.

In the first month of fighting, Iraq occupied about 10,000 square miles (26,000 sq km) of Iranian territory along a front running 375 miles (600 km) north to south (see Map 19.1). However, Iraqi casualties were higher than anticipated, and the Iranian resistance was much stiffer than expected. Husayn had completely miscalculated the effect that the invasion would have on the Iranian population. Rather than turning against the Khomeini regime, they rallied to it, displaying a degree of patriotism and loyalty that enabled the government to weather the initial setbacks and to regroup for a counteroffensive. Moreover, the military arsenal that the shah had accumulated was in some respects superior to Iraq's, and the Iranian armed forces were not nearly as decimated by the turmoil of the revolution as Husayn had been led to believe. Between November 1981 and May 1982, Iran mounted a series of counterattacks that drove the Iraqi forces back across the border and placed Iraq on the defensive. For the next six years, the war was fought mainly on Iraqi soil, and there were moments when it appeared that either the port city of Basra or the capital, Baghdad, would fall to Iran. But for most of the period from 1982 to 1988, the conflict settled into a dreary war of attrition punctuated by episodic Iranian offensives spearheaded by waves of human attackers that resulted in appalling casualties.

The war was not confined to the ground. Iraqi aircraft raided Iranian cities in an attempt to demoralize the population. In return, the Iranian air force destroyed the port installations at Basra, put the southern oil fields out of commission, and made damaging strikes on the important fields in the north. This severely crippled Iraq's oil industry and thus reduced the country's income at a time of vast military expenditures. In 1984 the war of attrition spread to the shipping lanes of the Persian Gulf when Iraq, in an attempt to reduce Iran's oil-exporting ability, started to attack tankers bound for Iranian ports. Iran retaliated with attacks against ships that traded with Kuwait and Saudi Arabia, Iraq's major Gulf allies.

With its oil-exporting capacity limited, Iraq was forced to borrow abroad to finance its war effort. Kuwait and Saudi Arabia were the major lenders, and together they supplied Iraq with between $50 and $60 billion worth of assistance during the war. Iraq's growing economic dependence on the pro-Western Arab Gulf states prompted Husayn's regime to modify its attitude toward U.S. allies in the region. Baghdad changed its rejectionist stance toward Israel and restored cordial relations with Egypt. In return, Egypt supplied Iraq with ammunition, spare military parts, and military advisers.

Throughout the war, the Soviet Union was Iraq's major arms supplier. But Western powers also came to Baghdad's aid. France, which was deeply involved in several large development projects in Iraq, provided Husayn's forces with Mirage jets and Super-Etendard war planes equipped with Exocet missiles. In 1984 diplomatic relations between Washington and Baghdad, severed in 1967, were restored, and the United States started to provide Iraq with military intelligence. The United States also pressured its

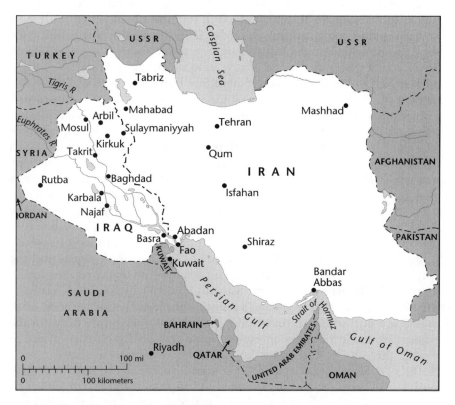

Map 19.1   Iraq and Iran in the 1980s

allies not to sell weapons to Iran and, in the final year of the war, campaigned for an embargo against Iranian oil. When Iran stepped up its attacks on Kuwaiti shipping in 1987, the United States allowed Kuwait's vessels to fly the U.S. flag, thus making an attack on them equivalent to an attack on a U.S. ship. Washington also reinforced its naval presence in the Gulf, and on several occasions in 1987 and 1988, U.S. gunboats engaged in direct military actions against Iran.

Although the U.S. government and media directed nearly hysterical criticism toward Saddam Husayn and his regime during the 1990–1991 crisis, we should recall how crucial U.S. assistance to Iraq was during the earlier war. For the United States in the 1980s, the demon of the Middle East was Ayatollah Khomeini, not Saddam Husayn, and Washington was willing to ignore the brutality of Husayn's regime in order to prevent the spread of the kind of Islamic radicalism and anti-U.S. sentiment represented by Khomeini. What was at stake for the United States in this war, as in that of 1991, was not human rights but oil reserves. The pro-Western Arab Gulf states controlled over half the world's known supply of oil. If Iraq were defeated, then it seemed likely that the Gulf states would either fall to Iran or at the very least come within Iran's orbit. This was an alarming prospect for the U.S. government, and it therefore lent its support to Iraq. The United States' military and diplomatic intervention on behalf of Husayn's government played an important role in persuading Iran's leaders to seek an end to the war.

In spring 1988 the Iranians launched a final offensive that succeeded in capturing the Kurdish town of Halabja in northern Iraq. The Iraqi air force responded by bombing the town with poison gas, killing at least 5,000 of its civilian inhabitants. This was not the first instance of Iraq's use of chemical weapons in the conflict, but the regime's decision to deploy them against its own population was a sign of the ruthlessness with which it was prepared to conduct the war. Iraq's possession of chemical weapons and the possibility that it might launch missiles armed with poison gas at Iranian population centers was another factor in persuading the Khomeini regime to accept a truce.

On August 20, 1988, a UN-sponsored cease-fire took effect, and the long war finally ended. Neither side had achieved its objectives. Instead of toppling the Iranian government, Saddam Husayn's invasion had strengthened it. And Ayatollah Khomeini's assertion that Iran would never agree to a truce as long as Husayn remained in power had to be reversed. As for the border dispute, it remained unresolved until 1990, when Husayn offered to restore the Algiers Agreement he had publicly torn up a decade earlier. Nothing, it seemed, had changed. The costs of achieving so little were staggering. Iran's war dead were estimated at 262,000, Iraq's at 105,000. The economic impact of the war on Iraq was devastating: The port facilities at Basra were destroyed, the ambitious civilian development projects had been abandoned, and austerity measures had been adopted. Moreover, Iraq emerged from the conflict with a huge foreign debt, estimated at $80 billion, over half of which was owed to the Arab Gulf states. The requirements of servicing the debt limited the funds that Iraq could devote to much-needed reconstruction.

Although the Kurds remained defiant, the war solidified sentiments of Iraqi national identity among the bulk of the population. Because of the regime's concern over the loyalty of the Shiʿas, it blended measures of conciliation toward the community with its continued policies of repression. Greater numbers of Shiʿas were appointed to high-ranking posts within the Baʿth Party and the armed forces, and President Husayn sought to project an image of himself as a concerned Muslim by visiting the Shiʿa holy sites and assuring the population that the Baʿth upheld the principles of Islam. The vast majority of Iraq's Shiʿas chose to side with their Arab identity over their religious affiliation and remained loyal to the government during the war. It was evident that they had no desire to come under Iranian domination.

Over the course of the war, Iraq's armed forces grew from 190,000 to over 1 million, and the country became a major regional military power. It developed a burgeoning armaments industry capable of producing everything from light arms and ammunition to Scud missiles and chemical weapons. With materials and equipment acquired primarily from European firms, Iraqi scientists were working intently on the development of nuclear capability. As the armed forces became the most important institution within the state, Iraqi society became militarized. The government glorified military virtues, and Husayn's daily television appearances wearing an officer's uniform served to emphasize his close ties to the armed forces. His control of the military strengthened his grip on total power. However, despite the participation of all sectors of Iraqi society in the war effort, Husayn's power base remained narrow, and he continued to appoint mainly members of his extended family and trusted long-term associates to sensitive positions within the armed forces, the security services, and the RCC. The war also intensified the personality cult that was built up around Husayn. So numerous were the posters and statues of the president that some Iraqis joked that the true population of their country was 28 million—14 million people and 14 million statues of Saddam Husayn.

Assessments of Iraq's economic position in 1988 concluded that the country's prospects for recovery were far from hopeless. If expenditures on the military were reduced and the substantial revenue from oil exports channeled into reconstruction, then Iraq stood a good chance of being able to meet its debts and attain a modest level of economic growth. But the regime gave rearmament priority over reconstruction; during the two-year period from 1988 to 1989, Iraq spent $10 billion on military equipment. It was partly because of these vast expenditures on the military that Husayn was moved to seek Iraq's economic recovery through the annexation of Kuwait in 1990. This adventure proved even more devastating to Iraq than the ill-conceived war with Iran had been.

Conclusion

In the writings of its cofounder, Michel Aflaq, the Baᶜth Party was defined in romantic and stirring language. It was to be an instrument for social justice and a vanguard organization with the eternal mission of bringing about Arab unity. The Baᶜth's platform offered the appealing vision of an Arab renaissance, and the party attracted young Arabs of the post-independence era eager for a cause and for the restoration of Arab dignity. However, Aflaq's intentions for the party were thwarted as it divided into regional groupings and quarreling factions. This was most evident in Syria and Iraq, where the Baᶜth came under the control of ambitious men who used its apparatus and ideology to serve their own ends. For al-Asad and Husayn, the Baᶜth became an instrument of control and indoctrination that assured the survival

The unveiling of a monumental portrait of President Saddam Husayn of Iraq during ceremonies in 1990 to celebrate his fifty-third birthday. (AP/Wide World Photos)

of their regimes. Both leaders justified their rule in the name of Baʿthist principles, but instead of using the party's ideology to prepare the foundations of Arab unity, they used it to criticize one another and to buttress their individual claims to regional supremacy. In the hands of al-Asad and Husayn, the Baʿth lost its Pan-Arab mission and developed rival Syrian and Iraqi branches, each of which sought to undermine the other. One of the victims of their rivalry was Aflaq himself. Expelled from Syria by a Baʿth regime that no longer needed him but feared his appeal, he was welcomed by Husayn, who trumpeted his presence in Baghdad as proof that the Iraqi Baʿth had remained true to the principles of the party's founder.

Both regimes practiced a combination of political repression and social reform. The extent of the reforms should not be underestimated. As was the case in Iran under the last shah, though, the emergence of a more literate and more prosperous population was not accompanied by a corresponding increase in opportunities for political organization or free intellectual expression. Syria and Iraq were ruled by authoritarian dictators backed by the power of the Baᶜth Party, the armed forces, and networks of internal security agencies. These were the institutions Hafiz al-Asad and Saddam Husayn had manipulated as they rose from impoverished peasants to national presidents, and they continued to rely on them for the perpetuation of their rule.

Notes

1. The comparison originates with Patrick Seale, *Asad of Syria: The Struggle for the Middle East* (Berkeley, 1989), p. 98.

2. Ibid., p. 339.

3. Hanna Batatu, *The Old Social Classes and the Revolutionary Movements of Iraq* (Princeton, 1982), p. 1088.

4. Cited in Marion Farouk-Sluglett and Peter Sluglett, *Iraq Since 1958: From Revolution to Dictatorship* (London, 1990), p. 180.

5. The quotations in this paragraph are cited in Dilip Hiro, *The Longest War: The Iran-Iraq Military Conflict* (London, 1990), pp. 34–35.

The Iranian Revolution and the Resurgence of Islam

⟨|⟩
⟨|⟩

20

The Iranian revolution of 1979 was of profound significance not only for Iran but for the Middle East as a whole, for Islamic states throughout the world, and for outside powers dealing with the Middle East. Within Iran, the revolution has been called "a cataclysmic event" that transformed the country's political, social, economic, and legal structure.[1] It overthrew the shah and led to the establishment of a republic; it replaced secular laws with Islamic codes of law; and it ousted the shah's hand-picked political and military leaders and set up a new elite.

The success of the revolution provided encouragement to those Muslims everywhere who were disenchanted with Western models of development and who longed for a restoration of Islamic institutions through which they hoped a prosperous and positive future could be built. But the rulers of Middle Eastern states did not share in the popular euphoria the revolution generated. The emergence in Iran of a militant Islamic Republic caused tremors among conservative monarchs and reformist dictators alike, and Iran became isolated in the Middle East. And finally, the revolution destroyed the foundations on which U.S. policy in the Persian Gulf had been built. The shah was the United States' strongest ally in the oil-rich Gulf; he received billions of dollars worth of U.S. arms in order to enable his country to protect U.S. interests and to discourage Soviet adventurism. With the onset of the revolution, Iran's military arsenal came into the hands of a regime that renounced its ties with the United States, condemned Israel, and pledged to eradicate U.S. influence in the region. During the decade after 1979, the United States' attempts to recover its position were awkward and bumbling, tending to worsen rather than improve its relationship with the new forces emerging from the revolution.

The Stages of Revolution in Iran

Stirrings of Opposition

In 1975 the regime of Muhammad Reza Shah took steps to further consolidate its control over the lives of the Iranian people. It abandoned the existing two-party system and introduced a single political organization, the Resurgence Party. Through the Resurgence Party and its affiliated organizations, the regime attempted to gain control of groups that had managed to retain a certain degree of autonomy from the government, especially the bazaar merchants and the ulama. The government tried to force the party apparatus into the bazaars and launched a simultaneous attack on the religious establishment by seeking to reduce the role of Islam in daily life and glorifying the monarchy at the expense of Islamic norms of identity. For example, in a measure that was so provocative as to be a challenge to the role of Islam, the shah replaced the Islamic calendar with a royal calendar that dated from the reign of Cyrus the Great. Such measures antagonized both the bazaar merchants and the religious establishment and activated the traditional alliance between them. Yet the government's totalitarian control of society appeared to be so all-embracing as to provide a secure foundation for the perpetuation of the monarchy.

However, cracks in the structure of royal absolutism were evident even in the period of its greatest strength. One of the regime's failings was in the area of economic management. Following the dramatic rise in oil prices in 1973 and 1974, the government indulged in wasteful spending that generated runaway inflation and showed the extent to which the benefits of the oil wealth were unevenly distributed. On the one hand, the privileged factions within Iranian society—developers, certain business people, and the intermediaries who arranged contracts with foreign firms—made vast fortunes during the 1970s. The shah's family and their retainers skimmed millions of dollars from the national wealth to support their lavish style of living. On the other hand, for the urban middle classes, the inflationary spiral sent the cost of living soaring and threatened their economic livelihood. The first public expressions of discontent came from members of this group.

The shah's reliance on foreign experts was another cause of popular opposition to his regime. With the purchase of advanced weapons systems and the inauguration of large-scale development projects, the regime was compelled to recruit ever-increasing numbers of foreign technicians and military advisers; by 1977 there were more than 60,000 of them in the country. To a broad cross-section of Iranian opinion, the presence of so many non-Muslim foreigners acted as a constant reminder of the shah's rush to copy the West and his dependence on the agents of Western imperialism. Slogans denouncing the shah's ties to the West would be prominent during the months of revolutionary protest.

A channel for the expression of grievances became available in 1977 when human rights organizations such as Amnesty International publicized the Iranian regime's violations of human rights and its use of torture on political prisoners. With the inauguration of President Carter in 1977, the U.S. administration began to pressure the shah to liberalize his regime. The shah, not wanting to jeopardize his relationship with Washington and his access to

U.S. military equipment, relaxed police controls, introduced court reforms for the trials of political dissidents, and released some 300 political prisoners. This modest shift in the regime's policies emboldened the opposition to speak out.

The leading voices in the first public expression of protest were the Westernized urban professionals and students from the new secular universities. They were joined by groups from the traditional sector of urban society, namely, the bazaar merchants and the students from the theological seminaries. Forming themselves into professional associations and student organizations, the protesters published pamphlets and distributed manifestos criticizing the regime's violation of human rights and demanding freedom of press and assembly. As the published criticism of the regime mounted, the opposition escalated its activities by resurrecting old political organizations and forming new ones. Although a variety of opposition parties soon emerged, the two most important were the Freedom Movement of Iran and the militant wing of the ulama.

Mehdi Bazargan (b. 1906), who founded the Freedom Movement in 1961, was representative of the forces of the liberal opposition that rallied to his organization. Educated as an engineer in Paris, Bazargan was a reformist politician who had supported Mosaddiq against the shah in the early 1950s. Although Bazargan believed that Iran should have a secular government, he did not advocate the abandonment of Islam. He saw Islam as a vital component of Iran's national culture and opposed the shah's relentless pursuit of Western values. Bazargan insisted that Islam itself was a reformist ideology and that it should be incorporated into a modernization program that was progressive yet distinctly Iranian. During the first phase of the revolution, Bazargan and his colleagues favored the restoration of the 1906 constitution and the establishment of a constitutional monarchy headed by the shah. They saw that change was coming to Iran, and they expected to play a leading role in determining its direction. They were to be disappointed.

The most influential ideologue in Bazargan's wing of the Freedom Movement was Ali Sharicati (1933–1977), a Paris-educated intellectual and teacher whose contributions to the protest movement of the 1970s were of the utmost significance. While studying for his doctorate in Paris, Sharicati participated in student politics and immersed himself in the works of Jean-Paul Sartre, Frantz Fanon, and Che Guevara among others. Upon his return to Iran, his radical outlook made it difficult for him to secure a teaching position, and he eventually became a lecturer at a religious meeting hall in Tehran. The lectures he delivered between his appointment in 1967 and his arrest in 1972 were circulated widely both in print and on cassettes.

Influenced by the achievements of the Algerian and Cuban revolutions but totally opposed to the secularism associated with those movements, Sharicati advanced a reformist doctrine that brought together an unlikely combination of Marxism, Shiʿism, revolutionism, and Iranian patriotism. The core of his message was that Shiʿism was an activist faith that required its adherents to oppose injustice and to assert their cultural heritage in the face of Western models of development. His doctrines had a religious orientation but showed no sympathy to those members of the ulama who practiced a stagnant religious scholasticism. In Shariʿati's view the apolitical ulama failed to recognize the essence of Shiʿa Islam as represented by Ali and Husayn, the historical Imams who achieved martyrdom in their struggles against the oppressors of their era. Shariʿati proposed a kind of "secular faith" that was dynamic, challenging, and inspiring; it called for action and for change, yet it was anchored in the culturally familiar framework of Shiʿa Islam. Denouncing the censorship, secularism, and corruption of the shah's regime in the mid-1970s, Shariʿati's call for action was immensely popular among high school and university students in that it provided them with "an ideology that fulfilled both their desire to remain loyal to their faith and their urge to undertake a revolution."[2] Shariʿati's mysterious death in London in 1977 was attributed to SAVAK and added to his luster as a martyr for the cause he had so passionately and persuasively advocated. As revealed in the writings and beliefs of Bazargan and Shariʿati, there existed a strong current of Islamic-oriented activism among the lay political and intellectual figures associated with the Freedom Movement.

The professional religious establishment did not have a common plan of action toward the shah's regime. Indeed, a large section of leading ulama believed that it was not the clergy's place to partake in political activities. A second group were moderate reformers whose objectives generally accorded with the program of Bazargan and the Freedom Movement—the restoration of the constitution and the establishment of a constitutional monarchy under the shah. A third wing within the religious establishment was more militant and more intransigent. This group was not content with the simple rearrangement of government that would be brought about by the restoration of the constitution. Instead, its members demanded fundamental change by calling for the overthrow of the monarchy and the creation of an Islamic state controlled by the ulama. This group was led by Ayatollah Ruhollah Khomeini, the central figure in the revolution, the inspirational force whose uncompromising stance and skillful blending of ideologies drew all the opposition forces to his side.

Khomeini (1902–1989) was trained at the Islamic seminary in Qum and then became an instructor there. He distrusted the policies of Reza Shah and his son, believing that both monarchs were determined to break the power of the ulama and to secularize Iranian society. In 1963 Khomeini was arrested for publicly accusing the shah of introducing policies that were incompatible with the principles of Islam. When he continued to criticize the regime after his release, he was again arrested and exiled to Turkey in 1964 (see Chapter 14). After a year in Turkey, he was permitted to reside in the

Shi‘a holy city of Najaf in Iraq, remaining there until his removal to the suburbs of Paris in 1978.

During his exile, he continued to speak out against the shah and his government. The lectures and sermons he delivered in Iraq were recorded, and the tapes were smuggled into Iran, where they circulated widely and kept Khomeini's name in the public eye as one of the most outspoken opponents of the regime. Khomeini's statements acquired credibility not only because of his courageous stand but also because he had maintained a network of former students who, in the 1960s and 1970s, rose to positions of prominence in the Iranian religious establishment. This range of well-placed disciples disseminated his various proclamations and prevented Khomeini's exile from isolating him from the Iranian people.

One of Khomeini's most persistent charges was that the shah was selling Iran to foreign, especially U.S., interests and that this was tantamount to the destruction of Iran's Islamic identity. Khomeini's proposals for a resolution to the ills Iran was suffering under the rule of the shah were contained in a series of lectures published in 1971 as a book, *Vilayati-i Faqih: Hukomat-i Islami* (Government of the Islamic jurist). One scholar has argued that the work was more than a guide for the reorganization of society; it was also "a handbook for revolution."[3] In it, Khomeini argued that an Islamic state modeled on the Quran and the community of the Prophet could realistically be created and that the men of religion, because of their knowledge of Islamic law, should manage the affairs of state. Khomeini further argued that the institution of monarchy was alien to Islam, and he called for the overthrow of the shah's regime through the creation of a parallel Islamic government that would mobilize the population to rise up against injustice and tyranny. Khomeini's demand for the shah's ouster and the establishment of a government run by the ulama was not fully accepted by the Freedom Movement and other elements of the opposition who hoped for a more secular government. However, as the revolution gained momentum, Khomeini's program attracted a growing measure of support. He stood for a religiously based political activism that transcended generations and classes because it was embedded in Iranian society at large. He tapped the shared heritage of religious protest based on antiimperial sentiments that had its roots in the tobacco protest of 1891, in the constitutional revolution of 1905–1911, and in the resistance that Khomeini himself had offered in 1963.

From Protest to Revolution

The year 1978 marked the transformation of the opposition to the shah from a moderate reformist movement of the professional middle classes to a popular Islamic revolution inspired by Khomeini and supported by the urban masses. The transformation was hastened by the brutal response of the shah's forces to the unarmed protest of the Iranian people.

In January 1978 an official government newspaper published a scandalous and far-fetched attack on Khomeini. The article prompted the students and bazaar merchants in Qum to mount a demonstration denouncing the shah's regime. Army units forcefully broke up the demonstration, killing several students in the process. The deaths at Qum introduced a new dimension to the opposition movement and gave it a decidedly Islamic coloring. It was customary in Islamic societies for friends and relatives to gather forty days after the death of a loved one to commemorate his or her passing. This custom was used with consummate political skill in the course of the revolution. The leading *ayatollah*s and other opposition members called on the Iranian people to observe the fortieth day of the deaths at Qum by attending mosque services. In this way, the rhythm of political protest was placed within the framework of Shiᶜa Islamic rituals, thus granting the religious establishment implicit authority to guide and direct the protest. On February 18, 1978, forty days after the Qum incident, memorial services and peaceful demonstrations took place in all of Iran's major cities. However, the protests turned violent in the city of Tabriz, and the government sent in tanks to quell the disturbances. Over 100 demonstrators died. In commemoration of their martyrdom, another round of memorial services was held forty days later, on March 29, and once again some of the processions turned violent when the crowds attacked such symbols of the shah's regime as luxury hotels, liquor stores, and movie houses that showed pornographic films. Dozens of demonstrators were killed by the forces of the regime, and the opposition movement again asked the country to honor the dead by another memorial service held on May 10. On this third occasion, the process of demonstrations, violence, and death was repeated.

At this point, in summer 1978, the shah's government adopted a new economic policy that was both a political and an economic disaster. In order to reduce inflationary pressures, the government decided to slow down the economy. The regime imposed wage freezes, canceled dozens of construction projects, and introduced a general austerity program. These policies very quickly created a recession that led to unemployment among urban workers and eventually to widespread labor unrest. Many of the urban workers were recent migrants from the countryside living in crowded shantytowns in and around Tehran. Dislocated from their rural existence and not yet fully incorporated into urban life, they were receptive to the calls for protest issued by the spokesmen of Islam.

The recession was a direct result of the regime's policy, and it brought the urban working classes into the streets to join the students and merchants who had been bearing the brunt of the shah's repression. The demonstrators' cries took on a more radical tone as they replaced the calls for the restoration of the constitution with demands for the death of the shah and appeals for the return of Khomeini. The government responded by declaring martial law and banning street demonstrations. The ban was ignored, and on Friday, September 8, 1978, the capital city of Tehran exploded in a series of confrontations between protesters from all classes of society and the armed forces of the government. The military deployed all the means at its disposal, from tanks to helicopter gunships, to break up the crowds. Hundreds of unarmed students, workers, and other civilians lost their lives. The episode became known as Black Friday and marked a turning point in the mobilization of public opinion against the shah's regime. In the words of one historian, Black Friday "placed a sea of blood between the shah and the people."[4] The regime's brutal response drove the masses firmly into Khomeini's camp and forced the Freedom Movement leaders to endorse his call for the overthrow of the shah if they wished to retain any degree of authority in the rapidly escalating confrontation. Black Friday was followed by a wave of strikes in such sensitive industries as the oil refineries and the oil fields. Labor protests reached a peak in October and led to the shutdown of most large industries and to the paralysis of Iran's economy.

The shah behaved indecisively during the latter stages of the revolution. Unable to make up his own mind about what course of action to follow and uncertain how much support he had from Washington for a total crackdown on the protesters, he vacillated, alternately offering concessions and ordering the deployment of force. It was later disclosed that Muhammad Reza Shah was terminally ill with cancer at the time. Although his illness may have affected his judgment, he was not known for decisiveness at times of crisis, and the lack of determination that he displayed from above only fueled the momentum of protest from below.

The culmination of the revolutionary protest movement occurred in December, during the ten days of Muharram, the customary period of ritual mourning for the death of Imam Husayn. Muharram was the most important ceremony in the Shiʿa calendar, and it was used on this occasion to place the antiregime protests firmly within a religious framework. Beginning on December 2, thousands upon thousands of protesters defied the regime's ban on demonstrations and took to the streets of Tehran. Donning white shrouds of martyrdom signifying their willingness to emulate the sacrifices of Ali and Husayn, who had died resisting the tyranny of their era, the marchers waved banners denouncing the shah and his U.S. ally and demanding the return of Khomeini. An estimated 700 protesters were killed during the first three days of Muharram, but still the demonstrations continued, culminating in a huge procession of some 2 million people in Tehran on December 12.

During the Muharram demonstrations, the military foundation on which the shah's regime rested began to crumble. Conscript troops, recoiling at the constant killing of unarmed students, shopkeepers, and workers, deserted their units, joined the demonstrators, and, according to some reports, fired shots at their commanding officers. In these desperate circumstances, Shapour Bakhtiar, a moderate Freedom Movement politician, agreed to become prime minister on the condition that the shah leave the country. But it was too late for the moderation of a figure like Bakhtiar. He was denounced by his colleagues in the Freedom Movement and by Khomeini himself, who issued a proclamation stating that any government appointed by the shah was illegal and that to serve it was to betray Islam.

On January 16, 1979, Muhammad Reza Shah left Iran on what was called an extended vacation. He died a year later, an exile in Egypt. On February 1, Ayatollah Khomeini arrived in triumph, welcomed by a huge crowd. An unarmed popular revolution inspired and guided by an elderly member of the religious establishment had toppled the king of kings and brought an end to the Pahlavi dynasty.

Consolidation of the Revolution and the Establishment of the Islamic Republic

By the time of Khomeini's return to Iran, the state, the army, and the internal security forces had disintegrated; the economy had collapsed; and organizations from the political left to the far right had begun a contest for power. It was a truly revolutionary situation—tumultuous, chaotic, its outcome anything but certain. These circumstances prevailed until 1982, inflamed by the struggle between secular and religious forces, by the existence of rival centers of power, and by the emergence of autonomous revolutionary organizations. The common thread running through these early years of turmoil was the conflict over the future orientation of Iranian society: Was it to come under the control of the religious establishment and become an Islamic theocracy, or was it to emerge as a constitutional regime under moderate reformers of the Bazargan mold? The resolution of this conflict cost thousands of lives and resulted in the total domination of the religious establishment over Iranian life.

The task of governing was made more difficult by the existence of two rival centers of authority. Khomeini, true to his word that any officials who accepted an appointment from the shah should be regarded as traitors to Islam, refused to recognize Prime Minister Bakhtiar's authority and forced his resignation in early 1979. He then named his own prime minister, Mehdi Bazargan (whose career was discussed in the previous section). Bazargan's task was to restore administrative order and economic stability. He and his cabinet of lay moderates sought to rein in the revolutionary organizations and encourage the formation of secular governing institutions. However, the scope of Bazargan's government was limited by the powers invested in a parallel ruling organization known as the Council of the Islamic Republic. Composed mainly of ulama and subject to guidance by Khomeini, the council was the supreme administrative and legislative body in the country.

It issued laws and decrees and had the power to veto policies proposed by Bazargan's government. The overarching authority of the council made it impossible for Bazargan to implement his program, and he resigned in November 1979, frustrated over clerical opposition to his domestic policies and to his attempts to maintain a semblance of cordial relations with the United States.

The emergence of autonomous revolutionary organizations posed a further challenge to the authority of Bazargan's government. As the central state disintegrated in the final weeks of the shah's regime, local committees were formed to carry out the basic tasks of security and administration. Headed in many instances by Khomeini's supporters among the ulama, the committees were used to expand the influence of the militant religious establishment throughout the country. In May 1979 Khomeini ordered the formation of the Revolutionary Guards, an armed force that was distinct from the regular military. Made up largely of impoverished young men from the urban centers, the Revolutionary Guards were deployed against opponents of the revolution and played an important role in the victory of Khomeini's coalition.

Another set of organizations that functioned outside the control of the government were the revolutionary tribunals. Established in February 1979, the tribunals were staffed by religious judges who passed sentences on former officials of the shah's government and others accused of counterrevolutionary activities. The desire for vengeance against officials of the shah's regime ran deep, and by the end of 1979 the revolutionary tribunals had ordered the executions of a former prime minister, several ex-parliamentarians, and hundreds of SAVAK agents and high-ranking military officers.

In order to provide an organizational structure for the ideology of Islamic revolution, a group of *ayatollahs* close to Khomeini formed the Islamic Republic Party (IRP) in mid-1979. The IRP sought to mobilize popular support for the Islamic Republic and to discredit the secular moderates. With its close connections to the national network of ulama, who in turn had regular and direct access to the population through the mosques, the IRP rapidly became the major political force within Iran. The IRP's powers of persuasion were increased by its ability to call upon the Revolutionary Guards to break up opposition rallies and to secure the arrest and detention of opposition figures.

Although the collapse of the shah's regime gave rise to an array of competing political groups that covered the full political spectrum from Marxists to militant clerics, the main contenders for power were the IRP and various strands of the Freedom Movement. The IRP had the support of the majority of the ulama and of the urban and rural masses, who had much to gain from a radical transformation of the political and social structure of Iran and who could identify with Khomeini's calls for the implementation of a program of Islamic social justice. The Freedom Movement politicians appealed to the middle-class technocrats and professionals, to some members of the bazaar, to segments within the Westernized universities, and to all who opposed the prospect of ulama dominance of government. Their constituency's link to the Western-oriented elements of society contributed to their defeat.

The steps that led to the establishment of a new Islamic order in Iran began with a national referendum in March 1979 that approved the replacement of the monarchy with an Islamic Republic. The results of this referendum inaugurated a struggle to define the constitutional meaning of the term *Islamic Republic*. In June 1979 Bazargan's government drafted a constitution that endorsed the principle of an Islamic state but did not grant any special administrative or judicial powers to the religious establishment. The government's draft was then submitted for debate to a popularly elected Assembly of Experts, the majority of whom were ulama. Khomeini personally addressed the first gathering of the assembly and informed the delegates that the constitution should be based "one hundred per cent on Islam."[5] In the course of its deliberations, the Assembly of Experts completely restructured the government's original draft, producing a constitution that required all of Iran's laws and regulations to be based on Islamic rules and standards. This condition made it possible for the ulama to become the dominant governing authorities within the state. The outcome of the constitutional debate launched Iran on the path of full political, legal, and social Islamization and may be considered every bit as revolutionary a development as the overthrow of the shah.

The constitution provided for a directly elected president, a prime minister appointed by the president, and a single-chamber national assembly, or Majlis, elected by the people. But the decisions of these institutions were subject to review by a twelve-member Council of Guardians. All laws and regulations approved by the Majlis had to be submitted to the council, which had the power to approve or reject them on the basis of their conformity to Islamic standards. The constitution also adopted the principle known as *vilayat-i faqih,* the governance of the Islamic jurist on behalf of the Hidden Imam. Khomeini himself was entrusted with the responsibility of serving as the ruling jurist. It was the most powerful position in the governmental structure. The position was to be held by "an honest, virtuous, well-informed, courageous, efficient administrator and religious jurist" who would serve as the leader of the people in the absence of the Hidden Twelfth Imam. Among the wide-ranging constitutional powers granted to the Islamic jurist was the right to appoint half the members of the Council of Guardians and to appoint and dismiss the commander in chief of the armed forces and the Revolutionary Guards as well as the commanders of the army, navy, and air force. In addition, the Islamic jurist was empowered to rule on the qualifications of candidates for president and to confirm the president's election. The creation of the position of supreme Islamic jurist was a triumph for Khomeini's long-standing belief that a truly Islamic state could be ensured only by the governance of the religious establishment. If, as the 1979 constitution stated, the Islamic Republic of Iran was a system based on the fundamental role of divine inspiration in the interpretation of laws, then only those who had mastered Islamic jurisprudence were qualified to administer the laws. The Iranian revolution elevated the men of religion from their previous status as interpreters of the divine will for secular monarchs to the status of rulers themselves.

The revised constitution was approved in a national referendum held in late 1979, and the first president of the Islamic Republic, Abol Hasan Bani-Sadr, was elected in 1980. Bani-Sadr (b. 1933) became a devotee of Khomeini while studying in Paris and served as his contact with the Western press during the *ayatollah*'s stay in the French capital. Although Bani-Sadr was committed to the preservation of Iran's Islamic cultural identity, he nevertheless favored secular government and opposed the growing dominance of the religious establishment. His resounding election victory was the result of his close personal association with Khomeini, not of his political ideas. His short and chaotic presidency was devoted to attempts to stop the ulama takeover of Iranian government, to curb the excesses of the Revolutionary Guards, and to bring the local committees and the revolutionary tribunals under the authority of the central government.

Bani-Sadr not only faced an imposing array of domestic issues, he also had to deal with two difficult foreign matters. In November 1979, youthful supporters of Khomeini occupied the U.S. embassy in Tehran and took hostage 57 U.S. foreign service personnel, holding them for 444 days. The drawn-out hostage issue embroiled Iran in a bitter dispute with the United States that poisoned relations between the two countries and contributed to the buildup of intense animosity toward Khomeini's regime on the part of the U.S. public. An ill-conceived and poorly executed attempt by the U.S. armed forces to rescue the hostages further inflamed Iranian opinion against the United States, destroyed President Jimmy Carter's reelection hopes, and undermined President Bani-Sadr's attempts to achieve a negotiated settlement to the crisis. To compound the president's difficulties, Iraq launched its invasion of Iran in late 1980, forcing Iran to wage a war for its survival at the same time that the revolutionary tribunals were purging the armed forces.

Although Bani-Sadr was supported by segments of the professional middle class, Khomeini and the Islamic Republican Party could call upon more widespread and more ruthless support within Iranian society. The secular middle-class reformers, who had once expected to dominate the post-shah era, were frightened into flight or silence. Bani-Sadr thus became politically isolated, and Khomeini finally abandoned him by allowing him to be impeached in 1981. Within two years, the revolution had devoured its first prime minister and its first president, both of whom advocated some form of restrictions on the ulama's control over the machinery of government. The departure of Bazargan and Bani-Sadr left the field clear for Khomeini and the IRP to consolidate their grip on power.

But no sooner had the Islamic Republic defeated its moderate secular challengers then it faced a new wave of opposition from the militant Islamic Left. During the second half of 1981, a wave of terrorist bombings carried out by the Mujahedin-i Khalq killed dozens of religious and political leaders and threatened to destabilize the regime. The government responded to the attacks of the Mujahedin with mass arrests and executions of such intensity that they constituted a reign of terror. According to one historian, the leftist threat led the government to intensify its efforts to impose ideological conformity over society as a whole.[6] The regime instituted a series of loyalty tests for civil servants, teachers, and other state employees. All of Iran's universities and colleges had been shut down in 1980 in order to undergo Islamization. During the closure, faculty were purged, curricula were redesigned to emphasize Islamic values, and textbooks were modified. When the universities started to reopen in 1982, the government made sure that only students with solid Islamic credentials and no records of leftist political activity were admitted. This policy resulted in a substantial drop in overall enrollments and a dramatic reduction in the number of female students: Tehran University declined from 17,000 students before the revolution to around 4,500 in 1983, and the proportion of women enrolled dropped from 40 percent of the total in the late 1970s to 10 percent.

By 1982 the Islamic Republic had turned back the challenges from both the Center and the Left and had secured its control over Iranian political life. The regime then turned its attention to economic recovery, the restoration of administrative efficiency, and the prosecution of the war with Iraq. Iraq's invasion in 1980 served to rally support for Khomeini and the Islamic Republic. Sentiments of Iranian patriotism mingled with pride in defending the cause of Islam against the regime of Saddam Husayn to generate widespread feelings of loyalty to the new republic and to the Islamic principles for which it stood. The war also enabled the government to expand its authority by recruiting thousands of young men for service in the Revolutionary Guards and the regular armed services. If the conflict enabled Khomeini and his supporters to consolidate the Islamic revolution, their political triumph was achieved at a very high price. Over 260,000 Iranians were killed during the war, and another 1.6 million were made homeless; the cities along the Iraqi border were reduced to rubble, and port installations, oil refineries, irrigation networks, roads, and bridges were destroyed. Iran faced a reconstruction challenge of immense proportions. Unlike Iraq, the government of Iran financed the war out of its current reserves rather than borrowing huge sums abroad. Although this policy created severe economic hardships for the population, Iran emerged from the war without the crippling indebtedness of Iraq and with a newfound sense of self-reliance born out of self-sacrifice. But the people expected rewards for their self-sacrifice. If the regime was to survive, it had to provide Iranians with social and economic benefits. For this to occur, the leadership would have to overcome the disagreements on economic policy that so divided its members.

The Islamization of Iranian Society

Because of the demands of the war, the government postponed decisions on how Islamic laws and standards were to be introduced and applied. From the first days of Khomeini's rule, though, certain objectives were established. Primary among them was the achievement of the Islamic principles of social justice and the equitable distribution of wealth. In the economic sphere the attempt to achieve these goals resulted in an expansion of the role of the state at the expense of private enterprise. The government nationalized banks and insurance companies as well as large industrial complexes. But there were sharp disagreements between supporters of capitalism and advocates of state control of the economy. As a result of these divergent views, the regime had not formulated a coherent economic policy by the time of Khomeini's death in 1989.

In the countryside, the early months of revolutionary turmoil witnessed the spontaneous seizure of land by the peasants and the confiscation of large landholdings by local revolutionary courts. The government endeavored to gain control of the situation by proclaiming a sweeping land reform law that provided for the confiscation of middle and large holdings and their distribution to landless peasants. The response to this law revealed the intricacies of Islamic jurisprudence and the difficulties that would be faced in attempting to implement it. Although the intent of the land reform law was to further social justice, certain members of the religious establishment—some ulama were large landowners—spoke out against it on the grounds that Islamic jurisprudence also defended the right of private property. The Council of Guardians vetoed the legislation, and the Iranian countryside remained chaotic for most of the 1980s. Rulings that protected the vested interests of the ulama and evidence of a marked improvement in the well-being of some *mujtahids* and *ayatollahs* aroused public suspicions that representatives of the religious establishment were gaining undue benefits from their exercise of political power. These suspicions were encapsulated in a popular song that has a low-ranking member of the ulama saying, "My poor old mule died last week; so to replace him I bought a Mercedes Benz."[7]

In other spheres of governmental responsibility, the process of Islamization took place more rapidly. There was, for example, a dramatic reorientation of the qualifications for the judiciary. In a reversal of legislation passed under Reza Shah in the 1930s that stipulated that only judges who had Western law degrees would be allowed to hear cases, the Islamic Republic of the 1980s decreed that judgeships would be awarded only to individuals with competence in Islamic law. Secular judges who lacked such competence were to be transferred, retired, or dismissed. In 1982 Khomeini insisted that Iran's courts discard all secular legal codes and base their decisions solely on Islamic regulations. This ruling necessitated an extensive review and augmentation of Islamic law, which was not specific in all areas of legal transactions and processes.

Additional Islamization occurred in the realm of officially approved social behavior. A dress code requiring all women, including female civil servants, to wear the loose-fitting garments and head scarf known as *hijab* was introduced in 1980. The university women who donned *hijab* clothing during the revolutionary days of 1978 as an assertion of cultural identity and revolutionary solidarity surely did not anticipate that they would later be subject to laws that required them to wear those same garments or face arrest and a year in jail. The regime further sought to purify society by implementing measures that ranged from banning music and dancing in public places to cracking down on drug dealers to razing Tehran's red-light district.

In its foreign relations, Iran was isolated in the Middle East and the international community throughout the 1980s. Statements by Khomeini and other high-ranking religious leaders claiming that the goal of the Iranian revolution was to establish a universal Islamic order alarmed the leaders of the Arab states, who feared for the security of their own regimes. Iran's intent to export its revolution was illustrated by its support of radical Shiᶜa groups in Lebanon who seized U.S. and European hostages. Thus, with the exception of Syria and Libya, the Arab states sided with Iraq in the Iran-Iraq conflict.

One of the goals of the revolution was to end Iran's dependence on the United States and to assert an independent foreign policy that was, in Khomeini's phrase, "neither East nor West." The Iranian leadership was also distrustful of Soviet motives in the Middle East and had no intention of substituting Moscow's embrace for that of Washington. For its part, the United States was at a loss over how to deal with revolutionary Iran. On the one hand, the Reagan administration of the 1980s sought to contain the spread of Islamic fervor and anti-U.S. sentiment associated with the Khomeini regime. But on the other hand, the administration recognized the economic and geopolitical significance of Iran and searched for avenues through which normal relations could be established with Tehran. This search led to the bizarre and inept episode subsequently known as Irangate or Contragate.

During 1985 and 1986, the United States, which was leading the campaign to impose an international arms embargo on Iran, secretly sold thousands of antitank missiles and tons of military spare parts to Tehran, mainly by using Israel as an intermediary. The purpose of the operation was to improve relations with Iran and to persuade the Khomeini regime to pressure

Representatives of three disparate and ultimately conflicting visions of the Iranian revolution. On the left is the young secular reformer, the Paris-educated first president of the Islamic Republic, Abol Hasan Bani-Sadr; in the center is the 1950s-era constitutional liberal Mehdi Bazargan, first prime minister of the republic; and on the right is Ayatollah Ruhollah Khomeini, the uncompromising spokesman of the religious establishment. (Courtesy of Nikki R. Keddie)

pro-Iranian groups to release the U.S. hostages they held in Lebanon. The operation failed miserably; three hostages were released but additional ones were taken, yet Iran received a windfall of weaponry and spare parts. Moreover, the revelation that the secret arms sales had been arranged by a small group of officials in the White House and the National Security Agency without the knowledge or approval of the State Department caused a domestic scandal in the United States that tarnished the Reagan presidency. And finally, the willingness of Washington to deal secretly with the Khomeini regime while publicly denouncing that same regime prompted the

United States's Arab allies in the Gulf to question the sincerity of U.S. diplomacy. The Irangate affair represented another example of the difficulty the U.S. government had in coping with the complexities of change created by the Iranian revolution.

With the end of the war with Iraq in 1988, the regime was forced to consider whether foreign firms should be allowed to participate in rebuilding the country or whether to continue on the path of total self-reliance. Although relations with the United States remained strained, Tehran did restore diplomatic relations with the major states of Western Europe and toned down its calls for the establishment of an Islamic order in the Middle East.

The revolutionary impulse within Iran had moderated by the late 1980s, and a certain accommodation was achieved between the requirements of piety in the workplace and the need for managerial competence. Iranian politics developed a pattern of "authoritarian populism" centered on Khomeini's personal charisma and his constitutional powers as supreme Islamic jurist.[8] Khomeini commanded a large base of mass support by addressing Iran's political, social, and economic issues in terms of Islamic ideology, an ideology that the population understood and endorsed. But the use of Islamic doctrine did not imply the desire for a simple return to the past. To portray the revolution, as many U.S. commentators did, as backward-looking and disembodied from the realities of everyday Iranian life is to miss its significance. The goals of the leaders, and certainly of the masses who supported them, were to improve the quality of life in the present. Social justice and cultural integrity went hand in hand. The mass revolutionary uprising against the shah's oppressive government and the privileged elite who benefited from it was motivated by hopes for a better economic future. Khomeini did not use his enormous constitutional powers as supreme Islamic jurist to establish a direct personal dictatorship; rather, he acted as a guide, offering decisions on major questions and avoiding involvement in routine administrative matters. He ruled by balancing various government factions against one another, making sure that no single group gained dominance. This may have been one reason the Islamic Republic Party was abruptly dissolved in 1987; it had served its purpose of establishing clerical authority and was abolished before it became a rival center of power. At times, Khomeini refused to make decisions on vital issues, a practice that kept his lieutenants guessing as to his wishes and paralyzed the operations of the government.

Although political life in the Islamic Republic was markedly different from what it had been under the shah, freedom of expression and choice were nonetheless constrained. The requirement that candidates for the Majlis had to be approved by the Council of Guardians ensured that no opponents of the regime would be elected to the national assembly. Nevertheless, the candidates did offer voters a choice, and debate within the Majlis was spirited even though the discussion of certain topics was prohibited. In addition, the very existence of relatively free elections represented a marked change from the shah's regime. The Islamic revolution ushered in a period of mass politics in which popular opinion, expressed at the polls, played a role that it had previously been denied.

During its first decade, the Islamic Republic did not employ a centralized security agency. However, correct political and social behavior was enforced by the Revolutionary Guards and bands of young men who roughed up, arrested, and occasionally executed individuals who were suspected of opposing the regime or who were identified as engaging in practices contrary to Islamic norms. The menacing shadow of SAVAK had been removed, but it was replaced with the equally menacing possibility of arbitrary punishment meted out by organizations operating outside the authority of the state but with the state's tacit approval.

In June 1989 Khomeini's death triggered great outpourings of popular grief. The question of succession had been settled in advance, and there was a smooth transition of power to Ayatollah Ali Khamenei as ruling Islamic jurist. By this time, all of the leading positions in government were held by members of the religious establishment; Khomeini's goal of consolidating the political authority of the ulama had been achieved. A deep divide still separated the proponents of religious and secular institutions, but the regime of the *ayatollah*s was widely accepted, if not always well liked. It remained to be seen how effectively that regime would function in the absence of the charismatic individual who had been responsible for its creation.

The Revival of Islam

An Overview

Although the Islamic revolution in Iran was by no means the first manifestation of Islamic-oriented political activity in the 1970s, the impact that it made called attention to the existence of Islamic movements in other countries. There can be no precise date for the emergence of a phenomenon such as the Islamic resurgence, but most observers have identified the resounding Arab defeat in the June War with Israel as the point at which disillusionment with borrowed ideologies and cultures became pronounced. During the 1970s and 1980s, the Islamic states of the Middle East—and beyond—experienced an outgrowth of popular demands to restore Islam to a central role in political and social life. Although the resurgence of Islam occurred in virtually every Islamic country, the forces that gave rise to it were specific to individual states. The movement should therefore be seen as a phenomenon that had its origins in the context of local conditions even though it acquired certain transnational features.

The first challenge facing the historian of this subject is deciding what to call it. Some Western scholars and journalists use the term *fundamentalism,* often, though not always, in a pejorative manner. But in the strictest historical sense, fundamentalism refers to a specific movement of American evangelical Protestantism in the early 1920s and is unsuitable as a defining label for Islamic groups. This book will employ the terms *Islamism, political Islam,* and *Islamists* to describe the contemporary current of Islamic activism and those who participated in it.

Some Western writers have characterized Islamists as fanatics or backward-looking reactionaries. That is an inaccurate portrayal of the movement and of the majority of the people who are sympathetic to it. The driving force behind the Islamic resurgence was not a rejection of change; rather, it was a rejection of the Middle East's dependence on Western and other alien models of development. The Islamic resurgence was also motivated by a rejection of the assumptions on which Western development theories were based. These theories equated modernization with secularization and suggested that societies would become modern only as they freed themselves from their traditional religious faiths. The Western experience in which church and state became separated and society became generally secular was posited as the only viable path to true modernity. But to many Muslims who reflected on the course of their modern history, this path had not only been forced on them, it had failed them.

As we have seen in earlier chapters, a dominant theme of nineteenth- and twentieth-century Middle Eastern history was the attempt by certain rulers to adopt Western technology, ideology, culture, and institutions. From the military uniforms of Sultan Selim III's new army to the weapons of Muhammad Ali's Egyptian forces, from Isma῾il's opera house and school system to the Ottoman constitution, and from Atatürk's relentless secularization policies to Muhammad Reza Shah's program of economic development, the inspiration was Western, not Islamic. The objective of these and other rulers was to imitate the West because Western products, techniques, or political institutions appeared to be superior.

Yet the end result of the nineteenth-century reforms was the defeat of the Ottoman Empire and the occupation of Arab-Islamic lands by Britain and France. The two European powers sought to generate a European model of political development by imposing Western-style parliamentary systems on Egypt and the Arab mandates. The systems failed, largely because they had not evolved out of the social and political fabric of the states on which they were imposed and because of their cynical manipulation by the imperial powers, and they were swept aside following World War II. In the 1950s and 1960s, Nasser and his imitators throughout the Arab world endeavored to create social equality and economic development through the adoption of socialist doctrines; Nasser was careful to label them Arab socialism in an attempt to disguise their foreign origins. Nasser and his admirers also emphasized Pan-Arab nationalism as the ideology that would lead the Arabs to unity, dignity, and victory over Israel. But Arab unity was never realized, and Arab socialism tended to produce bloated bureaucracies and inefficient economies. The ideologies of the Nasser era were already losing their power when they were dealt a devastating blow by the humiliating defeat of Egypt, Syria, and Jordan in the June War of 1967. Many Muslim Arabs regarded the defeat as more than a military disaster; they saw it as God's punishment to Muslims for straying from the divine path set forth in the Quran and the shariᶜah.

In addition to adopting foreign institutions, the Muslim states of the Middle East were also inundated with foreign products, and their inhabitants were urged to practice Western patterns of consumption that often seemed to contradict Islamic mores, to say nothing about common sense. The duty-free shops in the airports of even the most conservative Gulf states did a thriving business in packaged alcoholic beverages, and the presence of a bottle of Johnnie Walker Black Label scotch in the sitting room became, for some, a symbol of middle-class success. A sociologist's portrait of an Egyptian peasant relaxing with his family after a grueling day's work in the fields shows the jarring intrusion of foreign values into the Middle East during the 1970s: The peasant is watching Egyptian television on the set his son has purchased with money earned by working abroad. The program on the screen is *Dallas*. During commercial breaks, he "is told in English that he should be drinking Schweppes or in dubbed Arabic that he should use deodorant, and that all his problems are caused by having too many children—a total package of imported ideas."⁹ This sort of situation caused some Muslims to reflect on the dangers—and the folly—of relying on external cultural values.

As a result of the failure of imported, secular models to bring economic progress, political freedoms, or social justice, many Middle Eastern Muslims began to question their leaders' reliance on foreign practices and to reexamine their own personal values. By departing from an integral Islamic order, an order in which political, social, and economic activities were conducted according to the *shariᶜah,* their leaders had, many Muslims believed, contributed to the weakness of Islamic society as a whole. Muslims who held this view asserted that Islam contained the necessary ingredients for modern development. To be healthy, political and economic life should be derived from the moral values rooted in Islam, not from Western consumerism and materialism. Muslims undertook a renewed effort to find Islamic solutions to the problems that confronted them in their daily lives and troubled their societies as a whole.

However, it should be pointed out that for the vast majority of Muslims, the rural peasantry and the urban poor, Islam had remained a constant feature of their existence. They had not participated in the debates over socialism and capitalism, nationalism and Baᶜthism. As illiterate or semiliterate members of society, the Muslim masses had little reason to question the role of Islam in their lives. They continued to be strongly influenced by the rudiments of Islamic instruction they received in childhood, by the oral transmission of stories and legends about the heroic age of Islam, and by the general Islamic value system that shaped their outlook.

What was new about the Islamic resurgence of the 1970s and 1980s was the participation of members of literate urban society in a general movement to assert Islamic cultural authenticity. Among ordinary men and women, the Islamic resurgence was manifested by increased attendance at mosque services, by the adoption of Islamic dress codes, including the growing of beards by men and the wearing of *hijab* clothing by women. One educated Egyptian woman explained to a foreign visitor that wearing proper Islamic dress helped her overcome the frustrations of daily living: "We have problems with housing, with budgets, with the schools, with transportation, with electricity, butagas and water, and the telephone doesn't work. When we put on *ziyy shari* [lawful dress], we feel that at least here is one problem we can solve for our families and society for ourselves. At least we've done something."¹⁰ Other examples of the Islamic resurgence included an enormous increase in the publication of religious materials, a growth in the popularity of televised sermons, and a willingness to deposit funds in so-called Islamic banks that did not pay interest.

A significant component of the Islamic resurgence was a demand for the return of the *shariᶜah*. The Western legal codes that had been adopted piecemeal by the Ottoman Empire and Egypt during the nineteenth and early twentieth centuries drastically reduced the scope of *shariᶜah* jurisdiction in civil law. In 1949 an Egyptian jurist, Abd al-Raziq al-Sanhuri, framed a new Egyptian civil code drawing on examples from existing Egyptian legislation, from other contemporary codes, and from the *shariᶜah*. Although al-Sanhuri attempted to select rules of foreign origin on the basis of their conformity to the *shariᶜah*, the completed code was more French than Islamic. Al-Sanhuri also drew up civil codes for Iraq and Kuwait. The legal reforms of the post–World War II era made inroads into the last vestiges of *shariᶜah*.

Family law, or the law of personal status, was an even more sensitive issue because it touched the population directly and because it was regarded as the very heart of the *shariᶜah*. Yet even in this sphere of activity, rulers in Turkey, Iran, Iraq, Syria, and Egypt introduced legislation that altered the *shariᶜah* provisions dealing with the status of women. Such legislation contributed to the popular opinion that the proper order of state and society was being undermined by leaders who chose to ignore the *shariᶜah* and to impose statutes of Western origin. Thus, the very essence of Islamic society, rule by divine law, was eliminated. During the period of malaise that set in after 1967, militants and ordinary citizens alike expressed a desire for the reestablishment of the *shariᶜah*.

In the 1970s Islam was increasingly used as a political tool. As the populations of Islamic states came to demand greater adherence to *shariʿah*-inspired policies on the part of their rulers, political leaders sought to rally mass support through the manipulation of Islamic symbols. We have seen how the opposition in Syria criticized President al-Asad by calling him a heretic. Similarly, Ayatollah Khomeini was able to rally the Iranian people against the shah by using Islamic symbols and slogans. In the Iranian protest movement as in others, the instruments of modern communications assisted the spread of a religiously based message; the cassette recordings of the speeches of Khomeini and Shariʿati played an important role in expanding the audience of the two men. Rulers also used Islamic symbols to bolster their legitimacy. With the exception of Atatürk, no modern Muslim ruler has openly disavowed Islam. On the contrary, political leaders have sought to associate themselves with Islamic activities and have been quick to portray their domestic opponents as imperfect Muslims. The late shah of Iran tried to calm the growing opposition to his rule by proclaiming his attachment to Islam and his closeness to God. As the war clouds gathered over the Persian Gulf in early 1991, Saddam Husayn of Iraq attempted to rally international Islamic opinion to his side by presenting the U.S.-led UN coalition as an anti-Islamic campaign and calling on Muslims to wage a *jihad* throughout the world. Thus, Islamic symbols could become powerful mobilizing agents for opposition movements and incumbent regimes alike.

The Case of Egypt

Although the Islamic movement in Egypt during the 1970s and 1980s was grounded in the distinctive circumstances of Egyptian history, it exhibited many of the features that characterized the Islamic resurgence as a whole. (This period of Egyptian history has been discussed in Chapter 18 but is presented here with an emphasis on the components of the Islamic resurgence.) When President Anwar Sadat assumed the presidency in 1970, he feared that elements of the political Left posed the greatest threat to his tenuous hold on power. He sought to counter this threat by allowing representatives of what was known as "the Islamic tendency" to return to the political arena. Sadat released long-imprisoned members of the Muslim Brotherhood and authorized the brotherhood to publish its periodical, *al-Daʿwa* (The call), which rapidly achieved a circulation of over 100,000. In addition, Sadat used Islamic symbols to bolster his political legitimacy. He gave himself the title "the believer-president" and used the Egyptian media to cultivate an image of personal piety.

By permitting Islamic issues and symbols to become a prominent part of public discourse, Sadat unleashed forces that came to pose a major challenge to his regime. Despite his attempts to portray himself as a pious Muslim, his lavish style of living, his and his wife's preference for European designer clothes, and his agreement to a treaty with Israel all served to make him a target of criticism for the Islamic forces he had originally tried to manipulate. In addition, the failure of Sadat's *infitah,* or open-door economic policy, to benefit the majority after 1973 led to widespread opposition to his regime. The most militant opposition was organized by Egyptian youth and was expressed in Islamic terms.

The Egyptian situation during the 1970s differed from Iran's in that the Egyptian religious establishment had been largely taken over by the state during the Nasser era. The ulama were state employees, and their tendency to mouth the slogans of the regime caused Egyptians to refer to them as "pulpit parrots" and to regard them with a decided cynicism. Moreover, the Sunni Egyptian religious officials did not receive the same veneration as the Iranian *ayatollahs,* who were the representatives of the Hidden Imam and were therefore empowered to interpret God's commands. Since the Egyptian religious establishment was not independent of the state, the Islamic opposition in Egypt originated among lay members of society. Two dimensions of Islamic protest against Sadat's regime concern us here: The first is the university student movement; the second is the violent opposition on the part of organizations determined to overthrow the regime and replace it with an Islamic government.

As the hopes kindled by the relative success of the 1973 war with Israel began to recede in the bleak economic failure of the *infitah,* students in Egypt's teeming university campuses began to express their discontent through the formation of Islamic associations. Between 1974 and 1979, and again in the late 1980s and early 1990s, Islamic student associations gained control of most of the student organizations of Egypt's major universities. In part, the success of the Islamic student associations rested with their ability to identify the unsuitable conditions of campus life, to propose changes to them, and to place those changes within an Islamic frame of reference. For example, the groups campaigned for separate classrooms for male and female students on the grounds that the existing overcrowded circumstances subjected female students to harassment. They also encouraged the adoption of Islamic attire and sought to ban alcohol and Western music concerts from the campuses. In addition, Islamic student associations formed off-campus study groups, distributed free copies of professors' lecture booklets, and offered a sense of belonging to the thousands of young people who had come from small towns and villages to the large cities.

The attraction of the Islamic student groups rested in part with their ability to provide services and acceptable social settings in which young Muslims could meet. But the associations also offered hope that society could be changed and student prospects improved. The lack of employment opportunities for even the most successful students engendered a bitterness toward Sadat's regime: "Once the ex-student has acquired a diploma . . . he will then work each morning as an underpaid state employee, and spend the afternoon moonlighting as an amateur plumber, [as] a taxi driver who knows neither the streets nor the routes, or [as] some sort of jobber."[11] In drawing attention to the intolerable conditions on the university campuses and the bleak futures of university graduates, and in proposing to change those circumstances by the Islamization of society, the Islamic student organizations touched a raw nerve and became a potent opposition force.

The second dimension to Egypt's Islamic protest movement was provided by militant underground organizations. By the late 1970s, there were as many as twenty such groups operating in Egypt, but two of them—al-Takfir wa al-Hijrah and al-Jihad—achieved special notoriety. Although there were differences between the two organizations, both of them found their ideological inspiration in the writings of Sayyid Qutb, a member of the Muslim Brotherhood who was executed by the Nasser regime in 1966. His *Ma'alim fi al-Tariq* (Signposts on the road), written while Qutb was in prison and published in 1964, stated that the primary function of government was to ensure the enforcement of God's law. As long as rulers carried out that function, it was incumbent upon Muslims to obey them. But once rulers ceased to base their legislation on the *shari'ah,* they and their governments were no longer Islamic—they were *jahiliyyah,* ignorant of Islam. Qutb argued that true Muslims were bound to disobey *jahiliyyah* governments and to destroy them by whatever means necessary in order to restore the *shari'ah.* Such governments, because they were non-Islamic, were legitimate objects of *jihad,* sacred struggle in the cause of Islam. In Qutb's view, the Nasser regime was in a state of *jahiliyyah;* in the view of his younger disciples, Sadat's government fell into the same category.

The programs of al-Takfir and al-Jihad called for the violent overthrow of Sadat's impious regime by a vanguard of purified Muslims who would then restore the *shari'ah.* Interviews conducted by Egyptian scholars revealed that the membership of the organizations, though comprising a share of semiliterate slum dwellers, was dominated by university students and recent graduates, many of whom had achieved entry into the most demanding— and the most secular—faculties, such as medicine, pharmacy, and engineering. These students and graduates tended to come from small towns and villages to urban universities, where they experienced the alienation of city life. They turned to the Islamic associations of their upbringing as an anchor in a society they found morally confusing and economically unpromising. Their disillusionment over their prospects for employment and their search for an Islamic alternative to the society in which they should have achieved status and opportunity, but had not, stood as a glaring condemnation of the failure of the state to offer them hope for the future.

In 1977, members of al-Takfir wa al-Hijrah took hostage a former minister of religious endowments in order to force the release of imprisoned members of their organization. When the government refused to deal with the kidnappers, they killed their hostage. The regime retaliated by arresting and executing the leaders of al-Takfir and imprisoning scores of young Islamic militants. From that point until the death of Sadat, his regime and the Islamic organizations were in open confrontation. When Egypt signed the treaty with Israel in 1979, the leaders of al-Jihad condemned Sadat for surrendering Jerusalem to the Jews. The organization claimed that Sadat was an infidel, that he was in a state of *jahiliyyah* and was a ruler to whom the duty of *jihad* applied. His assassination in October 1981 by members of al-Jihad was intended to remove a non-Islamic despot and to usher in a popular revolution that would lead to the establishment of a proper Islamic state. Although there were disturbances in several cities following Sadat's death, there were no mass uprisings and the central state survived intact.

Under President Mubarak, the Islamic organizations continued their activities, and Egyptian society at large continued to demand the restoration of Islam to a prominent position in public life. Although the violence of the radical minority groups subsided during the 1980s, the attraction of Islam as a mainstream opposition movement increased. The Muslim Brotherhood, once the spearhead of Islamic militancy, became the representative of the moderate, centrist Islamic political movement. It expanded its influence on university campuses and gained control of the boards of the leading professional organizations (physicians, lawyers, and engineers). In keeping with its original mission, the brotherhood also worked with volunteer organizations engaged in medical, educational, and social welfare activities. Although the regime prohibited any religious organization from becoming a recognized political party, some members of the Muslim Brotherhood gained parliamentary seats by running as independents. By the late 1980s, deputies from the brotherhood and sympathizers from the legal parties formed the largest opposition bloc in parliament. This provided them with a public forum in which to express their demands for the revision of Egypt's secular statutes. The government responded to these pressures by pledging to review existing laws to see that they conformed to the *shariʿah* and by banning alcohol in all nontourist areas. Such gestures may have demonstrated the government's awareness of the latent power of the Islamic impulse within society, but they did nothing to resolve the causes of popular disaffection that led to the Islamic resurgence in the first place. As the regime tinkered ineffectively at the edges of Egypt's problems, ever-greater numbers of Egyptians embraced the possibility of an Islamic-inspired solution to the economic hardships, social malaise, and cultural alienation for which the secular state was held responsible.

Conclusion

The revolution that swept aside the regime of Muhammad Reza Shah in the final months of 1978 has been described as "one of the greatest populist explosions in human history."[12] During the Muharram demonstrations of December, millions of Iranians joined in protest marches against the shah. Denouncing the secular, authoritarian, and corrupt monarchy of the Pahlavis and its U.S. sponsors, the demonstrators demanded the return of Ayatollah Khomeini and the creation of an Islamic government, a combination they believed would bring about social justice, economic equality, political freedom, and sovereign independence. The Shiᶜa religious network, though battered by five decades of Pahlavi secularism and oppression, had remained intact and was available to direct the popular protest and to ensure that it was expressed through an Islamic idiom. Two intertwining sentiments were at work in the revolution: a desire for social, political, and economic change; and a belief that such change could be effected only by the renewal of an Islamic order.

The desire for the reconstitution of Islamic cultural traditions cut across classes and generations, yet there was a decided difference of opinion on the degree to which historical Islamic institutions should be implemented. Moderate liberal reformers favored the restoration of Islamic cultural values in combination with secular governing institutions. But they were overwhelmed by the religious establishment and the popular support the ulama obtained for revolutionary change.

Although Iran provides a unique example of a Muslim religious establishment's using Islam to bring about revolutionary political and social transformation, it was not the only case of Islamic protest against existing regimes. In all Islamic states, from Indonesia to Morocco, the 1970s and 1980s witnessed popular demands for the restoration of the *shariᶜah* and the renewal of the Islamic heritage. The failure of the independent regimes of the post–World War II era to solve pressing social and economic problems through the imitation of foreign models of development created a growing sense of popular disillusionment with external ideologies. Members of the general public, through such gestures as wearing Islamic dress, expressed their desire for the restoration of an Islamic social order, an order in which religion governed human relations and in which rulers were expected to govern in accordance with the principles of divine law. The belief in the need to restore an Islamic social order went beyond a popular desire to assert the authenticity of Islamic cultural traditions; it was also a belief that the essence of Islam was a divinely ordained system. In copying Western institutions, Muslims had abandoned the pattern of existence that God had commanded them to follow. Only by restoring, in a modern context, the divinely ordained social order would Muslim states experience prosperity and harmony.

The strength of the Islamic resurgence, and evidence that it was more than a passing phenomenon, was demonstrated in the Sudan, where Islamists seized power in 1989, and in the populous North African Arab state of Algeria. During the first round of Algerian parliamentary elections, held in December 1991, the voters rejected the National Liberation Front that had ruled the country as a single party for nearly thirty years and gave 82 percent of the seats to the Islamic Salvation Front, an avowedly religious party that pledged to reinstitute the *shariʿah*. The Islamic Salvation Front was expected to win the runoff elections scheduled for January 1992 and to gain a decisive parliamentary majority. However, the military intervened and declared the elections null and void, plunging that country into a horrible period of bloodshed and chaos. Nevertheless, supporters of the Islamic movement in the Middle East received the news of the Algerian election results with great enthusiasm and predicted that they would be repeated elsewhere in the Islamic world.

Notes

1. Shaul Bakhash, *The Reign of the Ayatollahs: Iran and the Islamic Revolution* (New York, 1986), p. 4.

2. Mangol Bayat, "Islam in Pahlavi and Post-Pahlavi Iran: A Cultural Revolution?" in John L. Esposito, ed., *Islam and Development: Religion and Sociopolitical Change* (Syracuse, 1980), p. 100.

3. Bakhash, *The Reign of the Ayatollahs*, p. 38.

4. Ervand Abrahamian, *Iran Between Two Revolutions* (Princeton, 1982), p. 516.

5. Cited in the introduction by Rouhollah K. Ramazani to the publication of the constitution of the Islamic Republic of Iran in *Middle East Journal*, vol. 34 (Spring 1980), p. 182. Future references to the Iranian constitution will be to this edition.

6. Bakhash, *The Reign of the Ayatollahs*, pp. 225–226.

7. Cited in Moojan Momen, *An Introduction to Shiʿi Islam: The History and Doctrines of Twelver Shiʿsm* (New Haven, 1985), p. 207.

8. See Richard W. Cottam, "Inside Revolutionary Iran," *Middle East Journal*, vol. 43 (Spring 1989), pp. 168–185.

9. Fadwa El Guindi, "The Killing of Sadat and After: A Current Assessment of Egypt's Islamic Movement," *Middle East Insight*, vol. 2 (January-February 1982), cited in John L. Esposito, *Islam and Politics* (Syracuse, 1984), p. 205.

10. John Alden Williams, "Veiling in Egypt as a Political and Social Phenomenon," in John L. Esposito, ed., *Islam and Development: Religion and Sociopolitical Change* (Syracuse, 1980), p. 83.

11. Gilles Kepel, *The Prophet and Pharaoh: Muslim Extremism in Egypt*, translated by Jon Rothschild (London, 1985), p. 135.

12. Cottam, "Inside Revolutionary Iran," p. 168.

The Arabian Peninsula in the Petroleum Era | 21

In the immediate post–World War II years, the states of the Arabian Peninsula were marginal to the main political and diplomatic issues that dominated the Middle East. Impoverished, sparsely populated, and ruled by traditional monarchs with few resources, they were of little international concern except to Britain, which had secured treaty relations with them in order to protect the route to India, and to a few Western companies that had begun exploring for oil in the 1930s. Within three decades, however, these desert states had achieved the highest per capita incomes in the world and become crucial participants in the global economy.

Oil was the resource that transformed the Arabian Peninsula from an isolated preserve of Britain to an area of world attention. The oil wealth was used on the one hand to generate enormous material and social changes in the producing states and on the other hand to prevent changes in the existing political order. The oil states presented seemingly contradictory patterns of modernization and conservatism, of rapid development coupled with political restrictions and the preservation of monarchical rule. Envied and often reviled by their more radical Arab neighbors, they were also courted by the rulers of these same states for their ability to provide copious financial assistance. For the most prosperous oil-producing states, financial aid was a tool of diplomacy designed to silence potential critics and keep restless neighbors from acts of aggression. Despite their vast wealth, the oil-producing states were unable to translate their economic power into military strength. Lacking population reserves and industrial technology, they were forced to depend on external patrons to protect their independence. The external power most willing and able to offer military assistance was the United States; but the United States also provided military and economic aid to Israel. How could the Arab oil producers balance their dependence on U.S. military protection with their responsibilities as Arab states? Even within the Arab and Islamic worlds, their position was precarious. How could they, as conservative monarchies, be sympathetic toward the social revolutions in Egypt, Syria, and Iraq or toward the Islamic revolution that swept non-Arab Iran? Yet how could they ignore these neighbors, with their large armies and their rhetoric of social egalitarianism? These were but a few of the dilemmas the states of the Arabian Peninsula faced as they went from isolated poverty to international financial prominence.

The Kingdom of Saudi Arabia

Patterns of Rule and Foreign Policy to 1973

Unlike the Pahlavi dynasty of Iran or the Hashimite monarchies of Iraq and Jordan, the al-Saʿud family had deep roots in the history of the country over which it ruled. The Saʿudis joined their tribal military forces with the puritanical Islamic ideology of Muhammad ibn Abd al-Wahhab in the eighteenth century to form a confederation that seized control of the holy cities of Mecca and Medina from the Ottoman authorities. Although defeated by Muhammad Ali of Egypt, the family retained a regional power base and reemerged in the twentieth century under the dynamic leadership of Abd al-Aziz ibn al-Saʿud, who created the kingdom that bore his family name (see Chapters 7 and 11).

King Ibn Saʿud introduced significant changes into the lives of his subjects, not the least of which was the establishment of a central government in place of regional tribal confederations. Yet even as he forged a state, Ibn Saʿud continued to adhere to a patriarchal style of rule. He made all policy decisions, large and small, and the institutions of government reflected his dominance. At the time of his death in 1953, the kingdom had no constitution, no codes of governmental procedure, no political parties, and no institutionalized forms of consultation. Islam was the ideology through which Ibn Saʿud legitimized the right of his family to rule. The Quran was the constitution, and the *shariʿah* was the law.

The kingdom's founder was succeeded by one of his many sons, Saʿud, the least competent of the four sons who have ruled since his death. King Saʿud's reign (1953–1964) coincided with the emergence of Egyptian president Nasser's appeal to secular Pan-Arabism and socialism, doctrines that posed a challenge to the Islamic and monarchical foundations on which Saʿudi rule rested. In addition, domestic changes created by the expansion of the petroleum industry and the wealth it generated further threatened the conservative social and political order that was the basis of the royal family's support. King Saʿud was ill equipped to deal with these challenges. He opted for hostility toward Nasser during the peak of the Egyptian president's popularity, a policy that isolated the kingdom in the Arab world and made its royal family a target of Nasser's attacks on "feudal reactionaries." Moreover, King Saʿud made no distinction between the state treasury and the royal purse, squandering millions of dollars on personal indulgences. His financial irresponsibility drove the state to the brink of bankruptcy, his lack of leadership in foreign policy exposed the kingdom to attack from the radical Arab states, and his behavior became an embarrassment to the royal family. In 1964 a coalition of family members deposed him in favor of Crown Prince Faysal.

Faysal's reign (1964–1975) transformed Saudi Arabia's administration, armed forces, educational system, and regional stature. Faysal made the fateful decision in 1973 to introduce the oil embargo, a decision that had the unanticipated results of turning the desert kingdom into a global financial power and making it an object of intense international scrutiny. In some ways, Faysal's modernization program was a reflection of the policies adopted by the Ottoman and Egyptian reformers of the nineteenth century. The king sought to broaden the role of government in order to be able to manage effectively the economic development of the country and to administer the far-reaching social welfare programs he wished to establish.

In order to train individuals to staff the new positions in the bureaucracy, Faysal began a program of educational expansion. New university campuses, both religious and secular, were constructed, and thousands of young Saudis were sent abroad to study, mainly at U.S. universities. Faysal then made sure that the new ministries and service agencies were staffed by graduates from the local and foreign universities. Although the new Western-educated elite achieved wider managerial responsibilities, they were excluded from the decisionmaking process. The king and selected members of the royal family, operating in conditions of extreme secrecy, determined the direction of state policy. Members of the new administrative elite were frustrated by their lack of participation in decisionmaking, yet they were nonetheless co-opted into accepting the traditional political order: They were awarded high offices within the bureaucracy and benefited from the wealth and prestige that went with their positions. As long as the Saudi royal system provided them with rewards for their advanced educational training, they were prepared to support that system and to accept the political constraints it embodied.

Yemen as an Issue in
Saudi Foreign and Domestic Policy

The most persistent and most immediately threatening foreign policy issue facing the Saudi regime from the early 1960s to the late 1970s was related to developments in the neighboring country of Yemen (see Map 21.1). In September 1962, factions within the Yemeni armed forces carried out a coup against the monarch, Imam Muhammad al-Badr. Inspired and supported by Nasser, the coup leaders abolished the monarchy and proclaimed the existence of the Yemen Arab Republic. However, the rebels had failed to capture Imam Muhammad, and when he surfaced in the northern region of the country and began rallying tribes in support of his return to the throne, Yemen was plunged into civil war. Neither the republicans nor the royalists

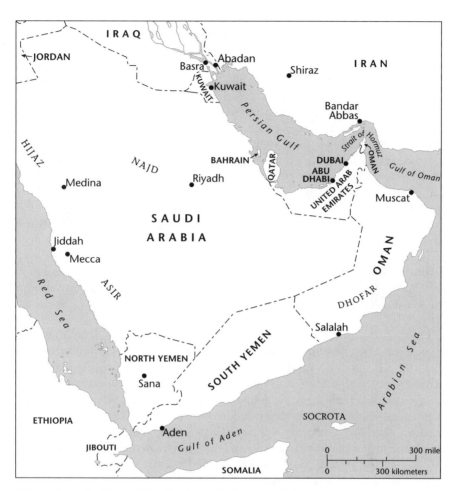

Map 21.1 Arabia and the Persian Gulf in the Mid-1970s

could achieve victory, and each party turned to outside powers for support, thereby transforming a civil war in the southern tip of Arabia into a regional conflict.

As discussed in Chapter 15, the republican regime of Abdallah al-Sallal received military assistance from Nasser, whereas the royalists in the north were aided by the Saudi government. Egyptian intervention was direct and substantial; by 1966, Egyptian forces in Yemen numbered nearly 70,000, and on several occasions the Egyptian air force bombed Saudi border towns. King Faysal refused to commit Saudi troops to the conflict for fear they would be defeated, and Saudi aid was therefore confined to providing subsidies and weapons to the royalist forces. Although the immediate Egyptian threat to the Saudi regime was ended by Nasser's agreement to withdraw his troops following the June War, developments in south Arabia continued to threaten the security of the Saudi monarchy.

In 1967 Britain withdrew from the Aden Protectorate and was immediately replaced by a Marxist National Liberation Front that established the People's Democratic Republic of South Yemen and pledged its support for the overthrow of all the traditional monarchies in the Arabian Peninsula. The Saudi regime thus faced two hostile Yemens, both of them with radical governments, both of them supported by the Soviet Union, and both of them committed to the establishment of republican forms of rule. King Faysal responded to this danger by mending fences with the northern Yemen Arab Republic and attempting to foment discord between it and the People's Republic of the south. Faysal's policy created an extremely complicated set of circumstances in which the northern republic accepted Saudi economic assistance and sometimes engaged in armed clashes with the People's Republic yet at other times pursued the goal of unifying the two Yemens. Although the north and south signed a unity agreement in 1979, their turbulent domestic politics prevented its implementation. Throughout the 1980s, the two Yemens viewed one another, and Saudi Arabia, with suspicion.

The radicalization of the Yemens and the emergence of popular liberation movements elsewhere in the peninsula prompted King Faysal to increase the size and efficiency of Saudi Arabia's armed forces. The confrontation in Yemen revealed that the Saudi military was not a credible deterrent against Egyptian and Yemeni aggression and raised the possibility that it might not even be capable of putting down a determined internal uprising. The government therefore embarked on an intensive program to expand the kingdom's military capability. The defense budget increased to over $2 billion in 1970 and rose steadily in the years that followed. During the 1970s, the Saudis allocated between 35 and 40 percent of their total annual revenues to defense and security expenditures. This percentage remained constant even as Saudi revenues soared, so that in the fiscal year 1975–76 the kingdom allocated nearly $36 billion for defense and security purposes. The government endeavored to acquire the most sophisticated military technology that could be purchased, giving special priority to the air force, regardless of whether the Saudi forces had the capability to operate and maintain it. The main beneficiary of this military spending spree was the United States, which concluded several lucrative weapons system contracts with the Saudis in the 1970s and 1980s.

The royal family was fully aware that young military officers had led the coups that overthrew the kings of Egypt and Iraq. The regime therefore kept the armed forces under close supervision and made sure that senior officers were appointed from among the Sa⁣ᶜudi family. Despite the vast sums devoted to the military, the kingdom was unable to build an armed force that could compare with that of either Iraq or Iran, the two most powerful potential regional antagonists. In any crisis that depended on military might alone, the Saudi state was bound to be ineffective. This was demonstrated by the Iraqi invasion of Kuwait in 1990 and the Saudis' speedy request for direct U.S. military assistance.

The Oil Embargo of 1973 and Its Consequences

In order to understand the extent to which the oil embargo and the oil price increases of 1973 changed the world economy and catapulted Saudi Arabia into prominence as a global financial power, we should review the arrangements that existed between the Saudis and the foreign oil companies prior to 1973. The kingdom's first oil concession was granted by Ibn Saᶜud in 1933 to the Standard Oil Company of California (later reorganized as the Arabian American Oil Company, ARAMCO), which acquired the right to extract and transport whatever petroleum was found within its concession in exchange for the construction of a refinery and the payment of royalties amounting to four gold shillings per ton of crude oil. The terms of the concession were immensely favorable to ARAMCO. Oil was discovered in the eastern province of Dahran in 1938, but major commercial production did not take place until after World War II. During the 1950s, the concession agreements were modified so that Saudi Arabia and most other Middle Eastern oil producers received 50 percent of the profits from the foreign companies. However, the oil-producing countries had little say in determining prices or production levels. ARAMCO emerged as a giant multinational corporation that controlled not only the exploration and extraction of Saudi oil but also its refining, marketing, and pricing.

In an attempt to gain a greater measure of control over pricing policies, representatives from five of the major producing countries—Iran, Iraq, Kuwait, Saudi Arabia, and Venezuela—founded the Organization of Petroleum Exporting Countries in 1960. The organization later expanded to include thirteen nations. A parallel group, the Organization of Arab Petroleum Exporting Countries (OAPEC), composed solely of Arab oil exporters, was created in 1968. The impulse behind the formation of the two organizations was a desire on the part of the member states to assert control of their most valuable natural resource. For the Middle Eastern states in particular, the issue was independence. OPEC was founded in the Nasser era, and one of the principal goals of Nasserism was to break out of the constraints of postwar neocolonialism that found the Western powers still manipulating the diplomatic and economic affairs of the Arab world. OPEC's immediate objective was to utilize the collective-bargaining power of its member states to pressure the Western oil companies to increase oil prices. But as long as the world supply of oil was plentiful, OPEC had limited success in its efforts to change the policies and attitudes of the oil companies.

Abundant, low-cost oil was the energy source that fueled the postwar recovery of Europe and Japan and assured the economic prominence of the United States. With the rise of gasoline-fueled automobiles and diesel-powered trains and the mounting use of oil to supply energy for industry, economies that had previously been based on coal were transformed to depend on oil. This transformation was based on the assumption that oil would always be readily available and moderately priced. During the late 1960s and early 1970s, the assumption was borne out as the industrial states enjoyed a period of rapid economic growth made possible by an ever-increasing supply of cheap oil. However, the industrial world's avid consumption of oil made it more dependent on Middle Eastern petroleum producers. As world demand for oil rose, the Middle East came to supply an ever-greater percentage of the demand. This was especially true for Japan and Western Europe, areas that either had no oil of their own or had oil that was extremely costly to extract (as in the case of the North Sea reserves). As a result of this reliance on low-cost petroleum, Saudi Arabia supplied 21.6 percent of Europe's oil requirements in 1972 and 13 percent of the world's total production of crude oil in 1973. Even the United States, a major producer and the world's largest consumer of petroleum, became dependent on imported oil. Saudi Arabia's share of U.S. oil imports in 1973 was 8.1 percent.[1]

In these circumstances of growing U.S., European, and Japanese dependence on Middle Eastern petroleum, a gradual restructuring of the industry started to take place. Led by demands from the shah of Iran, prices began to edge upward in the late 1960s, and some of the producing countries attained partial control over pricing and production levels. Despite these changes, the world was unprepared for the decision of the Arab producers to deploy their oil weapon as an instrument of diplomacy. In the midst of the Arab-Israeli war of October 1973, the United States engaged in an extensive airlift of military supplies to Israel, and President Richard Nixon requested that Congress approve a $2.2 billion appropriation for military assistance to Israel. Saudi Arabia responded to these actions by declaring an embargo on all oil shipments to the United States and the Netherlands (the latter was targeted primarily because of Rotterdam's importance as a port of entry and distribution center for oil destined for other parts of Europe). In addition, the Saudis and other Arab oil producers announced that they would cut back on oil production and reduce the amounts available to the consuming countries. These announcements created panic and confusion within the industrial states. A scramble to purchase non-Arab oil took place, and prices began to rise. In November 1973 the political leverage of the oil weapon became apparent as the European Economic Community and Japan both issued statements affirming Palestinian rights and urging Israeli withdrawal from the territories occupied in 1967. In the months that followed, previously underpriced petroleum began to find its true market value. OPEC set the price at $11.65 per barrel effective January 1, 1974; a year earlier the price had been $2.74. The effect of the price increases on Saudi revenues was dramatic. In the year before the price hikes, the kingdom earned $6.4 billion in oil revenues; in the fiscal year 1974–75, Saudi revenues skyrocketed by 330 percent to $27.7 billion. During 1981, when oil prices peaked at $34 per barrel, Saudi Arabia's oil revenues were an astounding $102 billion. The kingdom was awash in funds.

The embargo of 1973 set in motion a series of other significant developments within the petroleum industry, most notably the increased participation by OPEC countries in the ownership of oil-producing operations and their involvement in such downstream activities as refining, distributing, and marketing. However, the giant foreign oil companies did not disappear. They provided the technology and expertise on which the producers still depended, and their services were retained through lease-back arrangements and joint ventures with the local national oil companies. ARAMCO thus remained a prominent factor in the national life of Saudi Arabia.

Rapid Development After 1973

As the major Arab oil producer and a world petroleum and financial power, Saudi Arabia's regional and international stature was transformed after 1973. The kingdom could no longer avoid involvement in the Arab-Israeli issue and tried to maintain a balance between its desire not to alienate the United States, a major consumer of oil and supplier of military equipment, and its need to maintain common cause with the Palestinians and the regimes that supported them. The judicious distribution of oil wealth became an important instrument of Saudi diplomacy; Syria and the PLO received generous financial support from the Saudis in exchange for muting their criticism of the royal regime and its ties to the United States. Although the Saudi government preferred to buy off potential enemies rather than fight them, it viewed the Iranian revolution of 1979 as such a major threat that it embarked on another huge arms buildup. Billions of Saudi petrodollars were used to purchase sophisticated military equipment, to construct elaborate air-defense systems, and to increase the size of the domestic security agencies as well as the regular army, navy, and air force. Once again, the United States acted as the major arms supplier to the kingdom.

In addition to devoting huge sums to defense, King Faysal and his successors decided to use the kingdom's abundant oil wealth to launch a massive program of economic and social development. Members of the royal family tended to view the transformation of the country as a single procedure, a kind of technical exercise that would instantly transform underdevelopment into modernity. They therefore believed that it could be undertaken without upsetting the conservative social structure and Islamic value system on which the regime's authority depended. This assumption overlooked the possible changes in attitude that might be generated by the importation of foreign workers and technology and the creation of an indigenous, university-educated middle class.[2]

The implementation of the new development plans had just begun when King Faysal was assassinated in 1975 by one of his nephews. His successor, Khalid (1975–1982), was an inexperienced administrator and often in poor health. He delegated much of his authority to Crown Prince Fahd, who assumed major responsibility for the kingdom's affairs and became king after Khalid's death. Faysal was the last of the Saᶜudi monarchs to exercise full royal decisionmaking powers; his successors ruled through collective agreements reached among leading members of the royal family, a process that occasionally made it difficult to set clear policy directions.

But the existence of tensions within the ruling family did not prevent Saudi Arabia from embarking on an unprecedented decade of development that included expansion in all areas of the country's infrastructure, from transportation and communications to petroleum facilities, from the construction of architecturally stunning university campuses to the creation of desalinization plants and secondary industries. Material development and social change also brought pressures for political change.

One potential source for new ideas was represented by the large number of foreign workers employed in the kingdom to offset Saudi Arabia's acute shortage of manpower. Population statistics on the number of native Saudis are much disputed, especially because the government was in the habit of inflating them for planning and security purposes. Estimates of the native Saudi population for the year 1980 range from 4.59 million to 11.5 million. Nadav Safran's investigation into the subject led him to favor the lower figures, and his own estimate for the year 1980 is 5 million.[3] Imported labor was essential to carry out the infrastructure transformation the Saudi leadership envisaged. By 1980 there were 2.1 million foreign workers in the country with some 400,000 dependents. The largest group, about 1 million, came from North Yemen. Egyptians and Palestinians from Jordan and the occupied territories numbered about 200,000 each, and there were over 50,000 Asians, mainly Filipinos and Pakistanis. Of the 100,000 Westerners resident in the country, about 40,000 were from the United States and 25,000 from Britain. The presence of such large numbers of foreigners, many of whom held values that differed from those on which the Saudi royal order rested and who practiced patterns of living that were contrary to Islamic principles, led the regime to attempt to isolate its foreign residents. Westerners were concentrated mainly in the huge ARAMCO compound near the eastern oil fields. Other foreigners were closely monitored by Saudi security agencies and were quickly deported if they showed signs of troublesome activity.

Saudi Arabia's rapid modernization created a new indigenous middle-class elite of teachers, civil servants, private businessmen, and military officers. Despite this elite's education and its growing responsibility in managing the machinery of government, its members were excluded from participation in political life. The royal family maintained its tight control over decisionmaking and refused to sanction political parties, labor unions, or other interest groups. In the early 1980s, King Fahd proclaimed, as had Faysal and Khalid earlier, his intention of introducing a basic charter of rights and establishing a national consultative chamber. However, the king did not act on these promises. By refusing to share power or to open up the political process, the royal family ran the risk of alienating the new middle class that was a product of the regime's program of rapid modernization. The regime hoped to survive by rewarding the new elite with well-paying positions and providing the population at large with generous social welfare services.

In some respects, the Saudi Arabia of the early 1980s appeared similar to Iran in the final years of the shah's rule. Both countries experienced extensive economic, educational, and military development without a corresponding change in politics. The emerging Western-educated elite were denied channels through which to express their aspirations or their grievances. However, there existed a marked difference in the ways in which the shah and the Saudi royal family related to the official religious establishments of their two countries. This difference helps explain the stability of the Saudi system through the 1980s.

Islam and the Saudi State

Saudi Arabia projected to the outside world the image of a puritanical Islamic regime. Ibn Sa‘ud had consolidated his power by blending the strict creed of Wahhabi Islam with the fighting prowess of the Bedouin tribesmen. The rule of his successors was legitimized by their defense of Islamic beliefs and values. The House of Sa‘ud was allowed to govern because it claimed to be bound by the Quran and the *shari‘ah* and committed to enforcing them. King Faysal, justifying his decision not to issue a charter of rights, stated that "Sa‘udi Arabia has no need for a constitution because it has the Quran, which is the oldest and most efficient constitution in the world."[4] By posing as the protector of Islam, the royal family justified its monopoly of power.

Even during the period of rapid social and economic change inaugurated by Faysal and continued by his successors, the royal family's association with Islam remained its principal legitimizing factor. This association was made possible by the existence of a mutually beneficial relationship between the monarchy and the religious establishment. The relationship was established by Ibn Sa‘ud, who gradually eased the ulama out of policymaking authority and placed them on the payroll of the state. The ulama accepted their incorporation into the state bureaucracy and acknowledged the Saᶜudis' right to rule. In exchange, they were permitted to retain extensive influence over education, the legal system, and the supervision of public morality. In contrast to the situation in Nasser's Egypt, the ulama in Saudi Arabia continued to have recognized authority in important spheres of public activity; and in contrast to the situation in the shah's Iran, they were not independent of the state but neither were they attacked by it. Their status was respected, and the Saudi kings made a point of seeking their approval for policies that might affect the Islamic standing of the royal family. However, the ulama were not instrumental in the formulation of state policy as a whole.

The ulama could accept their exclusion from the realm of foreign policy and petroleum development because of the leverage they retained in their traditional spheres of activity. They had the power to withhold approval of sensitive domestic policies and thus to call into question the Islamic legitimacy of such policies and of the ruling house that proposed them. This power, and the favorable concessions it could bring from the state, was evident during Faysal's tenure as crown prince and king. Faysal introduced sweeping educational changes, but he allowed the ulama to set the moral tone of the system, agreeing to the inclusion of courses in Islamic religion at all levels of instruction. In 1960 Faysal's plan to introduce public education for females met with strong opposition from the religious establishment. Faysal insisted on the adoption of his policy, but he permitted the ulama to supervise the classroom arrangements and he appointed members of the religious establishment to pivotal positions in the Ministry of Education. The modernization of the Saudi educational program was carefully designed to cater to ulama preferences on curriculum content, the separation of sexes in the classrooms even in the "secular" universities, and the provision of mosque facilities within the new campuses. Another example of the concessions the ulama could wrest from the royal family arose from Faysal's proposal to bring television to the kingdom in 1963. Although the religious establishment objected to this innovation, Faysal introduced it anyway. But as a compromise he permitted the ulama to monitor the programming.

The ulama also retained a central role in the supervision of public behavior. They controlled the Morality Police, an organization that assumed increasing power after King Faysal's death. Originally responsible for ensuring the observance of such Islamic practices as the closure of shops during the hours of prayer and the wearing of proper attire by women, the Morality Police were allowed in the early 1980s to expand their authority to monitor the activities of foreigners resident in the kingdom and to propagate Islamic doctrines among the rural population. The religious establishment was also in charge of the annual pilgrimage, a ritual that emphasized the Islamic character of the kingdom. Thus, the royal family determined overall policy but granted the ulama sufficient authority to satisfy their demands and to guarantee their support for the House of Saᶜud as legitimate Islamic rulers.

Although the regime endeavored to project an image of piety, the behavior of individual princes tarnished the reputation of the royal family as a whole and made a mockery of its claims to conform to the standards of Islamic behavior. As the family grew and became more diverse—there were approximately 5,000 royal princes by the early 1980s—it lost the single-minded sense of purpose that had been its strength, and it proved unable or unwilling to control the activities of all of its members. The gap between the image of public morality and the reality of private behavior led opponents of the regime to accuse it of hypocrisy.

The most vivid example of religiously based discontent within the kingdom was the seizure of the Grand Mosque of Mecca in 1979. The seizure was led by Juhayman al-Utaybi, a former officer in the National Guard. Inspired by Wahhabi doctrine and disillusioned over what he saw as the corruption and materialism of the Saudi rulers, Juhayman attracted a following among youths, many of them university dropouts, who had been marginalized by modernization. During the pilgrimage in November 1979, Juhayman and a few hundred well-armed supporters occupied the Grand Mosque in Mecca and used the mosque's public address system to broadcast accusations of corruption against the government and the ulama. The occupation lasted for two weeks, during which the government sought and eventually obtained a decree from the ulama authorizing the use of armed force to break the siege. Dislodging the determined occupiers without destroying the holiest shrine in Islam proved a difficult task and cost many lives on both sides. Juhayman finally surrendered, and he and his surviving followers were later executed. His movement received no overt support within the country, but it alarmed the Saudi authorities because it represented a failure of their domestic intelligence services and damaged the reputation of the regime.

The Mecca incident revealed the vulnerability of the royal family to charges of impiety. The accusations of corruption Juhayman's followers broadcast during the siege did not go unnoticed. The scandalous and offensive behavior of some of the wealthy princes threatened to make the royal family appear unfaithful to the Islamic standards it used to legitimize its right to rule. If the family could not live up to the Islamic principles it professed to defend, then it might be deemed unworthy of the ulama's support; and the withdrawal of the religious establishment's backing might embolden the new middle classes to demand a voice in the decisionmaking councils of the kingdom.

Kuwait, Oman, and the Smaller Gulf States

At the head of the Persian Gulf, tucked between Saudi Arabia and Iraq, lies the state of Kuwait, one of the wealthiest nations in the world during the 1970s and 1980s. The southern end of the Gulf is dominated by Oman, a large and geographically diverse country also rich in petroleum resources. In between these two states are several small desert principalities—Bahrain,

Qatar, and the seven members of the United Arab Emirates (UAE). Beneath the sands and seas of Saudi Arabia and these eleven Gulf states lies 50 percent of the world's proven reserves of oil. Because of their petroleum resources, the states of the Gulf have been transformed from local subsistence economies with marginal diplomatic status into enormously wealthy states with substantial international influence. The affluence the Gulf states have acquired since the 1950s has helped enable their ruling families to strengthen their political authority. In an age that has largely abandoned the concept of government directed by hereditary royal families, the Gulf states stand out as exceptions.

Most of the family dynasties that ruled the Gulf states in the early 1990s were established in the mid-eighteenth century. Their survival and their acquisition of power was facilitated by a combination of British imperialism, oil concession agreements, and the vast revenues that began in the post–World War II era. During the nineteenth century, Britain sought to protect the route to India by keeping European powers and the Ottomans out of the Gulf. It accomplished this objective through a series of treaties that bound the states of the region to agree that they would not enter into diplomatic relations with other powers without Britain's consent. In return, Britain pledged to protect the Gulf states from external aggression. Most of these treaties remained in effect, with modifications, until 1971 and secured Britain's dominant role in the Gulf. At the time the agreements were concluded, the Gulf rulers were scarcely more than tribal chieftains who had been empowered by local tribal leaders and merchants to negotiate with foreign powers on their behalf. However, Britain's policy of treating these rulers as heads of state—even if subservient ones—institutionalized their authority and gave them a recognized ruling identity. As signatories to the treaties, the rulers were expected to enforce the terms of the agreements and to assume the responsibilities imposed upon them.

The arrival in the 1930s of Western oil companies seeking concessions further consolidated the authority of the ruling families. In each state it was the reigning prince who negotiated directly with the companies and who signed the concessions. When commercial oil production began after 1945, the prince and his family reaped the benefits; his name, or his father's or uncle's or brother's, was on the concession agreement. The signatory represented the state, and when the oil wealth poured in, there was no distinction between the state and the ruler. Although there were certain variations to this historical pattern, most Gulf states took such a course.

Kuwait: Petroleum Giant

Kuwait was settled in the early eighteenth century by tribes migrating from the Najd region of Arabia. By 1756 Kuwait had become an autonomous principality headed by the al-Sabah family, whose rule continued into the

1990s. Kuwait, like most of the Gulf states, looked to the sea, and its economy was based on commerce, shipbuilding, and, above all, pearling. Kuwait City was the best harbor on the Gulf, and the merchants of the region developed it as a center for trade between India and parts of the Middle East. These activities brought wealth to the Kuwaiti merchant community, which then subsidized the al-Sabah ruling family. Before the existence of oil revenues, the rulers had little income of their own. They depended on the merchants to maintain them, in exchange for which they allowed the merchants to have a voice in decisionmaking.

The Ottoman sultans acknowledged the autonomy of the al-Sabah rulers but nevertheless claimed sovereignty over the territory of Kuwait, regarding it as the southernmost administrative unit of the province of Basra. As with many of their distant and loosely held lands, the Ottomans did not directly enforce their claim to Kuwait and were content to rely on the al-Sabah rulers to maintain order in their portion of the Gulf. This situation prevailed until the nineteenth century and the arrival of the British, with their policy of extracting treaties of protection from the Gulf rulers. In 1897, in a move designed to prevent Kuwait from falling within the British sphere of influence, Sultan Abdul Hamid II appointed its ruler, Mubarak I, to the post of district administrator. The appointment implied Mubarak's subordination to the Ottoman governor of Basra, a status he resisted by appealing to the British for assistance against the Ottoman attempts at control.

Britain responded with a show of naval force, a provocation the Ottomans could meet only with angry protests. Mubarak I then signed a treaty with the British (1899) in which he pledged not to enter into negotiations with other states before obtaining British approval; Britain had no such reciprocal obligations. On the eve of World War I, the British became concerned over German ambitions in the territory stretching from Baghdad to the Gulf and decided that an agreement with the Ottomans to secure future interests in that region was more important than exclusive control of Kuwait. In the Anglo-Ottoman Convention of 1913, Britain relinquished its hold on Kuwait in exchange for the right to participate in railroad development south of Baghdad and for an Ottoman pledge to withdraw from certain territories on the western shore of the Gulf. The convention recognized Kuwait as an autonomous Ottoman administrative district and referred to the al-Sabah ruler as an Ottoman district supervisor.

Ottoman suzerainty over Kuwait was short-lived. When the Ottomans allied with Germany in World War I, Britain considered the 1913 convention to be invalidated and proclaimed Kuwait an independent principality under British protection. It remained so until independence in 1961. At the end of the war, the British drew the frontiers separating Kuwait from the new mandate state of Iraq, unwittingly laying the groundwork for future controversies.

During the 1920s and 1930s, Kuwait experienced a wrenching economic decline that turned it into one of the most impoverished countries in the world. The pearling industry was undercut by the worldwide depression and then virtually destroyed by the introduction of the cultured pearl. Kuwait's plunge into poverty was halted by the arrival of the international oil companies. In 1934 the ruler, Ahmad al-Jabir al-Sabah (1921–1950), signed an agreement with Gulf Oil and British Petroleum authorizing them to become equal owners in a concession known as the Kuwait Oil Company. Within four years, the exploration teams discovered one of the largest pools of oil in the world. Commercial oil exports began in 1946, generating an income in that year of $760,000. By 1953, oil revenues were $169 million, and after the price increases of 1973, they rose dramatically, reaching $21.7 billion in 1980. Petroleum income thrust the former backwater pearling state of less than 1 million native inhabitants into prominence as a major financial power.

Kuwait in the oil age has been characterized by immense changes, four of which deserve special attention: a reversal in the financial and political relationship between the amir (the title of the ruler after independence in 1961) and the merchant community; the creation of a welfare state; the reliance on imported labor; and Kuwait's assumption of a new role as a player in Middle Eastern diplomacy and a focus of concern for the Western industrial powers.

Kuwait was fortunate in having Amir Abdallah al-Salim al-Sabah (1950–1965) to guide it through the first phase of change generated by oil wealth. Abdallah was a cautious and frugal ruler who negotiated independence from Britain in 1961, who defused the lure of Nasserism by creating a national assembly in 1962, and who understood that Kuwaiti oil revenues would better serve future generations by being invested rather than squandered on the ruling family. The major political challenge Abdallah faced was to resolve the changing pattern of relationships between the al-Sabah ruling family and the merchants who had previously been its financial patrons. As the ruling family's immense wealth freed it from dependence on the merchant community's monetary contributions, the family tended to exclude the merchants from its decisionmaking councils. In the face of merchant protests over their declining political fortunes, Amir Abdallah reached an agreement with them. He pledged to guarantee the leading merchant families a substantial share of the oil wealth that accrued to him as ruler. In exchange, the merchants renounced their claims to political power; they withdrew from political life in order to preserve their financial well-being. This process was in marked contrast to the relationships that emerged between the bourgeoisie and the monarchs in Western Europe.

Amir Abdallah sought to provide a limited forum for political discussion by the creation of an elected national assembly, which first convened in 1963. During the years of the assembly's existence (it was dissolved from 1976 to 1981 and again from 1986 to 1992), it was the only such body in the Gulf and exemplified Kuwait's unique political life. Although the franchise was severely restricted—only adult Kuwaiti males whose ancestors were resident in the country before 1920 could vote—and the size of the assembly was limited to fifty deputies, the very presence of the body gave Kuwait a special character. The regime's toleration of a moderate opposition in the national assembly and of a relatively free press and publishing industry made Kuwait the most intellectually vibrant and politically diverse state in the Gulf during the 1960s and 1970s.

However, the existence of a national assembly did not restrict the political authority of the ruling family. Although the institutions of constitutional democracy were in place, genuine power was reserved for the amir and his relatives. Key government posts ranging from the prime ministership to the most sensitive cabinet positions were held by members of the al-Sabah family, and state policy was determined in family councils, not through debate in the national assembly. Insofar as Kuwaitis participated in government, they did so through their positions in the civil service. Kuwait, like Saudi Arabia, rewarded its educated citizens with appointments to the bureaucracy and access to the generous benefits that were associated with such posts. The practice created overstaffing and inefficiency, but it also blunted political dissent by making officeholders part of the system.

The fragility of Kuwaiti democratic institutions was made clear during the ministerial crises of 1985 and 1986. In 1985 the national assembly exposed the financial corruption of the al-Sabah minister of justice and forced his resignation. The assembly also pressured another al-Sabah cabinet minister, who had probably used his position for personal gain, to resign. The ruling family would not tolerate this second challenge to its authority, and in 1986 the amir dissolved the national assembly and imposed press censorship. Promises to reconvene the assembly were not implemented until late 1992. The abrupt termination of Kuwait's experiment in limited representation demonstrated the al-Sabah family's power.

The second characteristic of Kuwait in the oil era was its ability to provide its citizens with a cradle-to-grave welfare system unequaled anywhere else in the world. Amir Abdallah and his successors, Amir Sabah al-Salim al-Sabah (1965–1977) and Amir Jabir Ahmad al-Sabah (1977–), distributed their oil wealth as a form of royal largesse. Their policies brought Kuwaiti citizens such benefits as free education, health care, transportation, and housing. Donors and recipients alike regarded these privileges as grants from the ruling family to its subjects. The citizens of Kuwait paid no taxes; they were part of a special society that received welfare benefits without contributing to them. As was the case in Saudi Arabia, the ruling family gave education a high priority in its welfare expenditures and poured huge sums of money into developing an advanced educational system. Kuwait University, founded in 1966, had an enrollment of about 10,000 students in the late 1980s, half of whom were women. Yet the Kuwaiti constitution denied women the right to vote, a restriction that highlighted the discrepancy between social development and political participation that was evident in Saudi Arabia and Iran as well as in other Gulf states.

Also like Saudi Arabia and most other Gulf states, Kuwait depended on a foreign work force to develop its petroleum industry and supporting infrastructure. By 1965, foreign residents outnumbered Kuwaitis, and by the mid-1980s it was estimated that out of the country's total population of 1.5 million, 60 percent were foreigners. The foreign domination of the Kuwaiti work force ranged across the employment spectrum from managers and professionals to blue-collar workers and menial laborers. Palestinians from the West Bank and Jordan constituted the largest group of non-Kuwaitis, numbering between 300,000 and 400,000 in the mid-1980s. The Kuwaiti government did not extend to the foreign workers the same benefits it granted Kuwaitis: Foreigners were denied the right to own land or homes and were subject to deportation without notice. The discrepancy between the privileged Kuwaitis and the expatriate workers was a source of tension within the country, especially at times of regional crisis.

Kuwait's reliance on the external world for its development and prosperity extended beyond the work force. The country was dependent on the West and Japan as markets for its oil; as sources for the technology and equipment that extracted the oil; and as suppliers of the expertise that planned, built, and operated its airports, university campuses, hospitals, and communications systems. Moreover, Kuwait's continued prosperity rested to a large extent upon other countries' stock markets and real estate values. Because Kuwait could not spend the vast revenues it accumulated after 1973, the government embarked on a program of overseas investment. The program was so successful that by the mid-1980s Kuwait's income from investments exceeded the revenue it earned from oil exports. The country's mix of investment income and oil revenue earned it the name "Kuwait Incorporated," a label that was not intended as a compliment.

The fourth characteristic of Kuwait in the oil age had several dimensions: To the industrial powers of the world, Kuwait was a stable monarchy with enormous oil reserves and vast overseas investments, all of which deserved protection; to its immediate powerful neighbors—Saudi Arabia, Iraq, and Iran—it was a state to be courted and possibly annexed; and to other states of the region, it was a potential source of largesse and an object of criticism. The amirs of Kuwait tried to balance these various challenges and opportunities. On the one hand, they maintained cordial relations with the states that purchased their country's petroleum. But on the other hand, they sought to preserve Kuwait's independence and their own rule by providing generous foreign aid to potential regional enemies. The government was sensitive to the presence of nearly 400,000 Palestinians in Kuwait and gave extensive financial assistance to the PLO and the Arab states bordering Israel. During the Iran-Iraq war, Kuwait provided Arab Iraq with billions of dollars worth of direct and indirect economic assistance. However, as demonstrated by the Iraqi invasion of Kuwait in 1990, the use of oil revenues as an instrument of diplomacy was no substitute for a credible military force, and a military was one institution that Kuwait's money could not create.

Oman

Oman commands a strategic position at the juncture of the Gulf of Oman and the Arabian Sea. Its Persian Gulf territory includes the Musandam Peninsula, the finger of land that juts into the Strait of Hormuz. Tankers transport most of the Gulf's oil through this narrow strait. Oman differs in several ways from the other Gulf states. It is a large and geographically diverse country with an agricultural base lacking in the desert principalities. Although the other Gulf states have a Sunni Muslim majority, most Omanis belong to the Ibadi sect of Islam. Oman is further distinguished from its neighbors by its nineteenth century history as a leading commercial power.

In 1744 the present ruling family, the Al Bu Saᶜid, established an independent dynasty in Oman. During the first half of the nineteenth century, the reigning sultan created a maritime empire that stretched from the east African coast to present-day Pakistan. Oman's most valuable overseas possession was Zanzibar, and in the 1850s the sultan established his residence there. With the arrival of European steamships and the suppression of the slave trade, Oman's economy declined sharply. The Al Bu Saᶜid sultans, forced by Britain to abandon Zanzibar, reestablished the royal residence in Muscat. By the end of the nineteenth century, Oman's rulers lost control of the interior of the country and were reduced to accepting loans from the British government to maintain their power on the coast. Although Oman did not surrender its independence to Britain, the sultans signed several treaties with British representatives and relied heavily on British advice and assistance.

For the first sixty years of the twentieth century, Oman was an isolated, impoverished, and inward-looking country. During the long reign of Sultan Saᶜid ibn Taymur (1932–1970), the British assisted the royal forces in regaining control over the tribal interior. Once his country was reunited, Sultan Saᶜid left the capital of Muscat and settled in a distant coastal town in Dhofar province. Ruling in a despotic, anachronistic manner, he lived as a virtual recluse, and his country became as isolated as he was. Even after oil exports began in 1964, Sultan Saᶜid refused to change his habits or his conservative policies. Toward the end of his reign, there were only three schools in the country and 6 miles (9.6 km) of paved roads.

In 1970 the sultan was overthrown in a palace coup led by his son Qabus, who then assumed the office of sultan. The most pressing domestic issue facing the new ruler was an expanding rebellion in the province of Dhofar. The rebellion had begun in 1964 as a popular protest against Saᶜid's autocratic and neglectful rule, but in the late 1960s Marxist groups took over the leadership and expanded the scope of the movement to embrace anti-monarchical, antiimperial goals. The Dhofar rebellion became a rallying point for republican forces throughout the Arabian Peninsula. China and the Soviet Union provided assistance to the rebels, and South Yemen offered sanctuary to those who fled the sultan's forces. Sultan Qabus received help from his fellow monarchs, the shah of Iran and the king of Jordan, both of whom sent contingents of troops to contain the spread of republicanism. In an attempt to win the loyalty of Dhofar's population, Qabus directed large sums of development funds to projects located in the province. His policy of reconciliation succeeded in defusing the rebellion, and a combined Iranian and Omani offensive defeated the rebel forces and reestablished the sultan's rule in 1976.

Sultan Qabus was educated in England and was determined to transform his nation. Although Oman's oil revenues—$1.7 billion in 1978—were much lower than Kuwait's, they were sufficient to enable Qabus to launch an extensive program of infrastructure development. Schools and highways were quickly constructed, and the capital city, Muscat, underwent a rapid change in appearance. Within a decade of coming to power, Qabus succeeded in raising the standard of living of the population as a whole and generating widespread support for his rule. However, with almost no trained personnel of its own, Oman was forced to employ large numbers of foreign workers and managers to carry out its modernization program. Like Kuwait, Oman had to rely on foreign expertise and labor for its continued development.

Sultan Qabus endeavored to implement an ambitious program of material change while retaining all the traditional powers of the sultan. Although the machinery of government became more complex after 1970, Qabus continued to rule as an absolute monarch. Oman had neither a constitution nor a legislature; all power was concentrated in the person of the sultan. The ministries were headed mainly by members of the Al Bu Saʿid ruling family, and the sultan himself served as prime minister. Whether this absolutist system could survive in an era of rapid social and material change was the subject of considerable debate. But the sultan, who was born in 1940 and could rule into the next century, showed no inclination to allow his increasingly educated population to participate in the political affairs of Oman.

The Smaller States of the Gulf

There are nine political entities squeezed along the shore of the Persian Gulf between Oman and the island nation of Bahrain. All of them were under British tutelage from the nineteenth century until their independence in 1971. Seven of the states—Abu Dhabi, Dubai, Sharja, Ajman, Umm al-Qaiwain, Fujairah, and Ras al-Khaimah—became part of a federated state, the United Arab Emirates, in 1971, whereas Bahrain and Qatar chose to remain distinct, independent nations.

Britain's announcement in 1968 that it would withdraw from all its bases east of Suez within three years caused alarm rather than enthusiasm among the rulers of the small Gulf principalities. Britain may have been a restrictive patron, but it was also a protective one. As long as Britain maintained treaty relations with the rulers, their domestic status was secure and their territorial integrity assured. However, once the British intention to withdraw protection became known, Iran and Saudi Arabia sought to expand their influence over their weaker neighbors. Iran claimed sovereignty over Bahrain, and the shah's military occupied three small islands in the Strait of Hormuz in 1971. The withdrawal of the Western imperial power threatened to open the door for regional powers to make imperial claims of their own.

In the period between 1968 and 1971, British representatives presided over intensive and often difficult negotiations that resolved the most pressing tensions and preserved the separate identity of the Gulf states. In a referendum conducted by the United Nations, the population of Bahrain voted for independence rather than absorption into Iran. The shah agreed to drop his territorial claims on condition that Bahrain not join any union or federation. Qatar, a small but enormously wealthy oil state, also chose independence; the seven former trucial states were brought together in the UAE federation. Bahrain, Qatar, and the UAE all obtained formal independence in 1971.

Although the three political units possessed distinctive cultural, governmental, and religious identities, they generally followed the pattern of development that prevailed in Kuwait. Each state, including the seven members of the UAE, was headed by a ruling family that concentrated political power in the hands of the amir and his relatives. During the boom years of the 1970s, all three states embarked on spending sprees that transformed their material and social foundations yet left their traditional political institutions intact. As their petroleum wealth thrust them into regional prominence, they had to deal with the impact of regional tensions on their newly aware populations. These included popular attitudes to the Arab-Israeli conflict as well as to such crucial issues as political representation within a monarchical system and religious versus national identity. Qatar, with a majority of its population professing the Wahhabi version of Islam, was drawn to Saudi Arabia as a regional patron; Bahrain, 70 percent of whose population was Shiᶜa, also turned to Saudi Arabia for protection against revolutionary Iran, which resurrected claims to Bahrain and called upon its Shiᶜa population to overthrow the Sunni ruler.

Bahrain, which started to export oil in 1934, was the first Arab Gulf state to develop a petroleum-based economy. At a time when its neighbors were suffering from the collapse of the pearling industry, Bahrain was earning oil revenues that it used to train an indigenous labor force, establish a public education system, and sponsor the first Arabic-language newspaper in the region. Although Bahrain's oil revenues in the 1970s were less than those of Qatar or the UAE, its head start in development made it a more politically and socially complex state. It had a comparatively moderate reliance on imported labor: Approximately 30 percent of Bahrain's total population in the mid-1980s was foreign; by contrast, Qatar and the UAE relied so heavily on foreign labor and management that approximately 80 percent of the total population of each state consisted of resident aliens. Within the UAE, there existed a substantial imbalance among the federated states. Abu Dhabi, by far the largest and wealthiest member of the federation, was an important world petroleum power in the 1970s, and its amir served as president of the UAE. Two other oil-exporting states, Dubai and to a lesser extent Sharja, also played prominent roles in UAE governance. In 1984 a fourth member of the UAE, Ras al-Khaimah, began to export oil. The other states within the federation had meager subsistence economies that were subsidized by revenue-sharing agreements with the oil-producing members. Fueled by the sudden and substantial revenues that poured in after 1973, the entire federation went on a ten-year spending spree that made it the focus of attention for a broad spectrum of development operations, not all of which were reliable. Yet despite the tremendous changes and challenges generated by oil wealth, the seven states of the UAE as well as Qatar and Bahrain remained under the political control of nine traditional ruling families.

Conclusion

The oil embargo of 1973 was a momentous event for the states of the Arabian Peninsula as well as for the world economy. Arab oil producers discovered that their petroleum could be used as a diplomatic weapon in the Arab-Israeli conflict, and oil consumers were brought to a sudden recognition of their growing dependence on Middle Eastern oil. By withholding their oil from the market, the producing states were given an opportunity to discover the true value of their most precious resource. During the final months of 1973, consuming countries were willing to pay several times the set price for non-Arab oil. When the Arab producers reentered the marketplace in January 1974, they joined with their OPEC partners to set the price of a barrel of oil at $11.65, a dramatic increase from the $2.74 price of a year earlier. Until 1982, the price of oil rose steadily, bringing enormous wealth and enhanced status to the producing states.

Oil revenues fueled a development boom of unprecedented proportions among the states of the Arabian Peninsula. Yet amid the glittering material improvements and the disruptive social changes, political power remained in the hands of hereditary dynasties. The dominant ruling families attempted to preserve their authority by preventing the emergence of representative assemblies and mass politics. They muted discontent by the skillful distribution of oil income, providing well-paying jobs for the educated elite and generous welfare systems for the population as a whole. This technique created remarkable political stability and assured the survival of the ruling families. It did not, however, resolve problems, but merely postponed them.

Notes

1. Nadav Safran, *Saudi Arabia: The Ceaseless Quest for Security* (Ithaca, 1988), pp. 161–162.
2. Ibid., p. 172.
3. Ibid., pp. 223, 477. The figures on foreign workers are also from Safran.
4. Cited in Mordechai Abir, *Saudi Arabia in the Oil Era: Regime and Elites, Conflict and Collaboration* (Boulder, 1988), p. 97.

Challenges to the Existing Order: The Palestinian Uprising and the Gulf War

22

⟨|⟩
⟨|⟩

From 1987 to 1991 the Middle East was rocked by a series of internal crises and an external intervention that had momentous consequences for the future of the region. The Palestinian inhabitants of the West Bank and Gaza Strip participated in a mass uprising to bring an end to the Israeli occupation and establish an independent Palestinian state. The uprising, called the *intifada*, endured for nearly five years and forced Israel to recognize the impact of occupation on the Palestinians. A second internal regional crisis occurred in 1990 with the Iraqi invasion and annexation of Kuwait. This crisis quickly became internationalized into the Gulf War, which saw the devastation of Iraq by the armed forces of a U.S.-led coalition. Uncontested U.S. military intervention in the Middle East was made possible by a fundamental change in the international balance of power as a result of the end of the cold war and the collapse of the Soviet Union. In the aftermath of the Gulf War, Iraq continued to be crippled by the enforcement of tough economic sanctions and the occasional U.S. aerial bombardment. The war also had a lingering impact on Kuwait and Saudi Arabia, bringing the policies and behavior of the ruling families under closer scrutiny and unleashing demands for a greater degree of openness in the decisionmaking processes of the two states.

The *Intifada* from 1987 to 1991

Israeli Politics and the Occupied Territories

During the decade following the ill-conceived invasion of Lebanon in 1982, Israeli society experienced a polarization that was reflected in the fragmentation of the country's political life. In the elections of 1984 and 1988, numerous small parties at both extremes of the political spectrum attracted enough voters to deny the two main political groupings, Labor and Likud, the opportunity to form majority governments. The two parties were therefore forced to govern together in what was optimistically called a National Unity government but was in reality a situation of political paralysis.

The National Unity governments were divided by the different positions Labor and Likud held in regard to the occupied territories. The Labor Party favored territorial compromise, whereas Likud was adamantly opposed to relinquishing any portion of the Gaza Strip or the West Bank. Likud's position was forcefully represented by its leader, Yitzhak Shamir, who served as Israel's prime minister from 1986 to 1992. Born in Poland in 1915, Shamir immigrated to Palestine at the age of twenty and was quickly attracted to Jabotinsky's maximalist version of Zionism. He joined the Irgun in 1937 and later became one of the leaders of the Stern Gang, a terrorist organization responsible for carrying out attacks on Palestinians and British officials. Like his Likud predecessor, Menachem Begin, Shamir believed that all the lands of biblical Israel should be incorporated into the Jewish state. As prime minister, he intensified the construction of Israeli settlements in the West Bank and Gaza Strip and committed the government to a policy of incorporating the territories into Israel.

In addition to constructing new settlements, the Likud-dominated governments of the 1980s sought to prepare the way for the annexation of the territories by adopting measures designed to isolate and subjugate the Palestinian inhabitants. The Israeli state stepped up its practice of confiscating plots of Arab land, and the Israeli security services deported an increasing number of suspected political activists. Administrative detention, a practice that permitted Palestinians to be arrested without a warrant and held for up to six months without being charged, was employed with greater frequency. The occupation intruded on the daily lives of Palestinians in countless ways: They were required to carry identity cards and pay special taxes; they had to overcome a maze of bureaucratic obstacles and security checks to obtain the most basic licenses and business permits; and they were arrested, imprisoned, and sometimes tortured by the Israeli authorities at the slightest suspicion of political activism. One Palestinian academic explained the cumulative effect of Likud's policies as follows: "The denial of natural rights and more harsh treatment caused eventually an awareness that 'we are occupied.' Everyone felt threatened. Your national existence was targeted. This realization finally sunk into the consciousness of Palestinians, so the occupation was resisted."[1] The resistance took the form of a sustained popular uprising that was on the one hand a rejection of the Israeli occupation and on the other an affirmation of the Palestinian people's right to national self-determination.

The Localized Beginnings

The Palestinian uprising, or *intifada,* began in Gaza on December 9, 1987, following a road accident involving an Israeli military vehicle that killed four

Palestinians and injured several others. Thousands of Palestinians gathered to protest the incident, and when the Israeli army shot and killed some of the demonstrators, all of Gaza burst into open revolt. Within a few days, the West Bank was also engulfed in the uprising, as thousands of demonstrators carrying stones, slingshots, and gasoline bombs confronted the Israeli armed forces.

During its first few weeks, the *intifada*—which means a shaking off—was a spontaneous rebellion fueled by the anger of the discontented young people of the occupied territories. However, as the movement gathered momentum, it broadened to include all strata of Palestinian society, and an underground local leadership endeavored to coordinate the uprising. The Unified National Leadership (UNL), as it came to be known, was composed of a small group of individuals representing the major local factions of the PLO. Beginning in January 1988, the UNL issued sequentially numbered leaflets containing instructions for protest activities ranging from general strikes to street demonstrations. The discipline with which the Palestinians carried out the UNL's instructions was a measure of their support for the leaders and their determination to continue the uprising.

The objectives of the *intifada* were contained in a fourteen-point program drawn up by a group of prominent Palestinians and endorsed by the UNL. The program demanded that Israel stop building settlements and confiscating Arab lands and that it cancel the special taxes and restrictions that applied only to Palestinians. In addition, the program called upon Israel to recognize an independent Palestinian state under the leadership of the PLO. To achieve these goals, the *intifada* leaders employed tactics designed to make the continued occupation a financial burden for Israel. Thus, during the first three years of the uprising, Palestinians engaged in a campaign of civil disobedience that included general strikes, shop closures, and a refusal to pay Israeli taxes. In addition, the Palestinians attempted to make the Gaza Strip and the West Bank economically self-sufficient by boycotting Israeli goods and relying as much as possible on homegrown produce and locally manufactured goods. The violence that was an integral part of the civil disobedience consisted mainly of mass demonstrations and stone throwing. The Palestinians made a conscious decision at the beginning of the uprising to disavow the use of guns and knives. But as the *intifada* dragged on into the early 1990s, stabbings and shootings became more widespread. Israelis were not the only targets of the *intifada*. Palestinians who worked for Israel as informants were also singled out for revenge. Underground tribunals sentenced dozens of Palestinian collaborators to death, and local villagers beat and murdered many more.

As the uprising gained momentum, new organizations formed as rivals of the UNL, the most significant of which was the Islamic Resistance Movement, known widely by its Arabic acronym, Hamas. An offshoot of the

Gaza branch of the Muslim Brotherhood, Hamas came into existence in 1988. Its leadership was dominated by young, university-educated individuals, mainly of refugee camp origin, who represented a new, socially mobilized strata of Palestinian society. They challenged the local PLO-oriented Unified National Leadership, which contained a significant element of established notable families, for control of the uprising and for the loyalties of the Palestinians participating in it.

In contrast to the PLO, with its secular nationalism, Hamas framed its program and its call to action in Islamic terms. In its charter of 1988, Hamas referred to itself as a Palestinian resistance movement that takes Islam as a way of life. The charter sacralized the land of Palestine, defining it as an Islamic *waqf*, no part of which could be abandoned or conceded. This definition made it impossible for Hamas to accept the two-state solution gradually endorsed by the PLO. Working through such grassroots organizations as charitable societies, Islamic and secular educational institutions, and a network of mosques under its control, Hamas emerged in the early 1990s as a viable political alternative to the local PLO. Its support base, originally centered in Gaza, expanded to the West Bank during the latter part of the decade.

The Israeli government made a concerted effort to crush the uprising. The violence of the youthful stone throwers was met by the violence of the well-armed Israeli military. Television images of Israeli troops shooting at unarmed teenagers contributed to mounting criticism of the Israeli government both at home and abroad. The military also employed collective punishment on a broad scale, demolishing the homes of suspected stone throwers, placing entire villages under twenty-four-hour curfew for several days at a time, cutting off water and electricity, and closing the West Bank schools and universities. In an effort to undermine the Palestinians' efforts to gain economic self-sufficiency, Israeli troops and settlers uprooted fruit and olive trees and destroyed private vegetable gardens. However, according to Robert Hunter, Israel's use of collective punishment only caused participation in the *intifada* to increase. Israeli retaliation affected all Palestinians in the Gaza Strip and the West Bank and led Palestinian society to unite in common opposition to the occupation. But opposition had a price: By the end of 1990, the uprising had cost the lives of an estimated 1,025 Palestinians, including 250 alleged collaborators killed by the forces of the uprising, and 56 Israelis. Over 37,000 Arabs had been wounded and between 35,000 and 40,000 arrested. It was at this point—late 1990—that the intensity of the uprising began to diminish. Although it continued sporadically until spring 1992, the cooperation among all segments of Palestinian society that had sustained the *intifada* for its first two years started to evaporate in the face of Israeli countermeasures and internal divisions among Palestinians.

The International Dimension of the *Intifada*

The *intifada* began as a purely local Palestinian response to unbearable local conditions and was not inspired by the external PLO leadership in Tunis. Indeed, the *intifada* was an expression of dissatisfaction by the Palestinians of the West Bank and Gaza Strip with the PLO and its chairman, Yasir Arafat. To the Palestinians living under occupation, the PLO of the 1980s appeared to be more concerned with exile politics than with their plight. Yet no matter how disillusioned the Palestinians in the territories may have been with the PLO, they continued to regard it as their legitimate representative to the international community. Once the uprising began, links were forged between the external PLO and the occupied territories, and Arafat embarked on a new round of diplomacy.

Arafat recognized that in order for an independent Palestinian state to come into existence, Israel would have to abandon its hope of annexing the occupied territories. The only outside power capable of persuading Israel to modify its policies and enter into negotiations was the United States. However, the United States would not exercise its influence in this matter until the PLO recognized the state of Israel, something it had steadfastly refused to do. Under pressure to act on behalf of the Palestinians of the *intifada*, Arafat worked successfully to change the PLO's position. In fall 1988 he made a historic announcement that contained the following major points: The PLO accepted Israel's right to exist as a state; the PLO renounced the use of terrorism and agreed that UN Resolutions 242 and 338 should serve as the basis for an international peace conference; the PLO proclaimed an independent Palestinian state in the West Bank and Gaza Strip with East Jerusalem as its capital. Arafat's program represented the so-called two-state compromise: The PLO dropped its earlier insistence that all of Palestine should be liberated and acknowledged Israel's right to exist in its pre-1967 borders.

Arafat's compromise ushered in a series of U.S.-PLO negotiations conducted through the U.S. embassy in Tunis. The purpose of the discussions was to establish a basis for the entry of the United States into the peace process as a mediator between Israel and the PLO. However, the refusal of Prime Minister Shamir's government to consider any change in the status of the occupied territories undermined the efforts. This phase of U.S.-PLO relations collapsed completely when a splinter group within the PLO tried to mount a raid into Israel, thus calling into question the sincerity of Arafat's renunciation of terrorism. U.S. president Bush, bowing to domestic pressure from Israel's supporters, broke off negotiations with the PLO in 1990.

Arafat's diplomacy in support of the *intifada* had failed miserably. Counting on the ability of the United States to influence Israel, he had recognized Israel's right to exist without receiving any concessions in return. Abandoned by Washington in summer 1990, Arafat made the fateful decision to associate the PLO with the Iraqi regime of Saddam Husayn.

The Gulf Crisis of 1990–1991

Iraq's Invasion of Kuwait and the U.S.-Led Response

On August 2, 1990, the armed forces of Iraq invaded Kuwait; six days later, the Iraqi government announced that Kuwait had been annexed as the nineteenth province of Iraq. These actions precipitated an international crisis that culminated in a U.S.-led war against Iraq in January and February 1991. The full ramifications of that war will not be known for several years, but its immediate effects were abundantly evident: the devastation of Iraq, the creation of a refugee problem of momentous proportions, and the emergence of the United States as an uncontested superpower in the Middle East.

The crisis that led to the Gulf War was regional in nature and unfolded against the backdrop of the developments discussed earlier in this chapter. The failure of the Palestinian *intifada* to bring about a change in Israel's relentless settlement policy, the impending immigration of hundreds of thousands of Soviet Jews to Israel, the collapse of the Soviet Union, and the emergence of the United States—the ally of Israel—as the sole superpower all combined to create an atmosphere of frustration and uncertainty within the Arab world. In these circumstances, the aggressive propaganda campaign Saddam Husayn launched against Israel and the United States in early 1990 found a receptive Arab audience and enhanced the Iraqi leader's prestige as the only national leader who unequivocally championed the Palestinian cause. Husayn justified Iraq's ongoing military buildup with the argument that the only way to force Israel to recognize Palestinian rights was for the Arab states to achieve military parity with Israel. He warned that Iraq would retaliate against any Israeli attack on an Arab state and turn Israel into an inferno. These challenges to Israeli intransigence in the occupied territories were welcome in many quarters of the Arab world, especially among the Palestinians, and enhanced Iraq's standing within Arab circles opposed to the status quo.

To the rising Iraqi-Israeli tensions were added the specific disputes between Iraq and Kuwait, some of them of long-standing, others of more recent origin. The most enduring disagreement was caused by Iraq's refusal to recognize the legitimacy of the border dividing the two states. When British officials defined the Iraq-Kuwait border in 1923, they gave Kuwait more territory in the north than the Kuwaiti rulers traditionally controlled. This was not a reward to Kuwait but rather a deliberate British attempt to restrict Iraq's access to the Persian Gulf. By granting Iraq only 36 miles (58 km) of coastline, all of which was poorly suited to the development of modern port facilities, Britain intended to prevent the country from becoming a major Gulf naval power. Deprived of the opportunity to construct deep-water ports, Iraq was forced to rely on the port of Basra which was located over 50 miles (80 km) inland up the tortuous and much-disputed Shatt al-Arab waterway. Beginning with the reign of Faysal I, Iraqi governments disputed the border and refused to recognize the existence of the state of Kuwait until 1963. Even then, Iraq did not acknowledge the permanence of the British-drawn border, and official Iraqi propaganda continued to maintain that Kuwait was a part of Basra province.

Immediate economic and strategic considerations also played a role in Husayn's decision to annex Kuwait in summer 1990. The costly conflict with Iran had left Iraq with an enormous burden of debt, some $60 billion of which was owed to Kuwait and Saudi Arabia (see Chapter 19). Iraq constantly pressured Kuwait to forgive the debt, claiming that the Iraqi "defense" of the Arab Gulf states against Iran was an act of sacrifice in the name of Arab brotherhood. Iraq also accused Kuwait of extracting more than its share of oil from the Rumeila oil field, a petroleum deposit that straddled the border between the two states. According to Iraq's charges, Kuwait had been wrongfully exploiting the Rumeila field since 1980 and had "stolen" $2.4 billion worth of Iraqi oil. The most significant point of contention between the two countries was oil production. Iraq was dependent on oil revenues to finance its postwar recovery and its military buildup and therefore favored setting oil prices at the highest possible level. Each member of OPEC was assigned a production quota designed to maintain the price of oil at $18 a barrel. However, Kuwait and the UAE persisted in exceeding their assigned quotas and were accused by Iraq and other oil producers of flooding the market and causing a drop in the price of oil. Iraq's foreign minister pointed out that every $1 per barrel drop in the price of oil cost Iraq $1 billion in annual revenues. With the price of oil hovering around $12 per barrel in 1990, Iraq put tremendous pressure on Kuwait to abide by its OPEC production quota. In a skillfully waged propaganda war, the Iraqi regime placed Kuwait's oil policies within the context of the Arab-Israeli conflict. Iraqi spokesmen pointed out that the only beneficiaries of low oil prices were the Western consumer nations and Kuwait itself, which earned more from its investments in the Western economies than it did from petroleum. Kuwait was thus portrayed as a traitor state, a willing participant in the U.S.-Israeli alliance directed against the economic recovery of Iraq and the welfare of the entire Arab nation.

And finally, the destruction of the port of Basra and the blocking of the Shatt al-Arab waterway during the war with Iran left Iraq virtually landlocked and forced the country to rely on pipelines through Turkey and Saudi Arabia for the export of its oil. Pipelines were an uncertain means of export because they could be shut down at any time by the states through which they passed. Iraqi leaders were convinced that the future economic well-being of their country depended upon the acquisition of territory suitable for the construction of deep-water port facilities, and they contended that Kuwait's long-standing refusal to cede one of its offshore islands to Iraq for use as a port was but another example of the Kuwaiti royal family's support of U.S. imperialism.

In July 1990 Kuwait acknowledged that it had been overproducing oil and agreed to abide by the OPEC quota. Nevertheless, Baghdad claimed that Kuwait's overproduction, its use of the Rumeila oil field, and its refusal to cancel Iraq's debts amounted to economic warfare against Iraq. The August 1990 invasion was, according to Baghdad, a justifiable retaliation. The annexation of Kuwait promised to solve Iraq's most pressing economic problems: Access to the Gulf would be assured; the debt to Kuwait would be terminated; and funds for reconstruction and military procurement would become abundantly available. In addition, Iraq and Kuwait together possessed 20 percent of proven world oil reserves, a factor that alone would give the new, greater Iraq enormous influence within the petroleum industry. But Iraq was also a major military power, and that, in combination with its potential economic might, placed it in a position to dominate the Persian Gulf and to shape the oil policies of the producing states.

When Husayn ordered his troops into Kuwait, he had little reason to anticipate an aggressive U.S. response. Up to the eve of the invasion, the Bush administration courted Iraq, providing it with billions of dollars worth of agricultural credits and turning a blind eye to its human rights abuses and its nuclear weapons program. However, Washington was horrified at the prospect of Husayn's exercising control over the oil-producing Gulf and was quick to intervene after the occupation of Kuwait.

The first phase of the United States' military response was defensive; it was undertaken to protect Saudi Arabia from Iraqi aggression. Some policymakers thought at the time that Iraq's invasion of Kuwait was but a prelude to an attack on Saudi Arabia, and the Saudi armed forces, despite the billions of dollars the Saudis had spent on weapons, were no match for the larger and more experienced Iraqi military machine. The Saudi government therefore issued a formal invitation to the United States to send troops to defend the kingdom. Operation Desert Shield was set in motion, and by October 1990 over 200,000 U.S. troops were stationed in Saudi Arabia.

In the meantime the Bush administration set about building an international coalition against Iraq. Working through the UN Security Council, which played an especially active role in the crisis, the United States pushed through resolutions demanding Iraq's withdrawal from Kuwait and imposing a trade embargo on all goods to and from Iraq and Kuwait. Britain, France, Italy, the Netherlands, and Canada committed forces to Operation Desert Shield, and the Soviet Union, in a demonstration of post–cold war diplomacy, joined in the international criticism of Iraq and suspended arms shipments to Baghdad.

In an attempt to limit Arab condemnation of its military intervention in Arabia, the United States sought to persuade Arab countries outside the Gulf to support Operation Desert Shield. The Arab response to the U.S. diplomatic initiatives was divided. Egypt endorsed the intervention and sent troops to join the coalition. Syria, in a reversal of its long-standing anti-U.S.

policy, also agreed to participate in the operation. Both states were handsomely rewarded for their cooperation: The United States canceled $7 billion of Egypt's military debts, and Syria received generous loans from Saudi Arabia and the European Community. However, one of Washington's most durable Arab allies, King Husayn of Jordan, condemned the intervention and refused to join the coalition. King Husayn's stance was largely determined by the pressure he felt from the Palestinian community that made up a majority of Jordan's population. Among the Palestinians, Saddam Husayn's defiance of the United States, Israel's most important ally, was popular. The PLO voted against the Arab League resolution condemning the Iraqi invasion, but as the crisis intensified, the organization tried to cover its diplomatic flanks and termed the invasion illegal. Yet there was no denying that many Palestinians in the West Bank and Gaza Strip were attracted by Saddam Husayn's claim to be their liberator and openly sided with Iraq during the war.

Throughout the Arab world, the Gulf crisis generated anxiety and ambivalence. Although Iraq's occupation of Kuwait was generally condemned, the arrival of a major U.S. military force to reverse the occupation was extremely unpopular. The U.S. intervention tapped a deep source of Arab resentment that focused on the United States' double standard in the Middle East. Arabs noted that though Washington was quick to enforce UN resolutions against Iraq, it had not tried to compel Israel to obey UN resolutions pertaining to the West Bank and Gaza Strip. A reminder of the harshness of the Israeli occupation occurred on October 8, 1990, when Israeli police, in the bloodiest day of the *intifada,* responded to a Palestinian demonstration by killing twenty people and wounding scores of others. The Palestinians had been protesting plans by an Israeli fringe group to reclaim the Haram al-Sharif and to construct a Jewish temple on the site of Jerusalem's holiest Islamic shrines. The incident of the Temple Mount embarrassed the United States' Arab allies and provided Iraq with a potent propaganda weapon. Saddam Husayn drew a connection between the occupation of Kuwait and the Israeli occupation of the West Bank and Gaza Strip. As the crisis unfolded, the Iraqi president stated that Israel's withdrawal from the occupied territories was a necessary precondition for Iraq's evacuation of Kuwait. Although the United States denied that the two occupations were linked in any way, Saddam Husayn's tactics brought renewed attention to the Palestinian situation and to Washington's support of Israel.

The occupation of Kuwait also brought to the surface sentiments that were not entirely sympathetic to the Arab Gulf rulers. In the view of many Arabs, the Gulf states were unnatural entities whose borders and ruling families had been determined by Britain to serve British interests. The words of an Egyptian diplomat illustrate the ambivalence Iraq's actions evoked: "The invasion is a black and white situation. We condemn it. But the reasons for the invasion are not so black and white."[2] To many Arabs, it seemed unfair that the ruling families of the Gulf should benefit from a geological quirk that gave them control of over 30 percent of the world's petroleum reserves. The families' personal fortunes, their abilities to establish extensive social welfare systems, and their exclusion of foreign workers from citizenship aroused envy and resentment in other areas of the Arab world. From this perspective, Iraq's occupation of Kuwait represented a blow to the legacy of imperialism and a humbling of the arrogant Kuwaitis.

From Desert Shield to Desert Storm

By autumn 1990 the objectives of Operation Desert Shield had been achieved: The coalition forces stationed in Saudi Arabia were more than sufficient to protect the kingdom from invasion, and the UN-imposed economic sanctions were beginning to restrict Iraq's imports and exports. Under these circumstances, some U.S. policymakers suggested that a peaceful resolution of the crisis could be attained by the continued enforcement of the sanctions, which, they argued, would create such economic hardships for Iraq that it would eventually be forced to adhere to the UN resolutions and withdraw from Kuwait. Others within the Washington establishment argued that the embargo was only moderately effective and that it would become even less so with the passage of time. The merits of the arguments presented on Capitol Hill mattered little—President Bush had already made the decision to go to war. In early November he ordered U.S. forces in Arabia to be doubled to 400,000 troops and announced the need for the coalition to develop an offensive military option. During the same month, the UN Security Council passed a resolution setting January 15, 1991, as the deadline for the complete withdrawal of Iraqi forces from Kuwait. The resolution authorized the "use of all necessary means" to enforce Iraq's pullout after January 15. The operation that had been mounted for the defense of Saudi Arabia was being transformed into an offensive campaign for the liberation of Kuwait. By January 1991 the number of U.S. troops had risen to over 500,000, and Operation Desert Shield was poised to become Desert Storm.

The Bush administration justified its change of policy by emphasizing the moral responsibility of liberating Kuwait and of denying Iraq the fruits of its aggression. The administration also went to great lengths to portray Saddam Husayn as a source of evil whose crimes must not go unpunished. Bush's personalization of his animosity toward the Iraqi leader was reminiscent of British prime minister Eden's fixation on Nasser during the Suez Crisis of 1956. Bush compared the Iraqi president to Hitler and stressed the need to destroy his regime. The vilification of Husayn was so intense and the focus on him so concentrated that he, and he alone, was made out to be the embodiment of the Iraqi nation. By concentrating on the figure of Husayn, the U.S. administration gained popular support for military action directed against a ruthless individual ruler without having to explain the possible impact of such a war on the people of Iraq.

Behind the rhetoric about the liberation of Kuwait and the cruelty of Husayn lay a more practical motive for military action. The rulers of the Arab Gulf states provided the United States and Europe with dependable access to reasonably priced oil. From the perspective of the Western oil-con-suming nations, the stability of the Arab Gulf monarchies and their contin-ued willingness to sell oil to the West were essential to Western economic well-being. Moreover, the Gulf rulers' practice of reinvesting their oil profits in the West was vital to the health of the Western economies. Saudi Arabia, Kuwait, and the UAE had combined investments in the West totaling be-tween $200 and $300 billion. U.S. interests were well served by the existing economic and political order in the Gulf; Husayn's Iraq posed a threat to that order. For example, in a speech delivered in early 1990, Husayn called upon the Arab states to reinvest their oil profits in Arab economies, not in foreign ones. With the Iraqi annexation of Kuwait, the possibility emerged that Kuwait's investments would be redirected, that Kuwait's oil would be withheld from the market to achieve political concessions from the West, and that other oil-producing Gulf states might be persuaded to reconsider their accommodating policies toward the Western consuming nations. The U.S. administration could not allow Iraq to disrupt the favorable existing order in such a manner.

The UN deadline of January 15, 1991, passed without an Iraqi with-drawal from Kuwait. On January 16 the air war against Iraq began. For forty-two consecutive days and nights, the coalition forces subjected Iraq to the most intensive air bombardment in military history. Although the bombing campaign concentrated primarily on military targets, it also de-stroyed facilities on which civilian life depended—power-generating plants, communications centers, water mains, highways, bridges, and railroads. The entire infrastructure of Iraq was rendered inoperable. Iraqi forces in Kuwait were also heavily bombed, and the resulting damage to Kuwaiti installations was extensive.

Iraq was virtually defenseless against the bombing. Its air defenses were put out of action early in the campaign, and its air force was not ordered into combat. In these circumstances, the regime had recourse to a tactic de-signed to broaden the war and cause confusion among the coalition mem-bers. Iraq launched over thirty Scud missiles at Israel, twelve of which landed in downtown Haifa and Tel Aviv. At the time, it was feared that the missiles were armed with poison chemicals, and the Israeli government is-sued gas masks to all its citizens—but not to the Palestinians in the occupied territories—and urged them to remain indoors for long periods of time. The specter of the inhabitants of the Jewish state becoming the victims of chem-ical warfare was a chilling one and resurrected memories of the Holocaust. However, the Iraqi missiles were armed with conventional warheads and caused little material damage in Israel. But the attacks did threaten the cohesion of the coalition so painstakingly constructed by the United States. If Israel chose to retaliate against Iraq, it was likely that the Arab partners in the coalition would withdraw because they could not allow themselves to be part of a U.S.-Israeli alliance against an Arab state. Israel did not normally remain passive when threatened by its Arab enemies, and an attack of this psychological magnitude seemed sure to generate a swift military response. But in this instance U.S. pressure was successful in persuading the Israeli government to keep its air force out of the conflict.

Throughout the relentless bombing campaign, U.S. military commanders repeatedly warned that Iraq remained well armed and that the ground war to retake Kuwait would be difficult. It was launched on February 24 and lasted only 100 hours. Evidence released after the war revealed that U.S. reports grossly inflated the size and the abilities of the Iraqi military in order to justify the massive force deployed against Iraq. The Iraqi conscript troops who had managed to survive the bombings were poorly supplied and thoroughly demoralized. When the coalition forces entered Kuwait, the Iraqi army began a disorderly retreat back across the border toward Basra. The ground war quickly became a rout: Thousands of Iraqi soldiers surrendered and thousands more were killed by U.S. aircraft in scenes of horrible carnage along the road to Basra, known to the survivors as "the highway of death." According to the correspondent of the London *Observer,* the assault was so severe that it constituted "one of the most terrible harassments of a retreating army from the air in the history of warfare."[3] On February 27, 1991, Bush proclaimed the liberation of Kuwait and ordered the U.S. and coalition forces to suspend offensive operations. The president's decision to halt Operation Desert Storm without ensuring the overthrow of Saddam Husayn and his regime became the subject of much controversy in the months that followed.

The Uprisings

The cease-fire did not end the agony of the Iraqi people. In a spontaneous outburst of anger and resentment, segments of the Iraqi population rose up against the regime that had led the country into two devastating wars. The rebellion began in the Shiʿa south and soon spread to the Kurds in the north. In both regions the uprisings experienced early successes that were followed by crushing defeats.

In the south the rebellion was triggered by the retreating soldiers, who felt that the government had abandoned them once Operation Desert Storm was launched. The disaffected troops were joined by civilian opponents of the government, and this combination of forces took control of most of the southern cities, including Basra and the holy Shiʿa shrines of Karbala and Najaf, during the first two weeks of March 1991. Although the revolt had Shiᶜa overtones, it did not represent a movement among the Shiᶜa for union with Iran. Rather, it was a rejection of the regime and the hardships to which Husayn's disastrous policies had subjected the inhabitants of southern Iraq. In town after town, demonstrators attacked the Baᶜth Party buildings, the offices of the Baᶜth-appointed mayors, and the headquarters of the secret police. Mass revenge killings of Baᶜthist officials occurred throughout the course of the uprising.

Because the uprising in the south was spontaneous, it lacked organization, leadership, and objectives. In the chaotic circumstances of a true popular rebellion, the rebel forces in one town were usually unaware of events in neighboring towns. This lack of coordination facilitated the government's efforts to put down the uprising. Although the Iraqi army had been battered, it remained far stronger than the poorly armed civilian rebels; and although elements of the army participated in the rebellion, substantial units remained loyal to the regime. By the end of March, the Iraqi military had crushed the rebellion and begun the mass executions of rebels.

A similar scenario unfolded in the Kurdish territories of northern Iraq. Aware of the enormity of the army's defeat in Kuwait and of the spread of the rebellion in the south, Kurdish leaders decided that this was the opportune moment to seize the autonomy for which they had so frequently struggled. During a two-week period in March, Kurdish forces took control of the major cities and towns in the north. More experienced and better organized than the southern rebels, the Kurds set up municipal administrations in the captured cities and enunciated a program that had wide appeal: democracy for Iraq and autonomy for Kurdistan. However, when the Iraqi army turned its attention from the south to the north, the Kurdish rebellion disintegrated.

At the approach of the regular army, the Kurdish fighters retreated to the mountains. This induced panic among the unprotected civilian population, and they began to flee their towns and villages. The flight became a mass exodus as an estimated 2 million Kurds headed toward the Turkish and Iranian borders. The most often stated reason for the Kurds' flight was their fear of extermination at the hands of a regime that had used poison gas against the Kurdish town of Halabja in 1988 (see Chapter 19). The Kurdish flight constituted another tragedy of the Gulf War. Hundreds of thousands of Kurdish refugees became trapped in the harsh mountain climate of April, living in makeshift camps and surviving on the meager supplies provided by overstretched international relief agencies. At least 20,000 refugees, mainly infants, children, and the elderly, perished. In May 1991, U.S. and European troops entered northern Iraq and established "safe-haven" zones to which the Kurds could return under foreign protection. However, the majority of the Kurdish refugees were so fearful of reprisals from the regime that they remained in the camps for months.

The Formal Cease-fire Document

On April 3, 1991, after more than a month of negotiations, the UN Security Council adopted Resolution 687 setting forth the terms for a formal cease-fire in the Gulf War. Iraq officially accepted the terms on April 6. Part of the lengthy and complex resolution aimed at reducing Iraq's military capabilities by requiring Baghdad to destroy all its chemical and biological weapons as well as its ballistic missiles. Iraq was given fifteen days to provide the UN with a description of the locations and amounts of such weapons and was called on to pledge never to acquire them again. The inspection of Iraq's armament factories and the supervision of the destruction of the banned weapons was to be carried out by UN inspection units working in cooperation with the International Atomic Energy Agency.

The cease-fire resolution also punished Iraq for the invasion of Kuwait and attempted to prevent its recurrence. Iraq was required to return property stolen from Kuwait during the occupation and to contribute to a fund created to pay compensation for war damage claims against the Iraqi government. In addition, both Iraq and Kuwait had to accept any modifications in the boundary between them that might be proposed by a new UN commission. The commission's report, delivered in 1993, was punitive toward Iraq. It moved Kuwait's boundary 570 meters north, thus giving Kuwait possession of six additional wells in the Rumeila oil field and portions of the Iraqi naval base at Umm Qasr. In addition to the restrictions in the cease-fire document, the United States and its allies took steps to prevent a recurrence of Iraqi attacks on the Kurds and the Shiᶜa. In April 1991 Iraq was ordered not to fly any aircraft north of the thirty-sixth parallel; and in August 1992 the same prohibition was put in place for all flights south of the thirty-second parallel (see Map 22.1). Although Iraq insisted that the no-fly zones constituted an infringement on its sovereignty and from time to time tested the allies' resolve to enforce them, the constant presence of allied air patrols in the zones effectively deterred the regime from carrying out air attacks against the Kurds and the Shiᶜa.

And finally, the cease-fire document offered a gradual easing of the trade sanctions against Iraq. The embargo on food imports and other emergency civilian goods was lifted immediately. The resolution further stipulated that if Iraq handed over all its weapons of mass destruction and its nuclear, biological, and chemical materials to the UN inspection unit by mid-May 1991, then the ban on Iraqi exports, including oil, would also be lifted. These terms were important: They defined the actions Iraq had to take in order to begin earning the petroleum revenue that was vital for the reconstruction of the country's devastated infrastructure. If Iraq did not take the required actions, the UN Security Council could maintain the economic sanctions. Unfortunately for the people of Iraq, the sanctions were still in place in 1999.

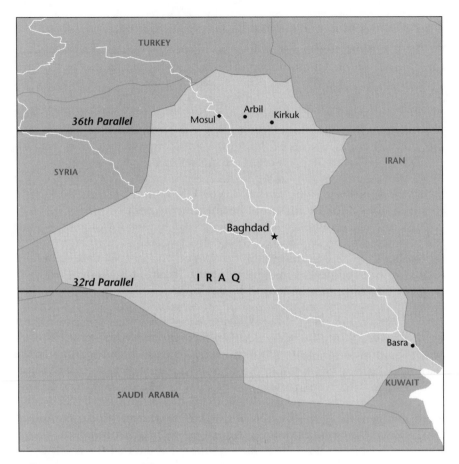

Map 22.1 The No-Fly Zones Imposed on Iraq in 1991 and 1992

The Aftermath of the Gulf War

The words of an experienced observer of Middle Eastern affairs can serve to place the impact of the Gulf War in its regional and global contexts:

> This war has been an unmitigated disaster for millions of people in the Middle East and beyond. The many tens of thousands killed, the billions of dollars of property destruction, the millions of displaced persons and disrupted lives, the uncounted thousands with permanent physical and psychological scars, and the badly damaged economies are far more devastating than anything that has happened in the region in this century. . . . The political, social and economic consequences of the U.S. assault on Iraq, and the Iraqi regime's consequent assault on its own people, will afflict the region and the world well into the next century.[4]

Only time can test the accuracy of this dark prediction. However, it is possible to give an accounting of the immediate consequences of the Gulf War on the Middle Eastern states and peoples it most directly affected.

Iraq: The Prolonged Postwar Period

The loss of life in Iraq will probably never be known for certain. Estimates range from no more than 10,000 to 100,000 individuals. The higher numbers seem more realistic, and it is likely that at least 82,000 Iraqi soldiers and 7,000 civilians were killed in the air and ground wars. By contrast, the coalition lost 139 soldiers in combat, 79 of whom were Americans. An additional 6,000 Iraqis were killed during the uprising in the south, and over 20,000 Kurds died from exposure and disease during their flight.

Despite the hardships that his decisions had inflicted on the population of Iraq, Saddam Husayn remained defiant in the face of the UN cease-fire resolution and U.S. threats to resume the conflict. The UN weapons inspection units, known as UN Special Commission on Iraq (UNSCOM), revealed the immensity of Iraq's chemical production and nuclear research programs and discovered that the country was much closer to achieving nuclear capability than had previously been thought. The regime resented the presence of the UN personnel, and until late 1998 Iraqi authorities practiced deception and engaged in a series of confrontations with the inspection units, refusing to provide them with access to several of the sites they wished to examine. Although tons of Iraq's conventional military arsenal were destroyed, the Security Council, and the United States in particular, remained convinced that the regime was successfully concealing its chemical and biological stores and the laboratories that produced them. Because of the combination of Iraqi deceit and U.S. suspicions, the Security Council determined that the regime had not complied with the terms of the cease-fire and therefore refused to lift the trade embargo. The only imports permitted into Iraq were food, medicine, and other items classified as humanitarian aid.

Finally, in 1996, a food-for-oil agreement was reached that allowed Iraq to sell $2 billion worth of oil every six months (the amount was raised to $5.8 billion in 1998) in order to purchase humanitarian supplies. However, Iraq's control over the proceeds of the sales was severely restricted. The proceeds were placed in a UN-controlled bank account and their distribution went first to meet Iraq's cease-fire obligations. Thus, 30 percent of the funds from the sales were used to pay Iraq's war reparations, another amount was designated for humanitarian supplies for the Kurds in the north, and still more was used to pay for UN operations in Iraq. By the time the Security Council had parceled out these funds, the amount remaining to alleviate the suffering of the Iraqi people was pitifully inadequate.

The effects of the prolonged sanctions on the people of Iraq were devastating. During the war, the coalition's bombs had destroyed or disabled virtually the entire civilian infrastructure of the country. Water purification plants, sewage treatment systems, electrical power stations, and irrigation systems were all either in ruins or able to function at only a fraction of their full capacity. Although the bridges and government buildings in Baghdad were rapidly rebuilt and essential services were sufficiently restored to enable the city to function, the sanctions continued to have disastrous effects. Because of a shortage of basic medical supplies and foodstuffs, malnutrition and disease, especially among children, increased throughout the country. Reports from UN agencies showed that child mortality had increased fivefold in the years from 1991 to 1996. Of particular concern was the health risk posed by the inadequate water treatment plants and sewage systems. The water purification system was not restored to its prewar capacity and lacked sufficient supplies of chlorine, which Iraq was forbidden to import because it was regarded as a chemical agent with potential military use. Sewage plants ceased chemical treatments completely and dumped raw sewage into the Tigris and Euphrates Rivers. The contaminated water supply was responsible for much of the disease that ravaged Iraq's child population. Food shortages were another basic problem, and the population was kept alive only by a tightly managed government food-rationing program.

Rampant inflation and currency devaluation reduced Iraq's once formidable middle class to poverty, and widespread unemployment contributed to a rise in crime and prostitution. Iraq's isolation deprived its professional classes of access to publications from outside the country and denied the country's emerging generation any familiarity with computers, the Internet, or satellite television. The humanitarian disaster created by the sanctions prompted some Western critics to question the morality of the collective punishment that was being inflicted upon Iraqi civilians and to doubt the logic behind the policy of holding "the welfare of a nation hostage to the good behavior of a dictator."[5]

Whether out of humanitarian considerations or, more likely, a desire for economic advantage, some of the permanent members of the Security Council raised discussions in the late 1990s about easing the sanctions. Within the framework of the oil-for-peace arrangement, France had emerged as Iraq's leading trading partner; China and Russia also engaged in trade with Iraq and were eager to expand their opportunities. Even some of the Arab states, most notably Egypt, that had been part of the coalition against Iraq participated fully in the trade allowed under the oil-for-peace agreement. Other indications suggested that Arab relations with the Iraqi regime were improving, and Iraqi officials visited Syria and Egypt on several occasions. As the possibility of ending the sanctions gained momentum, the United States became isolated in its insistence on retaining them. It was at this juncture, in late 1998, that the United States and Britain resumed the bombing campaign against Iraq (see Chapter 24).

Despite rumors of attempted coups and assassination plots, Saddam Husayn retained his firm grip on power. The ruthlessness with which he treated suspected opponents and the elaborate security measures with which he surrounded himself discouraged dissent within the ruling elite. Meanwhile, the population at large was more concerned with basic physical and economic survival than with a possible change in the regime. It has often been pointed out that in cases of economic embargo, the elite at whom the sanctions are directed are the least likely to suffer their effects. That was certainly the case in Iraq. While the population struggled to survive, lavish new presidential palaces sprouted in Baghdad and the countryside. A wealthy group of sanction busters within the elite, led by Husayn's two sons, managed to smuggle oil out of the country and import expensive consumer items. They were noted for their conspicuous presence in Baghdad's most expensive restaurants and nightclubs. The regime was totally unrepentant for the havoc wrought by its initiatives and was committed to staying in power at all costs.

Kuwait and Saudi Arabia: The Impact of the Decline in World Oil Prices

Before discussing the impact of the Gulf war on Kuwait and Saudi Arabia, we need to examine a trend that began before the war but that would have a profound effect on the abilities of these two states to maintain political stability following it. The soaring oil prices of the 1970s peaked at $41 per barrel in 1982, then began a gradual decline that culminated in a crash in 1986, when the price fell to $10 per barrel. From 1986 to the late 1990s, prices remained at less than $20. This decline in oil prices affected all petroleum-producing countries, but it had a particularly devastating impact on the Gulf states, which were almost entirely dependent on oil revenues, and an even greater impact on Kuwait and Saudi Arabia because of their responsibilities for Gulf War–related costs that totaled nearly $100 billion.

As discussed in Chapter 21, the ruling families of the Gulf region were able to enhance their power and retain their monopoly over the decision-making process because they could use enormous oil revenues to finance lavish social programs that bought popular loyalty and political quiescence. In the post–Gulf War situation, as populations grew and revenues declined, citizens of the Gulf states retained the expectations they had acquired during the twenty years of the oil boom, namely, that the state was responsible for providing them with a comfortable standard of living, free access to medical and educational facilities, and a host of other privileges. How could the ruling families of the Gulf keep their exclusive control of political power and economic resources if they were incapable of delivering the services their citizens had come to expect as a right? This question applied to all the Gulf monarchies, but it was particularly pressing in Kuwait and Saudi Arabia, where public criticism of the ruling families reached unprecedented levels in the postwar period.

Kuwait suffered severe damage from the Iraqi occupation and the coalition's liberation. Iraqi troops looted the country during the occupation and engaged in the wanton destruction of hotels and public buildings. Iraq also practiced environmental warfare, loosing on the northern Persian Gulf two of the largest oil spills ever recorded. And on the eve of their retreat, Iraqi forces dynamited 85 percent of Kuwait's 950 oil wells, leaving them blazing infernos pouring acrid black smoke into the air. As the equivalent of 2 million barrels of oil a day burned, the sky above Kuwait darkened and the entire country was turned into an environmental catastrophe. Most of the fires were extinguished within a year, and oil production was restored to prewar capacity by 1993, much sooner than experts had predicted. But the expenses associated with the war and reconstruction were enormous. Kuwait paid between $16 and $20 billion as its share for the costs of Operation Desert Storm and spent another $65 billion on reconstruction. Because the country had received no oil revenues at all for two years, the only way it could finance these expenses was by liquidating some of the $100 billion it had invested abroad. Moreover, with oil income still down after 1992, the Kuwaiti government began to run a series of deficit budgets in order to maintain its social services. It made up the deficits by continuing to draw down its overseas investments, a practice that could not go on indefinitely.

The reputation and credibility of Kuwait's ruling family suffered as a result of the war. While the Kuwaiti population was forced to endure occupation and warfare, the al-Sabah royal family passed the crisis in a luxury hotel in Saudi Arabia. Upon returning to Kuwait, the amir and his government appeared to give a higher priority to refurbishing the royal palace than to restoring essential services to the population at large. Beyond the ruling family's behavior during and after the war, deeper popular discontent centered on the regime's lack of accountability, especially for its mismanagement of Kuwait's oil and investment revenues. In 1992 financial scandals involving the loss of several billions of dollars were disclosed, and Kuwaitis were angered at the squandering of the revenues on which their social welfare system depended. In response to this combination of incompetence and insensitivity, the first weeks of the postwar era were marked by popular demonstrations for the establishment of democratic institutions. Although the al-Sabah family showed little understanding of the postwar expectations of its population for greater participation in decisionmaking, it finally bowed to pressure from within and from Washington and announced the restoration of the national assembly. Elections to the assembly were held in October 1992 and produced unexpected results. In a stunning rebuke of the royal family, the opposition captured thirty-five of the fifty seats in the assembly. The outcome of the election was all the more striking given that the electorate was still confined to the privileged few of Kuwaiti society—males over the age of twenty-one who could prove that their families had resided in the country before 1920. The restoration of the assembly and of electoral politics went a long way toward satisfying Kuwaitis' demands for popular representation.

However, the election results did not guarantee a smooth transition to democratic rule. It was questionable whether the members of the opposition could work together effectively. They included nineteen adherents of Islamic groups who called for the *shariʿah* to become the sole source of legislation and several businessmen and intellectuals committed to a more secular process of democratization.

Even with a national assembly dominated by opponents of the regime's policies, the al-Sabah family retained its intimate identification with and control of the state. The crown prince continued to serve as prime minister, and members of the al-Sabah family held the key cabinet posts. However, in a departure from previous practice, six members of the assembly were brought into the cabinet, and government accountability was more closely monitored than it had been previously.

Saudi Arabia also felt the pressures of close scrutiny by the Western media, declining revenues and increasing expenditures, and criticism of its policies from segments of the population. The direct costs of the war for the Saudis have been estimated at $55 billion, a sum that was financed, as in Kuwait, by liquidating foreign investments. Because of the decline in oil revenues, the kingdom had been running deficit budgets since the late 1980s. It continued to do so following the Gulf War, drawing down its reserves to dangerously low levels. Even so, the government could not maintain its social services at their prewar levels, nor could it provide the same degree of employment opportunities that it had previously.

The deteriorating economic situation, the continued presence of foreign troops on Saudi soil, and concerns about the government's financial management practices and its pro-Western orientation gave rise to protests from groups associated with secular-liberal interests on one side and Islamist activists on the other. A secular-liberal group of businessmen and writers signed a petition in late 1990 requesting the establishment of a consultative council, greater freedom of the press, and a change in the status of women. This last issue was highlighted by a November 1990 incident that received wide coverage in the Western media, whose reporters were on hand to cover the Gulf crisis. Forty Saudi women, most of them teachers in women's schools, defied the existing convention prohibiting women from driving by forming a convoy of cars and driving them through the streets of Riyadh. The government, challenged by the Islamic establishment to take action, placed the women under house arrest, confiscated their passports, and released them from their jobs. Although they were later reinstated, their actions resulted in the government's turning what had been an unwritten social convention into a formal law banning women from driving and in presenting to the world an example of the exceptionally restrictive regulations governing women's roles in Saudi Arabia.

Islamists also presented a petition to the king requesting some of the same reforms that the secular-liberal group had, but they framed their demands in terms of the need to observe the *sharicah* and to grant the ulama a greater role in the decisionmaking process. Another faction of Islamic activists outside official ulama circles voiced their complaints much more forcefully. Composed of thousands of young middle-class urban dwellers worried about their future in the declining economy, these activists went further in accusing the government of failing to observe Islamic tenets. They claimed that by inviting Western troops to protect it, the royal family had shown its inability to defend the holy sites of Islam, and that by continuing to rely on the presence of non-Muslim U.S. troops after the war, the ruling house revealed its total dependence on the West. These activists also condemned the spread of Western cultural influences and demanded that the state cut its ties with the West and reshape its policies and practices to conform to Islamic guidelines.

Under attack from both secularists and Islamists, King Fahd introduced new laws for the governing of the kingdom in March 1992. In the Basic Law of Government, the king reaffirmed the centrality of the House of Sacud to the affairs of state. The law stated that monarchy was the form of Saudi government and that succession passed through the sons of Abd al-Aziz ibn Sacud and their male descendants. The law also introduced sweeping changes in the process by which the king was chosen and expanded the pool of princes eligible for the throne, thus making it possible for one of the younger, foreign-educated princes to succeed Fahd. Notably absent from the Basic Law was any mention of civil or political rights or any suggestion that the government intended to address the question of the status of women. The Basic Law was not truly innovative and tended to reinforce the political and social status quo.

However, in a second measure, the king departed from tradition by authorizing the creation of the long-postponed consultative council (see Chapter 21) and appointing its sixty members. The council was empowered to provide advice to the king in several general areas. Because its deliberations and recommendations were confidential, it was impossible to know to what degree, if any, the council's advice influenced the royal court or the policies of state. In 1997 King Fahd renewed the council's mandate and expanded it to ninety members. The new council represented a cross section of educated Saudi society and included businessmen, ulama, two members of the Shica community, and several former high-ranking bureaucrats. It was a highly educated group, with 64 percent of its members holding doctoral degrees, most of them from international universities.[6] In one sense, the renewal and expansion of the council can be viewed as an exercise in royal cooptation designed to broaden the political base of the monarchy. But from another perspective, the king's decision to continue the consultative process may represent an evolutionary step in the Saudi political process.

The reforms did not placate the young Islamists, who continued to claim that affairs of state were not being conducted in accordance with true Islamic principles. In response, the ruling family insisted, as it always had, that the monarchy existed because it was Islamic and because it was guided in all matters by its adherence to Islam. This claim to Islamic legitimacy opened the door for critics to examine the degree to which Islam truly was the guiding principle of the regime. The Islamists found the regime wanting, and they questioned the legitimacy of the monarch with the same Islamic rhetoric that the king used to defend it. This confrontation could not be easily resolved, but its resolution was central to the kingdom's ability to introduce peaceful change.

Yemen

Although Yemen was distant from the field of battle, peninsular rivalries ensnared that country in the demographic repercussions of the Gulf War. Throughout the 1980s, up to 1 million Yemeni workers were employed in Saudi Arabia; their remittances accounted for over 40 percent of the gross domestic products of both North and South Yemen. In May 1990, on the eve of Iraq's invasion of Kuwait, years of on-again, off-again negotiations between North and South Yemen culminated in the unification of the two states as the Republic of Yemen. The new state faced not only the usual problems generated by a merger, such as the allocation of cabinet portfolios and the integration of armed forces, but it also had to attempt to unify the socialist economy of the south with the free market northern economy. Just as the newly unified state was coming to grips with these foundational issues, Iraq annexed Kuwait. Yemen attempted to remain neutral in the ensuing crisis, refusing to condemn the Iraqi invasion and withholding its support from the decision to send Arab forces to join the allied coalition. This stance prompted Saudi Arabia to begin expelling Yemeni workers, and in the months that followed some 800,000 of them returned to Yemen. The Gulf states followed Saudi Arabia's example, expelling an additional 50,000 Yemeni workers. This put a severe strain on the resources of the Yemeni state; it had simultaneously experienced a sudden population increase of nearly 1 million people and a precipitous decline in revenues as the remittances came to a halt and the Gulf states canceled their financial assistance programs. Although its economy suffered badly, Yemen managed to provide for the returning workers.

However, its survival as a unified state came into question when a secessionist movement of southern politicians and military officers plunged the country into civil war in summer 1994. The brief but brutal conflict resulted in a military victory for forces from the north and the restoration of a fully unified Yemen, an outcome that was widely supported by the populations of both regions. Having survived the influx of expelled workers and the effects of civil war with both its unity and its fledgling democratic institutions intact, Yemen, with its agricultural potential, its large population (12 million in the mid-1990s), and its nascent petroleum industry, was positioned to play a more prominent and assertive role in regional politics than it had in the past.

The Refugees

The invasion of Kuwait and the war that followed displaced hundreds of thousands of individuals and created a refugee problem of tragic proportions. A government's choice of ally during the crisis could directly affect the status of its citizens working within one of the neighboring countries. Egypt's decision to join the U.S.-led coalition brought about the expulsion and flight of over 300,000 Egyptian workers from Iraq; and, as we have seen in the section above, when Yemen chose not to endorse the coalition, Saudi Arabia expelled 800,000 Yemeni workers from the kingdom. The PLO's support of Iraq in the initial stages of the crisis had sobering repercussions for the organization itself as well as for Palestinians resident in the Arab Gulf states, especially in Kuwait. The PLO lost the subsidies that it had previously received from the Kuwaiti and Saudi governments, and the Palestinians lost their homes and their livelihoods. Prior to the Iraqi invasion, Kuwait had been home to a relatively prosperous Palestinian community numbering around 400,000; by the time the war was over, 350,000 Palestinians had fled Kuwait, and those who remained were subject to harassment for allegedly cooperating with the Iraqi occupiers.

Some of the refugees returned to the West Bank and Gaza Strip, but the majority remained in Jordan, where their presence had an unsettling economic and social impact. The vast majority of the refugees could not find employment in Jordan, and Jordan could not provide them with adequate relief assistance. As a result, several thousand uprooted Palestinians were once again forced to dwell in UN-sponsored refugee camps. The flood of refugees increased the Palestinian majority in Jordan and raised concerns among Jordanian officials that their country was becoming a surrogate Palestinian homeland.

Conclusion

The grievances that sparked the *intifada* in 1987 were similar to those that produced the Palestinian rebellion of 1936–1939, even though the two events were separated by more than fifty years. Both uprisings represented sustained popular expressions of resentment over occupation and dispossession. The Palestinian Arabs of the late 1930s feared that continued Jewish settlement would lead to the loss of their lands and their expulsion from Palestine. Their rebellion did not prevent those fears from being realized. The Palestinian Arabs of the late 1980s feared that continued Jewish settlement in the West Bank and Gaza Strip would lead to the further loss of their lands and the extinction of Palestinian national identity in the only territories where Palestinians still constituted a majority. Their uprising was an attempt to gain freedom from the hardships of occupation and recognition for Palestinian national rights. Although it did not achieve its full objectives, the *intifada* succeeded in revealing, both to Palestinians themselves and to Israelis, the depth of Palestinian nationalism.

Iraq, the product of Britain's imperial map making, was born without any previous national identity. In determining the frontiers of Iraq, Britain intentionally limited the new state's access to the Persian Gulf to prevent it from challenging Britain's extensive interests there. For more than thirty years, successive Iraqi governments refused to recognize the existence of Kuwait, the state that blocked Iraq from the Gulf. Saddam Husayn's decision to invade Kuwait in 1990 was but the most extreme of several previous efforts by Iraqi governments to modify the restrictive frontier.

The huge scale of the coalition's response to the Iraqi invasion was unprecedented in the post–World War II era. When the war against Iraq began, President Bush expressed his hope that a new world order would emerge out of the conflict. But in effect, the United States and its coalition partners intervened in an inter-Arab crisis, not to create a new world order, but to prevent Iraq from overturning the existing economic and political order, from which the Western economies derived extensive benefits. The state that challenged the old order in the Middle East was annihilated by U.S. firepower, whereas the ruling families that traditionally supported the existing system were rewarded with U.S. protection. The awesome display of U.S. military technology during the Gulf War, combined with the collapse of the Soviet Union, elevated the United States to unilateral hegemony in the Middle East. This development made those rulers who wished to preserve the existing order increasingly dependent on the United States.

However, as we will see in the following chapter, the combined effects of the *intifada* and the Gulf War set in motion a series of events that did open the possibility for the emergence of a new order elsewhere in the Middle East.

Notes

1. Cited in F. Robert Hunter, *The Palestinian Uprising: A War by Other Means,* 2nd ed. (Berkeley, 1993), p. 47.

2. Cited in Dilip Hiro, *Desert Shield to Desert Storm: The Second Gulf War* (New York, 1992), p. 101.

3. Cited in ibid., p. 387.

4. Eric Hooglund, "The Other Face of War," *Middle East Report,* vol. 21 (July–August 1991), pp. 11–12.

5. Roger Normand, "Iraqi Sanctions, Human Rights, and Humanitarian Law," *Middle East Report,* vol. 26 (July–September 1996), p. 42.

6. R. Hrair Dekmejian, "Saudi Arabia's Consultative Council," *Middle East Journal,* vol. 52 (Spring 1998), p. 210.

A Peace So Near, A Peace So Far: Israeli-Palestinian Relations Since the Gulf War

23

⟨⟩
⟨⟩

In devoting a separate chapter to Palestinian-Israeli relations in the 1990s, this work seeks neither to reify nor to isolate that subject. We acknowledge that the Arab-Israeli conflict was but one of several sources of regional instability during the period and that the launching of the Oslo peace process was far from being the only major development in the Middle East of the 1990s. Nevertheless, the rise and fall of the peace process was a momentous occurrence and deserves the careful attention of historians of the modern Middle East. The first agreement in the process, known as Oslo I, was concluded outside the glare of media scrutiny in secret face-to-face meetings between Palestinian and Israeli officials, and its disclosure took the world by surprise. It set the stage for additional steps toward the normalization of relations between Israel and its Arab neighbors, the most important of which was a full treaty of peace and mutual recognition between Jordan and Israel. It led also to the return of Yasir Arafat to Palestine and his assumption of full authority over a small portion of the West Bank and the Gaza Strip. But Oslo I and the agreements that followed it produced darker moments as well. They contributed to the assassination of an Israeli prime minister by a Jewish Israeli citizen and thus exposed the deep divisions within Israeli society over the future direction of the state and its role in the occupied territories. They revealed similar divisions within Palestinian society as Arafat, a virtual outsider, sought to suppress any local rivals, including the Hamas leadership, for control of the Palestinian ministate in the making by transforming the democratic framework envisaged by the Palestinians into an authoritarian apparatus controlled by his personal security forces. This chapter examines the key developments that opened up the possibilities of a peaceful settlement between Palestinians and Israelis but turned instead into a hostile impasse. In so doing, the chapter attempts to show the linkages between the *intifada,* the Gulf War, and the proposals for peace. The chapter also seeks to identify those currents within Palestinian and Israeli society that generated the early momentum for a peaceful settlement and those that contributed to the breakdown of negotiations.

The Road to the Oslo Peace Accords

The Madrid Conference of 1991

The effect of the Palestinian *intifada* on Israeli society, the dominance of U.S. power in the world, and the election of a Labor government in Israel formed part of a series of interconnected developments that contributed to a stunning breakthrough in Palestinian-Israeli relations. In the aftermath of the Gulf War, the Bush administration embarked on an extensive effort to achieve a resolution of the Arab-Israeli conflict. Washington had doubtless promised its Arab coalition partners that it would address the issue once the war with Iraq was over. Moreover, the logic of the liberation of Kuwait— that a people had the right to live free from occupation—offered a compelling reason to seek a settlement of the Israeli-Palestinian question. The proposed instrument of conflict resolution was an international peace conference jointly sponsored by the United States and the Soviet Union. The historic gathering opened in Madrid on October 30, 1991. In the short term, the Madrid Conference was more about public gestures than substantive discussions, and subsequent events have tended to relegate it to the background. However, the gathering at Madrid should not be overlooked; it was a significant step in bringing Israelis and Palestinians to a new level of contact. It brought together, for the first time, representatives from Israel, the Palestinian community, and the neighboring Arab states that had not yet recognized Israel's right to exist—Jordan, Lebanon, and Syria—to discuss peace. And the negotiating sessions that it set in motion conferred a sense of normalcy to the practice of Israeli and Palestinian spokespersons engaging in face-to-face meetings. The Madrid Conference also focused attention on the Palestinian delegation, which was composed of "insiders," that is, Palestinians who lived and worked in the occupied territories. They presented their case with clarity and in tones of relative moderation and made the aging PLO exile leadership appear politically stale and out of touch with the realities of life in the occupied territories.

Between December 1991 and spring 1993, the Arab and Israeli delegations met several more times in Moscow and Washington. In these post-Madrid meetings, the sticking point was, as it had been in all discussions since 1967, Israeli settlement policies in the occupied territories. But this time, the U.S. administration adopted a firm stance against continued settlement activity.

In 1990, in the midst of the *intifada* and on the eve of the Gulf War, Israel embarked on the most ambitious program of settlement construction in the occupied territories it had yet undertaken. The settlement program continued during the Madrid conference and the subsequent peace talks. In the opinion of the Bush administration, Israel's provocative actions in the occupied territories constituted the main obstacle to a successful outcome of the peace process. Israel's refusal to heed U.S. requests to freeze the settlements embroiled the two countries in a bitter dispute that finally drove President Bush to take a step that no U.S. president before him had taken: He linked U.S. financial aid to Israel to Israel's willingness to curb the settlements in the West Bank and Gaza Strip. The policy that Bush adopted was not new—every U.S. administration since 1967 had expressed its opposition to Israeli settlements in the occupied territories—but Bush was the first to enforce that policy.

The U.S.-Israeli dispute reached a climax in February 1992, when the United States announced that it would not approve a $10 billion loan guarantee to Israel unless Israel agreed to a freeze on the construction of all settlements in the West Bank and the Gaza Strip. Israel's Prime Minister Shamir was defiant and insisted that his government would never back down in its determination to populate the occupied territories with Jewish settlers. Shamir's uncompromising attitude caused the most serious strain in U.S.-Israeli relations since Israel's formation.

Despite Shamir's defiant rhetoric, Israel badly needed the U.S. loan guarantee so that it could borrow money on the international markets to help defray the costs of absorbing the new wave of Jewish immigration from the former Soviet Union. Israel planned to use the borrowed funds for housing construction and other measures required by the immigrants. Without the loans, Israel could not afford to finance its settlement policies in the occupied territories and at the same time prepare for the influx of Soviet immigrants.

All of the controversies associated with Shamir's government received intense public scrutiny during the buildup to Israel's national elections scheduled for June 1992. The elections pitted Shamir's Likud bloc against a Labor Party led by former Prime Minister Yitzhak Rabin. In a bitterly fought campaign, Shamir stressed Likud's commitment to Greater Israel, whereas Rabin expressed a vague but conciliatory position on the future of the occupied territories and pledged to restore friendly relations with the United States. The Israeli public rejected Shamir's ideological hard line and gave Rabin's Labor Party an overwhelming victory. The election results created an intriguing historical irony: Twenty-five years to the month after Rabin, as chief of staff of the Israeli army, commanded the campaign that captured the West Bank and Gaza Strip, he was given a popular mandate to negotiate a resolution of the problems caused by Israel's continued occupation of those same territories.

Rabin was no dove (as defense minister he had recently been charged with crushing the *intifada*), but he was willing to support measures designed to restore good relations with the United States. Immediately after forming a government, he announced a freeze on all settlements that were planned but not yet under construction. However, he also stated that all buildings currently under construction, even if only at the excavation stage, would be completed. That was far from the total freeze demanded by Washington, but it was enough to persuade the Bush administration that it should encourage Rabin's moderation. When the new Israeli Prime Minister made his first state visit to the United States in 1992, President Bush announced the authorization of the contentious $10 billion loan guarantee. In taking this action, the United States surrendered some of its financial leverage over Israel without gaining a complete freeze on Israeli settlements.

During his first weeks in office, Rabin proclaimed his willingness to meet personally with Arab heads of state and, in a departure from long-standing Israeli policy, indicated that his government would not be averse to negotiating with Palestinians who were directly affiliated with the PLO. Palestinian leaders showed cautious optimism toward the new Israeli government, but they reserved judgment on its policies until it produced concrete proposals for compromise on the West Bank and Gaza Strip. After twenty-five years of Israeli occupation and five years of Palestinian rebellion, the gap between Israeli policy and Palestinian aspirations was as wide as ever.

Israel and the PLO: The Breakthrough of 1993

In late summer 1993 Arab and Israeli delegates gathered in Washington to attend the eleventh round of the peace talks begun two years earlier in Madrid. The talks had become stalemated, and little was expected of this new session. For that very reason, the sudden disclosure of a secret agreement reached between representatives of the Israeli government and the PLO took the world by surprise. It was an astounding document, stunning both for its unexpectedness and its contents: The agreement provided for mutual recognition between Israel and the PLO and laid the foundations for Palestinian autonomy in the West Bank and Gaza Strip.

The circumstances that brought Israeli and PLO officials together in a series of clandestine meetings outside Oslo, Norway, in the winter and spring of 1993 originated outside normal diplomatic channels. In the course of conducting studies in the occupied territories, the director of a Norwegian research institute discovered that certain well-placed Palestinians and Israeli government officials were receptive to the idea of direct PLO-Israeli negotiations. Following an exchange of information, the Norwegian government volunteered to provide facilities for secret talks, and the two parties agreed to participate. From this uncertain beginning emerged the agreements that had the potential to change the political landscape of the Middle East. The reasons that prompted the two parties to depart so sharply from their established positions rested with a combination of factors.

Following the Gulf War of 1991, the PLO entered a period of political and economic disarray. As its funds dried up, the organization was forced to close offices and cultural centers and to dismiss large numbers of functionaries. Yasir Arafat's tilt toward Iraq cost the organization dearly and led to criticism of his leadership. Within the occupied territories, and especially in the Gaza Strip, the PLO's claim to political primacy came under renewed challenge from Hamas. The PLO leaders, fearful of being overtaken by the appeal of Hamas, looked to negotiations with Israel as a way of retaining their dominance. The attitude of the U.S. government was another factor that drove the PLO to explore direct talks with the Israelis. The new administration of President Bill Clinton was preoccupied with domestic affairs and had a distinctly pro-Israeli bias that made it unwilling to push Israel to make concessions as President Bush had done.

Faced with a deteriorating financial base, declining popular support, and an indifferent U.S. administration, the PLO leaders were desperate for a diplomatic triumph that would revive the organization's reputation and solidify their positions. It was evident to them, and most especially to Arafat, that the years of rejectionism and maximalist demands had failed to bring about the creation of a Palestinian state; the Norway meetings presented an opportunity, very possibly the last one their generation would have, to salvage something from their efforts—even if it meant accepting less than they had previously called for.

From the perspective of the new Israeli government, the prospect of endless violence and occupation was unacceptable. The *intifada* had shown the Israeli public the depth of Palestinian nationalism and had served to make many Israelis aware, for the first time, of the oppressive features of the occupation. Prime Minister Rabin had been elected on a modest peace platform but had devoted much of his first year in office to quelling Palestinian resistance organized by Hamas sympathizers. The growing strength of Hamas, with its ties to other Islamic opposition groups throughout the region, concerned the Israeli leaders and gave them cause to consider negotiations with the PLO as a means of defusing the discontent from which Hamas drew its strength.

The two agreements hammered out in the forests near Oslo were unprecedented. The first was a document of mutual recognition in which Israel recognized the PLO as the legitimate representative of the Palestinian people and, in return, the PLO unequivocally recognized Israel's right to exist in peace and security, renounced the use of terror and violence, and pledged to remove the clauses in the PLO Charter that called for the elimination of the state of Israel.

The second agreement, formally known as the Declaration of Principles on Palestinian Self-Rule but commonly referred to as Oslo I, outlined a five-year program for interim Palestinian autonomy in the occupied territories.

Although Israel would retain overall sovereignty throughout the term of the agreement, the period was divided into several stages, each of which granted increasing administrative responsibility to the Palestinians. During the first stage, Israeli troops were to withdraw from the Gaza Strip and the West Bank town of Jericho, and Palestinian authorities were to assume immediate administrative control of the two areas. In the next phase, an elected Palestinian Council was to assume responsibility for education, health, social welfare, tourism, cultural affairs, and direct taxation throughout the entire West Bank and Gaza Strip. At the same time, the Israeli armed forces were to be redeployed outside the populated areas of the West Bank; the Israeli military would, however, continue to be responsible for the security of Israeli settlers throughout the territories. It needs to be emphasized that Oslo I was not a peace treaty but an interim agreement that was to lead in stages to a final peace settlement. According to the schedule set forth at the time, the interim negotiations would conclude in 1998 with a permanent agreement based on UN Security Council Resolutions 242 and 338. Like most of the deadlines established in Oslo I, this one has been delayed.

The declaration postponed a number of crucial issues for later discussions, prominent among them the future status of East Jerusalem and the Israeli settlements, the fate of Palestinian refugees living abroad, and the question of Palestinian sovereignty. Yet for all the hard bargaining still to come, it appeared that Israelis and Palestinians had, through direct negotiations, taken a major step toward peaceful coexistence.

As the two parties to the agreement worked out last-minute details, the rest of the world scrambled to catch up. Arab leaders, though upset at their total exclusion from the Norway talks, cautiously endorsed the proposal. Although the agreement had caught the United States off-guard, President Clinton pledged his country's moral and financial support and agreed to reestablish formal contacts with the PLO. It was ironic that a U.S. president who had shown little interest in Middle Eastern diplomacy was granted the opportunity to preside over the ratification of what might turn out to be the most significant Arab-Israeli agreement of the modern era.

On September 13, 1993, Israeli and PLO leaders assembled on the White House lawn to participate in a ceremony that would have been unimaginable a few weeks earlier. It began with the signing of the autonomy agreement and then moved to a round of speeches. When Yitzhak Rabin stepped to the podium, he admitted that as a former soldier he was not entirely comfortable with the agreement. However, Rabin eventually found words suitable for the occasion, proclaiming "Enough of blood and tears. Enough!" Yasir Arafat, for so long denied permission to enter the United States, now stood in the shadow of the White House and expressed the hope that the agreement would bring a new era of peace and equal rights; then, addressing the people of Israel, he assured them that the exercise of Palestinian sovereignty and the removal of Palestinian feelings of injustice would be the strongest guarantees of Israeli security. The speeches were followed by a defining moment when the two former enemies, PLO Chairman Arafat and Israeli Prime Minister Rabin, exchanged a handshake of reconciliation. It seemed at the time to represent one of those instances when historical patterns are overturned and new beginnings made possible.

The Promising Beginnings of the Oslo Peace Process

Despite intense opposition to Oslo I from prominent Israeli and Palestinian figures and despite frustrating delays and frequent setbacks in the negotiating process, the overall momentum toward a negotiated settlement was maintained for two years following the signing ceremony. The challenge facing the two parties centered on the need to add specific details to the general principles and vague guidelines of the 1993 accords. This challenge was partially addressed in two agreements signed in 1994 dealing with economic relations and the transfer of administrative authority from Israel to the Palestinians in Gaza and Jericho. Crucial to the successful implementation of Oslo I was the establishment of a self-governing Palestinian authority. Both sides understood that Arafat and the PLO would constitute the leadership of any such authority. For Israelis, this meant allowing an individual and an organization that they had come to associate with the destruction of their state to return to Palestine. In the optimism of the time, these reservations were put aside, and in July 1994 Yasir Arafat, amid tumultuous rejoicing, established residence in Gaza and began to put in place the rudiments of an administrative and security structure. The broader regional impact of Oslo I was made dramatically evident in fall 1994, when Israel and Jordan signed a treaty of peace and mutual recognition, and President Clinton made an unprecedented visit to Syria in hopes of persuading Hafiz al-Asad to open negotiations with Israel. It appeared that the opportunity for a resolution of the entire Arab-Israeli conflict was tantalizingly near at hand.

The final agreement of the two-year period following Oslo I was signed in September 1995. Although it appeared to represent a logical outcome of the accords that had preceded it, this agreement, in combination with other developments to be discussed below, can be identified as a key factor in solidifying opposition to the peace process. Known formally as the Interim Agreement but commonly referred to as Oslo II, the 1995 document spelled out in excruciating detail (it was more than 350 pages long) the stages of Israeli military redeployment in the West Bank, the process by which power would be transferred to Palestinian civil authority, and several other long- and short-term matters. But it was the clauses on redeployment and the limitations imposed on Palestinian authority that drew the most criticism. As shown in Map 23.1, Oslo II divided the West Bank into three zones and specified a phased redeployment of the IDF from each zone. However, the extent of power was to vary from zone to zone. The end re-

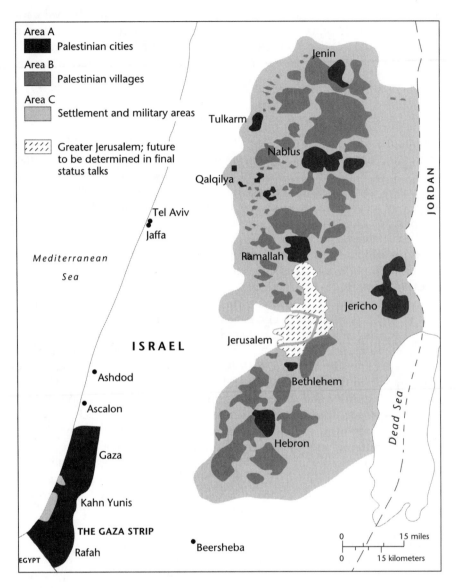

Map 23.1   The Territorial Provisions of Oslo II, 1995

sult was that the Palestinian authority would have direct control of Area A, 3 percent of the West Bank; it would control some municipal functions and would share control with Israel in Area B, 24 percent of the territory; and Israel would retain total control of Area C, an area that made up 74 percent of the West Bank and included all of the 145 settlements in the territory.

At the beginning of the Oslo peace process, Palestinian criticism of Arafat and the accords had been downplayed in the euphoria over the apparent breakthrough to a peaceful resolution of the conflict. But the clauses and maps of Oslo II made it impossible to sustain the pretense that the PLO had done anything other than negotiate from a position of weakness and that it had received anything other than the peace of the weak. To the Palestinians who had applauded Oslo I and the promise it had seemed to hold, Oslo II looked more like a step toward the creation of Palestinian bantustans on the West Bank than the recognition of Palestinian statehood, and increasing numbers of them began to gravitate toward opposition groups.

Problems with the Oslo Process: Two Perspectives

Palestinian.　Even as the White House hosted official ceremonies of public self-congratulation for Arab and Israeli leaders at each conclusive stage of their negotiations, Palestinians continued to suffer through the hard realities of Israeli military occupation, land expropriation, and settler violence. The peace process notwithstanding, Rabin had ended the freeze on settlement construction, and Israel confiscated 20,000 acres of Palestinian-owned land on the West Bank between 1993 and 1995. Some of the confiscated lands became part of an elaborate and expensive system of bypass roads that enabled Israelis to commute from West Bank settlements to major cities in Israel without having to come into contact with the Arab inhabitants of the occupied territories. The bypass roads also served to further fragment the West Bank Palestinian community by cutting villages off from their hinterlands and by disrupting established communication networks.

Even the establishment of a Palestinian self-governing authority brought as much disappointment as it did satisfaction because the qualities that made Yasir Arafat a successful exile resistance leader did not always serve him well as a civil administrator. From the moment he arrived in Gaza in 1994, Arafat endeavored to monopolize the decisionmaking process in the Palestinian National Authority (PNA). To limit the potential for the formation of opposition groups, Arafat appointed to the top posts in the PNA his loyal associates from among the former PLO exiles in Tunis. Those among the local Palestinian elite who had risen to prominence through their role in the *intifada* and who were sensitive to the needs and aspirations of the Palestinian population were largely bypassed in favor of the exile politicians. The result was increased tension between the outsiders, disdainfully referred to as "the Tunisians" by the local Palestinian population, and the resident elite, who were systematically excluded from positions of authority.

This situation did not noticeably change with the election of a Palestinian Council in 1996. Palestinians throughout the occupied territories turned out in large numbers to cast their votes for the council of eighty-eight representatives and for the head of the PNA. Although some local opposition candidates were elected, Arafat's supporters won a comfortable majority, and Arafat himself was chosen president. He then simply ignored the new council and proceeded to set up an authoritarian regime buttressed by an elaborate hierarchy of security forces. As many as seven different security services, numbering upwards of 40,000 men and ranging from uniformed presidential guards to ordinary policemen, were deployed on behalf of the regime. They silenced Arafat's opponents through arbitrary arrests, brutal interrogation methods, and the enforcement of press censorship. Palestinians began to feel that the PNA was becoming as oppressive as the Israeli occupation forces had been.

The deteriorating economic situation in the occupied territories after 1993 further alienated the Palestinian community from the peace accords. Instead of ushering in a period of economic prosperity, the peace process brought increased impoverishment to the occupied territories. Per capita income steadily declined and savings were depleted; by the late 1990s, Palestinian economic conditions were worse than they had been at any time during the Israeli occupation. This was caused in part by Israel's practice of sealing off the territories in response to terrorist activities and thus denying Palestinians access to the Israeli labor market on which they had become dependent. The corruption within Arafat's circle also contributed to the economic malaise. Profiteering and the establishment of monopolies on the sale of basic commodities were common practices among the PLO leaders from Tunis. Arafat himself exercised personal control over the foreign aid donated to the PNA, using it to pay his security forces and top-heavy bureaucracy instead of channeling it into infrastructure development. As the oppressive burden of economic hardship spread throughout the occupied territories, increasing numbers of Palestinians became disillusioned with the peace process and with Arafat's one-man rule.

Hamas was the main beneficiary of the growing disenchantment with the PNA. From the moment Oslo I was signed, Hamas leaders vowed to oppose it. Their opposition was grounded in the Hamas charter (see Chapter 22). If Palestine was defined as an indivisible Islamic territory, then recognition of Israeli sovereignty over any portion of it constituted a betrayal of Hamas's guiding principle of restoring the land to Islamic rule. At the more material level of the struggle for power and resources in the occupied territories, the Hamas leadership resented Arafat's takeover of the PNA and his promotion of external PLO figures to positions of authority. They felt the outsiders were reaping the benefits of the sacrifices Hamas members had made during the *intifada*. This sentiment was shared in many quarters of Palestinian society and enabled Hamas to consolidate its position as a legitimate home-grown opposition movement to Arafat and "the Tunisians." Hamas was firmly rooted in the shared hardships and poverty that Palestinians had experienced under Israeli occupation and was more directly involved in grassroots social welfare activities than were the PNA ministries.

At its most extreme, Hamas's rejection of the entire Oslo peace process was manifested in suicide bombings directed at Israeli civilians in the larger cities. A series of such attacks took place in late 1994 and early 1995, killing dozens of Israelis. The objective of the bombings was to sabotage the peace negotiations by turning the Israeli public against Rabin and the Labor government that had endorsed Oslo I.

Arafat's regime proved particularly vulnerable in its relationship to Hamas. The Israeli response to the bombings was to pressure Arafat to undertake more rigorous security measures in the areas under PNA control; he was expected to deploy his police forces in the slums of Gaza to protect the streets of West Jerusalem and Tel Aviv. Israel made it clear that if Arafat failed to rein in Hamas militants, he would prove himself to be an unreliable partner in the peace process, and negotiations would cease. In short, Israel encouraged Arafat to become the authoritarian ruler he was already inclined to be. Yet in complying with Israeli demands and conducting raids against Hamas organizations and jailing hundreds of suspected activists, Arafat undermined his credibility and turned Palestinians against his administration.

Israeli.   In the aftermath of the signing of Oslo I in 1993, the majority of Israelis were prepared to give Rabin's peace initiative a chance to succeed. However, the Hamas bombings and the prospect of the eventual establishment of an independent Palestinian state brought to the forefront of public concerns the sensitive issue of security, an issue that had served to unify the diverse strands of Israeli society since the formation of the state. If the Oslo Accords did not lead to security, then the peace process was not worth pursuing.

Opposition to the Oslo process was increasingly framed in religious terms. Like Hamas's founders, Jewish religious spokesmen presented a vision of the West Bank as sacred land and argued that any Israeli withdrawal would constitute a surrender of the biblical heritage of the Jewish people. To those who shared this vision, the Oslo compromise giving up portions of the West Bank in exchange for peace was more than a security risk; it was a violation of God's covenant and of a divinely presented opportunity to restore the connection between the Jews and the land God had promised them. In 1995 a group of rabbis placed the religious imperative above the laws of the state by issuing a decree instructing soldiers to resist orders to evacuate army bases in the West Bank. Orthodox and nationalist organizations vilified Prime Minister Rabin, and with each Hamas bombing, other segments of the population began to question the risks to which Rabin's peace process exposed Israel.

Israeli militants, like their counterparts in Hamas, resorted to violence to express their opposition to the Oslo Accords. In February 1994 Baruch Goldstein turned an automatic weapon on a large gathering of Palestinians praying in the Mosque of Abraham near the West Bank city of Hebron, killing twenty-nine of them before he himself was killed. Goldstein had been a member of a militant settler group, and his murderous assault brought to the surface a threatening current within Israeli society. On the evening of November 4, 1995, that current manifested itself in a sudden and tragic moment. As Prime Minister Rabin was leaving a large peace rally in Tel Aviv, he was assassinated by Yigal Amir, a young Israeli student in an institute of Jewish religious studies.

Israel briefly ceased its internal strife to mourn Rabin and to ponder the forces that had spawned his assassin. Subsequent investigations showed that Amir had received a devoutly Jewish religious education and that he acted out of the conviction that Jewish law required the death of any Jew who turned Jewish land over to the enemy. Once again, Israeli society seemed to be torn from within, and the question of which of the competing ideological forces would control the future direction of the country was prominently raised. It remained a critical question in the election to choose a new prime minister and, in the process, to determine whether the Oslo Accords would survive Rabin's death.

The assassination of Rabin left negotiations between Israel and the Palestinians suspended. But developments in the two years following Oslo I had revealed the lack of mutual trust that still divided the two peoples: There existed among Israelis a lingering suspicion that Palestinians were unreliable terrorists, and among Palestinians, a suspicion that the Israelis were determined expansionists.

The Unraveling of the Oslo Peace Process

Yigal Amir and other like-minded Israelis were not the only individuals who sought to destroy the peace process. During the interval between Rabin's assassination and the Israeli elections of May 1996, Hamas carried out another round of suicide bombings in Jerusalem and Tel Aviv that caused public opinion to shift away from support for the peace process. The Israeli government responded with a demonstration of its dominance over the Palestinians, sealing off the occupied territories, placing many West Bank towns under curfew, and causing increased economic distress within the Palestinian community. This crackdown, in turn, fed the atmosphere of hopelessness and despair among the Palestinians and led more and more of them to turn away from Arafat and the unsatisfactory status quo that he represented.

In this atmosphere of heightened tension, Israelis went to the polls and, by the narrowest of margins, chose as their new prime minister Binyamin Netanyahu, the leader of the Likud coalition. Netanyahu had campaigned on a pledge to "slow down" the peace process. Subsequent events showed that what he meant by that phrase was to end the process as it had been defined by the Oslo Accords. Yigal Amir's bullets and the bombs of Hamas had, it seemed, achieved their intended results.

Netanyahu formed a coalition government that has been called "one of the most conservative and religiously-oriented in the history of Israel."[1] It was also one of the most inept. During its first two-and-a-half years in office, it lurched from one self-induced crisis to another, barely managing to survive. In his need to conciliate the religious and nationalist elements upon which his coalition government depended, Netanyahu adopted hard-line policies toward the occupied territories. He refused to acknowledge any connection between land and peace, assuring Israelis that they could have security, settlements, and peaceful coexistence with the Palestinians. At the same time, he inaugurated a new round of provocative settlement activities—initiating the construction of new settlements and expanding existing ones—that seemed to invite Palestinian retaliation. It has been estimated that as many as 5,000 housing units were under construction in the West Bank during 1997. The low prices of government-subsidized housing in the occupied territories proved attractive, and the Israeli population in the West Bank and Gaza Strip increased by 10 percent in 1997. By the end of 1998 some 350,000 Israelis resided in areas that had been taken in the June War: 180,000 in annexed East Jerusalem, 164,000 in the West Bank, and 5,500 in the Gaza Strip.[2]

The most controversial of the several settlement projects was the start of a large settlement project in Arab East Jerusalem in violation of the Oslo Accords, which stated that no change in the status quo of that city should take place until final negotiations. The encroachment on Arab East Jerusalem was intended partly to satisfy the religious elements of Netanyahu's constituency, who insisted on the incorporation of all of biblical Jerusalem into the Israeli state. It was also intended to show Palestinians that their hopes of having an independent Palestinian state with East Jerusalem as its capital would never be realized. The late Prime Minister Menachem Begin's efforts to create "facts on the ground" found its fulfillment in the Netanyahu government's concerted attempts to predetermine the contours of any final status agreement in such a way that a pronounced Israeli demographic component, with the necessary security apparatus, would have to be taken into consideration and in such a way that any future Palestinian autonomy would be limited to fragmented and disconnected sections of isolated enclaves. At the same time that it promoted settlement activities in the occupied territories, Netanyahu's government stalled on carrying out the full range of troop redeployments agreed to in the Oslo Accords.

The intensified Israeli settlement activities exposed the most serious flaw in the entire Oslo process, namely, the imbalance of power between the two parties. The Oslo negotiation process was not carried out between equals. Israel was the occupying power, and Oslo I consigned the Palestinians to the status of the occupied for at least the full five years of the interim agreement. Moreover, because the Oslo agreements were made by the PLO and Israel alone, they fell completely outside the domain of the United Nations and were not subject to any UN resolutions or enforcement mechanisms. Although the United States, as the moral guarantor of the Oslo Accords, could and did raise objections to Israel's land confiscation, increased settlement activities, and refusal to redeploy its troops, Washington showed no inclination to back up its objections with anything more than rhetoric. Thus, Israel could ignore the terms of Oslo I with impunity, whereas the Palestinians had no choice but to bow to superior Israeli power.

The Israeli provocations caused a sadly familiar pattern to repeat itself: Hamas responded with another suicide bombing in summer 1997; Israel then sealed off the occupied territories more tightly than ever and demanded that Arafat and the PNA increase their efforts to arrest Hamas activists. Arafat, his credibility rapidly declining, was reduced to acting as Israel's policeman in PNA territory, to complaining fruitlessly about Israel's refusal to implement the Oslo redeployments, and to making provocative statements intended to disguise his inability to exercise substantial influence on the erosion of the peace process. The continued deterioration of Palestinian-Israeli relations raised the possibility of a major armed confrontation more violent and deadly than the *intifada* had been.

U.S. Intervention and the Wye Accords of 1998

As tensions increased, the Clinton administration assumed a more direct role in the stagnant peace process. Throughout 1998 the United States engaged in constant efforts to persuade the two parties to restart negotiations. The administration was particularly annoyed at Netanyahu's refusal to comply with the troop redeployments specified in Oslo I, and U.S. Secretary of State Madeleine Albright used strong language to publicly condemn Israel's lack of compromise. Continuing U.S. pressure finally succeeded in bringing Netanyahu and Arafat together at the Wye River estate in Maryland.

After days of bitter haggling and intense involvement by President Clinton, Arafat and Netanyahu signed a set of agreements known as the Wye Accords. They represented a very minor achievement, merely elaborating on the original Oslo agreement in which Israel had accepted the principle of exchanging occupied land for peace, in this case a withdrawal of its military from an additional 13 percent of the West Bank, and the PLO had renounced the use of terrorism.

What was lacking in the Wye Accords was the spirit of a partnership for peace that had characterized the atmosphere of Oslo I. Upon Netanyahu's return to Israel, he attempted to disassociate himself from the agreement he had just signed, stating publicly that he had only yielded to U.S. pressure in making the concessions at Wye. And Minister of Defense Ariel Sharon, who had been rehabilitated from his disgrace in the Lebanon invasion of 1982, called upon Israelis to seize as many hills as they could before a final settlement was negotiated. Several groups heeded his call and set up makeshift trailer settlements on West Bank hilltops—scarcely the way for the government of Israel to build a bridge of trust with the Palestinians. Arafat, for his part, had to convince the Palestinians that the territorial provisions of the Wye Accords were truly interim stages and not a foreshadowing of a final agreement that would leave Palestinians in control of only 14 percent of the West Bank. He also faced resistance to the security measures he had pledged to enforce and to the methods his police employed in carrying them out. Arafat, too, blamed the Americans for forcing him into concessions, and he expressed as much distrust of Netanyahu as the Israeli prime minister did of him.

The Fall of the Netanyahu Government and the Elections of 1999

The most significant aspect of the Wye Accords was not the agreement itself but, rather, Netanyahu's reluctant acceptance of the principle of exchanging occupied land for peace and security. However much he sought to distance himself from this portion of the Accords, the fact remained that he had accepted it on behalf of Israel. In doing so, he created deep rifts within the ruling Likud coalition, which had consistently demanded the establishment of Greater Israel and denounced all compromises on withdrawal from West Bank territory. As his government teetered on the brink of collapse, Netanyahu sought to appease his critics on the religious right with an announcement that Israel would suspend its scheduled withdrawal from an additional 13 percent of the West Bank. This was a violation of the Wye Accords he had signed only a month earlier. Riddled by dissension within and pressured by the United States from without, the Netanyahu government fell in December 1998 during a raucous session of the Knesset, which rejected the Wye Accords and voted to dissolve itself. Netanyahu's coalition of rightists and nationalists simply could not endorse the principle of returning occupied land to the Palestinians. At the same time, political moderates and leftists condemned Netanyahu for failing to implement the Wye agreement. Netanyahu's attempt to satisfy the United States and the Israeli moderates by signing the Wye Accords and to mollify the religious Right by refusing to carry them out had failed. He now had to submit his government's record to the Israeli electorate.

Although we have so far concentrated on Israeli-Palestinian relations, it should be noted that Likud's domestic policies also contributed to its downfall. Netanyahu's failure to further the peace process cost Israel the economic gains it had made in the immediate aftermath of Oslo I. Unemployment continued to rise and with it constant labor unrest. In the bitter contest over the role of religion in the state, Netanyahu catered to the religious Right. The government posed as the protector of Israel's Jewish identity in the face of secular assaults from within Israel and from the homogenizing effects of globalization on cultural distinctiveness in general. In a gesture of support for the religious conservatives, Netanyahu allowed the Knesset to debate a proposed Conversion Bill that would provide the Orthodox rabbinical establishment with greater power in determining who was a Jew in Israel. His government also increased state subsidies to ultra-Orthodox educational and social programs. Netanyahu's courting of the religious Right led secular Israelis to view him as a figure who was prepared to tilt Israel toward becoming a state controlled by Orthodox religious circles and served to intensify the cultural war that was already dividing Israeli society.

The election campaign, vituperative even by Israeli standards, pitted Netanyahu and his Likud bloc against Ehud Barak, a former army chief of staff, and his expanded Labor coalition known as One Israel. When Israelis went to the polls on May 17, 1999, they delivered a harsh verdict on Netanyahu's leadership. Barak received 56 percent of the votes for prime minister to Netanyahu's 44 percent. In the context of Israeli politics, this constituted a landslide victory for Barak and showed that Israelis had become disenchanted with Netanyahu's political machinations, with the divisiveness associated with his leadership, and with his failure to pursue a true peace agreement with the Palestinians.

Israel's new prime minister has been described as a dovish hawk in the image of his mentor, the late Yitzhak Rabin. Barak endorsed the resumption of peace negotiations with the Palestinians and recognized the need for compromise. He wished to avoid the confrontational posture adopted by his predecessor and to employ a more conciliatory approach to the Palestinian leadership. But as a career military man and the most decorated soldier in Israeli history, he possessed a keen sense of Israel's security needs and was expected to be a tough negotiator.

If Barak's victory represented the desires of the majority of Israelis for a revival of the peace process, the results of elections to the Knesset revealed a society deeply divided on domestic issues. Beginning with the elections of 1996, Israeli voters cast two ballots, one for prime minister and another for the party list. In the 1999 elections, an unprecedented thirty-three parties received official authorization to field candidates, and fifteen of these parties ended up with representation in the Knesset. The problem this proliferation of parties presented to the formation of a stable governing coalition was compounded by several competing domestic agendas among them. For example, the two parties that made the biggest gains in the Knesset held firm—and opposing—views on the role of religion in the state. One was a new rigorously secular party, Shinui, and the other was Shas, an ultra-Orthodox religious party that became the third largest party in the Knesset. Shas did not object to the peace process, but it rejected the concept of a secular legal system and insisted instead that Israel should be governed by Jewish law. The growth of these two parties suggested that the issue of peace with the Palestinians was less divisive than the differences between secular and religious sectors of Israeli society.

In seeking to rise above this rift and pose as the leader of all of Israel, Barak formed a coalition that included not just Labor's natural center-left partners but also Shas. This raised the possibility that Barak would be forced to make the same kind of domestic religious concessions that all of his predecessors had made in order to achieve consensus on such other issues as peace, economic policy, and social programs. Israel's electoral system, instead of providing the foundation for unified government under a popularly acclaimed prime minister, appeared to contain the seeds for further factionalism and stalemate.

Conclusion

The divergent domestic objectives of the parties within Barak's governing coalition were representative of the larger domestic controversy surrounding the direction of Israeli society and the meaning of a Jewish state. One component of this controversy, the hard-edged religious nationalist current, was represented by the settler groups, who had turned the grave site of Baruch Goldstein into a shrine and who demonstrated against any redeployment of Israeli forces in the West Bank by waving placards that read "All of Israel is ours." A much different current existed at the opposite end of the social and cultural spectrum. It was represented in part by the activists in the Peace Now movement and other organizations that called for a return of at least a large part of the occupied territories in exchange for peace. This current also included those who frequented the beaches and nightclubs of Tel Aviv, who were more interested in consumerism than in colonizing the West Bank, who held a more secular view of the application of religious law in public life, and who yearned for Israel to become what they thought of as a normal nation. Their outlook found one expression in central Tel Aviv in the wee hours of an April morning when thousands of them gathered to celebrate the announcement of the first-place prize awarded the Israeli transsexual singer, Dana International, in the Eurovision Song Contest of 1998. The nation was as divided over this prize as it was over the actions of its militant settlers and uncompromising rabbis. The struggle for the soul of Israel continues, and in its outcome rests the future of the peace process and thus of Palestinians as well as Israelis.

Notes

1. Baruch Kimmerling, "On Elections in Israel," *Middle East Report,* vol. 26 (October-December 1996), p. 18.

2. Geoffrey Aronson, "Obstacles to Peace," *Le Monde Diplomatic,* November 1998, p. 6.

Patterns of Continuity and Change in the Central Middle East Since the Gulf War

24

⟨I⟩
⟨I⟩

Any attempt to interpret the recent history of the Middle East runs the risk of being overtaken by rapidly changing events. Trends that appear to be of major significance at one moment can quickly be rendered peripheral by new and unexpected occurrences. Still, it is possible to identify those developments of the 1990s that were singularly important at the time and are likely to be of historical significance in the years to come.

In the preceding two chapters we have discussed some of the major post–Gulf War developments in Iraq and the Arabian peninsula and have examined the twists and turns of Israeli-Palestinian relations. This chapter focuses on Turkey, Iran, Egypt, and Islamic Central Asia; it begins with an overview of U.S. policy in the Middle East.

The years after the Gulf War were unsettled ones for the peoples and states of the central Middle East. Popular disaffection with the ruling elites spread throughout the region, whether in Islamic Iran, secular Turkey, or authoritarian Egypt. In Turkey and Egypt, this disaffection found expression in the renewed growth of Islamist movements; in Iran, on the other hand, discontent with the rule of the ulama led to an increasing desire for more pluralism and a certain attraction, especially among youth, to Western culture.

America's Moment in the Middle East

As the post-Ottoman era opened in the 1920s with British and French attempts to shape the Arab Middle East to serve their own interests, so too did the post–cold war period begin with the United States seeking to do the same. The three pillars of U.S. cold war policy toward the Middle East since the 1950s had been assuring the security and prosperity of Israel, containing Soviet ambitions, and securing access to the petroleum resources of

Patterns of Continuity and Change | 501

the oil-producing states. Although there may be much to criticize about the assumptions on which this policy was based and the ways and means through which it was pursued, there could be no question that in the aftermath of the Gulf War of 1991, America had emerged triumphant. In summing up the previous forty years of U.S. Middle East diplomacy, Michael Hudson wrote in 1996: "The Soviet Union is gone, Israel has not only survived but has become a regional superpower, pan-Arabism is a spent force, and Arab oil (most of it, anyway) is in the hands of friendly, dependent regimes. Defense of the Middle East has succeeded, and America has achieved hegemony."[1]

With its dominance unrivaled, the question of how the United States would conduct itself and what it would consider to be its primary interests and responsibilities in the region became critically important. Continuity with previous policy goals was evident in the retention of a strong U.S. commitment to Israel's security and well-being, especially during the Clinton administration. In order to promote regional stability, the United States also became deeply involved in efforts to secure a peaceful resolution of the Arab-Israeli conflict, a subject examined in Chapter 23.

The Policy of Dual Containment

One of the primary objectives of the Gulf War of 1991 was to maintain access to Middle Eastern oil. The United States continued to pursue policies designed to continue that access throughout the 1990s, but in a manner that differed markedly from the late cold war years. Instead of relying on a local power to serve as a surrogate enforcer of U.S. Gulf policy, as it had done with the shah's Iran before the revolution of 1979 and with Saddam Husayn's Iraq during the Iran-Iraq War, the United States appointed itself as the protector of the Gulf. U.S. ships patrolled the waters east of Suez, its warplanes made daily surveillance flights over Iraq, and its troops remained permanently stationed in the region.

This was part of a policy called dual containment, which represented U.S. efforts to isolate both Iraq and Iran through tough economic sanctions against the former and more modest restrictions against the latter. In Washington's opinion, Iran represented a destabilizing force in the region, and until it modified its conduct it was to be economically isolated. The U.S. policy establishment maintained that Iran would use the funds from its energy sales to acquire weapons of mass destruction. To keep Iran's revenues down, the U.S. government barred American companies from undertaking any trading and investment activities in the country, and in 1996 Washington took the extreme step of authorizing sanctions against any foreign companies investing more than $20 million in Iran. This step was taken just as the political climate in Iran was changing (see the discussion of Iran in the section "Turkey and Iran: Nations at a Crossroads") and the country was emerging from its self-imposed isolation and actively seeking foreign investment. European companies were outraged at Washington's threats and proceeded to ignore them, directly investing billions of dollars in Iranian energy development. American oil companies, displeased with the total ban on U.S. investment activities, lobbied hard for the administration to change its policy. The Clinton administration's refusal to moderate its stance toward a country as large and energy-rich as Iran appeared short-sighted, especially at a time when the Caspian energy basin was opening up to international investment and Iran was seeking to become the primary transit corridor for Caspian oil and gas (see the discussion of regional competition in the section "Expanding the Middle East: The Regional Reintegration of Central Asia and Transcaucasia").

U.S. containment efforts against Iraq were much more aggressive than those used against Iran. Washington insisted on maintaining the crippling economic sanctions imposed in 1990 until Iraq was deemed to be in full compliance with UN Security Council Resolution 687, which called for the destruction, under international supervision, of Iraq's entire arsenal of chemical and biological weapons and the missiles capable of delivering them (see Chapter 22). The United States insisted that Iraq continued to possess undiscovered stores of weapons of mass destruction and that if the sanctions were lifted, Iraq would use its oil revenues to rearm and again become a threat to the American order in the Gulf.

Despite Iraq's lack of full cooperation, UNSCOM had managed to set up an elaborate monitoring system and had made substantial progress in its disarmament efforts. This all came to an end in December 1998, when one of the periodic crises over UNSCOM's right of access escalated into armed conflict. President Husayn demanded an end to sanctions before he would allow UNSCOM to proceed further with its work. The United States and Britain responded with a concentrated three-day bombing campaign that was, according to U.S. officials, designed to "degrade" Iraq's military capabilities. Its unspoken objective was to weaken the Iraqi regime and produce the overthrow of Saddam Husayn. What had been begun as a quick-strike mission turned into a destructive war of attrition that was still ongoing in early 1999. It was fueled by the U.S. administration's desire to topple the Iraqi regime and by President Husayn's continued defiance. Claiming, as he often had, that the no-fly zones constituted a violation of Iraq's sovereignty, Husayn ordered the air defense systems in the zones to fire on U.S. and British aircraft (see Map 22.1). In turn, the allied pilots were instructed to retaliate, and they did so almost daily. Although these retaliatory air strikes severely crippled the Iraqi air defense systems, the bombing campaign as a whole appeared to negate much of what the U.S. sought to achieve in the region.

For one thing, the UNSCOM monitoring system was destroyed, and it was unlikely that Iraq would allow any kind of arms inspection unit into the country in the near future; for another, Saddam Husayn's grip on power was not noticeably weakened. In addition, the bombing was denounced by America's European allies (with the exception of Britain), it divided the UN Security Council, and it effectively broke up the fragile consensus on the need to maintain economic sanctions as France and Russia called for their termination. Moreover, the bombing of Iraq was an embarrassment to America's Arab allies, particularly as Arab popular opinion openly expressed its anger over the suffering of the Iraqi people. This was as true in Egypt as it was in the Gulf monarchies, where popular resentment at U.S. actions threatened to undermine the very rulers the United States was trying to protect.

Dual containment was in itself a poorly conceived strategy, and its manifestation in the ceaseless bombing of Iraq revealed a bankrupt U.S. policy that substituted force for diplomacy. However much Washington tried to blame Saddam Husayn for the confrontation, Arab public opinion saw little more than an imperious superpower unilaterally deploying its vast military arsenal against an Arab country while ignoring Israel's ongoing violations of the peace accords signed with the Palestinians.

Political Islam and Democratization

One of the platforms in U.S. President Bill Clinton's foreign policy was combating terrorism. Because of the earlier actions of Iran and the terrorist acts committed by a few Islamic organizations, the United States tended to equate the terrorism of a small minority as representative of the attitudes of Islamic activists throughout the world, ignoring the vast majority of Islamists peacefully working for domestic reforms within their respective countries. By constructing a policy framework that viewed all Islamic movements within the narrow context of U.S. security interests and antiterrorist measures, the United States distanced itself from the genuine popular movements within Islamic states and created barriers to its ability to work with the forces that might well shape the future of global Islam. This attitude was compounded by the U.S. popular press, which continued to concentrate on negative stereotypes of Muslims, and by discussions that took place in some Washington and academic circles to the effect that the containment of Islam might replace the containment of the Soviet Union as an organizing theme of U.S. policy. Although such thinking did not become official policy, there could be little doubt that the United States was uncomfortable with political Islam. In part this was because few U.S. officials acknowledged one of the primary causes that nurtured it: the intrusive U.S. presence in the Middle East and U.S. support for oppressive and unpopular regimes.

As political Islam, with its anti-Western and specifically anti-American rhetoric, became the driving force of opposition movements in the Arab

Middle East, the United States became trapped in a contradiction between its expressed goals and its actual policies. Although claiming to favor the establishment of democracy and political pluralism throughout the region, the United States did not pursue this objective. With the exceptions of Israel and Turkey, U.S. allies in the region were undemocratic regimes, some of which possessed very little political legitimacy. The popular forces opposed to those regimes, most often Islamic-oriented and suspicious of U.S. policy, would, in certain states, probably obtain a majority of votes in free and open elections. Therefore, the United States was reduced to ignoring its stated preference for institutionalizing democracy and to shoring up authoritarian rulers who accepted U.S. hegemony in the Middle East but whose domestic policies threatened to promote popular upheavals against them and their superpower ally.

Given the absolute dominance of the United States and its enormous military and economic resources, America's moment in the Middle East was not likely to end soon. But the Middle East that was being shaped by the short-sighted policies pursued during that "moment" might very well turn out to be a region in which America's interests were severely compromised.

Turkey and Iran: Nations at a Crossroads

This book has often compared and contrasted developments in these two states, the most populous non-Arab countries in the Middle Eastern region. During the 1990s, both of them appeared to depart from the historical patterns that had characterized them for the previous twenty years. An Islamist prime minister was elected in secular Turkey, and in Iran, a restive youth population turned away from the Islamicization program imposed by the ulama-led government and embraced aspects of secular Western popular culture.

Political Islam and the Military: Challenge to Turkish Democracy

Ever since the military intervened in politics to curtail the activities of the political left in 1980–1983 (see Chapter 14), Turkey's governing coalitions have been dominated by centrist or right of center parties. This trend continued in the early 1990s under the rightist True Path Party, headed in 1993 by Tansu Ciller, Turkey's first female prime minister. The True Path Party maintained the economic orientation toward a free-market economy that had begun in the 1980s and that facilitated the emergence of a new class of very wealthy entrepreneurs. These new rich embarked on a binge of conspicuous consumption, flaunting their wealth with cars, clothes, and entertainment. The policies of the True Path Party were obviously beneficial for the group that became known as "the have lots."

But the prosperity of the private sector did not affect all of its participants equally. In order to establish free-market principles, the state reduced its subsidies to the agricultural sector, a practice that led to increased migration from the countryside to the larger cities. Nor did the working classes gain from the influx of wealth into Turkey. Restrictions had been introduced on collective bargaining rights, strikes were forbidden, and, as a result, workers' wages were depressed at a time of increasing prosperity for the business elite. The huge income disparities in Turkey were reflected in a deepening political divide within the population. Whereas the pro-business True Path coalition satisfied those at the top, the masses of workers and peasants were attracted to Islamic-oriented parties.

The success of the Islamic parties in the 1990s had its origins in the antileftist measures adopted during the 1980–1983 military intervention. Reasoning that greater exposure to religion would serve as a counterweight to leftist ideologies, the High Command introduced compulsory courses in religion in the primary and middle schools. In addition, they expanded the network of religious schools that trained students to carry out basic ulama functions as prayer leaders and mosque preachers. These religious schools proved to be attractive sources of education and future jobs for the children of lower-class families in central Anatolia, and by the early 1990s, the schools had an enrollment of approximately 300,000 students. The Directorate of Religious Affairs, the agency charged with administering state-approved Islamic activities, grew into a large bureaucratic organization that received an annual budget of $262 million in 1994. In subsidizing and officially sanctioning the emergence of a new religious establishment, the government intended to control Islamic organizations and use them to serve its own ends. This was a risky undertaking, for there was no guarantee that the graduates of the religious schools, or the ulama who taught in them, wished to be contained within the confines of what the government deemed to be permissible Islamic political behavior.

The attempt to create a safe Islamic outlet backfired in the 1990s as the void left by the repression of the political Left was filled by Islamic-oriented political groups that offered the only remaining challenge to the comfortable alliance between the existing political establishment and business interests. The largest and best-organized of the Islamist parties was the Welfare Party, led by Necettin Erbakan. Campaigning for the establishment of a just order, the Welfare Party directed its message to the inhabitants of the poor neighborhoods surrounding the major cities and to the small provincial cities.

The steady growth in the Welfare Party's support culminated in the 1995 elections to the National Assembly, in which it received 21 percent of the popular vote, more than any other party in Turkey's fragmented political system. Necettin Erbakan became the prime minister in a coalition government and embarked on a program to emphasize the Islamic character of

Turkey. He upset the secular establishment by his state visit to the Islamic Republic of Iran, his encouragement of women to wear head scarves, and his practice of appointing Islamist sympathizers to key positions in the bureaucracy. One of the principles of Atatürk, the foundational concept of secularism, seemed to be in danger of being overturned. The military, which regarded itself as the guardian of Atatürk's legacy, did not stand idly by.

The High Command chose to make its stand against Erbakan and the Welfare Party over the issue of religious education. In 1996 the military demanded that the National Assembly pass a bill requiring students to spend more time in public schools before being allowed to enroll in a religious school. Prime Minister Erbakan refused to support the bill, and when it passed, the military pressured him into resigning. If this was not the direct intervention of the military into the realm of civilian political life, it was perilously close. A further attempt to drive Islamic organizations from the political arena was made in the 1998 decision by the Constitutional Court, Turkey's highest judicial authority, to ban the Welfare Party and to bar seven of its members, including former prime minister Erbakan, from political activity for five years. According to the court, Welfare's policies violated laws that prohibited any efforts to change the secular character of the Turkish Republic.

In defending the secular legacy of Atatürk, the military may have ignored another central principle of his heritage, namely, democracy. While concentrating solely on its concerns for the proper role of Islam in a constitutionally defined secular state, the High Command overlooked the equally critical question of the role of the military in a constitutionally defined democratic republic. The line between civilian and military control over decisionmaking was stretched even thinner in the state's response to Kurdish nationalist activities.

Kurdish Nationalism and the State: A Further Challenge to Democracy

A constant pattern running through the history of the Turkish Republic has been the conflict between the Kurdish desire for a form of cultural and political autonomy and the efforts of the Turkish state to prevent that autonomy (see Chapter 10). Starting in 1984, the conflict reached a new level of intensity with the launching of a widespread Kurdish insurrection that was met with an all-out show of force by the Turkish military. This confrontation showed no signs of abating in the late 1990s.

The Kurds are an ethnic minority within Turkey, numbering between 10 million and 12 million people, roughly 20 percent of the population. However, in the southeast portion of the country, where the Kurds are concentrated, they form a majority (see Map 24.1). This region has been the homeland of the Kurdish people for centuries, and it was their shared geo-

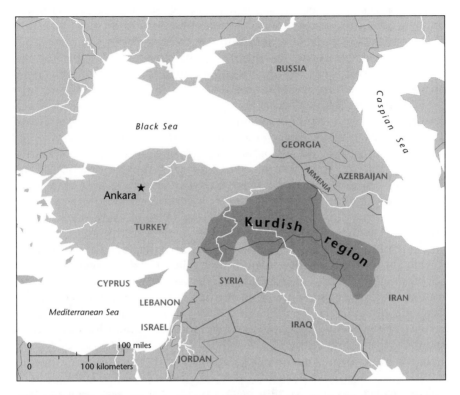

Map 24.1 Kurdish Homelands. The shaded area indicates the region where Kurds form a majority of the population. The region extends across four sovereign states.

graphical space and their distinct language that gave them a sense of communal identity. From the time of Atatürk to the present, the Turkish state endeavored to repress Kurdish identity by ignoring its existence. Official policy encouraged Kurds to assimilate into the dominant Turkish ethnicity, and most of those who did so were able to participate fully in government and politics. Those who did not were excluded from the national life of the state.

The insurrection that began in 1984 was organized by a militant organization within the Kurdish nationalist movement, the Kurdistan Workers' Party (PKK). Although the PKK issued a range of minimal and maximal demands, its basic objective was to achieve the recognition of Kurdish political and cultural autonomy within the framework and boundaries of the Turkish state. This was a form of federalism in which Kurdish would be the language used in the school system, the courts, and the media. To achieve its goals, the PKK leadership endorsed terrorism as a legitimate tactic. Targeting such representatives of the state as schoolteachers, civil servants, and government buildings, the PKK engaged in a campaign of assassination and destruction that made normal life in the Kurdish provinces impossible. Businesses shut down, government operations came to a halt, and southeastern Turkey, already an impoverished region, became even further distanced from the prosperity enjoyed by the consuming classes of the large cities.

Successive governments exacerbated the devastation of the Kurdish provinces by their response to the insurgency. From the perspective of Turkey's civilian and military establishment, the Kurdish uprising represented a threat to the integrity of the state and the Kemalist legacy of a Turkish nation, and they were determined to crush it. Throughout the 1990s, the government placed most of the Kurdish regions under a state of emergency and gave the armed forces a free hand to undertake whatever measures they deemed necessary in the circumstances. Those measures were severe by any standard. The military adopted a scorched-earth policy that included the concentration of heavy firepower on civilian areas, the forced deportation of the inhabitants of entire villages and the demolition of the vacated dwellings, the burning of vast areas of crops and forests, and the mounting of two large-scale operations into northern Iraq to strike at the PKK organizations that had located there after the Gulf War of 1991. It has been estimated that by the late 1990s, the military had destroyed more than 2,300 Kurdish villages and more than 2 million Kurds had fled or been forcefully relocated.

The threat to democratic principles was evident in the attitude of the military High Command toward the conduct of the Kurdish campaign. The military argued that the Kurdish issue was strictly a military issue and that only military means could resolve it. Exercising pressure within the political system, the military sought to persuade the civilian politicians to give it a free hand in the campaign against the Kurds. These efforts were successful, and by the late 1990s, the High Command increasingly took charge of policy as well as operations in matters involving the Kurds. For example, the High Command did not inform the prime minister in advance about a large cross-border operation into northern Iraq in late 1998, an arrogant act that showed civilian control of the military, and thus of policymaking, was slipping away.

Turkey's Troubled Foreign Relations

Turkey's membership in NATO, its reliance on military and economic assistance from the West, its extensive foreign trade with Western Europe, and its firm support for the allied coalition during the 1991 Gulf War underscored the close connection between the country's foreign relations and its economic development. Turkey's development strategies were oriented toward Western Europe, and its governing circles anticipated that it would become a full member of the European Union (EU), the unified economic bloc that was nearing completion in the late 1990s. However, Turkey's military campaign against the Kurds and the domestic security measures that accompanied it generated widespread European criticism that Turkey was engaged in human rights violations. European economists also questioned whether Turkey's economy was sufficiently developed to enable the country to participate in the European Union without large subsidies from the more prosperous member states.

In late 1997 the European Union not only rejected Turkey's application for membership but also stated that it would not encourage Turkey to plan on joining the EU in the future. The Turkish government was furious and immediately froze its relations with the EU. Turkish politicians accused the organization of having an anti-Islamic bias, pointing out that Greece, which was a member and which strongly opposed Turkey's entry into the EU, had economic problems similar to Turkey's.

At the time of this writing, it did not appear possible for Turkey to reorient its economy away from Europe despite nationalist and Islamic desires to do so. Turkey did, however, work to strengthen its ties to the United States and to seek new regional alignments, one of which was with Israel. The Turkish and Israeli armed forces carried out joint military exercises, and the two states began discussions about forging a long-term military alliance.

Turkey's regional relations, and its reputation in Europe, continued to be troubled by the festering Cyprus question (see Chapter 14). Negotiations to unite the Turkish and Greek portions of the island broke down in 1998, largely because the leadership of the Turkish Republic of Northern Cyprus refused to surrender any of the republic's sovereignty. Turkey continued to maintain a force of 35,000 troops in the north and remained the only country to recognize the existence of the Republic of Northern Cyprus. The failure of negotiations to obtain any degree of cooperation raised tensions on the island and created an explosive situation.

Turkey in 1999 was faced with an increasingly fragmented political system, the growing popularity of Islamic parties, a full-blown armed insurrection in the Kurdish provinces, and a military High Command that edged ever closer to controlling domestic policies.

Iran in the 1990s

Whereas the political opposition in Turkey expressed itself in Islamic terms, a different pattern emerged in Iran, where secular behavior and an admiration for Western popular culture became the means by which segments of the urban population expressed resentment at the intrusive Islamicization policies of the government.

In the years following Ayatollah Khomeini's death in 1989, popular pressure and economic necessity compelled the regime to moderate certain of its policies. Khomeini's successor as supreme Islamic jurist, Ayatollah Khamenei, and Iran's president, Ali Akbar Rafsanjani (1989–1997), formed an uneasy alliance through which they attempted to prevent the more radical ulama from gaining greater control of the state. In 1989 they engineered a series of constitutional amendments that eliminated the post of prime minister and increased the scope of presidential authority. The amendments did not, however, diminish the power of the supreme Islamic jurist, who retained ultimate authority over the armed forces, the making of war and peace, the direction of foreign policy, and the right to intervene in the domestic legislative process whenever he chose.

With the backing of the supreme jurist, President Rafsanjani introduced modifications in Iran's domestic and foreign policies. The economy had been slow to recover from the long war with Iraq, and the country suffered from widespread unemployment, declining standards of living, reduced oil revenues, and an alarmingly high annual population increase of 3.9 percent. The deteriorating economic situation caused the greatest hardships among the urban poor and the lower middle classes, the very groups that had comprised the regime's original base of popular support. Rafsanjani sought to restore confidence in the government by privatizing most of the companies that had been nationalized in the first years of the Islamic Republic and bringing in qualified technocrats to manage the economy.

Economic necessity also drove the government's attempts to end the county's diplomatic isolation. During the Gulf crisis of 1990–1991, Iran reestablished diplomatic relations with Saudi Arabia and endeavored to improve its regional reputation with assertions that its revolution was not exportable. In a major departure from Khomeini's policies, the government applied for a loan from the International Monetary Fund and encouraged foreign investment. In addition, as we will see in the section on Central Asia, the breakup of the Soviet Union and the emergence of a new constellation of Islamic states along Iran's northern borders presented the country with opportunities to expand its regional influence.

The changes introduced by Rafsanjani and his supporters met with resistance and intensified the struggle over the future direction of the Islamic Republic. On one side were ulama like Rafsanjani, who were committed to the survival of the Islamic Republic but sought to reorient the government's policies to accommodate the realities of a global economy and the demands of efficient government. Opposing them were groups of radical ulama who wished to deepen the Islamicization of society, to perpetuate their control of government, and to ensure that the constitutional prerogatives of the supreme Islamic jurist remained intact. The contest between these clashing viewpoints was played out in the Majlis, which became an important arena for the airing of diverse opinions. Because Majlis sessions were broadcast live on the radio, they provided the population with one of its few opportunities to hear public opposition to the government and open disagreement on a range of economic and social issues. The debates in the Majlis contributed to popular awareness that the government's positions need not go unchallenged and that dissent was present within the ranks of the ulama.

President Rafsanjani's economic opening to the outside world and his government's more relaxed enforcement of some of the regulations on social behavior were in part responses to popular disillusionment with the performance of the ulama as rulers of the country. Public displeasure was evident in the results of parliamentary elections, in which the proportion of ulama among the elected deputies declined steadily from a high of nearly 50 percent in 1980 to 24 percent in 1992. The sentiments that lay behind this voting pattern were given full expression in the presidential elections of 1997.

The Significance of the Presidential Elections of 1997

The government's policies of moderation may have been more in keeping with popular sentiments than it anticipated. In the presidential elections of 1997, the government's candidate for president, who was backed by the supreme Islamic jurist, suffered a resounding defeat at the hands of an independent candidate, Muhammad Khatami, who campaigned on a platform of tolerance, social reform, and a greater role for women in public life. Khatami's victory was a stinging rebuke of the regime; he received 69 percent of the vote and had particularly strong support from two segments of the population that felt excluded by the practices of the Islamic Republic: youth and women. The enthusiastic support for Khatami of these two constituencies, and especially of the youth, had important implications for the future. Between 60 and 70 percent of Iran's population was estimated to be twenty-five years old or younger.

Too young to have experienced the shah's regime or the revolution that overthrew it, they did not embrace the aggressive anti-Western attitudes of the ruling ulama and resented the restrictions that government-imposed Islamicization brought to their daily lives. They objected to the social codes that classified any public contact between unmarried or unrelated men and women as a violation of public morality; they detested the nightly patrols of police and religious vigilantes, who roamed the urban quarters searching for people listening to forbidden Western music or watching imported videos or satellite television. Even before the election of Khatami, individuals had engaged in countless gestures of defiance against the social strictures. In the capital city, Tehran, underground entrepreneurs did a thriving business providing foreign videos and alcoholic beverages to those who could afford them, and ill-concealed satellite TV dishes sprouted from many rooftops. Khatami's promise of tolerance struck a responsive chord among Iran's younger population, especially urban dwellers, and they participated actively in the campaign that elected him.

The figure on whom so many hopes rested was a member of the ulama, but an exceptionally worldly one. Although his education had included the customary courses in theological studies at Qum, he had also received university degrees in philosophy and education. Like many of the reformist ulama, he was committed to the concept of the Islamic Republic and to the preservation of an Islamic frame of reference in political and social life. But he recognized that in order to sustain the gains of the revolution, it was necessary to broaden the appeal of the Islamic Republic by winning the support of the groups dissatisfied with its policies. He wished to include women and young people within the structure of the Islamic system rather than having them campaign against it as alienated outsiders. During his first year in office, he succeeded in securing greater freedom of the press and media and in restraining the activities of the units that enforced the codes on social morality.

As Khatami attempted to broaden his base of popular support, he became locked in a political struggle with the entrenched radical ulama, who did not wish to lose their grip on power and the access to material benefits that it brought. This struggle, as with so much of the politics of the Islamic Republic, was reflected in the differing views that Khatami and his opponents held toward Iranian-U.S. relations. U.S. attempts to contain Iran and to use economic sanctions against it have been discussed earlier in this chapter. In a gesture designed to soften Washington's stance, Khatami, in early 1998, took an unprecedented step for an Iranian president in the postrevolutionary era: He agreed to an interview on CNN for the express purpose of addressing the U.S. public directly. In the course of the interview, he called for a dialogue between Iran and the people of the United States and suggested that negotiations between the two countries were possible. The tensions within the Iranian ulama leadership were revealed shortly after the interview, when supreme Islamic jurist Khamenei delivered a widely publicized sermon in which he denounced the United States and denied that Iran had any intention of becoming reconciled with it. Khamenei's sentiments showed the existence of a wide gap between the popularly elected president and the closed, self-selective circle of ulama who controlled the levers of power and determined the official policy of the state. It was not clear, in early 1999, how that gap could be successfully bridged. Nor could the full extent of popular dissatisfaction with the regime be accurately determined, though the 1997 election results did show that Khatami received a majority of votes in the countryside as well as in the cities.

The problems facing the ulama ruling elite in Iran were similar to the problems facing the secular regimes in the region. A restless young population, alienated by state control, economic mismanagement, and poor employment prospects, blamed the existing regime for denying them a future. But, for example, in Egypt and to a lesser extent Turkey, disaffected elements of the population demanded the restoration of Islamic government and *shariʿah* law to achieve social justice and economic opportunity. Was it conceivable that the opposition forces in Iran would demand an end to ulama control of government and a greater measure of secular legislation to achieve the same goals? As deeply as the ideology of revolutionary Shi'ism had been implanted in the Iranian body politic since 1979, the hard reality was that it had not fulfilled its promises of improving the lives of those at the lower end of the economic scale. And for many Iranians in the middle and upper classes, the policies of the Islamic Republic were isolating and incompatible with the kinds of lives they wished to lead in the new millennium.

The Persistence of Political Islam: The Example of Egypt

Overview

Radical political Islam achieved its first victory in the Islamic revolution that swept the ulama to power in Iran in 1979. At the time, most observers considered this to be an episodic event attributable to the particular circumstances prevailing in Iran and to the role of Shi'a Islam in that country. Although it is true that the origins and outcome of the Iranian revolution must be viewed in terms of conditions specific to that country, it is also true that in the years since 1979 political Islam has spread well beyond the borders of Iran and has become one of the most enduring Middle Eastern phenomena of the final two decades of the twentieth century. As governments such as that of Turkey, or authoritarian leaders like Anwar Sadat of Egypt, moved to silence the political Left, they compelled opposition groups to channel their activities through religious associations or parties of the Right. Thus by the 1990s, the only credible opposition to failing regimes came from Islamists, either as official parties, as was the case with the Welfare Party in Turkey, or as militant radical minorities, or, most often, as moderate centrists who worked within the system to rebuild and reform society. Egypt, which experienced simultaneous movements of violent and moderate Islamists, offers a revealing case study of the interaction between a failed authoritarian regime and its Islamic opposition.

Failings of the Mubarak Government

Scholarly accounts of Egypt in the 1990s frequently use such words as *stalemate, stagnation, corruption,* and *authoritarianism* to describe the regime of President Husni Mubarak. Given these characterizations of the government, it is no wonder that the Egyptian population's dissatisfaction with its ruling elite, already present in the late 1980s (see Chapter 18), intensified and that popular organizations did what they could to reorder society in ways that the government was unwilling and unable to undertake.

Although the United States rewarded Egypt for its participation in the allied coalition during the Gulf War by forgiving half its debt and maintaining an annual $2.3 billion aid package, the economic performance of the Mubarak government remained dismal. The government was unable to privatize the inefficient state-owned industries, largely for the reasons discussed in Chapter 18. As a result, Egypt's productive capacity remained low, and it was unable to compete in an increasingly globalized marketplace. With economic stagnation came rising unemployment, a decline in real wages, and a growing income gap between the few thousand well-off Egyptians and the population at large. The hopelessness of the situation for the younger generation was represented by figures showing that fewer than half of the nearly 500,000 Egyptians who entered the labor force each year could secure employment.

Popular resentment over the bleak economic outlook was compounded by the continued political failings of the regime and its determination to limit the opportunities for political participation. Mubarak cast aside the liberalizing tendencies of his early presidency in favor of one-party, one-man rule. The government restructured the election laws to ensure that no popularly supported opposition parties could win seats in the People's Assembly. Thus, in the 1995 parliamentary elections, fraud, vote rigging, and restricted campaign opportunities for opposition parties resulted in the ruling National Democratic Party (NDP) party winning 94 percent of the seats, far more than the 68 percent it had won in the more open 1987 elections. In addition, the likelihood that Mubarak would, at age seventy-one, seek a fourth six-year term as president gave the regime an authoritarian cast. Further tensions were created by Mubarak's refusal to fill the office of vice-president, thus leaving the question of an orderly succession unresolved. Mubarak's lack of inspirational leadership (see Chapter 18) had been somewhat alleviated by the belief that although he might have been dull, he was at least honest. However, by the early 1990s, rumors of corruption within the president's immediate family made him appear no better than other officials within the political class and increased the already deep disillusionment with the regime.

The Popular Response: Two Versions of Islamic Activism

The popular Egyptian response to economic stagnation, political repression, and regime corruption centered on two distinctive approaches to Islamic activism, which arose simultaneously. In the first of them, Islamic militants launched a full-scale armed insurrection against the regime with the intent of overthrowing it. The other, and more significant, approach was carried out by volunteer organizations working within the existing system. These organizations succeeded in institutionalizing Islamic revivalism within mainstream Egyptian society, a process that has been termed a "quiet revolution."

In 1992 a series of intermittent clashes between young Islamic radicals and government security forces erupted into a full-scale insurgency against the regime. The causes of the insurgency were social and economic, but the insurgents framed their cause in language reminiscent of the Islamic movements of the 1970s: The government's failure to implement Islamic law made Egypt an atheist state, they argued, and all true Muslims were obligated to wage *jihad* against it. The insurgency was generally uncoordinated, but its inspiration came from al-Jamaʿat Islamiyyah, an umbrella organization that embraced a variety of clandestine radical Islamic organizations, each of which conducted its operations independently. In addition to assassinating dozens of policemen and minor government officials, the radicals sought to bring down the regime by disrupting the tourist industry and thus creating further economic difficulties. Tourism was a crucial source of foreign currency, contributing $3 billion annually to the Egyptian economy and employing, directly and indirectly, millions of Egyptians. The most devastating incident of the radicals' campaign occurred in fall 1997, when Islamic extremists massacred more than sixty foreign tourists near the city of Luxor. The threat of becoming victims of violence did frighten off tourists, and by the late 1990s, Egypt's annual revenue from tourism had fallen to less than $2 billion. The radicals also took their campaign into the heart of Cairo, attacking groups of tourists and carrying out a highly publicized and widely condemned assassination of Faraj Fuda, a prominent secular commentator and critic of Islamic militancy.

In seeking reasons for the exceptional violence perpetrated by the 1990s insurgents, researchers discovered that their demographic profile differed from their counterparts of the 1970s (see Chapter 20). The radicals of the 1990s were likely to be younger and poorer and to include far fewer university-educated participants. Theirs was a revolt of the downtrodden from the neglected rural areas and the slums and shantytowns of the major cities where municipal services were nonexistent, a revolt of those who suffered most from the country's deteriorating economic situation. They were far more radicalized and desperate than the frustrated middle-class university graduates who had formed the backbone of the organizations of the 1970s.

The Mubarak government responded to the radical threat with a brutal counterinsurgency campaign. Security forces raided Cairo neighborhoods and swept through villages in Middle and Upper (southern) Egypt, where the insurgency was most widely supported. The security forces made massive arrests of extremists and sympathizers, and often of their friends and relatives, in a campaign of intimidation and government violence that made no pretense of observing human rights and the rule of law. An antiterrorism law allowed the state to try civilians suspected of terrorist activities in military courts, whose verdicts had no right of appeal. During the 1990s nearly 100 civilians were sentenced to death by the military courts alone, and thousands more were detained under emergency powers. By the late 1990s the government's draconian measures had enabled the security forces to quell the radicals' activities in Cairo, but the insurgency continued to smolder on in the southern provinces.

At the same time that the extremists were attempting to overthrow the government by force, another form of Islamic activism was gaining momentum in Egypt that had far more profound implications than the uncoordinated violence of the young radicals. This activism was moderate, conservative, and often apolitical; it represented the desire of the population at large to participate in the political process and to build a new society based on democracy, respect for human rights, and social justice, an objective that was such a prominent feature of the Quranic revelations. This centrist activism cannot be called a movement in that it had no single coordinating organization but consisted instead of the actions of separate groups within diverse sectors of Egyptian society. Yet for all its spontaneity and diversity, the success of moderate activism did owe much to the organizational capacity of that most resilient of modern Egyptian organizations, the Muslim Brotherhood. When President Sadat allowed the brotherhood to resurface in the 1970s, it adopted a centrist and reformist stance and demonstrated a willingness to work within the system. By the 1990s the brotherhood and several other middle-class volunteer organizations had established a network of charitable institutions, clinics, hospitals, day care centers, and legal aid societies that by their very presence testified to the failings of the existing system. Motivated more by a social than a strictly religious agenda, the moderate activists sought to integrate general Islamic principles with responsible social reform. Their activities were designed to demonstrate the relevance of Islam to contemporary social and economic conditions, and, by implication, they highlighted the regime's inadequacies in dealing with those conditions.

The difference between the Islamist activities of the 1970s and the so-called quiet revolution of the 1990s was the manner in which the latter became deeply institutionalized within mainstream Egyptian society. For example, members of the Muslim Brotherhood and other Islamic moderates gained dominance in the professional syndicates of lawyers, doctors, engineers, and journalists. Further evidence of the extent of the quiet revolution was found in the proliferation of private mosques and Islamic schools outside the direct supervision of the government. Most scholars of the moderate Islamist phenomenon argue that it embraced individuals from all social classes and age groups and was inclusive of women. Although social activism was at the forefront of moderate Islamism, it also had religious dimensions that manifested themselves in increased participation in Quran study groups and a resurgence of Sufism.

Although the moderate Islamists did not contest the authority of the state, their growing numbers, their call for democracy, and their efficient alternative social welfare programs represented a challenge to a regime that was determined to prevent the emergence of viable opposition groups.

Accordingly, the regime used the climate of crisis created by the radical insurgents to crack down on the moderates as well, arresting journalists and prominent individuals associated with the centrists, limiting their access to the media, and censoring their publications. In seeking to explain the regime's assault on the moderate Islamists as well as the violent militants, historian Raymond William Baker has argued that the violent minority could be contained by force, whereas, by contrast, "much more damaging to a dependent, corrupt, and unimaginative political order is the emergence of a social and political force, grounded in widely shared religious and cultural values, that by its very presence in the public arena constitutes a devastating critique of the existing system."[2] To Baker, the attack on the peaceful Islamic centrists highlighted not only the regime's failings but also its lack of legitimacy. The government's attempts to limit the growing influence of the moderate Islamists only served to put it at odds with a mainstream social-religious popular movement and to isolate it further from the majority of its citizens.

Expanding the Middle East: The Regional Reintegration of Central Asia and Transcaucasia

The collapse of the Soviet Union in 1991 was accompanied by the sudden and unexpected independence of five Islamic republics in Central Asia and several smaller states in Transcaucasia, the most important of which for this discussion was the Islamic republic of Azerbaijan (see Map 24.2). My purpose here is not to examine the domestic politics and the tangled ethnic rivalries of the new republics but, rather, to explore the impact that their emergence as independent polities has had on the Middle Eastern region, especially Turkey and Iran, and the significance that their vast energy reserves has had in shaping regional diplomacy. In broad terms, the three major driving forces behind the emerging linkages between Central Asia and the Middle East are ethnicity, interregional rivalry, and petroleum. Islam has also been a factor in facilitating contacts, but it has not been as uniformly determinative as the other three.

Background

From the beginning of the adoption of Islam by the population of Central Asia in the late eighth century, the region became an integral part of both formal intellectual and popular Islamic–Middle Eastern civilization. As Chapter 2 of this book pointed out, the Central Asian cities of Samarkand and Bukhara were centers of high Islamic culture, and scholars from those and other Central Asian cities made significant contributions to scientific and *shari*ᶜ*ah* studies that permanently enriched Islamic civilization as a

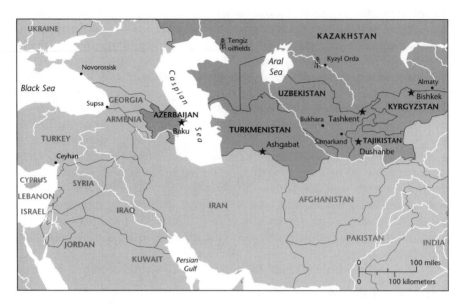

Map 24.2   Azerbaijan and Islamic Central Asia in the 1990s

whole. Islamic Central Asia was oriented westward toward the Middle East and the Islamic centers there, rather than toward China, and the contributions of its scholars, rulers, and ulama became part of the Middle Eastern Islamic tradition.

The great westward Turkish migrations of the eleventh through the thirteenth centuries that culminated in the formation of the Ottoman Empire left in their wake a largely Turkic-speaking Central Asian population whose rulers and scholars adopted Persian as the language of high culture. But this process of change only reinforced the region's linkages to the Islamic Middle East rather than to the Far East. However, beginning in the second half of the nineteenth century, czarist Russia incorporated Transcaucasia and Central Asia into its growing colonial empire, gradually cutting those areas off from their traditional ties to the Middle East. With the Soviet takeover in the early 1920s, the economies and politics of the region were completely reoriented toward Moscow, and during the seventy years of Soviet rule Transcaucasia and Central Asia were isolated from their neighboring Islamic states.

Unprepared for the independence they suddenly acquired in 1991, the new Islamic republics faced problems similar to those confronted decades earlier by the former Arab provinces of the Ottoman Empire: They had to determine symbols of national identity, to formulate independent foreign policies, and to develop institutions for self-governance, and they had to conduct these tasks within borders artificially drawn by their former Soviet rulers to serve the needs of Moscow, not of the local populations. A further similarity to the situation faced by the former Arab provinces was the prominence of a ruling elite trained under the collapsed imperial system. With the exception of Tajikistan, the presidents of the new Islamic republics were the same ex-communist officials appointed during the Soviet era. Their style of rule has been called secular authoritarianism, and they have not encouraged the creation of democratic institutions.

Regional Competition for Influence in the New Republics

Any discussion of the attempts of Middle Eastern states to acquire influence in Transcaucasia and Central Asia must take into consideration the prominent role that Russia continued to play in the affairs of the new Islamic republics. The Russian armed forces maintained a presence in the new states, and Russia sought to become a major economic beneficiary of the energy wealth of the region. Thus Turkey and Iran, the two principal competitors for influence in Central Asia, had always to conduct their policies with an eye to the sensitivities of Moscow.

A further constraining factor for outside powers was the complexity of the ethnic and religious composition of the new states. The languages of Azerbaijan and four of the five Central Asian republics are Turkic, whereas Tajikistan is a Persian-speaking country. However, the inhabitants of Turkic Azerbaijan are mainly Shi^{c}a Muslims, whereas the population of Persian Tajikistan embraces the Sunni version of the faith. These and a host of unresolved ethnic tensions contributed to a volatile mix that made it difficult for external states to establish consistent relations with the region.

When the Central Asian republics became independent in 1991, Turkish governing and business circles reacted with unrestrained enthusiasm. The cultural and ethnic ties that Turkey shared with the Islamic republics generated unrealistic expectations for the creation of an exclusive Turkish sphere of influence stretching from Azerbaijan to Kyrgyzstan. Turkey's elite proposed that the Kemalist model of development was the most suitable one for the new states to emulate, and they tried to present Turkey as the intermediary through which Central Asia could build contacts with the West and as the conduit through which Western aid could flow into the region. In the period immediately following independence, delegations of Turkish foreign service officers and businessmen descended upon the new states, and Turkey in turn hosted state visits for the Central Asian presidents.

However, once the initial euphoria of rediscovered cultural ties subsided, the Central Asian leaders made it clear that they did not wish to fall under Turkish domination and that they could not entirely break away from their reliance on Russia. While all parties accepted the new realism, Turkey nevertheless continued to pursue activities that accelerated the linkages of Central Asia to the Middle East. For example, Turkey established regular airline service to the leading Central Asian capitals, provided fellowships at Turkish universities for Central Asian students, and broadcast Turkish-language programs into the region by satellite. Turkey's policies toward Central Asia were designed not only to expand its role as a regional power but also to preempt Iran's efforts to establish its own presence in the region.

By all accounts, Iran's policies toward Central Asia and Azerbaijan were pragmatic and were not dominated by attempts to export the ideology of revolutionary Islam. Iran's main advantage in its competition with Turkey was geographical. Iran presented itself as possessing the most direct transportation route from landlocked Central Asia to the Persian Gulf and the Indian Ocean and attempted to tie itself to the new Islamic republics through the construction of a network of road and railway systems. In seeking to become Central Asia's principal trading outlet, Iran hoped to break out of its regional isolation and to establish its own sphere of economic influence.

Even though Iran did not attempt to impose its version of political Islam on the new states, Iran's form of ulama-dominated government alienated Central Asia's secular rulers and reduced Iran's appeal. In addition, Iran's militant anti-Western stance was not popular among the new republics, whose leaders hoped to establish positive relations with the West and to become the beneficiaries of Western economic and technical assistance. Yet despite the difficulties the two outside states encountered, the combined efforts of Iran and Turkey drew them into Central Asia and at the same time pulled that region into renewed contact with its historic Middle Eastern orientation.

The Islamic Factor

During the seventy years of Soviet rule over Central Asia and Transcaucasia, Moscow pursued a policy of religious suppression and forced secularization. With independence and the new freedom to practice their faith openly, the Muslim population embarked on a journey of religious rediscovery. Central Asian Islam was characterized as much by the diversity of practices as it was by unity, and it is generally acknowledged that at the time of independence Islam served more as a factor of ethnic and national identity than as a guiding religious doctrine. To Central Asia's neighboring Islamic states, the situation appeared to offer an unparalleled opportunity to shape the reemergent faith in their own image, and they became engaged in competition to capture the souls as well as the markets of the Islamic republics.

Notwithstanding its pragmatic policies toward the region, Iran nevertheless endeavored to appeal to the long-suppressed Islamic sentiments of the Central Asian peoples, especially in Persian-speaking Tajikistan, where Tehran sponsored the construction of new mosques and Islamic educational institutions. Iran also provided Tajikistan with Persian-language textbooks and thousands of copies of the Quran, and it embarked on an ambitious program of beaming radio and television broadcasts into Tajikistan.

Iran's activities spurred Saudi Arabia into an Islamic campaign of its own. Viewing itself as the center of true universal Sunni Islam, Saudi Arabia sought to counter the influence of Iranian Shiʿism in Central Asia through a parallel program of Islamic guidance by subsidizing the construction of mosques and providing ulama to instruct the population on the intricacies of Sunni doctrine and ritual. To the Saudi authorities, Central Asia offered a unique opportunity to revitalize a slumbering Islam and to bring its population into the mainstream of the Sunni *ummah*.

Although the Muslims of Central Asia and Azerbaijan showed a receptiveness toward their newfound freedom to practice their religion and to engage in the annual pilgrimage to Mecca, the secular ruling authorities discouraged any mingling of Islam and politics. Yet even as the rulers sought to prevent the formation of Islamic political organizations, they had to demonstrate a certain sensitivity to their citizens' resurgent Islamic sensibilities. One of the most striking examples of a ruler's response to popular sentiment was the action of President Saparmurad Niyazov of Turkmenistan, who replaced a prominent statue of Lenin with one of himself in the guise of a pilgrim to Mecca. Although it would be an exaggeration to assert that an Islamic revival was sweeping through the Muslim states of Central Asia, it was evident that the people's eagerness to recover their Islamic heritage and to learn more about it enhanced the contacts between those states and the Middle East.

Energy Resources:
The Driving Force for Reintegration

Ethnic and religious affinities and the preemptive contest between Turkey and Iran contributed to drawing Central Asia into the wider Middle Eastern world, but none of these factors played as dramatic a role as did the competition over energy rights and transportation routes. Beneath the waters of the Caspian Sea and in the countries bordering it rested the largest untapped pool of oil and natural gas in the world, estimated by some to reach the staggering total of a probable 200 billion barrels of oil. The main beneficiaries of this geological gift were Kazakhstan and Azerbaijan, with enormous oil reserves; Turkmenistan, which is the fourth largest gas producer in the world and also possesses substantial oil resources; and Uzbekistan, another world leader in gas production and a country where new deposits of oil are being discovered at a rapid rate.

The exploitation of a portion of these energy resources has a long history. From the 1880s to 1910, Baku, the capital city of Azerbaijan, was the site of the first big oil boom outside the United States and was one of the world's two main sources of petroleum. Although the Soviets continued to exploit and develop the energy resources of Central Asia, they preferred to concentrate exploration and production activities in Siberia and other areas of Slavic Russia. As a result, the enormous extent of the region's oil and gas reserves was not fully appreciated until independence, when foreign companies descended upon the area like vultures.

The competition between and among U.S., European, and Asian firms for exploration and concession rights took place in a free-wheeling atmosphere of deal making and breaking that involved oil executives and lobbyists, opportunistic Russian entrepreneurs, local officials looking for their cut, and the usual array of hustlers and fast-buck artists. During this oil rush of the 1990s, petroleum companies invested billions of dollars for rights to exploit the energy resources.

These investments had the potential to yield huge profits, but they also entailed substantial risks, the most significant of which was determining how to transport the resources out of landlocked Central Asia and into the world market. This was the issue that had the greatest potential to draw the new republics into the Middle East and to determine their relationships with Iran and Turkey. The resolution to the problem of transport would be the construction of pipelines, but each proposed route had certain disadvantages. It is beyond the scope of this book to examine all the proposals and counterproposals put forth, but we will discuss briefly the main possibilities in order to suggest the interplay between politics and economics in this high-stakes competition.

The existing pipelines all ran north through Russian territory, and one proposal was to upgrade and expand these lines to transport the energy from Azerbaijan and Kazakhstan to the Black Sea ports of Novorossisk in Russia and Supsa in Georgia. Once the oil reached these ports, tankers would carry it through the Turkish Straits. However, Turkish authorities objected on environmental and safety grounds to such heavy tanker traffic through the already congested shipping lanes of the Straits. The Turkish concerns were legitimate, but they were also colored by Ankara's preference for the construction of a pipeline from Supsa to the southern Turkish port of Ceyhan, which would provide Turkey with substantial transit fees (see Map 24.2). Each of these proposals was costly, and the pipelines would pass through politically unstable regions—the Kurdish territory of Turkey, the breakaway Russian republic of Chechnya, and the ethnically troubled state of Georgia. A far less expensive and much more secure alternative for the transport of the energy resources of Azerbaijan and Kazakhstan involved tying into Iran's existing pipeline network and sending oil to its Persian Gulf ports, which were already well equipped with the means to export petroleum. But this seemingly sensible concept caused a clash between pragmatic financial planning and international politics. The United States, in its determination to isolate Iran and to deny it economic benefits, strongly opposed the project, much to the consternation of U.S. and international petroleum companies. During the late 1990s, Washington's objections held sway, but the project made such sound economic sense that some of the companies contemplated defying U.S. objections.

All of the factors discussed in this section—competition for regional influence and markets, petroleum export routes, religious and ethnic ties, and historical tradition—seemed likely to draw the Islamic republics closer to the Middle East and possibly over the long run to make them once again an integral part of the region.

Conclusion: Connecting Threads

For the central Arab states, the events discussed in the final chapters of this book are more than just a part of the late-twentieth-century history of the Middle East; they are also an integral part of the legacy spawned by the dismemberment of the Ottoman Empire earlier in the century. The end of the Ottoman order created new Arab states separated by new borders drawn by British and French officials to serve European imperial interests. In the intervening decades, Arab leaders have had to cope with the consequences of those borders and have at times devoted considerable energy to altering them. The patterns of post-Ottoman history in the Arab Middle East have been shaped in part by responses to externally imposed conditions that were ill-suited to the needs of the region's inhabitants.

In seeking to reshape their societies in a manner more appropriate to popular needs, the first wave of reformers in the era of independence, represented by Nasser and his imitators, introduced planned economies, new social welfare systems, land reform policies, and expanded educational opportunities, and they entered into formal and informal alliances with the Soviet Union. But the state-run enterprises turned out to be inefficient, and the next generation of Arab rulers encouraged limited free-market economies while maintaining the state-run factories, an awkward combination that did not serve their people well in an increasingly globalized economy. Moreover, the new educational systems, especially in Egypt, quickly became overcrowded, and the employment expectations of university graduates went unfulfilled; the welfare systems proved too costly for some states but were politically impossible to cancel; and in 1991 the Soviet Union ceased to exist, forcing all states of the region to deal with the reality of hegemonic U.S. power.

The political promise of a new era of populism vanished with the establishment of authoritarian single-party regimes dominated by one-man rule. This trend began in the 1950s and continues to the present. Indeed, one of the striking patterns of the post–Gulf War period is how little that conflict altered the political contours of the region. Not only did Saddam Husayn remain in power in Iraq, but the same aging leadership held sway in Syria, Egypt, and many of the Gulf monarchies; and Yasir Arafat, at age seventy and after thirty years as chairman of the PLO, has become a virtual dictator in the region under his administrative control as head of the Palestinian National Authority. Some observers suggested that the proliferation of volunteer organizations in several Arab states during the early 1990s was a sign of approaching political liberalization, but the evidence does not support this contention. The continued suppression of personal freedoms and political liberties by ossified regimes that lack legitimacy does not hold the promise of a peaceful transition of power in such states as Egypt, Syria, Iraq, and the Gulf monarchies. The perpetuation of authoritarianism only serves to feed the growth of Islamist activities as other avenues for the expression of opposition are increasingly closed.

Outside the Arab states, Iran entered the twentieth year of its successful Islamic revolution unable to avoid the intrusion of worldly matters. To the population at large, and especially to the country's large and restive youth population, the government's failure to ensure economic well-being mattered more than its ideology. The regime of the ulama also faced opposition to its intrusive Islamicization activities and its restrictive and insular cultural policies. This is not to say that the powerful attraction of Shiʿism, which has been such a prominent feature of modern Iranian history, is diminishing or that secularism is on the rise. Rather, it is to suggest that the Iranian government, like all others, must satisfy the material as well as the spiritual needs of its people. In its failure to translate revolutionary Shiʿa rhetoric and anti-U.S. sloganeering into material well-being, the current regime has generated a current of opposition that looks to alternative forms of government and seeks greater freedom of expression. The Islamic Republic is at a critical juncture in its relatively short history.

Turkey, which had undergone a successful transition from a single to a multiparty political system in 1950, found itself confronting political paralysis in the 1990s, ironically because of the existence of too many parties. The proliferation of parties reflected the failure of the mainstream political groupings to satisfy popular aspirations. As a result, individuals gave their support to parties with more narrowly focused agendas, including Islamist organizations. With no party able to acquire a majority of seats in the National Assembly, Turkey stumbled from one coalition government to another. The Turkish military had intervened in the past to prevent political chaos, and it was becoming once again increasingly involved in the civil affairs of state.

The Middle East region as a whole and individual states within it have previously confronted and survived unsettled moments in their history. But it is difficult to recall a period prior to the late 1990s when popular discontent was so widespread, when so many authoritarian rulers in key states had held onto power for so long and were simultaneously reaching the age when their rule must end, or when a single outside power—the United States—exercised such exclusive domination and aroused such deep-seated resentment. The purpose of this book is to deal with the past, not the future, but it is difficult to examine the recent past without expressing reservations about the prospects for Middle Eastern peace and stability in the early years of the new century.

Notes

1. Michael C. Hudson, "To Play the Hegemon: Fifty Years of US Policy Toward the Middle East," *The Middle East Journal*, vol. 50 (Summer 1996), p. 336.

2. Raymond William Baker, "Invidious Comparisons: Realism, Postmodern Globalism, and Centrist Islamic Movements in Egypt," in John L. Esposito, ed., *Political Islam: Revolution, Radicalism, or Reform?* (Boulder, 1997), p. 128.

Glossary

Aliyah: Literally "the act of going up," as in ascending to Jerusalem; the term designates Jewish immigration to Palestine or Israel.

Amir: Military commander, governor, minor ruler; in Syria and Lebanon, a hereditary title carried within certain distinguished Arab families.

Ashkenazim: Jews whose recent ancestors were of East European origin and generally spoke Yiddish.

Askeri: Literally, "the military"; used to distinguish the Ottoman ruling elite from the ordinary tax-paying subjects of the empire.

A'yan: Notable persons; term for prominent urban Arab and Turkish notables.

Ayatollah: Title given to the most eminent Shiᶜa legal experts.

Bey: Title for senior officials in the Ottoman service beneath the rank of pasha; carried over in post-Ottoman society as a term of respect.

Caliph: The successor to the Prophet as the head of the universal Islamic community; the institution was known as the caliphate.

Capitulations: Commercial treaties between the Ottoman Empire and the states of western Europe granting Europeans favorable tariffs and extraterritorial privileges.

Derebey: Rural Anatolian notable.

Devshirme: The Ottoman levy of Christian youths of Balkan origin to be trained for service in the administration or the military.

Dhimmi: A protected non-Muslim living under Muslim rule.

Divan: The Ottoman council of state presided over by the grand vizier (q.v.).

Fatwa: The opinion of a mufti or a *mujtahid* (q.v.) on a point of Islamic law.

Feddan: A unit of land measurement equal to 1.04 acres (.416 ha).

Fellah (pl. *fellahin*): peasant; farmer.

Ghazi: A Muslim frontier warrior fighting against non-Muslims to extend the territories of Islam; *ghazi*s played a significant role in the rise of the Ottoman Empire.

Ghulam: Male slave in the service of the state; the slave soldiers of the Safavid Empire.

Grand vizier: The highest-ranking administrative official in the Ottoman Empire.

Hadith: A verified account of a statement or action of the Prophet Muhammad; the corpus of *hadith* is one of the main sources of Islamic law.

Hajj: The ritual obligation of pilgrimage to Mecca; it is one of the five pillars of Islam.

Hijrah: The emigration of Muhammad and his followers from Mecca to Medina in 622; the event marks the year 1 of the Muslim calendar.

Ijma: Consensus of legal scholars or of the Muslim community as a whole on a matter of religious law.

Ijtihad: The exercise of informed human reason in deciding matters of Islamic law.

Imam: The leader of the Islamic public prayers; the title of some Muslim rulers. In Shiᶜism, the divinely guided head of the community who is regarded as infallible by virtue of his direct descent from the Prophet Muhammad.

Infitah: Literally, "opening." Term used to designate the policy of economic liberalization introduced into Egypt in the 1970s.

Intifada: From a word meaning to be shaken off. Name given to the Palestinian protest movement that began in 1987 against Israeli occupation of the West Bank and the Gaza Strip.

Ismaᶜilis (or "Seveners"): A branch of the Shiᶜa who consider the line of Imams to be unbroken from Ali to the present; the Agha Khan is presently the divinely guided head of this community.

Jahiliyyah: "The days of ignorance," referring to the times before Muhammad received God's revelations. Some contemporary Muslim activists accuse their leaders of being in a state of *jahiliyyah,* that is, of neglecting to rule according to Islamic principles.

Janissary: The Ottoman infantry corps recruited mainly through the *devshirme* (q.v.).

Jihad: The exertion of effort in the cause of Islam; an inner struggle against impious temptations; religiously sanctioned warfare by Muslims against non-Muslims.

Jizyah: Poll tax paid by non-Muslim subjects of the Islamic state.

Kaᶜba: The most sacred Islamic shrine; located in Mecca, it is the object of the *hajj* (q.v.).

Madrasah: A college whose primary purpose is the teaching of Islamic law and related religious subjects.

Mahdi: A divinely guided figure who is expected to appear in the last days and establish the rule of Islam on earth; Muhammad Ahmad of the Sudan assumed the title during his rebellion against the Egyptians.

Majlis: Council, parliament.

Marja al-taqlid: The source of emulation; in Shiᶜism, the term designates a learned scholar of Islamic law whose legal opinions are binding on all Muslims who have accepted him as their spiritual guide.

Millet: A recognized religious community in the Ottoman Empire; the Ottomans administered their non-Muslim subjects through the *millet*s and allowed them a large measure of internal autonomy in religious and legal affairs.

Mufti: An expert in Islamic law qualified to give authoritative legal opinions known as *fatwa*s (q.v.); muftis were members of the ulama establishment and ranked above *qadi*s (q.v.).

Mujtahid: One who is recognized as competent to exercise *ijtihad* (q.v.).

Pasha: The highest Ottoman official title; it was granted both to civilian administrators and military commanders. Like the term *bey* (q.v.), it survived the Ottoman era and came to be used as a term of respect in Turkish and Arab society.

Qadi: A judge in a court administering religious law.

Qiyas: Analogical reasoning or deduction based on the Quran or *hadith* (q.v.); one of the sources for the *shariᶜah*.

Qizilbash: Shiᶜa tribal warriors, mainly of Turkish origin, whose military triumphs played a crucial part in the rise of the Safavid Empire. The name means the red-headed ones and derives from the colorful headgear worn by the tribesmen.

Quran: The holy scripture of Islam; the book containing the revelations of God to Muhammad.

Rashidun: "The rightly guided ones," a title given to the first four caliphs.

Salafiyyah: From an Arabic word meaning ancestor, with special reference to the pious Muslims who lived at the time of the Prophet and the Rashidun (q.v.). Salafiyyah is the early twentieth-century Islamic reform movement that called for a return to the principles followed by the venerable ancestors.

Salat: Obligatory Muslim ritual prayer; one of the five pillars of Islam.

Sawm: Fasting; the obligatory duty for all Muslims to fast from dawn to dusk during the month of Ramadan; one of the five pillars of Islam.

Sephardim: Jews whose ancestors came from Spain and spoke Ladino among themselves; later also loosely applied to "Oriental" Jews from the Middle East and North Africa to distinguish them from Jews of East European background.

Shahadah: The obligatory Muslim profession of faith asserting belief in one God and in God's designation of Muhammad as his Prophet; one of the five pillars of Islam.

Shahanshah: Meaning king of kings, the term denotes the ancient Iranian concept of an all-powerful monarch.

Shariᶜah: Literally, "path" or "way." The divinely ordained law of Islam that governs all aspects of Muslim behavior.

Sharif: Term given to individuals claiming direct descent from Muhammad.

Shaykh: A tribal leader; head of a village or religious order; term of respect for an elder.

Shaykh al-Islam: The head of the Islamic religious establishment in the Ottoman Empire.

Shiᶜa: The group of Muslims who regard Ali and his descendants as the only legitimate successors to the Prophet. In the Shiᶜa view, Ali and his line are divinely guided Imams.

Shiᶜism: The version of Islam practiced by the Shiᶜa; of the many branches of Shiᶜism, the two major groups are Seveners, or Ismaᶜilis (q.v.), and Twelvers.

Sipahi: Ottoman feudal cavalryman; holder of a *timar* (q.v.).

Sufism: Islamic mysticism.

Sultan: From a word meaning power, authority. Beginning in the tenth century, the term was used to designate the temporal sovereign as distinct from the caliph (q.v.). From the early sixteenth century to 1922, the Ottoman rulers united the two offices, combining in their persons the temporal power of sultan and the spiritual authority of caliph.

Sunnah: Custom; the practice of the Prophet and the early Islamic community that became an exemplary precedent for all Muslims.

Sunnis: Those who accept the *sunnah* and the historical succession of caliphs as opposed to the Shiᶜa; they are the majority of the Muslim community.

Sura: A chapter of the Quran.

Tariqah: A Sufi order or brotherhood.

Timar: The land and tax revenues that the Ottoman state granted to a *sipahi* (q.v.) in return for his military service.

Torah: The Five Books of Moses, or the Pentateuch. It contains the laws God revealed to the Jews, including the Ten Commandments and other comprehensive instructions on the proper ordering of state and society. It also includes God's promise to Abraham and his descendants that He will give the Jews the land of Israel.

Ulama (sing. **alim**): Literally, "those learned in the ways of Islam"; the collective term for the members of the Islamic religious establishment, including preachers, judges, teachers, scholars of religion, and administrators of the religious hierarchy.

Ummah: The universal Islamic community; in the twentieth century the term also came to mean nation.

Vilayat-i faqih: The exercise of governmental authority by an Islamic jurist; this principle was incorporated in the constitution of the Islamic Republic of Iran in 1979.

Waqf: Property or other revenue-yielding source endowed for a religious institution or charity. During the later Ottoman period, the practice of endowing *waqfs* for the benefit of private families became widespread. The income from *waqf* was exempt from taxation.

Yishuv: The name for the Jewish community in Palestine prior to the recognition of the modern state of Israel in 1948.

Za͓im: Leader; the term is specifically used to designate the political notables, or bosses, of Lebanon.

Zakat: The fixed share of income or property that all Muslims must pay as an alms tax; one of the five pillars of Islam.

Select Bibliography

This is intended primarily as an introductory bibliography of works in English to guide readers to the basic books on various aspects of Middle Eastern history. Each of the works listed here contains its own bibliography that readers seeking more specialized references may want to consult. The entries are more comprehensive for the period after 1800 than for the preceding centuries.

Periodicals

The *International Journal of Middle East Studies* (New York) is the scholarly journal of the Middle East Studies Association. It is comprehensive and multidisciplinary, publishing articles that embrace the full chronological scope of Middle Eastern studies from the rise of Islam to the present. The *Middle East Journal* (Washington, D.C.) treats contemporary affairs and foreign policy matters and has recently adopted the commendable practice of devoting entire issues to a single theme, for example, the twenty-fifth anniversary of the 1967 war or Iran ten years after the revolution. *Middle Eastern Studies* (London) and *Asian and African Studies* (Haifa) concentrate on modern history. *Middle East Report* (New York) offers a critical, left-of-center approach to a broad range of current events. The periodical's challenging and sometimes controversial coverage offers a perspective often at odds with official Washington policy.

For anyone seeking to follow current events in a systematic fashion, The *New York Times* is essential reading. The experienced Middle East correspondents of the *Manchester Guardian* provide the kind of critical in-depth analysis that is not always available in North American newspapers.

General Works on Islam and Middle Eastern History to 1700

Three outstanding overviews of Arab and Islamic history are now available. Marshall G. S. Hodgson, *The Venture of Islam: Conscience and History in a World Civilization,* 3 vols. (Chicago, 1974), places Islam in a global context and is one of the most stimulating and challenging explorations of Islamic history yet written. Ira M.

Lapidus, *A History of Islamic Societies* (New York, 1988), explores the shaping of Islamic civilization in all Islamic regions from the time of the Prophet to the twentieth century. Albert Hourani's masterful synthesis, *A History of the Arab Peoples* (Cambridge, Mass., 1991), treats the entire Arab world, emphasizing the development of social patterns and institutions. An additional survey of all the Islamic regions, John Obert Voll's *Islam: Continuity and Change in the Modern World* (Boulder, 1982), concentrates on the period after 1800.

The Quran is the essential foundation for an understanding of Islam. The translation used in this book is A. J. Arberry, *The Koran: Interpreted* (New York, 1955). P. M. Holt et al., eds., *The Cambridge History of Islam,* 2 vols. (Cambridge, 1970), is a conventional work but has the advantage of treating all aspects of Islamic civilization from the era of the Prophet to the twentieth century. Introductions to the faith and institutions of Islam include Malise Ruthven, *Islam in the World* (New York, 1984), a refreshing book that examines the impact of Islamic doctrines on Muslim patterns of living. H.A.R. Gibb, *Mohammedanism,* 2nd ed. (New York, 1970), despite its inappropriate title, remains useful. English-language surveys by Muslim writers include Fazlur Rahman, *Islam,* 2nd ed. (Chicago, 1979), and Seyyed Hossein Nasr, *Ideals and Realities of Islam* (Boston, 1972). A most helpful study of Shiᶜism is Moojan Momen, *An Introduction to Shiᶜi Islam: The History and Doctrines of Twelver Shiᶜism* (New Haven, 1985).

Any list of historical surveys must still include Bernard Lewis, *The Arabs in History,* rev. ed. (New York, 1966), a graceful and accessible synthesis. Marilyn R. Waldman presents a stimulating reappraisal of the periodization of Islamic history in her contribution, "The Islamic World," *New Encyclopaedia Britannica,* 15th ed. (Chicago, 1990), pp. 102–133. In a similar vein is Richard M. Eaton's *Islamic History as Global History* (Washington, D.C., 1990), a historiographical essay in the American Historical Association's series of studies on world and comparative history; Eaton's essay should be required reading for all who seek to understand the global significance of the consolidation of an Islamic civilization. The chronological underpinnings of the first 900 years of Islamic Middle Eastern history are provided by Hugh Kennedy, *The Prophet and the Age of the Caliphates: The Islamic Near East from the Sixth to the Eleventh Century* (London, 1986), and P. M. Holt, *The Age of the Crusaders: The Near East from the Eleventh Century to 1517* (London, 1986).

A more focused account of the origins and consolidation of Islamic society is W. Montgomery Watt's sympathetic but decidedly temporal biography of the Prophet, *Muhammad: Prophet and Statesman* (Oxford, 1991). The complexities of the interaction between Arabian Islam and its conquered territories are brought out in Fred M. Donner, *The Early Islamic Conquests* (Princeton, 1981), and Michael G. Morony, *Iraq After the Muslim Conquest* (Princeton, 1984). The development of the *shariᶜah* and the schools of jurisprudence is examined in N. J. Coulson, *The History of Islamic Law* (Edinburgh, 1964). An introduction to Islamic philosophy is found in W. M. Watt, *Islamic Philosophy and Theology* (Edinburgh, 1962). The consolidation of ulama educational institutions in the eleventh and twelfth centuries is the subject of George Makdisi, *The Rise of Colleges: Institutions of Higher Learning in Islam and the West* (Edinburgh, 1982). Sufism is the subject of Annemarie Schimmel, *Mystical Dimensions of Islam* (Chapel Hill, 1975). An informative and well-documented discussion of the agricultural revolution brought about by the transmission of East Indian crops to the Mediterranean basin through the trading network established under the Abbasids is Andrew M. Watson, *Agricultural Innovation in the Early Islamic World: The Diffusion of Crops and Farming Techniques, 700–1100* (Cambridge, 1983). Urban life and institutions are examined in Ira M. Lapidus, *Muslim Cities in the Later Middle Ages* (Cambridge, Mass., 1967). For the moment, the most satisfactory historical survey of the role of women in Middle Eastern Islamic societies is Leila Ahmed, *Women and Gender in Islam: Historical Roots of a Modern Debate* (New Haven, 1992). Not the least of this work's virtues is the author's refusal to be drawn into the "because of Islam" mode of explanation and to insist on placing the development of the status of Muslim women within the wider context of pre-Islamic Near Eastern practices.

General Works on Politics and Economics in the Modern Era

The two principal works on economic history are Roger Owen, *The Middle East in the World Economy, 1800–1914* (London, 1981), and Charles Issawi, *An Economic History of the Middle East and North Africa* (New York, 1982). Owen is arranged chronologically and by region and concentrates on Egypt and the Ottoman Empire; Issawi's organization is thematic, and he covers the area from Morocco through Iran. Issawi has also compiled four books of documents, readings, and commentary that are extremely valuable: *The Economic History of the Middle East, 1800–1914* (Chicago, 1966), which is primarily concerned with the Arab world; *The Economic History of Iran, 1800–1914* (Chicago, 1971); *The Economic History of Turkey, 1800–1914* (Chicago, 1980), which deals with the Ottoman Empire; and *The Fertile Crescent, 1800–1914: A Documentary Economic History* (New York, 1988). An important analysis of recent social and economic trends is Alan Richards and John Waterbury, *A Political Economy of the Middle East: State, Class, and Economic Development* (Boulder, 1990). Roger Owen and Şevket Pamak, *A History of Middle East Economies in the Twentieth Century* (London, 1998), is a very good introductory survey with both a country-specific and regional focus.

The work of Elie Kedourie provides a critical perspective on nineteenth- and twentieth-century Arab politics. Representative samples include his *The Chatham House Version and Other Middle-Eastern Studies* (London, 1970) and *Arabic Political Memoirs and Other Studies* (London, 1974). Roger Owen, *State, Power and Politics in the Making of the Modern Middle East* (London, 1992), employs a combination of narrative and thematic approaches to produce a sophisticated introductory political study of the region from World War I to the present. A masterful synthesis of the post-Ottoman period to the present and a work I highly recommend is Avi Shlaim, *War and Peace in the Middle East: A Concise History*, rev. ed. (New York, 1995). For studies of elites and politics, see Michael C. Hudson, *Arab Politics: The*

Search for Legitimacy (New Haven, 1977), which, in addition to its analysis of contemporary regimes, also provides sound historical background on the formation of the modern Arab states. Also recommended is James A. Bill and Robert Springborg, *Politics in the Middle East,* 3rd ed. (Glenview, Ill., 1990). Augustus Richard Norton, ed., *Civil Society in the Middle East,* 2 vols. (Leiden, 1995 and 1996), is an enormous undertaking that seeks to examine most of the countries of the Middle East and North Africa within the analytical framework of civil society, a concept on which the contributors do not have a shared definition but one that has nonetheless enabled them to produce some very important case studies of specific countries in the contemporary era.

The Ottoman Empire and Turkey

General Surveys and Specific Works on the Ottoman Empire to 1800

The most comprehensive and sophisticated analysis of the entire Ottoman era is Halil Inalcik and Donald Quataert, eds., *An Economic and Social History of the Ottoman Empire, 1300–1914* (Cambridge, 1994). A dauntingly thorough examination of the Ottoman centuries with rather less treatment of Turkey than is implied in the title is Stanford J. Shaw and Ezel Kural Shaw, *History of the Ottoman Empire and Modern Turkey,* 2 vols. (Cambridge, Mass., 1976, 1977). The Shaws' work contains a comprehensive bibliography. Roderic H. Davison, *Turkey* (Englewood Cliffs, N.J., 1968), is a very fine introductory survey that, in this case, delivers far more than the title promises: It treats the entire Ottoman era and is particularly strong on the nineteenth century. A concise analysis of Ottoman history and institutions from the foundation of the empire to the late eighteenth century is Norman Itzkowitz, *Ottoman Empire and Islamic Tradition* (New York, 1972). Halil Inalcik, *The Ottoman Empire: The Classical Age, 1300–1600* (London, 1973), is an essential work on political, economic, and religious institutions. The non-Muslim communities of the empire are examined in Benjamin Braude and Bernard Lewis, eds., *Christians and Jews in the Ottoman Empire: The Functioning of a Plural Society,* 2 vols. (New York, 1982), and the impact of and response to Ottoman rule in Europe is surveyed in L. S. Stavrianos, *The Balkans Since 1453* (New York, 1958). The grandeur and beauty of Ottoman architecture is captured in the text and illustrations of Godfrey Goodwin, *A History of Ottoman Architecture* (Baltimore, 1971).

From the Nineteenth Century to the End of the Empire

Bernard Lewis, *The Emergence of Modern Turkey,* 2nd ed. (London, 1968), treats the institutional and cultural impact of the reform movement from its beginnings through the Atatürk years. Other works that pursue this theme with a more limited focus include Stanford J. Shaw's detailed study, *Between Old and New: The Ottoman Empire Under Selim III, 1789–1807* (Cambridge, Mass., 1971); Roderic H. Davison's examination of the Tanzimat era, *Reform in the Ottoman Empire, 1856–1876*

(Princeton, 1963); Niyazi Berkes, *The Development of Secularism in Turkey* (Montreal, 1964), which is particularly strong on ideological currents; Şerif Mardin, *The Genesis of Young Ottoman Thought: A Study in the Modernization of Turkish Political Ideas* (Princeton, 1962); and two later and rather differently focused works by Carter V. Findley, *Bureaucratic Reform in the Ottoman Empire: The Sublime Porte, 1789–1922* (Princeton, 1980), and *Ottoman Civil Officialdom: A Social History* (Princeton, 1989). Important contributions on the role of the Ottoman—as well as the Egyptian, Iranian, and North African—religious establishment during the nineteenth-century transformation are found in Nikki R. Keddie, ed., *Scholars, Saints, and Sufis: Muslim Religious Institutions in the Middle East Since 1500* (Berkeley, 1972). A gap in the scholarly literature of the Ottoman transformation has been admirably filled by Zeynep Çelik, *The Remaking of Istanbul: Portrait of an Ottoman City in the Nineteenth Century* (Seattle, 1986).

A relatively recent historical approach to the Ottoman transformation stresses the detrimental impact of the penetration of European capital into the imperial domains and the consequences of the empire's incorporation into the global economy. Studies that adopt this approach include Şevket Pamuk, *The Ottoman Empire and European Capitalism, 1820–1913: Trade, Investment, and Production* (New York, 1987); Reçat Kasaba, *The Ottoman Empire and the World Economy: The Nineteenth Century* (Albany, 1988); and Huri Islamoğlu-Inan, ed., *The Ottoman Empire and the World-Economy* (Cambridge, 1987), in which the editor's introductory essay is especially helpful. Donald Quataert has addressed a long-standing gap in Ottoman studies in his *Ottoman Manufacturing in the Age of the Industrial Revolution* (Cambridge, 1993).

The diplomacy of the Eastern question is thoroughly covered, though from a decidedly European perspective, in M. S. Anderson, *The Eastern Question, 1774–1923* (New York, 1966). A fresh look at the Eastern Question, with a useful reminder that the Middle Eastern participants could manipulate diplomatic crises to their own benefit, is L. Carl Brown's lively *International Politics and the Middle East: Old Rules, Dangerous Game* (Princeton, 1984). A comprehensive collection of treaties, decrees, and diplomatic communications is J. C. Hurewitz, ed., *The Middle East and North Africa in World Politics: A Documentary Record:* vol. 1, *European Expansion, 1535–1914,* 2nd ed. (New Haven, 1975); vol. 2, *British-French Supremacy, 1914–1945* (New Haven, 1979).

The politics of the Arab lands under Ottoman administration is examined in P. M. Holt, *Egypt and the Fertile Crescent, 1516–1922: A Political History* (Ithaca, 1969). For the impact of the reform movement on the Arab provinces, see Moshe Maʿoz, *Ottoman Reform in Syria and Palestine, 1840–1861: The Impact of the Tanzimat on Politics and Society* (Oxford, 1968); John P. Spagnolo, *France and Ottoman Lebanon, 1861–1914* (London, 1977); Engin Akarli, *The Long Peace: Ottoman Lebanon, 1861–1920* (Berkeley, 1993); and William R. Polk and Richard L. Chambers, eds., *Beginnings of Modernization in the Middle East: The Nineteenth Century* (Chicago, 1968), which contains Albert Hourani's seminal article, "Ottoman Reform and the Politics of Notables." Works published after 1980 tend to focus on social and economic history; among them are Philip S. Khoury, *Urban Notables and Arab Nationalism: The Politics of Damascus, 1860–1920* (Cambridge, 1983); Linda Shatkowski Schilcher, *Families in Politics: Damascus Factions and Estates of the 18th and 19th Centuries* (Stuttgart, 1985); Leila Tarazi Fawaz, *Merchants and Migrants in Nineteenth Century Beirut* (Cambridge, Mass., 1983); and Beshara Doumani, *Rediscovering Palestine: The Merchants and Peasants of Jabal Nablus, 1700–1900* (Berkeley, 1995), which demonstrates the resilience and adaptability of a particular local economy in the face of Ottoman centralization and European commercial expansion. One of the few studies of Ottoman Arabia is William Ochsenwald, *Religion, Society, and the State in Arabia: The Hijaz Under Ottoman Control, 1804–1908* (Columbus, 1984). David Dean Commins, *Islamic Reform: Politics and Social Change in Late Ottoman Syria* (New York, 1990), examines social and intellectual currents among the Damascus ulama at the turn of the century.

The most significant recent contribution to the scholarship of the important Young Turk era is Hasan Kayalı, *Arabs and Young Turks: Ottomanism, Arabism, and Islamism in the Ottoman Empire, 1908–1918* (Berkeley, 1997), a work of historical revisionism that argues that the CUP was committed to Ottomanism and did not adopt a policy of Turkification. Ernest E. Ramsaur, *The Young Turks: Prelude to the Revolution of 1908* (Princeton, 1957), deals with the political and intellectual background to the 1908 revolt; and Feroz Ahmad, *The Young Turks: The Committee of Union and Progress in Turkish Politics, 1908–1914* (Oxford, 1969), is a study of the power struggles between the CUP and its opponents. The first articulation of Turkish nationalist sentiments is examined in Uriel Heyd, *Foundations of Turkish Nationalism: The Life and Teachings of Ziya Gökalp* (London, 1950), and Niyazi Berkes, ed. and trans., *Turkish Nationalism and Western Civilization: Selected Essays of Ziya Gökalp* (London, 1959).

Numerous works exist on the Arab attitude toward the Ottoman government during the Young Turk period. The pioneering study by George Antonius, *The Arab Awakening: The Story of the Arab National Movement* (London, 1938, and several subsequent editions), overestimates the pre–World War I force of Arab nationalism and anti-Ottoman sentiments but remains an eloquent statement of the Arab case from the perspective of the interwar era. C. Ernest Dawn's *From Ottomanism to Arabism: Essays on the Origins of Arab Nationalism* (Urbana, 1973), analyzes the social, economic, and political factors that led the majority of the Arab elite to support Ottomanism during World War I. Rashid Khalidi, et al., eds., *The Origins of Arab Nationalism* (New York, 1991), offers a reappraisal of the subject, focusing on the late Ottoman period.

The interests of the major powers, including the Ottoman Empire, during World War I, are surveyed in Marion Kent, ed., *The Great Powers and the End of the Ottoman Empire* (London, 1984). Britain's role in shaping the wartime agreements and the postwar settlement is carefully examined in Elie Kedourie, *England and the Middle East: The Destruction of the Ottoman Empire, 1914–1921* (London, 1987). The same subject is presented in David Fromkin's highly readable account, *A Peace to End All Peace: The Fall of the Ottoman Empire and the Creation of the Modern*

Middle East (New York, 1990). Detailed diplomatic histories of Britain's pursuit of its Indian and Persian Gulf interests are Briton Cooper Busch, *Britain and the Persian Gulf, 1894–1914* (Berkeley, 1967), and the same author's *Britain, India, and the Arabs, 1914–1921* (Berkeley, 1971). The neglected role of the Ottomans in Gulf history is treated in Frederick F. Anscombe, *The Ottoman Gulf: The Creation of Kuwait, Saudi Arabia, and Qatar* (New York, 1997). An account of Britain's efforts to organize the Middle East and an expression of regret at Britain's failure is Elizabeth Monroe, *Britain's Moment in the Middle East, 1914–1971*, 2nd ed. (London, 1981). French objectives are treated in Christopher M. Andrew and A. S. Kenya-Forstner, *The Climax of French Imperial Expansion, 1914–1924* (Stanford, 1981). The history of the Armenian community before, during, and immediately after the war is recounted in Richard G. Hovannisian, *Armenia on the Road to Independence, 1918* (Berkeley, 1967), and *The Republic of Armenia* (Berkeley, 1971). L. Carl Brown, ed., *Imperial Legacy: The Ottoman Imprint on the Balkans and the Middle East* (New York, 1996), is a collection of essays examining various aspects of the lasting institutional and ideological influence of the Ottoman centuries.

The Turkish Republic

A thorough political history from the end of the empire to the early 1990s is Feroz Ahmad, *The Making of Modern Turkey* (London, 1993). An excellent interpretive account is Eric J. Zürcher, *Turkey: A Modern History* (London, 1993), which demonstrates the continuities between the Young Turk and Republican periods. In addition to Lewis's *Emergence of Modern Turkey* and Berkes's *Development of Secularism in Turkey* cited above, studies of the Turkish independence movement and the Atatürk era include Lord Kinross, *Atatürk: A Biography of Mustafa Kemal, Father of Modern Turkey* (New York, 1965), and an intriguing if not entirely contextualized study by Vamik D. Volkan and Norman Itzkowitz, *The Immortal Atatürk: A Psychobiography* (Chicago, 1984). See also Ali Kazancigil and Ergun Özbudun, eds., *Atatürk: Founder of a State* (London, 1981), for a less adulatory perspective than is given in some works.

On the introduction of political pluralism after World War II, the pioneering study is Kemal Karpat, *Turkey's Politics: The Transition to a Multiparty System* (Princeton, 1959). It may be supplemented by Feroz Ahmad, *The Turkish Experiment in Democracy, 1950–1975* (Boulder, 1977), and William Hale, *The Political and Economic Development of Turkey* (New York, 1981). Walter F. Weiker, *The Modernization of Turkey: From Atatürk to the Present Day* (New York, 1981), emphasizes developments during the 1960s and 1970s and includes valuable statistical tables. Frank Tachau, *Turkey: The Politics of Authority, Democracy, and Development* (New York, 1984), treats the years from 1950 to 1980 in the thematic terms of the title, employing modernization as an analytical device. Another study by Walter F. Weiker, *The Turkish Revolution, 1960–1961* (Washington, D.C., 1963), discusses the military intervention and the trials of Menderes and the Democrats. Dankwart A. Rustow, *Turkey: America's Forgotten Ally* (New York, 1987), offers a succinct assessment of

Turkey in the 1970s and early 1980s; the analysis is soundly placed in the context of late Ottoman and early republican history. An interpretation of the 1980 military intervention is C. H. Dodd, *The Crisis of Turkish Democracy* (Beverley, UK, 1983). A sympathetic account of the entire Kurdish region is David McDowall, *A Modern History of the Kurds* (London, 1996); for the recent Turkish-Kurdish conflict, see Robert Olson, ed., *The Kurdish Nationalist Movement in the 1990s: Its Impact on Turkey and the Middle East* (Lexington, 1996).

Egypt

The most comprehensive and up-to-date treatment of modern Egypt is M. W. Daly, ed., *The Cambridge History of Egypt:* vol. 2, *Modern Egypt, from 1517 to the End of the Twentieth Century* (Cambridge, 1998), which incorporates recent historical interpretations in a series of chronologically ordered chapters by leading experts. Although not without its biases, P. J. Vatikiotis, *The History of Modern Egypt: From Muhammad Ali to Mubarak,* 4th ed. (Baltimore, 1991) remains an important survey. More general histories include Afaf Lutfi al-Sayyid Marsot, *A Short History of Modern Egypt* (New York, 1985), and Arthur Goldschmidt Jr., *Modern Egypt: The Formation of a Nation-State* (Boulder, 1991).

The Nineteenth Century to 1952

The important Muhammad Ali era is treated in Henry Dodwell, *The Founder of Modern Egypt* (Cambridge, 1931), and Afaf Lutfi al-Sayyid Marsot, *Egypt in the Reign of Muhammad Ali* (Cambridge, 1984). J. Heyworth-Dunne, *An Introduction to the History of Education in Modern Egypt* (London, 1939, 1968), is still valuable for its account of the educational missions to Europe. Khaled Fahmy, *All the Pasha's Men: Mehmed Ali, His Army, and the Making of Modern Egypt* (Cambridge, 1997), draws on a rich variety of Egyptian archival sources to examine Muhammad Ali's army from several different perspectives, ranging from the soldiers who resisted serving in it to the state that used it as an instrument of coercion. Kenneth M. Cuno, *The Pasha's Peasants: Land, Society, and Economy in Lower Egypt, 1740–1858* (Cambridge, 1992), offers a revisionist interpretation of rural landholding patterns before and during Muhammad Ali's reign. Studies that use Muhammad Ali's reforms as the starting point for more extended treatment of nineteenth-century Egypt include Roger Owen, *Cotton and the Egyptian Economy, 1820–1914* (Oxford, 1969); Gabriel Baer, *Studies in the Social History of Modern Egypt* (Chicago, 1969), and his *History of Land Ownership in Modern Egypt, 1800–1950* (London, 1962); and Judith Tucker, *Women in Nineteenth Century Egypt* (Cambridge, 1985).

F. Robert Hunter, *Egypt Under the Khedives, 1805–1879: From Household Government to Modern Bureaucracy* (Pittsburgh, 1984), is an important archival-based study on the evolution of governing institutions and the behavior of appointed officials. The Urabi rebellion is examined in Juan R. I. Cole, *Colonialism and Revolution in the Middle East: Social and Cultural Origins of Egypt's Urabi Movement*

(Princeton, 1993). The financial practices that contributed to Egypt's bankruptcy are examined in David Landes, *Bankers and Pashas: International Finance and Economic Imperialism in Egypt* (Cambridge, Mass., 1958). Egypt's pivotal role in the European scramble for colonies is treated in Ronald Robinson and John Gallagher, *Africa and the Victorians: The Official Mind of Imperialism* (New York, 1961).

An analysis of the changes introduced during the British occupation is Robert L. Tignor, *Modernization and British Colonial Rule in Egypt, 1882–1914* (Princeton, 1966). A critical study of Cromer and his policies is found in Afaf Lutfi al-Sayyid Marsot, *Egypt and Cromer: A Study in Anglo-Egyptian Relations* (London, 1968). The voice of Victorian imperialism rings loud and clear in Lord Cromer, *Modern Egypt*, 2 vols. (London, 1908). Anglo-Sudanese-Egyptian relations from the establishment of the condominium to Sudanese independence are thoroughly examined in M. W. Daly's two-volume study, *Empire on the Nile: The Anglo-Egyptian Sudan, 1898–1934* (Cambridge, 1986) and *Imperial Sudan: The Anglo-Egyptian Condominium, 1934–1956* (Cambridge, 1991). Changes in the judicial system and the rise of the legal profession are examined in Donald M. Reid, *Lawyers and Politics in the Arab World, 1880–1960* (Minneapolis, 1981), and Farhat J. Ziadeh, *Lawyers, the Rule of Law, and Liberalism in Modern Egypt* (Stanford, 1968).

The starting point for the study of the turn-of-the-century intellectual ferment in which Egypt played a leading part is the relevant chapters in Albert Hourani, *Arabic Thought in the Liberal Age, 1789–1939* (Oxford, 1970). More specialized works include Nadav Safran, *Egypt in Search of Political Community: An Analysis of the Intellectual and Political Evolution of Egypt, 1804–1952* (Cambridge, Mass., 1961); Jamal Mohammed Ahmed, *The Intellectual Origins of Egyptian Nationalism* (London, 1960); Nikki R. Keddie, *Sayyid Jamal al-Din "al-Afghani"* (Berkeley, 1972); and Malcolm H. Kerr, *Islamic Reform: The Political and Legal Theories of Muhammad Abduh and Rashid Rida* (Berkeley, 1966).

British policy in the years immediately after World War I is studied in John Darwin, *Britain, Egypt, and the Middle East: Imperial Policy in the Aftermath of War, 1918–1922* (New York, 1981). Egypt's interwar era has attracted considerable scholarly attention. For the politics of the period, see Marius Deeb, *Party Politics in Egypt: The Wafd and Its Rivals* (London, 1979), and Afaf Lutfi al-Sayyid Marsot, *Egypt's Liberal Experiment: 1922–1936* (Berkeley, 1977). The attempts by Egyptian entrepreneurs to overcome the disadvantages posed by the Capitulations are examined in Eric Davis, *Challenging Colonialism: Bank Misr and Egyptian Industrialization, 1920–1941* (Princeton, 1983), and Robert Vitalis, *When Capitalists Collide: Business Conflict and the End of Empire in Egypt* (Berkeley, 1995). The emergence of an organized labor movement and the role of workers in the politics of Egyptian nationalism are treated in a very fine study by Joel Beinin and Zachary Lockman, *Workers on the Nile: Nationalism, Communism, Islam, and the Egyptian Working Class, 1882–1954* (Princeton, 1987). The debate over Egypt's identity is analyzed in Israel Gershoni and James P. Jankowski, *Egypt, Islam, and the Arabs: The Search for Egyptian Nationhood, 1900–1930* (New York, 1986), and the same authors' *Redefining the Egyptian Nation, 1930–1945* (Cambridge, 1995). Margot Badran, *Feminists, Is-*

lam, and Nation: Gender and the Making of Modern Egypt (Princeton, 1995), focuses on the women's movement from the turn of the century to 1952 as represented by activists from the upper classes of society. The influence of a national university on Egypt's political and intellectual life is the subject of Donald Malcolm Reid, *Cairo University and the Making of Modern Egypt* (Cambridge, 1990). The best study of the Muslim Brotherhood is Richard P. Mitchell, *The Society of the Muslim Brothers* (London, 1969). On World War II in Egypt and the rest of the region, see George Kirk, *The Middle East in the War* (London, 1952). British policy in the immediate postwar era is thoroughly documented in Wm. Roger Louis, *The British Empire in the Middle East, 1945–1951: Arab Nationalism, the United States, and Postwar Imperialism* (Oxford, 1984).

From the Revolution of 1952

A good introductory overview is Derek Hopwood, *Egypt: Politics and Society, 1945–1984* (London, 1985). Among the many attempts to explain the Nasser era by studying the life of its dominant personality, P. J. Vatikiotis, *Nasser and His Generation* (New York, 1978); Jean Lacouture, *Nasser: A Biography* (New York, 1973); and Robert Stephens, *Nasser* (London, 1971), may be recommended. There are several good books on foreign policy matters. Egypt's relations with other Arab states are treated in A. I. Dawisha, *Egypt and the Arab World: The Elements of Foreign Policy* (New York, 1976), and Malcolm H. Kerr, *The Arab Cold War: Gamal Abd al-Nasir and His Rivals, 1958–1970*, 3rd ed. (London, 1971). The Egyptian-Soviet relationship is examined in Karen Dawisha, *Soviet Foreign Policy Towards Egypt* (New York, 1979), and Alvin Rubinstein, *Red Star on the Nile: The Soviet-Egyptian Influence Relationship Since the June War* (Princeton, 1977). The Suez crisis has received extensive treatment, and the following works are but a sampling of the material available: Hugh Thomas, *Suez* (New York, 1967); Kennett Love, *Suez—The Twice-Fought War: A History* (New York, 1969); Keith Kyle, *Suez* (New York, 1991); and Wm. Roger Louis and Roger Owen, eds., *Suez 1956: The Crisis and Its Consequences* (Oxford, 1989), which is a reassessment based on new documentary evidence. The 1967 war is analyzed in Nadav Safran, *From War to War: The Arab-Israeli Confrontation, 1948–1967* (New York, 1969). The best analysis of the circumstances leading up to the 1967 war is Richard B. Parker, *The Politics of Miscalculation in the Middle East* (Bloomington, 1993). A very good introductory survey of U.S. policy toward the Arab Middle East from the late 1940s to the early 1990s, with special emphasis on the effects of the cold war on America's diplomatic position on Israel and the Arab states, including the 1967 war, is Burton I. Kaufman, *The Arab Middle East and the United States: Inter-Arab Rivalry and Superpower Diplomacy* (New York, 1996).

A survey of economic change as a whole is Robert Mabro, *The Egyptian Economy, 1952–1972* (Oxford, 1974). Land reform is treated in Gabriel S. Saab, *The Egyptian Agrarian Reform, 1952–1962* (London, 1967). The uneven results of the land reform are studied in Leonard Binder, *In a Moment of Enthusiasm: Political Power and the Second Stratum in Egypt* (Chicago, 1978); Hamied Ansari, *Egypt: The Stalled So-*

ciety (Albany, 1986); and Robert Springborg, *Family, Power, and Politics in Egypt: Sayed Bey Marei—His Clan, Clients, and Cohorts* (Philadelphia, 1982), a fascinating account of how a member of the pre-1952 landed class retained his wealth and political influence during the Nasser and Sadat eras. Cynthia Nelson, *Doria Shafik, Egyptian Feminist: A Woman Apart* (Gainesville, Fla., 1996), is a superb study of a Parisian-educated activist who ought to have been welcomed by the Nasser regime but who was, instead, persecuted by it. A thorough and critical assessment of state policies for three decades after 1952 is found in John Waterbury, *The Egypt of Nasser and Sadat: The Political Economy of Two Regimes* (Princeton, 1983). See also Raymond William Baker, *Egypt's Uncertain Revolution Under Nasser and Sadat* (Cambridge, Mass., 1978), and Kirk J. Beattie, *Egypt During the Nasser Years: Ideology, Politics, and Civil Society* (Boulder, 1994).

Sadat is the subject of a scathing biography by Irene Beeson and David Hirst, *Sadat* (London, 1981); a more sympathetic approach is taken in Raphael Israeli, *Man of Defiance: A Political Biography of Anwar Sadat* (London, 1985). Sadat staked his own claim to a place in history in a self-serving autobiography, *In Search of Identity* (New York, 1978). William B. Quandt, *Camp David: Peacemaking and Politics* (Washington, D.C., 1986), is a thorough discussion of the intricacies involved in securing the Camp David Accords. A good discussion of a variety of the issues faced by the Sadat regime is John Waterbury, *Egypt: Burdens of the Past, Options for the Future* (Bloomington, 1978). The politicization of students under Nasser and Sadat is discussed in Ahmed Abdallah, *The Student Movement and National Politics in Egypt* (London, 1985). An excellent account of the Islamic opposition is Gilles Kepel, *The Prophet and Pharaoh: Muslim Extremism in Egypt,* trans. Jon Rothschild (London, 1985).

Robert Springborg, *Mubarak's Egypt: Fragmentation of the Political Order* (Boulder, 1989), examines the relationship between political authority and economic change during the first six years of Mubarak's presidency. Raymond William Baker, *Sadat and After: Struggles for Egypt's Soul* (Cambridge, Mass., 1990) examines alternative political groups and their plans for the resolution of Egypt's problems.

Syria

General histories include A. L. Tibawi, *A Modern History of Syria Including Lebanon and Palestine* (New York, 1969), and Tabitha Petran, *Syria* (New York, 1972). Previous studies of the mandate era have been superseded by Philip S. Khoury's splendid work, *Syria and the French Mandate: The Politics of Arab Nationalism, 1920–1945* (Princeton, 1987), but the insights in Albert Hourani, *Syria and Lebanon: A Political Essay* (London, 1946), remain valuable. A compact introductory survey of the period since independence is Derek Hopwood, *Syria, 1945–1986: Politics and Society* (London, 1988). The impact on Syrian politics of Nasser's Pan-Arab policies during the 1950s is treated in Patrick Seale, *The Struggle for Syria: A Study of Post-War Arab Politics, 1945–1958,* new ed. (New Haven, 1987). Nikolaos van Dam, *The Struggle for Power in Syria: Sectarianism, Regionalism, and Tribalism in Politics, 1961–1980,* 2nd ed. (New York, 1980), analyzes components of political life starting with the breakup of the UAR. Raymond A. Hinnebush has written several works on the Baᶜthist period, the most ambitious of which is *Authoritarian Power and State Formation in Baᶜthist Syria: Army, Party, and Peasant* (Boulder, 1990), a work that provides a political science perspective on the period 1950–1980. The Baᶜth Party is studied in John F. Devlin, *The Baᶜth Party: A History from Its Origins to 1966* (Stanford, 1976). The regionalist doctrine of the SSNP is examined in Labib Zuwiyya-Yamak, *The Syrian Social Nationalist Party: An Ideological Analysis* (Cambridge, Mass., 1966). A sympathetic portrait of Hafiz al-Asad is provided in the biography by Patrick Seale, *Asad of Syria: The Struggle for the Middle East* (Berkeley, 1989). An assessment of the Syrian president's policies and objectives is found in Moshe Macoz, *Asad, the Sphinx of Damascus: A Political Biography* (London, 1988), and in the same author's *Syria and Egypt: From War to Peacemaking* (Oxford, 1995).

Lebanon

The best historical survey of the nineteenth and twentieth centuries is Kamal S. Salibi, *The Modern History of Lebanon* (New York, 1965). Any bibliography of modern Lebanon must now include Elizabeth Picard's instructive and deeply engaged work, *Lebanon: A Shattered Country. Myths and Realities of the Wars in Lebanon,* trans. Franklin Philip (New York, 1996). An informative collection of essays on the working of the Lebanese system before the civil war is Leonard Binder, ed., *Politics in Lebanon* (New York, 1966). Michael Hudson, *The Precarious Republic* (New York, 1968), shows some of the stresses within the political structure at a time when it was being held up by others as a model of sectarian harmony. For developments leading up to the first phase of the civil war, one should consult Kamal S. Salibi, *Cross Roads to Civil War: Lebanon, 1958–1976* (Delmar, N.Y., 1976). An important interpretation of Lebanon's domestic situation as well as its place in the Middle East during the 1970s is Walid Khalidi, *Conflict and Violence in Lebanon: Confrontation in the Middle East* (Cambridge, Mass., 1979). An analysis of Israel's 1982 invasion is found in Itamar Rabinovich, *The War for Lebanon, 1970–1985,* rev. ed. (Ithaca, 1985). Helena Cobban, *The Making of Modern Lebanon* (London, 1985), is especially helpful for its coherent narrative of the years from the outbreak of the civil war to the immediate aftermath of the Israeli invasion. Among the several specific accounts of the civil war, useful perspectives are offered in Jonathan C. Randal, *Going All the Way: Christian Warlords, Israeli Adventurers, and the War in Lebanon* (New York, 1983), which is highly critical of the Maronites; Robert Fisk, *Pity the Nation: The Abduction of Lebanon* (New York, 1990), an account by an engaged observer who remained in the country throughout the turmoil; and Thomas L. Friedman, *From Beirut to Jerusalem* (New York, 1989), which contains effective anecdotes by the correspondent of the *New York Times.* Kamal Salibi, *A House of Many Mansions: The History of Lebanon Reconsidered* (Berkeley, 1988), examines the conflicting historical myths on which the various religious communities base their vision of Lebanon. The political awakening of the Shi^ca and the complexities of southern Lebanon are examined in Augustus Richard Norton, *Amal and the Shi^ca: Struggle for the Soul of Lebanon* (Austin, 1987).

Iraq

The best historical survey of Iraq is a very fine work by Phebe Marr, *The Modern History of Iraq* (Boulder, 1985). One of the most significant historical studies of any modern Middle Eastern state is Hanna Batatu, *The Old Social Classes and the Revolutionary Movements of Iraq: A Study of Iraq's Old Landed and Commercial Classes and of Its Communists, Ba^cthists, and Free Officers* (Princeton, 1982). Batatu's book is not for the beginner. Yitzhak Nakash, *The Shi^cis of Iraq* (Princeton, 1994), is a comprehensive and revisionist study of the subject from the mid-eighteenth century to 1958. Edith Penrose and E. F. *Iraq: International Relations and National Development* (London, 1978), deals with the mandate through the revolutionary era and is especially strong on economics and the petroleum industry. The early years of British control are treated in Peter Sluglett, *Britain in Iraq, 1914–1932* (London, 1976). Of the three books on Iraq by Majid Khadduri, the first, which examines the period from formal independence to the overthrow of the monarchy, is the best; it is *Independent Iraq, 1932–1958: A Study in Iraqi Politics,* 2nd ed. (London, 1960). The process of setting up a nationalist-oriented educational system is discussed in Reeva S. Simon, *Iraq Between the Two World Wars: Creation and Implementation of a Nationalist Ideology* (New York, 1986).

A detailed political history treating the period from the revolution to 1990, with considerable attention paid to the Saddam Husayn regime, is Marion Farouk-Sluglett and Peter Sluglett, *Iraq Since 1958: From Revolution to Dictatorship* (London, 1990). A very important and effectively illustrated study of the Ba^cthist regime and its attempts to use the pre-Islamic past to create a unifying secular culture is Amatzia Baram, *Culture, History, and Ideology in the Formation of Ba^cthist Iraq, 1968–1989* (New York, 1989). Samir al-Khalil, *Republic of Fear: Saddam's Iraq* (Berkeley, 1989), gained wide acclaim during the 1991 Gulf War, in large measure because it portrayed the Iraqi regime the way the U.S. public and administration wanted to see it. Although the spirit of the work has merit, some of its analysis of the Ba^cth Party must be treated with caution. The most satisfactory work on the Iran-Iraq war is Dilip Hiro, *The Longest War: The Iran-Iraq Military Conflict,* updated ed. (London, 1990).

A vast literature on Iraq's invasion of Kuwait and the resulting Gulf War of 1991 has already appeared, and many more studies are in preparation. Several of the instant books on the subject are marred by sensationalism and the absence of historical perspective. For the moment, the best accounts are Lawrence Freedman and Efraim Karsh, *The Gulf Conflict, 1990–1991: Diplomacy and War in the New World Order* (Princeton, 1993); Dilip Hiro, *Desert Shield to Desert Storm: The Second Gulf War* (New York, 1992); and a book compiled by the staff of *U.S. News and World Report, Triumph Without Victory: The History of the Persian Gulf War* (New York, 1993). A thoughtful collection of articles by distinguished contributors treating the regional and international ramifications of the war is found in Ibrahim Ibrahim, ed., *The Gulf Crisis: Background and Consequences* (Washington, D.C., 1992). The coverage in *Middle East Report* offers a stimulating alternative view to the explanations released by the Bush administration. Two excellent studies of the border disputes between Iraq and Kuwait are David H. Finnie, *Shifting Lines in the Sand: Kuwait's Elusive Frontier with Iraq* (Cambridge, Mass., 1992), and Richard Schofield, *Kuwait and Iraq: Historical Claims and Territorial Disputes,* 2nd ed. (London, 1993).

Jordan

Kamal Salibi, *The Modern History of Jordan* (London, 1994), is a basic introductory survey. Another broadly based study is Naseer H. Aruri, *Jordan: A Study in Political Development (1921–1965)* (The Hague, 1972). Mary C. Wilson's *King Abdullah, Britain, and the Making of Jordan* (Cambridge, 1987), examines the development of the state through the personality and ambitions of its ruler. A collection of essays by Uriel Dann, *Studies in the History of Transjordan, 1920–1949: The Making of a State* (Boulder, 1984), also concentrates on the reign of Abdullah, and his *King Hussein and the Challenge of Arab Radicalism: Jordan, 1955–1967* (New York, 1989), examines the crises generated by the spread of Nasserism.

Palestine and Israel

Zionism and the Mandate Period

A basic collection of documents is contained in Walter Laqueur, ed., *The Israel-Arab Reader: A Documentary History of the Middle East Conflict* (New York, 1969). For the history of Zionism and the development of Zionist ideology, see Shlomo Avineri, *The Making of Modern Zionism: The Intellectual Origins of the Jewish State* (New York, 1981); Ben Halpern, *The Idea of the Jewish State,* 2nd ed. (Cambridge, Mass., 1969); Arthur Hertzberg, ed., *The Zionist Idea* (New York, 1959); and Walter Laqueur, *A History of Zionism* (New York, 1972). A work that illuminates not only the life of its subject but also the history of political Zionism and the diplomacy of the mandate era is Jehuda Reinharz's excellent two-volume biography, *Chaim Weizmann: The Making of a Zionist Leader* (New York, 1985), and *Chaim Weizmann: The Making of a Statesman* (New York, 1993).

A comprehensive survey treating Palestine and Arab-Jewish relations from late Ottoman times to Oslo I is Charles D. Smith, *Palestine and the Arab-Israeli Conflict,* 3rd ed. (New York, 1996). A more detailed but less focused survey is Mark Tessler, *A History of the Israeli-Palestinian Conflict* (Bloomington, 1994). A revisionist approach that views the practices of the first and second aliyahs within the framework of a colonial enterprise is Gershon Shafir, *Land, Labor, and the Origins of the Israeli-Palestinian Conflict, 1882–1914,* updated ed. (Berkeley, 1996). Specific studies of the mandate, with strong emphasis on British policymaking, include Bernard

Wasserstein, *The British in Palestine: The Mandatory Government and the Arab-Jewish Conflict, 1917–1929* (London, 1978), which explains the machinery of government; and Christopher Sykes, *Cross Roads to Israel,* reprint (Bloomington, 1978). Barbara J. Smith, *The Roots of Separatism in Palestine: British Economic Policy, 1920–1929* (Syracuse, 1993), argues that Britain's economic policies facilitated the development of a separate Zionist economy as early as the 1920s. Zachary Lockman, *Comrades and Enemies: Arab and Jewish Workers in Palestine, 1906–1948* (Berkeley, 1996), examines the ways in which the mandate-era Zionist labor establishment was shaped by its internal debate on how to deal with Palestinian Arab workers and their unions. The final years of the mandate are examined in Michael Cohen, *Palestine, Retreat from the Mandate: The Making of British Policy, 1936–1945* (New York, 1978), and the same author's *Palestine and the Great Powers* (Princeton, 1982). The perspectives and policies of all the main participants are examined in Wm. Roger Louis and Robert W. Stookey, eds., *The End of the Palestine Mandate* (Austin, 1986). There is much that is still valuable in J. C. Hurewitz, *The Struggle for Palestine,* reprint (New York, 1968).

The best works on the development of Zionist institutions during the mandate are Noah Lucas, *The Modern History of Israel* (London, 1974), and Dan Horowitz and Moshe Lissak, *Origins of the Israeli Polity: Palestine Under the Mandate* (Chicago, 1978). The rise of political activity among the Palestinian notables is analyzed in great detail in Yehoshua Porath's two studies, *The Emergence of the Palestinian National Movement, 1918–1929* (London, 1973), and *The Palestinian Arab National Movement, 1929–1939: From Riots to Rebellion* (London, 1978). Philip Mattar, *The Mufti of Jerusalem: Al-Hajj Amin al-Husayni and the Palestinian National Movement* (New York, 1988), presents the mufti in the context of the politics of the notables. The emergence of Palestinian national identity is the subject of Muhammad Muslih, *The Origins of Palestinian Nationalism* (New York, 1990), and Rashid Khalidi, *Palestinian Identity: The Construction of Modern National Consciousness* (New York, 1997). Pamela Ann Smith's survey, *Palestine and the Palestinians, 1876–1983* (New York, 1984), is uneven but useful for its focus on the peasantry during the mandate. The thorny issue of population receives definitive treatment in Justin McCarthy, *The Population of Palestine: Population History and Statistics of the Late Ottoman Period and the Mandate* (New York, 1990). Another sensitive issue, the ownership of land, is examined in Kenneth W. Stein, *The Land Question in Palestine, 1917–1939* (Chapel Hill, 1984).

Israel and the Palestinians After 1948

In recent years, a lively and occasionally acrimonious debate has swept through Israeli scholarly circles as a result of the work of a group of so-called new historians who have challenged some of the long-accepted historical assumptions about Zionism and the early years of the Israeli state. Their work and that of other like-minded revisionist scholars may be sampled in Michael N. Barnett, ed., *Israel in Comparative Perspective: Challenging the Conventional Wisdom* (Albany, 1996). Two critical reappraisals of Israel's role in the events surrounding the war of 1948 by leading representatives of the new history are Avi Shlaim, *Collusion Across the Jordan: King Abdullah, the Zionist Movement, and the Partition of Palestine* (New York, 1988), and Ilan Pappé, *The Making of the Arab-Israeli Conflict, 1947–1951* (London, 1992). A spirited refutation of the new historians' methods, evidence, and motives is found in Efraim Karsh, *Fabricating Israeli History: The "New Historians"* (London, 1997).

In addition to Lucas's *Modern History of Israel,* cited above, Israeli institutions are treated in Yossi Beilin, *Israel: A Concise Political History* (New York, 1992); Nadav Safran, *Israel, the Embattled Ally* (Cambridge, Mass., 1981), a domestic history that nevertheless also emphasizes the development of the U.S.-Israeli relationship; and Howard M. Sachar's detailed studies, *A History of Israel from the Rise of Zionism to Our Time* (New York, 1976), and *A History of Israel from the Aftermath of the Yom Kippur War* (New York, 1987). A good introduction to the workings of the Israeli electoral and political systems is Gregory S. Mahler, *Israel: Government and Politics in a Maturing State* (San Diego, 1990). A more critical approach to the U.S.-Israeli relationship than Safran's is Cheryl A. Rubenberg, *Israel and the American National Interest: A Critical Examination* (Urbana, 1986). For the Palestinian community within Israel, see Ian S. Lustick, *Arabs in the Jewish State: Israel's Control of a National Minority* (Austin, 1980), which examines the system of controls Israel used to maintain the quiescence of its Arab citizens. Lustick has also examined the rise of militant Jewish settler groups with special emphasis on Gush Emunim in *For the Land and the Lord: Jewish Fundamentalism in Israel* (New York, 1988). Ilan Peleg, *Begin's Foreign Policy, 1977–1983: Israel's Move to the Right* (New York, 1987), is a critical interpretation of the role of the Right in influencing the Begin government's policies. Taking 1967 as their starting point, Dan Horowitz and Moshe Lissak examine twenty years of changes in Israel in *Trouble in Utopia: The Overburdened Polity of Israel* (Albany, 1989).

The reasons for the Palestinian exodus are carefully documented by Benny Morris, one of the new historians, in *The Birth of the Palestinian Refugee Problem, 1947–1949* (New York, 1988), which successfully refutes earlier explanations. The outstanding study of the PLO is Helena Cobban, *The Palestinian Liberation Organisation: People, Power, and Politics* (Cambridge, 1984). A good account of the emergence of Palestinian identity and the activities of the resistance movements in the years immediately following the 1967 war is William B. Quandt et al., *The Politics of Palestinian Nationalism* (Berkeley, 1973). On the Palestinian presence in Lebanon, see Rex Brynen, *Sanctuary and Survival: The PLO in Lebanon* (Boulder, 1990). An important study of politics and gender within the Palestinian community in Lebanon during the period 1968–1982 is Julie M. Peteet, *Gender in Crisis: Women and the Palestinian Resistance Movement* (New York, 1991). Indispensable for an understanding of conditions in the occupied territories after 1967 is Meron Benvenisti, *The West Bank Data Project: A Survey of Israel's Policies* (Washington, D.C., 1984), and later supplements. Other important studies of the occupied territories are Emile Sahliyeh, *In Search of Leadership: West Bank Politics Since 1967* (Washington, D.C., 1988), and Sarah Roy, *The Gaza Strip: The Political Economy of De-Development* (Washington, D.C., 1995).

A thorough study of the *intifada* is F. Robert Hunter, *The Palestinian Uprising: A War by Other Means,* 2nd ed. (Berkeley, 1993), a work that is enhanced by the author's interviews with Palestinians during the early phase of the uprising. A more recent account is Glen E. Robinson, *Building a Palestinian State: The Incomplete Revolution* (Bloomington, 1997), which connects the rise of a new Palestinian elite during the *intifada* with Arafat's oppressive policies as head of the PNA after 1994; Arafat had to crush this new elite if he was to survive politically. Robinson's work also includes an excellent analysis of Hamas. Another work on Hamas and other Palestinian Islamic activist organizations is Ziad Abu-Amr, *Islamic Fundamentalism in the West Bank and Gaza: Muslim Brotherhood and Islamic Jihad* (Bloomington, 1994). Joost R. Hiltermann, *Behind the Intifada: Labor and Women's Movements in the Occupied Territories* (Princeton, 1991) focuses on how the formation of trade unions and women's committees among Palestinians in the occupied territories contributed to the struggle for national liberation. A wide-ranging look at the effects of the uprising is Robert O. Freedman, ed., *The Intifada: Its Impact on Israel, the Arab World, and the Superpowers* (Miami, 1991).

A useful reference work for the period after Oslo I is Lawrence Joffe, *Kessing's Guide to the Mid-East Peace Process* (London, 1996), which reproduces the major documents, provides capsule biographies of the main participants, and offers an analysis of the peace process itself to mid-1996. An up-to-date work on the effects of the Oslo accords on the individual states of the region is Robert O. Freedman, ed., *The Middle East and the Peace Process: The Impact of the Oslo Accords* (Gainesville, Fla., 1998). For U.S. policy leading up to the peace process, the best work is William B. Quandt, *Peace Process: American Diplomacy and the Arab-Israeli Conflict Since 1967* (Washington, D.C., 1993).

The States of the Arabian Peninsula

The best starting point for a study of the Arabian Peninsula is the work of J. B. Kelly, *Britain and the Persian Gulf, 1795–1880* (London, 1968), and *Arabia, the Gulf, and the West* (London, 1980). The latter book treats oil, diplomacy, and internal developments in the twentieth century with a concentration on the 1970s; it is written with a decidedly bipolar worldview. Britain's role in the Gulf is also treated in Busch's *Britain and the Persian Gulf* and *Britain, India, and the Arabs*, both cited above, and, more recently, in John C. Wilkinson, *Arabia's Frontiers: The Story of Britain's Boundary Drawing in the Desert* (London, 1991).

For the early history of the Saudi state, see Christine Moss Helms, *The Cohesion of Saudi Arabia: Evolution of Political Identity* (London, 1981), and Joseph Kostiner, *The Making of Saudi Arabia, 1916–1936: From Chieftancy to Monarchical State* (New York, 1993). The ruling family is closely studied in David Holden and Richard Johns, *The House of Saud: The Rise and Rule of the Most Powerful Dynasty in the Arab World* (London, 1981). Nadav Safran, *Saudi Arabia: The Ceaseless Quest for Security* (Ithaca, 1988), concentrates on developments since 1970. Mordechai Abir, *Saudi Arabia in the Oil Era: Regime and Elites, Conflict and Collaboration* (Boulder, 1988), offers an important analysis of the new administrative elite and the tensions created by their continued exclusion from decisionmaking; Abir's sequel is an equally significant contribution, *Saudi Arabia: Government, Society, and the Gulf*

Crisis (New York, 1993). The excellent work by F. Gregory Gause III, *Oil Monarchies: Domestic and Security Challenges in the Arab Gulf States* (New York, 1994), offers a comparative reinterpretation of the bases of politics in the six Gulf monarchies during the period immediately before and after the Iraqi invasion of Kuwait.

For a history of Yemen, see Manfred W. Wenner, *Modern Yemen, 1918–1966* (Baltimore, 1968). Robert W. Stookey, *Yemen: The Politics of the Yemen Arab Republic* (Boulder, 1972), focuses on the period after 1962, as does Robert D. Burrowes, *The Yemen Arab Republic: The Politics of Development, 1962–1986* (Boulder, 1987). South Yemen is examined in Stookey's *South Yemen: A Marxist Republic in Arabia* (Boulder, 1982). See also Joseph Kostiner, *The Struggle for South Yemen* (New York, 1984), which studies the region during the final stages of British rule, and Robin Bidwell, *The Two Yemens* (London, 1983).

Several rich contributions on the history, culture, art, and geography of the Gulf are found in Alvin J. Cottrell, ed., *The Persian Gulf States: A General Survey* (Baltimore, 1980). Richard F. Nyrop, ed., *Persian Gulf States,* 2nd ed. (Washington, D.C., 1984), is a useful volume in the multidisciplinary Area Handbook series prepared by the American University. A good introductory survey is Rosemarie Said Zahlan, *The Making of the Modern Gulf States: Kuwait, Bahrain, Qatar, the United Arab Emirates and Oman* (London, 1989). More specific country studies include Jill Crystal, *Oil and Politics in the Gulf: Rulers and Merchants in Kuwait and Qatar,* updated ed. (Cambridge, 1995), and the same author's *Kuwait: The Transformation of an Oil State* (Boulder, 1992). On Oman, see Robert G. Landen, *Oman Since 1856: Disruptive Modernization in a Traditional Arab Society* (Princeton, 1967); John C. Wilkinson, *The Imamate Tradition of Oman* (Cambridge, 1987); J. E. Peterson, *Oman in the Twentieth Century: Political Foundations of an Emerging State* (London, 1978); and Carol J. Riphenburg, *Oman: Political Development in a Changing World* (Westport, Conn., 1998), a comprehensive analysis of Omani political culture and the social and economic changes that have influenced it, including Omani relations with its Gulf neighbors. The short history of the UAE is examined in Muhammad Morsy Abdullah, *The United Arab Emirates: A Modern History* (New York, 1978). For Qatar, see Rosemarie Said Zahlan, *The Creation of Qatar* (London, 1979).

A full history of the petroleum industry is found in Daniel Yergin, *The Prize: The Epic Quest for Oil, Money, and Power* (New York, 1991). Studies that concentrate on the Middle East include George W. Stocking, *Middle Eastern Oil* (Nashville, 1970), and Ian Skeet, *OPEC: Twenty-Five Years of Prices and Politics* (Cambridge, 1988). Joe Stork, *Middle East Oil and the Energy Crisis* (New York, 1975), is a critical account of the policies of the companies and the consuming nations.

Iran and Central Asia

From the Safavids to the Rise of the Pahlavi Dynasty

An introduction to the Mongol and Safavid periods is David Morgan's succinct survey, *Medieval Persia, 1040–1797* (London, 1988). For more detail and breadth on these eras, see the splendid work, Peter Jackson and Laurence Lockhart, eds., *The Cambridge*

History of Iran, vol. 6 (Cambridge, 1986). Another fine volume in this series, treating the political, diplomatic, economic, and cultural life of Iran from the fall of the Safavids to the revolution of 1979, is Peter Avery et al., eds., *The Cambridge History of Iran,* vol. 7 (Cambridge, 1991). A solid narrative account is Mehran Kamrava, *The Political History of Modern Iran: From Tribalism to Theocracy* (New York, 1992).

A very good introduction to modern Iranian history is Nikki R. Keddie, *Roots of Revolution: An Interpretive History of Modern Iran* (New Haven, 1981). One of the most lucid and perceptive studies of any transforming Middle Eastern society is Ervand Abrahamian's *Iran Between Two Revolutions* (Princeton, 1982). Although the author concentrates on the twentieth century and the growth of the political Left, he provides insightful comments on the Qajar period and on modern Iran as a whole. I have drawn extensively from this book and recommend it highly. Peter Avery, *Modern Iran* (London, 1965), is a solid study of the Qajar and Pahlavi periods.

More specific studies of the Qajar era include Hamid Algar's work on the oppositional role of the ulama, *Religion and State in Iran, 1785–1906* (Berkeley, 1969), and Abbas Amanat, *Pivot of the Universe: Nasir al-Din Shah and the Iranian Monarchy, 1831–1896* (Berkeley, 1997), a close study of the shah's traditional ruling style in a rapidly changing era. Ann K. S. Lambton, *Landlord and Peasant in Persia: A Study of Land Tenure and Land Revenue Administration* (London, 1953), is a pioneering study of rural conditions. Foreign policy is surveyed in Rouhollah Ramazani, *The Foreign Policy of Iran: A Developing Nation in World Affairs, 1500–1941* (Charlottesville, Va., 1966), and F. Kazemzadeh, *Russia and Britain in Persia, 1864–1914* (New Haven, 1968). Nikki Keddie's numerous contributions include a collection of essays, *Modern Iran: Religion, Politics, and Society* (London, 1980), and *Religion and Rebellion in Iran: The Tobacco Protest of 1891–1892* (London, 1966). Vanessa Martin, *Islam and Modernism: The Iranian Revolution of 1906* (Syracuse, 1989), studies the constitutional revolution.

The reforms of the first Pahlavi ruler, Reza Shah, are studied in Amin Banani, *The Modernization of Iran, 1921–1941* (Stanford, 1961). Shahrough Akhavi, *Religion and Politics in Contemporary Iran: Clergy-State Relations in the Pahlavi Period* (Albany, 1980), is an important examination of the religious institution and its survival during the reigns of two hostile rulers. On the development of an official ideology, see Richard W. Cottam, *Nationalism in Iran,* 2nd ed. (Pittsburgh, 1979). The domestic and international aspects of the Mosaddiq era are well covered in James A. Bill and Wm. Roger Lewis, eds., *Musaddiq, Iranian Nationalism, and Oil* (Austin, 1988), and the important work by Mostafa Elm, *Oil, Power, and Principle: Iran's Oil Nationalization and Its Aftermath* (Syracuse, 1992). For the patterns of political life under the last shah, see James A. Bill, *The Politics of Iran: Groups, Classes, and Modernization* (Columbus, 1972). Ann K. S. Lambton, *The Persian Land Reform, 1962–1966* (Oxford, 1969), is supplemented by the more up-to-date study by Eric J. Hooglund, *Land and Revolution in Iran, 1960–1980* (Austin, 1982). Pahlavi foreign policy is the subject of Rouhollah K. Ramazani, *Iran's Foreign Policy, 1941–1973* (Charlottesville, Va., 1975).

The Iranian revolution of 1978–1979 and its aftermath have been the subjects of numerous studies, and the list continues to grow. Only a sampling can be noted here. The best political and social analysis of the revolutionary regime from 1979 to the mid-1980s is Shaul Bakhash, *The Reign of the Ayatollahs: Iran and the Islamic Revolution* (New York, 1986). See also Nikki Keddie and Eric Hooglund, eds., *The Iranian Revolution and the Islamic Republic*, 2nd ed. (Syracuse, 1986); Mohsen M. Milani, *The Making of Iran's Islamic Revolution: From Monarchy to Islamic Republic*, 2nd ed. (Boulder, 1994); Said Amir Arjomand, *The Turban for the Crown: The Islamic Revolution in Iran* (New York, 1988); and Ervand Abrahamian, *Khomeinism: Essays on the Islamic Republic* (Berkeley, 1993), a stimulating work that situates Khomeini and his ideas in the realm of populism rather than rigid fundamentalism. Shireen T. Hunter has written a solid syntheis in *Iran After Khomeini* (New York, 1992). An outstanding and readily comprehensible study of contemporary Shiʿa Islam is found in Roy Mottahedeh's evocative work, *The Mantle of the Prophet: Religion and Politics in Iran* (New York, 1985). For a collection of the writings of Khomeini, see the work translated and annotated by Hamid Algar, *Islam and Revolution: Writings and Declarations of Imam Khomeini* (Berkeley, 1981). The foreign policy of the Islamic Republic is examined in Rouhollah K. Ramazani, *Revolutionary Iran: Challenge and Response in the Middle East* (Baltimore, 1986). Critical assessments of U.S. policy toward Iran are presented in James A. Bill, *The Eagle and the Lion: The Tragedy of American-Iranian Relations* (New Haven, 1988), and Richard W. Cottam, *Iran and the United States: A Cold War Case Study* (Pittsburgh, 1988).

The situation in independent Central Asia is so fluid that most books on the subject quickly become dated. Some of the best of the recent studies are Shireen T. Hunter, *Central Asia Since Independence* (London, 1996), which gives a thorough yet concise account of the post-Soviet years up to early 1996; David Menashri, ed., *Central Asia Meets the Middle East* (London, 1998), which contains useful contributions on the emerging regional linkages; and Martha Brill Olcott, *Central Asia's New States: Independence, Foreign Policy, and Regional Security* (Washington, D.C., 1996), which provides a political scientist's perspective on domestic and regional developments. One work that will not become dated is R. D. McChesney's *Central Asia: Foundations of Change* (Princeton, 1996), a superb interpretation of the broad themes of Central Asia's past and their connections to its future.

Intellectual and Religious Developments

A list of overviews of the history of ideas in the Arab provinces and Egypt during the nineteenth and twentieth centuries must begin with Hourani, *Arabic Thought in the Liberal Age, 1789–1939*, cited above. A fine study on the same subject is Majid Khadduri, *Political Trends in the Arab World: The Role of Ideas and Ideals in Politics* (Baltimore, 1970). An important study of the history and role of Arab journalism from its origins to 1945 is Ami Ayalon, *The Press in the Arab Middle East: A History* (New York, 1995). Sylvia G. Haim, ed., *Arab Nationalism: An Anthology* (Berkeley, 1962), includes translated selections from a variety of authors and a stimulating introductory essay by the editor. James Jankowski and Israel Gershoni, eds., *Rethinking Nationalism in the Arab Middle East* (New York, 1997), is a collection of essays that reexamines Arab nationalism in the light of recent theoretical studies on the subject of nationalism generally. Paul Salem, *Bitter Legacy: Ideology and Politics in the Arab World* (Syracuse, 1994), provides a critical reassessment of the dominant Arab ideologies from the turn of the twentieth century to the recent past and places them in a social and political context. William L. Cleveland, *The Making of an Arab Nationalist: Ottomanism and Arabism in the Life and Thought of Sati al-Husri* (Princeton, 1971), is an intellectual biography of the foremost theoretician of secular Pan-Arab nationalism. Cleveland's *Islam Against the West: Shakib Arslan and the Campaign for Islamic Nationalism* (Austin, 1985), examines the life and thought of an Arab activist who advocated the primacy of Islamic ties during the interwar era.

The Islamic resurgence has been the subject of numerous articles, monographs, and edited collections. Among the many edited works on the subject, John L. Esposito, ed., *Islam and Development: Religion and Sociopolitical Change* (Syracuse, 1980), contains several excellent essays that have stood the test of time, of which Michael Hudson's "Islam and Political Development" is worthy of special note. One of the most stimulating of the volumes on the Islamic revival is Barbara Freyer Stowasser, ed., *The Islamic Impulse* (Washington, D.C., 1989), which offers a variety of regional studies and theoretical perspectives. Nazih Ayubi, *Political Islam: Religion and Politics in the Arab World* (London, 1993), is an important work that combines an analysis of Islamic theory on religion, politics, and economics with six country-specific studies. In *Islam and Democracy* (New York, 1996), John L. Esposito and John O. Voll examine Islam as a social and political phenomenon and provide case studies from six countries, ranging from Algeria to Malaysia. Dale F. Eickelman and James Piscatori, an anthropologist and a political scientist respectively, have written a stimulating comparative work, *Muslim Politics* (Princeton, 1996), that raises questions about ideological politics in various regional settings. James P. Piscatori, *Islam in a World of Nation-States* (Cambridge, 1986), explores the significance of the revival of a universal religion in a world organized around a system of sovereign states. A variety of country-specific studies and theoretical issues are raised in John L. Esposito, ed., *Political Islam: Revolution, Radicalism, or Reform?* (Boulder, 1997), a work that also has a comprehensive up-to-date bibliography. Hamid Enayat, *Modern Islamic Political Thought* (Austin, 1982), and Emmanuel Sivan, *Radical Islam: Medieval Theology and Modern Politics,* 2nd ed. (New Haven, 1990), are sophisticated analyses. Samuel P. Huntington's controversial work, *Clash of Civilizations and the Remaking of World Order* (New York, 1996), posits a future confrontation between Islamic and Western civilizations. Huntington's premise, which first appeared in article format, is refuted in John L. Esposito, *The Islamic Threat: Myth or Reality?,* 2nd ed. (New York, 1995). A solid introductory study of the lives and writings of Muslim thinkers from al-Afghani to Khomeini is Ali Rahnema, ed., *Pioneers of Islamic Revival* (London, 1994). Two compilations of the writings of Muslims themselves on the topic are John J. Donohue and John L. Esposito, eds., *Islam in Transition: Muslim Perspectives* (New York, 1982), and John L. Esposito, ed., *Voices of Islam Resurgent* (New York, 1983). Studies that focus on modern Islamic law are J.N.D. Anderson, *Law Reform in the Muslim World* (London, 1976), and the very important work by Judith E. Tucker, *In the House of the Law: Gender and Islamic Law in Ottoman Syria and Palestine* (Berkeley, 1998).

Indigenous literature, including novels, can tell the historian much about a culture. The best starting point is the work of the Egyptian novelist Naguib Mahfouz, the first Arabic-language author to receive the Nobel Prize for literature (1988). Mahfouz's best-known work is the Cairo trilogy made up of *Palace Walk*, translated by William M. Hutchins and Olive E. Kenny (New York, 1990); *Palace of Desire*, translated by William M. Hutchins, Lorne M. Kenny, and Olive E. Kenny (New York, 1991); and *Sugar Street*, translated by William M. Hutchins and Angele B. Samaan (New York, 1992).

Index

Abbas I (khedive of Egypt), 92
Abbas I (Safavid shah), 55–56, 57
Abbas II (khedive of Egypt), 106–107
Abbasid dynasty, 17–19
  in conceptualizations of Islamic history,
    20–21, 22
  domains of, 23(map)
  economic prosperity of, 22, 24
  high culture in, 24
  Mongol destruction of, 22, 38
  Seljuk Turks and, 36–37
  Shiᶜas and Sunnis in, 36
  ulama and, 31
Abd al-Ilah (ruler of Iraq), 207, 208, 317,
  318
Abdallah (king of Jordan), 163, 209–211,
  321
Abd al-Rahman al-Azzam, 201
Abd al-Wahhab, Muhammad ibn, 120–121,
  437
Abduh, Muhammad, 108, 123, 124–125,
  230
Abdul Aziz, 85, 95
Abdul Hamid II, 85, 86, 89, 98
  al-Afghani and, 123
  authoritarian reforms, 117–118
  deposition of, 133
  Kuwait and, 449
  modernization reforms, 118–119
  opposition to, 131–132
  Pan-Islam doctrine and, 118, 128
  political repression and, 119–120,
    128
Abdullah. See Abdallah
Abdul Mejid, 177
al-Abid family, 137
Aboukir Bay, battle of, 65
Abu Bakr, 13
Abu Dhabi, 454, 456
Abu Talib, 8
Achemenid Empire, 2
Aᶜyans, 60

Adana, 72
Aden Protectorate, 225, 440
Adrianople, 77, 88
Adrianople, Treaty of, 77
al-Afghani, Jamal al-Din, 122–124
Aflaq, Michel, 316, 334, 387, 389, 407
Afrika Korps, 198
Aga Khan, 36
Agrarian reform
  in Egypt, 299, 309
  in Iraq, 319, 400
  See also Land reform
Agrarian Reform Law (Egypt), 299, 309
Agriculture
  Abbasids and, 22, 24
  in Egypt, 69–70
  in Greater Syria, Tanzimat reforms and,
    91
  See also Cotton industry
al-Ahdab, Khayr al-Din, 222
Ahmad Shah, 182
al-Ahram (newspaper), 106
Aida (Verdi), 96
AIOC. See Anglo-Iranian Oil Company
Ajman, 454
al-Alamain, 198
Alawites, 215, 386, 389, 394
Albright, Madeleine, 496
Al Bu Saᶜid family, 453
Aleppo, 213, 215, 216(map)
Alexander II (tsar of Russia), 235
Alexander the Great, 2
Alexandretta peninsula, 181, 219
Alexandria, 96, 97(photo), 199
Algeria, 434–435
Algiers, 42, 102
Algiers Agreement, 398, 403, 406
Ali (fourth caliph), 13, 15–16, 34–35
Ali Bey, 65
Ali Pasha, 82, 83
Allah, meaning of term, 9
Allenby, Edmund, 149–150, 193

Sinan, 42
Sino-Japanese War, 130
Sipahis, 47–48, 78
Slave armies
  Ottoman, 48
  Safavid, 55
Slaves. *See Devshirme* system; Slave armies
Smith, Charles, 257
Socialism. *See* Arab socialism
Social welfare
  in Kuwait, 451
Society of Friends (Philike Hetairia), 75, 76
South Yemen, People's Democratic Republic
  of, 440
Soviet Union
  Armenia and, 174
  collapse of, 359–360
  Egypt and, 307, 332, 364, 365–366
  emigration of Soviet Jews, 360
  Iran and, 187–181, 267, 268, 280, 291
  Iran-Iraq War and, 404
  Iraq and, 319, 402
  Madrid Conference and, 484
  October War and, 365–366
  Suez Canal crisis and, 303–304
  Syria and, 392
  Turkey and, 267–268, 291
Spain, 21–22
Stalingrad, battle of, 198
Standard Oil Company of California, 441.
    See also Arabian American Oil
    Company
Standard Oil of California, 227
State capitalism
  Iranian, 186
  Turkish, 180
State of Syria, 215. *See also* Syria
Stern, Abraham, 256
Stern Gang, 256, 459
Student associations. *See* Islamic student
    associations
Sudan
  British-Egyptian conquest of, 105
  Egypt and, 68–69, 72, 300
  Islamism and, 434
  Mahdiyyah rebellion and, 105, 121–122
Suez Canal
  construction of, 96–97
  crisis of 1956, 301, 302–304
  Ferdinand de Lesseps and, 94
  Great Britain and, 99, 194
  June War and, 331, 332
  nationalization of, 302

October War and, 365
World War I and, 149
Suez City, 303
Sufism
  Abd al-Wahhab on, 120
  history and development of, 31–32
Süleyman the Magnificent, 44, 57
al-Sulh, Riyadh, 224
Sultanate, 47, 49
  abolished, 175
  constitution of 1876 and, 85–86
Sunnah, 29, 34
Sunnis/Sunnism
  Abbasids and, 36
  in Central Asian republics, 519
  historical breach with Shiʿism, 34–35
  in Iraq, 57–58, 317
  Kurds and, 320
  in Lebanon, 220, 221, 222, 325
  Safavid Shiʿism and, 54–55, 57–58
  Seljuk Turks and, 36, 37
  succession of Rashidun caliphs and, 34
  in Syria, 215, 217, 388, 389
Supplementary Fundamental Laws (Iran),
    142, 184
Supreme Muslim Council (Palestine), 243,
    250
Supsa, 522
Sykes-Picot Agreement, 159–160
Syria
  under al-Asad, 385, 386–395
  Alexandretta peninsula and, 181, 219
  Arab Christian awakening and, 126–127
  Arab-Israeli War of 1948, 260
  under Baʿthist regimes, 387, 389
  constitution of 1973, 388
  corruption in, 390
  destruction of Hama, 394–395
  education in, 391
  Egypt and, 72, 74, 316–317
  as French mandate, 212, 213–218,
    222–223, 224–225
  Gulf War and, 465–466
  Ibrahim and, 89, 90
  illiteracy in, 391
  independence and, 223, 224–225
  Iran-Iraq War and, 393
  Islamic opposition to al-Asad, 394–395
  Israeli-Palestinian conflict and, 328
  June War and, 329, 331, 332, 333, 388
  Lebanon and, 375, 379, 380, 393
  military, expansion of, 386, 392
  military forces of, 217